Pregnancy
in Adolescence
Needs, Problems, and Man.

Pregnancy in Adolescence
Needs, Problems, and Management

Edited by
Irving R. Stuart, Ph.D.
Lehman College of the City University of New York
and
Carl F. Wells, Ph.D.
Lehman College of the City University of New York

VNR VAN NOSTRAND REINHOLD COMPANY
NEW YORK CINCINNATI TORONTO LONDON MELBOURNE

Copyright © 1982 by Van Nostrand Reinhold Company

Library of Congress Catalog Card Number: 81-10421
ISBN: 0-422-21225-9

Manufactured in the United States of America

Published by Van Nostrand Reinhold Company
135 West 50th Street, New York, N.Y. 10020

Van Nostrand Reinhold Limited
1410 Birchmount Road
Scarborough, Ontario M1P 2E7, Canada

Van Nostrand Reinhold Australia Pty. Ltd.
17 Queen Street
Mitcham, Victoria 3132, Australia

Van Nostrand Reinhold Company Limited
Molly Millars Lane
Wokingham, Berkshire, England

15 14 13 12 11 10 9 8 7 6 5 4 3 2 1

Library of Congress Cataloging in Publication Data

Main entry under title:

Pregnancy in adolescence.

  Includes index.
  1. Adolescent mothers—United States. 2. Adolescent mothers—Legal status, laws, etc.—United States. 3. Pregnancy, Adolescent—United States. 4. Pregnancy, Adolescent—Psychological aspects. I. Stuart, Irving R. II. Wells, Carl F. [DNLM: 1. Pregnancy in adolescence. WS 462 P923]
HQ759.4.P73   362.7'96   81-10421
ISBN 0-442-21225-9   AACR2

Contributors

Ager, Joel W., Ph.D.,
Professor, Center for Health Research,
College of Nursing, Wayne State University,
Detroit, Mich.

Agronow, Samuel J., Ph.D.,
Research Associate, C.S. Mott Center for
Human Growth and Development, School of
Medicine, Wayne State University, Detroit,
Mich.

Authier, Jerry, Ph.D.,
Associate Professor of Medical Psychology,
Department of Family Practice, University of
Nebraska College of Medicine, Omaha, Neb.

Authier, Karen, M.S.W., A.C.S.W.,
Director of Social Services, Assistant
Professor, Psychiatric Social Work, Nebraska
Psychiatric Institute, University of Nebraska
College of Medicine, Omaha, Neb.

Beckstein, Douglas, B.A.,
Program Associate, Center for Population
Options, Washington, D.C.

Bierman, Babette R., M.S.W., L.C.S.W.,
Clinical Psychiatric Social Worker, The Johns
Hopkins Center for Teen-Aged Parents and
their Infants, Johns Hopkins University,
Baltimore, Md.

Bracken, Maryann, M.A.,
Associate in Research, Department of
Pediatrics, Yale University Medical School,
New Haven, Conn.

Bracken, Michael B., Ph.D.,
Senior Research Associate in Epidemiology,
Obstetrics, and Gynecology; Director,
Perinatal Epidemiology Unit, Yale University
Medical School, New Haven, Conn.

Cooper, Elizabeth, C.N.M., M.S.,
Director, Nurse-Midwifery, Clinical
Associate, Department of Obstetrics and
Gynecology, The University of Rochester
School of Medicine and Dentistry, Rochester,
N.Y.

Covan, Frederick L., Ph.D.,
Chief Psychologist, Bellevue Psychiatric
Hospital, New York, N.Y.

Darabi, Katherine F., Ph.D.,
Assistant Professor of Public Health, Center
for Population and Family Health, College of
Physicians and Surgeons of Columbia
University, New York, N.Y.

DeRose, Ann M., M.Ed.,
Principal, Lee Adolescent Mothers Program
(LAMP), Fort Myers, Fla.

Dryfoos, Joy G., M.A.,
Fellow, The Alan Guttmacher Institute, New
York, N.Y.

Eisman, Howard D., Ph.D.,
Chief Psychologist, Coney Island Hospital,
Brooklyn, N.Y. Formerly, Associate Director,
Somerville Guidance Center.

Fine, Paul M., M.D.,
Director, Division of Child and Adolescent
Psychiatry, Department of Psychiatry,
Creighton University School of Medicine,
Omaha, Neb.

Graham, Elizabeth, M.S.W.,
Executive Director, Northside Center for
Child Development, New York, N.Y.

Greer, Joanne G., Ph.D.,
Deputy Chief, National Center for the
Prevention and Control of Rape, National
Institute of Mental Health, Rockville, Md.

Greydanus, Donald E., M.D.,
Director, Adolescent Medical Clinic, Division
of Biosocial Pediatrics and Adolescent
Medicine, School of Medicine and Dentistry,
The University of Rochester Medical Center,
Rochester, N.Y.

Jekel, James F., M.D., M.P.H.,
Professor of Public Health, Department of
Epidemiology and Public Health, Yale
University Medical School, New Haven,
Conn.

Klerman, Lorraine V., Dr., P.H.,
Associate Professor, Public Health, The
Florence Heller Graduate School for
Advanced Studies in Social Welfare, Brandeis
University, Waltham, Mass.

Lightman, Ernie S., **Ph.D.**,
Associate Professor, **Faculty of Social Work**,
University of Toronto, Toronto, Ontario,
Canada.

Mindick, Burton, Ph.D.,
Research Associate, Department of Human
Development and Family Studies, Visiting
Assistant Professor, Department of Human
Service Studies, College of Human Ecology,
Cornell University, Ithaca, N.Y.

Neuhoff, Sol D., M.D.,
Physician in Charge, Adolescent Obstetrics
and Gynecology, Department of Obstetrics
and Gynecology, Brookdale Hospital Medical
Center, Brooklyn, N.Y.; Clinical Instructor,
Department of Obstetrics and Gynecology,
State University of New York, Downstate
Medical Center, Brooklyn, N.Y.

Olson, Lucy, Ph.D.,
Department of Psychiatry, University of
Massachusetts, School of Medicine,
Northampton, Mass.

Oskamp, Stuart, Ph.D.,
Professor, Psychology, Claremont Graduate
Schools, Claremont, Calif.

Pape, Mary, M.S.,
Educational Therapist, Uta Halee Girls
Village, Omaha, Neb.

Paul, Eve W., J.D.,
Vice-President for Legal Affairs, Planned
Parenthood Federation of America Inc., New
York, N.Y.

Philliber, Susan Gustavus, Ph.D.,
Associate Professor, Center for Population
and Family Health, College of Physicians
and Surgeons, Columbia University, New
York, N.Y.

Rogel, Mary J., Ph.D.,
Director, Young Adult and Adolescent
Decision Making About Contraception
Project, Laboratory for the Study of
Adolescence, Michael Reese Hospital and
Medical Center, Chicago, Ill.

Rollins, Joan, Ph.D.,
Professor, Department of Psychology, Rhode
Island College, Providence, R.I.

Sacker, Ira M., M.D.,
Chief, Adolescent Medical Program,
Brookdale Hospital Medical Center,
Brooklyn, N.Y.; Assistant Professor
Department of Pediatrics, State University of
New York, Downstate Medical Center,
Brooklyn, N.Y.

Scales, Peter, Ph.D.,
Senior Research Analyst, Mathtech Inc.;
Director, Project on Barriers to Sex
Education, Washington, D.C.

Schaap, Paula, J.D.,
Legal Consultant, Planned Parenthood
Federation of America, Inc., New York,
N.Y.

Schlesinger, Benjamin, Ph.D.,
Professor, Faculty of Social Work, University
of Toronto, Toronto, Ontario, Canada.

Shea, Fredericka P., M.S.,
Associate Professor, Center for Health
Research, College of Nursing, Wayne State
University, Detroit, Mich.

Streett, Rosalie, B.S.,
Parenting Education Specialist, The Johns
Hopkins Center for Teen-Aged Parents and
their Infants, The Johns Hopkins University,
Baltimore, Maryland.

Zuehlke, Martha E., M.D.,
Clinical Director, Young Adult and
Adolescent Decision Making About
Contraception Project, Laboratory for the
Study of Adolescence, Michael Reese
Hospital and Medical Center, Chicago, Ill.;
Director, Child Psychiatry Liaison Service,
Department of Psychiatry, Michael Reese
Hospital and Medical Center, Chicago,
Illinois.

About the Editors

Irving R. Stuart, Ph.D. is Professor of Psychology, Herbert H. Lehman College, City University of New York. He has taught at Hunter College . . . served as a psychologist with the Department of Personnel Service at Brooklyn College, CUNY . . . completed a Fellowship at the Marriage Council of Philadelphia . . . and conducted a private practice in family and adolescent therapy for many years. Author of numerous research articles on personality formation and child development, Dr. Stuart has also co-edited books on the effects of family disruption on children's behavior, interpersonal relations in interracial marriages, and other topics. Among his books is *Self-Destructive Behavior in Children and Adolescents,* co-edited by Carl F. Wells and published by Van Nostrand Reinhold.

Carl F. Wells, Ph.D. is Associate Professor in the Department of Psychology, Herbert H. Lehman College, CUNY. He has been a member of the Department of Psychiatry, Albert Einstein College of Medicine . . . a consultant to the Family Treatment Unit at Creedmoor State Hospital, New York . . . and Research Director at New York Services for Orthopedically Handicapped. Currently on the Board of Directors of — and also Director of Research for — Save A Marriage, Inc., Dr. Wells has written articles and lectured on multiple family therapy, family interaction and marital therapy, and related subjects.

Preface

It is no surprise to those in the mental health services, or to professionals in gynecological and obstetrical specialties, nursing, and population research, that national statistics indicate that teenage pregnancy has reached alarming proportions during the past decade. Not only are two-thirds of young unmarried American women experiencing coitus by age nineteen, but one million teenage girls become pregnant each year; four out of every ten become pregnant; and three out of ten married teens with babies had conceived prior to marriage.

The cumulative result of these sexual and pregnancy experiences is manifested in the form of legal conflicts regarding the status of adolescent mothers and the rights of their children; heated controversy about abortion—whether supported with public funds or not; disagreements regarding policy on family planning and contraceptive advice programs; and dismay over the financial cost to taxpayers and the human suffering and deprivation.

This volume offers a group of original contributions prepared expressly for it and solicited by the editors from among the most distinguished leaders in the field. In selecting the contributions, the editors have focused on the salient problems of the subject and on creative, innovative approaches to solutions rather than merely on reviews of the existing literature or historical accounts.

The purpose of the book is to provide a reference text for teachers and students in such fields as human sexuality, population research, adolescent behavior and psychology, family interaction, adolescent health, parenting, psychology of self-destructive behavior, and counseling and intervention techniques. An equally important purpose is to offer an organized presentation of programs and techniques for the clinical practitioner working with adolescents. The experienced professional as well as the novice will find much useful material in this volume. While the majority of chapters have direct relevance and application to programs for adolescents, theoretical foundations have not been neglected. There is much here which takes from, and gives to, personality theory, attitude and attribution theories, self theories, and family systems approaches.

The book is divided into four sections. This is not entirely satisfactory to us, since we recognize the difficulty in making certain distinctions which the titles of the sections convey. It is somewhat artificial to make a clear separation between preventive and treatment aspects contained in several of the chapters placed in different sections. In a similar vein, those articles based on empirical research that also contain suggestions pertinent to program planning cannot be easily assigned to a particular part of the book. Thus alerted, the reader can be given a brief outline without being misled by the titles of the four parts of the book.

Part I, *Legal Considerations* reviews the contemporary legal status of teenagers and the effects of pregnancy and motherhood on the rights of the mothers and their illegitimate children.

Part II, *Needs,* surveys a broad range of conditions faced by these young people. Not only are the social and medical perspectives reviewed, but those social networks considered essential for the well-being of the teenagers are examined. Several chapters are devoted to studies of the factors contributing to contraceptor failure in a knowledgeable population.

Part III, *Problems,* presents the broad range of factors that affect teenagers, both before and after conception.

Part IV, *Management,* addresses itself to a wide variety of problems professionals have encountered and dealt with among populations of pregnant adolescents.

We wish to thank each of the contributors for taking time from their heavy schedules to write their chapters. We also thank them for their patience with the editors.

We also wish to express our appreciation for the assistance and patience of Susan Munger and Alberta Gordon, our editors on the staff of the publisher.

I.R.S.   White Plains
C.F.W.   New York City

Introduction

Adolescent Pregnancy: An Overview of the Current Status of the Problem

Carl F. Wells, Ph.D.

The increasing number of adolescents who become pregnant each year has been a topic of serious concern among health professionals for more than a decade. The subject has become more than an irritating curiosity, it is now a "social problem." According to some accounts in the mass media, adolescent pregnancy has reached epidemic proportions.

Indicative of the growing concern is the fact that in 1978 Congress passed legislation entitled The Adolescent Health Services, and Pregnancy Prevention and Care Act. Among other things, this legislation created an Office of Adolescent Pregnancy Programs to award and monitor grants to adolescent pregnancy programs. The movement at the federal level may have been prompted by the increasing evidence accumulated by social scientists regarding the rise in teenage sexual activity and pregnancy.

Cause for continuing concern are the results of the most recent large-scale survey of teenage sexual behavior (Zelnik and Kantner, 1980). The results provide no consolation or reasons for optimism regarding the future. The survey findings indicate an increase in premarital adolescent pregnancy since the previous two similar surveys in 1971 and 1976 by the same investigators. The realities of adolescent pregnancy are overwhelming. Annually, 1.1 million teenagers, or 11 percent of all teenage females in the country become pregnant. About 750,000 of the pregnancies are unintended and lead to approximately 400,000 abortions, about 30 percent of all abortions in the country.

When examined closely the statistics do not reveal any simple answers to account for the rise in premarital pregnancy. Rather, it becomes apparent that there are many interacting variables that must be taken into account, and that the statistics also reflect certain social changes in our culture. What are the causes and consequences of the increase in pregnancy among teenagers? What can we do to diminish the harmful effects?

The present book confronts some of the many complex questions which seem to abound in this area and brings the greater clarity needed to implement techniques for diminishing and possibly eliminating the costly consequences of unwanted pregnancy. It is beyond the scope of this book to deal with the many philosophical questions and value-laden issues existing in this area of human behavior. However, our contributors all are keenly aware of the ethical and moral issues; and although it is not their concern to directly deal with them, they often point out the significant influence of prevailing and frequently conflicting societal attitudes.

Thus the present volume attempts to deal with the more specific questions regarding teenage pregnancy that are amenable to research; and to discuss the implications of consistent findings in the field for policy planning and implementation. It may appear to some readers that this is an approach which leans toward a pragmatic problem-solving view at the expense of required theory building. It should be stated that the decision of the editors in choosing a focus has indeed been along the path of applied research and program planning. The contributors were instructed to give priority to material that would be most useful to the professionals working directly with teenagers.

Perhaps it bears repeating at this point that even though "there is nothing so practical as a good theory," theory construction and applied research or observations of the raw material of human behavior are inseparable. This holds true especially in the social sciences. It seems to me that understanding of the phenomenon of adolescent pregnancy is at that stage where we are still codifying the available research findings; we are not yet at a point where we have sufficiently explored the boundaries of this terrain. Therefore, we should be cautious about premature theorizing and the possibility of neglecting new approaches.

THE NATURE AND SCOPE OF THE PROBLEM

So many people are personally affected by adolescent pregnancy in today's world that it makes sense to outline the nature of the problem by thinking of the reaction of the intelligent layperson when confronted with the facts regarding the rise in teenage pregnancy as reported in the media. We can speculate with some confidence that the individual's response soon becomes a series of questions such as those posed below. The questions give evidence of the complexity of the problem; they also provide a framework setting forth the task for professionals hoping to supply responsive answers and eventual solutions to this major social problem.

Is there more sexual activity among teenagers these days? Is the increase due to the ready availability of contraceptives? If they are using contraceptives, why the increase in pregnancy? Which teenagers are sexually active—those in rural areas, minority group members, middle-class suburban kids, neurotic problem kids, those from broken homes? If the statistics show an increase in abortion, does it mean that adolescents are not worried about becoming pregnant when they have intercourse? What happens to the pregnant teenagers who do not have abortions?

There are also many questions raised about the role of the family and society at large such as: What are we teaching these kids, or not teaching them? Maybe the sex education in schools is inadequate. Are the parents of these teenagers responsible? We deplore the extent to which aggression and violence are depicted in

movies and television and the effect on children; what about the tremendous increase of sexual material in the mass media and the impact on teenagers?

Then there are the questions regarding the future: Is this a temporary situation
or will there continue to be an increase in teenage sexual activity and pregnancy?
What can be done effectively to deal with this problem?

Finally, we must include those questions which indicate a doubt whether in
fact there is a problem. Does adolescent pregnancy affect the general public, and
if so, how? What are the costs to the taxpayer? Is something happening to the
American family or is it merely experiencing an anticipated change from the out-
moded form of the traditional family structure? If teenagers are having out-of-
wedlock children and prefer to remain single mothers, is this just one of the results of the women's liberation movement? Is it liberating, and for whom?

The present book attempts to answer the majority of the questions posed
above. The contributors, as experts in their respective fields, deal with the questions directly in most instances and with the more philosophical, ethical issues
either directly or indirectly. We present in this volume relevant chapters in the
four parts of the book which deal with the results of studies telling us how many
and which teenagers are sexually active, becoming pregnant, and the nature of
contraceptive practice. Several chapters deal with the type of care the teenager
needs after becoming pregnant and with innovative programs for the new young
mother.

Considerable coverge is provided to the issues inherent in the relationship of
the teenager and her family which reflects the growing awareness in the field of
the important influences at work in this part of the adolescent's life space. An
additional critical aspect of the topic is discussed in several chapters devoted to
adolescent contraceptive behavior and the decision-making process. The growing recognition of the importance of the male partner is reflected in several chapters which mention his influence on decisions about contraceptive use and
termination of pregnancy.

RESPONSES TO THE MULTIFACETED PROBLEM: THE ORGANIZATION OF THIS VOLUME

The legal aspects of teenage pregnancy must not be ignored in consideration of
any intervention with adolescents both prior to and after any pregnancies. It is
not only in the arena of the abortion controversy that attention has been given to
the rights of teenagers; but greater attention is now paid to the legal rights of
children in all aspects of their relationships with parents and other adults.

Thus we have regarded it vital to devote Part I of the present volume to a chapter which outlines legal rights and responsibilities as a background for the more
familiar aspects of our topic presented in subsequent chatpers. Eve Paul and
Paula Schaap review the legal issues involved and point out that it is important

for a counselor working with teenagers to be sufficiently knowledgeable so that the rights of both the woman and her child may be protected. They carefully review the legal decisions and thinking centering around the issue of parental consent for abortion, and point out that an important derivative issue is still to be argued before the Supreme Court. The authors also provide guidelines for consent for medical treatment of the teenager. The important issue of financial support of the teenager and her child is examined as are questions about the rights of the illegitimate child and the putative father. The authors conclude their chapter with discussion of the legal considerations for teenagers who wish to keep their child, those who place the child for adoption, and those who put the child in foster care placements.

The second part of this book (Part II), which we call "Needs," includes a comprehensive overview of the topic of adolescent pregnancy by Joy Dryfoos. She provides answers at a general level to several of the commonly asked questions listed in the preceding section regarding how many adolescents are getting pregnant, and who they are. She uses available statistics to show that effective use of clinics and contraceptives does have an impact. Dryfoos emphasizes the well-documented finding that the level of knowledge about reproduction that teenagers have is certainly insufficient to protect them from unwanted pregnancy. She also notes that parents do not know much more than their children. Consistent with these facts, she outlines interventions based on education and family-planning services which are appropriate at different stages of development of the child. The author closes by reminding the reader we have reason to be optimistic—with respect to fertility control, specific programs have made a difference in the past and can do so in the future.

The question of how health professionals can help meet the needs of the adolescent at risk is approached by Donald Greydanus in the second chapter of Part II. Dr. Greydanus notes that attitudes toward sexuality have changed dramatically in the last 50 years and that if children and parents are taught to respect and accept their own sexuality, the concept of responsible sex functioning can make sense to the teenager. Within a framework which underlines the developmental stage of the adolescent and the need for establishing a good one-to-one relationship, the author stresses the need for the health professional to be knowledgeable regarding the contraceptive alternatives. There is no ideal contraceptive for all individuals. The author presents an overview of available contraceptive methods noting the accompanying advantages and disadvantages.

For the teenager who becomes pregnant, proper prenatal care is a vital necessity. Elizabeth Cooper (Chapter 4) reminds us that teenagers are too often not getting the care they require. She refers to the fact that most studies show that many teenagers deliver their babies without any care at all, despite the generally accepted view that pregnancy in the teenage years may be dangerous for both mother and baby. The author outlines the ideal prenatal program. An important component of the program is the nurse-midwife who can be an ideal care provider for the pregnant teenager. As with most of the contributions in this book, Cooper underlines the importance of education for the adolescent; in this instance education about self-care during pregnancy and in preparation for being a good mother.

An additional dimension of the topic of "needs of the pregnant adolescent" is the concern of Fine and Pape (Chapter 5) who stress the necessity of accurate diagnosis, especially family diagnosis, in order to guide adolescents making decisions affecting a pregnancy. These authors point out that pregnancy has special implications for each stage of adolescence; each stage requires specific help. Their cognizance of the importance of the girl's relationship to her family leads them to a discussion of the parameters of family diagnosis and the kinds of goals that can be realistically aimed for by the professional. Several brief case illustrations are presented to stress the urgency of taking into consideration the personal needs, ecological networks (such as family and peer group relationships), and professional service networks when working with adolescents.

The section of the book which we have referred to as "Problems, Before and After Pregnancy" (Part III) is comprised of several chapters dealing with a variety of crucial variables, such as medical problems of pregnancy, failure to use contraception, and personality factors that may be implicated in contraceptive behavior.

Sacker and Neuhoff (Chapter 6) discuss the medical problems that may be significantly associated with adolescent pregnancy. They give the reader a balanced and objective view of the various possible risks to the adolescent and her baby. They point out the difference between chronological age and gynecologic age indicating that biologic maturity plays an important role in pregnancy outcome. They are also concerned with the psychosocial risk factors and thus give us a picture of the bleak future facing many adolescent mothers and of the difficulties in the development of their children.

The question of the role played by personality factors in adolescent pregnancy continues to be largely unanswered. Although the need for more individualized approaches in counseling and educating the adolescent is recognized and echoed by professionals in the field, to date there have been too few studies which attempt to elucidate the influence of personality on contraceptive behavior and pregnancy resolution. We have included several contributions which are in the direction of filling this gap in our knowledge.

Mindick and Oskamp (Chapter 7) are interested in the personality characteristics that are influential determinants of contraceptive behavior. They point out that we are no longer dealing with a problem that is characteristic of certain segments of the population, and that reliance on only demographic descriptions is now quite unsatisfactory as a way of understanding behavior in this area. They also question the view that adolescent pregnancy is a product of severe psycho-

pathology. A theoretical model which seeks to explain effectiveness or ineffectiveness in the planning of births is presented. Effective birth planning, it is
maintained, ". . . is related to adequate socialization, positive self-concept, a
disposition to seek and use knowledge, and a willingness to look ahead and plan
for future contingencies." The authors describe a longitudinal predictive study
used, in part, to validate the theory. The results showed several significant differences between the successful and unsuccessful adolescents as predicted by the
personality indices, but the attitude measures used did not yield significant differences. These authors found in an additional investigation that side effects from
use of contraception, rather than being a cause of discontinuation of the birth
control and unintended pregnancy, are frequently simply mediating variables between these negative outcomes and personality characteristics. One major conclusion of Mindick and Oskamp is that identification of high-risk patients in
clinic settings is possible before an unwanted pregnancy and that prevention
strategies can be individualized.

We continue the exploration of the influence of personality variables on contraceptive behavior with the discussion by Olson and Rollins (Chapter 8) of the
"psychological barriers" that may prevent teenagers from effectively using birth
control. They describe a study they conducted to determine the extent to which
various birth-control devices are perceived as accessible, or their "psychological
availability." The results show that actual availability of contraceptives is not an
accurate index of their psychological availability, nor of their use. The authors
note that family-planning programs must take into account the cognitive, attitudinal, and motivational factors related to contraceptive behavior if they are to be
effective.

The contribution by Rogel, Zuehlke, and Petersen (Chapter 9) also explores
various influences on adolescent contraceptive behavior. Within a framework
outlining the various factors which at times have been shown to play a part in
birth control, the authors note the value of using a decision-making analysis in
understanding why some teenagers contracept and others do not. They also note
that the peer group seems to be particularly influential in the teenager's sexual
life and is a major source of information. Not an unexpected finding for adolescents.

Some studies have shown that the problem of unplanned pregnancies is in part
a problem of communication (between sexual partners and interpersonal communication skills in general). The latter part of the Rogel, Zuehlke, and Petersen
chapter describes the development of a primary prevention project based on the
premise that professionals must be aware of the many factors influencing behavior in the target population. The theoretical framework for the intervention project was based on a cost/benefit analysis of contraceptive behavior. The approach
provided some additional insight regarding why teenagers become pregnant.

Consistent with the earlier chapters in this volume which emphasize personality factors, the cost/benefit approach forces us to pay close attention to how the adolescents perceive and interpret their own experiences. It also merits emphasis that the application of the prior research findings to the development of the curriculum for the intervention project in the Rogel et al. study demonstrates the practicality of good theorizing.

The final chapter in this section of the book deals with the critical decision faced by pregnant adolescents of whether to deliver or abort. Klerman, Bracken, Jekel, and Bracken (Chapter 10), after reviewing the present knowledge regarding adolescent abortion, report the results of their own study of the delivery-abortion decision. Seven variables discriminated between the group of teenagers deciding to deliver and the group that decided to abort. The two groups did not differ on the measures of psychological functioning used in this study. One of the variables that showed a significant association with the pregnancy resolution decision was the adolescent's relationship with her sexual partner. Another discriminating variable was the "attitude toward abortion." The authors observe that the findings strongly suggest that the pregnancy resolution decision is related, for the most part, to circumstances surrounding the particular pregnancy. This view is supported by the findings of other studies, too, that adolescents often reverse their decisions (about whether to deliver or abort) from pregnancy to pregnancy.

The final section of this book (Part IV) is comprised of chapters concerned with applied problems and direct intervention programs—the "Management" section. The section opens with the Ager, Shea, and Agronow paper (Chapter 11) which discusses the findings of their study of 143 teens in a birth-control program followed over an 18-month period. The authors found that about 40 percent of the subjects continued on an effective method of birth control over the 18-month period. For those who discontinued contraception, the most frequent reason given was side effects of the pill, either experienced or feared. The writers indicate that a useful strategy within teen contraceptive programs may be to systematically prepare the teens for those situations and experiences known to cause them to terminate use of effective birth-control methods—for example, by using film dramatizations. They conclude by underlining the need for improved program procedures to prevent contraceptive discontinuance.

The role of the male partner has rarely been considered in discussions of teenage pregnancy. The contribution by Scales and Beckstein (Chapter 12) is devoted to this important facet of our topic. These authors suggest that as the pill became the method of choice, and contraception became more "politicized" as one consequence of the women's liberation movement, men were excluded from the mainstream of family-planning services. The chapter traces the developments which have led to remedying the neglect of the role of males and the more recent interest in men in this field. The authors address the salient issues with respect to male sexuality and the factors that must be taken into account in successful birth-control programs—such as male sexual myths, and the male influence on the decision-making process in contraceptive use and pregnancy resolution. The list provided of the "Best Educational Materials for Teenage Men and Men's Program Staff" at the end of the chapter is a valuable resource for many readers.

The growing recognition of the significance of the relationship of the teenager to her family relative to unplanned pregnancy is underlined here by the contribution of Authier and Authier (Chapter 13) on intervention with the families of pregnant adolescents. Here we have another valuable approach to answering questions about which individuals get pregnant. The writers briefly review for us some basic concepts used by family theorists who view the family as a dynamic system of complex relationships among its members. They point out the significance of family homeostasis, family rules, family myths, and family developmental stage as these concepts are used relative to the phenomenon of adolescent pregnancy. This sets the stage for the discussion of treatment of the pregnancy as a family crisis and of the intervention techniques that are useful within this approach to resolution of the problem. The authors also give attention to the needs of the family as well as to those of the adolescent—another often neglected aspect of the topic.

It may be that some segments of the public believe that adolescents who become pregnant are severely disturbed—neurotic or psychotic. This answer to the question of who becomes pregnant is rarely given by professionals these days. Perhaps because it is inconceivable that such a vast number of teenagers throughout the nation could be so afflicted; or more likely an explanation is that experienced professionals do not see other symptoms indicative of severe pathology in the vast majority of pregnant teenagers with whom they work. Nevertheless, as depicted in most of the preceding contributions reviewed, we cannot ignore the critical role often played by emotional factors in contraceptive behavior and in pregnancy resolution decisions. The paper by Eisman and Covan (Chapter 14) reminds us that there are a substantial number of cases where the pregnancy is a consequence of rather severe emotional problems of the youngster. The authors discuss the use of pregnancy by some adolescents as an attempt to resolve interpersonal and intrapsychic conflicts. The discussion is based on their clinical experience and they present several case illustrations of emotionally disturbed pregnant adolescents. They stress the importance of the family situation and emphasize family therapy as a major modality when possible when working with disturbed adolescents.

The most recent statistics indicate that over 90 percent of unwed teenage mothers are retaining custody of their infants. At the same time there is undeniable evidence that many of these young mothers, their families, and their infants suffer serious deprivations because of the birth and retention of the infant. The chapter by Ann DeRose (Chapter 15) describes a program developed as an attempt to ameliorate some of the harmful consequences of pregnancy for adolescents. The author traces the development of the school-based program aimed at preventing the pregnant adolescent who does not choose abortion from being forced to drop out of school. She gives a detailed account of the curriculum and also provides suggestions, based on her experience, for those interested in initiating a similar program.

The unmarried adolescent who chooses to give birth to the child has not always completed making the decisions related to the pregnancy. Many of these youngsters are uncertain about whether to raise their child or to give it up for adoption or foster care. Lightman and Schlesinger (Chapter 16) develop profiles of the adolescents making use of maternity homes who keep their infants and those who surrender them for adoption. They also suggest various services to provide for the needs of these groups of teenagers.

Addressing the plight of the pregnant young girl who cannot bring herself to abort but is not willing to mother her child, Joanne Greer (Chapter 17) advocates a return to the routine and serious consideration of adoptive placement for the infant. She briefly describes the counseling needs of the young mother of an infant placed for adoption. The author also stresses the point that if the reasons for unintended pregnancy in teenagers are so varied, there must be varied approaches to case management strategy. In her concluding remarks, Greer cites the results of a study by Schlesinger and his conclusions presented at the American Orthopsychiatric Association meeting in 1980 noting that the wrong girls (those least likely to be adequate mothers) were keeping their babies as compared to those girls who relinquished babies for adoption.

An additional contribution in this section of the book concerned with methods of preventing the harmful consequences of early motherhood is the paper by Bierman and Streett (Chapter 18). Based on their experiences at The Johns Hopkins Center for Teenaged Parents and Their Infants the writers stress the importance of recognizing the needs of the teenage mother lest these interfere with them being adequate mothers to their infants. Case illustrations are used effectively to indicate how the needs of the mother at various ages of the girls may be detrimental if adequate professional help is not provided.

The final chapter of this volume deals with still another aspect of teenage pregnancy—the problem of rapid repeat pregnancies. Darabi, Graham, and Philliber (Chapter 19) believe that to plan more effective postpartum counseling programs, characteristics of teenagers at greatest risk of rapid subsequent pregnancies need to be identified. The authors studied minority group adolescents who delivered their first child on the wards of a New York hospital and report that in their sample 76 percent had not experienced a subsequent birth within 30 months after their first. Two variables seem to be important in explaining the repeat pregnancy or repeat childbearing in these youngsters: these are, living arrangements and whether there is return to school after the first child is born.

CONCLUSION

As noted earlier in this chapter, the present volume attempts to answer many of the questions commonly raised about adolescent pregnancy. It may be useful at this point to briefly summarize the present state of knowledge and the kind of information we still need to acquire regarding unintended teenage pregnancy.

The present contributions add to the existing literature and together present an unambiguous answer to those questions about whether there is really a problem—unfortunately, an affirmative answer. Available studies leave no doubt about the seriousness of the medical risks associated with teenage pregnancy. There is increased incidence of infant mortality, prematurity, and the neurological impairments often linked with prematurity. The medical risks are also greater for the young mother than for older women who become pregnant. Early childbearing often leads to rapid subsequent pregnancies and thus increased obstetrical risk for the teenager. Several chapters in this book deal in detail with the risks involved to infant and mother and with the kinds of programs needed to minimize the dangers for adolescents who choose to carry to term.

In addition to the medical risks there are often severe social and psychological consequences of early pregnancy reported by many studies. The sudden change in status from being a child to a mother brings critical disruptions and dislocations in the youngster's life and development. Generally, there is an interruption or permanent cessation of the girl's education; and this usually produces serious limitations on career choice and earning power. The state of pregnancy often leads to bad marriages and/or severe marital problems and divorce, which in turn may cause psychological distress, loss of self-esteem, and further self-destructive behavior. Several chapters of this book describe intervention programs aimed at helping the teenager avoid these pitfalls.

Although we do not devote space in this book to the financial costs to the taxpaying public because of the great number of adolescent pregnancies, it should be remembered that this, too, constitutes a major problem. It is especially significant when we realize how frequently early motherhood leads to the vicious cycle of loss of opportunity and dependency on welfare—and is passed to subsequent generations. It must be noted also that family-planning programs (especially if ineffective) supported by public funds drain money from other needed public programs.

One category of questions regarding adolescent pregnancy, noted above, has to do with the girl's relationship to her family. A recurrent theme of much of the recent literature has been that the adolescent's conflicts, interpersonal and intrapsychic, are important determinants of her pregnancy. Another growing area of interest is the topic of the family's reaction to the youngster's pregnancy—how does the family handle the crisis and what are the effects on the family? Some of our contributors pay particular attention to these questions. For the most part, the indications are that sacrifices have to be made to accommodate the new mother and her child in the family structure. There are, however, some writers who point out that there may be beneficial consequences for the family. For example, Furstenberg (1980) states that the pregnancy has some, ". . . redeeming features for the family, such as building family morale, intensifying family exchanges, and filling the empty nest." (p. 84) I wonder whether these redeeming features are really worth the other costs that are involved; the benefits mentioned by Furstenberg could be accomplished by means other than the pregnancy of a teenager. Furstenberg's comment must be understood as made within a context where he advocates that greater attention be given to the family's role and that we need more information about the impact of early childbearing on the family.

The persistent questions about which adolescents become pregnant remain incompletely answered. The results of the latest Zelnik and Kantner (1980) survey provide some important information and partial answers. The available preliminary report of their findings indicates that the rate of premarital pregnancies among teenage women almost doubled between 1971 and 1979. The increase is attributed to the growing number of teenagers who are sexually active; the proportion of teenagers living in metropolitan areas who have had sexual experience increased from 30 percent in 1971 to 50 percent in 1979. Almost all of the increase since the 1976 survey is due to greater sexual activity on the part of white adolescents. The average age at which women begin intercourse has remained around 16 since 1971.

The available statistics also indicate that it is younger adolescents, regardless of race, who are at greater risk of becoming pregnant. The research also confirms our commonsense thinking that those youngsters who have never used contraception, or discontinued contraception, or use ineffective contraceptive methods are more likely to become pregnant. Many of the authors in this book go beyond these general findings which fail to account for the behavioral factors responsible for nonuse or ineffective use of contraception. It is well established that in large numbers of cases it is due to more than just ignorance of biological facts or of availability of contraceptives.

Work in this field has progressed from collecting the basic statistical and demographic data to the stage where we have begun to focus on the behavior of the individuals and systematically search for causal factors. Some examples of the latter type of inquiry are: the work of researchers who conceptualize women as "contraceptive risk-takers" and study the steps involved in their decision-making processes (Luker, 1975); the investigation of "psychological barriers" to effective birth control by Olson and Rollins reported in this volume; the cost/benefit approach applied to adolescent decision making used by Rogel et al., also in this volume; the investigation of personality traits associated with contraceptive practice described here by Mindick and Oskamp; and the Klerman et al. study of the decision to deliver or abort. These approaches have in common a close contact with the adolescents, usually by way of interview, in order to better understand their behavior. There is also greater opportunity for serendipitous findings to appear.

As we have gained greater understanding of the sexual and contraceptive behavior of teenagers we have also acquired new opportunities to explore the possibilities of new preventive and remedial programs. For example, having learned that a lack of communication between the teenager and her partner, or her mother, is often a causal factor in failure to use birth control, we can teach youngsters how to communicate more effectively. Schinke and Gilchrist (1977) used an interpersonal skill training program with a group of 13- to 19-year-old adolescents and they are optimistic about the efficacy of the approach in preventing pregnancies due to teenagers' deficits in such skills.

It has also been shown that for many adolescents the lack of realistic career opportunities and their low self-esteem push them in the direction of early motherhood. Therefore, good sex-education programs these days incorporate discussions of careers for women as alternatives to the career of motherhood.

In this brief summary of the state of our knowledge, and our look at the many forces that impinge on the individual teenager and affect her decision making, we cannot ignore the major changes that have occurred in society. As noted earlier in this chapter, television and the other mass media have greatly increased their use of sexual material. Teenagers have been exposed to a tremendous bombardment of explicit and implicit sexual material over the last decade—without being offered any meaningful guidelines on how to interpret this material or on how it applies to their own lives. In addition to the increase in open sexuality there have been rapid changes in women's attitudes toward the role of women in society. One major change is the movement toward equality with men including the area of sexual behavior. Therefore, there is now greater independence and freedom for women to make their own decisions about when, where, and with whom to have sex. There is also greater individual freedom about living together rather than marriage, and also about choosing to be a single parent. If these are the social realities confronting today's adolescents, it is little wonder that there is an increase in sexual activity. But it is not mandatory that there be a concurrent increase in unwanted pregnancies! Pregnancy for the young adolescent is not freedom; it all too often becomes a confining cage robbing the youngster of her opportunity for self-realization and greater happiness. Adolescents need to be taught (by methods better than those used today) the meaning of freedom and how to make responsible decisions.

It will become apparent to the reader that despite being faced with the complex problems of adolescent pregnancy and the human misery generated by this aspect of human behavior, there is no apathy or defeatism expressed by the contributors to this volume. Rather, it seems to me, there is a sense of slowly gathering strength and of optimism. I detect an attitude of "we already know much, we know what we need to find out, and we know what we need to try." Expressed somewhat differently, it appears to me that we are ready for the types of research that study individuals more intensively, and study the many implicated variables in an interactive manner. We are ready for the blending of social science perspectives which will allow us to account for the variances within our subgroups of subjects. I think we are moving toward a greater understanding of the individual teenager and that we will soon be able to develop a "profile of the teenager at risk" for pregnancy and a description of her decision making. Then we can apply our knowlege to more precisely fit our intervention methods to the individuals needing them.

REFERENCES

Furstenberg, F.F., Jr. Burdens and benefits: The impact of early childbearing on the family. *Journal of Social Issues* 1980, 36, 64–87.

Luker, K. *Taking Chances: Abortion and the decision not to contracept.* Berkeley: University of California Press, 1975.

Schinke, S.P. and Gilchrist, L.D. Adolescent pregnancy: An interpersonal skill training approach to prevention. *Social Work in Health Care* 3 (2), Winter 1977.

Zelnik, M. and Kantner, J.F. Sexual activity, contraceptive use and pregnancy among metropolitan-area teenagers: 1971–1979. *Family Planning Perspectives* 1980, 12, 230–237.

Contents

Pregnancy
in Adolescence
Needs, Problems, and Management

Part I
Legal Considerations

1.
Legal Rights and Responsibilities of Pregnant Teenagers and Their Children*

Eve W. Paul, J.D.,
Vice-President for Legal Affairs,
Planned Parenthood Federation of America, Inc.
New York, N.Y.

and

Paula Schaap, J.D.,
Legal Consultant,
Planned Parenthood Federation of America, Inc.
New York, N.Y.

Teenage pregnancy poses many legal problems. The initial question which must be asked is whether the woman wants to have the child at all. The United States Supreme Court has stated that teenagers, as well as adults, have a fundamental constitutional right of privacy which includes the right to decide to have an abortion. Many unmarried teenagers will exercise the right to terminate their pregnancies. We will discuss attempts being made to restrict the teenager's right to obtain an abortion without getting consent from, or notifying, her parents.

If a teenager decides to carry her pregnancy to term, other legal issues arise. The teenager's need for medical care and her ability to obtain such care on her own consent are discussed in this chapter. Financial support, either from parents or through public assistance programs, is essential for teenage parents. The issue of the rights of illegitimate children, including their right to support from their fathers, is also dealt with. Finally, we discuss what happens when a teenage parent is unable to care for his or her child. Adoption and foster care are two alternatives, but each may result in termination of the natural parent's rights.

It is, therefore, crucial that the teenage parent be aware of the laws in these areas.

*The authors wish to express their thanks to Martin Guggenheim, Clinical Professor of Law at New York University, who reviewed the manuscript.

3

INTRODUCTION

When a teenager becomes pregnant the decisions that she makes during and after her pregnancy are critically affected by statutes and court decisions. Some of the questions which a teenager and her counselor may have to deal with that require legal answers include: Can she obtain an abortion without parental consent or notification? How does she surrender her child for adoption? What are the rights of the father of the child? Whose obligation is the child's support?

The answers to most of these questions are governed by domestic relations law which varies from state to state. There are limitations, however, to the states' sovereignty in this area; most significantly, rulings by the United States Supreme Court on constitutional issues protect the rights of the teenager and her child. In addition, domestic relations law has recently undergone important changes. Evolving psychological theories and the changing condition of women and children in American society have affected state courts and legislatures to varying degrees. A counselor who is assisting teenage parents or prospective parents must be careful, therefore, when a legal problem has been identified, to consult a local attorney.

The term "teenagers" is used here as referring to someone under 18, which is today the legal age of majority in almost all states. (Alabama, Nebraska, and Wyoming retain 19 as the age of majority; that age is still 21 in Colorado, for most purposes, and in Pennsylvania.)

The law generally does not allow minors to exercise the full legal rights enjoyed by adults. The traditional view was that children were totally subject to their parents' wishes (Wald, 1979). The rationale was that children are not capable of forming mature, reasoned decisions and must be protected from their own inexperience. Parents were given a large degree of control over their children's persons and property. Minors could not enter into many kinds of contracts. Some of the disabilities of minority have come under attack by proponents of children's rights (Sussman, 1977). Their criticism is that the law's treatment of children goes beyond protecting them, and indeed deprives them of important rights. Until recently, minors were not entitled to be represented by counsel in criminal trials; they still do not have the right to counsel in custody proceedings. In addition, the critics argue, parents do not always have their children's best interests at heart: in some circumstances the parents' wishes may directly conflict with their child's needs (Westman, 1979). Indeed, some children are victims of child abuse and incest. Courts and legislatures have in recent years greatly expanded the rights of young people.

It is important for the counselor to be able to identify the legal issues that arise in the context of teenage pregnancy, so that the rights of both the woman and her child are protected. This article will identify a number of those issues and discuss current trends in the law.

THE TEENAGE WOMAN'S RIGHT TO AN ABORTION

Abortion and the Supreme Court

For teenagers, the controversy over abortion centers mainly around the issue of parental consent. A woman's right to an abortion has been bitterly contested by antiabortion groups since the United States Supreme Court's landmark decisions, in 1973, of *Roe v. Wade*, 410 U.S. 113 and *Doe v. Bolton*, 410 U.S. 179. In those cases, the Court stated that the fundamental constitutional right of privacy protects the right of a woman, in consultation with her physician, to decide to terminate her pregnancy. In the first trimester of pregnancy, states may not restrict this right except by requiring that the procedure be performed by a licensed physician. After the first trimester and until the fetus becomes viable, states may restrict abortion, but only to protect the health of the pregnant woman. After viability, states may restrict and even prohibit abortion except if it is necessary to protect the woman's life or health. In *Roe* and *Doe*, the Supreme Court left open the question of whether a minor has a constitutional right to obtain an abortion.

Several years later, the question of a minor woman's right to an abortion came to the Court in the case of *Planned Parenthood of Central Missouri v. Danforth*, 428 U.S. 52 (1976). The Missouri statute challenged in that case required parental consent to a minor's abortion. The Court held that a minor has a fundamental right of privacy and a state cannot allow a third party, even a parent, to veto the minor's abortion decision.

Many legislatures continued to try to limit the right of teenagers to an abortion. A statute was enacted in Massachusetts which required parental consent for an unmarried minor's abortion, but provided that a judge could grant consent if the parents refused. The statute would have required the teenager to inform her parents of her pregnancy since the court order would be available only after her parents refused consent. This statute was challenged in *Bellotti v. Baird*, 443 U.S. 622 (1979), and the Supreme Court declared it unconstitutional.

While the *Bellotti* decision was essentially favorable for the teenage woman, it also left some confusion in its wake. Although eight Justices agreed that the law was unconstitutional, they did not agree on the basis for the ruling. The Supreme Court handed down two separate opinions, each signed by four Justices.

The opinion written by Justice John Paul Stevens viewed the use of a court order as a tantamount to a third-party veto which the Court had found unconstitutional in *Planned Parenthood v. Danforth*. He noted that the need to seek a court order would impose a burden on the minor woman, perhaps as great a burden as having to seek parental consent (443 U.S. at 655).

Justice Lewis F. Powell's opinion was less protective of the teenager's right to an abortion. Although he wrote that "every minor must have the opportunity—if she so desires—to go directly to a court without first consulting or notifying her parents," Justice Powell nevertheless said that the rights of children cannot be equated to the rights of adults because of the "peculiar vulnerability of children" (443 U.S. at 634). His opinion outlined a statute which could pass constitutional muster. If the minor was unwilling or unable to seek parental consent, she would have to be able to demonstrate to a court or administrative agency either that she was mature enough to make the decision to have the abortion on her own, or, even if she was not mature, that an abortion would be in her best interest.

It is not clear how the statute proposed by Justice Powell would be implemented. One of its main problems is that it lengthens the time before a teenager can obtain an abortion. Studies have shown that a higher proportion of teenagers seek abortions late in their pregnancy than do adults (Department of Health, Education, and Welfare, 1977). The medical risks of abortion increase dramatically the later it is performed (Cates, 1977). Such a statute, therefore, would appear not to be in the best interest of the teenager. Massachusetts has enacted a new statute along the lines set forth in Justice Powell's opinion. The statute is now being challenged in the courts; a preliminary injunction has been denied.

The *Bellotti* decision did not definitively answer the question of whether a statute which requires only parental notification would be constitutional.[1] A case dealing with this issue, *H___ L___ v. Matheson*, 101 S. Ct. 1164, was decided by the Supreme Court in 1981. A requirement of parental notification before an abortion can be performed may be as detrimental as a requirement of parental consent, since many teenagers do not wish their parents to learn of their pregnancy at all, and may be driven to illegal practitioners. In *H___ L___*, the Supreme Court upheld, at least with respect to minors who are immature and dependent on their parents, a Utah requirement that parents be notified before an abortion is performed. The Court gave strong indications that it might reach a contrary result for emancipated minors and mature minors and in cases where it could be shown that notifying the parents would put the minor at risk.

While the law for minors seeking abortions is not settled, it is clear that a state cannot require parental consent without providing an alternative procedure for the minor woman (Paul and Pilpel, 1979). Although the Supreme Court has never considered the issue, it seems clear from the rationale of its decisions, as well as from lower court holdings in Maryland and Michigan,

---

[1]At the time of this writing, Maryland, Montana, and Utah have statutes requiring that parents be notified before an abortion is performed on their minor daughter; in Maryland, notification may be waived if the physician believes that it might result in physical or emotional abuse of the pregnant minor.

that parents cannot *compel* a minor to have an abortion. The minor's right to choose includes the right to carry her pregnancy to term (*In re* Smith, 295 A.2d 238 [Md. App. 1972]).

Medicaid Funding for Abortions

Although statutes which have attempted to limit a woman's right to abortion have been declared unconstitutional in virtually all cases, the Supreme Court has applied a different standard to statutes limiting federal funds available for abortion for indigent women.

Starting in 1976, Congress has each year passed an amendment to the annual health and welfare appropriations bill severely limiting the availability of Medicaid funds for abortion (Law, 1978). These amendments are known as the "Hyde Amendments" after their chief sponsor, Congressman Henry Hyde of Illinois. Under the Hyde Amendment, states may continue to fund abortions, but the federal government pays its share only in very limited circumstances. The most recent form of the Hyde Amendment provides that abortions will be funded only if the woman's life is in danger, or if the pregnancy resulted from rape or incest, promptly reported (Appropriations—Fiscal Year 1980—Continuance, Pub. L. No. 96-123 §109, 93 Stat. 926 [1979]). The Hyde Amendments were challenged as unconstitutional in *Harris v. McRae,* 100 S. Ct. 2671 (1980), but the Supreme Court sustained them. As in three prior Medicaid abortion cases which dealt with the obligation of states to fund abortions, (*Beal v. Doe,* 432 U.S. 438 [1977]; *Maher v. Roe,* 432 U.S. 464 [1977]; *Poelker v. Doe,* 432 U.S. 519 [1977]), the Court again said that while the government cannot unduly burden a woman's decision to have an abortion, it can choose to fund childbirth and not abortion.

For those women without funds for an abortion, the Supreme Court opinions are potentially devastating (Law, 1978). Many teenagers are eligible for Medicaid either through their families or, if they are living on their own, because of their limited earning capacity. A number of states, however, may continue to provide Medicaid abortions from state funds either by choice or under court order.[2] Unfortunately, this will not be of much help to a teenager

---

[2]At the time of the Supreme Court's opinion in *Harris v. McRae,* a number of states were under court order to fund all medically necessary abortions. These states included: California, Connecticut, Georgia, Illinois, Louisiana, Minnesota, Missouri, New Jersey, Ohio, Pennsylvania, Virginia, West Virginia, and Wisconsin. Each one of these orders must be challenged and vacated before these states can refuse to fund abortion.

In three states—Massachusetts, New Jersey, and California—a right to Medicaid reimbursement for abortions has been asserted under the *state* constitution. These cases are still in litigation.

As of this writing, the states that continue to pay voluntarily are Alaska, Colorado, Hawaii, Maryland, Michigan, New York, North Carolina, Oregon, Washington, and the District of Co-

who lives in a state which does not provide Medicaid abortions, if she does not meet the Hyde Amendment requirements. Under the Supreme Court case of *Shapiro v. Thompson,* 394 U.S. 618 (1969), states cannot require an individual to reside in that state for a specified period of time before qualifying for public assistance. The states can require, however, that the individual seeking Medicaid funding be a bona fide resident of the state. Residency requirements vary and some states are more lenient than others. A teenager who needs a funded abortion may, therefore, face a number of obstacles in seeking to effectuate her decision.

One alternative that may be open to teenagers is the rape exception to the Hyde Amendment. Many teenage pregnancies are the result of statutory (rather than forcible) rape. Each state has its own definition of statutory rape, setting the age under which even consensual intercourse is deemed rape; the age of the male is also a factor. A teenager who is the victim of statutory rape must promptly report the rape to the police or a public health agency to protect her right to Medicaid funding for an abortion (Benshoof and Donovan, 1979).

CARE OF MOTHER AND CHILD

Emancipation

It is possible for a minor to become emancipated from her parents and assume the rights and obligations of adulthood before reaching the age of majority. Traditionally, a minor was emancipated by marriage, entry into the armed forces, or when he/she left home and became self-supporting (Clark, 1968). The borderline cases occur when a minor is still living at home, but providing most of her own support, or when the parents supply some support while the minor lives on her own (Cady, 1979). Court decisions in this area vary from state to state and depend on the circumstances of the case. *(See, Parker v. Stage,* 43 N.Y. 2d 128, 371 N.E. 2d 513, 400 N.Y.S. 2d 794 [1977]; *Brunswick v. La Prise,* 262 A. 2d 366 [Me. 1970].) In response to the uncertainty of these situations, California and Connecticut recently enacted comprehensive bills dealing with emanicipation. (Cal. Civil Code §60-70 West Cum. Supp. [1980]; Conn. Pub. Acts 79-397 [1979]; Blackburn [1980].)

Whether a teenager has been legally emancipated will affect her life in a number of ways, including her ability to consent to medical care for herself and her child, her ability to obtain support from her parents, and eligibility

---

lumbia. The status of payment for abortion under Medicaid is subject to change within relative short time periods. The Hyde Amendment itself, as an amendment to an appropriations bill, must be voted upon yearly, and could fail to pass or be modified each year.

for public assistance. The legal effect of emancipation is to remove the disabilities of minority; for example, an emancipated minor can enter into contracts or receive medical care without her parents' consent. Emancipation is not necessarily total; a minor may be considered emancipated for some purposes and not for others (Sussman, 1977).

Medical Care

Consent to Medical Care. Traditionally, a minor could not consent to his/her own medical care. There were always exceptions to this general rule, however. A physician can treat a minor without parental consent in an emergency, when the minor is emancipated, or when a minor is "neglected" in that her parents are not willing to consent to necessary medical care (Brown and Truitt, 1979). Technically, a physician could be liable for assault and battery or negligence if he/she provided care for a minor without obtaining parental consent, unless one of these exceptions applied. No case has been found, however, holding a physician liable when the minor was over 15, the treatment was for the minor's benefit, and the minor gave his/her consent (Brenner, Pilpel, and Paul, 1978).

In recent years, many state legislatures have enacted statutes that allow minors to consent for certain types of medical treatment or for medical care generally. Many of these statutes provide a minimum age at which a minor can consent. For example, Alabama allows all minors 14 and older to consent to medical care (Ala. Code. tit. 22 §8-4 [1977]); Massachusetts allows minors 12 years and older to consent to treatment for drug addiction. (Mass. Ann. Laws. ch. 112 §12E [Michie/Law Co-op 1974].)

Many statutes also provide that a married minor may consent to medical care for herself, her spouse and her child. (Colo. Rev. Stat. §13-22-103 [Cum. Supp. 1979]; Ind. Code Ann. §16-8-4-1 [Burns 1973].)

In many states, minors may consent for medical care during pregnancy and for medical care of the child after birth. (Cal. Civil Code §34.5 [West Cum. Supp. 1980]; N.J. Stat. Ann. §19:17A-1 [West 1979].) By December, 1975, 31 states had enacted legislation enabling women under 18 to consent for pregnancy-connected care. By statute in every state, a minor may consent to treatment for venereal disease. (e.g. Ala. Code tit. 22 §8-6 [1977]; Ind. Code Ann. §16-8-5-1 [Burns 1973].) In some states, minors can consent to treatment for drug addiction (Colo. Rev. Stat. §13-22-102 [1973]; Minn. Stat. Ann. §144.343 [West Cum. Supp. 1979]), or alcohol abuse. (Ill. Ann. Stat. ch. 111 §4504 [Smith-Hurd Supp. 1980]; Minn. Stat. Ann. §144.343 [West Cum. Supp. 1979].)

Another category of minors who may give effective consent to medical treatment are "mature minors." The mature minor doctrine was created by case law (judge-made law) and some states have codified the rule by statute. Under this doctrine a physician may treat a minor on his/her own consent if the minor can understand the nature and consequences of the medical procedure, and it is for the minor's benefit (Brown and Truitt, 1979).

When a pregnant teenager needs medical care, and is unwilling to consult with her parents, a counselor should determine the following:

1. Is the teenager emancipated by marriage or otherwise? If so, she can consent to medical care for herself, her spouse, and her child. If the teenager is emancipated she will be responsible for the cost of medical care.

2. If she is not emancipated, does the state have a "mature minor" doctrine which will allow her to consent to treatment? If so, she can consent if she is sufficiently old and intelligent to understand the proposed treatment (Westman, 1979).

3. Is there a state statute that covers the minor's specific medical problem, e.g., pregnancy, venereal disease, or drug addiction? As noted, many states permit a minor to consent to all aspects of pregnancy-related care.

4. Does the minor have a constitutional right to the treatment sought, such as abortion or contraception?

As a practical matter, it is important to remember that, although a minor may have the right to obtain medical care on her own consent, a private hospital or physician may require parental consent as a condition of treatment. Few hospitals will admit an unmarried minor without the consent of her parents.

Financing Medical Care—Medicaid. The Medicaid program is a joint federal-state program. If a state decides to participate—all states except Arizona participate in Medicaid—it must provide certain services in order to qualify for federal funds. These mandatory services include inpatient hospital, outpatient, physician, x-ray, and laboratory, nursing home, EPSDT (Early and Periodic Screening, Diagnosis, and Treatment of Children under 21), and family-planning services (Butler, 1974). An individual's eligibility for Medicaid is determined by his/her income level. The "categorically needy"—those for whom Medicaid is mandatory—are patients who qualify for public assistance: SSI (Supplemental Security Income), or AFDC (Aid to Families with Dependent Children) (McCormick, 1977). The states may, but are not compelled to, provide services for the "medically needy." The medically needy are those whose income is in excess of the state ceiling for welfare payments, but whose medical expenses are large enough to reduce their income below the state welfare eligibility level. (Butler, 1974).

A teenager may qualify for Medicaid on her own or her family may be entitled to Medicaid. Even if the family is not entitled to welfare benefits, medical costs of the pregnancy and care of the infant may bring the family's income within the Medicaid-eligible range. A local legal services office or the state Medicaid office should be consulted as to eligibility requirements and application procedures.

The early and periodic screening diagnosis and treatment program (EPSDT) is of special interest to young women and their children. The program was enacted to screen eligible children under 21 for medical problems, and to provide comprehensive diagnosis and treatment for all medical conditions found. Unfortunately, EPSDT has not had the beneficial effect that was envisioned. There has been a shortage of providers willing to provide comprehensive screening, particularly in rural areas, and many of the state Medicaid programs have proved unwilling or unable to advertise and successfully implement the program. In 1979, Congress once again revised the program, providing for stronger enforcement measures and penalties for failure to comply (Rosenbaum, 1980). It remains to be seen whether this will effectively increase the number of families and children served by EPSDT.

In 1978, Congress passed the Adolescent Pregnancies Act, authorizing the Secretary of Health, Education, and Welfare (now Health and Human Services) to make grants for the provision of adolescent services (Title VI of Pub.L. No. 95-626, 42 U.S.C. 300a-21 et seq.). The act opens with a summary of congressional committee findings that adolescents are at especially high risk of unwanted pregnancy. It notes that "pregnancy and childbirth among adolescents, particularly young adolescents, often result in severe adverse health, social and economic consequences."

When eligible young people are unable to pay for services without financial assistance from their parents or legal guardians, and are unwilling to seek that assistance, DHEW regulations issued under the statute (effective July 23, 1979) require DHEW grantees to provide services gratis, regardless of the annual income of the parents or guardians.

Counselors should determine whether an EPSDT or Adolescent Pregnancies program is available in their area and assist eligible teenagers and their children to avail themselves of its services.

Financial Support of the Teenager and Her Child

Parental Support. In many states, a teenager's parents are liable for her support until she reaches 21, even though, in most states, the legal age of majority is 18. Usually, the father is primarily liable for his children's support, while the mother is liable only if the father is unable to provide support (Clark, 1968). There is a movement to change this inequality; some states now hold both parents liable.* (Ill. Ann. Stat. ch. 23 §10-2 [Smith-Hurd Supp. 1980]; *Pendexter v. Pendexter*, 363 A.2d 743 [Me. 1976].) In addition, a recent Supreme Court case, *Orr v. Orr*, 440 U.S. 268 (1979), held unconstitutional an Alabama law that imposed the obligation to pay alimony on the husband only. This case may affect many domestic relations laws that distinguish between male and female roles without a rational basis for the distinction. Thus, the holding in *Orr* may hasten the equalization of a mother's and father's duty to support their offspring.

The common-law duty of support is often enforceable by criminal statutes. (S.C. Code §20-7-40 [Cum. Supp. 1979].) The minor can also sue her father (and possibly her mother) for support. If her parents are divorced or separated, the separation agreement or divorce decree will usually provide for support payments. A delinquent parent is subject to a number of sanctions upon failure to comply with the terms of the agreement or decree (Clark, 1968). Many states have enacted the Uniform Support of Dependents Law to facilitate the enforcement of support obligations both within the state and across state lines.

What happens if the minor daughter has left her parents' home? If she is married, she is emancipated from her parents' control, and she and her spouse have a reciprocal duty to support each other and their child. The parents of a married teenager do not have a duty to support her. If she is emancipated through court order or by her acts—by becoming self-supporting, for example—she can usually no longer look to her parents for support. (*Parker v. Stage*, 43 N.Y. 2d 128, 371 N.E. 2d 513, 400 N.Y.S. 2d 794 [1977].) This is not always true, however; some courts have held that parents were liable for the support of minor children who live apart from them. (*Brunswick v. La Prise*, 262 A.2d 366 [Me. 1970].) If the parent has abandoned or neglected his child, he is still liable for the child's support (Clark, 1968).

Father's Support for his Child. As stated, if the minor woman is married, her spouse must support her and their child. If the infant is illegitimate, the parents are still liable for its support. (Ill. Ann. Stat. ch. 106 3/4 §52 [Smith-Hurd Supp. 1980]; N.J. Stat. Ann. §9:16-2 [West, 1976].) Before the father of an illegitimate child may be held liable for support, however, paternity must be proved. The question of paternity proceedings will be dealt with in the section on illegitimate children.

Aid to Families with Dependent Children. AFDC provides payments to families with dependent children when one parent is incapacitated or absent.

---

*In New York State, for example, both parents are equally and concurrently responsible for the support of their child, based on their ability to contribute financially.

Some states also provide AFDC benefits when the wage-earner is unemployed. (72 U.S.C.A. §§606 and 607 [Cum. Supp. 1980].) Courts have held that parents cannot receive AFDC payments on behalf of their minor child when that child is emancipated. (*Lawson v. Brown*, 349 F. Supp. 203 [W.D. Va. 1972]; *Daniels v. Thompson*, 269 A.2d 437 [D.C. App. 1970].) Of course, a teenager, whether she is emancipated or not, can receive AFDC payments for her child. The fact that a minor daughter received AFDC payments for her child does not, in itself, mean that she is emancipated. One case has held that the father of a teenager who received AFDC benefits was still liable for her support. (*French v. French* [Mo. Ct. App. 4/15/80], *Family Law Reporter*, 1980, 6, 2471).

Can a teenager who is pregnant, but has no other children, receive AFDC benefits during her pregnancy? The United States Supreme Court answered that the states may provide such benefits but they do not have to. (*Burns v. Alcala*, 420 U.S. 575 [1975].) The Court ruled that the state could provide AFDC benefits for pregnant women with children while denying them to pregnant women without children.

STATUS OF THE CHILD

Illegitimacy

Rights of the Illegitimate Child. An illegitimate child is defined as a child who is conceived and born out of wedlock (Clark, 1968). The chances that an illegitimate child will have a teenage mother are high; 50 percent of all out-of-wedlock births are to teenagers (*11 Million Teenagers*, Alan Guttmacher Institute, 1976).

Illegitimacy presents special problems for both the parents and child because illegitimates are often discriminated against in society and under the law. The Supreme Court has dealt with the special problems of illegitimates in a long line of cases. Unfortunately, the decisions have been conflicting and have not established a clear standard which a court can use when determining the constitutionality of a statute affecting illegitimate children. The Court has, however, upheld the right of illegitimate children to be supported by their fathers and has gone far towards eliminating the old distinctions that once made illegitimate children "second-class citizens."

A state cannot completely cut off the right of illegitimate children to inherit property from their fathers (*Trimble v. Gordon*, 430 U.S. 762 [1977]; *Labine v. Vincent*, 401 U.S. 532 [1971].) However, the Supreme Court upheld a New York law providing that an illegitimate child can inherit from his father only if the father has initiated legitimation proceedings. (*Lalli v. Lalli*, 439 U.S. 259 [1978].)

An illegitimate child can recover for the wrongful death of his mother (*Levy v. Louisiana,* 391 U.S. 68 [1968]), but not his father unless the father has legitimated his child. (*Parham v. Hughes,* 441 U.S. 347 [1979].) The child can recover under the Worker's Compensation Act. (*Weber v. Aetna Casualty & Surety Co.,* 406 U.S. 164 [1972].) Provisions of the Social Security Act which favored the claims of legitimate children over illegitimate children when they became eligible for benefits were declared unconstitutional. (*Griffin v. Richardson,* 346 F. Supp. 1226 [D. Md.], *aff'd,* 409 U.S. 1069 [1972]; *Davis v. Richardson,* 342 F. Supp. 588 [D. Conn.], *aff'd,* 409 U.S. 1069 [1972]; *but see, Mathews v. Lucas,* 427 U.S. 495 [1976].)

Perhaps most important is the issue of support for the illegitimate child. In 1973, the Supreme Court held that a Texas statute which did not permit illegitimate children to recover support from their fathers violated the Equal Protection clause of the Constitution. (*Gomez v. Perez,* 409 U.S. 535 [1973].) A number of states have statutes making parents liable for the support of their illegitimate children. (Ill. Ann. Stat. ch. 106 3/4 § 52 (Smith-Hurd Supp. 1980); N.J. Stat. Ann. § 9:16-2 [West 1976].)

Putative Fathers—Legitimation and Paternity Proceedings

Marriage of an illegitimate child's parents, even after birth, legitimates the child (Clark, 1968). Marriage may not be possible or desirable, particularly for teenagers. In order to hold the father liable for support, in cases where the parents do not marry, either there must be some acknowledgment by the father, or a judicial determination that the child is his. This can be accomplished either by a legitimation procedure or a paternity suit.

The procedure for legitimating a child is set out by statute. It generally requires the filing of a signed, acknowledged statement of paternity by the father. (Mich. Comp. Laws Ann. § 702.83 [1980].) Arizona and Oregon are exceptions to this rule. In these states, illegitimate children are automatically accorded the same status as legitimate children. (Ariz. Rev. Stat. Ann. § 8-601 [Cum. Supp. 1979]; Or. Rev. Stat. § 109.060 [1975].) The father must be careful to follow the statutory procedure since these statutes are often strictly enforced. The result may be that a parent who intended to legitimate his child will not succeed because of failure to comply with statutory technicalities (Clark, 1968).

If the father is unwilling to acknowledge his child, the mother may initiate a paternity suit. In some states, paternity suits have a quasi-criminal quality with the state prosecuting the alleged father while in other states they are civil proceedings. It is not uncommon for a state to have both types of proceedings. (Clark, 1968; Idaho Code §§ 7-1101—7-1123 [1979].)

In a typical quasi-criminal paternity suit, the mother makes a complaint to a judicial officer who issues a warrant for the father's arrest. The father may post a bond for his release. The trial may be before a jury; the father is held liable for support if paternity is established. In the civil version the mother, rather than the state, is the plaintiff (Clark, 1968).

For both legitimation and paternity suits, it is important to remember that there are limits on the time period after the child's birth during which the action may be brought. A mother or father considering either alternative should be advised to seek legal counsel promptly.

Some states have adopted the Uniform Parentage Act to clarify and protect the parent-child relationship. Recently, the Colorado Supreme Court struck down as an unconstitutional gender-based discrimination a portion of that act which denies a man legal standing to assert that he is the father of a child born to a woman during her marriage to another man. The court held that the man was entitled to "judicial access to establish a constitutionally significant relationship." (*R. McG. and C. W. v. J.W. and W.W., Family Law Reporter*, 1980, *6*, 2834.)

CUSTODY OF THE CHILD

"Best Interests of the Child" Standard

If a teenager is unable to care for her child, the alternatives may be adoption or foster care. Each of these situations involves legal rights and responsibilities of which the teenager should be aware.

Traditionally, courts have been extremely reluctant to sever the parent-child relationship. The degree of parental unfitness or abandonment had to be high before the court would terminate the parent's rights or prefer a stranger to the parent in a custody proceeding (Clark, 1968). This was because the courts considered that, no matter how difficult the situation, it was still preferable for children to be with their natural parent. This legal assumption was challenged by a provocative text, *Beyond the Best Interests of the Child* (Goldstein, Freud, and Solnit, 1973). The authors discussed the needs of children to have a continuous supportive relationship with a "psychological" parent and disputed the prevailing wisdom that placement with the natural parent was presumptively correct.

The effect of this book is noticeable in recent court decisions. Now, opinions often discuss the "best interests of the child" as being of paramount importance. (In re J.O.L. II [D.C. Ct. App. 12/10/79], *Family Law Reporter*, 1980, *6*, 2163; *Bennett v. Jeffreys*, 40 N.Y.2d 543, 356 N.E.2d 277, 387 N.Y.S.2d 821 (1976). Nevertheless, the courts are still sensitive to the rights of the natural parent. At the same time, another set of parents—adoptive and foster—have asserted their rights to be heard in custody proceedings (Howe,

1979). The conflict between the needs of the natural parent, adoptive and foster parents, and the child are discussed in the following sections.

Termination of Parental Rights

Voluntary Termination. A parent may agree to terminate his right to custody of his child by placing the child for adoption. Some states hold parents liable for support even after the child is surrendered, until the child is adopted. (*Commonwealth v. Woolf* [Pa. Super. Ct. 3/21/80], *Family Law Reporter*, 1980, 6, 2410; Colo. Rev. Stat. § 14-7-101 [1973].) Many jurisdictions, however, provide that the agency assumes the parental role once the child is surrendered. (*Smith v. OFFER*, 431 U.S. 816, 827, n.19 [1977].)

Involuntary Termination. Involuntary termination of parental rights is accomplished by a court order through what is usually designated a "guardianship" hearing. Guardianship proceedings seek to make a child eligible for adoption without requiring consent from the natural parents. The most common grounds for guardianship are abandonment, failure to support, or an unlikelihood of the parent and child being reunited in the foreseeable future. Many of the statutes which provide for termination do not give parents clear notice of the conduct that will result in termination of their rights. (Browning and Weiner, 1979; *Linn v. Linn* [Neb. Sup. Ct. 1/3/80], *Family Law Reporter*, 1980, 6, 2197.) In addition, the standard of proof necessary to show parental misconduct varies widely. Some courts require only a "preponderance of the evidence," (*In re Minor*, 393 N.E.2d 379, *Family Law Reporter*, 1980, 5, 2566 [Mass. 1979]; *In re B.E., B.L. & L.S.M.* [S.D. Sup. Ct. 12/31/79], *Family Law Reporter*, 1980, 6, 2213), the usual standard for civil cases, while others require clear and convincing evidence (*In re G.M.* [Text Sup. Ct. 3/19/80], *Family Law Reporter*, 1980, 6, 2349), or even proof beyond a reasonable doubt. (*In re Angelia M.P.* [Calif. Ct. App. 5/1/80], *Family Law Reporter*, 1980, 6, 2492.) The preponderance of the evidence standard means that the judge or jury must determine that the majority of the evidence presented supports a finding of parental unfitness. "Clear and convincing" and "beyond a reasonable doubt" require substantially more proof; beyond a reasonable doubt is the standard needed to convict someone of a crime.

It is important for teenagers to understand that their actions may result in an involuntary termination of their relationship to their child. If, for example, a teenager leaves her child with a relative and does not remain in contact with the child, grounds for abandonment may be found and her rights may be terminated.

Adoption

Notice and Consent. Adoption severs all rights and obligations of natural parents to their children. It is, therefore, a serious proceeding requiring protection of the natural parents' rights. Notice of adoption proceedings must be provided to the parents. Notice may be waived by a parent, but such a waiver may be invalid when the parent is a minor (Clark, 1968). Many states also provide for notice to the putative father (N.Y. Domestic Relations Law 111-a [McKinney Cum. Supp. 1979].) Those that do not will probably change their adoption statutes in line with the recent Supreme Court ruling of *Caban v. Mohammed*, 441 U.S. 380 (1979).

Parents must consent to the adoption of their children. If a parent withholds her consent she can effectively block the adoption unless there are grounds for involuntary termination of parental rights. The procedure varies from state to state, and often depends on whether the placement is done privately or through an agency. Consent is not required, however, if the parent abandoned the child, if parental rights were terminated in a guardianship hearing, or if the parent wilfully failed to perform his obligations. A minor is capable of giving consent for the adoption of her child. (Clark 1968; N.J. Stat. Ann. § 9:3-19-1 [West, 1976].)

The Supreme Court has decided two cases dealing with the issue of obtaining consent for adoption from the father of an illegitimate child. In 1978, in *Quilloin v. Walcott*, 434 U.S. 246 (1978), the Court upheld a Georgia statute that provided that an illegitimate child could be adopted without the putative father's consent. One year later, in *Caban v. Mohammed*, 441 U.S. 380 (1979), the Court invalidated a New York statute that required only the mother's consent when an illegitimate child was to be adopted. The facts in *Quilloin* and *Caban* differed and may account for the seemingly inconsistent holdings. In *Quilloin*, the father had not legitimated his child and had shown limited interest in him. The natural father in *Caban*, however, had been in continual contact with his children and had also petitioned the court to adopt them. Read together, *Quilloin* and *Caban* seem to say that the putative father's consent is mandatory only where the father has been in contact with his children and has evidenced an interest in their welfare.

Revocation of Consent. Once a teenager has decided to place her child for adoption, is it final? Generally, yes, but there are instances where the natural parent has been allowed to revoke her consent. The teenager should not be encouraged to rely on these cases since each case is decided on its own facts and it is difficult to predict how a judge would rule. Nevertheless, if a teenager can show real and pressing circumstances that led her to give consent and she has changed her mind, the revocation should be attempted promptly with legal assistance.

Fraud, duress, or undue influence exercised on the natural parent may always be shown as a reason for revocation of consent (Clark, 1968). Minority of the parent is usually not, of itself, sufficient justification for revocation, although it may be considered as a factor by the court. (*In re Adoption of Holman*, 80 Ariz. 201, 295 P.2d 372 [1956].)

Absent a showing of fraud, duress, or undue influence, the courts are divided as to when consent may be revoked. The best interests of the child may support a revocation, but it may also cause the court to refuse to accept the withdrawal of consent. This is particularly true when the child is already with the adoptive parents and has formed emotional bonds with his new family. (*Matter of Adoption of Gibson*, 239 N.W.2d 540 [Iowa 1976]; *Re Adoption of Anderson*, 235 Minn. 192, 50 N.W.2d 278 [1951].)

Some courts allow parents to revoke their consent arbitrarily (*Re Adoption of One Child*, 154 N.J. Super. 513, 381 A.2d 1232 [1977]; *Small v. Andrews*, 530 P.2d 540 [Or. App. 1975]), while others require that good cause be shown. (*Re S.*, 572 P.2d 1370 [Utah 1977].) Reasons for withdrawal which have been found sufficient range from a simple change of mind (*Re Adoption of Thompson*, 178 Kan. 127, 283 P.2d 493 [1955]); to the fact that consent was given while the natural parent was under emotional strain. (*Re Adoption of Vaida*, 34 Or. App. 631, 579 P.2d 313 [1978]; *Warner v. Ward*, 401 S.W.2d 62 [Ky. 1966].) In other cases, however, courts have rejected similar reasons for revocation. (*William v. Pope*, 281 Ala. 416, 203 So.2d 271 [1967]; *Hendrix v. Hunter*, 99 Ga. App. 785, 110 S.E.2d 35 [1959]; *Re Fusco*, 50 Del. 241, 127 A.2d 468 [1956].)

The timing of the revocation may influence the court's decision. Courts have allowed parents to revoke even after the child was placed with his adoptive parents. (People *ex rel. Scarpetta v. Spence-Chapin Adoption Service*, 28 N.Y.2d 185, 269 N.E.2d 787, 321 N.Y.S.2d 65, *cert den.*, 404 U.S. 805 [1971].) It may help the natural parent if she petitions for revocation soon after her child has been placed. (*Re D.L.F.*, 85 S.D. 44, 176 N.W.2d 486 [1970].) Some courts, however, will not allow revocation once the child has been placed, either because they reason that the adoptive parents have relied on the natural parent's consent (*Rhodes v. Shirley*, 234 Ind. 587, 129 N.E.2d 60 [1955]), or because the child has remained with the adoptive parents long enough to form attachments. (In re *Child*, 295 N.E.2d 693 [Mass. App. 1973].)

Courts have also examined the care given to the child by the natural parent prior to her surrendering the child for adoption and the natural parent's present ability to support her child. Where the natural parent has not visited her child, or is considered too young or financially insecure to care for her child, the court will often refuse to allow her to revoke her consent. (*Adoption of Curtis,* 195 Cal. App.2d 179, 15 Cal. Rptr. 331 [1961]). On the other hand, evidence that the parent cared for her child before surrendering him, or that she has matured and is capable of supporting her child will often be considered in her favor. (*Guardianship of M.,* 66 Cal. App.3d 254, 135 Cal. Rptr. 866 [1977]; *Graves v. Graves,* 51 Ala. App. 601, 288 So.2d 142 (1973).

A teenager who wishes to revoke her consent to an adoption should consider why she wishes to revoke and her present ability to care for her child. She should be encouraged to speak to an attorney to determine if, in her state, she has good grounds for revocation.

Foster Care

If a teenager is unable to care for her child, but is not willing to place the child for adoption, foster care is one alternative. Placing a child into foster care may not be as final as adoption, but it does have far-reaching effects on the parent-child relationship and should not be treated lightly.

Foster-care systems are envisioned as "temporary" homes for children. Parental rights are not terminated and the expectation is that the parent and child will be reunited once the parent's disability ends. (*Smith v. OFFER,* 431 U.S. 816, 833 (1977).) Studies have found, however, that foster care is not a temporary situation for the majority of children. In addition, a significant percentage of children in foster care do not remain with one family, but are subjected to two or more placements (Levine, 1973). This will often have a disruptive effect on the child's development.

The difficulties of foster care are further complicated by the uncertain status of both the foster parent and the natural parent. The foster parent is responsible for the day-to-day management of the child's affairs. The natural parent, however, has not surrendered her right to the child and is expected to plan for the child's future welfare. (*Smith v. OFFER,* 431 U.S. at 827-28). This conflict is particularly apparent when foster parents seek to retain custody or to adopt their foster children.

In the past, foster parents' rights were rarely considered. The courts were protective of the natural parents' rights, and the foster parents had to show that the natural parent was unfit before they could prevail. The modern trend, however, is to place greater emphasis on the needs of the child and to recognize the validity of the emotional relationship between the child and the foster parent (Goodman, 1978).

Thus, the New York Court of Appeals held that, depending on the circumstances, foster parents could be allowed visitation rights after the child was returned to his natural parents. (*In re Melissa M.* [N.Y. Fam. Ct. 12/17/79], *Family Law Reporter,* 1980, *6,* 2144.) A New Jersey court allowed foster parents to intervene in parental rights termination proceedings, noting that "(t)he trend appears to be that foster parents should have standing in court on matters affecting their foster children." (*In re J.A.T. & J.T.T.* [N.J. Juv. & Dom. Rel. Ct. 10/10/79], *Family Law Reporter*, 1980, *6*, 2172.) Statutes also provide that foster parents who have retained custody for a certain period of time will have preference in adoption proceedings. (N.J. Stat. Ann. § 30:4C-26.7 [West Cum. Supp. 1980]; *In re M.D.H.* [Mo. Ct. App. 2/25/80], *Family Law Reporter*, 1980, *6*, 2378.)

For the teenage parent, the significance of these legal developments is that her rights may not supersede a foster parent's. If she wishes to ensure that her relationship continues with her child, she must maintain contact with him/her. The teenager should also be taking affirmative steps towards becoming capable of supporting her child at some future time.

CONCLUSION

The pregnant adolescent needs guidance through a maze of complex laws that add to the difficulties of her situation.

If she chooses to terminate her pregnancy, and if her parents are not supportive, she may require assistance to obtain an abortion without parental consent or notification. Additionally, she may need help to pay for the abortion.

If she decides to carry the pregnancy to term, she may require assistance in obtaining medical care and financial support for herself and her child. Possible sources of support will include her parents, the father of the child, and various governmental programs.

The status and rights of the child will also need clarification. A different approach will be appropriate depending on whether the teenager wishes to keep the child or place it for adoption or foster care. In all of these situations, care is required to protect the rights of both mother and child.

REFERENCES

Books and Articles

Benshoof, J. and Donovan, P. Statutory rape: Does it offer teenagers a chance to get Medicaid abortions? *Family Planning/Population Reporter*, 1979, **8**, 30–32.

Blackburn, M. Teen-agers leave home—legally. *New York Times*, February 20, 1980, C9, col. 1.

Brenner, N. G., Pilpel, H. F., and Paul, E. W. Summary and analysis of state laws relating to contraceptive and abortion services to minors. *Family Planning, Contraception, Voluntary Sterilization and Abortion: An Analysis of Laws and Policies in the United States, Each State and Jurisdiction.* U.S. Department of Health, Education, and Welfare (1978).

Brown, R. and Truitt, R. The right of minors to medical treatment. *De Paul Law Review*, 1979, **28**, 289–320.

Browning, C. M. and Weiner, M. L. The right to family integrity: A substantive due process approach to state removal and termination proceedings. *Georgetown Law Journal*, 1979, **68**, 213–248.

Butler, P. The Medicaid program: Current statutory requirements and judicial interpretations. *Clearinghouse Review*, 1974, **8**, 7–18.

Cady, F. Emancipation of minors. *Connecticut Law Review*, 1979, **12**, 62–91.

Cates, W., *et al.* The effect of delay and method choice on the risk of abortion morbidity. *Family Planning Perspectives*, 1977, **9**, 266–273.

Clark, H. H. Constitutional protection of the illegitimate child? *University of California at Davis Law Review*, 1979, **12**, 383–411.

Clark, H. H. *The Law of Domestic Relations in the United States.* St. Paul, Minn.: West (1968).

Department of Health, Education, and Welfare. *Decision Memorandum (Shuck Report).* (1977).

11 million teenagers. New York: Alan Guttmacher Institute (1976).

Goldstein, J., Freud, A., and Solnit, A. J. *Beyond the Best Interests of the Child.* Free Press: New York (1973).

Goodman, J. F. Family law—foster care and adoption. *Annual Survey of American Law*, 1978, 411–430.

Howe, R. W. Development of a model act to free children for permanent placement: A case study in law and social planning. *Family Law Quarterly*, 1979, **13**, 257–344.

Law, S. Reproductive freedom issues in legal services practice. *Clearinghouse Review*, 1978, **12**, 389–403.

Levine, R. S. Caveat parens: A demystification of the child protection system. *University of Pittsburgh Law Review*, 1973, **35**, 1–52.

McCormick, H. L. *Medicare and Medicaid Claims and Procedures.* St. Paul, Minn.: West (1977).

Paul, E. W. and Pilpel, H. F. Teenagers and pregnancy: The law in 1979. *Family Planning Perspectives*, 1979, **11**, 297–302.

Rosenbaum, S., The Medicaid early and periodic diagnosis and treatment program: HEW's new regulations. *Clearinghouse Review*, 1980, **13**, 742–748.

Sussman, A. *The Rights of Young People.* New York: Avon (1977).

Wald, M. S. Children's Rights: A Framework for Analysis. *University of California at Davis Law Review*, 1979, **12**, 255–282.

Westman, J. *Child Advocacy.* New York: Macmillan (1979).

Cases

Adoption of Curtis, 195 Cal. App.2d 179, 15 Cal. Rptr. 331 (1961).

Beal v. Doe, 432 U.S. 438 (1977).

Bellotti v. Baird, 443 U.S. 622 (1979).

Bennett v. Jeffreys, 40 N.Y.2d 543, 356 N.E.2d 277, 387 N.Y.S.2d 821 (1976).
Brunswick v. La Prise, 262 A.2d 366 (Me. 1970).
Burns v. Alcala, 420 U.S. 575 (1975).
Caban v. Mohammed, 441 U.S. 380 (1979).
Commonwealth v. Woolf, (Pa. Super. Ct. 3/21/80), *Family Law Reporter*, 1980, **6**, 2410.
Daniels v. Thompson, 269 A.2d 437 (D.C. App. 1970).
Davis v. Richardson, 342 F. Supp. 588 (D. Conn.) aff'd, 409 U.S. 1069 (1972).
Doe v. Bolton, 410 U.S. 179 (1973).
French v. French, (Mo. Ct. App. 4/15/80), *Family Law Reporter*, 1980, **6**, 2471.
Gomez v. Perez, 409 U.S. 535 (1973).
Graves v. Graves, 51 Ala. App. 601, 288 So.2d 142 (1973).
Griffin v. Richardson, 346 F. Supp. 1226 (D. Md.), aff'd, 409 U.S. 1069 (1972).
Guardianship of M., 66 Cal. App.3d 254, 135 Cal. Rptr. 866 (1977).
H.L. v. Matheson, No. 101 S. Ct. 1164 (1980).
Harris v. McRae, 100 S. Ct. 2671 (1980).
Hendrix v. Hunter, 99 Ga. App. 785, 110 S.E.2d 35 (1959).
In re Adoption of Holman, 80 Ariz. 201, 295 P.2d 372 (1956).
In re Angelia M.P., (Calif. Ct. App. 5/1/80), *Family Law Reporter*, 1980, **6**, 2492.
In re B.E., B.L., & L.S.M., (S.D. Sup. Ct. 12/31/79), *Family Law Reporter*, 1980, **6**, 2213.
In re Child, 295 N.E.2d 693 (Mass. App. 1973).
In re G.M., (Tex. Sup. Ct. 3/19/80), *Family Law Reporter*, 1980, **6**, 2349.
In J.A.T. & J.T.T., (N.J. Juv. & Dom. Rel. Ct. 10/10/79), *Family Law Reporter*, 1980, **6**, 2172.
In re J.O.L. II, (D.C. Ct. App. 12/10/79), *Family Law Reporter*, 1980, **6**, 2163.
In re, M.D.H. (Mo. Ct. App. 2/25/80), *Family Law Reporter*, 1980, **6**, 2378.
In re Melissa M., (N.Y. Fam. Ct. 12/17/79), *Family Law Reporter*, 1980, **6**, 2144.
In re Minor 393 N.E. 2d 379 (Mass. 1979), *Family Law Reporter*, 1980, **5**, 2566.
In re Smith, 295 A.2d 238 (Md. App. 1972).
Labine v. Vincent, 401 U.S. 532 (1971).
Lalli v. Lalli, 439 U.S. 259 (1978).
Lawson v. Brown, 349 F. Supp. 203 (W.D. Va. 1972).
Levy v. Louisiana, 391 U.S. 68 (1968).
Linn v. Linn, (Neb. Sup. Ct. 1/3/80), *Family Law Reporter*, 1980, **6**, 2197.
Maher v. Roe, 432 U.S. 464 (1977).
Mathews v. Lucas, 427 U.S. 495 (1976).
Matter of Adoption of Gibson, 239 N.W.2d 540 (Iowa 1976).
Orr v. Orr, 440 U.S. 268 (1979).
Parham v. Hughes, 441 U.S. 347 (1979).
Parker v. Stage, 43 N.Y.2d 128, 371 N.E.2d 513, 400 N.Y.S.2d 794 (1977).
Pendexter v. Pendexter, 363 A.2d 743 (Me. 1976).
People ex rel. Scarpetta v. Spence-Chapin Adoption Service, 28 N.Y.2d 185, 269 N.E.2d 787, 321 N.Y.S.2d 65, *cert den.*, 404 U.S. 805 (1971).
Planned Parenthood of Central Missouri v. Danforth, 428 U.S. 52 (1976).
Poelker v. Doe, 432 U.S. 519 (1977).

Quilloin v. Walcott, 434 U.S. 246 (1978).
Re Adoption of Anderson, 235 Minn. 192, 50 N.W.2d 278 (1951).
Re Adoption of One Child, 154 N.J. Super, 513, 381 A2d 1232 (1977).
Re Adoption of Thompson, 178 Kan. 127, 283 P.2d 493 (1955).
Re Adoption of Vaida, 34 Or. App. 631, 579 P.2d 313 (1978).
Re D.L.F., 85 S.D. 44, 176 N.W.2d 486 (1970).
Re Fusco, 50 Del. 241, 127 A.2d 468 (1956).
Re S., 572 P.2d 1370 (Utah 1977).
Rhodes v. Shirley, 234 Ind. 587, 129 N.E.2d 60 (1955).
Roe v. Wade, 410 U.S. 113 (1973).
Shapiro v. Thompson, 394 U.S. 618 (1969).
Small v. Andrews, 530 P.2d 540 (Or. App. 1975).
Smith v. OFFER, 431 U.S. 816 (1977).
Taylor v. Hill, 420 F. Supp. 1020 (D. N.C. 1976), aff'd, 430 U.S. 961 (1977).
Trimble v. Gordon, 430 U.S. 762 (1977).
Warner v. Ward, 401 S.W.2d 62 (Ky. 1966).
Williams v. Pope, 281 Ala. 416, 203 So.2d 271 (1967).
Weber v. Aetna Casualty & Surety Co., 406 U.S. 164 (1972).

Statutes

Ala. Code tit. 22 § 8-4 (1977).
Ala. Code tit. 22 § 8-6 (1977).
Appropriations—Fiscal Year 1980—Continuance, Pub. L. No. 96-123 § 109, 93 stat. 926 (1979).
Ariz. Rev. Stat. Ann. § 8-601 (Cum. Supp. 1979).
Cal. Civil Code § 34.5 (West Cum. Supp. 1980).
Cal. Civil Code §§ 60–70 (West Cum. Supp. 1980).
Colo. Rev. Stat. § 13-22-102 (1973).
Colo. Rev. Stat. § 13-22-103 (Cum. Supp. 1979).
Colo. Rev. Stat. § 14-7-101 (1973).
Conn. Pub. Acts 79-397 (1979).
Idaho Code §§ 7-11014–7-1123 (1979).
Ill. Ann. Stat. ch. 23 § 10-2 (Smith-Hurd Supp. 1980).
Ill. Ann. Stat. ch. 106 3/4 § 52 (Smith-Hurd Supp. 1980).
Ill. Ann. Stat. ch. 111 § 4504 (Smith-Hurd Supp. 1980).
Ind. Code Ann. § 16-8-4-1 (Burns 1973).
Ind. Code Ann. § 16-8-5-1 (Burns 1973).
Mass. Ann. Laws ch. 112 § 12E (Michie/Law. Co-op. 1975).
Mich. Comp. Laws Ann. § 702.83 (1980).
Minn. Stat. Ann. § 144.343 (West Cum. Supp. 1979).
N.J. Stat. Ann. § 9:3-19.1 (West 1976).
N.J. Stat. Ann. § 9:16-2 (West 1976).
N.J. Stat. Ann. § 19:17A-1 (West 1979).
N.J. Stat. Ann. § 30:4C-26.7 (West Cum. Supp. 1980).

N.Y. Domestic Relations Law § 111-a (McKinney Cum. Supp. 1979).
Or. Rev. Stat. § 109.060 (1975).
S.C. Code § 20-7-40 (Cum. Supp. 1979).
Title IV-A, Social Security Act, 42 U.S.C.A. §§ 606 § 607 (Cum. Supp. 1980).
Title VI, Pub. L. No. 95-626, 42 U.S.C.A. § 300-a-2/et seq.

Part II
Needs

2.
The Epidemiology of Adolescent Pregnancy: Incidence, Outcomes, and Interventions

Joy Dryfoos, M.A.,
Fellow, The Alan Guttmacher Institute,
New York, N.Y.

The incidence of adolescent pregnancy is continuing to rise; in 1978, more than 1.1 million pregnancies were experienced by women under age 20. Only one-fourth of the conceptions were intended at the time and 38 percent were terminated by abortion. Young, unmarried, and minority youngsters experienced the greatest difficulty with fertility control. Those who became mothers encountered a myriad of negative consequences.

The statistics of adolescent pregnancy reflect a number of conflicting trends: a significant increase in early initiation of premarital sexual activity and a drop in marriage rates; increased use of contraception and a slight turning away from the most effective methods; a public opinion in support of sex education and an abysmal lack of knowledge about reproduction; better access to abortion and more controversy surrounding its availability.

Adolescents will require a wide array of interventions if they are expected to control their fertility. They need to be given adequate information by their parents and their schools at early ages, they need to have access to more effective and safe contraceptive methods, and to go to family planning clinics and abortion services with high-quality medical and counselling components. Most of all, adolescents, especially those who are disadvantaged, need to be assured that the society really can deliver alternatives to pregnancy such as higher education, skilled employment, and regular income.

Since the mid-1970s, increasing attention has been directed toward the problem of adolescent pregnancies, with the oft-repeated indicator: more than 1 million pregnancies to women under 20. Much of the attention seems to focus on adolescent mothers, yet in reality there are 50,000 fewer births to teenaged mothers now than a decade ago. Indeed, there are more pregnancies occurring to the nation's 10 million adolescent women, but they are much more likely to be terminated by abortion than ever before. The increase in the number of pregnancies, and especially of unintended pregnancies, may be attributed to the marked increase in early initiation of sexual intercourse. More youngsters are at risk of pregnancy each year. At the same time, the rate of pregnancy among sexually active adolescents has decreased slightly as might be expected given the improved access to effective contraceptive methods.

Perhaps the level of interest in adolescent pregnancy has heightened because the adolescents who do become mothers are more likely than ever to be white, very young, and unmarried. Black youngsters have long suffered the consequences of out-of-wedlock motherhood: poverty, educational and occupational disadvantage, marital instability, and other negative outcomes. Society has dealt with the the problem of black illegitimacy by attributing it to "their culture"; it was assumed that the so-called black matriarchy would absorb the out-of-wedlock children into existing family units. As white youngsters experienced earlier sexual initiation and discovered the negative consequences, suddenly early adolescent childbearing achieved problem status. This fact became ever more evident because most, but not all, older women appeared to have their fertility well under control.

For the first time, legislation was passed by Congress in 1978 to address the specific problem of adolescent pregnancy: *The Adolescent Health Services, and Pregnancy Prevention and Care Act*, Title IV of the Health Services and Centers Amendments (P.L. 95-626). Under this act, an Office of Adolescent Pregnancy Programs was organized in the Health Services Administration of the Department of Health and Human Services, to administer grants to comprehensive adolescent pregnancy programs that could offer a wide range of linked curative services in one site. An innovative program at Johns Hopkins Hospital was considered to be a model for comprehensive services for adolescent mothers (Select Committee, 1978). Agencies with the capacity to provide prenatal and postnatal care, delivery, infant care, parenting classes, access to continuation of schooling, and job counseling were encouraged to apply for federal funds. A very large number of proposals were received by the Office of Adolescent Pregnancy Programs; only four received grants in the first year. While a maximum of $60 million was authorized for these services when the legislation was passed by Congress, the actual appropriation was $1 million in the first year and only $10 million in the most recent year, a clear indication of the low priority the program has received.

During the same period, Congress has recognized the importance of expanding the scope of family-planning services for adolescents and improving sex-education programs. Family-planning clinics are supported with project grants through Title X of the *Public Health Service Act* (P.L 94-63); the appropriation was $166 million for 1981 with $10 million earmarked for expansion of adolescent services. These funds are administered by the Bureau of Community Health Services in the Health Services Administration. Title X funds also support the Center for Population Research of the National Institute of Child Health and Human Development, National Institutes of Health. In 1981, $79 million was appropriated to the CPR primarily for research and training on contraceptive methods and reproductive physiology, with small amounts for behavioral and social science research. Medicaid (Title XIX) and other social services moneys (Title XX of the Social Services Act), state funds and fees are also used for family-planning services. Curriculum development in family-life education and other sex education programs are supported through the Department of Education as well as the Office of Health Education in the Centers for Disease Control.

Within the government, a number of programs exist that impact on adolescent health and well-being; like many social efforts, the programs are fragmentary and uncoordinated. Yet, there is recognition at the highest levels of decision making that the problem of adolescent pregnancy cannot be resolved *post facto* and that early intervention is necessary to assist adolescents to prevent pregnancy and to handle their sexuality in a responsible way. At the same time, the society appears to be ambivalent about who is responsible for intervening in the lives of its children—schools, parents, courts, clinics? People who work with youngsters are confronted daily with evidence of early sexual initiation and the conflicts produced by the mixed messages of the society. Many adults are reluctant to acknowledge the sexual behavior of their children or others, and these attitudes are reflected, for example, in school boards that resist sex education programs.

In order to deal with this subject, it is important to have an understanding of the facts: who is getting pregnant, why, what are the results, what are the problems, and what are some approaches to the solution of the problems. It cannot be said about the problem of adolescent pregnancy that there is a lack of research. Much information has been produced by the Johns Hopkins studies of Adolescent Sexuality, Contraception and Pregnancy, projectible national sample surveys conducted among females aged 15 to 19 in 1971, 1976, and 1979 (metropolitan areas only), and among males 17 to 21 in 1979. Melvin Zelnik and John Kantner, principal investigators, have written extensively on the subject (Zelnik and Kantner, 1977, 1978, 1980). Since the mid-1970s, the Center for Population Research has supported numerous research endeavors on the determinants and consequences of adolescent childbearing and its societal costs (Baldwin and Cain, 1980). Many of the contractors used existing data bases so that the various Health Interview Surveys, Current Population Reports from the Bureau of the Census, the Collaborative Perinatal Project Study, National Longitudinal Study of the Labor Market Experiences of Young Women, Project Talent, and other survey data have been analyzed in detail to extract meaningful relationships between behavioral, social, and economic variables and maternity at an early age (Chilman, 1980). The data presented in this chapter relies heavily on these sources, as well as on vital statistics and special studies of family-planning services and abortion providers conducted by The Alan Guttmacher Institute.

ADOLESCENT PREGNANCY: INCIDENCE AND TRENDS

Who is getting pregnant?

In 1978, more than 1.1 million U.S. adolescent women aged 15 to 19 experienced a pregnancy (Table 2-1). Only about one-quarter of these pregnancies were intended. The pregnancies resulted in 543,000 births, 419,000 abortions, and an estimated 150,000 miscarriages and other fetal deaths. Thus, fewer than half of all pregnancies to adolescents ended in a live birth and 38 percent were terminated by an induced abortion.

Marital status had a significant effect on the incidence and wantedness of pregnancies and the outcomes. About 35 percent of all adolescent pregnancies occurred to married adolescents; these pregnancies, as would be expected, were more likely to have been intended and to have resulted in live births: just about half were intended and more than three-fourths ended in live births. During the year, unmarried adolescents had 721,000 pregnancies; only 14 percent were intended and one-third ended in live births. As a result, births to married adolescents accounted for 56 percent of all adolescent births while abortions to married adolescents accounted for 6 percent of all adolescent abortions. Not all of the births to married adolescents were conceived postmaritally. Fully 60 percent of the in-wedlock births were the result of

Table 2-1. Number of pregnancies to adolescents and percent intended, according to outcomes (births, abortions, and miscarriages), and marital status, 1978 (numbers in thousands)

OUTCOME	NUMBER TO WOMEN 15–19			PERCENT INTENDED		
	TOTAL	MARRIED	UNMARRIED	TOTAL	MARRIED	UNMARRIED
Total pregnancies	1,112	391	721	26.5	49.1	14.3
Births	543	303	240	45.3	52.8	35.8
Abortions	419	25	394	0.0	0.0	0.0
Miscarriages	150	63	87	32.7	50.8	19.5

Source: Births—NCHS, *Monthly Vital Statistics Report*, Vol. 29, No. 1, 1980, Tables 2 and 13.
Abortions—Number from The Alan Guttmacher Institute unpublished survey for 1978; characteristics extrapolated from Center for Disease Control, *Abortion Surveillance, Annual Summary*, Atlanta, 1980, Tables 6, 8, and 10.
Miscarriages—Estimated: 20 percent of births and 10 percent of abortions.
Intentions, Married—Special tabulations of 1976 National Survey of Family Growth, NCHS.
Intentions, Unmarried—Projected for 1978 from M. Zelnik and J. F. Kantner, "First Pregnancies to Woman Aged 15–19: 1976 and 1971", *Family Planning Perspectives*, 10:11, 1978, Table 5.

premarital conceptions (Zelnik and Kantner, 1978), suggesting the possibility that in one year as many as 182,000 teenagers were forced to get married because of impending maternity. Thus of all births to adolescents in 1978, 422,000 births, 78 percent, were actually conceived out of wedlock.

The age distribution of pregnant adolescents is significant: while a pregnancy to a 15-year-old may carry with it markedly higher health risks, age 18 or 19 may represent an optimum time for the safety and well-being of the mother and the baby. Most of the expressed concern focuses on very early pregnancy, usually defined as occurring at age 17 or under. As would be expected, the younger women who became pregnant were more frequently unmarried and few intended to become pregnant. Table 2-2 shows that 458,000 adolescents aged 17 or less became pregnant in 1978 and, of these, 214,000 became mothers. About 60 percent of the young mothers were not married when they delivered. These young unmarried women were more likely to carry their pregnancies to term than the unmarried women aged 18 and 19; 52 percent of the pregnancies to unmarried 15- to 17-year-olds terminated in abortion compared to 57 percent of unmarried 18- to 19-year-olds. These age differentials in abortion suggest that the younger adolescents might have encountered greater difficulties obtaining abortions than those who are 18 and over.

The number of pregnancies has been related to the number of women to derive pregnancy rates (events per 1000 women aged 15 to 19) according to outcome and race (Table 2-3). In 1978, nonwhite adolescent women experienced much higher pregnancy rates than white adolescents: about 19 percent of all nonwhite unmarried women aged 15 to 19—almost 1 in 5—experienced a pregnancy compared to 9 percent (1 in 11) of all white women in that cohort. Though nonwhite abortion rates were almost twice as high, the white youngsters were more likely to resolve their pregnancies with abortion. Nonwhite adolescents had a higher incidence of unintended pregnancy and childbearing than white adolescents; 16 percent of all nonwhite adolescent women experienced an unintended pregnancy in 1978 as did 7 percent of white adolescents.

In addition to the pregnancies experienced by women aged 15 to 19, about 30,000 girls younger than 15 also conceived during 1978, resulting in 11,000 births, 15,000 abortions, and 4,000 miscarriages. Virtually none of these pregnancies were intentional. This group of youngsters carries with it the highest risk of negative health, social and economic consequences to the mother and the baby. While the incidence is very low—there are about 4 million 13- and 14-year-old girls—the impact of pregnancy on the individual is dramatic, particularly among the girls who become mothers.

In summary, more than 800,000 unintended pregnancies were experienced by women aged 19 or less in 1978; 1 in 13 adolescents either had an abortion

Table 2-2. Number of pregnancies to adolescents and percent distribution by outcome according to age and marital status, 1978 (numbers in thousands).

	AGE 14 OR LESS			AGE 15 TO 17			AGE 18-19		
	TOTAL	MARRIED	UNMARRIED	TOTAL	MARRIED	UNMARRIED	TOTAL	MARRIED	UNMARRIED
Pregnancies									
Number	30	*	30	428	103	325	685	289	396
Percent	100.0		100.0	100.0	100.0	100.0	100.0	100.0	100.0
Percent									
Births	36.7		36.7	47.4	83.5	36.0	49.8	75.4	31.1
Abortions	50.0		50.0	39.3	**	51.7	36.6	8.7	57.0
Miscarriages	13.3		13.3	13.3	16.5	12.3	13.6	15.9	11.9

*Less than 1,000
**Less than 0.5%

Source: See Table 2-1.

Table 2-3. Number of pregnancies and pregnancy rates (events per 1000 women aged 15–19) according to outcome and race, 1978.

OUTCOME	NUMBER OF EVENTS (IN THOUSANDS)			RATES PER 1000 WOMEN AGED 15–19		
	TOTAL	WHITE	NONWHITE	TOTAL	WHITE	NONWHITE
Pregnancies	1,112	796	316	107	91	192
Birth	543	380	163	52	44	99
Abortion	419	309	110	40	35	67
Miscarriage	150	107	43	14	12	26
Unintended pregnancies	817	562	255	79	65	155
Unintended births	297	185	112	29	21	68
Number of woman	10,357	8,711	1,646			

Source: See Table 2-1.

or bore an unwanted child. About 300,000 babies were born to young mothers who did not intend to become pregnant at the time of conception. Being young, unmarried and/or black increased the chances of an early unplanned pregnancy.

The impact of unintended childbearing on the child, the mother, the father, and the society is well-documented and measurable in terms of behavioral problems, economic deprivation, marital disruption, educational gaps, and welfare costs (Chilman, 1980; Select committee, 1978). The impact of unintended pregnancies terminated by abortion on the pregnant youngster, the male partner, and the society is less directly measurable. From an individual and societal point of view, it is surely more beneficial for a youngster to be able to terminate an undesired pregnancy to avoid premature motherhood. However, as a long-term policy, one would not advocate that abortion be used as the primary means of birth prevention, an occurrence which could become a norm, if current trends continue.

Trends in Adolescent Pregnancy

Changes in the incidence of pregnancy to adolescent women during the past decade reflect the impact of conflicting trends: the increase in early sexual activity, along with greater permissiveness about sexual matters; the decrease in early marriages; the legalization of abortion in 1973; and the availability of family-planning services. In regard to birth rates, shown in Table 2-4, the greatest increase in the rates has been among unmarried 15- to 17-year old

Table 2-4. Birth rates according to race and marital status, 1968, 1973 and 1978.

| | WHITE | | | | NONWHITE | | | |
| | TOTAL | | UNMARRIED | | TOTAL | | UNMARRIED | |
YEAR	15–17	18–19	15–17	18–19	15–17	18–19	15–17	18–19
1978	25.4	70.1	10.5	19.5	72.3	139.9	64.9	116.3
1973	29.5	79.6	8.5	15.0	91.6	163.7	76.5	114.6
1968	25.7	102.0	6.2	16.8	94.1	196.6	67.3	114.8
% change 1968-1978	−0.1	−31.3	+69.4	+16.1	−23.2	−28.8	−3.6	+1.3

Source: 1973, 1968—Stephanie J. Ventura, *Teen-age Childbearing: U.S., 1966–1975. Monthly Vital Statistics Report*, National Center for Health Statistics, September 1977. 1978—NCHS, *Monthly Vital Statistics Report*, Vol. 29, No. 1, 1980, Tables 4 and 13.

white women. Marital fertility has declined markedly over the past decade among all adolescents, yet race differentials remain high.

Abortion data were not available until 1973. Before that time, many women of all ages apparently obtained illegal abortions but there were no age-specific estimates for that period. In 1973, 232,000 women aged 15 to 19 were reported to have obtained legal abortions. Altogether, there were 604,000 births to women aged 15 to 19 and about 980,000 adolescent pregnancies in that year; 24 percent of the pregnancies were terminated by abortion. Each year since 1973, the number of pregnancies has increased as has the proportion of the pregnancies that were terminated by abortion; in 1978, the proportion reached 38 percent, a 14-point increase. Actually, the number of adolescent births declined 11 percent between 1973 and 1978 while the number of abortions increased by 81 percent.

DETERMINANTS OF PREGNANCY

Premarital Intercourse

The high rates of premarital pregnancy reflect the fact that more than 4 out of 10 unmarried adolescent girls have experienced sexual intercourse at least once (Zelnik and Kantner, 1980). This behavior represents a major social change in American society, a change observed closely by the adolescents themselves (and a few social scientists), but not well understood or accepted by the great American public. While it was known from the Kinsey studies and others that premarital coitus occurred among certain unique subsets of the population, early sexual initiation is now becoming the norm among teenagers. During the decade of the 1970s, a major shift occurred: in 1971, about 27 percent of unmarried adolescents reported that they had experienced intercourse compared to 42 percent in 1979, more than a 50 percent change in the proportion (Zelnik and Kantner, 1980). The mean age of first intercourse, 16.2 years, decreased slightly over the decade because the increase in sexual activity was greater among younger adolescents than among older adolescents. As shown in Table 2-5, about 14 percent of 15-year-olds reported intercourse in 1971 and 21 percent in 1979 (a 51 percent increase), while 47 percent of 19-year-olds reported intercourse in the earlier study and 63 percent in 1979 (a 34 percent increase).

The most marked change was among white youngsters. A very high proportion of black adolescents were sexually active in both studies (51 percent in 1971 and 63 percent in 1979); during the same period the proportion of white adolescents who were sexually active almost doubled from 21 percent to 40 percent.

Male adolescents have not been studied with the same thoroughness as females. In general, it has been assumed that boys initiate sexual intercourse

Table 2-5. Percent of never-married women aged 15–19 who ever had intercourse, by age and race, 1979 and 1979.

AGE	1979			1971			PERCENT CHANGE 1971–1979		
	TOTAL	WHITE	NONWHITE	TOTAL	WHITE	NONWHITE	TOTAL	WHITE	NONWHITE
15–19	42.4	39.9	62.8	26.8	21.4	51.2	58.2	86.4	22.7
15	20.8	18.3	40.9	13.8	10.9	30.5	50.7	67.9	34.1
16	34.9	33.8	48.1	21.2	16.9	46.2	64.6	100.0	4.1
17	46.2	44.1	70.5	26.6	21.8	58.8	73.7	102.3	19.9
18	53.3	50.0	75.2	36.8	32.3	62.7	44.8	54.8	19.9
19	62.6	59.0	88.3	46.8	39.4	76.2	33.8	49.7	15.9

Source: 1971: Melvin Zelnik and John F. Kantner, "Sexual and Contraceptive Experience of Young Unmarried Women in the U.S.," 1976 and 1971, *Family Planning Perspectives*, Vol. 9, No. 2, March/April 1977, Table 1, p. 56.
1979: Extrapolated to U.S. total from Melvin Zelnik and John F. Kantner, "Sexual Activity, Contraceptive Use and Pregnancy Among Metropolitan-Area Teenagers," *Family Planning Perspectives*, Vol. 12, No. 5, September/October, 1980. (Published 1979 figures were for metropolitan areas only.)

earlier and in larger numbers than girls. However, the recent Johns Hopkins study found that only 55 percent of urban 17- to 19-year-old males were sexually active, about 10 percentage points more than their female counterparts (Zelnik and Kantner, 1980). (This seems like a low estimate; for the purposes of planning services, it has previously been assumed that about 60 to 65 percent of males aged 15 to 19 were sexually active.) (AGI, 1976)

Applying rates of sexual activity to the adolescent population yields estimates of the numbers of adolescents who are sexually active and therefore at risk of pregnancy. In 1978, about 4.8 million U.S. women aged 15 to 19 were at risk; 4 million of them were unmarried (AGI, 1980). Their potential partners included about 6 million sexually active males, aged 15 to 19, almost all of whom were unmarried (plus, of course, older men). Thus the nation contained about 11 million youngsters who were participating in sexual relations, many of whom were very young and ignorant of the possible consequences of their sexual activities.

Using estimates of the number of adolescent females who are sexually active as a denominator yields more accurate pregnancy rates for unmarried adolescents. In 1978, about 18 percent of all sexually active unmarried adolescents, one in six, were pregnant as were 48 percent of married adolescents. Altogether, 23 percent of all sexually active adolescents who were at risk of pregnancy did become so, a very slight decrease from previous years.

Having experienced sexual intercourse once may seem like a poor description of a sexually active person. In the Johns Hopkins study in 1976, almost half of the sexually experienced adolescent women had not had intercourse the 4 weeks preceding the interview. Only one-fourth had sex three or more times during a month and 18 percent had never had more than three partners. White adolescents reported higher frequencies of intercourse and more partners than their black peers. (Zelnik and Kantner, 1977). Having sex the first time is the most important event, and once that bridge is crossed, the youngster is likely to be available for other experiences, whether they occur that month or that year.

It is significant that the risk of unintended pregnancy appears to be very high at the onset of sexual activity. Of those adolescents who experienced a premarital pregnancy, 22 percent became pregnant within 1 month of initiation of sexual intercourse and 50 percent within 6 months (Zabin, Kantner, and Zelnik, 1979). Many became pregnant the first time they had intercourse, demonstrating how high the probabilities of pregnancy are for unprotected intercourse among young fecund women. The younger the girl, the shorter the time-span between initiation and pregnancy. The reason for this unhappy consequence is that half of all adolescents do not use contraception at the time of first intercourse (Zelnik and Kantner, 1980). The mean time between intercourse and contraceptive use may be more than a year, as has been demonstrated, ample time to become pregnant. The rationalization for not using contraception presented by most of these young women is that they did not expect to have intercourse. This denial syndrome has resulted in countless unintended pregnancies and hundreds of thousands of unwanted babies.

The evidence is clear that the use of effective contraception makes a difference: only 6 percent of adolescents who always used a medical method of contraception experienced a premarital pregnancy compared ot 58 percent of adolescents who never used any method at all (Zelnik and Kantner, 1978). Thus, consistent users of effective methods were 10 times better protected against pregnancy than nonusers.

Use of Contraception and Clinics

Most sexually active adolescents have used some method of contraception during their brief sexual careers. A 1979 profile of use at last intercourse shows about one-third were using pills and IUDs, 20 percent were using diaphragms, condoms, or foam, 17 percent were using the least effective methods (withdrawal, rhythm, douche) and 30 percent were using no method (AGI, 1981). Pill use among sexually active adolescents increased dramatically between 1971 and 1976, but as a result of the negative publicity accorded to the long-term effects of pill use, a slight downturn was evidenced by 1979. The use of condoms and withdrawal showed marked increases, while diaphragm use more than doubled (from 1 to 2.5 percent).

The safety and effectiveness of methods are subjects of considerable controversy, with repeated "scare" stories about the pill, recalls of the Dalkon Shield, and other problems. Many clinicians prefer to prescribe diaphragms to youngsters; high success rates have been reported by one doctor who took the time to teach each patient how to use the method (Lane, et al., 1976). In some circles, natural family-planning methods are being promoted. This requires a daily regimen of self-examination and sophisticated knowledge of the reproductive system. Family-planning clinic personnel strictly enforce informed consent procedures and tell patients about possible side effects and long-term consequences of each method. Among clinic patients, however, there has been little observable increase in diaphragm use or natural methods, a large drop-off in IUD use, and little change in pill use. More than three-fourths of all adolescent clinic patients still opt for pills.

Family-planning clinics in the U.S. served 1½ million patients under 20 years of age in 1978, one-third of the total case load of 4.5 million (Secretary of Health and Human Services, 1980). Organized clinic services are available for women of all ages in 5000 clinics located in most parts of the country, operated by health departments, Planned Parenthood affiliates, hospitals, poverty programs, free clinics, and other types of agencies. About 40 percent of all adolescent patients were served by health departments, 30 percent by

Planned Parenthood affiliates, 10 percent by hospitals and the rest by other facilities.

It is of some interest that local health departments now provide family-planning services to more than two out of five of the young patients. When federal funds for birth-control programs first became available about a decade ago, many local boards of health were reluctant to initiate what they regarded as a potentially controversial service, fearing the wrath of the community if they did so. Yet after programs were initiated, little resistance was encountered and in fact, many health departments which formerly limited their services to sanitation and immunization, began to offer preventive health services for the first time. The diffusion of family-planning services among traditional health agencies is an interesting example of the strength of consumer demand and acceptance overcoming the timidity of local health officials. At first, health departments offered contraception to married women only. However, these barriers have almost all disappeared and health-department clinics are among the most successful at serving adolescents.

Many agencies offer special programs for teenagers in their family planning clinics: designated sessions with specially trained counselors; peer discussion groups; male involvement activities; novel outreach approaches in schools, social clubs, the workplace and street corners. Television, posters, radio, and other media efforts are being developed. However, areas which appear to be the most successful at serving at-risk adolescents are those with the most accessible services for women of all ages, rather than those with specialized teen programs (Dryfoos and Heisler, 1978). In interviews, all but the youngest adolescents claimed that they required no special treatment but wanted to receive services without "hassle" and long waiting times, with privacy and confidentiality (URSA, 1976). These are the same attributes that older women mention most often, particularly waiting times, which can consume up to 4 hours in some clinics.

In 1979, an extensive evaluation of clinic services for adolescents was conducted by DHEW as part of its initiative on adolescent pregnancy. (Coughlin, 1978) An internal review team strongly recommended the strengthening of the counseling component in family-planning clinics. They found that most clinic sites offered counseling that was limited to information and education about birth-control methods, a medical history review or update, preparation for pelvic examination, and selection of a contraceptive method. Additional components recommended included more in-depth counseling to identify problems and assist teens with their concerns about contraception, sexuality, and their lives in general, and to strengthen teen-agers decision-making skills in resolving their problems.

The assessment team also commented on the importance of involving parents in this process and the need of parents for help in communicating with their children. In their interviews with parents, they found that a majority rejected the idea that parental consent should be required before teenagers could go to clinics; the parents feared that some teenagers would be deprived of needed services.

Despite the parental attitudes described above, a recent survey found that 44 percent of abortion clinics and 20 percent of family-planning clincs require parental consent or notification before a teenager can be served (Torres, 1980). However, the circumstances under which these policies are applied may differ widely and in some instances not affect availability of services. Less than half of the restrictive family-planning clinics have procedures that actually require the patient to bring her parent to the clinic (typical of hospitals); the remainder are more lenient in enforcing the policies. Access to abortion services is more limited for adolescents, not only because of parental consent requirements, but also due to other barriers such as distance and cost.

The abortion delivery system is somewhat different from the family-planning delivery system. While contraceptive care was largely added onto the service roster of established agencies after federal funds became available (in health departments, in particular), more than two-thirds of all abortions are performed by recently organized freestanding clinics. Many are operated for profit, yet because of the volume of procedures they perform, these clinics are able to provide abortions at a lower cost than hospitals (about $165 compared to $250 plus physician's fee in hospitals) (Lindheim, 1979). The 522 abortion clinics, the preferred locus for adolescents seeking pregnancy termination, are located primarily in metropolitan areas. Because of cost, lack of interest, and policy shifts, as well as negative community pressures, hospitals play a decreasing role in abortion provision.

Private physicians may also provide their adolescent patients with family-planning care and even perform abortions when necessary. This is one subject about which research is limited. From rough estimates, it has been assumed that 1.3 million adolescents received family-planning care from a local private physician in 1978 (Secretary, Health, Education, and Welfare, 1979). It is known that about half of all sexually active adolescent pill users received their first prescription from a private physician. There is a great deal of mobility between sources of care; some youngsters prefer the anonymity of the clinic for an initial visit and after that go to their own physician. Others switch from physicians to clinics. Many use no source for contraception and their initial visit for fertility-related care is an abortion clinic or a prenatal clinic.

Not all physicians welcome unmarried adolescents as contraceptive patients; in a survey of Arizona doctors, more than one-fifth would never serve a minor without parental consent, and only 31 percent would always do so (Jenkins-Reed, 1979). Even for minors with parental consent, only 62 percent of the doctors would always serve them.

Knowledge About Reproduction

Why do some girls get pregnant at very early ages while other manage to survive their adolescent years without that experience? About one-fourth of the adolescent pregnancies are intended and reflect conscious decisions by young women, mostly married and aged 18 or 19 to begin their families. Unintended pregnancies, occurring more frequently among younger unmarried women, can result from the failure of even effective contraceptive methods, the use of ineffective methods, or the lack of contraception entirely. In order to use contraception effectively, it is necessary to have at least a rudimentary knowledge of reproduction and contraception.

Studies have shown repeatedly that the level of knowledge about reproduction among adolescents is inadequate to insure protection against unwanted pregnancy. Only two out of five adolescent women know the time of the month when they are at the greatest risk of pregnancy (two weeks after the period begins) (Zelnik and Kantner, 1977). Those who are sexually active have only a slightly higher level of knowledge than those who are not, and sex education courses appear to make little difference. Parents are not much better informed than their children; in one highly educated group, only 65 percent of respondents age 20 and over were able to answer the question about time of risk correctly (Columbus, 1979). Even if parents are willing to inform their children about human sexuality and reproduction, they are often ill-equipped. It has been shown that well-educated young parents, who were themselves the product of the sixties' generation, are reluctant to talk to their children about sex.

An important determinant of unintended pregnancy, it may be concluded, is sheer ignorance. The lack of sufficient knowledge to initiate and maintain adequate fertility control appears across a broad spectrum of young people. This seems ironic in a society where everyone is exposed to blatant and overt sexuality at very early ages.

The determinants of childbearing are not the same as the determinants of abortion seeking. In regard to childbearing, race and poverty are still clear predictors of early maternity, even in light of changing norms among non-poor, white adolescents. A number of psychological studies have identified other characteristics of unmarried adolescent childbearers controlling for social and economic variables (Chilman, 1980). These young mothers tend to have lower self-esteem and to do less well in school. It is not yet clear whether these youngsters drop out of school because they are pregnant, or become pregnant so they can have an excuse to drop out of school, or drop out of school first, and then become pregnant. It appears, however, that those who are less connected to the school system and have little faith that their education will give them further options, are more likely to become mothers.

Pregnant adolescents who opt for abortion are somewhat different from those who carry to term; they come from higher status families, are less religious, and are unmarried. A reasonable assumption may be that the decision to have an abortion is also determined by accessibility: knowledge that abortion is a viable legal alternative, awareness of the location of an abortion provider, and the means to travel to that place and to pay for the procedure.

In 1980, the Supreme Court ruled that the so-called Hyde Amendment restrictions, prohibiting Medicaid funding for abortions except under extreme circumstances, could be enforced by states. The climate produced by the debate about public funding for abortions could have an effect on adolescents' possibilities of obtaining abortions, both directly, by limiting subsidization for those who are eligible, and indirectly, by creating an aura of disapproval and confusion as to the legality of the procedure.

UNMET NEEDS: POSSIBLE INTERVENTIONS

If more than 10 percent of all adolescent females are experiencing a pregnancy each year, and if three-quarters of these pregnancies are unintended, it is clear that additional interventions are required. These interventions are needed at many stages of development:

- Young children need to know about family life, reproduction, and sexuality;
- Prepubescent children need to know about contraception, pregnancy, and abortion;
- Young adolescents need help in understanding their sexual feelings and deciding about their sexual behavior;
- Sexually active youngsters need access to family-planning services and counseling;
- Pregnant youngsters need access to pregnancy counseling, abortion services, maternal, and child-health services and other kinds of care.

Early Sex Education

Perhaps the greatest unmet need is at the earliest stages. To state the obvious, if youngsters were well informed about reproduction, contraception, and the consequences of unintended childbearing before the option of sexual intercourse was even presented to them, perhaps the decisions they would make would be more rational (e.g., either to protect themselves from pregnancy or not to have intercourse).

This means that parents, schools, churches, and the society in general, will have to be willing to acknowledge that human sexuality is a subject that needs more open discussion, at least as open as in the pornographic magazines, suggestive songs, and lurid movies that are currently the instructors of youth. The subject matter is already available; some high schools have offered sex education for decades and new curricula for elementary and high-school students are being developed on sex and family-life education in many parts of the country. Opinion polls show that most parents agree that sex education should be taught in schools. Yet, as was pointed out above, youngsters still lack essential information and in many communities, school boards resist the initiation of even the blandest social hygiene approaches. Given the emerging patterns of early and unprotected intercourse, sex education without information about contraception and abortion is clearly inadequate.

One approach to young people that has been underutilized is through the media. In only a few instances has television been used to either recruit patients for family-planning clinics or inform them about reproduction or contraception. At the same time, the subject of teenage pregnancy has received dramatic coverage in a series of TV movies and soap operas. Advertising of contraceptive methods is not allowed, not because of law but because of the negative policies of TV networks. Again, the double standard is obvious (as it must be to young people), that various sprays for feminine hygiene are acceptable to show on the TV screen, but condoms are not.

America's youngsters are considered to be a prime market for "hucksters"; it is interesting to postulate what would happen to the adolescent pregnancy rate if condoms were marketed with the same enthusiasm as rock-and-roll tapes. Left to advertising agencies, there is a risk that contraceptive methods could be sold to young people without adequate attention to taste and accuracy of claims. Preventing unintended adolescent pregnancy is certainly in the public interest and it therefore follows that public interest advertising could be directed toward assisting youth with fertility control. In the same vein, if children grew up with the same exposure to contraceptive advertising that they do to toothpaste ads, it would be more likely that they would use contraception the first time they were ready to initiate sexual activity, the key moment at which the practice of pregnancy prevention must begin.

Expansion of Family Planning Clinic Outreach

This emphasis on the earlier years should not imply that everything that is needed by adolescents in later years is available to them. While 1½ million sexually active adolescents used family-planning clinics in 1978, and about 1.3 million went to their private physicians, still at least 2 million youngsters who are at risk of unintended pregnancy did not use medically supervised contraception and, in fact, as has been pointed out, 30 percent of sexually active adolescents used no method at all. To reach all these young people, family-planning programs will have to broaden their outreach efforts to recruit more adolescent patients and to encourage initiation of clinic use closer to the time of initiation of sexual intercourse. (Currently, a lapse of a year between first intercourse and the initial clinic visit is typical.) Most clinics are organized to enroll medical patients only; visits that do not result in a physical examination and prescription have not generally been subsidized by public funds. This policy discourages family-planning agencies from recruiting patients who desire family-planning counseling with the effect of limiting clinic use to those who are already sexually active. This policy is currently undergoing examination with a view toward broader usage of the clinic sites for education and counseling about all aspects of fertility control for young people and for the community at large.

Youth-serving agencies of all kinds—YM and YWCAs, 4-H Clubs, scouts, church groups, mental-health clinics, community health centers, as well as schools, must become more aware of their clients' needs for assistance in the area of sexual development. Along with all the interest and involvement in communication techniques, values-clarification, decision-making skills, there must be recognition that young people also need and want to confront the difficult questions of sex and maturation directly and honestly. They are acutely aware of the omission of this subject in school curricula and youth programs. In the adolescent's view, when adults—parents, teachers, group-workers, counselors—"cop out" on the matter, then they lose the right to be indignant about adolescent behavior and its consequences.

Access to Abortion Services

While more than 400,000 adolescents obtained legal abortions in 1978, others, who wanted to terminate their unintended pregnancies, were unable to do so. As shown in Table 2-1, almost 300,000 unintended births occurred to adolescent mothers; it is not unreasonable to assume that about half of those women would have preferred to terminate their pregnancies if this option had been available to them. Geographic accessibility remains a major factor in abortion availability (unlike family planning). In many parts of the country, few abortion facilities have been identified; there are still 300 metropolitan counties and 2087 nonmetropolitan counties with no facilities, and many contain large numbers of women who need abortions (Seims, 1980). Even in communities with available abortion facilities, adolescents may be deprived of access to pregnancy termination because of real or perceived barriers such as parental consent or parental notification requirements.

Programs for Adolescent Mothers, Fathers and their Babies

The recent Title IV legislation directed toward enhancing the outcomes of adolescent pregnancies has received only minimal funding and in all probability will not be renewed in 1981. Thus, despite a lot of publicity, little progress has been made toward helping young mothers, fathers, and their babies deal with a myriad of health, social, and economic problems, exacerbated in a time of unemployment and inflation. In one view, the problems of adolescent childbearing cannot be separated from the problems of race and poverty; they all lead to disadvantage, and in combination, produce negative and long-lasting consequences for all members of the family—the grandparents, mother, father, and the offspring.

An adolescent girl is told that she should not get pregnant because if she does, she will have to stay home and take care of the baby and be deprived of further education, skilled employment, and high income. That offer can only make sense to a youngster who believes that the job and the money are really options. If the options do not exist, and for many minority youngsters they do not, then who is to say what rational behavior should be.

High-quality programs directed toward pregnant teen-agers and young parent to help them improve their parenting skills, stay in school, find gainful employment, and other forms of assistance are essential. Only about 20 percent of teenage parents were receiving these much needed services in a recent year (Goldstein and Wallace, 1978). However, as with sex education, early intervention would have a much greater cost-benefit. The promise of gainful employment and higher incomes may be as effective pregnancy-prevention measures as the use of contraception.

The Future

The prevention of unintended pregnancy is stil an inexact science. Without better contraceptive technology, the goal that every pregnancy be planned and wanted cannot be reached. Even the most effective methods can fail; women of all ages experience some anxiety at having to choose between safety and efficacy. Sterilization is now the method of choice among almost one-third of married couples, but this is surely not a method for youngsters. If sexually active adolescents are to be expected to exercise fertility control, either new methods will be required or existing methods, such as the pill, modified to assure long-term viability.

More adolescents use contraception and visit family-planning clinics all the time; they demonstrate an increasing sense of responsibility for their sexual behavior. Yet, there remains a sizable group who know about contraception, have access to clinics, are aware of the consequences of pregnancy, and still have intercourse without protection. Until these youngsters begin to practice birth control, the prognosis for the elimination of unintended adolescent pregnancy is not good. Several approaches have been proposed here; to support programs to help disadvantaged adolescents realize their life's options; to educate parents so the parents can talk to their children; to involve all youth-serving agencies in counseling and referral; to use media to legitimate the family-planning program and to popularize condoms; to expand outreach in family-planning clinics and assure better access to abortion providers; and to eliminate barriers to clinic use such as parental consent requirements. The implementation of these approaches is dependent on a combination of federal support and community acceptance.

The future for fertility control among adolescents may be jeopardized by the implementation of other approaches that deny federal support and obstruct community acceptance in the guise of protecting parents' rights and keeping the American family structure intact. Partisans of these objectives often regard premarital intercourse as immoral and propose abstention as the primary solution to adolescent pregnancy. Harassment of clinic personnel, denial of funds for programs, passage of restrictive local ordinances, and even abortion clinic burnings have been attributed to antiabortion and antibirth-control groups who share those views.

The problem of adolescent pregnancy is not a phenomenon isolated from the problems of the society as a whole. Its solution, to the degree possible, is highly dependent on how the society responds to a wide range of diverse needs and intense pressures. At least it can be said about fertility control that specific programs have made a difference in the past, and that with more support they can make a difference in the future.

REFERENCES

1. Alan Guttmacher Institute (AGI). *Teenage Pregnancy: The Problem That Hasn't Gone Away*, 1981.
2. Alan Guttmacher Institute (AGI). *11 Million Teenagers*. New York, 1976.
3. Baldwin, Wendy and Virginia Cain. "The Children of Teenage Parents." *Family Planning Perspectives*. Vol. **12**, No. 1, January/February, 1980.
4. Chilman, Catherine. (ed.) *Adolescent Pregnancy and Childbearing*. Washington, D.C.; U.S. Government Printing Office, 1980.
5. "Columbus Alive," Responsive Television, Station QUBE, Columbus, Ohio, September 25, 1979.
6. Coughlin, Dennis J. *Family Planning and the Teenager: A Service Delivery Assessment*. Report presented to Secretary of DHEW (Califano), November, 1978.
7. Dryfoos, Joy and Toni Heisler. "Contraceptive Services for Adolescents: An Overview." *Family Planning Perspectives*. Vol **10**, No. 4, July/August 1978.

8. Goldstein, Hyman and Helen M. Wallace. "Services for and Needs of Pregnant Teenagers in Large Cities of the U.S., 1976." *Public Health Reports*. January/February 1978, Vol. **93**, No. 1.
9. Jenkins-Reed, Emily and Jane A. Canby. *Family Planning in Arizona, 1977: Needs Assessment*. Arizona Family Planning Council, January, 1979.
10. Lane, Mary, Rosalind Arceo, and Aquiles J. Sobrero. "Successful Use of the Diaphragm and Jelly by a Young Population: Report of a Clinical Study." *Family Planning Perspectives*, Vol. **8**, No. 2, March/April 1976.
11. Lindheim, Barbara. "Services, Policies and Costs in U.S. Abortion Facilities." *Family Planning Perspectives*. Vol. **11**: No. 2, 283, 1979.
12. Secretary of Health and Human Services. *Five-Year Plan for Family Planning Services and Population Research*. Submitted to Congress, May, 1980.
13. Secretary of Health, Education, and Welfare. *Five-Year Plan for Family Planning Services and Population Research*. Submitted to Congress, September 1979.
14. Seim, Sara. "Abortion Availability in the U.S." *Family Planning Perspectives*. Vol. **12**, No. 2, March/April, 1980.
15. Select Committee on Population. *Fertility and Contraception in America: Adolescent and Pre-Adolescent Pregnancy*. USGPO, Washington, 1978, Vol. **II**, No. 3, pp. 203–217.
16. Torres, Aida. "Telling Parents About Adolescents' Use of Family Planning and Abortion Services: Clinic Policies and Teenage Behavior." *Family Planning Perspectives*. Vol. **12**, No. 6, November/December, 1980.
17. Urban and Rural Systems Associates (URSA). *Improving Family Planning Services for Teenagers*. Report to DHEW, June, 1976.
18. Zabin, Laurie Schwab, John F. Kantner, and Melvin Zelnik. "The Risk of Adolescent Pregnancy in the First Months of Intercourse." *Family Planning Perspectives*, Vol. **II**, No. 4, July/August 1979.
19. Zelnik, Melvin and John F. Kantner. "Sexual Activity, Contraceptive Use and Pregnancy Among Metropolitan-Area Teenagers: 1971–1979." *Family Planning Perspectives*. Vol. **12**, No. 5, September/October 1980.
20. Zelnik, Melvin and John F. Kantner. "Contraceptive Patterns and Premarital Pregnancy Among Women Aged 15–19 in 1976." *Family Planning Perspectives*, Vol. **10**, No. 3, May/June, 1978.
21. Zelnik, Melvin and John F. Kantner. "First Pregnancies to Women Aged 15–19: 1976 and 1971." *Family Planning Perspectives*, Vol. **10**, No. 1, January/February 1978, Table 12, p. 17.
22. Zelnik, Melvin and John F. Kantner. "Sexual and Contraceptive Experience of Young Unmarried Women in the U.S., 1976 and 1971." *Family Planning Perspectives*. Vol. **9**, No. 2, March/April 1977.

3.
The Health System's Responsibility to the Adolescent at Risk

Donald E. Greydanus, M.D.,
Director, Adolescent Medical Clinic,
Department of Pediatrics,
University of Rochester Medical Center,
Rochester, New York

It is the premise of this chapter that health-care professionals should provide counseling about sexuality and information about contraception to teenagers, particularly those at risk for pregnancy. Thus, basic concepts of adolescence and adolescent sexuality are reviewed. It is stressed that parents, as well as their children, be taught such aspects of normal sexuality. Teenagers, as well as their parents, should be prepared for the inevitable changes of adolescence long before puberty is achieved. Sex education is the responsibility of parents, along with the health-care profession. Fundamental to any such educational achievement, however, is establishment of adequate rapport with youth.

All methods of contraception can be presented by the counselor (whether social worker, psychologist, physician, or other). Such discussions imply neither acceptance nor rejection of teenage coital activity, but are specifically designed to reduce the large numbers of teenage pregnancies and sexually transmitted diseases currently noted. We should remember that we are not transferring our own morality onto our patients (or clients), but are helping them understand and then deal with their own specific views.

Abstinence or barrier methods (as condom or diaphram with vaginal contraceptives) can always be emphasized, but oral contraception remains the most common of the effective methods. Effective methods also include the minipill, intrauterine device, medroxyprogesterone acetate, and postcoital contraceptives. Methods which are generally not recommended for teenagers include rhythm (periodic abstinence), coitus interruptus, lactation, and douching. Sterilization and abortion are not considered in this section.

INTRODUCTION

When the health-care professional attempts to deal with a phenomenon as complex as teenage pregnancy and its prevention, it is best to first consider the underlying process of adolescence and adolescent sexuality. The teenager is that special individual who is undergoing a dramatic change, from childhood to adulthood. Puberty thrusts a willing or unwilling child into a new phase of growth and development. This person is given a finite number of years to become an autonomous adult, functioning at intellectual, vocational, and sexual levels which are acceptable to society. Separation from parents, rapidly changing physique, peer-group influences, increasing educational requirements, emerging sexuality, and other factors, clash and force him/her to react to many biological, cognitive, and sociocultural influences. What has transpired during childhood combines with current adolescent conditions to determine how the youth will react to this inevitable process of adolescence.

The health-care system must react by attempting to help the youth cross the oft uncertain bridge from childhood to adulthood and offer as much support as possible. A major contribution stems from the basic recognition that all youth must come to grips with their own concepts of sexuality. Humans are indeed sexual beings, that is, they derive physical response and pleasure from physical contact with themselves and others. Thus, erections are noted in utero, masturbation is common in the 2–4-year-old, genital exploration of playmates is often reported in latency-age children—these and other observations or situations acquaint the child with some sexuality concepts and help explain his/her natural curiosity about sexuality related phenomena. The reaction to this can have considerable influence on the child. Parents' failure to acknowledge the existence of sexuality, religious constraints placed on it, and mass media exploitation of sexuality all clearly exert their impact on the child. When the biological clock of time causes the inevitable sex hormonal changes, failure to recognize and deal with these issues can be detrimental to the whole process of adolescence itself.

A major responsibility of the health system is to educate the child and his/her parents to deal with such issues as directly as possible. Understanding and acceptance of normal human sexuality concepts should start from infancy and proceed through all phases of life, including childhood, adolescence, and adulthood.

In this regard, it is helpful to consider normal adolescent sexuality, as it relates to the three psychological states of adolescence—early, middle, and late. Early adolescence is defined by pubertal influences—specific body changes, usually occurring between ages 11–14 years. The youth typically is concerned about body issues, begins to emancipate or separate from parents, and identifies with extraparental figures. During this time, the same gender peer group becomes important. Males have several male friends or may join some type of "gang," and girls develop a few very close friends. Masturbation and homosexual feelings or experiences often occur at this time. Guilt over such feelings or thoughts can have considerable negative impact on the early adolescent's growth and development.

Middle adolescence is characterized by completion of most pubertal events, usually between 14–17 years of age. The youth tends to turn away from body concerns and grapple with more basic concepts of development—further emancipation from parents, peer group influences, and heterosexual thoughts and experiences. Masturbatory action continues, homosexuality declines, and heterosexual experimentation becomes the norm or, or least, the desire. Family and youth must be educated to the realization that such processes are normal and, indeed, inevitable. The actual expression of heterosexual feelings is dependent on a wide range of factors—pubertal development, sociocultural background, religious beliefs, opportunity, self-image, and many others. Many youth experiment with various sexual activities, including masturbation, kissing, petting, oral-genital sex, and even coitus. The consequences of such action may include guilt, sexually transmitted diseases, and pregnancy. Though few would feel that middle adolescents are prepared for "significant" sexuality and its results, the health system should acknowledge its existence, attempt to prevent as much of it as possible, and deal directly with these consequences.

Late adolescence is seen in the youth who has finished most of the biological changes, has accepted himself/herself intellectually and sexually, and now becomes more invested in acquiring vocational skills and an adult sexual role. This is the last phase of adolescence, and prepares the individual for an adult life-style. Various heterosexual activities occur, as noted with middle adolescence. Masturbatory activity remains common, and in a few, a homosexual life-style may displace or alternate with heterosexuality.

As health professionals, what can we do to assist this process from childhood through the various phases of adolescence? As noted, education of the youth and family is important. Sexuality is a basic part of the individual and begins in infancy.[1] Discussion of these ideas with parents and even children should take place. Activity which is common to children, as masturbation or curiosity about genitals, should be reviewed from a broad perspective. Parents should be taught to give children some range of freedom, with limits determined by society and their own moral views. Discussions with children should be directed at their specific cognitive level. Physicians can examine the child's external genitalia, including this as part of each well-child visit. Children can be taught the correct names of genital parts. Giving these parts "special" names and ignoring "normal" activity only serves to teach children that genitals and sexuality are dirty, unclean, or somehow "forbidden." Parents' attitudes can be explored so that the child enters adolescence without being taught (overtly or covertly) negative facts and attitudes about normal sexuality.

It can be noted that attitudes toward sexuality have changed dramatically over the past 50 years. Masturbation, for example, tends to be viewed in this modern era as a harmless, physiologic process, yet centuries of negative attitudes remain,[2] and children (or youth) are often given mixed messages concerning this aspect. Civilization has always tended to conclude that masturbatory activity or "excess" coital activity would impair its survival—these beliefs remain as many parents continue to condemn or ignore such acts. Again, open discussions to explore one's feelings can be helpful. Any professional can aid with this, whether physician, psychologist, social worker, teacher, or other.

If the child and parents have been taught to accept and respect their own sexuality, within the confines of society and their own moral judgments, then the teenager will be better prepared to acknowledge and understand his/her own emerging views and concepts regarding sexual function. The concept of responsible sex functioning can then be put into proper perspective. Indeed, the future adult personality is intimately related to how these concepts develop in childhood and adolescence.[3]

Teenagers must go through early, middle, and late adolescence and deal with these issues. Whether or not it is "normal" for teenagers to be sexually active is difficult to know. The earlier maturation noted during the past 100 years, a changing societal attitude toward sex, and other factors certainly have contributed to the observation that many teenagers have coitus, with resultant increased risk for sexually transmitted diseases and pregnancy.[4] The realization that many million teenagers are sexually active and that there are 1 million pregnant youth and many million cases of teenage venereal disease each year is a startling concept for health professionals.[5-8] These problems are noted among all youth, whether early, middle, or late adolescents. Medical and psychosocial risks to pregnant youth do exist,[9-15] and will be discussed elsewhere in this book.

Thus, prevention of teenage pregnancy and sexually transmitted diseases would seem to be the goal of most professionals dealing with youth. Again, we return to the previous theme as to what can be done by the health system. Preparation of the child has been mentioned. What about the teenager? Our responsibility involves learning to develop rapport with the teenager and then seeking to provide education about the risks of coital activity and methods of preventing some of these consequences. Professionals at all levels can provide education, but having an effective relationship with the youth is also important and perhaps more fundamental. These concepts will be explored in this chapter.

Failure to Use Contraceptives

Clearly not all teenagers can be helped to avoid pregnancy. The causes of teenage pregnancy are complex and will be discussed in other sections of this book. Some youth want to become pregnant,[16] and do not heed any advice to avoid coital activity or utilize effective contraception. There are many motivating factors for adolescent coital patterns and developmental influences can be enormous.[17] Early adolescents often become pregnant to forge closer ties to their mothers or simply to try out their new bodies. Many are simply not cognitively able to understand aspects of pregnancy prevention or of pregnancy itself. Many young pregnant teenagers draw their fetuses as stick figures outside their own bodies.[18] Magical thinking is often noted in this group and convinces them that they will not get "caught." The younger the teenager, the more ineffectively they tend to use contraceptives.[19] Many simply fail to acknowledge the consequences of their sexual activity.[20]

Middle adolescents may refuse contraception and become pregnant because of oedipal conflicts, desire for autonomy, and a need to manipulate parents or sex partner. Providing contraception to these individuals can be a very difficult task.[21] The pregnancy may be part of a general reaction to unpleasant life circumstances and thus prevention of the pregnancy must start with improving the many detrimental socioeconomic problems they face.[22] Older adolescents become pregnant for reasons similar to adults, but early and middle adolescent issues may also surface. Many youth are at high risk for contraceptive failure—this group certainly needs further identification.[23,24]

Though health professionals will encounter some youth unwilling or unable to avoid pregnancy, this does not mean a pessimistic picture need be painted. Many youth do wish, and can be motivated to avoid pregnancy, and the health professional who develops an awareness of the needs of teenagers and an ability to interact with them, can be very effective in this regard.[25] Such an awareness involves assessing the psychosocial and physiological maturity of the youth and interaction on the level of the particular teenager, whether he/she is in early, middle, or late adolescence and is normally or abnormally developed.[26,27]

Such a view of adolescence implies that the teenager is often capable of understanding aspects of his/her own health care and that such an understanding is very important. It is critical to provide youth with as much help with their health needs as possible.

One aspect of this is for the health professional to begin during older childhood or early adolescence to deal with the patient on an individual basis. We, as health-care professionals, tend to deal primarily with the parents when caring for a child. Physicians especially develop a primary physician-parent relationship and secondary physician-child relationship. In this transactional health-care model, decisions about the child are made between parents and physician, with the child allowed little control in this process.[28]

However, all members of the health-care system must change this level of interaction when the patient (or "client") is a teen-ager. It is often difficult to work with youth unless a primary physician-adolescent relationship is developed in which one works directly with the youth in a one-on-one, confidential manner. The professional attempts to show the youth that he/she is interested in them and is not a mere extension of the parent. Thus, the youth is seen alone on most or all occasions and encouraged to speak openly. Complete confidentiality cannot be promised, but guidelines can be established by the worker at the very onset of the initial meeting. Parents are not ignored but are informed of this attempt to allow their son/daughter new freedom in growth and development. A secondary physician-parent relationship then ensues. Younger teenagers may be hesitant to accept this, while older teenagers usually do.

Sex Education for Youth

Once the professional has gained the teenager's confidence, it becomes possible to assess the individual's level of sexuality and how he/she can be helped to avoid the consequences of irresponsible coital activity. We are not their parents and should not tell them what to do or what not to do from a moral point of view. Our role is to aid them to reach sufficient maturity to make their own responsible decisions. This is especially true for middle adolescents, who are emancipating from their parents and eager for the advice of their peer group and *some* extraparental adults. The advice of peers is often wrong, while our own advice about sexuality and other matters should be as accurate as possible. Teenagers frequently relate peer-supported myths about sex, pregnancy, and contraception.[29] We should attempt to take the time to educate our youth about the basic, true concepts, or find others who can do so.

The health-care system becomes, then, responsible along with the parents for the sex education of teenagers. This subject of sex education is, of course, a highly charged and sensitive one in our current era. However, such education is the duty of both parents and professionals who come in contact with teenagers. Parents must be urged to teach their own concepts of morality and sexuality to their children. Most parents, in fact, want this duty,[30] and one can educate them to accomplish it. Knowledgeable, interested parents can be very effective educators,[31,32] and should realize that no communication about sexuality is a very specific, often negative type of communication.[33] Such communication and education begins early, since sexuality begins early. Sole reliance on school-based educational programs is not effective.[34] Knowledge itself does not lead to sexual experimentation, but ignorance can increase the teenager's risk for an unwanted pregnancy.[35] All types of educational techniques should be used, including classrooms and even the mass media.[36,37] Sex education and counseling should be the duty of all trained health-care professionals working with youth.[38]

Another concept to emphasize is that such interaction is a combined effort of all such health-care profesionals—psychologists, social workers, physicians, and others. Programs which report the best success in dealing with sexually active teenagers and reducing pregnancy in youth are those which consist of many professional individuals working together to establish rapport with their patients and counseling them over a prolonged period of time.[39-42] Programs which also seek the enhancement of life opportunities for children and teenagers are necessary.[43] Such an undertaking, however, is difficult though important. This discussion now turns to a look at what contraceptives are available to youth.

Contraception for the Adolescent at Risk

Thus, counseling about contraception should be the responsibility of *any* health-care professional who works with sexually active teenagers. Prescription of medical methods of contraception is done by a physician, but there are simply too many youth at risk and too few physicians trained in this specific area to be of value to the millions of involved teenagers. Just as the physician should not hand out contraception without added counseling about sexuality, the counselor should not deal with issues of sexuality without providing contraceptive information. Too many youth use no contraception or rely on poor methods.[44,45] Too many youth are sexually active for months before attending a medical clinic seeking specific contraception,[46] and so many become pregnant within 6 months of coital initiation (some even within 1 month).[47]

The value of effective contraception is clear. Zelnik and Kantner have estimated that an additional 680,000 teenagers would become pregnant annually without contraception, and if all youth used effective contraceptive methods there would be at least 300,000 less teenage pregnancies each year.[48] Legal barriers for teenage contraception have been widely removed and virtually any sexually active teenager wishing contraception can now receive it in a confidential manner.[49-51]

Thus, the goal of many health professionals seems clear—to knowledgeably provide advice to the interested youth. The challenge in this regard is posed to all. We must remember that the patient is choosing to be sexually active or to avoid coitus and to use a contraceptive method or not. Our own moral views should not interfere with this process.[52] The professional who looks within himself/herself and finds there are specific views which significantly affect his/her advice or relationship to the youth should refer this patient or client to other sources. Granting neutral advice or recommending a specific contraceptive method does not necessarily imply acceptance or approval of the youth's coital activity or manner of sexual expression. Many times, we lose sight of this concept.

It must also be admitted that not all our prejudice can be removed, but we must attempt its elimination in ourselves and in our colleagues who deal with youth. Not infrequently, one can note anger or disgust on the part of some professionals dealing with a youth who is pregnant or has a sexually transmitted disease. Then a condescending attitude or even a rough pelvic examination or other prejudicial measures are noted. Such must be eliminated as much as possible.

Professional advice to the teenager concerning contraception must also be based on a knowledgeable review of all methods available to the patient and his/her sex partner (Table 3-1). There is no ideal contraceptive method for all individuals,[53] and a "supermarket" or "cafeterialike" approach is useful, with all available methods being presented.[54] In addition, methods chosen at one time can always be changed at a later date—the patient's choice always remains in a state of flux, and his/her counselor or advisor can help with this. For example, the birth-control pill may be the best alternative for a 16-year-old sexually active youth who refuses barrier and other methods; however, she may change her mind at age 18 with further personal growth and maturity. Advice to the youth is given within the framework that adolescence represents only part (but a significant part) of her total reproductive life.

Table 3-1. Methods of contraception.

A. Abstinence
B. Barrier Methods
   1. Diaphragm
   2. Vaginal contraceptives
   3. Condom
   4. Combinations
C. Rhythm Methods
   1. Periodic abstinence
   2. Basal body temperature method
   3. Mucus method of Billings
   4. Combinations
D. Oral Contraceptives ("Medical Contraception")
E. Intrauterine Devices
F. Postcoital Contraception
G. Injectable Contraceptives
H. Miscellaneous
   1. Coitus interruptus
   2. Lactation
   3. Noncoital sex
   4. Douche
   5. Homosexuality
   6. Sterilization
   7. Abortion

Also, counselors should include the patient's sex partner, if at all feasible. Counseling the "couple" may be more effective than the one partner alone. Any advice or actual prescription should be vigorously followed up to allow the youth to reflect on current choices and attitudes, to incorporate life changes in the decision, and to allow continued ventilation about the whole process of adolescent sexuality. The young teenager especially needs careful professional supervision and frequent counseling.

An overview of contraceptive methods is now presented.

A. Abstinence. Any discussion of contraception should include exploration of the reasons for the youth's sexual activity and abstinence can certainly be offered as a viable option. Many teen-agers elect not to be sexually active and many others are only sporadically sexually active. Some youth have an initial coital experience so they will not be accused of being "virginal" by peer groups, and then refrain for a prolonged period of time from coitus. Patterns are varied, and thus it is important to obtain a careful sex history. Whatever the previous pattern, the counselor should remind the patient that coital experience is not necessary and can be postponed without psychological or physiologic risk. Youths caught up in middle-adolescent sexual concepts may need this reassurance. Here good rapport with the patient is critical, as is a confidential relationship. Question should be directed to the quality of the peer-group influence, especially with the middle adolescent. Rape or domination by an older teenager or adult may be operational in a particular early adolescent.

Previous sexual activity, regardless of the initiating factors, may lower the youth's self-worth, leading to further risk for pregnancy (because of a failure for adequate self-care). The greater the psychosocial maturity, the more success one can have in this approach of offering abstinence as a real method. Alternatives to sexual activity can be presented, as well as ways to improve the patient's life opportunities. Patients should not engage in careless sex as a reaction to depression or dissatisfaction with their life. This is not to make the choice for him/her, but to allow him/her to explore all options.

Many, however, have chosen a coital pattern and will need a careful matching with other specific contraceptive methods. If poor methods are being used, advice to use an effective method is important. Time is needed to educate the youth concerning what methods he/she can rely on and what present unacceptably high pregnancy risks. The youth should be told that unprotected sex carries a very high pregnancy rate. However, magical thinking is noted in so many teenagers, giving them a false sense of security and a false idea that contraceptive methods are not needed for them.

B. Barrier Methods. *1. Diaphragm.* The diaphragm is a rubber cap with a metallic rim.[55] After contraceptive gel or cream is added, it is placed in the vagina prior to coitus. Pregnancy is prevented because the diaphragm blocks entry of sperm into the uterus and because there is killing of the sperm by the jelly or cream. Once the coital act has occurred, more vaginal contraceptive jelly must be added if further coital activity takes place, and the diaphragm should not be removed until six hours after the last encounter.

It is a potentially effective and safe method which should be offered to all females, allowing them to take an active part in their own pregnancy protection. The diaphragm is easily carried around, is relatively inexpensive, and the jelly or cream does offer some limited protection from certain sexually transmitted diseases. A trained health professional can easily fit the patient with the proper sized diaphragm. It is also useful for the many individuals having infrequent or sporadic sex. Side effects are limited to an occasional buring of the vagina because of allergy to rubber or vaginal contraceptives. The male does not usually know the diaphragm is in place and only rarely complains of penile discomfort upon contact with the contraceptive jelly or cream. It is also useful when waiting to switch or begin other methods. Older teenagers are usually more capable of using this method properly than the younger ones.

There are however many disadvantages, and the majority of teen-agers simply will not use it or use it ineffectively. Many youth will not accept the genital intimacy needed with its use. The individual must become very familiar with their bodies and must undergo a careful pelvic examination to be fitted with the proper size. A change in weight of 5 to 10 pounds may necessitate a new fitting. Many youth will not accept the need to carefully prepare for each coital act, and feel that they are thereby expressing an unacceptably high interest in sex and sexual pleasure. Also, vigorous sex play can dislodge the diaphragm, reducing its effectiveness.

Unfortunately, many health-care professionals do not have much faith in this method and do not advocate it very strongly for their patients or clients. Though it is true that large-scale studies indicate it is not as good as the pill, it may be a very effective method in the adequately screened and carefully followed female adolescent. The diaphragm should not be ignored by the patient or the counselor and when the patient is prepared to try it, adequate counseling must be available. It is clearly the safest method, apart from abstinence, which the teenage girl can use, especially if she cannot rely upon her partner. Combining it with the condom can allow the couple to alternate and share their contraceptive responsibility.

2. *Vaginal contraceptives.*[55] Vaginal contraceptives are agents which the girl can place in her vagina prior to coitus in an attempt to reduce the pregnancy risk. There are many types, including tablets, foaming powders, suppositories, pastes, creams, jellies, and others. Variations include a water-soluble plastic film and agents which swell within the vagina. These agents usually contain chemicals which are spermicidal—that is, they kill the sperm.

High pregnancy rates are usually noted if these agents are used alone, but when combined with other methods (diaphragm or condom), they can be very effective.

Other advantages are that the girl can take responsibility to protect herself, she does not need a prescription, she will have relatively few side effects, will have partial protection from some forms of sexually transmitted diseases, will have a lubricant to relieve any painful coital activity, and will be using a relatively inexpensive method. It is also useful for those with infrequent sex, and it allows mutual sharing of contraceptive responsibility if the male uses a condom.

However, there are many disadvantages. As noted with the diaphragm, many will not accept it at all or use it poorly. There is also some fear on the part of patients (and even some health-care professionals) that such spermicidal agents may harm the fetus. Fortunately, there is no evidence to support such concerns. Again, it is important to find out what the youth knows, from whom they have learned their information, and give them accurate data. Counseling should attempt to expose the many myths teenagers (and others) have about sexuality (including contraceptive methods).

3. Condoms.[55] Just as the teenage father is often forgotten when we deal with the teenage mother,[56,57] so the sexually active teenage male is often forgotten or ignored when contraceptive advice or information is given. The reasons for male sexuality are many, as noted with the female, and refusal to accept contraception can be based on various psychological factors.[58] We need to educate our teenage males from an early age about normal, responsible male sexuality. This knowledge, as noted also with the female, tends to be very limited.[59] Many will refuse to participate, but some will accept the role of contraceptive responsibility. Currently, their options are limited to abstinence, condoms, noncoital sex, or coitus interruptus. As noted previously, counseling both partners together increases the chance to explain these options and the responsibility the male partner has. Also, compliance is often related to the level of psychosocial maturity.

Advantages of the condom often include the fact that it can be a good method which the male can use, and the fact that it produces some protection from giving or receiving sexually transmitted diseases. There are no side effects, and no prescription is needed. The condom must be placed on the erect penis prior to penetration, and after ejaculation carefully removed. Contraception is afforded since sperm is prevented from entering the uterus. Condoms do reduce penile sensation a bit, but this can be used to treat one of the most common sex dysfunctions noted in teenage males—premature ejaculation. Lubricated condoms may relieve dyspareunia or the problem of the female partner having pain with intercourse. If she placed the condom on the male penis, sexual pleasure is enhanced and male compliance increases.

Though the condom or prophylactic ("rubber") is common in many parts of the world, American youth often do not use it. There are many reasons for this, including the need for proper technique with each coital act, possible disruption of foreplay, or decreased penile sensation, cost, and even the stigmata of promiscuity which condoms seem to have. As is true with any contraceptive method, religious beliefs may prevent its acceptance and utilization. Other reasons for its nonuse include the refusal of many males to accept the responsibility for contraception, the failure of pharmacists to allow easy access to the many types of high-quality condoms available, and the failure of health-care professionals to effectively advocate this method. The female partner can be counseled that refusal by the male partner to use the condom may indicate an eventual failure to accept appropriate responsibility should pregnancy or sexually transmitted diseases occur.

C. Rhythm Methods. There are various rhythm methods which are based on avoidance of sex around the estimated time of ovulation. Usually, unacceptably high rates of pregnancy occur, partially because teenagers often have irregular menstrual periods, and thus have difficulty in estimating when ovulation occurs. Also, many teenagers are ignorant of when they are "safe," and many are not capable of accepting the self-intimacy which may be required, or following the necessary steps month after month.

Methods used to predict ovulation include careful measurement of body temperature, estimation based on menstrual regularity, changes in cervical or vaginal fluid, or combinations of these methods.[52] None of these methods have been shown to be of value for most teenagers, for the reasons already listed. There is current enthusiasm among some to teach women avoidance of sex during the time that cervical mucus or fluid is of the consistency of raw egg whites; however, though this Billings method of contraception may be of value to a few older teenagers capable of following the necessary steps, most youth will not be able to utilize this consistently as a reliable method. However, those with a high level of psychosocial maturity and high degree of motivation may wish to use this technique, with or without other methods.

D. Oral Contraceptives. Oral contraceptives or birth-control pills have been available since 1960 and now represent the most common and most effective of the "medical" or "chemical" methods of contraception.[60,61] These pills are made of an estrogen-compound with a progesterone-compound and work in many ways, including specific and reliable inhibition of ovulation, thus making pregnancy impossible if the pills are taken as directed. If the teenager is having regular menstruation and is motivated to take the pills daily, she has virtually a 100-percent chance of not becoming pregnant, despite her coital activity. It is an especially good method when she has frequent sex and cannot rely on her partner(s) for contraceptive help. There is no current evidence that the pill causes breast or genital cancer, and there may even be improvement noted with painful menstrual cramps (dysmenorrhea) and with certain breast or ovarian disorders.

Before any youth is started on the pill, a careful medical history and thorough physical examination (with pelvic examination) must be done by a trained professional. The carefully screened youth will usually have minimal difficulty on the pill. Common side effects may include nausea, emesis, edema, mild hypertension, tender and/or congested breasts, headaches, acne, weight gain (up to 5 or 10 pounds), menstrual irregularities, and others. Most of these problems are mild and do not necessitate cessation of the pill. Careful follow-up by the clinician is imperative to reduce morbidity associated with the pill.

Sometimes medical screening identifies a medical problem which the pill is known to worsen in some situations. Counseling can include discussion of these conditions. Absolute contraindications to pill use include a history of thromboembolism, active liver disease, pregnancy, vaginal bleeding of unknown etiology, breast cancer, and certain other types of cancer. The pill is never given to patients who have these situations. Many other conditions occur which are termed *relative* contraindications—disorders which the pill can worsen, but physican and patient may decide that pregnancy would be a far worse risk. There are many such problems, including menstrual irregularity, migraine headaches, epilepsy, diabetes mellitus, heart disease, kidney disorder, and others. A careful discussion should occur between patient and physician (or counselor) to decide if the pill is really the best contraceptive method available to her.

Since there are so many potential problems associated with the pill, many feel it has no role with teenagers. However, this method is safe for most youth, if taken under careful medical supervision. In addition, it should be only prescribed if other methods (as the barrier types) are not accepted. Very careful follow-up is imperative, and the patient who is unable or unwilling to work closely with her physican and counselor should probably not stay on the pill. Also, the need to take the pills daily is important. If the individual begins to skip the pill, menstrual irregularity and pregnancy often occur. If the pregnant youth inadvertently takes the pill, fetal anomalies may result.

Finally, another reason for close physician and/or counselor follow-up of the individual on the pill is to allow continued discussion of her fears about this method of contraception. Frequently, a lay article or peer advice about the pill may worry the patient and she may then need the benefit of further counseling. If her fears continue, then other forms of contraception should again be sought. It is my own opinion that the teenager should be on this method only as long as it takes for her to decide on another method, such as the barrier types. It should, however, be available to the carefully screened youth—the choice is the patient's and, as previously noted, our responsibility is to give accurate, not prejudicial advice.

E. Miscellaneous.[60,61] The minipill is a progesterone-only compound which does not cause many of the side effects associated with the combined pill. However, it has a higher pregnancy rate and causes unacceptable menstrual abnormalities in many. The intrauterine device (IUD) is a metallic or plastic device which is placed by a health-care professional within the uterus. It is an effective method which works, not by stopping ovulation per se, but by preventing the conceptus from implanting or becoming established on the uterine wall. Many devices given to teenagers have copper added, increasing its contraceptive potential. Once it is inserted, the female need do nothing, and this is an obvious advantage. It is usually removed every two to three years. However, many women will not accept it because of increased menstrual bleeding, increased menstrual pain, and the risk of genital infections if she acquires gonorrhea from her partner. There are other problems associated with the IUD, and yet it can be a safe, effective method, particularly suited for some women—even teenagers.

There is a "morning-after" pill which can be given in certain emergency situations, as with rape. *Diethylstilbestrol* is the only type of this postcoital contraceptive currently approved by the Food and Drug Administration (FDA). There is also an injection available to women for contraceptive purposes. An intramuscular injection of *Depo-medroxyprogesterone acetate* every 3 months will prevent pregnancy just as effectively as any of the many brands of birth-control pills. Many women do develop menstrual irregularities and resumption of regular menstruation may take several months after cessation of this injectable contraceptive. Such a method has been recommended for some mentally retarded or psychotic teenagers who are at risk for pregnancy.[62]

Coitus interruptus is not recommended as a sole contraceptive method due to the great deal of control needed by the male. Younger teen-age males especially would find this method very difficult to do consistently. Lactation does delay the onset of menstruation after delivery, but not predictably so, and pregnancy occurs in many women while still nursing their babies. The fact that a youth has been pregnant and is now at risk again should be a stimulus to get her onto effective contraception as quickly as possible— whether she is nursing or not. As previously noted, *noncoital sex* may be discussed during the counseling session and the health-care professional should be prepared to nonjudgmentally explore the youth's feelings in this regard. Douching is also not a good method since sperm reaches the uterus relatively quickly postejaculation and immediate removal of all sperm is usually not possible or practical.

Though homosexuality may be a life-style chosen by some older youth, it should not be viewed as a contraceptive method in itself. Sterilization clearly is a very effective type of contraception,[1,61] but the current legal climate which exists has made such a process not possible in most cases. Sterilizing teenagers is a very emotional issue, and legal as well as medical counsel would be required. It is usually only done in a few older teenagers in select cases. Finally, though abortion is a common method of contraception for some youth,[63-65] it will not be discussed in this chapter.

CONCLUSION

The theme of this chapter is that the health-care professional should provide accurate contraceptive information to his/her adolescent patient/client. Though abstinence or barrier methods of contraception are recommended by most counselors, all methods (table) should be discussed, and the ideal is a careful match of the patient with a method most suited and acceptable to him/her. Indeed, this is a most basic responsibility which the health-care professional has toward the adolescent at risk for pregnancy.

REFERENCES

1. Litt, I.F., and Cohen, M.I. Adolescent sexuality. *Adv. Pediatr.* **26**:119–36 (1979).
2. Greydanus, D.E. and Geller, B. Masturbation. Historic perspective. *N.Y.S. J. Med.*, **80**(12):1892–1896 (1980).
3. Greenspan, S.I. Sexuality and psychic structure—the adolescent level of organization. *Psychiatr. Clin. No. Am.* **3**(1):45–60 (1980).
4. Katchadourian, H. Adolescent sexuality. *Pediatr. Clin. No. Am.* **27**(1):17–28 (1980).
5. *11 Million Teenagers, What Can be Done about the Epidemic of Adolescent Pregnancies in the United States?* The Alan Guttmacher Institute. New York: Planned Parenthood Federation of America, 1976.
6. Jaffe, F.S. and Dryfoos, J.G. Fertility control services for adolescents: Access and utilization. *Fam. Plann. Perspect.* **8**(4):172–5 (1976)
7. Zelnik, M. and Kantner, J.F. Sexual and contraceptive experience of young, unmarried women in the United States, 1976 and 1971. *Fam. Plann. Perspect.* **9**:55–71 (1977).
8. Zelnik, M., Kim, Y.J., and Kantner, J.F. Probabilities of intercourse and conception among U.S. teenage women, 1971 and 1976. *Fam. Plann. Perspect.* **11**:178–9 (1979).

9. Furstenberg, F.F. Jr. The social consequences of teenage parenthood. *Fam. Plann. Perspect.* **8**:148–64 (1976).
10. Card, J.J. and Wise, L.L. Teenage mothers and teenage fathers: The impact of early childbearing on the parents' personal and professional lives. *Fam. Plann. Perspect.* **10**:199–207 (1977).
11. Moore, K.A. and Waite, L.J. Early child-bearing and educational attainment. *Fam. Plann. Perspect.* **9**(5):220–5 (1977).
12. Osofsky, J.D and Osofsky, H.J. Teenage pregnancy—psychosocial considerations. *Clin. Obstet. Gynecol.* **21**(4):1161–73 (1978).
13. McCarthy, J. and Menkins, J. Marriage, remarriage, marital disruption and age at first birth. *Fam. Plann. Perspect.* **11**:21–30 (1979).
14. Baldwin, W. and Cain, V.S. The children of teenage parents. *Fam. Plann. Perspect.* **12**(1):34–43 (1980).
15. Elster, A.B. and McAnarney, E.R. Medical and psychosocial risks of pregnancy and childbearing during adolescence. *Pediatr. Ann.* **9**(3): 11–20 (1980).
16. Ryan, G.M. and Sweeney, P.J. Attitudes of adolescents toward pregnancy and contraception. *Am. J. Obstet. Gynecol.* **137**:358–66, (1980).
17. Cohen, M.W. and Friedman, S.B. Nonsexual motivation of adolescent sexual behavior. *Med. Asp. Hum. Sex.* **9**(9):9–31 (1975).
18. Hatcher, S.L. Understanding adolescent pregnancy and abortion. *Prim. Care* **3**(3):407–25 (1976).
19. Statement on teenage pregnancy. Committee on Adolescence. Am. Acad. Pediatr. *Pediatrics* **63**(5):795–7 (1979).
20. Nadelson, C.C., Notman, M.T., and Gillon, J.W. Sexual knowledge and attitudes of adolescents: Relationship to contraceptive use. *Obstet. Gynecol.* **55**(3):340–5 (1980).
21. McAnarney, E.R. and Greydanus, D.E. Adolescent pregnancy—a multifaceted problem. *Pediatr. Rev.* **1**(4):123–6 (1979).
22. Wright, C.H. Teenage pregnancy, a national disaster: A significant factor in black teenage unemployment. *J. Nat. Med. Assoc.* **70**(9):685–7 (1978).
23. Brandt, C.L., Kane, F.J. Jr., and Moan, C.A. Pregnant adolescents: Some psychosocial factors. *Psychosomatics* **19**:790–3 (1978).
24. Litt, I.F., Cuskey, W.R., and Rudd, S. Identifying adolescents at risk for non-compliance with contraceptive therapy. *J. Pediatr.* **96**(4):742–5 (1980).
25. *Adolescent Perinatal Health. A Guidebook for Services.* Chicago: The American College of Obstetricians and Gynecologists, 1979.
26. Greenberger, E. and Sørensen, A.B. Toward a concept of psychosocial maturity. *J. Youth Adol.* **3**(4):329–58 (1974).
27. Greydanus, D.E. and McAnarney, E.R. The value of the Tanner staging. *J. Curr. Adol. Med.* **2**:(2):21–5 (1980).
28. Greydanus, D.E. and Hofmann, A.D. A perspective on the brittle teenage diabetic. *J. Fam. Pract.* **9**(6):1007–12 (1979).
29. Rauh, J.L. and Jensen. G.D. Counseling adolescents on sex problems. *Interact* **1**(4):1–12 (1977).
30. General Mills. *Family Health in an Era of Stress.* Minneapolis, 1979.

31. Scales, P. How we guarantee the ineffectivenes of sex education. *SIECUS Report* **6**(4):1–3 (1978).
32. Fox, G.L. The family's influence on adolescent sexual behavior. *Child. Today* **8**:21–36 (1976).
33. Drake, L.W., Nederlander, C., and Mercier, R.G. Sexual assertiveness training for adolescents. *J. Curr. Adol. Med.* **2**(5):47–9 (1980).
34. Klerman, L.V. (ed.). Adolescent pregnancy: A new look at a continuing problem. *Am. J. Publ. Hlth.* **70**(8):776–8 (1980).
35. Scales, P. Teenage pregnancy—what next? *J. Curr. Adol. Med.* **2**(6):43–7 (1980).
36. Hutchinson, J. Using TV to recruit family planning patients. *Fam. Plann. Perspect.* **2**(:2):8–11 (1970)
37. Hein, K. Impact of mass media on adolescent sexual behavior. *Am. J. Dis. Child.* **134**:133–4 (1980).
38. Perry, R.W. Jr. and Perry, E.C. Sex education and counseling in office practice: Is it for everyone? *Contin. Educ.* **12**(1):78–80 (1980).
39. Edwards, L.E., Steinman, M.E., and Hakanson, E.Y. An experimental comprehensive high-school clinic. *Am. J. Publ. Hlth.* **67**(8):765–6 (1977).
40. Hardy, J.B., Welcher, D.W., Stanley, J., et al. Long range outcome of adolescent pregnancy. *Clin. Obstet. Gynecol.* **21**(4):1215–32 (1978).
41. Brann, E.A., Edwards, L., Callicott, T. et al. Strategies for the prevention of pregnancy in adolescents. *Adv. Plann. Parent.* **14**:68–76 (1979).
42. Hallum, A.V. Jr. Teenage pregnancy—a liability to our future. *J. Med. Assoc. Ga.* **68**:396–8 (1979).
43. Chilman, C.S. Teenage pregnancy: A research review. *Soc. Work* **24**:492–8 (1979).
44. Finkel, M.L. and Finkel, D.J. Sexual and contraceptive knowledge, attitudes and behavior of adolescents. *Fam. Plann. Perspect.* **7**:256–70 (1975).
45. Zelnik, M. and Kantner, J.F. Contraceptive patterns and premarital pregnancy among women aged 15–19 in 1976. *Fam. Plann. Perspect.* **10**:135–42 (1978).
46. Baldwin, W. Adolescent pregnancy and childbearing: Growing concerns for Americans. *Pop. Bull.* **31**(2):3–24 (1977).
47. Zabin, L.S., Kantner, J.F., and Zelnik, M. The risk of adolescent pregnancy in the first months of intercourse. *Fam. Plann. Perspect.* **11**:215–22 (1979).
48. Zelnik, M. and Kantner, J.F. Sexuality, contraception and pregnancy among young unwed females in the United Sates. *In Commission on Population Growth and the American Future, Demographic and Social Aspects of Population Growth.* C.F. Westoff and R. Parke Jr. (Eds.), Vol. 1 of *Commission Research Reports.* Washington, D.C.: U.S.Government Printing Office, 1972, pp. 359–374.
49. Hofmann, A.D., Becker, R.D., and Gabriel, H.P. *The Hospitalized Adolescent.* New York: The Free Press, 1976, pp. 211–232.
50. Bodine, W. Minors and contraceptives: A constitutional issue. *Ecology Law Quart.* **3**:859 (1973).
51. Holden, A.R. *Legal Issues in Pediatrics and Adolescent Medicine.* New York: John Wiley & Sons, 1977.
52. Greydanus, D.E. and McAnarney, E.R. Contraception in the adolescent. *Pediatrics* **66**(3):475–6 (1980).

53. Sullivan, W.R. Contraception: Matching method and patient. *Contin. Educ.* **12**:(1):28–36 (1980).
54. Djerassi, C. The politics of contraception. The view from Beijing. *N. Engl. J. Med.* **303**(6):334–6 (1980).
55. Greydanus, D.E. Contraception in adolescence. An overview for the pediatrician. *Pediatr. Ann.* **9**(3):52–66 (1980).
56. Pannor, R. The forgotten man. *Nurs. Outlook* **18**(1):36–7 (1970).
57. Pannor, R., Evans, R.W., and Massarik, F. *The Unmarried Father.* New York: Springer Publishing Co., 1971.
58. Rothstein, A.A. Adolescent males, fatherhood and abortion. *J. Youth Adol.* **7**:203–14 (1978).
59. Freeman, E.W., Rickels, K., Huggins, G.R., et al. Adolescent contraceptive use: Comparisons of male and females attitudes and information. *Am. J. Publ. Hlth.* **70**(8):790–7 (1980).
60. Greydanus, D.E. and McAnarney, E.R. Contraception in the adolescent: Current concepts for the pediatrician. *Pediatrics* **65**(1):1–12 (1980).
61. Greydanus, D.E. Alternatives to adolescent pregnancy. A discussion of the contraceptive literature from 1960–1980. *Sem. Perinatol.,* **5**(1):53–90 (1981).
62. Medroxyprogesterone acetate (Depo-provera). Committee on Drugs, Am. Acad. Pediatr. *Pediatrics* **65***(1):A-74 (1980).*
63. Green, K.W. and Resnik, R. The abortion issue: Past, present and future. *Curr. Probl. Pediatr.* **7**(10):1–44 (1977).
64. Hanson, M.S. Abortion in teenagers. *Clin. Obstet. Gynecol.* **21**(4):1175–90 (1978).
65. Olson, L. Social and psychological correlates of pregnancy resolution among adolescent women. A review. *Am. J. Orthopsychol.* **50**(3):432–45 (1980).

4.
Prenatal Care for the Pregnant Adolescent

Elizabeth Cooper, C.N.M., M.S.,
Clinical Associate,
Department of Obstetrics and Gynecology,
University of Rochester School of Medicine and Dentistry

Prenatal care is essential in preventing the complications of pregnancy, especially in the adolescent, who may be at greater risk because of her biologic immaturity. In addition, her race and socioeconomic status may predispose her to problems such as hypertension, prematurity, and perinatal loss. Teenagers are best served by a multidisciplinary team because of their multifaceted needs. They especially need comprehensive care from caring individuals, with emphasis on education and counseling. Education should encompass preparation for labor, delivery, and infant care. Nutritional assessment and counseling are important in improving outcomes and preventing problems. Common complications of teenage pregnancy are discussed, including anemia, toxemia, venereal disease, and premature labor. Outreach to the adolescent at home is an essential part of prenatal care, as is provision in the program to meet the needs of the teenage father.

The importance of prenatal care in the prevention and early detection of the complications of pregnancy is an acknowledged fact. When the physical and psychosocial demands of pregnancy have been superimposed on the demands of adolescence, the need for good prenatal care is even more evident. In addition, most pregnant teenagers in the United States are lower socioeconomic nonwhites (Cutright, 1975), putting them into the class with the highest morbidity and mortality statistics.

Unfortunately, teenagers aren't getting the care they need. They register later in their pregnancies and are less compliant with keeping appointments than older women (Ryan and Schneider, 1978; Houde and Conway, 1976; Osofsky, 1968). Most studies show significant numbers of teenagers who deliver their babies without any care at all. What is it that prevents teenagers from getting care?

Allen (1980) points out that one reason for the delay in seeking care is denial and hiding of the unplanned pregnancy until it becomes physically obvious. He contends, however, that the single most important cause of the delay is the teenager's lack of participation in the health-care system. This seems to be true, since often the teenager who has already entered the system for contraceptive or mental-health care will have her pregnancy diagnosed earlier. Transportation problems may be responsible for some noncompliance, particularly among rural teenagers. Allen found that it was the lack of positive experiences in the health-care system which most determined failure to keep appointments.

It is generally accepted that pregnancy in the teenage years is dangerous for both mother and baby because of the reportedly increased incidence of complications. In 1978, Ryan reviewed several studies to show the wide variation in data on complications, and concluded that psychosocial factors may be more the cause of the problems than biologic immaturity, with the possible exception of cephalopelvic disproportion. Even though he found that hypertension, toxemia, prematurity, and low birth weight babies were common problems in his study group, he attributed this to the overall deficit in prenatal care. Of the 55 percent of his study group for whom he had data on prenatal care, 72 percent received either no care or care in the third trimester only.

Comprehensive programs have been developed which are geared to the pregnant teenager's special needs. Hardy et al. (1978) reported a decrease in prematurity rates in their program at Johns Hopkins. Doyle and Widhalm (1979) found that inner city teenagers attending a special midwife clinic had good maternal weight gains and a reduction in low birth weight babies, presumably reflecting an improved nutritional status. A statistical analysis of an antepartum program for teenagers showed bigger babies and better Apgar scores among the younger girls, and fewer urinary tract infections and cesarean sections (Smith et al., 1978).

This, then, is the challenge to the obstetrical care team. It is clear that without care pregnant teenagers, especially the younger ones, have higher risks of pregnancy-induced hypertension, toxemia, cephalopelvic disproportion, cesarean section, abruptio placenta, anemia, and urinary tract infections. Their babies are more likely to be premature, growth retarded, or die perinatally. With care, most of these complications can be reduced, and this chapter will address the major components of that care.

THE MULTIDISCIPLINARY TEAM

To begin, the ideal prenatal program should consist of several health professionals working together to correct the multidimensional problems which the pregnant teenager and her family present. Such a team should be comprised of physicians, nurse-midwives, nurse-practitioners, social workers and family counselors, nutritionists, and educators. These professionals should represent the disciplines of obstetrics, gynecology, pediatrics, mental health, and community health.

Coordination is a difficult goal for this team, but one which must be met if the pregnant teenager is not to "fall through the cracks." Regular, frequent planning meetings are essential, as is an atmosphere of collegiality and respect for each contributor on the team.

One of the most underutilized care providers is the Certified Nurse-Midwife, probably because of the small numbers of these professionals in the United States. Yet her family-centered approach to the low-risk obstetrical patient, and her emphasis on educational and emotional support both during and after the pregnancy, make her an ideal care provider to the pregnant teenager. Continuity of care is a hallmark of midwifery practice, and the ability to manage the birth with emphasis on nonintervention and maternal-infant bonding are also key reasons why nurse-midwives, where available, should be incorporated into the health-care team.

THE FIRST CONTACT

Eventually, and usually belatedly, the pregnant teenager presents for care. Her initial contacts with the system will largely determine her compliance and ultimately the outcome of her pregnancy. Her initial physical exam must, therefore, not be a traumatic experience if it can be avoided. For this reason, time for talking and discussion in a nonjudgmental atmosphere should precede getting undressed and undergoing poking and probing. This obvious fact is too often put aside because of the need to conserve the time of overworked professionals, but it demonstrates from the outset the amount of respect for the individual girl that the provider feels. Burst (1979) points out that the approach of the provider must be marked by enthusiasm, honesty, caring, and a nonjudgmental attitude. She emphasizes that the lack of an effective approach to the adolescent negates the value of the medical care. The physician or other provider must be a counselor and educator as well, with a sincere attitude and an assurance of confidentiality (Tyrer, Mazlen, and Bradshaw, 1978).

A family history must be obtained by a nurse or social worker, so that the psychosocial situation of the girl is well understood. Some girls are reluctant to give full details on an initial visit, so that follow-up on vague information needs to be done during subsequent visits when rapport has been established.

Once the psychosocial situation of the girl is known, her personal medical history and that of her family, needs to be obtained. Medical terms, such as "diabetes," may not be known by the teenager, so that colloquial terms like "high blood sugar" need to be used. It is a good idea to follow up this history on the second visit as well, so that the girl can check with her parents on those questions she is unsure of.

Of importance are the girl's habits such as smoking, drinking, and drug use. All are known to have negative effects on pregnancy and neonatal outcome. Smoking is common among teenagers today, but appropriate education about its hazards to the fetus will often motivate the girl to stop or cut back. The fetus is also susceptible to alcohol abuse, as has been extensively reported recently. History in this are is very difficult to obtain accurately, so there should be a high index of suspicion if the girls admits to drinking "sometimes." Again education is an important component in the prevention of fetal alcohol syndrome.

Menstrual history is obtained in order to date the pregnancy, but is often unreliable information. Few teenagers keep records of their menstrual periods. They know the general character of their menses, i.e., whether it occurs monthly, is heavy or light, and its usual duration. However, the girl is unlikely to recall the first day of the last menstrual period, especially if she is already five to six months pregnant. It may be more useful to ask when the girl believes she became pregnant, as many can recall more clearly the general date of that occasion. It is also helpful to relate the questioning to holidays, e.g. "Did you have a period around Thanksgiving? Around Christmas?"

Early examination is most helpful in accurately estimating the period of gestation, but when that is not possible because of late registration for care, an alternative is available. Ultrasound measurement of the fetus is an excellent, dependable method for dating the pregnancy and estimating the due date, if done prior to the 30th week of pregnancy. Thereafter, it becomes increasingly unreliable because fetal size in the third trimester is strongly influenced by genetic and environmental factors. Thus, a fetus may measure the size of 28 weeks gestation, when in reality it is a growth-retarded 31-week fetus. When such growth retardation is suspected, serial ultrasound measurements help the obstetrician closely follow the growth. Ultrasound is also useful in detecting placental abnormalities, twins, and miscarriages.

INITIAL PHYSICAL EXAMINATION

After obtaining all the necessary history, the pregnant girl should receive a complete physical examination and laboratory studies. The physical will include a pelvic examination to assess the health of the girl's reproductive system and estimate the duration of pregnancy. A pap smear and cultures for gonorrhea are obtained from the cervix. Blood tests will include a complete blood count to detect anemia or infection; blood type and Rh factor determination; serologic test for syphilis; screening for rubella immunity, and for sickle-cell anemia, and for tuberculosis. Urine samples are examined for signs of infection, diabetes, or kidney disease. A significant percentage of pregnant women may be found to have asymptomatic urinary tract infections by routine checks. Since such infections are related to an increased risk of premature labor, their detection is an important part of prenatal care.

The pelvic is that part of the exam most dreaded by teenagers and unfortunately, some girls may have been needlessly frightened by friends or family relating their negative experiences, or may have personally had a previous exam which they experienced as painful. A history of rape or incest, or of a previous painful sexual experience, should be known to the care provider before beginning this exam. Indeed, even with the most relaxed and gentle approach, some girls may repeatedly refuse to allow this portion of the exam.

The best approach is a good basic explanation of the anatomy to be examined, the instruments to be used, the tests to be taken, and ways the girl can help minimize any discomfort. Patience is called for and a slow manner is needed to allow the girl to be comfortable with the exam each step of the way. Use of a pediatric size speculum is helpful in very young or not sexually active girls.

After completing the initial exam, it is not enough to note that the teenager has dental caries on the record. As Anderson (1976) points out, comprehensive care of the teenager includes attention to all aspects of her health. Dental referral should be routine if the girl is not in ongoing care, even though no problems are noted. Comprehensive care entails viewing the teenager as a whole person, not just a pregnant girl, and treating not just obstetric but all aspects of her health problems. In an age of medical specialization, this is an important point which is often overlooked. Visual or hearing problems, severe acne or other dermatologic conditions, or serious medical problems require referral to appropriate specialists.

NUTRITION COUNSELING

No doubt the most difficult and important aspect of ongoing care for the pregnant adolescent is the provision of nutrition counseling. While the girl may be interested in changing her eating habits to ensure a healthy baby, eating patterns long established are some of the most difficult behavior to modify. In addition, teenagers are known to eat erratically, often skipping meals and snacking (Worthington, Vermeersch, and Williams, 1977). Most teenagers do not regularly cook for themselves, making parental involvement in the counseling process necessary. Some parents encourage their pregnant daughters to eat more, some less, and in the most disadvantaged families, no one takes any interest in the girl's diet. The influence of boyfriends and peers also cannot be underestimated. Many times I have heard a boyfriend say, "Isn't she getting too fat?" Education about the need of proper nutrition must extend to those with influence on the girl's behavior.

In order to achieve any success the care provider must adapt the prenatal dietary requirements to the girl's food preferences. For example, the girl can be taught that a milkshake is preferable to a coke from a nutritional standpoint. Most lower socioeconomic class girls will have little or no knowledge of the relative nutritional value of foods, making basic education in this area an essential starting point.

General dietary recommendations for the pregnant adolescent are increased over the adult pregnant woman because of the teenager's continued growth. Clearly, the younger the teenager and the closer in time to her menarche, the greater the nutritional needs. Most authors agree that increased calories, protein, iron, and calcium are the most important nutritional needs of pregnancy. (Worthington, et al., 1977; King and Jacobson, 1975).

Increased calories are necessary because of the energy demands of the growing fetus and of the growing teenager. Heald and Jacobsen (1980) recommend 2700 calories per day for adolescents ages 11–14, and 2400 calories per day for ages 15–18. Too often, the teenager's eating habits make it difficult for her to meet this need. Skipped meals, especially breakfast, may result in dizziness, fainting, nausea, and fatigue. Besides three meals each day, the girl should be urged to have between meal and bedtime snacks. If she feels too full or uncomfortable eating a full meal, then six small feedings are an equally good way of getting needed nutrients.

Of course, these extra calories should come from nutritious food. Usually, a natural increase in appetite will allow the girl to get the extra calories. She should be encouraged to choose from whole-grain bread and cereals, potatoes, pasta, fresh fruit, or milk products to satisfy her hunger. If the teenager seems to be loading up on sweets, it is often because she is not including other healthier sources of carbohydrates in her diet. Don't expect, however, compliance with a "no desserts or candy" diet. Instead recommend ice cream over cake, pudding over candy bars.

The majority of pregnant teenagers do not meet their protein needs. The development of the fetus and placenta, and the physiologic changes in the girl, such as an increased blood volume and larger uterus, require 80–100 grams of protein daily (Worthington et al., 1977.) To meet these needs the teenager should have daily a quart of milk, or its equivalent, 1–2 eggs, and two servings of meat, chicken, or fish. Beans, whole-grain cereals, and nuts are other sources of protein.

Many adolescents, especially the more disadvantaged, may not be used to eating some of these foods and hence dislike them. Milk intolerance is common—"I throw up when I drink milk." Yogurt and cottage cheese are unacceptable substitutes. So the care provider must patiently construct a diet which the pregnant teenager has some reasonable chance of following, and which meets her needs as clearly as possible. Milkshakes, pudding, hamburgers, peanut butter sandwiches, cheese pizza, and spaghetti are usually well liked.

It is important to praise the girl's efforts at diet modification and also those parts of her diet which are healthy. A negative approach—"stop eating junk food and eat liver once a week!"—will only result in her failure to keep appointments. Keeping diet diaries is helpful in letting the girl work out for herself those areas of her intake which could be improved, and provide the care provider with a more accurate picture of her dietary pattern. They are useful as well for positive reinforcement.

Iron supplements are routinely given, as well as vitamin supplements. The compliance with taking these is fair at best. Lost prescriptions, inability to swallow pills, or discontinuance from side effects, such as nausea or constipation, are common reasons why supplements cannot be depended on.

High-iron foods such as liver, eggs, iron fortified cereals, dried fruits, and dark green vegetables should be stressed. Anemia due to iron deficiency is one of the most common complications of teen-age pregnancy. This is discussed below.

Increased calcium needs can be met with milk, but an oral supplement may be needed if the girl refuses, or is unable to take any milk. Some green vegetables, such as broccoli, are also sources of calcium. For a summary of dietary recommendations of other vitamins and minerals the reader is referred to Heald and Jacobson's (1980) article or Worthington et al's. (1977) excellent book.

A nutritionist is an indispensable member of the multi-disciplinary team because of her special skills in counseling. An adolescent who is depressed and has no appetite is the most difficult problem with which the care provider must cope, and referral to a qualified professional will help a great deal.

COMMON COMPLICATIONS

As has already been stated, certain complications seem to occur most frequently in pregnant teenagers. Several of these are known or suspected to have a nutritional basis. Anemia, too much or too little weight gain, pregnancy-induced high blood pressure, toxemia, and fetal intrauterine growth retardation fall into this category.

Anemia normally occurs because of insufficient iron in the diet to meet the demands of pregnancy. Blood volume increases by 50 percent and iron is needed to make new red blood cells. In addition, the fetus stores iron during the last few months of the pregnancy in preparation for a diet of milk in the early months of life. Many teenage girls are slightly anemic to begin with because of their poor diets and their monthly loss of blood with menstruation. If not anemic, they may have depleted iron stores with which to meet the physiologic changes of pregnancy.

Rarer forms of anemia may also be found, so that it is essential to perform blood tests on anemic girls to ascertain whether that iron deficiency is the cause.

Treatment of anemia is directed at increasing dietary iron and adding oral supplements. Getting teenagers to comply with taking pills regularly is difficult, and at times iron may be given in liquid form with increased tolerance. In extreme cases which do not respond to dietary supplements, iron injections may be used. Anemia predisposes to hemorrhage and infection at the birth, and usually leaves the girl feeling weak and tired. In some disadvantaged girls, however, chronic anemia may be so long-standing that the girl has become adjusted to the state and denies any unusual symptoms.

Ideas about optimal weight gain in pregnancy have changed a great deal over the last 20 years. Even as recently as 1968, Osofsky recommended restricting caloric intake and holding weight gain to a certain maximum amount. He advocated use of diuretics as well to eliminate edema and prevent toxemia. However, since publication of results of a collaborative study, (National Research Council, 1970) it is now accepted that an optimal weight gain in pregnancy is about 25 pounds. An increasingly accepted theory is that toxemia of pregnancy is nutritionally induced. Although the actual pathophysiology of this illness is well understood, the etiology is still unknown, and the nutritional basis still unproven scientifically. It is an illness characterized by an increase in blood pressure, rapid fluid accumulation leading to edema and excessive weight gain, proteinuria, and an increased neurologic irritability. Left untreated, it may progress to seizures.

Pregnancy-induced hypertension is a more recently coined term applied to those cases where blood pressure rises during the pregnancy, but no other symptoms of toxemia are present. While it has been known that a slight increase in blood pressure near term is normal, the cause of this more marked elevation is unknown, although it is often found in conjunction with an excessive weight gain (50 pounds or greater). Hypertensive disorders of pregnancy are consistently reported as increased in the teen-age population, especially the younger ones, although the etiology is unknown.

For many teenagers, it is the failure to gain any weight that is more troubling, since in fact it reflects weight loss in the pregnant girl. This constant utilizing of fat and protein stores for energy because of inadequate diet produces a metabolic state which is most unfavorable to the developing fetus and, most especially, the fetal brain. In such cases, the fetuses may fail to grow to their potential and begin life moderately or severely malnourished. In very severe cases, labor may even be induced prematurely in order to remove the fetus from a potentially life-threatening environment. Ultrasound is helpful in detecting and following this condition. Heald and Jacobsen (1980) report some success in hospitalizing the teenagers who "fail to thrive" in pregnancy in their special clinic. They do comprehensive studies to determine the causes.

Prematurity remains the leading cause of perinatal death and its incidence is increased among teenagers, although the reasons for this are probably not related solely to age, but also to race and socioeconomic status. The care provider needs to take an aggressive approach to signs of premature labor. Sometimes it is difficult to differentiate from the usual aches and pains of pregnancy, but suspicion should be aroused if the girl complains of noting increasingly frequent and uncomfortable cramps prior to the last four weeks of pregnancy. This often indicates an overactive uterus getting ready for labor. If the cervix is found to be dilating early, another premonitory sign of labor, the girl may be confined to bedrest or treated with drugs in an attempt to stop the progress toward labor. Unfortunately, teenagers are often difficult to keep confined to bed at home, so that hospitalization may be necessary.

Urinary tract infections may predispose to premature labor, and because of their often asymptomatic nature, routine cultures should be performed. These infections are usually limited to bladder, and one of the most common symptoms, frequency of urination, is a normal phenomenon of pregnancy. Antibiotics which are safe to the fetus are used for treatment. Untreated, the infection may spread to the kidney, producing pain and fever, and often requiring hospitalization for treatment.

An additional common complication of teenage pregnancy is venereal disease. Gonorrhea is treated with penicillin, and the teenager who has been found to have the disease should be routinely recultured periodically to check for reinfection. Cultures should be taken both at the initial exam and 4–6 weeks before the due date. Any suspicious vaginal discharge should be cultured as well.

Genital herpes infection is an increasingly difficult problem. A small sore on the labia may not be reported by the girls, and usually subsides in 7–10 days. The lesions may be internal and go completely unnoticed. Active lesions at the time of labor may transmit the virus to the fetus as it passes through the birth canal. Herpes infection in the newborn is an extremely serious illness, often fatal. For this reason, if lesions are present at onset of labor, cesarean section is usually performed. Frequent cultures near term may be indicated, and labor is sometimes induced near term when the teenager is well, in order to avoid possible surgical delivery.

The herpes lesions usually itch at onset and are quite painful. No known treatment exists for this virus, although various measures may relieve some of the symptoms. Any complaints of perivaginal itching should be visually examined for signs of these small red sores.

Vaginitis is so common that it is considered more a "normal" discomfort of pregnancy than a complication. Changes in the vaginal cells during pregnancy make it especially susceptible to fungal or yeast infections. In addition, the parasite Trichomonas Vaginalis is a common pathogen in the sexually active girl. It may be transmitted by infected males and is difficult to eradicate with local treatment. Metronidazole, a highly effective oral drug, is contraindicated in pregnancy. Inspection of the vagina and examination of the discharge under a microscope will detect the causative organism and suggest the appropriate therapy. Follow-up is especially important with teenagers, as they are often noncompliant with drug requirements. On regular prenatal visits the care provider should ask about vaginal discharges, itching, or irritation, as many girls think these conditions are normal or neglect to report them. Chronically inflamed vaginal tissue is less elastic at birth and lacerations are more likely than with a healthy vagina.

Psychiatric problems can be seen in any pregnant woman, and teenagers are no exception. Depression can be severe, leading to lack of appetite, poor diet, and fetal malnutrition. When severe depression is noted, referral to appropriate mental-health professionals is imperative. Such girls may have profound disturbances postpartum with diminished mothering ability. Occasionally, a teenager may be psychotic and require hospitalization.

Educational Aspects

Much of the work of the care provider involves the health education of the pregnant teenager. At each prenatal visit, she should have an opportunity to ask questions about her concerns and to have them answered patiently without any condescension. Her questions can be stepping off points for more detailed teaching on the subject in which she is interested. For example, during the routine abdominal exam of each visit, during which the growth and position of the fetus is assessed, the girl may ask, "how big is my baby now?" Beyond a simple factual answer, a few minutes can be devoted to overall fetal growth and development, with use of appropriate visual aids. Many of the pamphlets available for prenatal patients are not wholly appropriate for teenage use, but those which picture fetal development will be valued. Such questions also provide opportunities to reemphasize some other health teaching such as nutrition and its relationship to fetal development. More formal educational lessons need to be incorporated into the prenatal program, but whenever the adolescent initiates the subject, she is most likely to be ready for learning.

Group sessions are excellent means of more organized teaching, especially if there is opportunity for open exchange among the girls. A comprehensive program should include teaching in the following areas:

1. Self-care during pregnancy, including hygiene, activities, nutrition, signs of problems;
2. Common discomforts of pregnancy, their causes and measures for their relief;

3. Preparation for labor and delivery including physical exercises;
4. Preparations for the baby and care of the newborn, including basic parenting skills;
5. Postpartum expectations for the first 6 weeks after the birth;
6. Methods of contraception.

Readiness for learning must be considered before wasting precious time. A teenager nearing her due date becomes focused on that event. Until she has the delivery behind her, she will be unreceptive to teaching about contraception or even infant care. The ideal time to teach care of the newborn is on the postpartum hospital unit when the girl is faced with handling her baby. Contraception is best taught in detail a few weeks postpartum after the early adjustment to motherhood has been coped with, and the motivation is strong not to repeat pregnancy too soon.

Since many pregnant teenagers are socioeconomically deprived, they may have serious hygiene problems. Daily bathing and frequent clothes laundering are luxuries often unavailable to them. For this reason a combined approach by the medical and the social work staff will be more likely to succeed. Getting a layette together may mean visits to community agencies, perhaps with the special help of a family worker. For the very young teenager especially, the added social assistance available in a comprehensive program is necessary to make adequate preparations for the baby.

Some teaching about the needs of the newborn can be done by pediatric nurse practitioners or pediatricians. These professionals should meet the pregnant girl as she nears delivery to discuss the health-care follow-up for the baby. Coordination of postpartum visits of the girl, with baby visits for the baby, help ensure better compliance for both. If the facilities are available, this combined visit routine for the teenager and the baby can continue at least through the first year of life. Unfortunately, even some of the most comprehensive programs do not have pediatric care as an integral part of the program. This is especially ironic since the adolescent is still considered a pediatric patient herself from most other standpoints.

Preparation for labor and the birth is an essential aspect of education. This is usually done by group teaching about the processes of labor, and training in relaxation exercises which will facilitate the birth. The girl should be encouraged to bring a "significant other" with her to attend these classes and to coach her in labor. This might be a boyfriend, sister, mother, or friend. Some girls are in such poor social situations that they have no one person available to support them during this critical time. In some communities, a childbirth education group will provide a "labor coach" for such teenagers. Such coaches may attend classes with the girl, or tutor her privately in the breathing techniques used to enhance relaxation and cooperation with the phenomenon of childbirth. These coaches then are "on call" and join the girl during labor to assist her.

With adequate teaching about the signs of labor, teenagers are less likely to make trips to the hospital in false labor, and are more likely to be cooperative and involved during the experience. Besides the use of charts and drawings to explain the birth process, films of actual births, and tours of the labor and delivery facilities help the girls feel more prepared and less frightened. Group discussion can help dispel myths and fears passed on by well-meaning relatives and friends. Furthermore, the teenager who participates in the birth process will enhance her own self-esteem, and need less drugs during labor, thus enhancing her baby's well-being. She will be more alert at the birth and more ready to bond to her newborn.

Some programs such as the Rochester Adolescent Maternity Program in Rochester, New York, stress ongoing group sessions for their clients. These groups can be used as vehicles for education, but also serve an important psychological function. The teenagers can discuss and work through some of their feelings about their pregnancies, themselves, and their parents. Ideally, the groups could be continued into the postpartum period and deal with the naturally conflicted feelings the girls will feel toward their infants and also teach them basic parenting skills.

COMMUNITY OUTREACH

It is not enough to just see the pregnant teenager in the clinic or office setting, because the view is necessarily skewed. An essential member of the multidisciplinary team is a community health nurse who can visit the girls at home during the pregnancy and after delivery. If continuity of care is practiced, then the nurse or midwife who is the primary contact for the girl at the teenage prenatal program also might visit at home. The community health nurse visit might occur toward the end of the pregnancy and be geared toward assessment of home preparations for the baby. After the birth, she can visit again to evaluate the infant's care and the teenager's mothering abilities.

The family counselor, an adjunct to social services, has been helpful in the Rochester Adolescent Maternity Program in making frequent visits to the very young teenagers and helping them mobilize their resources. These nonprofessional workers may provide transportation to get to appointments or to obtain equipment for the baby. Their goals are to assist the adolescent and her family to adjust to changes in roles and responsibilities resulting from the pregnancy and birth of the baby, and to assist in coordination of services with which the adolescent may be involved.

THE TEEN-AGE FATHER

No comprehensive program would be complete without involvement of the teenage father and attempts to meet some of his needs. This might be done by special groups for the boyfriends and by access to vocational counseling as appropriate. Involvement in the classes in preparation for the birth, and the classes in infant care, are other means to recognize his concerns and needs, and to make him feel an integral part of the prenatal program.

SUMMARY

Data is inconclusive about the risks of childbearing during adolescence. Elster and McAnarney (1980) contend that the older adolescent who receives *adequate* prenatal care does not experience more complications than adult women of the same race, parity, or socioeconomic status. But they question whether the younger adolescent aged 10–14 years may experience increased toxemia, prematurity, and perinatal mortality despite the care she receives.

Adequate prenatal care for teen-agers involves a team approach because of the multifaceted needs. Without mutual cooperation and consultation her prenatal care will be fragmented and incomplete. Prenatal care should teach the teenager how to care for herself and baby so as to prevent medical problems and increase the overall level of wellness. Further, it should early detect complications, both minor and major, and provide treatment with which the teenager can comply. Prenatal care for the birth should prepare her for the experience and help her fully cooperate to help herself.

Pregnancy, usually unsought, can become a growth experience for the teenager, enabling her to increase her self-esteem and thus to better mother her infant. Better mothering is the only hope for breaking the vicious cycle of poverty and illegitimacy which persists from one generation to the next. It is a challenging task which demands a multidisciplinary team who provide a unique brand of teenage care.

REFERENCES

Allen, J.E. and Bender, D. *Managing Teenage Pregnancy*. New York: Praeger, 1980.

Anderson, G.D. Comprehensive management of the pregnant teenager. *Contemporary Obstetrics and Gynecology,* 1976, **7** (2), 75–80.

Burst, H.V. Adolescent pregnancies and problems. *Journal of Nurse-Midwifery,* 1979, **24** (2), 19–24.

Cutright, P. The rise of teenage illegitimacy in the United States: 1940–1971. In J. Zackler and W. Brandstadt (Eds.), *The Teenage Pregnant Girl*. Springfield, Ill.: Charles C. Thomas, 1975.

Doyle, M.B. and Widhalm, M.V. Midwifing the adolescents at Lincoln Hospital's teenage clinics. *Journal of Nurse-Midwifery*, 1979, **24** (4), 27–32.

Elster, A.B. and McAnarney, E.R. Medical and psychosocial risks of pregnancy and childbearing during adolescence. *Pediatric Annals*, 1980, **9**, 89–94.

Hardy, J.B., Welcher, D.W., Stanley, J., and Dallas, J.R. Long-range outcome of adolescent pregnancy. *Clinical Obstetrics and Gynecology*, 1978, **21**, 1215–1232.

Heald, F.P. and Jacobsen, M.S. Nutritional needs of the pregnant adolescent. *Pediatric Annals*, 1980, **9**, 95–99.

Houde, C.T., and Conway, C.E. Teenage mothers: A clinical profile. *Contemporary Obstetrics and Gynecology*, 1976, **7**, 71–78.

King, J.C. and Jacobsen, H.N. Nutrition and pregnancy in adolescence. In J. Zackler and W. Brandstadt (Eds.), *The Teenage Pregnant Girl*. Springfield, Ill.: Charles C. Thomas, 1975.

National Research Council, Committee on Maternal Nutrition. *Maternal Nutrition and the Course of Pregnancy*. Washington: National Academy of Sciences, 1970.

Osofsky, H.J. *The Pregnant Teenager: A Medical, Educational, and Social Analysis*. Springfield, Ill.: Charles C. Thomas, 1968.

Ryan, G.M. Jr., and Schneider, J.M. Teenage obstetric complications. *Clinical Obstetrics and Gynecology*, 1978, **21**, 1191–1197.

Smith, P., Wait, R., Mumford, D., Nenny, S., and Hollins, B. The medical impact of an antepartum program for pregnant adolescents: A statistical analysis. *American Journal of Public Health*, 1978, **68** (2), 169–172.

Tyrer, LS., Mazlen, R.G., and Bradshaw, L.E. Meeting the special needs of pregnant teenagers. *Clinical Obstetrics and Gynecology*, 1978, **21**, 1199–1213.

Worthington, B.S., Vermeersch, J., and Williams, S.R. *Nutrition in Pregnancy and Lactation*. St. Louis: C.V. Mosby Co., 1977.

5.
Pregnant Teenagers in Need of Social Networks: Diagnostic Parameters

Paul Fine, M.D.,
Director, Division of Child and Adolescent Psychiatry,
Department of Psychiatry,
Creighton University School of Medicine,
Omaha, Nebraska

and

Mary Pape, M.S.,
Educational Therapist, Uta Halee Girls Village,
Omaha, Nebraska

Diagnosis for biological, personal, family and social factors guide pregnant adolescents toward adaptive decisions affecting health services. Needs are determined in context with obstetrical care and a secure place to live as first priorities.

Personal traits for evaluation include the process of adolescence, stages of pregnancy, personal assets and, in some cases, psychopathology. Adolescent pregnancies alter biorhythms and social relationships. Psychopathology can color these processes with depression, psychophysiologic disorders, anxiety-provoking inner conflicts, developmental disabilities, disruptive personality patterns, and disintegrations. Personal strengths and talents form a matrix to cope with adolescence, pregnancy, social changes, and emotional problems.

The family is the most consistent sociocultural group for help to cope with pregnancy. Each family transmits skills for intimate relationships, self-assertion, small-group living, friendships, and economic survival. Family diagnosis considers transgenerational patterns, extended relationships, functional integrity, structure, and dynamics. Pregnant adolescents from poorly functioning families may require help toward ancillary or substitute networks. Adolescents normally experience transitions from the family of origin to peer groups, marriage, and a family of choice. Family problems arise from social enmeshment, disengagement, distortion, disorganization, rigidity, or disintegration.

Professional networks cannot substitute for family networks. They can offer medical, nursing, counseling, mental health, educational, religious, institutional, and social services. This is done most effectively when there is sanction from the family and other personal networks. Accurate diagnoses and timing are essential for success.

Childbirth and child rearing remain a major function of the family in any society, and each pregnant woman requires love and support from her family within that society. Teenagers who become pregnant in modern society experience complications both in their adolescence and pregnancy. Pregnancies during adolescence present a challenge for support to the individual, the family and society.

Health practitioners require accurate, relevant diagnoses in order to guide adolescents toward constructive decisions affecting a pregnancy. Each diagnosis should include evaluations of the young person's physical and emotional adjustment to adolescence, her adjustment to pregnancy, personal strengths and weaknesses, and the social structure that surrounds her. The root meaning of the Greek word diagnosis, after all, is "knowing through."

Disturbed teenagers are less likely to make effective decisions concerning pregnancies, and are more likely to come from disturbed or disrupted families (Nix, 1979; Osofsky et al., 1973). Neurotic teenagers may act out self-defeating patterns which their families often tend to reinforce (Stone, 1975). Pregnancy is sometimes sought by adolescents from marginal or deviant families as a quick way to increase status or to get more love. Such pregnancies can become a one-way ticket into the "culture of poverty" (Fischman and Palley, 1978; Osofsky, 1968; Shaffer et al., 1978). These cases require more diagnostic emphasis on family structure. Poor planning, innocent passions, and bad luck are additional causes for unwanted pregnancies, more often than not among teenagers from functional middle-class families (Plionis, 1975). Not all adolescents experience pregnancies that are unplanned or unwelcome. In point of fact, there are families in this country among whom early pregnancies represent a positive expression of subcultural norms (Stack, 1972), and are not a function of race.

Each pregnant teenager is confronted with tasks of psychological maturation, to negotiate a new place in the family and a personal future. No decision concerning a typical adolexcent pregnancy is completely satisfactory. Continuation of the pregnancy carries adult responsibilities, abortion involves moral dilemmas, and giving the baby up for adoption triggers feelings of guilt and loss (Marens, 1966; Nadelson, 1975). Any one, or a combination of prenatal care, case work, family counseling, and behavioral or psychological therapy, therefore, has a role in every case. With diagnosis as an exercise in discovering effective priorities, therapy is offered most constructively if it is acceptable to the family and the social network (Magid, Gross, and Shuman,

1979; Enos and Hisanaga, 1979). Clinical experience indicates that each pregnant girl's state of adjustment assumes diagnostic precedence for purposes of treatment planning over other problems in need of attention.

STAGES OF ADOLESCENCE

Adolescence can be thought of as a psychosocial process containing psychological and social developmental tasks (Erikson, 1968). Psychologically, each girl must leave behind childhood while accepting adult abilities. This process is painful when childhood has been conflictual or if the future as an adult appears overwhelming (Blos, 1971). The emotional pain of adolescence can be analogized to mourning, mourning for the security of a lost childhood. The more the pain, the more need there is for help.

Major social tasks of adolescence include achieving a mature relationship with the family of origin, while at the same time practicing new roles in the peer group toward an adult "family of choice." Teenagers normally alternate between peer group and family in search of support; the more support, the easier the process (Jessor and Jessor, 1977).

The family shares adolescent developmental tasks and can also experience mourning. Family members give up a child to receive a contributing adult, and the family group experiences a restructuring of relationships. In our society, school and church can play an integrating role in these developmental processes. When the situation becomes difficult, however, help from friends and relatives from other families may become necessary, or from the helping professions (Josselyn, 1971).

Adolescence begins at puberty with the greatest magnitude of change occurring early (Tanner, 1961). Endocrine glands stimulate adult hair distribution, body contours, external genitalia, menarche, and richer affectional expression. Teenagers become sensitive, self-involved, and dependent. They reintegrate attractions, attachments, and emotions previously mastered in a child's body, but this time within the body of an adult, and still predominately focused on members of the family of origin.

Each adolescent's perception of time is metered biorhythmically by the brain through six behaviorally measured states of consciousness. These states include: (1) quiet-alert; (2) aroused or excited; (3) drowsy; (4) light sleep; (5) active sleep; and (6) deep sleep. Infants depend on adult guidance for balance among behavioral states (Wolff, 1966). School-aged children become expert and self-reliant about managing their bodies. Time perception is altered for young adolescents under the cyclic influence of hormones and they must refocus for balance. Pubescent girls usually depend on mature women to relearn balance but some get lost in the here and now.

Fluctuations between idealisms and disillusionment also add vulnerability to adolescence as formal operational thinking becomes available during this stage of life (Piaget, 1969). Disturbing new insights can include the eternity of time, the infinity of space, limitations of religion and of culture, and imperfections of the self, the family, and society (Coleman, 1978).

Early teenaged girls typically experiment with new personal abilities. Emotional defenses can be weak and conflicts near the surface. Childhood immaturities and adolescent confusion tend to predominate. Helpful personal or family insights sometimes are chieved with surprising ease at this stage, but they need to be worked through over time in a positive way.

Families are seldom fully prepared to reintegrate teenage children suddenly physically grown, freshly intuitive, and sexually mature. Concrete suggestions, reality testing, and predictable structure are required of the home in this developmental process. These supports are not always offered, and seldom are completely accepted. Encouragement, reassurance, and conflict resolution are more effective than probing, blaming, or self-condemnation. Clinicians who are consulted concerning the postpubescent adolescent stage can helpfully focus on individuation within the family. The child and other family members are all in need of help as they enter a maturational process.

Most girls are well advanced into adolescence between 14 and 16 years of age. Conflicts during this middle period generate from two ongoing developmental issues: (1) regressive needs for immature dependency as opposed to mature skills for social interdependency; and (2) immature attempts at sensual gratification as opposed to well-identified sexual and personal roles and values. Girls at this stage are able to contribute love, support, and practical abilities to the family, but they also can expose hypocrisies, put cherished family values to the test, and aggravate latent conflicts.

Conflict resolution is difficult for the families of midadolescents because these girls tend to act out internal conflicts within the home, but may seek problem resolution from the peer group. Clinicians most frequently are called upon to mediate family conflicts during this stage. Individual, family, and peer-group techniques are used for this purpose (Smith and Smith, 1976).

The final stage of adolescence is resolution. Sooner or later each girl steps away from the family emotionally, into young adult life. Some cultures encourage physical separation from the family to college, into marriage, or to a job in the city. Other families expect a more continuous and ongoing close relationship with the teenager at gradually increasing levels of maturity. As each woman leaves adolescence, she internalizes a gestalt for primary social skills. These skills equip her for life as an adult in small, intimate new family groups. Young women from stressful or complicated family situations may experience delays in resolution. They may seem to avoid responsibilities as they engage in a taxing psychological task of personal integration, with little room for other concerns. This phenomenon has been described as a psychosocial moratorium (Erikson, 1968). In this case, the clinician's normative goal is to facilitate personal integration.

PREGNANCY AND THE ADOLESCENT PROCESS

Pregnancy itself is a developmental process involving stages over the short course of nine months and, in the majority of cases, eventuating in parenthood as a long-range continuum. Each pregnancy involves serious life-shaping personal decisions. Approximately 1 million teenage, American girls become pregnant annually. Six hundred thousand of them carry to term (Arehart-Treichel, 1978). Of these, approximately 90 percent keep their infants (Chilman, 1979). Teenage mothers, preoccupied with their own personal development, experience higher risks for pediatric morbidity (Morris, 1980). Pregnant adolescents carry a higher risk for prematurity and for perinatal mortality which increases with a second child (Jekel et al., 1975). Their infants display more developmental abnormalities. There are indications that these problems correlate more with social and developmental factors than with the mother's physical immaturity (Levkoff, 1978; Kreutner and Hollingsworth, 1978). Higher levels of social stress, for example, have been correlated with an increase in premature deliveries (Newton, Webster, Binu, Maskrey, and Phillips, 1979).

Any realistic acceptance of pregnancy is grounded in personal maturity. Pregnancy, in common with adolescence, focuses attention for a woman onto her body and onto love relationships, with heightened intensity. Sexual union with a male calls for receptiveness, sharing, and some surrender of control. Pregnancy creates an intimate bond outside the family of origin. Conception shifts the focus to self-image, beauty, and sensitivity as a bearer of new life. Quickening introduces the woman to a vulnerable and dependent creature within, requiring conformity to another being's biorhythms and needs. Fantasies about the unseen fetus are a part of this process, as are thoughts about motherhood and the future. These realities of pregnancy are accepted most easily by a pregnant teenager who has achieved integrated capacities for trust, assertion, sensuality, and a purpose of life. As always, each integration incorporates experiences from the past, especially from childhood (Deutsch, 1945; Miller, 1976).

Pregnancy has special implications for each stage of adolescence. Postpubertal adolescents, closest to childhood, are least prepared for pregnancy. Pregnancy at this stage usually conflicts with age-appropriate developmental needs. A girl of this stage normally is preoccupied with personal development, especially her body. Emotions and fantasies concerning sex and pregnancy are not well differentiated. They are linked to parents and other family members as closely as to peers. Confrontations with the family can be precipitated by the pregnancy over a variety of unrelated issues. These confrontations frequently are premature, and may become chronic rather than lead to a healthy process of individuation.

Each stage of pregnancy for young adolescents requires specific help. During the first trimester reality testing is necessary with support toward personal acceptance, telling the family, and then adjusting the family routine to the requisites of pregnancy (Furstenberg, 1976). Techniques for relaxation, exercise, and to modulate biorhythms are always helpful.

Later stages are fraught with anxieties concerning disfigurement, guilt and shame, isolation from peers, abandonment by the family, and the physical hazards of childbirth. Following delivery or termination of the pregnancy, there are other disturbing realities. Loss of a fetus or infant may take years to work through. By the same token, a newborn may be perceived as a novelty rather than a person, and childbirth as an occasion to receive, rather than practice, mothering. The fact that early adolescent pregnancies are likely to occur in broken or disorganized homes makes tasks of maturation a problem for society at large.

When pregnancy occurs during midadolescence, fluctuations between regressive factors and maturity tend to predominate. Psychological needs and social networks are in transition. Dependency on the family can be perceived by the girl as regressive; to be resisted. Pregnancy pushes these frequently overconfident girls toward unrealistic commitments with boys who are equally immature. Narcissistic fantasies about the romance can then be cruelly exploited when effects of the pregnancy become obvious. Isolation from peer groups is a complication at this juncture. Girls of this age will benefit from contact with other pregnant adolescents. Individual counseling also is helpful to encourage personal development, for help with frustrations, and to accept realistic family supports.

Late adolescence is not always dystonic for pregnancy. Childbearing enhances individuation from parents. It can draw a girl closer to peers, to a mate, and toward a clear future, with motherhood as a focus for identity. Traumatic experiences during pregnancy, on the other hand, can isolate a girl socially, overwhelm her emotionally, and distance her from the support of a loving family. Direct counseling and education for parenting skills are indicated for late adolescents as well as counseling for her parents. Biology, in this case, does not allow a psychosocial moratorium. Girls of this age should be able to understand, and make rational decisions concerning, conception and contraception, motivations for pregnancy, marriage and motherhood, implications of adoption or abortion, options for the future, and the effects of pregnancy on their future.

PSYCHOPATHOLOGY

Serious emotional disorders are found among teenagers, as they are among any age group. These disorders are sometimes misidentified or overlooked as confusion accompanies pregnancy. As an approximate guideline, between 5 and 20 percent of adolescent pregnancies present serious problems in need of psychiatric treatment. Syndromes in need of diagnosis may include severe cases of (1) depression; (2) psychosomatic and psychophysiologic problems; (3) anxiety arising from internalized psychological conflicts; (4) developmental disabilities; (5) personality disintegration; and (6) disruptive personality patterns (Josselyn, 1971).

Professional judgments concerning the severity of mental illness are based on a life history of premorbid patterns, similar disorders in the family, previous episodes, dramatic changes in life adjustment, a current mental status examination, a thorough physical-medical evaluation and objective testing, including psychological testing (Chess and Hassibi, 1978). In each case the diagnostician should remember that most disordered behavior is reactive or transitory, or may represent a healthy response to abnormal situations. Also, the presence of one syndrome does not imply the absence of another.

Profound depression is a common life-threatening situation (Masterson, 1967). Ominous signs of depression include suicidal preoccupation, extreme weight loss, feelings of hopelessness and helplessness, anhedonia, early wakening, and a reversed day-night sleep cycle. Less obvious signs and symptoms can include accident proneness, obesity, encopresis, enuresis, skin disorders, separation anxiety, fatigue, irritability, and generalized unhappiness (Frommer, 1968; Malmquist, 1971). Depressive teenagers tend to have depressive mothers (Agras, 1959). Suicide attempts are more likely among those who come from disorganized homes or have absent fathers (Toolan, 1975).

Psychosomatic and psychophysiologic conditions are also frequently encountered during adolescence. Severe conditions may lead to dangerous physical-medical problems. Anorexia nervosa is a case in point. Fear of pregnancy is an underlying dynamic for many anorexic girls. By starving themselves they are able to maintain a low ratio of body fat, thereby inhibiting ovulation and even puberty. Anorexics suffer profound distortions of body image and of self-esteem (Bruch, 1973). They can literally starve themselves to death. Overeating, typically, alternates with starvation as a part of this syndrome.

Obesity and other nutritional disturbances can be serious when, rarely, pregnancy occurs.

More frequent psychosomatic conditions include simple obesity, epilepsy, asthma, and diabetes. In common with anorexia, these conditions respond well to relaxation training and biofeedback techniques. Family stability and cooperation, however, are essential for effective treatment.

Neurotic defenses and anxieties that underly them can explain many cases of irrational or disruptive behaviors and decisions affecting pregnancy. Serious neurotic problems reflect exaggerated inner needs to avoid anxiety. Neurotic defenses, including phobias, obsessions, compulsions, hysteria, and masochistic patterns, tend to be repetitious, inflexible, and maladaptive. They are seldom totally effective, with disruptive anxiety frequently breaking through. As a result, inflexible behavior alternates with overdependency or panic, poor decisions, and reluctance to accept care. Treatment usually relies on psychotherapy or behavioral techniques to resolve conflicts and reduce anxiety.

Developmental disabilities require specific diagnosis. They can include mental retardation, cerebral palsy, deafness, and blindness, conditions that usually are well diagnosed. Rare conditions such as Tourette's syndrome of progressive tics (Lucas, 1970) and autism, a profound disorder of language and attention (Wing, 1972), may require increased diagnostic alertness. Attention deficit syndromes and specific learning disabilities are less overt and, therefore, more commonly overlooked (Foulkes and Abrams, 1979).

Patients with severe developmental disabilities require special education and other environmental supports. Frustration is common among undiagnosed teenagers from this group, and problems are compounded when the child and family are judged, or blamed, for behaviors they have not been able to control.

Schizophrenia occurs in about .07 percent of the population (Kramer, Pollack, and Redick, 1961). It sometimes appears during childhood, but usually makes an unwelcomed entrance during adolescence or young adult life. There is an inborn predisposition for this disease. Early symptoms include panic, withdrawal, confusion, uncanny facial and body illusions, and delusions of persecution. Many of these symptoms are present in any group of adolescents, but they are not so severe or pervasive. Auditory hallucinations during the quiet-alert state are a strong indication of schizophrenia.

Severe personality disintegrations are also found among adolescents in the form of reactive and developmental psychoses. These illnesses usually resolve with appropriate support and, unlike schizophrenia, are not prognostic for life-long disabilities. Postpartum psychosis, for example, is diagnosed more commonly following out-of-wedlock deliveries (Kendell, 1978). Any psychosis, however, distorts decisions affecting pregnancy and motherhood. Treatment is required.

Drug and alcohol addition or abuse are dangerous situations for adolescents who are pregnant and can be catastrophic for the unborn child (Jones, Smith, Streissguth, and Myrianthopoulos, 1974). Emergency drug reactions usually present as organic brain syndromes with symptoms of restlessness, confusion, lethargy, and misperceptions of stimuli. Central nervous system depression can be a fatal aftermath of high doses of phencyclodine ("angel dust"), barbiturates ("downers"), narcotics, alcohol, and other sedatives, and following withdrawal from chronic barbiturate, amphetamine, narcotic, and alcohol intoxication. Emergency treatment at a hospital is essential for these cases (Hamburg, Kraemer, and Jahnke, 1975). Acute amphetamine intoxication ("uppers") mimics paranoid schizophrenia. Some anticholinergic hallucinogens are also life threatening at high doses. Dangerous toxic inhalents include insecticides, gasoline, and nail-polish remover. There are many other physical-medical causes of acute brain syndrome, and most instances of habitual drug use are undramatic correlates of family and individual life-styles and of maladaptive personality patterns (Fine, 1980).

A diagnosis of personality pattern disturbances is, in effect, a description of disruptive aspects of the individual's approach to life. There are indications that many children who experience multiple family disruptions and various forms of neglect and abuse develop personality pattern disturbances (Yarrow, 1964). Severe personality disturbances can be as disabling as any other form of emotional illness. They usually arise from learned distortions of primary social skills. Relating to other people, for example, can be distorted into withdrawal or physiologic conversation, retarding social, intellectual, emotional, and even physical development (Money, Wolff, and Annecills, 1972). Self-assertion can be distorted into attention demanding or protest behaviors or sometimes exaggerated into antisocial and aggressive patterns (Tizard and Rees, 1975). Intimacy and small-group living can be distorted into excessive competition or social manipulativeness. These patterns are diagnosed as psychopathology when they become habitual and disabling.

PERSONAL STRENGTHS

Pregnancy during adolescence usually evolves a crisis. Teenagers confronting this crisis require a diagnosis of constructive traits, coping skills, and emotional strengths. Supportive services can then be offered to reinforce personal assets and for syntonicity with personal styles. From this point of understanding coping is encouraged, practical alternatives suggested, and general support constructed.

Procedures to diagnose personal strengths parallel those for evaluating psychopathology but emphasize positive rather than negative traits. A history of temperament, talents, and constructive life experiences is obtained and compared with data about current successes and objective achievements. Some personal strengths are achieved by transcending crises. Others are acquired in the course of imperceptibly smooth life events. Personality strengths relate closely to personal styles. Both are organized developmentally in a hierarchy of social skills. Constructive skills evolve from stage appropriate life experiences, with a basis in genetics and temperament (Muller, 1969).

Social traits for evaluation include: (1) primary capacities for close interpersonal relationships; (2) self-control and abilities to accept or master the environment; (3) an internalized gestalt of norms and behaviors sufficient for life in complex intimate family groups; (4) secondary skills to function in larger social groups, regularly but with less intimacy; and (5) tertiary skills, including economic and political abilities acquired in still larger and more transient groups (Fine, 1973).

Capacities for intimate personal relationships are basic during pregnancy. Each pregnant teenager becomes symbiotically attached to the newborn fetus psychologically as well as physiologically, an attachment that must be worked through. Initially, experience for this process is acquired by prospective mothers during their own first three years of life, following delivery (Mahler, 1972). At that time attachment is followed by individuation and frequently painful realizations of personal separateness. Separation-individuation repeats serially throughout life with more or less success. The process is especially pronounced during adolescence, pregnancy, and maternity. Successes build strength for each future crisis of intimacy.

Romantic attachments are intensified during pregnancy, as are those for parents, the family, the obstetrician, and other helping professionals. Normal maturing girls are able to accept appropriate dependency. Those with weaker intrapersonal abilities may deny attachments, lose their sense of individual identity, or be overcome by anger as they realize separateness. In these cases it helps to gradually recognize competencies for intimacy, but not to force them. It can be assumed that each pregnant teenager will build from her unique personal and family style.

Mastery, self-assertion, and self-control are also essential for pregnant adolescents. During pregnancy intense affects are aroused, biorhythms are disrupted, and social frustrations are encountered. Strengths and skills for this particular set of challenges are acquired initially during the toddler period. New capacities blossom at that time and are reconciled with family demands for social conformity. Success in this process of training eventuates in social skills, that, in turn, can be reinforced throughout life by further successes. Disruptions, defeats, and inadequate guidance are likely to create a maladaptive cycle of ineffective assertion, poor self-image, and continued failure.

Some adolescents attempt to compensate for ineffective assertive skills by seeking dependency at any cost. These girls are sexually vulnerable, and may become pregnant. They are likely to transfer nonassertive dependencies onto helping professionals when pregnancy occurs (Deutsch, 1945). In these cases, professional help concentrates most effectively on competencies and personal styles for assertion, however subtle. Small successes that are recognized can restore morale.

Clinicians have found that norms for family life are also organized during the preschool years. These norms prepare the individual for situations concerning morals, emotions, modesty, sharing, self-expression, and sensuality and to reconcile conflicts as an inevitable part of intimate small-group life. A gestalt about family size, roles, routines, and authority ensues and is perceived as an inner conviction that is taken for granted as natural or normal. This "script" (Berne, 1972) is achieved during childhood but is reinforced during adolescence for life as an adult. Deeply held family values are a cornerstone for personal security during pregnancy, but the process for achieving it is complicated by pregnancy.

Early experiences with unresolved conflicts, guilt, shame, and doubt are a part of every family romance (Fenichel, 1945). These negative traits sometimes are acted out by teenagers to the dramatic exclusion of their more positive social skills. Some pregnant teenagers, for this reason, may seem to lack moral values or family norms. Clinicians are well advised in these cases to seek evidence of strengths and then to help clients identify and work through constructive new personal integration for intimate, small-group living. Psychological uncovering is unnecessary. Fundamental assumptions about life should not be challenged but can be modified. It is never basically helpful for a professional to side with a pregnant teenager against someone she loves.

Secondary social skills are essential to pregnant adolescents as they are for all young people. These skills are acquired initially at home, in the neighborhood, and at school during the middle years of childhood. Work, friendships, and some aspects of courting require secondary skills. Most tertiary skills come still later. Those economic and political abilities, removed from intimacy, also are essential for survival. Many adolescents from disrupted homes lack secondary and tertiary abilities, yet show little interest in acquiring skills since they are preoccupied with umet primary needs. Adequate secondary and tertiary skills can help these girls meet personal needs to compensate for more basic problems. When social, education, and other training programs are set up extra support, sensitivity, and patience are required. Such programs have better results when they are insulated from overwhelming agency, institutional, or family politics, and economic pressures (Fine and Taylor, 1972). As always, preexisting personal talents should be identified and reinforced.

THE FAMILY AND ECOLOGICAL NETWORKS FOR SUPPORT

Throughout history the family has been a consistent sociocultural matrix for the human life cycle (Washburn and Jay, 1968). to this day it is the most natural unit in which to help shape important personal decisions (Goldenberg and Goldenberg, 1980). Each adolescent pregnancy represents social activity with outcomes emerging from interpersonal networks (Macintyre, 1977). Families are always a part of these networks, and childbirth a central event for each family as well as for its daughters.

Empathy toward the family, and an attempt at diagnostic understanding, are necessary before seeking family support. Families maintain established, entrenched attitudes toward pregnancy. These attitudes resist change and they are crucial for acceptance. There are a limited number of options available to any family when presented with a gravid adolescent. The family can choose to encourage its offspring toward: (1) marriage or common-law marriage; (2) staying with the family; (3) independent living with single parenthood; (4) joining an established outside or nontraditional group or family; (5) placing the child for adoption; or (6) terminating the pregnancy. Family traditions, cohesion, and leadership are effected by any of these options.

Teen-agers are not good diagnosticians for their own families. As described earlier in this chapter, girls often deny or disengage from their families during adolescence. Personal strengths and weaknesses, however, continue to parallel family attitudes in a system of unconsciously shared, negative and positive, ideologies. Teenagers' perceptions of their families, often are immature, intense, and distorted. Most professionals in this situation attempt to understand their clients by comparing the adolescent's family to personal experiences. Such comparisons must be objectified to be useful, particularly when a teenager is at odds with her family, or if it is very different from that of her evaluator's. The most accurate way to define a family is on its own terms; as its leaders define it.

Each family has social structure on at least two levels, nuclear and extended. Nuclear families are defined as a combination of children and parents living under the same roof (Parsons, 1965). Extended families are larger inclusive groups, transgenerational, and related by kinship, common ancestry, adoption, or marriage (Schneider and Homans, 1955). Some nuclear families are relatively self-contained, particularly families that are geographically mobile and upward striving. Other nuclear families transact routinely with other more or less clearly defined units in the extended group. Small towns and other American subcultures experience this type of structure. Still other nuclear units function communally as a part of the extended family group. Diagnostically, family evaluations should be approached broadly (Fine, 1973).

Clinical evaluations of families rely on direct observations of transactions and shared tasks over time, conjointly, and in subgroups. Historical material, home visits, tapes, two-way mirror equipped interviewing rooms, and shared observations increase objectivity but require preparation and formal permission from family members. Formulations about the family, based in clinical material, include: (1) an estimate of the functional integrity of the family; (2) a description of the family structure and power relationships; and (3) affectional dynamics.

Functional families provide a safe and secure place to live, financial security, religious and ethical traditions, ethnic identity, the wisdom of elder members, intimacy, leaders, peers, and siblings. Pathological families cannot meet these needs and sometimes make destructive demands on members to hide family secrets, deny realities, or distort communications. Family therapies (Langsley and Kaplan, 1968; Satir, 1964) and network therapy (Reuveni, 1979) are available for dysfunctional families.

Structure supports the functional integrity of a family, both internally and as it faces the outside world. Normal family structures define boundaries, authority, leadership, rules, and roles. For clinical purposes, five general types of normal structures are described: (1) close relationships that are casually organized; (2) close relationships that are formally organized; (3) distant relationships that are casually organized; (4) distant relationships that are formally organized; and (5) combinations of organizations varying by age group throughout the extended family.

Structural qualities of a family usually stem from deeply held traditions. Pregnancies and teenagers both disrupt any family's structure. Normal families are upset by changes, but restitute with time and support (Kantor and Lehr, 1975). Professional services, whenever possible, should be offered in a manner that does not further challenge supportive family structure.

Some families are structured in ways that do not function well. Types of malfunctional family structures include: (1) enmeshed; (2) disengaged; (3) distorted; (4) disorganized; (5) rigid; and (6) disintegrating. Abnormal types occur in combinations and can vary during each family's life cycle. Directive therapies have been devised to improve pathological family structures (Minuchin, 1974) or power relationships (Haley, 1973). These healing techniques require training and experience for good results. Referrals for therapy may become necessary when the family is perceived to have become a danger to itself.

Enmeshed families deny differences among their members and demand emotional conformity. Psychological or actual incest is an extreme point of enmeshment. Disengagement, in contrast, describes a pathological avoidance of intimacy. Disengaged families may appear normal away from the home. In private, however, they are emotionally hollow. Pregnancy may sometimes occur when teenagers from these families seek intimacy outside the family. Distorted families maintain ineffective power and authority relationships. Young children, for example, may provide leadership in a distorted family, with parents dependent on the children and teenagers considered extraneous. Enmeshed, disengaged, and distorted families can all be rigid. Rigid families are compartmentalized, inflexible, and frequently authoritarian. Teenagers tend to rebel from them. Disorganized families, in contrast, lack predictable structures. Divorce and bereavement are examples of family disintegration, a loss of structure.

Family dynamics describe the interplay of passions in the family. Dynamics are subtle, elusive, and subconscious. They are passed on through generations, frequently involving the memory of absent or dead relatives. Diagnosis for family dynamics requires intuition as well as observation. All families, including single parent, blended and communal families, share common human passions and similar dynamics. Empathy with family groups can be an intense and even disturbing experience, with overinvolvement common. Discussing family dynamics with colleagues helps to objectify feelings relating to them (Whitaker and Malone, 1953).

Normal family dynamics include the love of a marital couple for each other and for their children, and the children's love for each other. Pseudo or false mutuality among family members, in contrast, are clearly abnormal, as are self-abasement or isolation. Negative passions among family members are not always destructive. Competition stimulates alliances for skills and achievement; envy and jealousy encourage emulation. Hostility clarifies boundaries; guilt defines limits.

Adolescent pregnancies arouse passions in almost any family. Early states of pregnancy typically elicit family denial. Middle stages are characterized by turmoil without insight and, when the baby is born, delivery can be marred by shared joyless feelings of loss and depression. Overwhelming eroticism, guilt, shame, and hostility in these cases can lead to regression and destructive dynamics including scapegoating, negative coalitions, and generalized misinterpretations by family members of each other's feelings and actions, sometimes based on events long past.

Family therapies to heal pathological dynamics are available. Most of these require a contract by the family with a therapist for intensive work over an extended period of time (Boszormenyi-Nagy and Framo, 1965; Pavenstadt, 1967) and are not designed to cope with a crisis. In the instance of adolescent pregnancy, general principles for emotional support are more immediately helpful. These principles include nonpossessive warmth, accurate empathy, genuine interest (Truax and Carkhuff, 1967), with a restoration of morale as the fundamental goal (Frank, 1971). Tracing extended family roots in a nonconflictual or existential manner has also been found useful (Bowen, 1978).

Each persons' web of relationships within the family is defined as their family network. Family networks normally enable pregnant teenagers to meet medical, educational, recreational, mental health, legal, religious, and other social needs. A significant proportion of teenagers prefer to rely on extended family networks during and after pregnancy (Zuckerman, Winsmore, and Alpert, 1979), and there is evidence that multiple cooperative parenting is conducive to good child care (Chodorow, 1978). Some isolated nuclear families structure extended networks with neighbors or in the community at large (Attneave, 1976).

Pregnant teenagers who are estranged from their families may require help to structure a relevant substitute family network. Substitue networks should be ecological, as close as practical to the community and, when possible, integrated with permanent family relationships (Christensen and Fine, 1979). Residence at a group home or foster home may be required, and sometimes other more restrictive settings, such as hospitals become necessary. These settings usually cannot meet their clients' needs for a home and family since, for a variety of reasons, most are organized along bureaucratic or institutional lines (Goffman, 1961). Teenagers frustrated in these settings are likely to regress, rebel, refuse care, or engage in antisocial activities (Fine and Offer, 1965). Placements in restrictive settings are most constructively kept short, under 3 months. Whenever possible, it is best for adolescents to reach network decisions in a family context, especialy decisions concerning marriage or termination of a pregnancy. Families normally understand the strengths and weaknesses of their members. Ordinarily, with appropriate support, they can be of help.

MATCHING NEEDS WITH PROFESSIONAL NETWORKS

A final step in diagnosis is to match each case with needed technical skills. Every community contains a variety of essential professions, usually organized in networks based on shared interests and skills. Professional networks are more goal focused and less personal than family networks (Auerswald, 1965). Clients are not members of professional networks. Immature pregnant teenagers normally rely on family or other personal-ecological networks for help to locate appropriate professional networks. Families require information to make these judgments.

Figure 5-1 diagrams a scheme for matching personal needs with professional services and family relationships. The circle on the left represents a variety of personal needs typical for a pregnant teenager. The overlapping

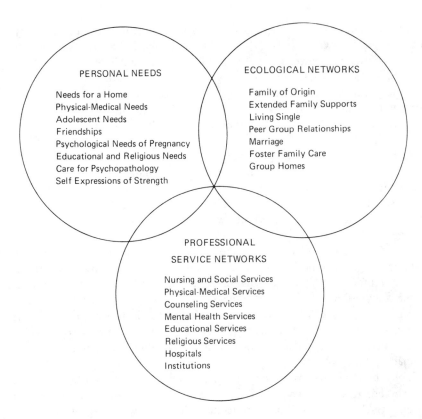

Figure 5-1. Matching personal needs of pregnant teenagers with professional services and family networks.

circle on the right represents primary ecological networks, and the circle below represents networks for professional services. Some personal needs are most appropriately filled by the family and other primary ecological networks. These needs include a home, intimacy, friendships, maturation, and self-expression. Professional services are ancillary in these instances. Another set of needs during pregnancy calls for professional expertise and leadership: this set of needs includes obstetrical care and can involve other medical specialities, nursing, special education, counseling, and social work, as well as religious, mental health, or institutional services. Team work and confidentiality among helping professions increases efficiency for service delivery but cannot substitute for an interface with primary ecological networks.

Technical services need not conflict with other personal and family needs. The following process for matching needs with professional networks is suggested: (1) formulate a set of case priorities based on screening and preliminary diagnoses of the pregnant teenager's biological, personal, family, and ecological-network needs; (2) scan the professional community for technical services necessary for the case and culturally acceptable to the patient and her family; (3) reestablish priorities for referral based on a realistic appraisal of timing for needs and acceptance of services; (4) suggest appropriate services and, on request, make referrals; and (5) work through the diagnostic relationship with the client and her family so that it does not become oppositional to other services that are required.

Each adolescent and her pregnancy are unique and, as with any human being, complicated. Diagnostic parameters offer guidelines for the clinician but intuition and flexibility are required in practice. Figure 5-2 summarizes diagnostic parameters, and the following cases are offered as examples for their use. These cases are composite with details disguised to preserve confidentiality.

Case #1—Shelly, at age 14, is the second daughter in a family of four children ranging from ages 11 to 21. Shelly's father is a military officer, recently retired. A 4-year-old daughter of her unmarried older sister also lives in the family home. Shelly is a good student but underachieves. She is friendly and popular at school. Her developmental history is unremarkable except for several changes in residence and her sister's pregnancy. Her mother suffers from rheumatoid arthritis, a painful condition which interferes with intimate marital relations.

Shelly became pregnant during a casual liaison with a classmate. Neither she nor her friend evidence an interest in marriage. Shelly has no signs of serious psychopathology. She is romantic, idealistic, worries about her family, and seems to be excessively close to her father. He, in turn, concentrates on his new job and hobbies. Shelly's parents maintain casual but constructive

A. Personal
   1. Adolescent stages
   2. Stages of pregnancy
   3. Psychopathology
   4. Personal strengths
B. Family/Network
   1. Culture
   2. Functional integrity
   3. Structure
   4. Dynamics
   5. Extrafamily relationships
C. Professional Services
   1. Technical skills
   2. Acceptability
   3. Timing and process

Figure 5-2. Summary of diagnostic parameters.

relationships with extended family on both sides. Members of the family accept Shelly's pregnancy philosophically and they say they will welcome another baby. Her mother is knowledgeable concerning the community and able to arrange appropriate services. Shelly copes with pregnancy by becoming more dependent; her older sister makes plans for independent living.

This case illustrates helping networks for a pregnant adolescent from a functional but enmeshed, isolated, middle-class family with intense and complicated dynamics. Goals for Shelly at her young age will be for her to mature and differentiate from her family while raising her baby in their home. The family will require encouragement to let her grow up.

Case #2—Linda, age 14, is the younger of two daughters. The family resides in a trailer court. Linda's father is an alcoholic who manages to hold a maintenance job. Her mother, with a history of psychiatric hospitalizations, works as a waitress. Linda, herself, has suffered psychophysiologic symptoms since early childhood. Her school performance is marginal. For at least 2 years she has evidenced a thought disorder with overwhelming anxieties and fears verging on paranoid delusions. She has been hospitalized twice but refuses psychotropic medications. Her life-style is disorganized and sexually promiscuous.

Linda says she decided to become pregnant because a baby will make her independent of her parents. She is in poor physical condition but does not follow through with medical care. Nor does she tell her parents or the putative father, a 30-year-old, married, policeman, about the pregnancy. Three months into her pregnancy she is admitted to a psychiatric unit in a state of acute alcohol and drug intoxication. She aborts spontaneously, mourns her loss passionately, but remains defiant and pathologically overinvolved with her family. Linda is sensitive, intuitive, and responds episodically to kindly support. She has a strong desire to be "normal" and independent.

This case illustrates a network for a severely disturbed, pregnant young adolescent with psychotic motivations. Her family is enmeshed and disorganized. She lacks normal relationships. Goals in this case include long-term contacts with social service and mental-health professionals, psychiatric treatment, vocational rehabilitation, and a supportive, realistic approach to her close-knit, but poorly functional family.

Case #3—Ellen, age 16, is the third child born to her mother, the product of a second marriage. Two older brothers are married and out of the home. Her mother maintains a companionable third marriage, but remains neurotically bound to her own compulsive mother and domineering father. Ellen has a long history of petty theft. Her biological father, abusive to her in childhood, left the family when she was 7. She habitually runs away from home, and has been sexually active for about 2 years. Two brief foster placements during her 15th year have not been constructive.

Ellen has spend seven months in her third, apparently successful, foster placement. She is settled and fond of her foster mother. Ellen is a good student with many friends. Unexpectedly, she becomes pregnant. The putative father is 18. Her biological family and foster mother both consider him a poor provider. Ellen uses her pregnancy neurotically to provoke anger from her boyfriend, foster mother, biological mother, and grandparents. She appears mildly depressed, accepts professional advice, but resists confiding in her parents. Ellen wants to raise her baby.

This case illustrates a moderately disrupted, pregnant, middle adolescent from a dysfunctional, rigidly distorted, extended family. A major goal is to reinforce Ellen's relationship with her foster mother, an experienced grandmother, who will help her learn self-care, parenting skills, and ways to cope with her family and boyfriend. Her foster mother also is available to help Ellen arrange appropriate professional services; this will require sanction from her biological family.

Case #4—Teena, age 16, lives with her widowed mother and a sister who is 13. A learning disabled older brother is living independently away from home. Teena's father, who was a computer operator, recently died suddenly from a heart attack. Teena's mother reports that she was "relieved" because her husband was "difficult to live with." A developmental history indicates that Teena was a "sweet" baby, a compliant child, and an excellent student during middle childhood. She ran away from home for the first time when she was 13, continues to run away and to date boys who are racially and ethnically unacceptable to her mother. After Teena complains about her home situation to her pastor he invites her, with reluctant permission from her mother, to live with his family and begins counseling the family.

Teena becomes pregnant while living in the pastor's home. She is not interested in marriage to the putative father, also 16. Her mother and grandparents are grossly disapproving. They demand an abortion. The pastor does not approve of abortion, but is unable to oppose the family. Teena returns home after the abortion. She is nervous and oversensitive. She seeks out a neighbor, a divorced mother of three, for advice and support. Her school work improves and she stops running away. In response to the pastor's insistence, Teena's mother agrees to one family therapy session. During this session family members accept some general advice concerning adolescents, but are not able to face fundamental issues.

This case illlustrates pregnancy in a teenager from a rigid, but disintegrating, disengaged family in crisis. Teena, along with her family, employs defenses of denial and displacement. Her pregnancy probably is accidental, stemming from ignorance and unmet needs for closeness. Teena will need to find help to cope with feelings about her abortion, to mature, and to mourn her father.

Case #5—Gloria, at age 17, has been married for six months; she is three months pregnant. Gloria and her husband, a 22-year-old construction worker, live in a small frame, cottage house. They appear to be coping well with marriage, their home, and the pregnancy.

Gloria was raised in a functional, nuclear, middle-class family with casual extended relationships. She experienced a happy, stable childhood, but her mother died suddenly when she was 13. Her father was not able to cope. At that point Gloria, overwhelmed by grief, became uncontrollably rebellious. Family disintegration ensued. Gloria was then placed in an adolescent group home where, over the course of a year, she was able to mourn her mother and regain control over her behaviors. In the course of time, Gloria's father remarried, the family reconstituted, and she was able to return home. She remained with her father until she was married, after graduation from high school.

Gloria maintains close relationships with her father and brother. She is polite, but cool, toward her stepmother and sister. She and her husband live next door to the group home, and maintain constructive long-term relationships with girls and staff she knew when she was in residence there. Gloria uses her parents' family doctor for obstetrical care.

This case illustrates a pregnant girl successfully maturing into young womanhood, who is able to construct family and other networks around herself.

Health services for each of the five representative situations presented above are determined by needs in context with physical-medical care and a secure place to live assuming first priorities. Stages of adolescence, requisites of pregnancy, personal strengths, and psychopathology influence each teenager's acceptance of obstetrical care and other essential services.

Confidentiality, civil rights, and personal strivings are respected in each case as social networks are evaluated to reinforce constructive, developmental patterns and cultural affiliations. The family and related ecological networks are indispensable supports for pregnancy during adolescence. These networks ordinarily complement helpful technical skills as they are offered by professional networks and teams.

SUMMARY

Diagnosis for biological, personal, family, and social factors guide pregnant adolescents toward adaptive decisions affecting health services. Needs are determined in context with obstetrical care and a secure place to live as first priorities.

Personal traits for evaluation include the process of adolescence, stages of pregnancy, personal assets and, in some cases, psychopathology. Adolescent pregnancies alter biorhythms and social relationships. Psychopathology can color these processes with depression, psychophysiologic disorders, anxiety provoking inner conflicts, developmental disabilities, disruptive personality patterns, and disintegrations. Personal strengths and talents form a matrix to cope with adolescence, pregnancy, social changes, and emotional problems. The family is the most consistent sociocultural group for help to cope with pregnancy. Each family transmits skills for intimate relationships, self-assertion, small-group living, friendships, and economic survival. Family diagnosis considers transgenerational patterns, extended relationships, functional integrity, structure, and dynamics. Pregnant adolescents from poorly functioning families may require help toward ancillary or substitute networks. Adolescents normally experience transitions from the family of origin to peer groups, marriage, and a family of choice. Family problems arise from social enmeshment, disengagement, distortion, disorganization, rigidity, or disintegration.

Professional networks cannot substitute for family networks. They can offer medical, nursing, counseling, mental health, educational, religious, institutional, and social services. This is done most effectively when there is sanction from the family and other personal networks. Accurate diagnoses and timing are essential for success.

BIBLIOGRAPHY

Agras, S. The relationship of school phobia to childhood depression. *American Journal of Psychiatry*, 1959, 116, 533–536.

Arehart-Treichel, J. America's teen pregnancy epidemic. *Science News*, 1978, 113 (18), 299.

Attneave, C. L. Y'all come! Social networks as a unit of intervention. In P. Guerin (Ed.), *Family Therapy, Theory and Practice*. New York: Gardner Press, 1976.

Auerswald, E. H. Interdisciplinary versus ecological approach. *Family Process*, 1965, 7, 202–215.

Berne, E. *What Do You Say After You Say Hello?* New York: Bantam Books, 1972.

Blos, P. The child analyst looks at the young adolescent. *Daedalus*, 1971, 100 (4), 961–978.

Boszormenyi-Nagy, I. and Framo, J. L. *Intensive Family Therapy*. New York: Hoeber Medical Division of Harper & Row, 1965.

Bowen, M. *Family Therapy in Clinical Practice*. New York: Jason Aronson, 1978.

Bruch, H. *Eating Disorders: Obesity, Anorexia and the Person Within*. New York: Basic Books, 1973.

Chess, S. and Hassibi, M. *Principles and Practice of Child Psychiatry*. New York: Plenum Press, 1978.

Chilman, C.S. Teenage pregnancy: A research review. *Social Work*, 1979, 24 (6), 492–498.

Chodorow, N. *The Reproduction of Mothering: Psychoanalysis and the Sociology of Gender*. Berkeley and Los Angeles: University of California Press, 1978.

Christensen, G. and Fine, P. Corrective socialization in foster care of children. *Child Psychiatry and Human Development, 1979*, **10** (1), 15–34.

Coleman, J. C. Current contradictions in adolescent theory. *Journal of Youth and Adolescence*, 1978, **7**, 1–11.

Deutsch, H. *The Psychology of Women: A Psychoanalytic Interpretation*, (Vol. 2). New York: Grune & Stratton, 1945.

Enos, R., & Hisanaga, M. Goal setting with pregnant teen-agers. *Child Welfare*, 1979, **58** (8), 541–552.

Erikson, E. H. *Identity: Youth and Crisis*. New York: W. W. Norton, 1968.

Fenichel, O. *The Psychoanalytic Theory of Neurosis*. New York: W. W. Norton, 1945.

Fine, P. Drug abuse in children and adolescents. In G. D. Maragos (Ed.), *Pediatric Emergencies in the Ambulatorium*. New Delhi, India: Interprint, 1980.

Fine, P. Family networks and child psychiatry in a community health project. *Journal of the American Academy of Child Psychiatry*, 1973, **12** (4), 675–689.

Fine, P. An appraisal of child psychiatry in a community health project: Relevance as a function of social context. *Journal of the American Academy of Child Psychiatry*, 1972, **11** (2), 279–293.

Fine P. and Offer, D. Periodic outbursts of antisocial behavior: Outbursts among adolescents in a general psychiatric hospital. *Archives of General Psychiatry*, 1965, **13**, 240–254.

Fine, P. and Taylor, W. R. Staff supports: Lessons from the child guidance and community mental health movements. *Child Psychiatry and Human Development*, 1972, **2** (4), 1976–184.

Fischman, S. M. and Palley, H. A. Adolescent unwed motherhoods: Implication for a national family policy. *Health and Social Work*, 1978, **3** (1), 30–46.

Foulkes, R. W. and Abrams, J. C. Some emotional factors in learning disabilities. *Academic Therapy*, 1979, **14** (5), 559–564.

Frank, J. Therapeutic factors in psychotherapy. *American Journal of Psychotherapy*, 1971, **25**, 350–361.

Frommer, E. A. Depressive illness in childhood. *British Journal of Psychiatry*, 1968, **2**, 117–136.

Furstenberg, F. F. *Unplanned Parenthood: the Social Consequences of Teenage Childbearing*. New York: Free Press, 1976.

Goffman, E. *Asylums*. New York: Anchor Books, 1961.

Goldenberg, I. and Goldenberg, H. *Family Therapy: an Overview*. Monterey, Calif.: Brooks/Cole Publishing, 1980.

Haley, J. *Uncommon Therapy: the Psychiatric Techniques of Milton Erikson*. New York: Ballantine Books, 1973.

Hamburg, B.A., Kraemer, H.S., and Jahnke, W. A. A hierarchy of drug use in adolescence: Behavioral and attitudinal correlates of substantial drug use. *American Journal of Psychiatry*, 1975, **132** (11), 1155–1163.

Jekel, J. F., Harrison, J. T., Bancroft, D. R. E., Tyler, N. C., and Klerman, L. V. A comparison of the health of index and subsequent babies born to school age mothers. *American Journal of Public Health*, 1975, **65** (4), 370–374.

Jessor, R. and Jessor, S. L. *Problem Behavior and Psychosocial Development: A Longitudinal Study of Youth*. New York: academic Press, 1977.

Jones, K. L., Smith, D. W., Streissguth, A. P., and Myrianthopoulos, N. C. Outcome in offspring of chronic alcoholic women. *Lancet*, 1974, **1**, 1076–1078.

Josselyn, I. M. *Adolescence*. New York: Harper & Row, 1971.

Kantor, D., and Lehr, W. *Inside the Family: Toward a Theory of Family Process*. San Francisco: Jossey-Bass, 1975.

Kendell, R. E. Childbirth as an aetiological agent. In M. Sandler (Ed.), *Mental Illness in Pregnancy and the Puerperium*. Oxford: Oxford University Press, 1978.

Kramer, M., Pollack, E. S., and Redick, R. W. Studies of the incidence and prevalence of hospitalized mental disorders in the United States: Current status and future goals. In P. H. Hock and J. Zubin (Eds.), *Comparative Epidemiology of Mental Disorders*. New York: Grune & Stratton, 1961.

Kreutner, A. K. K. and Hollingsworth, D. R. Pregnancy outcome. In A. K. K. Kreutner and D. R. Hollingsworth (Eds.) *Adolescent Obstetrics and Gynecology*. Chicago: Year Book Medical Publishers, 1978.

Langsley, D. G. and Kaplan, D. M. *The Treatment of Families in Crisis*. New York: Grune & Stratton, 1968.

Levkoff, A. H. Biologic, emotional and intellectual risks in teenage mothers and their babies. In A. K. K. Kreutner and D. R. Hollingsworth (Eds.), *Adolescent Obstetrics and Gynecology*. Chicago: Year Book Medical Publishers, 1978.

Lucas, A. R. Follow-up of tic syndrome, in Gilles de la Tourette's syndrome. In F. S. Abuzzahab and F. O. Anderson (Eds.), *International Registry*, (Vol. 1). St. Paul, Minn.: Mason Publishing, 1970, 13–17.

Macintyre, S. *Single and Pregnant*. New York: Prodist, 1977.

Magid, D. T., Gross, B. D., and Shuman, B. J. Preparing pregnant teenagers for parenthood. *Family Coordinator*, 1979, **28** (3), 359–362.

Mahler, M. S. On the first three subphases of the separation-individuation process. *International Journal of Psycho-Analysis*, 1972, **53**, 333–338.

Malmquist, C. P. Depression in childhood and adolescence. *New England Journal of Medicine*, 1971, **284**, 955–961.

Marens, A. E. The psychological effect of pregnancy on the adolescent girl. In F. P. Heald (Ed.), *Adolescent Gynecology*. Baltimore: Williams & Wilkins, 1966.

Masterson, J. E. *The Psychiatric Dilemna of Adolescence*. Boston: Little, Brown, 1967.

Miller, J. B. *Toward a New Psychology of Women*. Boston: Beacon Press, 1976.

Minuchin, S. *Families and Family Therapy*. Cambridge: Harvard Press, 1974.

Money, J., Wolff, G., and Annecills, C. Pain agnosia and self-injury in this syndrome of reversible somatotropin deficiency (psychosocial dwarfism). *Journal of Autism and Childhood Schizophrenia*, 1972, **2** (2), 127–139.

Morris, N. M. Pediatric health promotion through risk reduction. *Family and Community Health*, 1980, **3** (1), 63–76.

Muller, P. *The Tasks of Childhood*. New York: McGraw-Hill, 1969.

Nadelson, C. The pregnant teen-ager: Problems of choice in a developmental framework. *Psychiatric Opinion*, 1975, **12** (2), 6–12.

Newton, R. W., Webster, P. A. C., Binu, P. S., Maskrey, N. and Phillips, A. B. Psychosocial stress in pregnancy and its relation to the onset of premature labor. *British Medical Journal*, 1979, **2** (6187), 411–413.

Nix, L. M. Adolescent pregnancy programs. *Young Children*, 1979, **34** (4), 68–69.

Osofsky, H. J. *The Pregnant Teen-ager: A Medical, Educational, and Social Analysis* Springfield, Illinois: Charles C. Thomas, 1968.

Osofsky, J. J., Osofsky, J. D., Kendall, N., and Rajan, R. Adolescents as mothers: An interdisciplinary approach to a complex problem. *Journal of Youth and Adolescence*, 1973, **2** (3), 233–249.

Parsons, T. The normal American family. In S. Farber, P. Mustacchi, and R. H. L. Wilson (Eds.), *Man and Civilization: The Family's Search for Survival*. New York: McGraw-Hill, 1965.

Pavenstadt, E. (Ed.). *The Drifters: Children of Disorganized Lower-class Families*. Boston: Little, Brown, 1967.

Piaget, J. and Inhelder, B. *The Psychology of the Child*. New York: Basic Books, 1969.

Plionis, B. M. Adolescent pregnancy: Review of the literature. *Social Work*, 1975, **20** (4), 302–307.

Rueveni, U. *Networking Families in Crisis*. New York: Human Sciences Press, 1979.

Satir, V. *Conjoint Family Therapy*. Palo Alto, Calif.: Science and Behavior Books, 1964.

Schneider, D. M. and Homans, G. C. Kinship terminology and the American kinship system. *American Anthropology*, 1955, **57**, 1194–1208.

Shaffer, D., Pettigrew, A., Wolkind, S., and Zajicek, E. Psychiatric aspects of pregnancy in school girls: A review. *Psychological Medicine*, 1978, **8** (1), 119–130.

Smith, R. H. and Smith, A. R. Attachment and educational investment of adolescence. *Adolescence*, 1976, **11** (43), 394–357.

Stack, C. B. Black kindreds: Parenthood and personal kindreds among urban blacks. *Journal of Comparative Family Studies*, 1972, **3** (2), 194–206.

Stone, J. P. Some teen-agers are still having babies. *Psychiatric Opinion*, 1975, **12** (3), 29–35.

Tanner, J. M. The course of children's growth. *Education and physical growth*. London: University of London Press, & Blackwell Scientific, 1961, 14–38.

Tizard, B. and Rees, J. The effect of early institutional rearing on the behavior problems and affectional relationships of 4-year-old children. *Journal of Child Psychology and Psychiatry*, 1975, **16** (1), 61–73.

Toolan, J. M. Suicide in children and dolescents. *American Journal of Psychotherapy*, 1975, **29** (3), 339–344.

Truax, C. and Carkhuff, R. *Towards Effective Counseling and Psychotherapy*. Chicago: Aldine Publishing, 1967.

Washburn, S. L. and Jay, P. C. *Perspectives on Human Evolution*. New York: Holt, Rhinehart & Winston, 1968.

Whitaker, C. and Malone, T. P. *The Roots of Psychotherapy*. New York: Blakiston, 1953.

Wing, L. *Autistic Children*. New York: Brunner/Mazel, 1972.

Wolff, P. H. The causes, controls, and organization of behavior in the neonate. *Psychological Issues, Monograph no. 17*, New York: International Universities Press, 1966.

Yarrow, L. J. Separation from parents during early childhood. In M. L. Hoffman and

L. W. Hoffman (Eds.), *Review of Child Development Research*. New York: Russell Sage Foundation, 1964.

Zuckerman, B., Winsmore, G., and Alpert, J. J. A study of attitudes and support systems of inner city adolescent mothers. *The Journal of Pediatrics*, 1979, **95** (1), 122–125.

Part III
Problems

6.
Medical and Psychosocial Risk Factors in the Pregnant Adolescent

Ira M. Sacker, M.D.,
Chief, Adolescent Medical Program,
Brookdale Hospital Medical Center,
Brooklyn, New York

Assistant Professor,
Department of Pediatrics,
State University of New York,
Downstate Medical Center,
Brooklyn, New York

and

Sol D. Neuhoff, M.D.,
Physician in Charge, Adolescent Obstetrics and Gynecology,
Department of Obstetrics and Gynecology,
Brookdale Hospital Medical Center,
Brooklyn, New York

Clinical Instructor,
Department of Obstetrics and Gynecology,
State University of New York,
Downstate Medical Center,
Brooklyn, New York

The study of adolescent pregnancy must always include an understanding of its results. Medical and psychosocial consequences of teen-age pregnancy must not only be listed, but placed in appropriate perspective. In reviewing the literature and adding some further observations, we discuss the medical problems associated with adolescent pregnancy. Most significant and relevant are the problems of prematurity and toxemia. Generally, maternal and prenatal morbidity and mortality are increased. Increased incidence of cesarean section, although often mentioned, may not be that major a problem. Maternal anemia is also discussed. Psychosocial problems include not only the teenager's attitude toward her pregnancy with all its implications, but also many results of pregnancy as well. Income levels and educational attainments are shown to be less than expected for the adolescent mother. Repeat pregnancy is always something to be considered. Unfortunately, family instability and child abuse may be increased for the adolescent mother.

Understanding these issues will ultimately shape society's attitude toward adolescent pregnancy, and will determine whether and how far society will go in establishing programs for pregnancy prevention and provision of pregnancy related services to adolescents.

INTRODUCTION

Although reports of the obstetric performance of pregnant teenagers first emerged in the literature in significant numbers in the 1920s, pregnant adolescents and their problems have been of increasing interest and concern to professionals in the past few years. The literature is now replete with theories, assumptions, conjectures, comparisons, and in some instances, hard data relative to this area. However, a clear picture of which medical and psychosocial problems the adolescent will incur during her pregnancy, and which of these her newborn will be confronted with, does not emerge.

In view of the fact that the adolescent years (though relatively short in duration) encompass a wide range of maturational changes, the many studies of pregnancy in adolescence are not uniform and perforce do not reach similar conclusions. The scope of this chapter is much beyond any single study because each study usually confines itself to a unitary variable, such as age, race, socioeconomic subgrouping, and the like.

Adolescents are maturing earlier, and therefore becoming sexually active at an earlier age. Group pressure and earlier physical maturation have played a significant role in early sexual awareness and intimate physical contact. By age 15, two-thirds of the males in four studies admitted to being sexually active and reported more varied sexual patterns than females.[8,13,33,46] It should be borne in mind, that while the total number of years of adolescence is not great, a 17-year-old having her first baby is not exposed to the same risks as the 12-year-old with her first child.[8] It is not surprising that the literature in discussing these two separate cases arrives at different conclusions. The 12-year difference between a 21- and 33-year-old pregnant woman is not as significant from an obstetric and psychiatric point of view as a 5-year difference might be in an adolescent.

During the past decade the United States has noted a dramatic decrease in fertility rates. This has *not* been the case with adolescents under 17 years of age. The proportion of all babies that are born to teenagers has risen. In 1950, females under 20 years of age bore 12 percent of all children. In 1975, they bore 19 percent of all children and 35 percent of all first children. Another notable occurence is the increased portion of births that occur outside of marriage. In 1975, 14 percent of all babies were born to unmarried women, 52 percent of these out-of-wedlock births occurred to teenagers, and 39 percent of these teen-age births occurred outside of marriage.[3,8]

Aside from age, social factors such as race, educational attainment, marital status, and income level play an important role in determining the obstetric outcome of the individual teenager. For example, the single, black teenager having her third out-of-wedlock child and dependent upon public assistance cannot be compared with the intact white, recently married, financially supported 18- or 19-year-old who has completed high school and is expecting her first child.[30]

Interestingly, the pregnant adolescent, with increasing frequency, is keeping her baby and attempting to deal with the responsibilities and pressures of her new and often premature role. Abortion is likewise being chosen more frequently, and adoption is being seen much less as an alternative to keeping a baby. The more frequent choice of keeping one's child seems to represent a significant cultural change which is adding to the general alteration of the family unit.

Thus, in examining the literature, often we find ourselves comparing apples and pears. We will attempt to raise and clarify some of these confusing issues and, as a result, it is hoped that we will emerge with a clearer picture as to expectations of medical outcome when a pregnant teenager presents herself for treatment.

SCOPE AND LIMITATIONS

While it is not our purpose here to write a textbook on obstetrics, we will discuss those medical problems specifically related to adolescent pregnancy which have no bearing on adult pregnancy, and are rarely dealt with in adult obstetric literature. Also in our scope are preexisting medical problems that are affected differently by adolescent pregnancy than adult pregnancy, as well as maternal and neonatal medical problems resultant from pregnancy which, although present in the adult population, have singular implications or assume greater significance in the teenager.

Completely beyond the scope of this presentation are medical problems that simply coexist with, and are not affected by, pregnancy; be it adult or adolescent. In addition, conditions related to, affected by, or resultant from pregnancy, that pertain in equal importance to the adolescent and adult and have no special relationship to, or different incidence in, the teenage population, will not be discussed and might be mentioned only in passing. We limited ourselves when discussing medical problems of adolescent pregnancy to the immediate newborn period and have not included, for example, health of children of adolescent mothers once they enter school.

PREGNANCY

Pregnancy in general, is perceived by women, especially the adolescent, as a psychological crisis. It is an event of enormous personal impact that bridges the childless life and the "irreversible state of parenthood and in some sense assures one's immortality."[55]

In the early part of a typical pregnancy, a woman may become more regressed and introspective, acknowledging the idea that there exists a fetus in her body. She is concerned with the past, especially with her relationship towards her own mother. Her role is to move away from the dependent ties of her mother to form her own personal mothering identity. As the pregnancy reaches term, a more realistic plan is sought. This is usually accompanied by feelings of excitement as well as anxiety. Feelings of anxiety are usually focused on concern with labor and delivery as well as fantasies about the baby's well being.

During a normal pregnancy, especially the first, a woman may experience emotional lability with mood swings, irrational feelings of concern, bodily discomforts, and shifts in body image. She is quite dependent on environmental supports. With an adolescent, the above issues provide additional stress, since the process of establishing a sense of autonomy from one's mother may be nonexistent.

PREGNANT ADOLESCENT

When pregnancy occurs during adolescence, the typical drive of moving from a more dependent relationship to a more independent or more autonomous position is disrupted. This normal maturation process is halted with the acknowledgement of being pregnant, often leaving the adolescent regressed and dependent. An adolescent feels more ambivalent about leaving her environmental supports and the security of her family, which only adds to the conflict and anxiety of the situation. Parents show anger, disappointment, guilt, and hurt on being confronted with the pregnancy. Minority families do not accept the news any easier than do Caucasian or middle-class families.

An adolescent has many fantasies about childbirth and the baby itself. During the course of the pregnancy, she may have fantasies of sharing her love needs with the baby and expectations that the baby will fulfill these needs. This often creates feelings of anger and depression a few months after the baby's birth when the attention and support from the environment during the pregnancy is withdrawn. At this point the adolescent mother is confronted with the reality of caring for a very dependent and complex human being. The original fantasies of excitement and love are now changed, often permanently. She may feel that her years of being a teenager, free and having fun, are now gone, and she is left with new feelings and responsibilities of being a mother. It is not that surprising that a common response of female adolescents is an inability to resist pressure from the male. Although one should not see the female solely as the exploited victim of the male, if they were not pressured many women would probably wait until their latter teens to begin sexual activity. On many surveys, one-quarter of the adolescents felt that the females should have relations before age 18.[13,24,46]

Many adolescents have failed to put off immediate sexual gratification and assume responsibility for their actions. Some researchers feel this is due to the inability of adolescents to plan for the future and form positive directions for their lives. Many pregnant adolescents will say, "I don't really care if I'm pregnant; I wasn't doing much anyway." Poor self-image and lack of self-esteem seem to be likewise added incentives to early sexuality, pregnancy, and motherhood. The emptiness, worthlessness, and helplessness expressed by these individuals seem to increase the risk of pregnancy as an alternative to these feelings. The pregnant teenager is a girl who has a syndrome of failure—failure to fulfill her adolescent functions, remain in school, limit her family, establish stable values, and be self-supporting.[55]

According to reported statistics three-quarters of the pregnant adolescents in the United States are black and in the low socioeconomic class; a higher percentage are on welfare, are unmarried, and have repeated pregnancies during their adolescence. In one third of the cases, the adolescent has been raised by one parent and moved around repeatedly.[3,13,56]

An article by Matern in 1973 indicates that pregnant adolescents have a greater risk of drug and alcohol experimentation and habituation. In this study, the pregnant adolescent had an increased incidence of out-of-wedlock pregnancies and high rates of sexual promiscuity and prenatal and perinatal morbidity and mortality.

Zelnick and Kantner in 1972 studied sexual behavior in both black and white adolescents and their results indicate that black girls have earlier intercourse than white girls of a comparable socioeconomic group. The black adolescent becomes pregnant at an earlier age, and is much less likely to seek and use forms of contraception.[33]

Although many adolescents now appear to be street wise and/or sophisticated for their chronological age, there is a tremendous amount of misconception perpetuated from individual to individual. Surveys and questionnaires over the past five years reveal gaps in knowledge as regards human anatomy, contraception, ovulation, and pregnancy. Large groups of adolescents practice what we call "reverse rhythm"; believing the safest time for sexual intercourse is between menstrual periods and the time of least safety is at the end of their cycle. Others feel that if sexual relations occurred only occasionally, they would not become pregnant. Still others began to experience sexual activity prior to ovulation occurring, and therefore became convinced that no contraception was needed, and so greater risks were taken.

Many parents, likewise, appear to be living in the dark ages and grossly underestimate their son's or daughter's sexual experience. Surveys seem to suggest that many parent's estimates are so low as to indicate an almost massive denial of the existence of sexuality. This allows the parents to preserve the fantasy of their child staying out of trouble, and releases them from taking action in the prevention of potential pregnancy. Parents also reveal ambivalence with what to do even if they know their child is sexually active.[24]

MEDICAL PROBLEMS ASSOCIATED WITH ADOLESCENT PREGNANCY

Pre-existing Conditions

Maternal conditions existing prior to the onset of pregnancy, specifically mentioned when discussing adolescent pregnancy, have included smoking, alcohol ingestion, poor nutritional status, substance abuse, venereal disease, and anemia.

The reasons for these conditions include the current life-styles of teen-agers in our permissive society. Diet fads, experimentation with drugs, and sexual promiscuity all place the teen-ager at a disadvantage even before the onset of pregnancy.

Prenatal Conditions

Several of the aforementioned conditions are directly related to the maternal prenatal problems often cited in the literature on adolescent pregnancy. These include pregnancy-induced hypertensive diseases, anemia, excessive or poor weight gain, abnormal bleeding, premature labor, premature rupture of membranes, aburptio placenta, placenta previa, intrauterine growth retardation, spontaneous abortion, fetal death, urinary tract infection, and maternal mortality (see Table 6-1).

Many of these prenatal problems are clearly related to preexisting conditions in the adolescent. Poor nutritional status and anemia are the results of a preoccupation with smoking, diet fads, and substance abuse prior to pregnancy, causing weight problems and anemia during pregnancy. These conditions in turn, no doubt, play a significant role in the development of toxemia, premature labor, intrauterine growth retardation, and fetal death. Severe hypertensive disease, resultant eclampsia, bleeding assoicated or not with abrup-

Table 6-1. Placental, fetal, and neonatal disorders by maternal age: causes, frequency, and perinatal mortality.

COMPLICATION	AGE OF MOTHER		
	10–15	16–19	20–34
Premature rupture of membrane			
Numbe per 1,000 births	318	237	207
Death per 100 cases	0.8	0.9	1.6
Perinatal mortality	2.7	2.2	3.3
Amniotic fluid infection			
Number per 1,000 births	140	126	119
Deaths per 100 cases	8.7	4.1	4.2
Perinatal mortality	12.1	5.2	5.0
Major congenital anomalies			
Number per 1,000 births	48	43	45
Deaths per 100 cases	12.3	12.9	14.2
Perinatal mortality	5.9	5.5	6.4
Breech and/or forceps delivery			
Number per 1,000 births	31	32	37
Deaths per 100 cases	2.1	1.1	1.0
Perinatal mortality	0.7	0.3	0.4
Abruptio placentae			
Number per 1,000 births	26	13	22
Deaths per 100 cases	20.5	24.2	19.0
Perinatal mortality	5.4	3.2	4.1
Large placental infarcts			
Number per 1,000 births	26	29	34
Deaths per 100 cases	3.2	8.4	8.4
Perinatal mortality	0.8	2.4	2.9
Placental growth retardation			
Number per 1,000 births	24	12	10
Deaths per 100 cases	3.2	12.2	11.0
Perinatal mortality	3.8	1.4	1.1
Postnatal infections			
Number per 1,000 births	11	8	9
Deaths per 100 cases	50.0	62.1	42.5
Perinatal mortality	5.4	4.8	3.7
Hydramnios			
Number per 1,000 births	7	10	19
Deaths per 100 cases	0	4.4	1.0
Perinatal mortality	0	0.4	0.2
Umbilical-cord compression			
Number per 1,000 births	6	9	10
Deaths per 100 cases	11.1	8.4	11.1
Perinatal mortality	0.7	0.7	1.2

Table 6-1. (continued)

COMPLICATION	AGE OF MOTHER		
	10–15	16–19	20–34
Placenta previa			
Number per 1,000 births	3	3	7
Deaths per 100 cases	25.0	13.8	12.0
Perinatal mortality	0.7	0.4	0.9
Incompetent cervix			
Number per 1,000 births	1	3	5
Deaths per 100 cases	0	10.5	6.6
Perinatal mortality	0	0.4	0.3
RH erythroblastosis fetalis			
Number per 1,000 births	1	2	7
Deaths per 100 cases	0	5.3	27.8
Perinatal mortality	0	0.1	1.9
Other disorders			
Perinatal mortality	13.4	10.6	16.8
Total			
Perinatal mortality	51.7	37.6	48.2

From: The Infants of Adolescent Mothers. T.A. Merritt et al. *Pediatric Annals*, Vol. 9, p. 43.

tio placenta or placenta privia, and drug and alcohol abuse, coupled with their complications, will obviously increase maternal mortality rates.

Intrapartum Problems

Intrapartum problems mentioned in the literature on adolescent pregnancy have include cephalopelvic disproportion, prolonged or abrupt labors, lacerations, and malpresentations.

Simple biologic immaturity with incomplete development of the maternal pelvis in the very young adolescent, with or without excessive weight gain, can cause a baby too large to be delivered through a small pelvis, in addition to al the complications related to this condition.

Postpartum Complications

Placental problems, hemorrhage, and puerperal febrile morbidity have been mentioned in association with adolescent pregnancy (see Table 6-1). That these conditions are more prevalent among teenagers has been substantiated; however, no clear reasons for this prevalence have been offered.

Table 6-2. Summary of publications on medical aspects of early teenage pregnancies.

SAMPLE SIZE	AGE	BLACK (%)	SOCIOECON.	PRENATAL CARE	PERINATAL DEATH RATE	PREMAT. RATE	TOXEMIA (%)	CPD (%)	BREECH (%)	C-SECTION (%)
201	12–16	7.0	High	Ex'l.	15.0	70	3.8	2.0*	2.0	3.5
139	12–15	84.9	Low	Poor-fr.	67.0	129.5	—	4.8	—	5.0
3,995	12–19	51.9	Mix	?	25.2	128.0	6.0	2.5	3.4	3.6
1,083	12–16	60.6	Low	Poor-fr.	50	187	10.0	1.0	3.8	2.0
491	11–15	67.2	Low	Poor-fr.	43	170	—	—	—	—
636	11–14	88.2	Low	Poor-fr.	82	234	29.2	35.7†	—	3.4
137	12–14	99.4	Low	Poor	65.7	190	14.6	15.3†	—	4.4
291	10–16	99.0	Low	Poor	—	206	22.6	0.3*	3.4	1.3
400	10–16	99.0	Low	Good	—	112	14.0	0.75*	2.0	0.9
224	11–15	2.0	Low	Poor-fr.	—	170	36.0	—	4.8	3.2
634	12–16	99.2	Low	Fair	38.0	119	19.7	0.45*	2.5	0.6
2,404	11–15	100.0	Low	Good	15.0‡	135	5.3	2.5	1.4	2.7
4,403	11–15	100.0	Low	Poor	33.7‡	192	—	—	—	—
407	10–14	82.1	Mix	Mixed	55.6	150	—	—	—	—

*Indication for cesarian section.
†Bu pelvimetry.
‡Hebdomodal mortality rate (perinatal mortality rate in series A is 29.9)
From: Medical and Social Factors Affecting Early Teenage Pregnancy, A.B. Dott and A.T. Fort. *American Journal of Obstetrics and Gynecology*. Vol. 125, p. 534.

Table 6-3. Medical complications of early pregnancy and childbirth, selected studies, 1970–1975.

AUTHOR, DATE, & COUNTRY	STUDY POPULATION	MEDICAL COMPLICATIONS	
		MOTHERS	INFANTS
Akhter, 1974, Bangladesh	NR	anemia, preeclampsia and eclampsia, toxemia, cephalopelvic disproportion, difficult and obstructed labor	prematurity, low birthweight, and stillbirth
Akingba, 1974, Nigeria	hospital patients under 20	higher operative rates than for older women	higher stillbirth rates than for older women
Andrews, 1975, USA	hospital patients aged 20 or less	preeclampsia and eclampsia, premature rupture of membranes, uterine dystocia, infections, first and/ or third trimester bleeding	prematurity, asphyxia neonatorum, infections, hemolytic diseases
Chibungo, 1974, Zambia	hospital patients under 19	eclampsia, anemia, difficult labor	prematurity and stillbirth
Delgado Urdaneta et al., 1972, Venezuela	hospital patients under 17	no increase in maternal complications	low birthweight

116

Table 6-3. (continued)

AUTHOR, DATE, & COUNTRY	STUDY POPULATION	MEDICAL COMPLICATIONS	
		MOTHERS	INFANTS
Park, 1974, **Republic of Korea**	hospital patients aged 11–19	anemia, toxemia, preeclampsia	prematurity
Pauls, 1974, **Zaire**	young hospital patients	anemia, preeclampsia and eclampsia	prematurity and low birthweight high among all deliveries
Purandare & **Krishna,** 1974, **India**	hospital patients aged 20 or less	anemia, toxemia, cephalopelvic disproportion, spontaneous abortion	prematurity
Rauh, 1971 & 1973, **USA**	adolescent clinic patients	preeclampsia, severe anemia, third trimester bleeding	prematurity
Roopnarinesingh, 1970, **Jamaica**	mothers under 16	toxemia, hypertension, high operative rate	prematurity and low birthweight

NR = Not Reported
From: *Population Reports, Family Planning Programs.* Adolescent Ferility—Risks and Consequences. Series J. No. 10. 157–75 (1976).

Specific Medical Problems

Despite the catalogue of medical problems of the pregnant adolescent and her newborn which was presented briefly, two conditions are paramount as the major problems associated with adolescent pregnancy. The issues of hypertensive disorder in pregnancy:

Toxemia and Prematurity—(Low birth weight) predominate, not only because of their gravity but also the consensus in the literature seems to be that these two issues are especially relevant to adolescents (see Table 6-3). Most authors agree that the incidence of these two problems is greater in the adolescent than adult population (see Table 6-4).[28] The difference between the two populations in incidence of other medical complication, although present, is not nearly as impressive. We thus address these two issues first.

1. Hypertensive Disorders. These disorders were formerly considered separate although related diseases. New nomenclature demands that these related diseases now be consolidated under one name and be distinguishable as diseases along the spectrum of a pathologic process. Whereas once these diseases were considered preeclampsia, renal disease superimposed on preg-

Table 6-4. Comparison of incidence of complications in teen-age pregnancy in selected studies.

	TOXEMIA (%)	PREMATURITY (%)		PERINATAL LOSS (%)
National statistics	6-7	5-10		
Marcheti and Manaker (1950)	19.7	14.8		3.8
Aznar and Bennett (1960)	9.8	18.7		5.0
Israel (1963)	6.0	14.2		2.52
Hassan and Falls (1964)	8.8	10.7		2.5
Osofsky (1970)	13.7	8.0	(by weight)	0.9
		4.5	(by weight and dates)	
Dickens (1973)	5.0	8.0		1.0
Sarrel (1969)	5.0	10.8		0.8
Klerman and Jekel (1973)	13.9	11.7		1.1

From: Teenage mothers: A clinical profile. C.T. Houde and C.E. Conway, *Contemporary Ob/Gyn*, Vol. 7, p. 73.

nancy, and hypertension complicated by pregnancy, it is now recognized that these actually represent a spectrum of disease involving the placenta and kidney and the mother's kidney and vascular system. Although the exact etiology of so-called toxemia or preeclampsia remains unknown, we do know that this part of the hypertensive disease of pregnancy spectrum typically affects, although it is certainly not limited to, the young woman having her first pregnancy. Toxemia is a disease of late pregnancy characterized by a triad of hypertension, edema, and proteinuria, the ultimate stage of which terminates in generalized seizures known as eclampsia. The subject need not be reviewed here in detail and information can be obtained from any standard obstetrics text.

It is widely accepted that toxemia is a familiar, if not the most common, maternal complication of adolescent pregnancy[16,18,30,34,42,45,50] (see Table 6-5).

Most authors report a 5.1 to 35 percent incidence of toxemia in adolescents.[30,34,50,51] Recent studies have shown lower incidences (10%[59]–17%[37]) possibly because of the availability of prenatal care, better nutrition, and improved socioeconomic circumstances. In one group provided with unique prenatal care specifically geared to the adolescent, the incidence was 11.1 percent as compared with 16.7 percent in an adolescent control group.[9] Another study has reported an incidence of toxemia as high as 42 percent in

Table 6-5. Comparisons of rates of toxemia, teenage mothers, and control groups.*

	TEENAGE POPULATION		CONTROL POPULATION	
	TOXEMIA PREECLAMPSIA	UNCLASSIFIED TOXEMIA	TOXEMIA PREECLAMPSIA	UNCLASSIFIED TOXEMIA
STUDY	(PERCENT)	(PERCENT)	(PERCENT)	(PERCENT)
Jovanovic[4]	7.3		5.1	
Coates[9]	14.6		7.9	
Battaglia[62]				
Age under 13	29.2		11.2	
Age 15–19	21.1			
Marchetti[6]				
Age 13	42			
Age 16	16.1		6	
Lewis[23]				
Age 16	20			
Utian[76]	21	15	12	5
		(Total 35)		(Total 17)
Rauh[33]	25		7	

*Teenagers receiving comprehensive prenatal care
From: Obstetrical and medical problems of teenage pregnancy, R.C. Stepto et al. in *The Teenage Pregnant Girl*, J. Zackler and W. Brandstadt, p. 129. Charles C. Thomas, 1975.

girls under age 13.[34] Preeclampsia has been reported to be two[1,51] to five[27] times more frequent in adolescents than adults.

Although poor nutrition and inadequate prenatal care are known to be associated with toxemia of pregnancy, efforts to explain the higher incidence in adolescents will remain futile as long as the etiology of toxemia eludes us.

2. Cesarean Section. Many authors believe, and we concur, that the total incidence of cesarean section in adolescents is equal to or less than the occurrence in adults.[7,10,14,16.37,40,45,51,60] (see Table 6-7). This may be due to the virtual absence in adolescent pregnancy of such problems as malpresentations, placenta previa, and preexisting medical conditions such as Diabetes Mellitus. On the other hand, it seems universally agreed that younger adolescents, if not all teenagers, have a much higher incidence of cephalopelvic disproportion, or a bony pelvis which is too small to allow normal delivery.[14,16.18,21,45,46] Contracted pelvis, usually related to age, has been reported in between 10–40 percent of adolescents.[4,14,50] Since cephalopelvic disproportion is the major condition for cesarean section in all women, it should follow that studies would report increased incidence of cesarean section in teenagers. In fact, only one such study was found.[46] Reports, however, are difficult to compare. Cephalopelvic disproportion is a condition largely due to the immaturity of the pelvis in younger adolescents. In studying this condition, some reports may not have included significant numbers of younger adolescents, thus artificially decreasing their total cesarean section rate. Other series of cases may be weighted with 13- and 14-year-old girls who will have a higher incidence of cesarean section because of their often small and inadequate pelvis.

Related to the problem of cesarean section are the other abnormalities in

Table 6-6. Mortality rates* and low-birth-weight percentages by age groups.

AGE (YEARS)	NEONATAL MORTALITY RATE	FETAL MORTALITY RATE†	PERINATAL MORTALITY RATE	LOW BIRTH WEIGHT (%)
<17	22.9	17.9	40.3	15.8
17–19	22.1	18.0	39.8	15.4
20–34	16.7	16.8	33.2	14.4
35–39	14.3	50.8	64.4	18.5
40+	43.5	28.1	70.4	28.2
Entire group	19.2	18.4	37.2	15.1

*Expressed as mortality per 1000.
†Deaths of fetuses weighing <500 g are omitted.
From: Experience with Teenage Pregnancy, F.L. Hutchins et al. *Obstetrics and Gynecology*, Vol. 54, p. 3.

Table 6-7. Teenage cesarean section rate.

INVESTIGATOR	NUMBER OF PATIENTS IN CONTROL POPULATION	PERCENT CESAREAN SECTION	NUMBER OF TEENAGE PATIENTS	PERCENT CESAREAN SECTION	ABSOLUTE PERCENT DIFFERENCE (y)
Jovanovic[4]	9,536	5.1	1,033	3.2	−1.9
Jorgensen[26]	Unknown	8	350	14.4	+6.4
Coates[9]	2,968	5.4	137*	4.4	−1.0
Lewis[23]	8,366	6.5	102	3.9	−2.6

*14 years or less.
From: Obstetrical and medical problems of teenage pregnancy, R.C. Stepto et al. in *The Teenage Pregnant Girl,* J. Zackler and W. Brandstadt, p. 128.

labor and delivery, such as prolonged or severely shortened labors or lacerations. The literature in discussing these phenomena is paradoxical. Quotes of 15–43 percent labor and delivery complications[14,26,34,42,53] directly contradict reports that find no increase in problems of labor and delivery in teenagers.[7,12,4,51]

Maternal Problems

1. Prematurity-Low Birth Weight. This problem also encompasses several related but distinct processes. Firstly, from the maternal viewpoint, there is premature labor, or the onset of labor before 37 weeks of gestation. This condition has been shown to be more common in adolescent pregnancy.[40,45] The reasons for the latter are purely conjectural, but may be related to biologic immaturity of an adolescent mother, poor nutrition, anemia, inadequate prenatal care, smoking, and possible increase in maternal antenatal infection. It is important to note that premature labor will not always result in a low birth weight baby because the labor may cease spontaneously, or be inhibited medically by various means ranging from bed rest to specific drugs which inhibit uterine contractions.

Second in this group of problems is prematurity, the condition in which a baby is born prior to 37 weeks of pregnancy. This may result from uninhibited spontaneous premature labor, from deliberate induction of labor, or from cesarean section. Labor may have been induced or cesarean section performed because the physican had mistakenly believed that there was a mature infant in the uterus. More likely, the physician felt that delivery was indicated, regardless of a premature birth for the infant, for various reasons, including abruptio placenta, placenta previa, evidence of intrauterine fetal distress, premature rupture of membranes, etc. Any of these conditions might be critical enough for the physician to feel that continued intrauterine existence poses more hazards for the infant than closely monitored life in the hospital nursery.

Although placenta previa occurs less often in adolescents, abruptio placenta occurs more frequently because of its well-known relationship to toxemia.[16] Premature rupture of the membranes before the onset of labor and the attendant risks of serious fetal and maternal infection are more common in adolescents.[40,46,51]

Third in this set of problems is the concept of low birth weight, a medical term that is not synonymous with prematurity. The low birth weight baby is one that weighs less than 2500 grams. This term includes both the premature and the baby that is born small for gestational age, although it might very well be mature. That prematurity and resultant low birth weight are increased in adolescents is a well-established fact, and will be discussed shortly. Also more common to adolescence are small-for-gestational age-babies.[38] Low birth weight, the net result of premature labor, premature rupture of the membranes, and prematurity, is the major cause of perinatal morbidity and mortality, in adults as well as in adolescents. It may result in death, neurologic defects, seizures, mental retardation, cerebral palsy, learning problems, and stunted growth and development.[3,8,13,30,38,56]

A perusal of the literature on prematurity yields only one report to the effect that there is no increased incidence of low birth weight in adolescents,[38] and that particular study was for white mothers only. Most authors agree that prematurity (low birth weight) is a significant, if not the most acute, problem for infants born to teen-age mothers.[8,12,16,19,21,38,42,43,56,57] The single risk of teenage pregnancy, in a study done in Sweden, was prematurity.[12] An even more grave problem exists among nonwhites[38,55] and among the younger adolescent group (i.e., less than 15 years or low gynecologic age)[12,21,26,50,60,61] (see Figures 6-1 and 6-2). Reports range from 30 percent higher incidence of prematurity for adolescents to 200 or 260 percent.[1,2,3,7,9,12,23,35,50,52] Whereas the adult prematurity rate is 6–8 percent, that for adolescents has been reported between 10 and 31 percent.[1,7,17,21,26,28,30,45,51,52,54,54,55,56,59,60] Approximately 25 percent of all low birth weight babies are born to teenagers.[3,35,50] It seems quite obvious that teenagers are giving birth to smaller and more premature infants for reasons that are often enigmatic, but with sequelae that are dreadful.

2. Other Maternal Problems. The most frequently discussed problem in the literature germane to this topic is anemia. Anemia, and specifically iron-deficiency anemia, has been found to be one of the most common maternal complications of adolescent pregnancy.[2,23,28,42,50] Eleven to 43 percent of pregnant teenagers have been reported to be suffering from anemia,[3,7,50,59] and

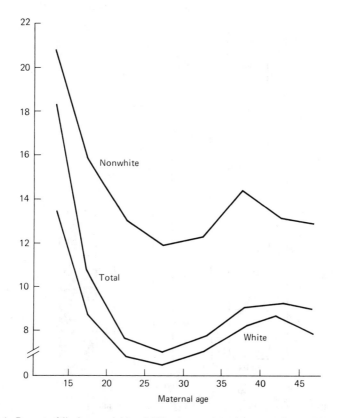

Figure 6-1. Percent of liveborn weighing 2,500 grams or less, by maternal age and race, U.S.A. 1968. From Pregnancy in adolescents: scope of the problem, G. Stickle and P. Ma. *Contemporary Obstetrics and Gynecology,* **5,** 88

these teenagers are 1.3 times more likely than adults to have this complication[1,3] (see Figure 6-5). Poor nutritional habits are overwhelmingly to blame for this condition, and it follows that with good prenatal care, adequate nutritional advice, and iron and vitamin supplementation, anemia in the pregnant adolescent should be brought down to acceptable levels.[51]

Antepartum hemorrhage is not a significant concern in teenagers,[40] and different authors have reported conflicting statistics regarding fetal distress during labor.[15,45]

Postpartum complications including temperature elevation and hemorrhage are probably not more common in teens[16,34,45] (see Figure 6-5). Other maternal, fetal, and infant problems which are not directly related to the adolescent and her pregnancy, such as preexisting medical conditions or substance abuse, are not discussed in detail here.

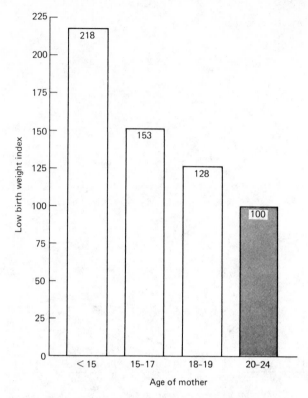

Figure 6-2. Risk of low birth weight (≤2,500 g) among babies born to teenage mothers and mothers aged 20-24, U.S., 1973 (Risk to babies of mothers 20-24 = 100). From Alan Guttmacher Institute. *11 Million Teenagers*, New York Planned Parenthood Federation of America, Inc., 1976, p. 22.

Infant Problems

Considerable attention has been focused on the problems of infants of adolescent mothers. Specifically mentioned have been low birth weight, small for gestational age, infections, congenital anomalies, asphyxia neonatorum, hypoglycemia, seizures, birth injuries, cerebral palsy, neurologic defects, and increased perinatal and neonatal mortality (see Table 6-1).

These conditions are often directly related to the problems previously mentioned. Premature labor and premature rupture of membranes will result in low birth weight babies. In addition, poor nutritional status and inadequate weight gain will result in small-for-gestational-age babies as well. The association between smoking and low birth weight has been given much attention in recent years. Drug ingestion and alcoholism have long been known to cause congenital anomalies. Syphilis in pregnancy will result in a malformed child or stillbirth. Low birth weight babies are subject to problems such as asphyxia, hypoglycemia, seizures, and birth injuries. Furthermore, all these neonatal complications often contribute to babies with resultant cerebral palsy and neurologic defects. With all these factors working against them, it is no wonder that these babies are more likely to die.

Gynecological Age and Teenage Offspring

1. Gynecological Age. Central to all maternal and neonatal conditions is the role of age per se. Is maternal age alone the source of all these problems? Is age, only when combined with other components, crucial to these conditions? Or are the other factors, independent of age, the sole determinants?

The concept that gynecologic age, i.e., the number of years from menarche, is more important than chronologic age has been mentioned.[51] Thus a 16-year-old who began her periods at age 15 is at greater risk for poor obstetric performance than her 14-year-old counterpart who had menarche at age 10.

This also is directly related to the concept of biologic immaturity, and its relationship is more obvious. The 16-year-old with a gynecologic age of 1 year is more biologically immature than the 14-year-old with a gynecologic age of 4 years. If we believe that biologic maturity plays a role in pregnancy outcome, and instances where it does will be shown, then gynecologic age becomes a much more important factor than a simple chronologic age.

2. Teenage Offspring Problems. Previously mentioned were the problems of neonates associated with prematurity (e.g. seizures, cerebral palsy, learning disabilities, mental retardation, and stunted growth and development). Neurologic defects, also a sequel of prematurity, have been shown to be 2–4 times more common in infants of adolescent mothers.[1,3,16,23,27,50] Neonatal depression, as evidenced by low Apgar scores, is also more common.[45] Congenital anomalies have either been reported in equal numbers to infants of adults[28,35,50,51,60] or less frequently.[16,26,38,57] Chromosomal abnormalities, known to be increased in the offspring of women more than 35 years of age, are less common in teenagers.[38] Only these anomalies associated with drug or alcohol ingestion might be more common in infants of teenage pregnancy, as the teenage population abuses these substances more frequently.[34]

Mortality

1. Perinatal. In light of the foregoing, a more detailed examination of the chances for the survival of an adolescent's offspring is in order. As has been already noted, the most important etiology for perinatal mortality at any age group is prematurity and low birth weight. Perinatal mortality actually encompasses two separate statistics including fetal death prior to labor and neonatal death when the baby is born alive. Therefore, the earlier statement that prematurity is the major contributing factor to perinatal mortality naturally refers to neonatal mortality, since prematurity should have no effect on the rate of babies dying before delivery. Fetal mortality, or still birth, is usually attributable to intrauterine distress, congenital anomalies, intrauterine infection, etc. Neonatal mortality is usually caused by the same processes in addition, and proportionally related, to prematurity.

Perinatal mortality has been found to be up to twice as common in teenagers, expecially younger ones, as in adults[27,44] (see Table 6-5). For black adolescents or those under 14 years of age, this rate is increased even more.[23,26] (see Figure 6-3). Biologic immaturity, although it must be considered, is not the prime factor contributing to perinatal mortality.

Controversy exists as to the still birth rate in teenagers. Some authors believe that the adolescent is more likely to experience late fetal demise,[1,27] while others contend that the adolescent is not at risk[38,44] (see Table 6-6). Personal experience confirms the latter view. Increase in parity or birth order, however, might put the fetus at even greater risk for demise.[1,8,22]

Most authors do agree, however, that infant mortality is 2–4 times more

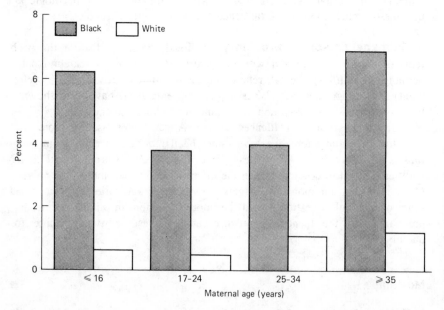

Figure 6-3. Distribution of perinatal deaths by maternal age. From Long range outcome of adolescent pregnancy, J.B. Hardy et al. *Clinical Obstetrics and Gynecology*, **21**, 1219.

likely to occur in teenagers as opposed to the adult population[1,2,3,11,26,38,50,53] (see Table 6-6).

Percentages of infants dying in their first year have been reported between 4 and 10 percent.[3,15,50,60]

2. Maternal. Next to preeclampsia the major medical consequence of teenage childbearing is the mortality of the mother.[30] Although the actual statistics remain quite small, the significance of this fact should not be undervalued. Maternal mortality rates are higher for the adolescent, perhaps as much as double the adult rate.[1,3,42,43,50] When the pregnancy is not the teenager's first, rates may climb even further,[28] and when the mother is younger than 15, the numbers are truly impressive, increasing the risk of mortality in the teenager by up to 10 times the risk in an adult.[2,3,8,30,42,44,50] Mortality may be due to a variety of reasons, some of which have already been discussed, including hypertensive disorders of pregnancy, increased cesarean section rates, and anemia (see Figure 6-4).

It is difficult to separate medical risk factors from the psychosocial, since they are interrelated. However, this report cannot be complete without focusing on the psychosocial effects on the pregnant adolescent.

PSYCHOSOCIAL RISK FACTORS

Education: Pregnancy—Motherhood—School Retention

Pregnancy and motherhood are major reasons for girls leaving school. Up to two thirds of all female school dropouts cite pregnancy and/or marriage as the reason for leaving. Title IV of the Education Amendments of 1972, effective July 12, 1975, prohibits schools which receive federal funds from excluding any student because of pregnancy or a pregnancy related condition. However, many schools exert intense pressures on pregnant adolescents while giving little emotional assistance. Few facilities and supportive services have been developed to ensure the right of education. The responsibilities involved with childbearing, and the economics involved, make it difficult for many of these mothers to remain in school. Opportunities for school-age parents vary considerably throughout the country.[13,24,55]

In two studies of over 200 adolescent mothers, 50 percent dropped out before termination of pregnancies. In exploring why adolescent girls drop out of school, the most common response is pregnancy or school-age marriage. Exploring this further, one notes that of young women in the 10th grade or lower who both marry and have a baby, over 70 percent leave school. Among those who marry but do not have a baby during the year at risk, close to 80 percent leave school. Many of these, however, are pregnant at the time.

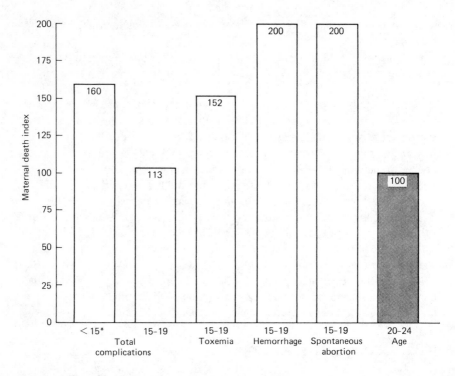

*Numbers too small to calculate ratios for individual complications.

Figure 6-4. Risk of fatal complications during pregnancy, labor and childbirth to teenage mothers and mothers 20-24, United States, 1974 (Risk to mothers 20-24 = 100). From Alan Guttmacher Institute: *11 Million Teenagers*, New York Planned Parenthood Federation of America, Inc., 1976.

Women, therefore, who are already married and do not have a child during that year, drop out more often than single women, but less than women who both marry and become mothers. Those who are neither wives nor mothers are most likely to remain in school; only 7–9 percent drop out. Those who become mothers, but do not marry, are nearly three times as likely to drop out. Those who marry but do not bear a child, (although some are pregnant), and those who both marry and bear a child, have the highest dropout rate; four out of five of these women quit school. Finally, little evidence is found to indicate that adolescent mothers are able to catch up later with their peers who delay childbearing. Rather, the earlier an adolescent leaves school the greater the risk of lifelong loss of schooling.[13,24,39,55]

Nearly half of the dropouts in these samples were moderately able students and seemed committed to obtaining a high-school diploma. With each subse-

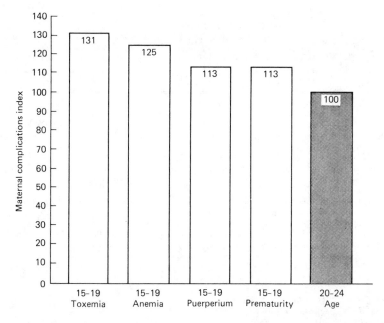

Figure 6-5. Risk of nonfatal complications of pregnancy, labor and childbirth to previously nulliparous 15-19-year-old mothers and 20-24-year-old mothers, United States, 1960s (Risk of complications to mothers 20-24 = 100). From Alan Guttmacher Institute. *11 Million Teenagers,* New York Planned Parenthood Federation of America, Inc., 1976, p. 23.

quent pregnancy the proportion of dropouts increased. And with those with three or more pregnancies, 85 percent had left school without first obtaining a high-school diploma. As a comparison, only one third of the young mothers who did not become pregnant again, failed to complete high school.

Impact of Early First Birth

Very few studies have focused on the importance of education to later economic and social status. The largest evaluation was performed by "National Longitudinal Study of the Labor Market Experiences of Young Women" (NLS) which clearly indicated that early childbearing is associated with major educational losses. In their study of 5000 young women between the ages of 14 and 24 (1968–1978), girls who bore a child at 15 years or younger completed only 9 years of school, on the average. Those who had a first child at 16 or 17 completed 10½ years, on the average.[39]

When the variables of family background, educational goals, and age at marriage were controlled for, young women who had their first child at age 15 or younger were found to complete 2 years less schooling on the average than women who were still childless at age 24. Therefore age at first birth is one of the strongest influences on schooling.

Since the presence of babies and young children seem to disrupt the lives of black women less than white women, it is now known that early childbearing interferes much less with black than white formal education. Among young black women, only those births occurring at the youngest ages are associated with educational losses.[8,39]

Early childbearing does have a strong negative effect on white women and a moderate negative effect on schooling of black women. Early marriage negatively affects the schooling of both whites and blacks.

The effect of early marriage on schooling has likewise proven to be statistically significant. An adolescent, who is both married and has a child, has a greater risk of dropping out of school at an earlier time. The adolescent who has a child, but does not marry, is only half as likely to drop out of school. The school-age mother is still more likely to leave school, whether married or not, compared to her adolescent counterpart who has not given birth.[8,13,24,39,46]

"Catching Up" on Schooling

The adolescent's ability to return to school after childbirth and catch up, has been a question only recently evaluated. Some reports seem to show that some progress in education does occur, but as a whole the young mother never quite catches up. In fact, the gap in educational completion between young mothers and young women who are childless at 18, 21, and 24 years of age increases as the childless women continue their education. In a few small studies of approximately 150 young mothers, upwards of 30 percent return to school, attend adult education classes or pass a high school equivalency examination. On retrospective analysis, however, less than 10 percent of the youngest adolescent mothers (17 years or under) are high-school graduates. Therefore, the earlier the birth the less the chance of school completion.[29]

Process of Educational Attainment

The factors which promote completion of a formal education are different in childbearing adolescents from those who postpone children. Those adolescents who postpone childbirth have a greater amount of self-motivation and support and/or help from others in their family or peer group. For the adolescent mother, family background, plays a unique and ever important role in school completion. "Those girls with a more advantaged family, few siblings, a father with a formal education, an intact family, have a better chance of being supported emotionally and having a family member accept some of the responsibilities of child rearing."[39,46,47]

Race seems to play a small and rather insignificant role on schooling. However, we have previously stated that adolescent childbirth does affect schooling, and early childbearing is more common among black adolescents in the United States. Theories reflecting this indicate that black adolescents actually suffer less of an educational disadvantage than white adolescents, since social mechanisms in black females, peer groups, and school systems in black neighborhoods are better established. Since childbearing may be more socially acceptable in black families, there is evidence to suggest that it is less disruptive to schooling and the overall lives of black adolescents as compared to their white adolescent peers. Only births occurring to the youngest black adolescents (17 years or less) are associated with any greater school disruption.

SOME SOCIOECONOMIC CONSIDERATIONS

Family Size

Numerous studies have reported that the earlier a woman begins her family the more children she is likely to have. This results not from a directed plan or desire, but from having more unplanned births. The New York Study of New Mothers in 1976 found that only 20 percent of the teenagers had planned their births as compared to 70 percent of the women who were 24–29 years of age. The teenage mother is less likely to intentionally choose motherhood as a priority for her first birth, and this pattern seems to repeat itself with later pregnancies. Early motherhood has a major effect on future options available for this person. Since childbirth interferes with the educational process, vocational opportunities are few and for poorly paid jobs. This increases the amount of available and nonproductive time, increasing the risks for subsequent pregnancies.[33,39]

In an extensive (2000) study of the NHL retrospective, 200 mothers aged 24 who became mothers at 15 years of age or younger had an average of 1.25 to 1.5 more children than women who gave birth at 21 to 24 years of age. In another large study (1500) of mothers aged 35 to 52 years, those women who gave birth at 15 years of age or younger had an average of three children more than women who were at least 24 years when they became mothers. In the same study, women whose first child was born when they were 16 or 17 years of age had an average of 2.7 more children than women who delayed childbearing until age 24. Overall, among women 35 to 52 years of age in this study, those mothers who had their first child at age 17 or younger had an average of 5 children each. These families were obviously exposed to extreme financial and emotional pressures at a time when most young people are just establishing independent identities and career goals.[39]

Family size has been found to be smaller among white women, better educated women, non-Catholics and women from more recent birth cohorts. Southern white women were found to have smaller families than Northern whites; farm background did not affect fertility. Black women who worked early in marriage had smaller families than those who were not employed. Employment early in marriage did not change fertility among white women once age at first birth and age at marriage were considered.

Child Development

The children of adolescent mothers have been described as being more dependent and distractible. They had more behavioral problems and were likely to be below the average mean percentile in height and weight. Hardy, from the Johns Hopkins' Child Development Study in 1976, reviewed the development of 525 children born to girls who were 16 years or less at the time of delivery. At age 4, 11 percent of the children scored 70 or below on IQ tests as compared to 2.6 percent at the general population of 4-year-olds. In the general population approximately 25 percent of 4-year-olds will have an IQ of 110 or above, only 5 percent of the children born to these young mothers tested that high. Hardy also reported that school failure and significant behavior disorders were also prevalent in the study sample. "Other serious problems such as child abuse, delinquent behavior and early pregnancies among the children themselves have been encountered."[8] Oppel and Rayston in 1971 suggested that the disabilities reflected in these children resulted from inadequate or inappropriate nurturing by the young mother.[8,30]

Separation and Divorce

Although many teenage pregnancies occur out-of-wedlock, the vast majority of these mothers are married by their early twenties. Young women are usually married within their first year following childbirth in most of the sampled populations.

Adolescent pregnancy and marriage is associated with a higher probability of marital dissolution. Regardless of the age of the mother at first childbirth and the timing of the birth, the younger the couple, measured by the wife's age, seems to be the critical determinant of separation and divorce. In controlling for age at first marriage, the only other factors found to predict marital stability were the number of years already married, race and parental socioeconomic status. White women were found to be less likely to separate or divorce than black women. Among black women, both early marriage and early parenthood suggest a higher probability of divorce or separation.[24,39,55]

Almost all studies showed that economic resources were strongly linked to marital stability. One study (French and Furstenberg in 1976) described the husband's reaction to the wife who accepted menial jobs which were poorly paying. He was depicted as being resentful and inadequate over his role of provider. He felt he was "being put down" for his inability to support his family. This hostility was built up over several months usually ending in separation or divorce. One out of every four women in this sample attributed the failure of her marriage to her husband's inability to support his family. Earning potential of the husband was based on whether he had completed high school and held a skilled or unskilled job. Lower status consisted of those individuals not completing high school and/or unskilled work. Higher status was composed of those males completing high school and/or holding skilled jobs. Among lower status males, there was a 45 percent probability of separation within two years of the wedding date, while only a 19 percent probability of marital dissolution within two years for the men classified as higher status. These statistics reflect the importance of the economic positions of the male who fathers a child out of wedlock or marries a single mother. A forced marriage due to pregnancy may prevent educational completion and limit the ability for economic advancement.[24,39,55]

This same study by Furstenberg followed these same women who were separated for the next five years. The data suggest that a high proportion of separated women will not remarry after their initial unsuccessful marital relationship. Another interesting aspect is that many of these women will never complete divorce proceedings, but will remain separated indefinitely. Many remained technically married even after 4 or more years of separation. These women showed no movement toward divorce, although they no longer considered their marriage to be binding or successful. Few of these had any plans to remarry.[24]

Child Abuse and Suicide

There are other risk factors resulting from teenage pregnancy which often go unreported. Both the risk of abuse for the child or suicide for the mother are plausible, since the teenage mother is often placed under intolerable stress as a result of raising a child. The child is often the scapegoat for the anger and guilt shared by the parents. The child is often unplanned, and this is coupled with lack of emotional and social support available to older mothers. The adolescent mother is generally less prepared for the demands of motherhood as well as marriage. Gabrielson and colleagues have reported that the incidence of suicide is more frequent among adolescent mothers than nonmothers, but it is unclear if both the pregnancy and suicide were related to early problems in the adolescent or her family.[8]

Employment and Earning Impact

Earnings are primarily a result of formal education and on-the-job experience. The girl who becomes pregnant as a teenager is forced to interrupt schooling and assume child-care responsibilities. Women with less schooling obtain jobs with lower socioeconomic status, make lower hourly wages, and earn less annually. This places her in a significantly poorer position to secure higher paying jobs. Many of these adolescent mothers were unable to find jobs at all, while others accepted the most menial type of work in order to make ends meet. Numerous studies reflect the lower family incomes of couples who married when the bride was already pregnant.

Poverty and welfare become the natural consequences of the early pregnancy and/or marriage. The greater the ability for a woman to delay childbirth the greater the overall effect of reducing the risks of poverty and welfare.[8,13,24,39,46,55]

COMPREHENSIVE PRENATAL AND FOLLOW-UP SERVICES

Of paramount importance is the availability and utilization of prenatal care. The premise that adolescents do not get adequate prenatal care, and that this is a major cause of medical problems in pregnancy, is one that is raised repeatedly in the literature.[11,12,14,15,16,25,32,38,41,45,49,50,52,57,58]

Many authors believe that where adequate prenatal care is provided, adolescents are at no greater risk than adults for most pregnancy complications.[6,9,15,20,21,23,28,29,36,45,50,51] Others believe that even good prenatal care cannot compensate for the inherent risks of adolescent pregnancy.[23,45,58]

Adolescents as a group are more likely not to seek or receive prenatal care for various reasons (discussed elsewhere in this book) including lack of availability and the lack of utilization. This can and ought to be corrected and attempts have been and are being made to rectify this deplorable situation. It must be mentioned, however, that despite the best intentions of health professionals, the adolescent who is more involved in drug and sexual experimentation and less concerned with maintaining good nutrition, is less likely to avail herself of good prenatal care, regardless of its availability. Ironically enough, the adolescent who is likely to utilize prenatal care is that very adolescent who is less likely to become pregnant initially.

As a group, adolescents recognize the social stigma of teen pregnancy and consequent dropping out of school. Reluctant to admit to pregnancy and its attendant social and physical complications, they deny themselves prenatal care and adequate nutrition in order to maintain the status quo and fit into their clothes a bit longer.[6]

Thus, on the one hand, lack of prenatal care is an integral part of the whole range of problems of adolescent pregnancy, and age, per se, is the prime factor. On the other hand, studies have shown that good prenatal care, despite age, can eliminate some of these problems and result in better outcomes. Better nutritional advice, nutritional and vitamin supplementation, counseling for substance abusers, and venereal disease diagnosis and treatment, might bring the incidence of such significant problems as preeclampsia and prematurity down to acceptable levels.

The same holds true for the infants as regards mortality and low birth weight.[23,32,44] In one study there was a 0.6 percent prenatal death rate for primigravid as opposed to 7.0 percent for secundigravid adolescents. Low birth weight risk was 10.7 percent for first, 21.2 percent for the second, and 42.8 percent for third babies born to adolescent mothers.[21]

This occurrence is a difficult one to explain, but two possible reasons may exist. The first is that socioeconomic status, which is so important in the outcome of adolescent pregnancy, becomes almost of necessity poorer with increased parity. Whereas an adolescent without a child to tend has the opportunity to go to school, obtain employment, and otherwise improve her situation, this becomes so much more unlikely when she has one and certainly two babies at home. In addition, any emphasis that the teenager might previously have placed on herself in obtaining good prenatal care and following sound nutritional and related advice, she might now direct at her new infant or infants. The second reason postulated for poorer tolerance of higher birth order pregnancy might be related to the concept of biologic maturity. Even if the body of the young adolescent may be able to withstand the physical and nutritional stresses of a pregnancy, it would probably become depleted of strength and important nutritional and vitamin stores. Instead of giving her body the chance to recuperate (and the adolescent may need a longer recuperative period than the adult), another pregnancy may put a stress to bear on the teenager that she simply cannot tolerate.

According to David Schwartz in his article *Perspectives on The Adolescent Pregnancy*:

Follow-up studies of adolescent pregnancies have shown that without appropriate comprehensive care, the long-term outlook for patients and their children remain bleak. Compared to controlled populations, the children's intellectual development and academic performance is impaired. The patients have more children at close intervals and with a higher perinatal mortality. The divorce rate is higher and marriages less stable with more frequent partner changes, especially in the first years following the delivery of their child when stability for the infant is so important. The patients themselves do not attain the satisfactory educational level necessary to enable them to pursue their vocation, or achieve financially meaningful employment. Economic deprivation is therefore perpetuated and aggravates the cycle. This totally unsatisfactory situation has prompted the observation that the adolescent pregnancy presents a syndrome of failure in so many of the aspects of healthy human development in our society.[46]

SUMMARY AND CONCLUSION:

In summary, whereas age might be the prime reason for adolescents performing poorly in pregnancy, equally important are such issues as utilization and availability of prenatal care, race, socioeconomic status, parity, and gynecologic age. Table 6-2 compares various studies by age, race, socioeconomic status, and prenatal care with prematurity and prenatal maturity rates, and as expected these rates differ markedly.

These may all represent additional problems for the adolescent age group simply because their youth places them at greater risk in these respects. However, they may also be exerting a critical influence on the pregnant adolescent independent of and in addition to her age.

CONCLUSION

Multiple factors, either separate and distinct or casually related, are known to exist in the teenager. These include low chronologic age (by definition), unsatisfactory socioeconomic conditions, poor or inadequate prenatal care, increased parity, and others. All of these play a role in causing or aggravating specific medical problems of adolescent pregnancy. Predominant among these, due to their impressively increased incidence, are preeclampsia and prematurity. Also significant are such problems as maternal and perinatal mortality, increased cesarean section rates, maternal anemia, neonatal neurologic deficits, and related problems. The attempt here has been to place these conditions in proper perspective.

Goals for the future ought to include prevention of adolescent pregnancy where feasible and appropriate, and improvement of socioeconomic conditions with provision of better prenatal care for teenagers that do become pregnant, and comprehensive continued care services.

BIBLIOGRAPHY

1. Adams, J.B. and Hatcher, R.A. The perplexing problem of teenage pregnancies. *Urban Health*, March: 26–49 (1977).
2. *Adolescent Perinatal Health: A Guideline for Services*. The American College of Obstetricians and Gynecologists, 1979.
3. Alan Guttmacher Institute. *11 Million Teenagers*. New York: New York Planned Parenthood Federation of America, Inc., 1976.
4. Aiman, James. X-Ray pelvimetry of the pregnant adolescent. *Obstetrics and Gynecology*, **48**:281–86 (1976).
5. Alkon, Ellen and Carlson, Gertrude. Low birth weight to girls enrolled in the Minneapolis pregnant school girl program. *Minnesota-Medicine*, November 822–5 (1979).

6. Anderson, Garland D. Comprehensive management of the pregnant teen-ager. *Contemporary Ob/Gyn*, **7**:75–80 (1976).

7. Arkutu, A.A. Pregnancy and labor in Tanzanian primigravidae aged 15 years and under. *Int. J. Gynaecol. Obstet.*, **16**:128–31 (1978).

8. Baldwin, Wendy, H. Adolescent pregnancy and childbearing—growing concerns of Americans. *The Population Bulletin*, **31**:(2) (Population Reference Bureau, Inc. Washington, D.C., 1976).

9. Berg, Marjorie, Taylor, Barbara, Edwards, Laura, and Haranson, Erick. Prenatal care for pregnant adolescents in a public high school. *The Journal of School Health*, January 32-5 (1979).

10. Beric, Berislav, Bregun, Nada, and Bujas, Milenko. Obstetric aspects of adolescent pregnancy and delivery. *Int. J. Gynaecol. Obstet.*, **15**:491–3 (1978).

11. Billung-Meyer, Jo. The single mother: Can we help? *The Canadian Nurse*, November: 26–8 (1979).

12. Bremberg, Sven. Pregnancy in Swedish teenagers. *Scandinavian J. Soc. Med.*, **5**:15-19 (1977).

13. Burst, Helen, V. Adolescent pregnancies and problems. *Journal of Nurse-Midwifery*, **24**2, 19–24 (1979).

14. Chanis, Margaret, O'Donohue, Nancy, and Stanford, Alicia. Adolescent pregnancy. *Journal of Nurse-Midwifery*, **24**:(3) 18–22 (1979).

15. Deschamps, J.P. and Valantin, G. Pregnancy in adolescents: Incidence and outcome in European countries. *J. Biosoc. Sci.*, Suppl. 5: 101–16 (1978).

16. Dott, Andrew B. and Fort, Arthur T., Medical and social factors affecting early teenage pregnancy. *Am. J Obstet. Gynecol.*, **125**:(4) 532–6 (1976).

17. Dryfoos, Joy G. Fertility in adolescence: The incidence and outcome of adolescent pregnancy in the United States. *J. Biosoc. Sci. Suppl.* **5**:85–99 (1978).

18. Duenhoelter, Johann, H. Jimenez, J., and Baumann, G. Pregnancy performance of patients under fifteen years of age. *Obstetrics and Gynecology* **46**:1 49–52 (1975).

19. Dwyer, John F. Managing the teenage pregnancy. *Ob-Gyn Observer* May (1975).

20. Efiong, E.I. and Banjoko, M.O. The obstetric performance of Nigerian primigravidae aged 16 and under. *Br. J. of Obstet. and Gyn.* **82**:228–33 (1975).

21. Elster, Arthur B. and McArnarnye, E.R. Medical and psychosocial risks of pregnancy and childbearing during adolescence. *Pediatric Annals* **9**:3 11–22 (1980).

22. Engstrom, Lars. Teenage pregnancy in developing countries: Fertility in adolescence. *J. Biosoc. Sci. Suppl.* **5**:117–26 (1978).

23. Fielding, J.E. Adolescent pregnancy revisited. *New England J. Medicine* **229**:16 893–6 (1978).

24. Furstenberg, Frank F., Jr. *Unplanned Parenthood: The Social Consequences of Teenage Pregnancy*, New York: The Free Press, Macmillan, October, 1976.

25. Hanse, C.M., Brown, M.L., and Trontell, M. Effects on pregnant adolescents of attending a special school. *J. Am. Dietetic Ass.* **68**:538–41 (1976).

26. Hardy, J.B., Welcher, D.W., Stanley, J., and Dallas, J.R. Long range outcome of adolescent pregnancy. *Clinical Obstetrics and Gynecology* **21**:4 1215–32 (1978).

27. Hertz, Dan. Psychological implications of adolescent pregnancy: Patterns of family interaction in adolescent mothers-to-be. *Psychosomatics* **18**:13–6 (1977).

28. Hofmann, Adele D. Adolescent pregnancy. *The Female Patient*, December 44–48 (1979).
29. Houde, C.T. and Conway, C.E. Teenage mothers: A clinical profile. *Contemporary Ob/Gyn* 7:71–78 (1976).
30. Hutchins, F.L., Jr. Teenage pregnancy and the black community. *J. Am. Med. Assn.* 70:857–9 (1978).
31. Hutchins, F.L., Kendall, N., and Rubino, J. Experience with teenage pregnancy. *Obstetrics and Gynecology* 54:1–5 (1979).
32. Jekel, J.F., Harrison, J.T., Bancroft, D.R., Tyler, N.C., and Klerman, L.V. A comparison of the health of index and subsequent babies born to school age mothers. *AJPH* 65:370–4 (1975).
33. Kantner, J.F. and Zelnik, M. Sexual experience of young unmarried women in the United States. *Family Planning Perspectives*, 4:(4) p.9, 1972.
34. Kreutner, A. Kessler, Karen, M.D., and Hollingsworth, Dorothy Reycroft, (eds.). *Adolescent Obstetrics and Gynecology*. Chicago, London: Year Book Medical Publishers, Inc. 1978.
35. Louten, R.C. and Cook. R.A. Teenage pregnancy in Maine. *J. of the Maine Medical Association*, 68:269–74, (1977).
36. McAnarney, E.R., Roghmann, Klaus, Adams, B.N., Tatelbaum, R.C., et al. Obstetric, neonatal and psychosocial outcome of pregnant adolescents. *Pediatrics*, 61:199–205 (1978).
37. McKilligin, H.B., Deliveries in teenagers data Newfoundland general hospital. *CMA Journal*, 118:1252–1254 (1978).
38. Merritt, T.A., Lawrence, R.A., and Naeye, R.L. The infants of adolescent mothers. *Pediatric Annals*, 9:32–51 (1980).
39. Moore, Kristin A., Hofferth, Sandra L., Caldwell, Steven B., and Waite, Linda J. *Teenage Motherhood: Social and Economic Consequences*, Washington, D.C.: The Urban Institute, January, 1979.
40. Ngoka, W.M. and Mati, J.K.G. Obstetric aspects of adolescent pregnancy. *The East African Medical Journal*, 57:124–30 (1980).
41. Plionis, B.M. Adolescent pregnancy: Review of the literature. *Social Work*, July 302–7 (1975).
42. Polley, M.J. Teen mothers: A status report. *J. of School Health*, October 466–9 (1979).
43. Population Reports, Family Planning Programs. Adolescent fertility—Risks and Consequences. Series J. No. 10. 157–75 (1976). U.S. Government Printing Office
44. Rothman, D. and Capell, P. Teenage pregnancy in England and Wales: Some demographic and medico-social aspects. *J. Biosoc. Sci.*, Suppl. 5:65–83 (1978).
45. Ryan, G.M. and Schneider, J.M. Teenage obstetric complications. *Clinical Obstetrics and Gynecology*, 21:1191–7 (1978).
46. Schwartz, D.B. Perspectives on adolescent pregnancy. *Wisconsin Med. J.*, 79:35–36 (1980).
47. Shaffer, D., Pettigrew, A., Wolkind, S., and Zajicek, E. Psychiatric aspects of pregnancy in schoolgirls: A review. *Psychological Medicine*, 8, 119–130, printed in Great Britain (1978).

48. Sherline, D.M. and A. Davidson, R. Adolescent pregnancy: The Jackson, Mississippi experience. *Am. J. Obstet. Gynecol.*, **132**:245–55 (1978).

49. Smith, P.B., Wait, R.B., Mumford, D.M., et al. The medical impact of an antepartum program for pregnant adolescents: A statistical analysis. *AJPH* **68**:169–72 (1978).

50. Smith, Peggy B. and Mumford, David M. (eds.) *Adolescent Pregnancy: Perspective the Health Professional.* Boston: G.K. Hall & Co. 1980.

51. Spellacy, W.N., Mahan, C.S., and Cruz, A.C. The adolescent's first pregnancy: A controlled study. *Southern Medical Journal*, **71**:768–71 (1978).

52. Steinman, M.D. Reaching and helping the adolescent who becomes pregnant. *Am. J. Maternal Child Nursing*, January/February 35–7 (1979).

53. Stickle, G. and Ma, P. Pregnancy in adolescents: Scope of the problem. *Contemporary Ob/Gyn*, **5**:85–91 (1975).

54 Sugar, Max. At-risk factors for the adolescent mother and her infant. *J. Youth and Adolescence*, **5**:251–70 (1976).

55. Turnbull, C.D. and de Haseth, L.C. Teenage pregnancy in North Carolina: A 10-year study. *North Carolina Med. J.*, **38**:701–6 (1977).

56. Ventura, S.J. Teenage Childbearing: United States, 1966–75. Monthly Vital Statistics Report Natality Statistics from the National Center for Health Statistics 26: November 5 (1977).

57. World Health Organization Technical Report Series No. 583: *Pregnancy and Abortion in Adolescence.* Geneva: World Health Organization, 1975.

58. Youngs, D.D. and Niebyl, J.R. Adolescent pregnancy and abortion. *Medical Clinics of North America*, **59**:1419–27 (1975).

59. Youngs, D.D., Niebyl, J.R., Blake, D.A., Shipp, D.A., et al. Experience with an adolescent pregnancy program, a preliminary report. Obstetrics and Gynecology, **50**:212–6 (1977).

60. Zackler, Jack M.D. and Brandstadt, Wayne M.D. (eds.). *The Teenage Pregnant Girl.* Springfield, Illinois: Charles C. Thomas., 1975.

61. Zlatnik, F.J. and Burmeister, L.F. Low "gynecologic age": An obstetric risk factor. *Am. J. Obstet. Gynecol.* **128**:183–6 (1977).

7.
Individual Differences Among Adolescent Contraceptors: Some Implications for Intervention

Burton Mindick, Ph.D.,
Cornell University;

and

Stuart Oskamp, Ph.D.,
Claremont Graduate School,
Faculty in Psychology

A model of adaptive coping is presented in outlining personality characteristics that are likely to lead to the successful practice of birth control. Elements distinguished are: (1) early relationships; (2) socialization processes; (3) the emergence of positive self-concept; (4) the disposition to cope cognitively; and (5) to plan for future goals.

Described are three major studies designed to test the theoretical model. The first two studies were longitudinal predictive researches that measure person and attitude variables in two samples containing nearly 1100 contraception clinic patients in metropolitan Southern California. After either two or three years of following up patients, various criteria of success or failure in birth planning within the samples were identified. When predictor measures were then correlated with the criterion outcomes, all elements of the model, especially, socialization, self-concept, cognitive coping, and planfulness were supported as personality characteristics that were significantly related to contraceptive practice.

Also described is a retrospective archival study of clinic records of physiological side effects experienced by patients in the populations studied. The physical problems were attributed to the contraceptive methods employed. Analyses that took account of the occurrence of method side effects, the criterion outcomes, and the likelihood of a causal relationship between the two, show a significant relationship betwen the premeasured person variables of the conceptual model described above and later side effects that lead to clinic attrition or to unwanted pregnancy. The research program in totality thus suggests an important role for cognizance of contraceptor personality char-

acteristics in interventions in the area of birth planning, and implications for prediction and prevention, and management are discussed.

There are many long-cherished or well-entrenched beliefs about the question of adolescent pregnancies. Some of these beliefs are not especially helpful to those who are interested either in preventing unwanted pregnancies or in assisting those who have already experienced such a pregnancy. In an attempt to familiarize the reader with the prevailing currents in the area, we begin by delineating some of these views, at the same time commenting on their limitations. But despite those limitations, it must be noted that many of these views are widely held in either the professional, the scholarly, the policy-making, or the lay community.

DEMOGRAPHIC DETERMINANTS?

Perhaps the oldest, and most prevalent of these views is the one which holds that excess fertility, or unwanted pregnancy among adolescents or adults is invariably a function of low socioeconomic or ethnic minority status. The study of fertility has long been the near-exclusive domain of demographers. Thus, at one point in time, it was demographic characteristics alone that were seen as correlates of fertility patterns. This research perspective implied that demographic characteristics were the *determinants* of fertility. Some large-scale research projects such as the Family Growth in Metropolitan America Study (Westoff, Potter, and Sagi, 1963) or the Indianapolis Study (Welpton and Kiser, 1963) had measured psychological variables, but the instruments employed were largely *ad hoc* metrics, and their inconclusive results gave rise to the still prevalent notion that psychological indices are of little use in understanding fertility. In the interim, there has been a decade of social psychological and personological research in the area, focusing especially on patterns of pregnancy and childbirth among teen-agers. This research generally does not explain all of the variance in the behavior observed, but it has proved its very considerable utility in understanding some of the important correlates and likely determinants of birth planning or the lack of it. Two areas that have proved to be especially fruitful in this kind of investigation have been attitude measurement and personality assessment.

Concurrent with the surge in psychological prediction of fertility has come the realization that the traditional demographic variables no longer demonstrate the same predictive validity that they once did. For nearly a decade now, demographers have noted "a convergence" of fertility patterns among various socioeconomic and ethnic groups, especially in urban areas (Sweet,

1974). In general, it has been shown that through contraception and abortion, fertility among adult women, has been reduced markedly compared with the 1950s and early 1960s. It is *adolescence* that remains the problem area with regard to unwanted pregnancy, and if Tietze (1978) is correct in projecting a 40 percent pregnancy rate for present cohorts of teen-age girls, it is quite evident that we are not dealing with a phenomenon that is peculiar to fractional ethnic or socioeconomic groups. Clearly then, sole reliance on demographic descriptors is increasingly unsatisfactory as a means of predicting, to say nothing of understanding scientifically, fertility related behavior, especially among the young.

PSYCHOPATHOLOGY?

Some of the earliest psychologically oriented research on problem fertility has centered on the hypothesis that deep-seated psychopathology is responsible for out-of-wedlock pregnancies, particularly where multiple conceptions occur in rapid succession. A number of the early psychiatric studies found considerable disturbance among women who fail in birth planning (Devereaux, 1965; Malmquist, Kiresuk and Spano, 1966), or who elect *not* to terminate such pregnancies in abortion (Kane and Lachenbruch, 1973). Often, such persons are seen as acting out repressed hostility against their parents (Wolf, 1973) or against themselves (Miller, 1973a).

The conclusions reached by these studies cannot be dismissed, although some of them were conducted using research methods that were not adequate to justify the generalizations drawn. There can, however, be little doubt that among a recognizable proportion of persons practicing contraception, considerable psychopathology in the form of hostility, masochism, and other forms of disturbance play their role in out-of-wedlock conceptions, especially where multiple pregnancies of this kind occur. Indeed, later we will have occasion to note the important relationship between inadequate contraception and inadequate adjustment. Thus, it is not surprising to find that in instances where severe pathology disrupts effective coping with life's challenges generally, it also disrupts fertility-related behavior as well.

Our question, however, is with the view that sees *all*, or even a very large proportion of excess fertility, especially among teenagers, as the product of severe psychopathology. Considering the nearly 1 million teenagers who annually become pregnant, and the above mentioned projection of a 40 percent pregnancy rate (Tietze, 1978) among adolescents before they outgrow their teens, it is hard to see "severe pathology" as the modal cause of the problem. The necessary corollary of such a view would be that nearly half of all American adolescents are markedly disturbed. This is a conclusion that might be reached from time to time by a long-suffering parent of a contemporary teenager. In the scientific community, however, the acceptance of such a generalization would require far better corroboration than has yet been supplied by the available research.

RELATIVELY RATIONAL DECISION-MAKING?

Another prevalent perspective on adolescent contraception practice, and the frequent failure thereof, takes the very opposite tack from those who attribute the problem to psychopathology. Rather than seeing the problem as *irrationality*, here the view is expressed that inadequate contraceptive practice, or failure to use birth control at all, is the result of "relatively rational decision making," albeit accompanied by a "discounted sense of risk" (Luker, 1975).

A prime exponent of this perspective is Luker (1975), who has concluded that many young women are quite knowledgeable about contraception and abortion. According to Luker, these women are concerned about health and other problems associated with contraception. Consequently, they discount the risks of possible conception, deciding that should pregnancy occur, abortion or giving birth are reasonably attractive alternatives to having practiced birth control in the first instance. This description of behavior argues for a causality that is the very opposite of psychopathology. Rather, it is suggested that an informed decision *not* to use birth control is being made consciously and rationally as well.

The empirical work on which Luker's conclusions are based, however, has several important methodological shortcomings, the most important of which are small sample size and purposive rather than random selection of subjects. But here again, there can be little doubt that for some women there is a kind of informed weighing of alternatives, and an eschewal of birth control in favor of freedom from contraception-related complications. The problem is that there is also little doubt that this is not the usual way of things for most young women, especially not for younger adolescents. Several studies suggest that during adolescence, knowledge about contraception and abortion is relatively poor. Estimates of the probabilities of conception are unwarrantedly low, and conscious (to say nothing of rational) decision making in this area is characteristically absent. This unholy trinity of poor knowledge, underestimation of pregnancy risk, and the lack of conscious decision making are especially typical of those who experience unwanted pregnancy. Thus, although Luker's "grounded theory" probably explains the contraceptive practice of some fraction of sexually active older women, this view, too, is unlikely to account for the mainstream of contemporary adolescents.

Indeed, all of the theories outlined above apply to some segment of the population we are considering here. The problem that is common to all three perspectives, however, is that increasingly they do not account for the large number of teenagers who either fail in the practice of birth control or who do not use birth control at all, but who cannot be classified as economically disadvantaged, as severely disturbed, or as balancing calculatedly and knowledgeably the risk of pregnancy against the risks of effective contraception. The question then becomes, what are the other determinants of the many conceptions that occur among the "middle range" of American adolescents, those factors which operate more normally rather than at the "extremes" described in the theories presented above?

A CONCEPTUAL MODEL OF ADAPTIVE BEHAVIOR

Over the past several years, the authors have reviewed a considerable body of literature in the area of birth planning (Mindick and Oskamp, 1979). This review has been supplemented by a careful reading of recent psychological literature, especially in the subareas of personology, social and applied psychology, and learning theory. Combining this theoretical material with the data derived from early data collection efforts in the area of birth planning, as well as field experience stemming from interactions with contraceptive staff and patients, Mindick (1978) has put forward a theory of adaptive behavior that seeks to explain effectiveness or ineffectiveness in the planning of births. Increasingly, the conceptualization appears to have explanatory power in other areas of human behavior as well, although a proper review of the relevant literature cannot be presented here.

The theory is most succinctly presented in the conceptual model shown in Figure 7-1. Stated very briefly, the model represents the view that optimally, early relationships result in processes of socialization and of self-concept that lead to a coping style that involves planfulness, as well as to seeking and utilizing information in successfully meeting the challenges of life. Or stated conversely, where early relationships result in inadequate socialization or low self-esteem (or both), individuals may fail to deal effectively with the social environment because of a coping style that does not look ahead and does not search for or use relevant knowledge.

This is a statement of the theory that underlies the research presented here and the strategies for prevention and management to be outlined later on. We might elaborate on this conceptualization or describe the model more fully, pointing out, for example that there are *feedback loops*, and elements of *bi-directional causality* that are not shown explicitly in the model, but that are inherent in the conceptualization. Space constraints, however, do not permit us this luxury, and we must content ourselves with the above statement, and a bare bones presentation of the literature that has suggested the schema offered here.

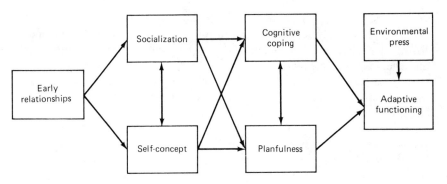

Figure 7-1. Proposed model of adaptive human functioning.

Socialization

The first concept in the model to be examined is *socialization*; and as long as two decades ago, Gough (1960) and Vincent (1961) had found lower levels of socialization (as determined by scores on the California Psychological Inventory) among women who had unplanned pregnancies. More recent studies have supported these findings. The current research has focused on a variety of different subareas, but all are related to the main theme of socialization.

The very transition from virginity to nonvirginity has been shown to be associated with attitudes favoring less "sexual regulation" by society (Miller, Note 1), and a more "anti-establishment value system" generally (Jessor and Jessor, 1975). The Jessors have also found that adolescentswho were moving toward their sexual debut had a more tolerant view of deviance generally, and had more friends who served as models for deviance than teenagers who remained virgins. Similarly, Vener and Stewart (1974) found that rise in adolescent sexual activity was related to greater use of alcohol and of illicit drugs, as well as to commission of a greater number of delinquent acts. The overall thrust of these findings strengthens the view that unmarried adolescents who initiate sexual activity, but who risk pregnancy through nonuse or inadequate use of contraception, are more likely to exhibit attitudes (Ball, 1973), psychometric scores (Gough, 1973 a;b), and overt behaviors (Vener and Stewart, 1974) indicative of inadequate socialization.

Personal Efficacy

In addition to socialization, a second dimension of personality that is related to adaptive behavior is personal efficacy. This general concept has been widely studied under several different names: competence (White, 1959), locus of control (Rotter, 1966), passivity or learned helplessness (Seligman,

1975), and self-efficacy (Bandura, 1977). Efficacy may be seen as an aspect of the broader concept of positive self-esteem, and not surprisingly, both of these personal characteristics have been hypothesized to be conducive to better contraceptive practice.

Quite a number of studies of the outcomes of birth-control usage have shown that perceived efficacy or self-esteem is higher among effective contraceptors than among women who conceived unwanted pregnancies or who were at risk of doing so (Ball, 1973; Goldsmith, Gabrielson, Gabrielson, Matthews, and Potts, 1972; Slagle, Arnold, and Glascock, Note 2; Slavin, 1975). In studies using the related concept of locus-of-control, sexually active unmarried female college students who used contraception were significantly more internal than nonusers (Lundy, 1972; MacDonald, 1970). Similarly, a number of early studies of low SES subjects found that an external perceived locus-of-control and feelings of powerlessness were associated with inconsistent or nonusage of birth control and with high fertility (Bauman and Udry, 1972; Groat and Neal, 1967; Kar, 1971; Keller, Sims, Henry, and Crawford, 1970). A few studies that measured perceived control using the Rotter (1966) scale, have not found significant relationships between internality-externality and contraception, but overall, the concept has proved quite useful in research in this area.

Planfulness

Closely associated with locus-of-control and efficacy are the ideas of planning and future-time perspective. As a matter of fact, some scales that purport to measure efficacy actually contain items that are more clearly indices of *planfulness* (cf. Rotter, 1966; Slagle et al., Note 2). Unless one sees life as consisting of a series of stimulus-response chains, it is evident that competent and efficacious behavior involves anticipation of future contingencies and planning activities to meet these contingencies. The importance of planfulness for adaptive functioning has already been stressed by Freud (1953); Lewin (1946) similarly spoke of the desirability of a capacity to integrate past experience and anticipations of the future into a phenomenological present consciousness that guides a person's actions. Besides being related to personal efficacy, planning (or more specifically future time perspective) has been shown to be positively correlated with socialization among young delinquent or nondelinquent males (Stein, Sarbin, and Kulik, 1968).

In the contraception area, Fawcett and Bornstein (1973) have reviewed a number of studies linking planfulness and contraceptive practices. One of the most commonly found relationships shows that aborters are low in impulse control or frustration tolerance (Cobliner, Schulman, and Smith, 1975; Noble, 1972; Rovinsky, 1972). Other studies have focused on contraceptive use or nonuse. Results have generally demonstrated that using birth control is associated significantly with sexual planfulness (Drucker, 1975; Keller et al., 1970), general future planning ability (Spain, 1977), future orientation (Kar, 1971), and longer future-time perspective (Mindick, Oskamp, and Berger, 1977).

Cognitive Coping

Related conceptually to both efficacy and to planfulness is another variable associated with individual differences, i.e., cognitive coping style. The "cognitive revolution" of recent years has brought with it a number of provocative perspectives: information processing, constructivism, Gibsonian perceptual realism, and especially, Neisser's (1976) revision of perceptual realism so as to include imagination and fantasy in personal transactions with the environment. Thus a broad array of elements can be included under the heading of cognition: information gathering and problem-solving skills, general intelligence, coping style, and specific measures of relevant knowledge.

In research on contraception, only a few investigators have focused on general cognitive skills, but two studies (Grunebaum and Abernethy, 1974; Steinlauf, 1977) have found successful contraceptive practice to be associated with marital or more general problem-solving abilities. Research attempting to relate I.Q. to the effective use of birth control has produced very mixed rather than clear-cut findings.

On the other hand, denial is a defense mechanism which essentially seeks to avoid cognitive modes of problem solving, and several studies have found significant correlations between ineffective contraception and various measures of the tendency to use denial in response to difficult life circumstances (Grunebaum and Abernethy, 1974; Miller, 1975; Mindick et al., 1977; Rader, Bekker, Brown and Richardt, 1978; Slavin, 1975).

But by far the most frequent operationalization of the cognitive dimensions found in the contraception literature is the measurement of relevant knowledge. Although this preocedure is far from ideal, it has been used most often in studying contraception. And although a few investigators have failed to find significant relationships, or have questioned their existence (Kane and Lachenbruch, 1973; Lehfeldt, 1971; Luker, 1975), there are many and varied studies showing a positive correlation between effective use of birth control and amount of knowledge about sexuality and contraception (Adler, Note 3; Furstenberg, Gordis, and Markowitz, 1969, Goldsmith et al., 1972; Gough, 1973a; Hagelis, 1973; Miller, 1975; Shipley, 1974).

METHODOLOGICAL IMPLICATIONS

With this discussion of cognition and its operationalizations in terms of sex and contraceptive knowledge, we conclude our highly schematic review of the general and birth-planning literature on four of the major components of the conceptual model presented earlier in this chapter. A fifth component, i.e., "early relationships," has not been treated in this section, because the connection between this concept and the others (e.g., socialization and self-concept) is too obvious to require elaboration. Although interpersonal relationships have been an important part of our focus in the empirical phase of the research, this is also true of other variables frequently studied in relation to fertility and contraception, including such elements as: demographic characteristics, attitudes, life events and transitions, as well as personal adjustment. Once again, however, space constraints dictate a narrowing of scope so as to target those aspects of the research that might prove most salient to prevention and management in the area of contraception.

What we regard as most salient in this context is the view stated earlier: that effective birth planning is related to adequate socialization, positive self-concept, a disposition to seek and use knowledge, and a willingness to look ahead and plan for future contingencies. Having stated this view, we recognize that a number of questions are likely to occur to the reader. Two of the most pressing are: (1) Considering the retrospective nature of much of the research cited here, is it not possible that the negative personality charactistics to which failure in contraception is attributed may be the *consequences* rather than the *antecedents* of unwanted contraception, and (2) if problems in contraception are indeed the result of personality dispositions, is there any likelihood at all of prevention and/or successful management?

We will attempt to deal with the second question in the discussion section of this chapter, but first we must reflect on the first question by pointing out that it was this very concern that influenced our decision to undertake a longitudinal predictive research methodology, rather than the simpler cross-sectional and retrospective approaches that have been used so commonly in other investigations. We recognized, for example, that having an unwanted conception might itself cause a narrowing of time horizon, or lead to a perceived lack of internal control. Worse still, because of researcher expectancies and the stigma associated with out-of-wedlock pregnancy, negative personality characteristics might easily be attributed to those who experience such pregnancies, especially, where subjective and post hoc assessment strategies are employed. it is precisely for these reasons that it was decided to employ the research methodology that we will now describe.

METHOD

Sampling

Participants in Study I were new intake patients who, during late 1973 and the first half of 1974, came to contraception clinics at four agencies affiliated with Planned Parenthood in the greater Los Angeles area. Random selection procedures were used in identifying patients who were then asked to take part in the research. The rate of refusal was only about 2 percent of those approached in both Study I and Study II, even though it was made clear to patients that research participation was voluntary and did not affect their eligibility to receive clinic services. The Study I Research Group consisted of 645 patients, all of whom were interviewed and tested during the waiting periods between the various clinic procedures, and carefully followed up for the next three years. In addition, all other new intake patients who came to the clinic during this period of time (i.e., those who had not been selected for the Research Group), became a Control Group (N=431) who were not tested, interviewed, nor specially followed up, except at one point during the following 3-year period.

Sites for Study II consisted of 11 different family-planning clinics, 4 of them, the same ones used in Study I. Two additional clinics run by Los Angeles Planned Parenthood were also included in the second study, as well as 5 public county-run clinics in different areas of Orange County (a part of greater Los Angeles). A consecutive sample of approximately 700 new contraceptive patients who had not reached their 20th birthday, was contacted at their intake visit during a period of six months starting early in 1977. Because of differences in the demographic characteristics of the patient populations, and in the follow-up procedures that we were allowed to use, only the private Planned Parenthood data are comparable to Study I. Therefore, findings for approximately 200 Orange County patients are not included here.

Description of the Research Groups

The Research Group patients in Study I included women of all ages within the childbearing years. Thus, ages ranged from 14 to 50, though most of the women were young, with a mean age of 21.6 years. Mean education was just under 12 years. There was a substantial proportion of ethinic minority group members: 18 percent Black, 19 percent Latin or Spanish surnamed, and 1 percent Asian. Family take-home pay, as reported to the clinic, averaged about $4500 per year for a mean family size of two persons, but there was a wide spread of income figures and many of these did not appear to be reliable. Only 25 percent of the sample were married, 62 percent were single, and 13 percent had been formerly married. Despite these figures on marital status, 50 percent had had one or more pregnancies, 19 percent had had at least one therapeutic abortion, and 35 percent had living children.

Fully 44 percent of these patients had *not* been using any birth-control method at all before their clinic intake visit, while 3 percent had been using pills, and 19 percent some other method. The method prescribed by the clinic doctors was overwhelmingly pills (83%), with 5 percent IUDs, 4 percent diaphragms, and 7 percent condoms and/or foam. Only 17 percent of the

patients said that they didn't want anymore children, while 63 percent said
they would like a child or children later on.

Study II, in contrast to Study I, focused exclusively on adolescent women.
Thus, participants averaged 17.8 years of age and had completed a mean of
11.2 years of school. They included 13 percent Blacks, 13 percent Latin or
Spanish surnamed, and 1 percent Asians—a somewhat lower percentage of
minority group members than in Study I. About 71 percent were still living
with their families. As a result of experience gained in Study I, we learned
that family income figures reported to the clinic were not always highly
reliable. As a consequence, it was decided to collect our own measures of
socioeconomic status. These indices include parental incomes, education, and
occupations. The data gathered showed an essentially rectangular distribution
of SES in the sample, with only the very lowest of the seven classifications
utilized showing underrepresentation.

As with the teenage portion of the Study I sample, almost all of the
patients were single—92 percent never-married, 7 percent married, and 1
percent separated or divorced. Also, much as before, 30 percent had been
pregnant, and 21 percent had had at least one therapeutic abortion. Eight
percent had living children, and only 6 percent had never had intercourse,
though 43 percent had never used birth control. Over half (62%) had not been
using contraception recently, while about 20 percent had been using pills and
about 18 percent some other method. Though three years had elapsed, the
contraceptive methods most frequently prescribed by clinic doctors had not
changed. The prescription was still predominantly the pill (81%) and the
proportion of patients using other forms of birth control did not differ from
that found in Study I by more than a few percentage points in any instance.
Also, as before, a heavy majority (72%) of these young women said they
wanted a child or children later on, while only 4 percent were definite in
wanting no more children.

Research Instruments

In both studies, data were gathered from clinic records, a variety of research
questionnaires, and personal interviews. Also, in both studies, a 15–20 minute interview was administered by specially trained female research staff
members, some of them graduate students, some of them regular clinic staff
members, a few who were both. Following the interview, subjects were asked
to complete three (in Study I) or four (in Study II) brief questionnaires, while
they were waiting during intervals between various clinic procedures.

In Study I, the sample included a number of Spanish-speaking patients.
Consequently, these women were interviewed and tested in Spanish. The
sample in Study II was younger and did not contain many Hispanic adoles-

cents who did not speak English. Hence all testing and interviewing was carried out in English. Several different sets of questionnaires were used during the course of the research, so that a greater number of predictive instruments could be tried out. As a result, the number of subjects varied widely for different measures. The instruments utilized in Study I were:

a. Future Events Test (FET), a measure of planfulness adapted from the work of Stein, Sarbin, and Kulik (1968);
b. Personal Values Abstract (PVA—Gough, 1972);
c. Rotter's (1966) Internal-External Locus-of-Control Scale;
d. Miller's (1973b) Personal Style Inventory (PSI), developed to measure personality variables related to pregnancy planning behaviors;
e. Miller's Sexual and Contraceptive Knowledge Questionnaire (no date);
f. A questionnaire on knowledge and attitudes concerning sexual and contraceptive matters, containing the most discriminating items, used by Goldsmith et al. (1972) with teenage Planned Parenthood patients;
g. Shipley-Hartford vocabulary scale, a brief measure of verbal intelligence (Buros, 1972, p.321)

In planning Study II, we were able to benefit from our experience in Study I. Rather than testing intact instruments, it was decided to test concepts measured convergently by several different scales. Specific scales and items were adapted or selected from our previous research and from studies by Ager (1973), Ball (1973), Bendig (1956), Cole (1975,) Goldsmith et al. (1972), Jessor and Jessor (1975), Kantner and Zelnik (1973), Kar (Note 4), Kothandapani (1971), Miller (Note 1), Rosenberg (1965), Rotter (1966), Slagle et al. (Note 2), Vener and Stewart (1974), and several other investigators. For each major concept to be investigated one or more scales was assembled, each containing 2–10 items. In the interest of brevity, details regarding scale reliability will be omitted here. The interested reader is directed to Mindick (1978), Oskamp and Mindick (1979), or Oskamp and Mindick (in press).

In Study I, the interview schedule included quite a diversity of topics. In Study II, interview subject matter was largely confined to family occupational, educational, and demographic information. Both interview schedules, however, required research personnel to rate their interviewees on a number of personal characteristics, especially those related to the conceptualization of adaptive coping presented earlier. Staff members were also asked to predict the likelihood of contraceptive success for each patient.

In addition to the ratings, material either in the questionnaire or in the interviews covered the following areas: (a) personality characteristics and related attitudes; (b) overt behaviors; (c) parental and peer relationships as well as communication regarding sex and birth control; and finally, (d) sexual and birth control knowledge, attitudes, behavioral intentions, and experiences. In both studies, presentation of questionnaires was alternated over the months of data collection according to a variety of different schedules, so that no single subject would be required to fill out all questionnaires. This helped lighten the patient's task so that the interview and questionnaires took most subjects only about an hour to complete. Hence, patient research participation rates ranged from 98 to 99 percent in the two studies.

Follow-Up Procedure and Criterion Classification

At several of the clinics studied, patients using oral contraceptives (about 80 percent of the Research Group in both studies) normally return about 3 months after intake to get another supply of pills. IUD patients are expected to return about one month after the IUD's insertion for a check on its placement. Diaphragm users and condom and/or foam patients are not expected to return until the time for regular medical exams. Most clinics scheduled return visits at six months and at one year after intake. Thereafter, patients might return at six-month or one-year intervals if they experienced contraception side effects, encountered other medical problems, or if they needed supplies. Follow-up letters were routinely sent by the clinic to the patients (unless they had specified no mail contacts) reminding clients to make appointments for regularly scheduled visits.

Additional follow-up procedures beyond those established by the regular clinic routine were instituted for patients in this research program. All non-returners who had agreed to allow mail contacts were sent a second letter by the research staff about two months after the regular clinic letter. It again reminded them about returning to the clinic, and it requested information about whether they were getting birth-control help elsewhere, or had decided to stop using contraception. Later, patients who had neither returned to the clinic nor answered the letters were followed up by telephone (if they had indicated that phone contacts were acceptable). Up to five phone calls at various hours were made, and if the patient was reached, a brief and diplomatic phone interview asked about her current contraceptive status using questions similar to those in the follow-up letter.

Based on these follow-up procedures, a criterion classification system was established involving several different measures of contraceptive success or failure. It included behavioral indices of patient attrition, amount of delay in return visits to the clinic, and various outcomes of the contraception program, especially the occurrence of an unwanted pregnancy. Also noted were any problems or side effects with the contraceptive method, any changes in method, and any conditions (unrelated to contraception) that required medical attention.

In Study I, criterion measures were determined for each patient at five different points after clinic intake (1–3 months, 6 months, one year, two years, and three years). The final three-year classification of criterion status, made about three and one-half years after clinic intake, showed the following distribution of categories for patients in the Research Group:

1. Unwanted pregnancies ($N=76$)—about 80 percent of these cases were opted for abortions;
2. Pregnancies in whiich wantedness was questionable ($N=15$)—all of these cases were dropped from further analyses to reduce error variance;
3. Wanted pregnancies ($N=22$);
4. Unknown status; no recent contact nor information to indicate classification in any other category ($N=272$);
4. Moved away, and no additional information ($N=27$);
6. Discontinued using birth control ($n=35$);
7. Getting birth control elsewhere ($N=98$);
8. Returned to clinic at about three years, but not completely regular and prompt for full three years ($N=44$);
9. Regular, prompt returners over whole 3-year period ($N=56$).

Two independent coders arrived at a 92 percent rate of agreement using this classification scheme. To correct for chance levels of agreement, a more precise index of intercoder reliability for nominal scale judgments ws computed, as recommended by Scott and Wertheimer (1972, p.194). For a random sample of 285 judgments by each rater, the value of the π coefficient was .905.

Several different comparisons have been made among the above criterion groups. The unwanted pregnancy group (No. 1 above) has been compared with the regular return group (No. 9 above), with all other patients (Nos. 3–9 above, except for group No. 2), and with the patients in groups 3, 7, 8, and 9 combined. This latter combined group were termed "birth planners" since they had successfully achieved their birth-control goals—that is, they either were known to have continued their contraceptive program successfully for three years without becoming pregnant, or to have purposively discontinued in order to have a child. It is this last and most clear-cut comparison, i.e., unwanted pregnancy group ($N=76$) vs. birth planners ($N=220$) that we will consider here, presenting results selected with a view to the concerns that underly this chapter and this volume in general.

SELECTED RESULTS OF STUDY I

Due to space limitations, only a few findings can be presented here. Complete results of Study I can be found in Mindick (1978), and of Study II in Oskamp and Mindick (1979).

Comparison of Contraceptive Success and Failure Groups

Table 7-1 shows significant differences between the birth planners, who, according to research criteria were considered successful contraceptors, and the unwanted pregnancy group, who had failed in their own undertaking of contraception and whose problems were not attributable to method failure. Because many directional hypotheses were made, the significance tests shown here are all one-tailed.

As displayed in Table 7-1, successful contraceptors were significantly older, had a higher educational attainment (attributable at least in part to their age), and were more likely to be married. They were also more likely to be Anglos, rather than blacks or Latins. Other demographic measures, e.g. family income, mean income per family member, etc., however, failed to distinguish the two groups.

A predictor that was notably better than these income measures was the Personal Values Abstract Socialization Scale on which women who later proved to be successful contraceptors had obtained higher scores at clinic intake. Also, good prediction was characteristic of the interviewer ratings made prospectively, in most instances as many as one to three years before the criterion outcomes of success or failure were determined. As hypothesized, women who later failed in contraception were seen at the outset of their birth-control program as significantly: more passive, having a more negative self-concept, more self-rejecting, more impulsive rather than planful, and possessed of more negative personality characteristics in general. It must also be noted that there was no evidence of prejudice among these interviewer ratings, even though there was a smaller proportion of ethnic minority group members in the success than in the failure group. A correlational analysis between interviewer ratings and ethnic background in the sample as a whole showed, if anything, a slight and nonsignificant tendency for interviewers to rate blacks and Latins more favorably than Anglos. Thus the more negative ratings of women in the pregnancy group do not appear to be attributable to racial or ethnic bias.

In addition to self-concept and socialization, two other components of the theoretical model, i.e., cognitive coping and planfulness, received support. To the degree that relevant knowledge may be considered an adequate index of a disposition toward coping cognitively, evidence for differential coping strategies is supplied by the highly significant disparity between the pregnancy and birth-planner groups in their mean scores on the measure of sex and contraceptive knowledge. As hypothesized, the birth planners had more accurate information in these two areas, despite the fact that the measure of verbal intelligence used in the study showed no significant difference between the two groups.

As for planfulness, convergent evidence was available in this particular

Table 7-1. Comparison of unwanted pregnancy group with birth planner group—Study 1.

MEASURE	UNWANTED PREGNANCY GROUP (N=76)		BIRTH PLANNER GROUP (N=220)		t (or X²)
	MEAN (SD)	N	MEAN (SD)	N	
Demographic Variables					
Age	20.24 (4.85)	76	21.74 (5.31)	220	2.17*
Highest grade completed	10.71 (2.84)	76	12.22 (2.39)	220	4.53***
Marital status					
Single or formerly married		64		156	X²=4.35*
Married		12		63	
Ethnic Background					
Anglo		34		159	X²=18.48***
Black		22		31	
Latin		18		27	
Personality Scales					
Socialization (Gough PVA)	18.94 (5.08)	32	21.57 (3.85)	60	2.78**
Interviewer Intake Ratings					
Negative self-concept scale	16.68 (4.37)	57	15.12 (4.09)	181	2.47**
Mean of 16 ratings (1=little—a pos. rating; 5=much—a neg. rating)	2.77 (0.65)	67	2.63 (0.60)	214	1.65*

Table 7-1. (continued)

MEASURE	UNWANTED PREGNANCY GROUP (N=76) MEAN (SD)	N	BIRTH PLANNER GROUP (N=220) MEAN (SD)	N	t (or X^2)
Avoids eye contact	2.55 (1.03)	67	2.31 (0.95)	214	1.76*
Passive, controlled by events	3.10 (0.65)	62	2.73 (0.81)	195	1.23***
Impulsive, not planful	2.89 (0.63)	55	2.69 (0.74)	189	1.81*
Loser, masochistic, self-rejecting	2.84 (0.91)	62	2.59 (0.82)	202	1.99*
Planfulness					
FET mean future age	30.25 (6.19)	47	35.34 (9.67)	167	3.41***
FET mean future extension	10.40 (4.31)	47	13.45 (6.45)	166	3.05**
FET density index	0.49 (0.26)	56	0.58 (0.21)	182	2.48**
PSI look-ahead scale (sum of GR, PFO, & V scales)	19.74 (4.37)	23	21.74 (4.45)	77	1.90*
Sexual and Contraceptive Knowledge					
Total adjusted errors on sex knowledge scale	3.87 (2.60)	49	2.42 (1.83)	125	4.18***
Contraceptive Attitudes					
How sure of continuing b.c. program (1-5; 5=very)	4.03 (0.73)	69	4.27 (0.64)	210	2.64**

*p<.05
**p<.01
***p<.001

area. The Future Events Test showed that the pregnancy group had a shorter future time perspective, whether measured in terms of the mean future age, or the mean future extension (i.e., number of years beyond the present age) at which they expected future events to occur. Likewise, three scales from the Personal Style Inventory (Planning and Future Orientation, Vigilance, and Graduated Response) were combined because of their conceptual commonality in terms of the planfulness-impulsiveness dimension; the resulting combined scale, called "look-ahead" (Kaplan, Note 5), revealed significant differences that paralleled those found with the Future Events Test. Results on these two scales, plus the predictive interviewer ratings on the planfulness-impulsiveness dimension, converged in supporting the view that the two groups differed in the expected direction in their ability to look ahead and plan.

Attitude measures utilized in this study did not fare as well as did the personality indices. Most of the attitude scales yielded results in the hypothesized direction, but most also fell short of significance. The one exception to this rule was a measurement of the patient's own certainty of continuing contraception, a kind of behavioral intention item. Here, patients who were later to succeed in their birth-control plans had been more certain of their success at clinic intake than were women who later failed.

The above findings, however, provided evidence suggesting the importance of the four major concepts investigated in this research as possible determinants of successful contraceptive practice and perhaps of other kinds of adaptive behavior as well. However, for several reasons, it was thought appropriate to replicate these findings. First, not all of the predictor variables studied had the success of those shown here. Second, the attitude area had, in our view, not been measured with sufficient precision, and this was also true for parent-child relationships. Finally, the evidence that the group at greatest risk were the adolescents suggested the need for additional research focusing on teenagers.

Follow-up and Criterion Classification—Study II

We have already described the sample drawn for Study II, as well as the methodology for interviewing and testing. The same general follow-up procedures used in Study II follow-up lasted for only two years (or for some patients, 18 months, depending on the date of initial intake) rather than three years.

After two years, final criterion classification for the 465 Planned Parenthood teenage patients was conducted—first through a check of clinic records, and then by mailing the same questionnaire used in Study I to patients who had not returned to the clinic for their one-year visit nor contacted the clinic subsequently. Because our experience in Study I showed that these young women were in a highly mobile period of their lives, it was decided that attempts to telephone the patients who had not returned the questionnaire would not be productive.

The final criterion classification was based largely on the 18-months return visit point, for which data were available on almost all patients. The same basic indices and categories of contraceptive success of failure were used as in Study I, with some minor refinements. Patients were classified into the following criterion categories:

1. Unwanted pregnancies ($N=47$);
2. Pregnancies where wantedness was questionable ($N=7$, including two cases of possible method failure)—omitted from further analyses;
3. Wanted pregnancies ($N=10$);
4. Unknown status; no recent contact nor information about criterion status ($N=216$);
5. Moved away, and no additional information ($N=5$);
6. miscellaneous communications, but no recent return to clinic ($N=6$).
7. Discontinued using birth control ($N=14$);
8. Getting birth control elsewhere ($N=25$);
9. Reported sexual abstinence as their latest method, and had not gotten pregnant since intake ($N=7$);
10. Returned to clinic at around 18 months, but not completely regular in all return visits ($N=41$);
11. Regular, prompt returners for full 18 months ($N=87$).

As in Study I, a criterion group of "birth planners" was defined, in this case made up of categories 3, 8, 9, 10, and 11 (combined $N=170$). Several comparisons were made in Study II, as in Study I. The contrast to be presented here is one which compares this "birth planner" group with a group of patients who had unwanted pregnancies or who had failed to return or even contact the clinic or the research team despite repeated inquiries. This latter group is quite comparable to the contraception "dropouts" often studied by other investigators. Since their dropping out occurred within 18 months after clinic intake, rather than after 3 years (the criterion used in Study I), concern about their being at risk of contraception failure was judged to be a more serious one.

SELECTED RESULTS OF STUDY II

Table 7-2 shows a variety of findings related to this comparison of the unwanted pregnancy and no-contact patients as distinguished from the birth planners. Because the results generally conform so closely with those obtained in Study I, we will describe them only very briefly.

Most of the demographic variables failed to differentiate those who were at

Table 7-2. Selected results comparing teenage birth planner group with unwanted pregnancy plus no contact groups—Study II.

MEASURE	BIRTH PLANNER GROUP (N=170)		UNWANTED PREGNANCY PLUS NO CONTACT GROUPS (N=229)		t
	MEAN (SD)	N	MEAN (SD)	N	
Age	17.80 (1.37)	170	17.89 (1.48)	229	.64[ns]
Race (1=white; 2=other)	1.11 (0.32)	169	1.20 (0.40)	226	2.40**
Latin Descent (2=no; 4=yes)	2.24 (0.62)	169	2.27 (0.66)	229	.46[ns]
Marital Status (1=single; 2=ever married)	1.07 (0.26)	169	1.08 (0.27)	227	.31[ns]
Anyone in family on welfare (1=yes; 2=no)	1.95 (0.21)	170	1.89 (0.32)	229	2.50**
Highest grade completed	11.29 (1.40)	169	11.18 (1.46)	228	.79[ns]
Highest grade patient expects to complete	14.57 (2.03)	169	13.90 (2.09)	220	3.19***
Patient yearly income to nearest $1000	2.62 (2.01)	66	3.31 (1.94)	68	2.02*[b]
Father SES based on job (1-7; 1=highest)	3.41 (1.58)	158	3.94 (1.62)	200	3.17***
Lived with both parents (1=yes; 9=no)	1.68 (2.24)	165	2.42 (3.06)	214	2.72**

Table 7-2. (continued)

MEASURE	BIRTH PLANNER GROUP (N=170)		UNWANTED PREGNANCY PLUS NO CONTACT GROUPS (N=229)		t
	MEAN (SD)	N	MEAN (SD)	N	
How many times patient used psychedelic drugs	0.36 (1.04)	69	1.62 (6.33)	85	1.81*
How many times patient used hard drugs	0.22 (1.24)	69	2.02 (8.16)	85	2.01*
No. of friends who used marijuana regularly (1-5; 5=nearly all)	2.70 (1.32)	69	3.19 (1.42)	88	2.25*
No. of friends who tried LSD or psychedelics (1-5; 5=all)	1.72 (0.80)	69	1.99 (1.07)	87	1.76*
Friends' models for deviance (7-35; 7=least)	18.00 (4.34)	68	19.40 (4.84)	83	1.85*
Self-competence (7-35; 35=most competent)	25.07 (4.09)	73	23.94 (3.79)	90	1.82*
Internality, system control (2-10; 10=most internal)	6.29 (1.76)	73	5.50 (1.72)	90	2.87**
Combined internality scale (12-60; 60=most internal)	43.00 (6.28)	73	40.67 (5.87)	89	2.43**
Academic and social activity (2-10; 2=least)	6.51 (2.06)	75	5.40 (2.37)	94	3.18***

	BIRTH PLANNER GROUP (N=170)		UNWANTED PREGNANCY PLUS NO CONTACT GROUPS (N=229)		
MEASURE	MEAN (SD)	N	MEAN (SD)	N	t
Own deviant behavior (low score=least)	28.71 (26.46)	41	53.53 (71.77)	46	2.19*
Avoids eye contact (1-5; 1=very little, a pos. rating)	1.62 (0.79)	164	1.96 (1.04)	215	3.57***
Feels inadequate (1-5; 1=very little, a pos. rating)	1.85 (0.93)	163	2.14 (1.07)	210	2.77**
Immature (1-5; 1=very little, a pos. rating)	1.81 (0.90)	165	2.12 (1.08)	209	3.10***
Passive, controlled by events (1-5; 1=very little, a pos. rating)	2.11 (1.24)	126	2.44 (1.25)	167	2.26*
Impulsive, not planful (1-5; 1=very little, a pos. rating)	2.09 (1.25)	111	2.37 (1.25)	145	1.75*
A loser, masochistic (1-5; 1=very little, a pos. rating)	1.86 (1.03)	111	2.22 (1.20)	152	2.57**
Ignorant or naive about sex (1-5; 1=very little, a pos. rating)	2.04 (0.99)	108	249 (1.24)	150	3.25***

161

Prediction about b.c. program (1-6; 1=success, very sure)	2.04 (0.92)	165	2.32 (1.15)	214	2.59**
Combined negative ratings by interviewer (13-66; 13=least neg.)	23.49 (9.20)	57	28.41 (12.00)	80	2.71**
Present age of FET respondents	17.15 (1.31)	72	17.63 (1.38)	91	2.23*[b]
Future Events Test Scores:					
No. of FET future events	11.22 (5.49)	76	9.66 (5.17)	97	1.92*
Sum of FET future events	417.00 (122.28)	66	362.07 (146.87)	84	2.44**
FET mean future extension	15.03 (3.93)	66	13.81 (5.00)	84	1.68*
No. of FET past events	2.22 (2.01)	76	2.89 (2.19)	97	2.05*[b]
Sum of FET past events	44.72 (27.74)	57	55.95 (34.02)	81	2.06*[b]

	Mean (SD)	N	Mean (SD)	N	t
Total correct on sex knowledge items 2-26	14.49 (3.60)	168	12.75 (4.25)	222	4.36***
Conventional attitudes about sex (2-10; 2=least)	5.77 (1.77)	71	5.02 (1.86)	93	2.62**
Factors making b.c. unnecessary (3-15; 3=least)	4.91 (1.64)	82	5.63 (1.76)	95	2.79**
Miscellaneous pro-b.c. behavior intentions (6-30; 6=least)	22.94 (3.41)	80	21.67 (3.80)	94	2.30*

[b] 2-tailed test (all others are 1-tailed)

*p< .05
**p< .01
***p< .001

risk, or who had unwanted conceptions, from those who used birth control successfully. Neither age, marital status, ethnic background, family income, average income per family member, nor several other demographic characteristics (not shown here) distinguished the two groups from one another. Significant differences did, however, appear in race, patient's personal income, welfare status, or the socioeconomic status attributable to father's occupation. The birth planners were more likely to be whites. They reported fewer family members on welfare, earned a higher personal income, and came from a family of origin whose father's occupation was apt to be of higher socioeconomic status.

Early Relationships

As for early relationships, it is evident that those in the at-risk or pregnancy group were more likely to have come from broken homes, and several other indices of parental relationships provided evidence of domestic difficulties.

Socialization

Overt behaviors rather than scale scores were emphasized in our examination of prosocial behavior in Study II. Table 7-2 shows that in the pregnancy and no-contact group there was, among other things:

1. Greater usage of psychedelic and other hard drugs;
2. A larger number of friends who used hard and psychedelic drugs and exhibited deviant behavior;
3. A greater amount of self-reported deviant behavior;
4. less in the way of academic activity or even social activity with peers.

Self-Concept and Planfulness

Among the personality scales, there was considerable replication of the findings of Study I with regard to perceived self-competence, locus-of-control, and future time perspective. Study II also showed significant differences betwen the two criterion groups in terms of *past* time perspective. In addition, interviewer's ratings of patient characteristics corresponded quite closely to those of Study I. This was especially true in relation to interviewer perceptions of patient feelings of inadequacy, passivity, and impulsiveness, once again providing convergent, multimethod evidence.

Cognitive Coping

This convergence was also found in three indices of cognitive coping: the interviewer ratings of sex and contraceptive knowledge, the paper-and-pencil measure of the same kind of knowledge, as well as the patient's declared aspirations for higher educational attainment (i.e., the highest grade the patient expected to complete). Thus, in Study II also, we see fairly strong support for four of the major components of the theoretical model, with some suggestions that both parent-child and later social relationship with peers may also be important variables in the contraception and general adaptive behavior equation.

In Study II, the attitude and behavioral intention measures with regard to sexuality and birth control also showed predictive utility. In addition, it must be noted that when the predictive power of the demographic measures (some of which were significant) was compared with that of the attitude and especially the personality measures, it became clear that the strength of association with the outcome variables was markedly stronger for the latter than the former. Stated succinctly, this simply means that although some patients of low-SES or ethnic minority background are likely to fail in contraception, it is *person variables* rather than ethinicity or SES that are more highly correlated with contraception success or lack of it.

CONTRACEPTION SIDE-EFFECTS STUDY

Although these findings of Study II and those of Study I reported earlier provided confirmation of research hypotheses, some important questions still remained. One of the most interesting of these questions arose in the course of the approximately seven years during which the research for Studies I and II took place, on occasions when the first author of this chapter spent considerable time examining the records of patients in the research program. Coding or checking the coding of others was the chief purpose of this archival search, but working with clinic records proved to be revealing in and of itself. It became apparent that in many instances, where unwanted pregnancy had occurred, files showed that the patient had first complained to the clinic regarding physiological problems she believed to be related to her birth-control method. Often shortly after such a complaint, method changes were made; but often, too, the patient discontinued contraception altogether. In many cases, pregnancy followed this lapse of contraception.

Here was clearly a potential rival hypothesis to that which posited a connection between personal characteristics and success in coping with contraception. If the problems were physical rather than psychological, and if physical problems led to failure in birth planning, psychological determinants of effective birth planning among adolescents might well be questioned. It was therefore decided to conduct a thorough search of the clinical records of all patients in Study II and patients aged 21 and under in Study I to see whether or not the side effects that preceded contraception failure were themselves related to patients' premeasured psychological characteristics, or whether side effects constituted an independent path of possible causality.

In the course of the archival research, patient records were scrutinized for the following information:

1. Birth-control side effects reported by patients at clinic intake;
2. Medical conditions unrelated to contraception reported at intake;
3. Contraceptive method first prescribed by the clinic;
4. Subsequent contraceptive methods used by the patient;
5. Timing (relative to clinic intake) of changes in method;
6. Contraceptive side effects reported by patients during the birth control program;
7. Medical conditions unrelated to birth control reported during the contraception program;
8. Timing (relative to clinic intake) of side effects and other medical problems;
9. Supply visits, medical visits, and communications by the patient to the clinic.

We have noted earlier that more than 80 percent of the time, the contraceptive method prescribed by the clinic was the pill. Interestingly, as many as 50 kinds of problems attributed by patients to birth-control usage were distinguished in our search, although modally it was breakthrough bleeding, amenorrhea, and other menstruation-related difficulties that were the object of patient concern.

In the first stage of the side-effects study, the approach was simply to tabulate the total number of side effects experienced by adolescent patients in Study I beginning with clinic intake to an end-point 4 years after their first day at the clinic. The next step was then to deteremine from clinic records which side effects appeared to lead to negative contraception outcomes, i.e., pregnancy or clinic attrition. Such determinations were made based on inferences derived from patient statements as well as the timing of clinic attrition in relation to occurrence of the side effect. Coders making these determinations were of course blind as to the premeasurement data on all patients.

Further methodological details of this first stage of the side-effects study, and complete results cannot be presented here. The interested reader is referred to Mindick and Oskamp (1980). But, summarizing the findings briefly, we may say that generally, several of the personal characteristics that had been measured at clinic intake and had been shown to be related to the criterion outcomes were also related to side effects reported by contraceptive patients generally. When attention was focused on side effects that led to negative contraceptive outcomes (i.e., clinic attrition or unwanted pregnancy), the relationship was even more marked. Thus, compared with all *other* patients, women who, during the course of their contraception programs, experienced negative outcomes that were apparently related to birth-control side effects: (1) had been rated by research interviewers at clinic intake more negatively on the average on the various personality indices utilized, especially; (2) on the negative self-concept scale. Such women (3) had displayed less test-measured sex and contraceptive knowledge and; (4) had showed a shorter future-time perspective. There was no significant evidence with regard to socialization and early relationships in this comparison, though women in the sample generally who experienced more side effects (irrespective of contraception program outcome) came from families that were significantly more often not intact, and these patients gave indications of having uneasy relationships with parents generally, and with regard to norms of sexuality and birth-control usage specifically.

In the second part of the side-effects study where attention was focused on the adolescent sample drawn in Study II, even stronger findings were revealed as a result of two methodological refinements employed in coding the relationship between contraception side effects and negative contraception outcomes. The first refinement was to ask coders (who again were blind as to premeasurement data) to rate the likelihood of a causal relationship between a side effect and patient attrition or unwanted pregnancy. The second refinement was to consider for comparison with the rest of the sample only patients who had reported at least two instances of birth-control method problems which then appeared to lead to a negative contraception outcome. The net effect of these two procedures was to define a criterion group that had had considerable physiological difficulty with contraception, and for whom the likelihood was strong that method problems caused the dropping of birth control and/or pregnancy. Thus, a correlational analysis that combined both criterion status and likelihood of causality was carried out. The results of this analysis showed that compared with other clinic patients, those who later dropped out of the program and/or experienced an unwanted pregnancy and were likely to have done so because of side effects, had responded to research measures taken on their first day at the clinic indicating that: (1) They had worse relationships with parents (this was found in two separate scales) and; (2) with peers; (3) they had come from single-parent households; and (4) their mothers were more likely to be divorced, deceased, or retired; (5) they had committed more delinquent acts; and (6) they had more close friends who drank or smoked marijuana; (7) they had lower scores on scales measuring self-assurance, optimism, self-competence, internality, self-esteem, and planfulness; and (8) they were rated more negatively by the research interviewers, especially with regard to passivity and impulsiveness. (9) These unsuccessful patients also rated themselves as having less information about sexuality and birth control. Results from the test of such knowledge employed in Study II converged with this self-report, although the correlation between the test score and the criterion outcome narrowly missed significane at the .05 level. (10) In the attitude area, scales assessing the patient's procontraception behavior intentions and attitudes based on friends' experience with birth control showed significant results in the expected direction.

As for the predictive value of contraceptor demographic characteristics, with the exception of age and marital status, demographic descriptors were noticeably absent from the list of significant variables utilized in the prediction equations resulting from both parts of the side-effects study.

Thus the overall conclusion drawn from all findings of the side-effects study was that it is highly likely that contraception side effects, rather than being an independent cause of birth-control discontinuation and unwanted pregnancy, frequently are simply mediating variables between these negative contraception outcomes and personality characteristics of the contraceptor.

DISCUSSION

The above findings and those from this research program broadly suggest an important role for person variables in the determination of effective contraception practice and perhaps in other areas of adjustment as well. We recognize, of course, that the entire research program has been correlational rather than experimental, and hence, inferring causality is quite risky. Nonetheless, it must be stated that nearly 10 years of research in this area have persuaded us that at least some significant portion of the variance in the behavior studied is attributable to personality. Tightly controlled experimental research in this area and many others involving real-world coping processes is a long way off. It may occur only infrequently as a result of the pragmatics of doing studies that manipulate independent variables in a nonlaboratory context, and the proverbial Pandora's box of ethical dilemmas that are opened by such research. Thus, we cannot afford to ignore the findings of correlational studies, especially if we are interested in the practicalities of prevention and management. It is to these very practicalities of intervention that we now turn our attention.

IMPLICATIONS OF THIS RESEARCH FOR PREDICTION AND PREVENTION

The results of this research program imply that the goal of identifying high-risk patients in clinic settings before, rather than after, an unwanted pregnancy is not a completely unattainable one. As a matter of fact during some of our contacts with experienced clinic personnel while planning this research program, we asked about characteristics of those who fail in contraception, and whether these characteristics can be recognized prospectively rather than retrospectively. We were pleased to find that clinic personnel singled out many of the same person variables that we were interested in studying. They stated that in many instances they could discriminate potentially successful from unsuccessful contraceptors on the basis of verbal inflections and response content as well as facial expressions and other aspects of body language. The record of their significant predictive success in both Studies I and II, and the Side Effects Study suggests that despite their lack of intensive formal psychological training, they had mastered important elements of clinical prediction. They were far from "predicting all of the people all of the time" (Bem and Funder, 1978), and their summary predictive judgments as to who would succeed and who would fail were not always above chance levels. But almost invariably, their ability to recognize personality traits that were indicative of later contraception outcomes were both remarkable and statistically significant. And when their judgments were combined by the research team into summary predictions and were merged with the psychometric indices employed in the study, the resulting levels of prediction were both statistically significant and pragmatically worthwhile, speaking in terms of cost-benefit ratios that could be reached if prediction can be coupled with effective prevention.

We, of course, do not mean to imply that every person who does not succeed in birth planning can be identified prospectively. Nor do we suggest that the model of adaptive behavior fits all those who succeed in the birth-control endeavor. There are of course two parties in the practice of birth control—both a male and a female; and like those of many other investigators, our attempts to study males have met with markedly less success than our attempts to study females. Also it is evident that there are several roads to both positive and negative birth-planning outcomes.

As a matter of fact, a reinterview study was conducted after Study I was completed, to examine more closely the processes through which adequate and inadequate contraception had taken place in the study population. Fifty-four women, among whom both contraceptive success and failure were represented, were interviewed, and were once again rated along a number of dimensions (for further details see Oskamp and Mindick, 1979). As a result of this substudy we concluded that successful contraceptors fell into three basic categories: (1) highly motivated, active women who seemed to have a clear sense of goals, and who perceived the link between behavior and attainment of their goals; (2) somewhat passive women who found birth control easy to use, and who took the pill regularly out of habit; and (3) women who were somewhat dependent, and who used contraception because they had been instructed to do so by a parent or a boyfriend.

Women who did not avoid unplanned pregnancies were also seen as divided into three basic categories. Graduate student interviewers saw these women as: (4) "careless or lazy" persons who found birth control "too much of a hassle," even if it meant simply going to the clinic to pick up a packet of pills; or (5) persons who wanted to avoid pregnancy, but who failed to reckon with their own impulsive behavior; and (6) persons who seemed unable to connect their stated goals with their own immediate behavior.

The reinterview study also distinguished a seventh category of contraceptors, a group that was termed "doubtfully successful." This classification included women who exhibited behavior patterns similar to those of patients in the failure category. But the "doubtfully successful" were seen as avoiding pregnancy as a result of luck (or perhaps, subfecundity), or involuntary abstinence from sex.

These findings (and the variety of personality characteristics they show) support other aspects of the research program. But they also remind us of Allport's strongly held view that it is not individual traits so much that affect behavior as the configuration of characteristics that are determinative. We may also add that situational determinants cannot be ignored; neither can we neglect the "personality of situations" (Bem and Funder, 1978) nor person X situation interactions (Karoly, 1980) when we consider the enterprises of intervention. Having offered these caveats, however, we may say that predicting the potential unsuccessful use of birth control on the basis of personal characteristics seems vindicated by the results of the research program described here.

As for prevention strategies that might be employed after high-risk patients have been identified, several approaches suggest themselves. Some of these approaches are general; some are specific. In the general category are those having to do with normal operating procedures used by various clinics. Some clinics, for example, follow up their intake patients quite carefully; others do not. Our experience has been that establishing rapport with patients at intake and providing close follow-up thereafter are both extremely important procedures. In Study I, rather than protesting the research procedures, many patients indicated that the study personnel made them feel "cared about," and it is notable that after one year of follow-up, clinic attrition was 11 percent lower in the Research Group than in the Control Group that was not tested and not followed up.

Prevention strategies can be individualized. At minimum, persons identified as being at higher risk can be encouraged to use an IUD, a birth-control method that requires somewhat less daily attention by the patient. Also, it is our view that personal characteristics are not immutable. Where patients are identified as being at risk, supplementary educational programs in human sexuality, contraception, and other relevant areas of knowledge can be given to patients. In some instances, self-concept and internality can be enhanced by allowing patients to have more input in making the choice of the kind of birth-control method to be prescribed. Having a caring staff member build a somewhat more personal relationship with an at-risk patient seems desirable, especially where the patient is a young adolescent who appears to be frightened, and likely to experience method side effects or unwanted pregnancy. All of these strategies suggest themselves as possible avenues of prevention. Especially where method side effects occur, it may be important to "flag" a patient's chart, assess the contraception program, and perhaps institute intervention procedures.

Implications of this Research for Management

As for patient management, the implications of this research program are manifold, although much depends on the resources and influence available to the professional who seeks to intervene. For example, Bronfenbrenner (1979) has suggested that both joint parent-child activity *and* the social networks in which the family is embedded have an important influence on sociocognitive development. Clearly, the practitioner cannot "reparent" the adolescent who, in many cases, is already a parent herself. But involving such teen-agers in joint and cooperative activity (perhaps with peers), giving her challenges at graded levels of difficulty where success is possible and is also recognized, building a sense of goal-directedness, and helping suggest the means to achieve goals, encouraging the adolescent to expand social networks that are supportive and involving, teaching cognitive coping strategies that can readily be employed (Karoly, 1980)—all of these are techniques of management that are suggested by our research and that of others.

The authors of this chapter are academics rather than practitioners, and the specific details of implementation must be left to others more skilled in arts required for patient management. We can only point in the directions suggested by the theory and the data—i.e., that the mainstream of American adolescents who encounter problems in contraception are not simply pathological misfits who are irredeemable. They simply are, more often than not, youngsters whose adjustment is less than it needs to be in the face of an environment in which sexual activity has increased considerably. (Zelnik and Kantner, 1973; 1977). The adolescents of whom we speak are not simply undifferentiated members of ethnic, racial, or socioeconomic subgroups who may be simplistically stereotyped as ineffective copers; they are individual human beings whose personal lives differ from one another, and who may require the kind of help in growing up that was not available in a family of origin that itself was not intact. Far from being knowledgeable about birth control, many of these young women lack some of the most basic information about both sexuality and contraception. They must receive this information if they are expected to cope successfully.

Thus, management, whether in the form of external or self-management techniques, or both, must pursue the direction of incorporating the adolescent within a network of peers that supports normative societal behavior, rather than leaving him/her isolated or at the mercy of those who advocate the kind of activity that leads to delinquency. Management must encourage the building of justifiable self-esteem as well as ". . . cognitive, affective, and instrumental repertoires in conjunction with the facilitative and nonfacilitative realities of the social milieu . . ." (Karoly, 1980). Management must help the adolescent set goals and understand the connection between aspiration and past as well as present behavior. The challenge offered to the practitioner by these goals is a rather considerable one. Some of the paths suggested are relatively untried, although others are already being incorporated into research or demonstration programs. We can only point to the enormous value of such attempts, and hope that research presented here may help expand understanding, and spark an idea or two for intervention.

REFERENCE NOTES

1. Miller, W.B. Some psychological factors predictive of undergraduate sexual and contraceptive behavior. Paper presented at the American Psychological Association Meeting, Washington, D.C., September, 1976.
2. Slagle, S.J., Arnold, C.B., and Glascock, E. Self-competence: A measure of relative risk of unwanted pregnancy. Paper presented at the 82nd Annual Convention of the American Psychological Association, New Orleans, 1974.
3. Adler, N.E. Factors affecting contraceptive use. Paper presented at the American Psychological Association Meeting, New Orleans, August, 1974.
4. Kar, S.B. Consistency between fertility attitudes and behavior: A conceptual model. Paper presented at the American Psychological Association Meeting, Washington, D.C., September, 1976.
5. Kaplan, S. On the fear of cognitive chaos. Paper presented at the meeting of the American Psychological Association, Washington, D.C., September, 1976.

References

Ager, J.W., Werley, H.H., and Shea, F.P. Correlates of continuance in a family planning program. *Journal of Obstetric, Gynecologic, and Neonatal Nursing*, 1973, **2**, 15–23.

Ball, G.W. *A Method of Identifying the Potential Unwed Adolescent*. Unpublished doctoral dissertation, University of California at Los Angeles, 1973.

Bandura, A. Self-efficacy: Toward a unifying theory of behavioral change. *Psychological Review*, 1977, **84**, 191–215.

Bauman, K.E. and Udry, J.R. Powerlessness and regularity of contraception in an urban Negro male sample. *Journal of Marriage and the Family*, 1972, **34**, 112–114.

Bem, D.J. and Funder, D.C. Predicting more of the people more of the time: Assessing the personality of situations. *Psychological Review*, 1978, **85**, 485–501.

Bendig, A.W. The development of a short form of the manifest anxiety scale. *Journal of Consulting Psychology*, 1956, **20**, 384.

Bronfenbrenner, U. *The Ecology of Human Development: Experiments by Nature and Design*. Cambridge, Massachusetts: Harvard U., 1979.

Buros, O.K. (Ed.) *The Seventh Mental Measurements Yearbook*. Highland Park, N.J. : Gryphon Press, 1972.

Cobliner, W.G., Schulman, H., and Smith, V. Patterns of contraceptive failures: The role of motivation re-examined. *Journal of Biosocial Science*, 1975, **7**, 307–318.

Cole, S.G. *Critical Factors in Family Planning Participation*. Final progress report for NICHD grant, Texas Christian University, 1975.

Devereaux, G. A psychoanalytic study of contraception. *Journal of Sex Research*, 1965, **1**, 105–112.

Drucker, C.A. *The Psychological Aspects of Contraceptive Choice Among Single Women*. Unpublished doctoral dissertation, Adelphi University, 1975.

Fawcett, J.T. and Bornstein, M.H. Modernization, individual modernity, and fertility. In J.T. Fawcett (Ed.), *Psychological perspectives on population*. New York: Basic Books, 1973.

Freud, S. Formulations regarding the two principles in mental functioning. In *Collected Papers* (Vol. 4). London: Hogarth, 1953.

Furstenberg, F., Jr., Gordis, J., and Markowitz, M. Birth control knowledge and attitudes among unmarried pregnant adolescents: A preliminary report. *Journal of Marriage and the Family*, 1969, **31**, 34–42.

Goldsmith, S., Gabrielson, M., Gabrielson, I., Matthews, V., and Potts, L. Teenagers, sex and contraception. *Family Planning Perspectives*, 1972, **4**, 32–38.

Gough, H.G. A factor analysis of contraceptive preferences. *Journal of Psychology*, 1973(a), **84**, 199–210.

Gough, H.G. Personality assessment in the study of population. In J.T. Fawcett (Ed.), *Psychological Perspectives on Population*. New York: Basic Books, 1973(b).

Gough, H.G. *Manual for the Personal Values Abstract*. Palo Alto, Calif.: Consulting Psychologists Press, 1972.

Gough, H.G. Theory and measurement of socialization. *Journal of Consulting Psychology*, 1960, **24**, 23–30.

Groat, H.T. and Neal, A.G. Social psychological correlates of urban fertility. *American Sociological Review*, 1967, **32**, 945–959.

Grunebaum, H. and Abernethy, V. Marital decision making as applied to family planning. *Journal of Sex and Marital Therapy*, 1974, **1**, 63–74.

Hagelis, J.P. *Unwed Adolescent Pregnancy and Contraceptive Practice*. Unpublished doctoral dissertation, California School of Professional Psychology, Los Angeles, 1973.

Jessor, S.L. and Jessor, R. Transition from virginity to nonvirginity among youth: A social-psychological study over time. *Developmental Psychology*. 1975, **11**, 473–484.

Kane, F.J., Jr. and Lachenbruch, P.A. Adolescent pregnancy: A study of aborters and non-aborters. *American Journal of Orthopsychiatry*, 1973, **43**, 796–803.

Kantner, J.F. and Zelnik, M. Contraception and pregnancy: Experience of young unmarried women in the United States. *Family Planning Perspectives*, 1973, **5**, 21–35.

Karoly, P. Person variables in therapeutic change and development. In P. Karoly and J.J. Steffen (Eds.) *Improving the Long-Term Effects of Psychotherapy*. New York: Gardner, 1980.

Kar, S.B. Individual aspirations as related to early and late acceptance of contraception. *The Journal of Social Psychology*, 1971, **83**, 235–245.

Keller, S.B., Sims, J.H., Henry, W.E., and Crawford, T.J. Psychological sources of "resistance" to family planning. *Merrill-Palmer Quarterly of Behavior and Development, 1970*, **16**, 286–302.

Kothandapani, V. *A Psychological Approach to the Prediction of Contraceptive Behavior*. Chapel Hill, N.C.: Carolina Population Center, 1971.

Lehfeldt, H. Psychology of contraceptive failure. *Medical Aspects of Human Sexuality*, 1971, **5**, 68–77.

Lewin, K. Behavior and development as a function of the total situation. In L. Carmichael (Ed.), *Manual of Child Psychology*. New York: Wiley, 1946.

Luker, K.C. *Taking Chances: Abortion and the Decision not to Contracept*. Berkeley: University of California Press, 1975.

Lundy, J.R. Some personality correlates of contraceptive use among unmarried female college students. *The Journal of Psychology*, 1972, **80**, 9–14.

MacDonald, A.P., Jr. Internal-external locus of control and the practice of birth control. *Psychological Reports*, 1970, **27**, 206.

Malmquist, C.P., Kiresuk, T.J., and Spano, R.M. Personality characteristics of women with repeated illegitimacies: Descriptive aspects. *American Journal of Orthopsychiatry*, 1966. **36**, 476–484.

Miller, W.B., Psychological antecedents to conception among abortion seekers. *Western Journal of Medicine*, 1975, **122**, 12–19.

Miller, W.B. Psychological vulnerability to unwanted pregnancy. *Family Planning Perspectives*, 1973(a), **5**, 199–201.

Miller, W.B. *The Personal Style Inventory*. Unpublished manuscript, Stanford University, 1973(b).

Miller, W.B. *Sexual and Contraceptive Knowledge Questionnaire*. Unpublished manuscript, Stanford University, no date.

Mindick, B. *Personality and Social Psychological Correlates of Success or Failure in Contraception: A Longitudinal Predictive Study*. Unpublished doctoral dissertation, Claremont Graduate School, Claremont, California, 1978.

Mindick, B. and Oskamp, S. *Contraception use Effectiveness: The Fit Between Method and User Characteristics*. Final Progress Report under Contract No. 1-HD-82842, submitted to the Center for Population Research, NICHD, 1980.

Mindick, B. and Oskamp, S. Longitudinal predictive research: An approach to methodological problems in studying contraception. *Journal of Population*, 1979, **2**, 259–276.

Mindick, B., Oskamp, S., and Berger, D.E. Prediction of success or failure in birth planning: An approach to prevention of individual and family stress. *American Journal of Community Psychology*, 1977, **5**, 447–459.

Neisser, U. *Cognition and Reality: Principles and Implications of Cognitive Psychology*. San Francisco: Freeman, 1976.

Noble, LD. *Personality Characteristics Associated with Contraceptive Behavior in Women Seeking Abortion under Liberalized California Law*. Unpublished doctoral dissertation, California School of Professional Psychology, San Francisco, 1972.

Oskamp, S. and Mindick, B. *Long-Term Study of Success in Contraceptive Planning*. Final Progress Report for Grant No. HD-08074-05. Submitted to National Institute of Child Health and Human Development, Bethesda, Md., 1979.

Oskamp, S. and Mindick, B. Longitudinal predictive study of success in birth-control programs. In M. Harway, and S. Mednick, *Longitudinal Research in the U.S.*, Vol. II, in press.

Rader, G.E., Bekker, L.D., Brown, L., and Richardt, C. Psychological correlates of unwanted pregnancy. *Journal of Abnormal Psychology*, 1978, **87**, 373–376.

Rosenberg, M. *Society and the Adolescent Self-Image*. Princeton, N.J.: Princeton University Press, 1965.

Rotter, J.B. Generalized expectancies for internal versus external control of reinforcement. *Psychological Monographs*, 1966, **80**, (1, Whole no. 609).

Rovinsky, J.J. Abortion recidivism: A problem in preventive medicine. *American Journal of Obstetrics and Gynecology*, 1972, **39**, 649–759.

Scott, W.A. and Wertheimer, M. *Introduction to Psychological Research*. New York: John Wiley & Sons, 1962.

Seligman, M.E.P. *Helplessness: On Depression, Development, and Death*. San Francisco, Calif.: Freeman, 1975.

Shipley, R.R. *Changes in Contraceptive Knowledge, Attitudes and Behavior in a College Current Health Problems Class*. Unpublished doctoral dissertation, Temple University, 1974.

Slavin, M.E. *Ego Functioning in Women who use Birth Control Effectively and Ineffectively*. Unpublished doctoral dissertation, Boston University School of Education, 1975.

Spain, J.S *Psychological Dimensions of Effective and Ineffective Contraceptive use in Adolescent Girls*. Unpublished doctoral dissertation, City University of New York, 1977.

Stein, K.B., Sarbin, T.R., and Kulik, J.A. Future time perspective. *Journal of Consulting and Clinical Psychology*, 1968, **32**, 357–264.

Steinlauf, B. *Attitudes and Cognitive Factors Associated with the Contraceptive Behavior of Young Women*. Unpublished doctoral dissertation, Wayne State University, 1977.

Sweet, J.A. Differentials in the rate of fertility decline: 1960–1970. *Family Planning Perspectives*, 1974, **6**, 103–107.

Tietze, C. Teenage pregnancies: Looking ahead to 1984. *Family Planning Perspectives*, 1978, **10**, 233–235.

Vener, A.M. and Steward, C.S. Adolescent sexual behavior in middle America revisited: 1970–1973. *Journal of Marriage and the Family*, 1974, **36**, 728–735.

Vincent, C.E. *Unmarried Mothers*. New York: Glencoe Free Press, 1961.

Westoff, C.F., Potter, R.G., and Sagi, P.C., *The Third Child*. Princeton: Princeton University, 1963.

Whelpton, P.K. and Kiser, C.V. (Eds.), *Social and Psychological Factors Affecting Fertility*. New York: Milbank Memorial Fund. 5 Vols., 1947–1958.

White, R.W. Motivation reconsidered: The concept of competence. *Psychological Review*, 1959, **66**, 297–33.

Wolf, S.R. Psychosexual problems associated with the contraceptive practices of abortion-seeking patients. *Medical Aspects of Human Sexuality*, 1973, **7**, 169–182.

Zelnik, M. and Kantner, J. Sexuality, contraception and pregnancy among young unwed females in the U.S. In C.F. Westoff and R. Parke, Jr. (Eds.), *Demographic and Social Aspects of Population Growth and American Future Resarch Report*, No. 1. Washington, D.C. : U.S. Government Printing Office, 1973.

Zelnik, M. and Kantner, J.F. Sexual and contraceptive experience of young unmarried women in the United States, 1976 and 1971. *Family Planning Perspectives*, 1977, **9**, 55–71.

ACKNOWLEDGMENTS

We are grateful for the help of countless people in carrying out this research: particulary the 2000 or so young women whose contraceptive progress we have studied; the scores of interviewers, coders, clinic staff members of Los Angeles and Pasadena Planned Parenthood, research assistants, and secretaries who have contributed to the work; and the Center for Population Research of NICHD which provided seven years of support under research grant HD08074 and contract No. 1-HD-82842. More extended reports of the results may be obtained from either author.

8.
Psychological Barriers to Contraceptive Use Among Adolescent Women

Lucy Olson, Ph.D.,
Department of Psychiatry,
University of Massachusetts;

and

Joan Rollins, Ph.D.,*
Rhode Island College

The present study explores several variables that are presumed to be associated with "psychological barriers" to contraceptive use among unmarried, adolescent women. An assumption underlying the study is that young people's beliefs concerning the availability and dangerousness of (or psychological barriers to) contraception, are directly related to contraceptive practice and thus also to pregnancy risk. Questionnaires, designed to tap teenage women's perceptions of the availability and dangerousness of various methods of contraception, were administered to 430 sexually active high-school and college students. Results indicate (1) that contraception is perceived as difficult to obtain by a substantial minority of both high-school and college women; and (2) that both groups consider prescription devices as hazardous to health. These findings are suggestive in light of the failure of large numbers of young people to use reliable family-planning methods. Implications for policies and programs addressing the problem of unwanted pregnancies to teenagers are discussed and recommendations for improved contraceptive practice are offered.

The past decade has witnessed a sharp drop in age at first intercourse and a dramatic rise in the incidence of premarital pregnancy among teenage women. Recent estimates indicate that one-fifth of all adolescent women in the U.S.

*The author gratefully acknowledges the assistance of Dr. Joan Rollins, Professor of Psychology, Rhode Island College.

have had sexual intercourse by age 16, and two thirds by age 19 (Zabin, Kantner, and Zelnik, 1979; Zelnik, Kim, and Kantner, 1979). Of these sexually active women, roughly one quarter become pregnant by age 17, and by age 19, more than a third have had a first premarital pregnancy (Zelnik, 1980). What this means is that one in ten women in the U.S. has at least one premarital pregnancy by age 17, and of those under 19, one-quarter become pregnant at some time (see especially, Zelnik, Kim, and Kantner, 1979).

The negative consequences of teenage childbearing have been widely documented both in the scientific literature and in the popular press and include social, economic, medical, and psychological problems for both the mother and her offspring. Even so, more than one million teenage women become pregnant each year. The high incidence of unwanted pregnancy to adolescent women—viewed by many as an "epidemic"—attests to the widespread failure of effective contraception among sexually active young people—this despite substantial increases both in the proportion of women who currently use any type of contraceptive technique and in the proportion of those who use birth control regularly and effectively. Indeed, the plain—and tragic—fact is that effective and consistent contraceptive use has failed to keep pace with the continuing problem of unwanted pregnancy among adolescent women.

In interpreting data on the prevalence of pregnancy risk to unmarried teenage women, allowance must be made for the increased rate of sexual intercourse among adolescent women generally, and especially among very young teenagers whose counterparts of an earlier era would never have been exposed to the risk of conception at such an early age. The pool of sexually active teenage women who are at risk of multiple and early pregnancies has increased tremendously, and were it not for the use of contraception, pregnancy rates would be far higher than they are.

In the light of the statistics cited above, it may seem surprising that the proportion of sexually active adolescent women who become pregnant each year has not increased over the past decade. Even if allowance is made for increased sexual activity, the rate of premarital pregnancy to blacks actually decreased somewhat. Yet the proportion of white teenagers who conceive premaritally increased during this same period even though whites showed lower levels of pregnancy risk at certain ages.

In their continuing analysis of data taken from national surveys of adolescent women in 1971 and 1976, Zelnik, Kantner, and their colleagues have shown that except for a slight increase in the proportion of women who conceive before age 16 (19 percent in 1976 and 18 percent in 1971), pregnancy rates have been dropping on average by about 5 percent each year (Zabin, Kantner, and Zelnik, 1979; Zelnik, 1979; Zelnik, 1980; Zelnik and Kantner, 1978; Zelnik and Kantner, 1979; Zelnik, Kim, and Kantner, 1979). This trend is largely due to the use of contraceptives. Forty-five percent of sexually active blacks under 16 became pregnant in 1971, contrasted with 34 percent in 1976, and there was a comparable decline in the proportion of black women under 19 who became pregnant between 1971 and 1976, from 61 percent to 53 percent, respectively. Among sexually active whites under 16, 23 percent became pregnant in 1971, contrasted with 17 percent in 1976. But among those 18–19 years old, there was no change: Approximately 31 percent became pregnant during both the first and second half of the decade.

But whatever declines have occurred in the rate of premarital pregnancy among teenage women are hardly reassuring and may appear insignificant when compared with the consistently high incidence of pregnancy in this population. The fact that more than 66 percent of all sexually active teenage women (i.e., over half of all sexually active black teenagers, and almost a fifth of all sexually active white adolescents) conceive each year, is both alarming and tragic. Ironically, existing contraceptive technology is capable of eliminating or substantially reducing this costly social—and human—problem. Birth-control devices are available to nearly all who seek them, and even nonprescription methods (e.g., condoms) are safe, easy to use, and highly effective. While many factors have been found to be associated with the nonuse or underutilization of contraception, the most obvious reason for the continued high rates of conception among unmarried teenage women is the failure to use contraception regularly, effectively, and early enough.

VARIABLES AFFECTING CONTRACEPTIVE USE

Before considering some of the factors that are associated with contraceptive behavior among adolescent women, a note of caution is in order: Statistics which reflect the prevalence of a given behavior frequently mask divergent, even conflicting, trends and patterns within different age levels, racial groups, geographic regions, and socioeconomic strata. It is often necessary, therefore, to disaggregate the data in order to understand what they describe and whether and under what conditions they apply. For example, while 20 percent of all adolescent women have had sexual intercourse by age 16, this statistic underestimates the proportion of black adolescents who are sexually experienced, for whom the rate (39 percent) is almost double the figure for all adolescents; and it slightly overestimates the prevalence of coital experience for whites in this age group (16 percent). Similarly, while two thirds of all adolescent women have had sexual intercourse by age 19, 60 percent of white women under 19 are sexually experienced, as contrasted with 83 percent of black women who are (Zelnik, Kim, and Kantner, 1979). Similar variations and disparities exist for geographical regions (e.g., higher rates of sexual activity and pregnancy are found in urban as compared with rural settings) and for social, economic, ethnic, religious, and other groups (Olson, 1980). The data may thus reflect quite discrepant behavior among different groups, and it is important to understand what is summarized in a given statistic.

Age

Many studies have reported on an association between age, contraceptive use, and pregnancy risk (see especially, AGI, 1976). Early age at first intercourse has been found to be a major factor in explaining pregnancy risk among unmarried adolescents. For example, adolescents 15 years of age or younger are twice as likely to become pregnant as those who wait until they are 18 or older (Zelnik, 1980). The obvious reason for this finding is that younger sexually active adolescents are far less likely to be protected during intercourse than are their older counterparts. Recent data suggest that approximately half of all first pregnancies to teenagers occur during the initial six months of sexual experience (ibid.). Forty percent of women aged 15 or younger never use contraception, contrasted with 25 percent of 18–19 year olds who never do. Apparently, early age at initiation of sexual intercourse and the associated nonuse of contraceptives largely account for early pregnancy risk to the younger adolescent. Moreover, while the probability of premarital conception increases during each successive year, the younger adolescent has a longer interval of exposure in which to become pregnant (whether for the first time or for repeat pregnancies).

Family-planning clinics report that there is a lag of two years, on average, between the time of first coitus and initiation of birth-control practice (Akpom, Akpom, and Davis, 1976). Not surprisingly, the all too frequent result of this delay is pregnancy. Older adolescents seem more likely than younger teenagers to be reached by family planning programs and to practice contraception effectively; but for a large proportion of younger women, contraception begins only after the first pregnancy, and risk of repeat pregnancy is also high (Zabin, Kantner, and Zelnik, 1979). For example, 64 percent of premarital repeat pregnancies to white adolescents and 44 percent of premarital repeat pregnancies to blacks occur to women who first conceived within 6 months of initial intercourse (ibid.). (Among blacks, the relation between age and contraceptive use is far stronger than for whites: 58 percent of blacks aged 15 or younger never use any form of contraception, contrasted with 20 percent of 18–19 year olds who never use contraception. Comparable statistics for whites reveal that 36 percent of the younger population never use contraception, compared with 28 percent of the older group who never use it [Zelnik, 1980].)

Delay among adolescent women in seeking professional family-planning services has been cited by many researchers as a key factor in accounting for the high risk of pregnancy. The reasons for this delay and the consequent failure to use birth control appear to be numerous and complex. In the following sections, we examine some of the possible explanations for the observed delay, nonuse, or underutilization of contraceptive devices among adolescent women.

KNOWLEDGE AND USE OF CONTRACEPTIVES

Research centering on the relationship between adolescents' knowledge of birth-control technology and their utilization of a method of contraception confirms the observation that while most sexually active young people know about contraception, this apparent knowledge does not reliably predict the actual use of birth control during coital activity (Dickens, Mudd, and Higgins, 1975; Jekel, 1977; Needle, 1977; Reichelt, 1978; Weichman and Ellis, 1969). Studies of college students have generally found both male and female undergraduates to be informed about contraception (Grinder and Schmitt, 1966; Needle, 1977). But explicit and consistent definitions of contraceptive knowledge are lacking, and students' evaluations of the extent of their knowledge may be inaccurate (see especially McCreary-Juhasz, 1967). Thus, it is uncertain, for example, whether students in fact have information that is necessary, pertinent, and useful for them in the effective practice of birth control.

Several authors (Bernard and Schwartz, 1977; McCreary-Juhasz, 1967) have suggested that students lack essential sexual and contraceptive information, and Bernard and Schwartz (op. cit.) imply that this ignorance may be a source of emotional problems as well as of contraceptive failure. Sexual and contraceptive education may thus serve the dual purpose of reducing pregnancy risk and contributing to young people's mental health.

While ignorance of contraception does not appear to be widespread among college students, a significant minority of sexually active undergraduates apparently feel inadequately informed about birth-control techniques. In Needle's (1977) survey of sexually experienced male and female college students, for example, 9 percent of the men and 7 percent of the women said they lacked information about contraception. An additional 26 percent of the men and 15 percent of the women claimed limited or difficult access to contraceptives (e.g., were ignorant of where to obtain birth control, didn't know they could get it, or believed it couldn't be purchased).

In the same survey, Needle also found that only three-fifths of male and female undergraduates used contraceptives during first intercourse (compared with two fifths of teenage women generally [Zelnik and Kantner, 1978]). This suggests that a substantial (and unexpected) proportion of older and presumably better educated adolescents are unprotected against pregnancy risk, some of them, for lack of adequate information. Like their noncollege counterparts, then, many college women risk having unwanted pregnancies. In light of the fact that more adolescent undergraduates engage in premarital sexual intercourse than in the past—and at earlier ages—the risk is comparably great for this population as for noncollege women.

COGNITIVE AND PSYCHOLOGICAL VARIABLES

Among younger, noncollege adolescents, misconceptions and misinformation about "the safe period" and risk associated with infrequent or episodic coitus, have also been cited as reasons for failure to use contraception (Marinoff, 1972; Kantner and Zelnik, 1976; Zelnik and Kantner, 1979). A number of investigators have suggested that lack of knowledge is actually part of a larger problem involving several cognitive, behavioral, and social dimensions (Baldwin and Staub, 1976; Cvetkovich et al., 1975, 1978, Mudd et al., 1978; Reichelt and Werley, 1975; Schinke et al., 1977). For example, Schinke and his colleagues explain contraceptive failure not in terms of a lack of information, but rather as a lack of cognitive and behavioral skills necessary to make appropriate use of this information. The authors argue that adolescents need to "personalize" the information and apply it specifically, directly, and concretely to their own situations.

A theoretical association between contraceptive behavior and level of cognitive and ego development has also been advanced by several authors (Cvetvich et al., op. cit.; Reiss et al., 1975). According to them, lack of psychological maturity and limited reasoning skills may act as a distorting filter for contraceptive information. This idea is compatible with a cognitive-developmental interpretation and, in fact, has been extended to a Piagetian framework. Thus, the younger adolescent who has not yet completed the transition from concrete to formal-operational thinking, may have little notion of the meanings and consequences of her sexual behavior and may be quite unprepared to plan for the future and take the necessary precautions against pregnancy. In Elkind's terms, the very immature and impulsive adolescent is likely to be dominated by a form of egocentric thinking (the "personal fable") which leads her to believe that she is invulnerable and that "it can't happen" to her. Such women (and their partners) may also fail to perceive possible behavioral alternatives that are available to them and take chances that their older counterparts would not take (Dembo and Lundell, 1979).

The cognitive problems of younger, adolescent women are complicated in sexual relations by the anxiety, conflict, and ambivalence that often accompany early premarital intercourse. Social disapproval of premarital coitus may also discourage adolescents from using contraceptives because their use would imply identification with, and responsibility for, actions that are not sanctioned by their communities. A risk-taking orientation may thus develop because acceptance of the involvement would threaten self-esteem and raise disturbing questions and doubts about personal and sexual identity, values, and level of commitment to the relationship. For many young adolescents, deliberate planning for sexual intercourse may be less acceptable and more problematic, both emotionally and cognitively, than taking steps to protect against pregnancy risk.

OTHER FACTORS ASSOCIATED WITH NONUSE OF CONTRACEPTION

Motivational problems and attitudinal resistance to contraceptive use have been associated with pressures and obstacles that are endemic to specific subgroups of teenage women. Recent investigations, employing a broad range of samples and methods, have emphasized the importance of such sociodemographic variables as social class, family background and structure, ethnic characteristics, educational achievement, religion, and geographic location in contraceptive practice (Dembo and Lundell, 1979; Evans, Selstad, and Welcher, 1976; Hornick, 1978; Menken, 1972; Olson, 1980; Phipps-Yonas, 1980; Reiss et al., 1975; Snyder and Spreitzer, 1976; Thompson and Spanier, 1978). Pregnancy risk has been found to be disproportionately great for teenagers from lower socioeconomic levels, who have minority group membership, and a history of low educational achievement and family discord. Moreover, in certain social milieux, single parenthood appears to be an acceptable alternative to middle-class expectations and values and it may effectively legitimate another (lower-class) life-style.

Yet, considering that among women who use contraceptives at all (approximately 40 percent [Zelnik and Kantner, 1978]), and that fewer than half as many (17 percent) are regular users, it is clear that no single group can account for the widespread failure of adolescent women to protect themselves against the risk of pregnancy. Finally, the notions that sexual intercourse should be "spontaneous," that birth control makes sexual relations less "romantic," and similar objections cannot explain repeated pregnancies and continued lack of family planning.

THE STUDY

In order to explore some of the possible reasons for nonuse or underutilization of birth control, the present study was undertaken as a first step in illuminating a variable which has appeared to be important to a fuller understanding of unwanted premarital pregnancy among teenagers: The variable we refer to is the "psychological availability" or "accessibility" of birth control, by which we mean the extent to which various birth-control devices are perceived as accessible to a given individual or group (as distinguished from the actual ease or difficulty that might be experienced in obtaining them). More specifically, the study was intended to reveal what kinds of psychological barriers there might be to the regular and reliable use of a method of contraception.

An assumption underlying this research was that young people's beliefs about the danger or health risks associated with contraceptive use and notions about the difficulty of obtaining contraception—regardless of the *actual* health risks or unavailability—could render contraception "psychologically unavailable" to them. A second assumption was that people's explanations of their nonuse of birth control as well as their attitudes about family planning generally, were part of a "belief system" which could create barriers to effective contraceptive practice and increase the likelihood of unwanted pregnancy.

Method

In order, then, to learn whether, and to what extent, "psychological barriers" to contraception exist for teenage women, data were collected from high-school and college students concerning their perceptions of the relative danger and availability of various methods of birth control. Questionnaires were administered to 430 sexually active, teenaged women, 150 of whom were drawn from either of two suburban, public high schools, and the other 280 of whom were undergraduates at a state college located in a southern New England city. In their sociodemographic characteristics, the samples of students were similar, reflecting the ethnic and cultural composition of the region. Thus, both samples were almost entirely white, predominantly Italian, Irish, or French-Canadian, and Catholic. The samples did differ, however, with respect to age and social class, with younger women from lower socioeconomic strata being more highly represented in the high school than the college samples.

The questionnaire used in this study was designed to tap, among other things, information concerning the respondents' perceptions of both the availability and dangerousness to physical health of various methods of contraception. Students recorded their responses on anonymous answer sheets. Questionnaires were administered to 15 to 18-year-old female high-school students who were enrolled in Health Education classes. Since these courses are required for all students, the samples probably yield a fair cross-section of the female high-school student body. At the college level, questionnaires were administered to female undergraduates, 18 to 20 years of age, enrolled in introductory psychology courses. (To the question, "Did you feel free in

answering these questions?" students responded overwhelmingly in the affirmative.)

FINDINGS

Perceived danger

Students were asked to rate various contraceptive devices (prescription and
nonprescription) on a five-point scale ranging from "Very Safe" to "Very
Dangerous" to general physical health and well-being—distinct from the
question of their efficacy in preventing pregnancy. The results are surprising
in that the majority of students in both samples did not appear to view any
method of contraception as "Very Safe" in this sense (see Table 8-1). Equally
surprising is the finding that, of the two samples, high school students judged
birth control as safer than the college students. Exceptions were the condom
and spermicidal foam which high-school students thought were somewhat
more dangerous than college women.

Table 8-1. High school and college women's judgments of the dangerousness of various contraceptive devices (in percent).

TYPE OF CONTRACEPTION	DANGEROUSNESS			
	VERY DANGEROUS	SOMEWHAT DANGEROUS	RATHER SAFE	VERY SAFE
Condom				
HS* (N=150)	9%	3%	38%	50%
COL** (N=280)	2%	7%	41%	50%
Foam				
HS	6%	22%	59%	13%
COL	8%	16%	58%	18%
Pill				
HS	9%	47%	38%	6%
COL	20%	53%	18%	8%
Diaphragm				
HS	3%	19%	75%	3%
COL	6%	24%	51%	18%
IUD				
HS	13%	38%	50%	0
COL	24%	48%	24%	4%
[Abortion				
HS	16%	26%	48%	10%]
COL	20%	43%	31%	5%]

Note: Numbers may not add to 100 due to rounding.
*High School
**College

The College Sample

Almost three-quarters of the college students thought the pill and IUD were "Somewhat" or "Very Dangerous." Not even abortion appeared to them to be as dangerous as these contraceptive methods, since only 62 percent placed this procedure in either of the "dangerous" categories (compared with 74 percent and 77 percent for the pill and IUD, respectively). Indeed, the college undergraduates appear to perceive the IUD as more dangerous than abortion. (Of course, it is impossible to be certain against what standard of dangerousness abortion and contraception are judged for these women.)

Of the prescription forms of contraception, the diaphragm was viewed by college women as the safest method, but it was believed dangerous by a significant minority of students: 30 percent considered the device dangerous, about the same proportion of those who thought foam dangerous (26%). A surprising 5 percent of the college undergraduates also considered the condom dangerous.

Table 8-2. High school and college women's judgments of the dangerousness of various contraceptive devices (in percent).[a]

	DANGEROUSNESS	
TYPE OF CONTRACEPTIVE DEVICE	VERY OR SOMEWHAT DANGEROUS	RATHER OR VERY SAFE
Condom		
HS* (N=150)	12%	88%
COL** (N=280)	9%	91%
Foam		
HS	28%	72%
COL	24%	76%
Pill		
HS	56%	44%
COL	73%	26%
Diaphragm		
HS	22%	78%
COL	30%	69%
IUD		
HS	51%	50%
COL	72%	28%
[Abortion		
HS	42%	58%]
COL	63%	36%]

Note: Numbers may not add to 100 due to rounding.
[a]Categories in Table 1 have been collapsed to yield a dichotomous variable.
  *High School
**College

The High School Sample

Similar patterns are found in the data from the high-school samples, though, as was pointed out earlier, these young people perceive all forms of contraception, especially the pill, IUD, and abortion as safer than do the college subjects. The pill is viewed as "Somewhat" to "Very Dangerous" by 55 percent of the high-school students, while the IUD is so judged by 41 percent (compared with roughly 75 percent of the college students who see both methods as dangerous.) The condom is believed dangerous by 12 percent of the high-school students (about one-half the number who view foam and the diaphragm as dangerous).

These data suggest that the methods of contraception which are most reliable and convenient are perceived by teenagers in the samples as mild to serious health hazards. Other methods are also thought to present risks to health by a significant minority of students. While the data do not show that perceived danger is directly related to actual failure to utilize contraception, one can speculate that the students' beliefs concerning the risks of contraception do have important implications for birth-control practice.

Perceived Availability

A second question that was asked of the students in the survey concerned the relative availability of the various methods of birth control. (See Table 8-2). Not surprisingly, the condom and spermicidal foam are perceived as easiest to obtain by both the high-school and college samples. Among the college students, about 80 percent rate these devices as "Somewhat Easy" to "Very Easy" to obtain. Three percent believe the condom, and 6 percent think foam difficult to obtain, a perplexing finding, considering that these methods are prominently displayed in drugstores throughout the nation.

A larger proportion of college women thought prescription devices difficult to obtain than thought nonprescription devices difficult to obtain: Roughly a fifth (22 percent) of these young people believed the pill to be difficult to obtain, and almost a third (30 percent) put the diaphragm in the "Difficult to Obtain" categories. Interestingly, abortions were viewed by 44 percent of the college students as easy to obtain. This proportion is comparable to the percentage of those who place the IUD or diaphragm in the "Easy" categories (41 and 43 percent, respectively). Thus, we may infer that the college students consider abortion about as easy to obtain as the IUD and diaphragm.

Among high-school students, the patterns in the data are similar, though the methods which in fact are easiest to obtain appear to be slightly less accessible to them than to the college students. Thus, condoms and foam are both thought difficult to obtain by 9 percent of the high-school students. The

Table 8-3. Psychological availability of contraception as assessed by the question: How easy or difficult to obtain are the following contraceptive devices? (In percent.)

			DIFFICULT		
TYPE OF CONTRACEPTION	VERY EASY	SOMEWHAT EASY	SOMEWHAT DIFFICULT	VERY DIFFICULT	DON'T KNOW
Condom					
HS* (NR=130)	53%	9%	3%	6%	28%
COL** (N=220)	69%	12%	2%	1%	15%
Foam					
HS	41%	25%	6%	3%	25%
COL	55%	24%	5%	1%	14%
Pill					
HS	9%	53%	13%	6%	19%
COL	30%	39%	17%	5%	9%
Diaphragm					
HS	13%	19%	31%	13%	25%
COL	14%	41%	25%	5%	15%
IUD					
HS	7%	16%	36%	10%	32%
COL	12%	37%	25%	9%	16%
Abortion					
HS	9%	25%	41%	34%	0%
COL (N=90)	12%	32%	33%	23%	1%

Note: Numbers may not add to 100 due to rounding.
*High School.
**College.

prescription methods with the exception of the pill and abortion, are all seen as more difficult to obtain for high-school students than for college students in the samples. Whereas 31 percent of the college women perceived the pill as difficult to obtain, only 19 percent of the high school women thought so. The sharpest distinction between the high-school and college samples appears to be in the perceived availability of abortion: For high-school students, abortion appears considerably less available than for college students (possibly because women under 18 in most states must have parental consent for the procedure). Seventy-five percent of high-school students put it in the "Difficult" categories, vs. 56 percent of college students who did.

These findings are consistent with the data on students' perceptions of the relative dangerousness of contraception. But wholly unexpected was the finding that high-school students who are younger and presumably less knowledgeable (though perhaps not less experienced) consider the most reliable forms of contraception more accessible than the college students.

Table 8-4. Psychological availability showing *easy* or difficult to obtain categories combined.

TYPE OF CONTRACEPTIVE	DIFFICULTY	
	EASY	DIFFICULT
Condom		
HS* (N=130)	62%	9%
COL** (N=220)	81%	3%
Foam		
HS	66%	9%
COL	79%	6%
Pill		
HS	62%	19%
COL	69%	22%
Diaphragm		
HS	32%	44%
COL	55%	30%
IUD		
HS	23%	46%
COL	49%	34%
Abortion		
HS	25%	75%
COL	44%	56%

Note: Numbers may not add to 100 due to rounding.
*High School.
**College.

Reasons for Unreliable Use or Nonutilization of Contraceptives

In a series of follow-up questions aimed at tapping the reasons why birth control is not used among college students, those who did not usually use contraceptives were asked to indicate their reasons. Only a small percentage (5%) indicated that inability to get them was a reason for not using contraceptives. The same number of students (5%) said they assumed their partner was using birth control. More than twice as many checked such reasons as not caring (11%), not wanting sex to seem planned (15%), not thinking of pregnancy (12%), and "trusting to luck" (12%).

A slightly higher proportion indicated that birth control was against their religion (15%), and 59 percent didn't expect to have sex. But, generally speaking, these data do not appear very illuminating with respect to the actual reasons for lack of contraceptive use. Apparently, most students in our sample felt that the reasons stated in the questionnaire did not apply to them. On this point, our results raise questions that require further research to answer.

Summary

Clearly, the actual availability of contraceptives is not an accurate index of their psychological availability—nor, apparently, of their actual use. (Over half the college sample [53%] indicated that they used no contraception at first intercourse.) Neither, however, is exposure to sex education classes an accurate index of the psychological availability of birth control. Over 80 percent of the women said they had had sex education or human biology courses.

The beliefs these young people have concerning the danger and un-availability of birth control, and their attitudes toward contraception, appear to be part of a deeply embedded belief system which is distinct from actual exposure to, and availability of, birth-control information and devices. The fact that for many teenagers, birth control is not perceived as safe or available, i.e., the fact that it is "psychologically unavailable," implies that these young people are more at risk of unwanted pregnancy than may be suspected.

CONCLUSION

While it may run against the American grain to suggest that some social problems have no clear and simple solutions, it must be pointed out that the problem of unwanted pregnancy cannot simply be laid to either lack of information or to actual inaccessibility of birth control. Therefore, solutions are not to be found merely in the provision of more information about, or even increased availability of, birth-control devices—though increased information about and availability of contraception are a first step in combating unwanted teenage pregnancy. Indeed, solutions will elude us until we have a better understanding of the beliefs, emotions, and attitudes that are tied to the use or nonuse of contraceptives.

Apparently, contraceptive programs must go much farther than merely disseminating information. Such programs must, in addition, provide opportunities for young people to explore their beliefs, attitudes, and values, and to consider their long-term goals. Since failure to use contraception is frequently attributable to lack of planning and forethought, contraceptive programs should focus on the necessity of planning, not only where a specific sexual relationship is concerned, but also for the more distant future. Clearly, underlying cognitive, attitudinal, and motivational characteristics must be addressed in any successful contraceptive program.

REFERENCES

Akpom, C.A., Akpom, K.L., and Davis, M. Prior sexual behavior of teenagers attending rap sessions for the first time. *Family Planning Perspectives*, 1976, **8**, 203–20.

The Alan Guttmacher Institute. *11 Million Teenagers*. New York: The Alan Guttmacher Institute, 1976.

Baldwin, B.A. and Staub, R.E. Peers as human sexuality outreach educators in the campus community. *Journal of American College Health Associations*, 1976, **24**, 290–293.

Bernard, H.S. and Schwartz, A.J. Impact of a human sexuality program on sex related knowledge, attitudes, behavior, and guilt of college undergraduates. *Journal of American College Health Associations*, 1977, **25**, 182–185.

Campbell, K. and Barnlund, D.C. Communication patterns and problems of pregnancy. *American Journal of Orthopsychiatry*, 1977, **47**, 134–139.

Cvetkovitch, G., et al. On the psychology of adolescents' use of contraceptives. *Journal of Sex Research*, 1975 **11**, 256–270.

Cvetkovich, G., Grote, B., Lieberman, E.J., and Miller, W. Sex role development and teenage fertility-related behavior. *Adolescence*, 1978, **13**, 231–236.

Daily, E. and Nicholas, N. Use of conception control methods before pregnancy terminating in a birth or a requested abortion in New York City municipal hospitals. *American Journal of Public Health,* 1972, **62**, 1544–1545.

Delamater, J. and Maccorquodale, P. Premarital contraceptive use: A test of two models. *Journal of Marriage and the Family*, 1978, 135–247.

Delcampo, R.L., Sporakowski, M.J., and Delcampo, D.S. Premarital sexual permissiveness and contraceptive knowledge: A biracial comparison of college students. *Journal of Sex Research*, 1976, **12**, 180–192.

Dembo, M.H. and Lundell, B. Factors affecting adolescent contraception practices: Implications for sex education. *Adolescence*, 1979, **14**, 21–30.

Dickens, H.O., Mudd, E.H., and Higgins, G.R. Teenagers, contraception, and pregnancy. *Journal of Marriage and Family Counseling*, 1975, 175–181.

Dickinson, G. Adolescent sex information sources: 1964–1974. *Adolescence*, 1978, **52**, 653–657.

Evans, J.R., Selstad, G., and Welcher, W.H. Teenagers: Fertility control behavior and attitudes before and after abortion, childbearing, or negative pregnancy test. *Family Planning Perspectives*, 1976, **8**, 192–200.

Goldsmith, S., Gabrielson, M.O., and Gabrielson, I. Teenagers, sex and contraception. *Family Planning Perspectives*, 1972, **4**, 32–38.

Grinder, R.E. and Schmitt, S.S. Coeds and contraceptive information. *Journal of Marriage and the Family,* 1966, **28**, 471–479.

Hornick, J.P. Premarital sexual attitudes and behavior. *The Sociological Quarterly*, 1978, **19**, 534–544.

Hottois, J. and Milner, N.A. *The Sex Education Controversy*. Lexington, Mass.: D.C. Heath, 1975.

Jekel, J.F. Primary or secondary prevention of adolescent pregnancies? *Journal of School Health*, 1977, **47**, 457–461.

Kantner, J. and Zelnik, M. Contraception and pregnancy: Experiences of young unmarried women in the U.S. *Family Planning Perspectives*, 1973, **5**, 21–35.

Lindemann, C. *Birth Control and Unmarried Young Women*. New York: Springer, 1974.

Marinoff, S.C. Contraception in adolescents. *Pediatric Clincs of North America*, 1972, **19**, 811–819.

McCreary-Juhasz, A. How accurate are student evaluations of the extent of their knowledge of human sexuality? *Journal of School Health*, 1967, **37**, 409–412.

Menken, J. The health and social consequences of teenage childbearing. *Family Planning Perspectives*, 1972, **4**, 45–53.

Morris, L. Estimating the need for planning services among unwed teenagers. *Family Planning Perspectives*, 1974, **6**, 91–97.

Mudd, E.H., Dickens, H.O., Garcia, C., Freeman, E., Huggins, G.R., and Logan J.J. Adolescent health services and contraceptive use. *American Journal of Orthopsychiatry*, 1978, **48**, 495–504.

Needle, R.H. Factors affecting contraceptive practices of high-school and college-age students. *Journal of School Health*, 1977, **24**, 106–111.

Olson, L. Social and psychological correlates of pregnancy resolution among adolescent women: A review. *American Journal of Orthopsychiatry*, 1980, **50**, 432–445.

Phipps-Yonas, S. Teenage pregnancy and motherhood: A review of the literature. *American Journal of Orthopsychiatry*, 1980, **50**, 403–431.

Presser, H.B. Social consequences of teenage childbearing. In W. Peterson and L. Day (Eds.), *Social Demography: The State of the Art*, Cambridge: Harvard University Press, 1977.

Rainwater, L. *Family Design*. Chicago: Aldine Publishing Co., 1965.

Rees, B. and Zimmerman, S. The effects of formal sex education on the sexual behaviors and attitudes of college students. *Journal of the American College Association*, 1974, **22**, 370–371.

Reichelt, P.A. Changes in sexual behavior among unmarried teenage women utilizating oral contraception. *Journal of Population*, 1978, **1**, 57–68.

Reichelt, P.A. The desirability of involving adolescents in sex education planning. *Journal of School Health*, 1977, 99–103.

Reichelt, P.A. and Werley, H.H. A sex information program for sexually active teenagers. *Journal of School Health*, 1975, **45**, 100–107.

Reichelt, P.A. and Werley, H.H. Contraception, abortion, and V.D. *Family Planning Perspectives*, 1976, **7**, 83–88.

Reiss, I.L., Banwart, A., and Foreman, H. Premarital contraceptive usage: A study and some theoretical explorations. *Journal of Marriage and the Family*, 1975, **37**, 619–630.

Schinke, S.P. and Gilchrist, L.D. Adolescent pregnancy: an interpersonal skill training approach to prevention. *Social Work in Health Care*, 3 (2), Winter 1977.

Settlage, S.F., Beroff, S., and Cooper, D. Sexual experience of younger teenage girls seeking contraception assistance for the first time. *Family Planning Perspectives*, 1973, **5**, 223–226.

Shah, F., Zelnik, M., and Kantner, J. Unprotected intercourse among unwed teenagers. *Family Planning Perspectives*, 1975, **7**, 39–44.

Snyder, E.E. and Spreitzer, E. Social correlates of attitudes toward sex education. *Education*, 1975, **96**, 222–225.

Sorensen, R. *Adolescent Sexuality in Contemporary America*. New York: World Publishers, 1973.

Spanier, G.B. Sex education and premarital sexual behavior among American college students. *Adolescence*, 1978, **13**, 659–674.

Thompson, L. and Spanier, G.B. Influence of parents, peers, and partners on the contraceptive use of college men and women. *Journal of Marriage and the Family*, 1978, 481–490.

Weichmann, G.H. and Ellis, A.L. A study of the effects of sex education on premarital petting and coital behavior. *Family Coordinator*, 1969, **18**, 231–234.

Zabin, L.S., Kantner, J.F., and Zelnik, M. The risk of adolescent pregnancy in the first months of intercourse. *Family Planning Perspectives*, 1979, **11**, 215–222.

Zelnik, M. Sex education and knowledge of pregnancy risk among U.S. teenage women. *Family Planning Perspectives*, 1979, **11**, 355–357.

Zelnik, M. Second pregnancies to premaritally pregnant teenagers. *Family Planning Perspectives*, 1980, **12**, 69–76.

Zelnik, M. and Kantner, J.F. Sexual and contraceptive experiences of young unmarried women in the U.S.: 1976 and 1971. *Family Planning Perspectives*, 1977, **9**, 55–71.

Zelnik, M. and Kantner, J.F. First pregnancies to women aged 15–19: 1976 and 1971. *Family Planning Perspectives*, 1978, **10**, 11–20. (a)

Zelnik, M. and Kantner, J.F. Contraceptive patterns and premarital pregnancy among women aged 15–19 in 1976. *Family Planning Perspectives*, 1978(b), **10**, 135–142.

Zelnik, M. and Kantner, J.F. Reasons for non-use of contraception by sexually-active women aged 15–19. *Family Planning Perspectives*, 1979, **11**, 289–296.

Zelnik, M., Kim, Y.J., and Kantner, J.F. Probabilities of intercourse and conception among U.S. teenage women, 1971–1976. *Family Planning Perspectives*, 1979, **11**, 177–183.

9.
Adolescent Contraceptive Behavior: Influences and Implications

Mary J. Rogel, Ph.D.

Martha E. Zuehlke, M.D.
Michael Reese Hospital and Medical Center,
Laboratory for the Study of Adolescence,
Chicago, Ill.

Factors associated with adolescent use and nonuse of contraception can be categorized in terms of demographic characteristics, intrapsychic factors (e.g., knowledge, attitudes, experiences, developmental stage, personality characteristics), and interpersonal factors. Examining these various factors, it is clear that no single factor or specific group of factors can adequately explain or predict adolescent contraceptive behavior. The relative importance of demographic, intrapsychic, and interpersonal factors varies across populations; and even within apparently similar populations, researchers report contradictory or disparate findings.

Keeping in mind a biopsychosocial developmental perspective helps to make sense out of this complexity. The factors being considered are both difficult to measure and not highly intercorrelated. Yet they are informative when considered as part of a matrix of life experiences through which the adolescent filters life experiences, which in turn influence the matrix. Thus, to understand adolescent contraceptive behavior, one would ideally consider each adolescent individually. As that is not often possible, an alternative is to focus on subpopulations of adolescents when developing interventions. An intervention that addresses real concerns of the target population is likely to be more effective than one that addresses concerns identified from a national or other large sample.

We describe one such attempt to develop an intervention program grounded in the unique characteristics and needs of a target population. The Young Adult and Adolescent Decision Making About Contraception (YADMAC) Project at Michael Reese Hospital and Medical Center in Chicago was developed to address the factors identified as important for contraceptive use, particularly first contraceptive use, in a target population of low-income, central-city residents at high risk for adolescent pregnancy. These factors are described along with the intervention based upon them. Special emphasis is placed on primary prevention. Thus our goal is to increase the number of adolescent girls using contraception before the occurrence of an unintended pregnancy (an issue of "recruitment"). However, we also address the need to continue and improve contraceptive use (an issue of "retention").

The fact of increasing teenage pregnancy and childbearing has been well documented. Efforts at ameliorating the negative consequences of teenaged childbearing are beginning to be successful (Bennett and Bardon, 1977); Schweitzer and Youngs, 1976). However, the more difficult task of primary prevention has not been as successful in delaying youthful childbearing as prenatal programs have been in improving their pregnancy outcomes. In this chapter we examine factors contributing to the use and nonuse of contraception by teenagers, and explore the implications of this information for the development of primary prevention programs to improve contraceptive use and reduce unintended pregnancies among teenagers.

INFLUENCES ON ADOLESCENT CONTRACEPTIVE USE

Cross-sectional and descriptive studies have been very helpful in identifying factors influencing teenage contraceptive use. Predictive longitudinal studies and qualitative investigations have deepened our understanding of why teens do or do not contracept. The factors that these studies have identified as being associated with adolescent contraceptive use can be categorized along several dimensions: demographic characteristics; intrapsychic factors, including knowledge, attitudes, experiences, developmental stage, and personality characteristics; and interpersonal factors. We omit discussion of external factors, such as geographic availability of contraceptive services.

Demographic Characteristics

Gender is the most outstanding demographic predictor of contraceptive behavior among teenagers, just as it is among adults. Our current cultural bias that contraception is the female's responsibility is reflected both in the preponderance of female over male contraceptive methods available, and in the relative absence of males as research subjects in studies of contraceptive attitude and use. In spite of an apparent convergence in rates of female and male sexual activity (MacCorquodale, in press), the disparity between male and female adolescents' contraceptive activity remains significant (Scales, 1977).

Studies that have looked at adolescent male contraceptors report mixed results. Finkel and Finkel (1978) reported that most of their male subjects did not take effective precautions against pregnancy at their last coitus prior to completing the questionnaire. More than half relied on withdrawal or douche or used nothing.

Cvetkovich et al. (1978) reported that about a third of the 16–17 year old males in their study used birth control because of their positive and responsible attitudes toward contraception. These males were aware of the risks of pregnancy with unprotected coitus and perceived birth control as available and convenient. Vadies and Hale (1977) suggested that more young males are coming to view contraception as a dual responsibility rather than only the responsibility of the female. This is fortunate in light of the finding by Cvetkovich and Grote (unpublished manuscript) that initiation and consistency of contraceptive use is strongly affected by the male's participation in the decision, except when the female partner was already using the pill, diaphragm, or IUD. The importance of the male's contribution to effective contraception stands in sharp contrast to societal messages that discourage them from participating in family planning (Scales, 1977).

When race and ethnic background were taken into account, Finkel and Finkel (1978) found that more black and Hispanic than white male teenagers used ineffective or no contraception. However, this may be explained by the greater use of reliable methods by their black or Hispanic female partners. A similar finding was reported by Zelnik and Kantner (1978): In their survey, more white teenagers than black teenagers used contraception on the occasion of first intercourse, but black teenagers were more likely to use the more effective medical methods (pill, IUD, and diaphragm) if they used any method. Since the medical methods are female methods, the male partners of teenage girls using these methods may tend to be lax in their contraceptive efforts.

Mindick, Oskamp, and Berger (1978) found no racial differences and no other meaningful social-demographic differences (e.g., age, income, religious preference) in the percentage of female contraceptive clinic users who returned as scheduled 6 months after beginning a contraceptive program (returning contraceptors) and those who did not return or who were unintentionally pregnant (problem contraceptors). Rogel et al. (1980b) similarly reported that none of the demographic variables they examined was a significant predictor of the timing of first contraceptive use.

Kantner and Zelnik (1973) identified household composition as another demographic variable predictive of contraceptive use. Teenage girls who lived alone or in father-absent households were more likely to contracept than those who lived with their fathers. However, Rogel et al. (1980b) did not find this to be a significant predictor in their sample.

While age is often linked theoretically to effectiveness of contraceptive use, there seems to be no real relationship between current age and use of birth control (Cvetkovich et al. 1978; Rogel et al., 1980). However, there may be a relationship between age at first intercourse and first use of contraception. Cvetkovich et al. (1978) reported that girls who were 16 years or older at first intercourse were better current contraceptors than girls who had first intercourse at age 15 or younger. Zelnik and Kantner (1977) reported that older girls were more likely than younger girls to use contraception at the time of first intercourse or within 1 year. Yet Rogel et al. (1980b) found that age at first intercourse was not a statistically significant predictor of first contraceptive use in their sample. Perhaps age is correlated with another factor that does predict how soon after first intercourse a girl will start using contraception. An explanation suggested by Cvetkovich et al. (1978), but not directly tested, is that this factor is psychological maturity.

Intrapsychic Factors

A wide range of intrapsychic factors has been associated with contraceptive use among female adolescents. These factors include knowledge, attitudes, and experience related to sex, birth control, and pregnancy; developmental factors or psychological maturity; and personality characteristics.

Knowledge, Attitudes, and Experience. Poor knowledge about sexual functioning and contraceptive alternatives is frequently identified as a factor in poor contraceptive behavior (Delcampo, Sporakowski, and Delcampo, 1976; Kantner and Zelnik, 1973; Meara, 1979; Mindick and Oskamp, 1977; Mindick, Oskamp, and Berger, 1978; Reichelt and Werley, 1976; Shah, Zelnik, and Kantner, 1975; Zelnik and Kantner, 1977). Among adolescents, misconceptions abound as to the safe time of the month, the birth process, age at which girls become fertile, and effective birth-control methods (Goldsmith et al., 1972; Shah, Zelnik, and Kantner, 1977).

Even among those teenagers who understand the need for contraception, many do not have accurate information (Diamond et al., 1973), and those who have access to the most complete information about birth control do not necessarily contracept well (Cvetkovich et al., 1975). Cvetkovich and Grote (1977) found no differences in knowledge about sex and contraception between good and poor contraceptive users. They also found that all of the sexually active youth shared similar kinds and numbers of myths. Evans, Selstad, and Welcher (1976) reported that even with motivating experiences such as a pregnancy scare, their teenagers often did not improve their contraceptive knowledge or use. The problem is clearly more complicated than simply lack of information.

Attitudes and experience related to sexual functioning also play a part in contraceptive behavior. In Mindick et al. (1978) returning contraceptors were less proud or happy about their first periods, were older at first coitus, had

had fewer partners, and expected to have intercourse less frequently in the coming month than the problem contraceptors. The returning contraceptors felt that the advantages of contraception outweighed the disadvantages and that contraception is effective in preventing pregnancy. They were more negative about pregnancy and more willing to stand up to disapproving peers and partners. Problem contraceptors were more likely than returning contraceptors to believe that oral contraceptives cause future infertility and that if teenage boys do not have sex when they "need" it, "they can almost go crazy."

The costs of using contraception may themselves be considered high. Many teenagers discontinue their birth-control method, or do not use birth control, because they fear unpleasant or dangerous side effects (Ager, Shea, and Agronow, 1979) while they do not express such fear about pregnancy. Many also discontinue contracepting altogether after experiencing undesirable side effects from a particular method (Ager et al, 1979). Similarly, Rogel et al. (1979) reported that the girls in their sample were reluctant to use contraception, which to them meant the pill, because of fears about its safety and side effects.

Interestingly, Zelnik and Kantner (1977) reported that girls who do not use birth control at first intercourse begin contracepting with a more effective method. This finding cannot be explained by age differences or by experience with pregnancy. Instead, it seems to be related to commitment to being sexually active. The less invested a girl is in sexual activity, the less likely she is to contracept and the more likely that contraception, if used, will be a male method.

Developmental and Personality Factors. The general consensus is that most teenagers who become pregnant are not pregnant intentionally. Indeed, more often it seems that they are pregnant from a failure to decide (Campbell, Townes, and Beach, 1975). Some have attributed this to the immature thought patterns of adolescents who are unable to tolerate delaying gratification or to think abstractly, especially in terms of future consequences (Cobliner, 1974; Crider, 1976; Pannor, Evans, and Massarik, 1971). Adelson (1975) reports that young adolescents rarely reason in cost-benefit terms, instead making their choices arbitrarily and impulsively. Hatcher (1973) found that a girl's experience of sexuality and pregnancy is greatly influenced by whether she is in early, middle, or late adolescence, indicating some changes in emotional and cognitive functioning during these years. It seems that those girls best able to use their experiences for positive growth are those who are already closest to maturity. These researchers assert that adolescents are poor contraceptors because their cognitive processes lead to unrealistic thinking, general lack of planning, and consequent risk taking (Cobliner, 1974; Hill, 1973).

Goldsmith et al. (1972) reported that those who feel they have more individual control over events in their lives are more likely to use birth control. Similarly, Mindick et al. (1978) reported that their returning contraceptors were more internal-oriented than the problem contraceptors on certain items, that they reported greater independence from social influences by friends and male partners, and that they had longer future-time perspectives. Cvetkovich et al. (1975) suggested that a "certain amount of individual differentiation is needed for effective contraceptive activity." (p.261)

Personal ambitions appear to be related to effective contraception by adolescents. Jekel, Klerman, and Bancroft (1973) reported that already-pregnant girls who stayed in school were less likely to become pregnant again by 15 months postpartum compared to those outside of school. Goldsmith et al. (1972) compared a contracepting group to maternity-home residents and abortion patients, and found that the contraceptors were "significantly more oriented toward higher education and the postponement of marriage." (p. 33).

Luker (1975) points out that numerous subjective factors may influence the psychologically healthy individual's behavior regarding pregnancy and contraception. Many independent adult women find it psychologically costly to use birth control. It may be even more costly for a younger person, still financially and emotionally dependent upon the family and insecure about the relatively new experience of romantic relationships. The use of contraception forces one to admit his or her sexuality, something many young people are not comfortable doing. Goldsmith et al. (1972) indicated that acceptance of one's own sexuality is a more important correlate of contraceptive use than other factors, such as exposure to sex education, knowledge of sex and contraception, and religious background. Ambivalence about acknowledging one's sexuality has been reported to interfere with successful contraception (Goldsmith et al., 1972; Rains, 1971; Baldwin, 1976). Risking pregnancy may be less psychologically stressful than admitting sexuality by contracepting.

Decision-making analyses of teenage contraceptive behavior provide important insights into why some teenagers contracept and others do not, and into what factors might affect the initiation of contraception. Cvetkovich (1980) compared the costs to first sex partners of using female-dependent medical methods to those of using the male-dependent condom. The personal, psychosocial, and financial costs to a teenager of obtaining the more effective female methods are considerable, especially compared to the costs of obtaining the condom; yet using the condom exacts a higher set of costs in that its use requires communication between the participants, while the use of female methods does not. Thus, the nature of the relationship and the girl's estimation of her personal risk of pregnancy affect whether and which contraceptive method will be used.

Rogel et al. (1980a) also applied a decision-making approach to explain why the girls in their sample tended to be poor contraceptors. They found that many of the girls considered the costs of contracepting to be higher than the costs of unintended pregnancy. Their poor knowledge of contraceptive alternatives, and their perception that opportunities for intercourse came up unexpectedly, made it difficult for them to be effective decision makers.

Interpersonal Factors

With whom and how the adolescent interacts with others, especially about sex-related topics, has a great impact on opinions and behavior. Several investigators have found that the attitudes of and interactions with parents, or the closest relative, affect contraceptive behavior. Jorgensen (1973) reported that the impact of the young girl's closest relative is more important than any other factor in her discontinuation of contraception. After studying 337 unmarried black teens, Furstenberg (1976) concluded that their experience with contraception was related to the way their mothers viewed sex. He also found that even limited instruction from the mother had a positive impact on the daughter's use of contraception. His finding is corroborated by Rogel et al. (1980b), who reported that knowledge of parents' experience with birth control was predictive of the daughter's use, independent of what that experience was. Sexually active girls who did not contracept did not know what their parents' experience had been.

Though communication is beneficial when it occurs, Torres (1978) found that if teenagers were required to inform their parents of their clinic attendance, many of them would stop attending the clinic. A substantial number would thus engage in unprotected intercourse.

The peer group seems to be particularly influential in the teenager's sexual life and to serve as a major source of information (Thornburg, 1972; Gebhard, 1977). Adolescents express concerns with the group's opinion about their sexual performance (Finkel and Finkel, 1975), and Spanier (1977) reports that the amount of sexual activity is influenced by peers. Mindick et al.'s (1978) returning contraceptors were more independent of the influences of peers and partners, while problem contraceptors turned to their friends for information and had more sexually experienced girl friends. Rogel et al. (1980a) also note the importance of modeling, since almost all of the girls in their sample, who were at high risk for unintended pregnancy, knew someone who had been pregnant as a teenager and who kept the baby. They also reported that the girls experienced strong internal and external pressures to keep the baby once they became pregnant, even though they believed that their significant others disapproved of teenage parenting.

How adolescents communicate with their sexual partners is also a factor determining sexual activity and contraceptive use (Cvetkovich, 1980; Scales, 1977). Female teenagers reported that they became sexually active because they could not say no, they wanted to please their boyfriends, or they felt it was expected of them (Cvetkovich and Grote, 1977). The males also reported difficulties communicating about sexual matters. Discussing the use of birth control before first coitus is very strongly related to actual use of birth control both at first coitus and for the duration of the relationship (Cvetkovich and Grote, unpublished manuscript). Campbell and Barnlund (1977) found significant differences in interpersonal communication patterns between never pregnant women and women who had had two or more unplanned pregnancies. They concluded that the problem of unplanned pregnancies is in part a problem of communication.

Conclusion

It is clear that to date no single factor or specific group of factors has been found that can adequately explain or predict adolescent contraceptive behavior. Within varied populations the relative importance of demographic, intrapsychic, and interpersonal influences varies such that no clear-cut conclusions can be drawn that have relevance for the adolescent population at large. Even within apparently similar populations, researchers report contradictory or disparate findings.

One way to understand this complexity is to keep in mind a developmental perspective. Personality and developmental characteristics are not easily measured, nor do they precisely correlate with age, gender, or experience. However, they do serve as a matrix through which life experiences are filtered, and may, therefore, be the primary factors that determine how particular demographic or interpersonal factors influence a given individual at a given point in time. Life experiences influence maturation at the same time that the meaning and import of life experiences are influenced by the level of psychological and physical maturation.

In assessing the relevant factors associated with contraceptive behavior in a given population, one must bear in mind the complete interplay of external and internal factors uniquely applicable to those adolescents' sexual and contraceptive behavior, so as to be most effective in utilizing interventions built around their demographic, intrapsychic, and interpersonal characteristics.

DEVELOPING PRIMARY PREVENTION PROGRAMS

While the influences on adolescent contraceptive use are obviously complex, it is possible to begin to untangle the factors affecting contraceptive use within a specific subpopulation. We feel that a primary intervention program that is to be effective must address the particular factors influencing behavior in its target audience, as well as addressing the more general factors affecting adolescent contraceptive use.

To illustrate how one can develop such a primary prevention program, we describe how we used information about our target population to develop the Young Adult and Adolescent Decision Making About Contraception (YAD-MAC) Project, a program designed to improve contraceptive use among teenage girls at high risk for unintended pregnancy. We are currently in the process of empirically evaluating the program's effectiveness.

We have used a three-stage process to develop and test the YADMAC Project. We began with an information-gathering survey of our target population. The purpose of the survey was twofold: (1) to help us better understand the teenagers and aspects of their lives especially relevant to contraception and childbearing; and (2) to inform the intervention. In Phase II, we used the information gathered in the survey to develop a curriculum. During Phase II we also trained a team of peer leaders and pilot-tested the project. Phase III is the experimental evaluation of the program.

THE YADMAC PROJECT

The theoretical framework of our study is based, in part, on Luker's (1975) study of adult abortion clinic patients to discover why they had become pregnant. Viewing behavior as rational and as drawing meaning from its context, Luker examined contraceptive use as the outcome of a cost-benefit process in which using contraception entails certain costs and benefits as does getting pregnant. Luker found that the women in her sample took chances and risked unwanted pregnancy when both their estimates of the costs of contraception and of the benefits of getting pregnant were high.

We were interested to learn whether teenagers engage in the same type of cost/benefit analyzing and risk-taking with respect to contraception and pregnancy. Hypothesizing that teenagers are not all that different from the older women studied by Luker, we found that a cost/benefit approach does provide some insight into why the teenagers in our target population became pregnant.

Characteristics of the Target Population

This study was undertaken because members of the Department of Obstetrics and Gynecology at Michael Reese Hospital and Medical Center were concerned about the number of teens having repeat deliveries and abortions (about 30 percent of the pregnant teenagers seen at the Medical Center). We thus identified our target population as the teenage girls in the catchment area for the Medical Center.

In the Phase I survey we interviewed 120 girls aged 12–19 who came to three clinics (Teen Family Planning, Prenatal, and Pediatric Acute Care) at the Medical Center between April and August 1979. The Acute Care Clinic was included so that we could have a comparison group of girls who had not come to the Medical Center for reproductive reasons. Using a semistructured interview protocol, we gathered information concerning demographic characteristics, intrapsychic factors, and interpersonal relationships. The sample reflected the South Side area in which the Medical Center is located, rather than the patient population it actually serves. Almost 87 percent of our subjects lived within 1 hour's travel time of the Medical Center by public transportation, and 98 percent were black.

Demographic Characteristics. The mean age for the girls in the survey sample was 16.6 years; and most of the girls we interviewed were 14 years and older. Religion and education were valued by most of the girls. The majority wanted to finish high school at least, and many of those who were not in school had already graduated. Family incomes were low, with families supported by welfare and/or by a wage-earner. Number of persons in the home ranged from 1 to 13 people, with 3 to 7 people in three-quarters of the families. While most of the girls lived with their mothers and not with their fathers, many of them had regular contact with their fathers. Four of the girls were married, and one had been previously married.

The girls in this sample, and in the target population, represent a group of teenagers at high risk for pregnancy while still teenagers. According to a recent Planned Parenthood report (MacClarence, no date), the areas of the city from which our sample was drawn had some of the highest adolescent birth rates in the city during 1976. MacClarence also noted that the rate of sexual activity is high in the population we have targeted. Thus, an understanding of why the teenagers do and do not contracept, and why they elect to carry their pregnancies to term, is essential to the development of an effective intervention program.

Intrapsychic Factors: Knowledge, Attitudes, and Experience. Because of our sampling procedure, the majority of girls were sexually active, as defined by having had intercourse at least once. Among sexually active girls, age at first intercourse ranged from a high of 18 years to a low of 9 years; the median age was 14.9 years old. First intercourse generally was not overtly planned. Over half of the girls had had only one sexual partner (who was often the current partner), and few had had more than three partners. They reported rather egalitarian sexual relationships, the majority saying that they and their boyfriends decided equally when to have sex. Those not deciding equally were split evenly between girls who said that they decided, and those who said that their boyfriends made the decision.

Though our sample does not seem to differ from a national probability sample of black teenagers in rate of sexual activity (Rogel et al., 1980a), their reported level of activity compared to older populations was very low. Whereas older populations report a minimum coital average of about twice per week (Kinsey, 1953; Ryder and Westoff, 1971), during the 2 months preceding the interview, one quarter of the sexually active girls had not had intercourse, and about half had had intercourse less than once a week. Intercourse was even less frequent when girls who were not currently pregnant were considered separately.

Though the girls reported sporadic intercourse, they also reported primarily positive attitudes about their sexual relationships. The majority reported that they never felt awkward or embarrassed when they had sex, that they never felt guilty about it, that having sex strengthened their relationships, that they looked forward to having sex, and that they felt good when they had sex. Yet, a large majority reported frequently feeling that sex had been forced upon them.

Of the 101 sexually active girls, pregnancy status ranged from 25 who had never been pregnant to one who was pregnant for the fourth time. Fully three-quarters of the sexually active girls had been, or were currently, pregnant. Allowing for differences created by our sampling procedure, the rate of pregnancy does not seem to differ from that in a national probability sample of black teenagers (Rogel et al., 1980a). The median age at first pregnancy was 15.6 years old, and 81 percent of first pregnancies occurred by age 17. Almost 44 percent of the ever-pregnant girls became pregnant for the first time within 1 year of becoming sexually active, and 93 percent became pregnant within 3 years of becoming sexually active. More than one quarter of the girls already had their desired number of children or would with the current pregnancy. Yet, of the girls who became pregnant, only four had wanted to become pregnant.

The high incidence of sexual activity and pregnancy in this sample raises the question of contraceptive use. The median age at which girls in this sample first used birth control was 15.8 years, almost identical to the median age at first pregnancy. The range of ages at first contraceptive use was broad, however, with some of the sexually active girls reporting use of birth control *prior* to first intercourse and others reporting never having used birth control. Over half had used birth control within 1 year of first intercourse.

The birth-control method most frequently used (ever and currently) was the pill. For most of the girls "birth control" meant "the pill," which they called "birth controls." They had little knowledge or experience with other methods of contraception. Abstinence was the second most popular method of birth control being used at the time of the interview.

Though most girls could correctly answer only two or three of six knowledge questions about birth control, the majority assessed their chances of getting pregnant when not using birth control as "very likely" or "a sure thing." The girls from the Pediatric Acute Care Clinic were least knowledgeable about their chances of getting pregnant. Yet one-third of the sexually active girls and close to twice as many of those who were not pregnant reported never using birth control.

The most frequent reasons for not using birth control fell into a category we call "abdicated responsibility." Examples include "just took a chance" and "didn't expect to have intercourse." Concerns about the safety and side effects of birth control were also mentioned frequently. These concerns were clearly directed toward the pill.

The reasons given by girls in our sample for not using contraception were somewhat different from those reported by Shah et al. (1975) for the 1971 national survey. The girls in their sample cited low risk of pregnancy as the major reason for not using birth control, whereas the girls in our sample cited fear of safety or side effects, just taking a chance, or being unprepared because intercourse was not expected. About two-thirds of our sample were concerned about safety and side effects, but only one-fifth of their sample were.

The girls in our sample had a better sense of their chances of becoming pregnant during unprotected intercourse compared to girls in the 1971 national survey (Kantner and Zelnik, 1973). Yet contraceptive use was poor in our sample. Usage levels for the pill were similar in both samples, but use of all other methods was lower in our sample than in the 1971 sample.

Intrapsychic Factors: Developmental and Personality Factors. In general, the girls tended to be moderately high in self-esteem as measured by the Rosenberg Self-Esteem Scale (1965), scoring higher than several comparison groups of teenagers (Rogel et al., 1980a). The girls' mean score on health-related locus of control (HLC) (Wallston et al., 1976) indicated a somewhat external orientation. Persons with external orientations tend to feel that they are ineffective agents in bringing about rewards for their own behavior.

Though the girls tended to be external in their expectations, about two-thirds disagreed or strongly disagreed with the statement, "Whether or not a girl gets pregnant depends mostly on luck," while about one-third were undecided or agreed. Neither did they equate womanhood and motherhood: most disagreed or strongly disagreed with the statement, "Having a baby makes a girl a real woman."

Most described their problem-solving style as active—doing something to solve the problem rather than letting their problems solve themselves. About half reported discussing their problems with their friends, though only a quarter said they and their friends think alike.

The decision-making approach gives us an appreciation of how the girls might view their own experiences. If we consider contraception and physical intimacy to be the balancing factors in a cost/benefit ratio, we see that both the costs of contraception and the benefits of physical intimacy are high. Furthermore, the opportunities for physical intimacy present themselves "unexpectedly," and the consequences of being pregnant are not seen as necessarily negative. Rather than pass up the opportunity for physical intimacy, many opt for taking their chances on not getting pregnant.

The perceived costs of contraception are inflated by the fact that many girls equate "birth control" and "the pill." They have almost no knowledge or experience with other methods of birth control. Therefore, their perceived options are severely limited. They recognize the pill as an effective contraceptive but are afraid to use it. Because they know so little about other methods, and consider those they know ineffective, they take their chances instead.

While the girls acknowledged that having unprotected intercourse carries a high risk of pregnancy, they do not seem to plan ahead enough to be prepared. Pregnancy seems to be something that "happens" to them, just as opportunities for intercourse "happen." This perspective is congruent with their tendency to be externally oriented on health-related locus of control. At the same time, they have many models for teenage parenting, and once they become pregnant they perceive a great deal of internal and external pressure to carry the pregnancy to term and keep the baby. They are morally opposed to abortion and consider raising the baby on welfare to be a more acceptable alternative. Further, they perceive their parents, boyfriends, and other important persons as agreeing with them. Thus, pregnancy seems to be an unintended, but acceptable, outcome of being sexually active.

Another factor encouraging risk-taking is the sporadic nature of their sexual activity and the feeling that, "If I can make it just this once, I'll be better prepared next time." For many girls, the "failure to decide" about birth control and pregnancy may actually represent the conflict they feel over: (1) their negative valuation of contraception (the pill); (2) their positive valuation of physical intimacy with their boyfriends; and (3) their ambivalent feelings about pregnancy.

Interpersonal Factors. In general, the girls considered themselves rather independent of their peers, saying that they stick with the group only some or none of the time. While interviewing, we were struck by the number of girls who volunteered that they had no friends or did not care what their friends thought.

The majority of girls reported their relationships with their families and with their mothers to be generally good. Over half expected that their lives would be somewhat or very much like their mothers' in about 15 years.

The majority of unmarried girls had a boyfriend at the time of the survey. Most had known their boyfriends or husbands for over a year and saw them daily or several times a week. These figures suggest that their relationships were relatively stable. When questioned about their future plans most thought that they would marry someday, although a sizable minority thought that they would not or were not sure.

The girls perceived their parents (usually mothers), boyfriends, and friends to be more in favor of birth control than they were themselves. They also reported the largest proportion of their parents and boyfriends as believing that, "any woman should be allowed to have an abortion." Their own attitude choices concerning abortion were evenly distributed among the four categories provided.

Yet the girls who had been, or were currently, pregnant reported themselves wanting an abortion more frequently than they thought their parents, boyfriends, or friends wanted them to. The ever-pregnant girls perceived others as wanting them to keep the baby as much or more than they themselves wanted to. Thus, they experienced a great deal of external pressure to carry their pregnancies to term. Most of this perceived pressure came from families and boyfriends rather than girl friends.

In addition to this perceived pressure, the girls seemed to have many models for adolescent pregnancy and childbearing. Most of the girls had a close friend who had been pregnant, and all knew someone close (friend, sister, other relative) who had been pregnant. Most of these close persons, the majority of whom were friends, kept their babies. Over half of the girls had sisters who had been pregnant, and almost all of the sisters had kept their babies. Further, most believed that their mothers and sisters had never had an abortion and had never had a baby who was raised by someone else.

Factors Affecting First Contraceptive Use

To understand the relative importance of demographic variables, intrapsychic factors, and interpersonal relationships on first use of contraception by girls in our target population, we performed a separate multiple regression analysis with variables from the survey that were related to timing of first contraceptive use, measured as time after first intercourse (Rogel et al., 1980b).

Intrapsychic and interpersonal factors were most predictive of how soon after first intercourse the girls began contracepting. The most important influence on the timing of first contraceptive use was the girl's own belief that pregnancy depends on luck. Girls who have a feeling of control over pregnancy contracepted sooner after first intercourse.

Modeling by peers was another important factor. Girls who did not have close friends who had been pregnant began contracepting earlier. Modeling of adolescent pregnancy and childbearing by a sister also entered the regression solution, but its influence was not statistically significant.

Two other variables that did contribute significantly to the solution were knowledge of parents' and siblings' experience with birth control and judged conflict over birth control. What the girls knew about the experience of family members concerning birth control was not important. What was important was that they knew something. Girls who did not know about their family members' experiences did not contracept at all or began two to five years after first intercourse, by which time they had already had a baby. Thus it seems that modeling of birth control use by family (even when the experiences were negative) was almost as important as lack of modeling of peer teenage pregnancy in encouraging early contraception. In this context, level of conflict about birth control understandably contributed to timing of first contraception.

A sixth variable entered the regression equation but did not contribute significantly to the solution: reaction to her boyfriend's disapproval of something the girl wished to do. Girls who could solicit and take into account the opinions and beliefs of their boyfriends contracepted earlier than girls who could not. This latter group of girls tended not to contracept at all.

Using these six variables and others significantly related to timing of first contraception, we were able to distinguish three groups of girls: contraceptors, late-contraceptors, and never-contraceptors. We initially divided contraceptors into early- and middle-contraceptors, respectively, those who began contracepting prior to first intercourse or within one month, and those who began contracepting one month to one year after first intercourse. However, we could find no meaningful differences between these groups and combined them. Late-contraceptors began contracepting 2–5 years after first intercourse; never-contraceptors have never used any type of birth control. Contraceptors believed that pregnancy did not depend on luck, and they judged their chances of getting pregnant when not using birth control to be about 80 percent. They further believed that using birth control (i.e., the pill) would not effect their future fertility. The girls in these groups tended not to have friends who had been pregnant, and they took their boyfriends' opinions into account when making decisions.

The late-contraceptors were in some ways similar to the earlier contraceptors, but they also demonstrated some differences. Like the earlier contraceptors, they believed that pregnancy did not depend on luck and that using birth control (pills) would not affect their future fertility. However, they judged their chances of getting pregnant when not using birth control to be about 90 percent. This high appraisal of their fertility is likely to be related to the fact that all of the late-contraceptors had had prior pregnancies. In addition, many of them had sisters who had been pregnant, and they knew what kind of experience their siblings had had with contraception. Like the earlier contraceptors, they took into account their boyfriends' opinions. It seemed that the motivation of the late-contraceptors was to space or limit the size of their families, while the motivation of the earlier contraceptors was to prevent pregnancies.

The never-contraceptors clearly differed from the contraceptors. They were undecided about whether pregnancy depends on luck, and about how using birth control would affect their future fertility. Understandably, they were judged to be conflicted about birth control. They considered their chances of getting pregnant when not using birth control to be only about 65 percent, and they did not know what kind of experiences their parents and siblings had had with contraception. Furthermore, they failed to take their boyfriends' opinions into account when they disagreed.

We suspect that noncontracepting girls (and boys) who can be assisted in the four areas we have identified will be able to begin contracepting earlier than they would if left to their own devices. Thus, we recommend that pregnancy prevention programs focus on these four goals: (1) enhancing a sense of control over pregnancy; (2) providing accurate information about birth control; (3) mobilizing peer influences in favor of birth control; and (4) encouraging communication about contraception within the family and within the peer group.

THE YADMAC INTERVENTION

In planning and implementing the YADMAC Project, our thinking was guided by the four needs revealed as relevant in our preliminary study of our population: (1) enhancing a sense of control over pregnancy; (2) providing accurate information about sexuality and birth control; (3) mobilizing peer influence in favor of postponing childbirth; and (4) encouraging communication about sexuality and contraception within a biopsychosocial perspective on development (Zuehlke et al., in press) to ensure that the technique we utilized in the intervention would impact appropriately on these girls. The maturational tasks and capacities within each of these spheres of development—the biological, the psychological, and the social—could then be consciously considered and incorporated into the format of our program.

We selected a peer-group format for our intervention to minimize the risk-taking involved for an individual adolescent wanting some information and making use of it, and to provide a setting in which needs for belonging, intimacy, and attachment might be met (therefore perhaps reducing the drive to sexual activity motivated by these needs). In addition to the peer-group format, we selected and trained adolescent girls from our target population to serve as peer-group leaders, making the *peer* aspect of the group more salient and providing the experience of a "successful" role model for knowledge and contraceptive use.

Adult staff members regularly attend the meetings to provide parent surrogates and adult role models of conscious information seeking and associated decision making, to ensure adherence to the curriculum, and to make empirical observations for later analysis of program effectiveness.

The duration of the program was decided by balancing the needs for enough time to develop some trust and comfort within the group (i.e., establish and consolidate interpersonal ties within the group), to foster a sense of identification with the group, to allow repetition of the information and practice of associated behaviors, and to allow time to cover material of special relevance to group members. The 12-week curriculum can be completed over the summer or within one school semester, and is a time period with which adolescents are familiar. Thus the form of the intervention itself attempts to respond to specific aspects of the adolescents' biopsychosocial development and to provide a setting that could encourage and enhance the developmental process.

The content of the curriculum and the format of the sessions were also determined by the needs outlined in our study and our use of a biopsychosocial perspective on development. We had a firm grasp of the dual problems of inadequate or inaccurate information and the apparent lack of use of information to guide sexual behavior. For this reason we decided to alternate the presentation of information with putting this information to use behaviorally. Not only can this approach enhance the assimilation of the particular information, but it can serve as practice for behavior and decision making outside the group in the adolescents' daily lives. The topics covered in the curriculum (Table 9-1) were partially determined on the basis of the findings from our study and also by our use of Luker's (1975) theoretical orientation about decision-making processes. We settled on a cost-benefit orientation for both the presentation of information and for the behavioral practice to provide a framework the adolescents could use to guide their own behavior in this area of their lives. The cost-benefit perspective also speaks directly to the original finding that a sense of control over the occurrence of pregnancy is highly correlated with successful contraceptive behavior. Our thinking was that if we could make a cost-benefit perspective comprehensive and useful to adolescents, we would foster their decision-making skills and, thus, their sense of control over their lives, including their sexual lives.

The information presented is repeated at various times and in various modalities in an attempt to meet the varied cognitive levels and psychological maturity of the girls. Repetition in different modalities not only increases retention of the material, but allows opportunities for processing the information at different levels (i.e., cognitive or intellectual, personal values, emotional consolidation, behavioral adoption). The inclusion of activities such as group discussion, brainstorming, handling contraceptive materials, and participating in and observing role-plays of relevant interactions not only makes

Table 9-1. Yadmac curriculum outline.

Week 1	Introduction, preassessments Videotape of peers in role play
Week 2	Making decisions, setting goals Film and video tape
Week 3	Birth Control—I Film of methods
Week 4	Birth Control—II Guest speaker—demonstration
Week 5	Costs and Benefits—I Role plays
Week 6	Abortion Guest speaker and role plays
Week 7	Teenage Pregnancy Guest speaker and film
Week 8	Teenage Parenting Film
Week 9	Costs and Benefits—II Role plays
Week 10	Others' Opinions Members bring boyfriends to group
Week 11	Looking to the future Role plays
Week 12	Summary and postassessments Refreshments

the process a more active and therefore more meaningful one to the girls, but it provides real practice for the skills we are attempting to enhance: conscious decision making about sexuality and contraception, and behaviors consistent with the decision made. Through the activities and the discussions following them, a real decision-making experience is possible. This is what we see as the central difference between our pilot program and other sex education programs.

The YADMAC Project is a hospital-based program. In addition to the peer leaders and staff members for each group of 10–15 girls, we have utilized other adults who actually serve adolescents within the Medical Center. These professional women, by virtue of participating, provide career role models and indirectly suggest options for the girls' futures. Directly, they are used to present information and reinforce the attitude that decisions can be appropriately made and acted on to postpone pregnancy until it is desired. Introduced to the girls in this setting of nonemergent needs, and a relaxed, unhurried atmosphere, these professionals can be seen as allies and familiar faces in the often intimidating and impersonal world of medical clinics. We anticipate that adolescent girls will be more likely to visit a clinic if they know and view a staff member there as interested and friendly.

Participation in our program is limited to adolescent girls between 12 and 19 who live within the Medical Center's catchment area. It is this population that we studied to prepare the intervention program and that we are appropriately addressing. A signed consent to participate is required from parent or guardian, but parents are not allowed to join the weekly sessions. In this way we attempt to raise the topic of sexuality and contraception in a way that does not imply or suggest the adolescents' actual activity. Rather, it is hoped to model a relatively neutral discussion that the adolescents can attempt at home with their families.

At the same time, we are attempting to speak to the needs for independence and psychological separation from the family that are major adolescent developmental tasks. Along these same lines the staff members present themselves as noncritical, but operate from a clearly expressed set of values that the girls can accept or reject. While we overtly support reserving sexual activity for meaningful and mutually gratifying relationships, and using contraceptives to delay childbearing until adulthood, we acknowledge that there are positive as well as negative consequences of these choices. We see the modeling of a clear set of values, and how one makes decisions and acts on them within a value system, as an important input to these girls' own development of a set of personal and usable values from which they can make conscious decisions about their behavior. At the same time we actively engage them in attempting to clarify their own values and to use these in a cost-benefit model of decision making. To give an example of how this might work, we would initiate a discussion about being sexually active as a teenager. The discussion would focus on a cost-benefit analysis of the decision to be sexually active. We encourage active participation from all group members, listening to the varied points of view, and helping the participants grasp the range of alternative choices that become apparent in such a discussion. In this way we are attempting to model and encourage the practice of conscious decision making in the context of personal values that relate to contraceptive use.

Finally, the curriculum is organized conceptually to move from discussions of sexual intimacy to discussions of pregnancy and the various aspects and alternatives confronting a pregnant teenager, all the while dealing with these issues in the context of a specific relationship and in the context of one's overall life plans and goals. Here, again, we are attempting to address particular aspects of adolescents' cognitive, emotional, and interpersonal growth in such a way as to be developmentally appropriate, at the same time that we encourage them to enhance their maturation.

The YADMAC Project to date seems to speak to the needs of girls not yet sexually active, as well as to already sexually active girls. This is a time in their lives when they have questions and few answers. The program gives them permission to ask questions about sexuality, contraception, pregnancy, parenting, and planning for their futures. It provides a forum where they can share their questions and their decisions relating to these topics. The topics and the questions, in this setting, are no longer taboo or humiliating, so the girls can more readily think about the issues, consider alternatives, and find support for their choices or at least for making a choice.

In addition to encouraging the girls to make their own personal choices, participation in the project facilitates communication with significant others— friends, boyfriends, parents, siblings—who are not directly involved in the group. In light of our findings from our survey concerning the importance of peer influence and input about contraceptive experiences (independent of the content of that input), we are enthusiastic about this "ripple-effect." Some of the girls have taken on the role of educator among their friends at school and in their neighborhoods. Their participation in the group seems to legitimate their information as well as their position of role model for decision making in this area. This is a most gratifying and unexpected behavioral outcome.

We have described a pilot intervention founded on an assessment of the literature to date, and on a specific study of the relevant factors in a given target population. To modify a behavior such as contraceptive behavior, with multiaxial determinants, multiple foci of intervention must be included or considered in order to be effective. The girls in our program live in neighbor- hoods with some of the highest rates of adolescent pregnancy in Chicago (MacClarence, no date). Some of the highest rates of unemployment, school dropouts, state dependency, drug and alcohol abuse, and violent crime also exist in these neighborhoods. Thus we are attempting to separate out one problem among many, and to apply an intervention that may not only be effective but may have relevance to other aspects of their development into maturity. The attempt to maintain a broad view of development from a biological, psychological, and social perspective provides us with a useful structure and a hopeful outlook. We frequently remind our girls, "Not to decide is only one way of deciding—and not a very good way." We are seeing that, given an opportunity and guidance, adolescent girls can be helped to make good and appropriate decisions.

REFERENCES

Adelson, E. *Sexuality and Psychoanalysis*. New York: Brunner & Mazel, 1975.
Ager, J.W., Jr., Shea, F., and Agronow, S. Consequences of teen contraceptive program dropout and of method discontinuance. Presented at the 87th Annual

Convention of the American Psychological Association, New York, September 4, 1979.

Baldwin, W.H., Adolescent pregnancy and childbearing—growing concerns for Americans. *Population Bulletin*, 1976, **31**, 3–36.

Bennett, V.C. and Bardon, J.I. The effects of a school program on teenage mothers and their children. *American Journal of Orthopsychiatry*, 1977, **47**, 671–678.

Campbell, B.K. and Barnlund, D.C. Communication patterns and problems of pregnancy. *American Journal of Orthopsychiatry*, 1977, **47**, 134–139.

Campbell, F.L., Townes, B.D., and Beach, L.R. Counseling for childbearing: Toward a calculus of conscious choice. Unpublished manuscript, University of Washington (DK-40), Seattle, Washington, 1975.

Cobliner, W.G. Pregnancy in the single adolescent girl: The role of cognitive functions. *Journal of Youth and Adolescence*, 1974, **3**, 17–29.

Crider, E.A. School-age pregnancy, childbearing, and childrearing: A research review. Bureau of Elementary and Secondary Education, U.S. Office of Education, November 19, 1976.

Cvetkovich, G. Towards a theory of psychosocial development and fertility control. Paper presented at the Annual Meeting of the American Psychological Association, Montreal, September 1980.

Cvetkovich, G. and Grote, B. Current research on adolescence and its program implications. Paper presented at the joint meeting of the Washington State Council on Family Planning and the Washington Alliance Concerned with School Aged Parents. Olympia, Washington, September 29, 1977.

Cvetkovich, G. and Grote, B. Male teenagers—Sexual debut, psychosocial development and contraceptive use. Unpublished manuscript. Washington University.

Cvetkovich, G., Grote, B., Bjorseth, A., and Sarkissian, J. On the psychology of adolescents' use of contraceptives. *The Journal of Sex Research*, 1975, **11**, 256–270.

Cvetkovich, G., Grote, B., Lieberman, E.J., and Miller, W.B. Sex role development and teenage fertility-related behavior. *Adolescence*, 1978, **13**, 231–236.

Delcampo, R.L., Sporakowski, M.J., and Delcampo, D.S. Premarital sexual permissiveness and contraceptive knowledge: A biracial comparison of college students. *The Journal of Sex Research*, 1976, **12**, 180–192.

Diamond, M., Steinhoff, P.G., Palmore, J.A., and Smith, R.G. Sexuality, birth control and abortion: A decision-making sequence. *Journal of Biosocial Science*, 1973, **5**, 347–361.

Evans, J.R., Selstad, G., and Welcher, W.H. Teenagers: Fertility control behavior and attitudes before and after abortion, childbearing, or negative pregnancy test. *Family Planning Perspectives*, 1976, **8**, 192–200.

Finkel, M.L. and Finkel, D.J. Male adolescent contraceptive utilization. *Adolescence*, 1978, **13**, 443–451.

Finkel, M.L. and Finkel, D.J. Sexual and contraceptive knowledge, attitudes, and behavior of male adolescents. *Family Planning Perspectives*, 1975, **7**, 256–260.

Furstenberg, F.F. The social consequences of teenage parenthood. *Family Planning Perspectives*, 1976, **7**, 149–150.

Gebhard, P.H. The acquisition of basic sex information. *Journal of Sex Research*, 1977, **13**, 148–169.

Goldsmith, S., Gabrielson, M.O., Gabrielson, I., Matthews, V., and Potts, L. Teenagers, sex, and contraception. *Family Planning Perspectives*, 1972, **4**, 32–42.

Hatcher, S.L.M. The adolescent experience of pregnancy and abortion: A developmental analysis. *Journal of Youth and Adolescence*, 1973, **2**, 53–102.

Hill, J.P. *Some Perspectives on Adolescence in American Society.* Position paper prepared for the Office of Child Development. DHEW mimeographed, Washington, D.C., May 1973.

Jekel, J.F., Klerman, L.V. and Bancroft, D.R. Factors associated with rapid subsequent pregnancies among school-age mothers. *American Journal of Public Health* 1973, **63**, 769–773.

Jorgensen, V. One year contraceptive follow-up of adolescent patients. *American Journal of Obstetrics and Gynecology*, 1973, **115**, 484–486.

Kantner, J.F. and Zelnik, M. Contraception and pregnancy: Experience of young unmarried women in the United States. *Family Planning Perspectives*, 1973, **5**, 21–35.

Kinsey, A.C., Pomeroy, W.B., Martin, C.E., and Gebhard, P.H. *Sexual Behavior in the Human Female.* Philadelphia: Saunders, 1953.

Luker, K. *Taking Chances: Abortion and the Decision not to Contracept.* Berkeley: University of California Press, 1975.

MacClarence, P. A demographic analysis of adolescent fertility: The case of Chicago, Illinois, 1970–1976. In Analysis of adolescent fertility in a metropolitan area: The Chicago example. Training and Research Center, Planned Parenthood Association—Chicago Area, 55 E. Jackson Boulevard, Chicago, Illinois 60604. n.d.

MacCorquodale, P. Premarital sexual behavior of contemporary youth. *Medical Aspects of Human Sexuality* (in press).

Meara, H. Adolescent cognition and contraception. Paper presented at the Annual Meeting of the American Psychological Association, New York, September 1979.

Mindick, B. and Oskamp, S. Teenage contraceptors in metropolitan Southern California. Early results. Paper presented at the meeting of the American Psychological Association, San Francisco, August 1977.

Mindick, B., Oskamp, S., and Berger, D.E. Prediction of adolescent contraceptive practice. Paper presented at the meeting of the American Psychological Association, Toronto, August 1978.

Pannor, R., Evans, B., and Massarik, F. *The Unmarried Father, New Approaches for Helping Unmarried Parents.* New York: Springer, 1971.

Rains, P.M. *Becoming an Unwed Mother.* Chicago: Aldine, Atherton, 1971.

Reichelt, P.A. and Werley, H.H. Sex knowledge of teenagers and the effect of an educational rap session, *Journal of Research and Development in Education*, 1976, **10**, 13–22.

Rogel, M.J., Petersen, A.C., Richards, M., Shelton, M., and Zuehlke, M.E. Contraceptive behavior in adolescence: A decision-making perspective. Paper presented at the Annual Meeting of the American Psychological Association, New York, September 1979.

Rogel, M.J., Zuehlke, M.E., Petersen, A.C., Tobin-Richards, M., and Shelton, M. Contraceptive behavior in adolescence: A decision-making perspective. *Journal of Youth and Adolescence*, 1980a, **9**, 491–506.

Rogel, M.J., Zuehlke, M.E., Weiss, C., Petersen, A.C., and Shelton, M. Factors differentiating early-, middle-, late-, and never-contraceptors. Paper presented at the Annual Meeting of the American Psychological Association, Montreal, September 1980b.

Rosenberg, M. *Society and the Adolescent Self-image*. Princeton, N.J.: Princeton University Press, 1965.

Ryder, N.B. and Westoff, C.F. *Reproduction in the United States: 1965*. Princeton, N.J.: Princeton University Press, 1971.

Scales, P. Males and morals: Teen-age contraceptive behavior and the double standard. *Family Coordinator*, 1977, **26**, 211–222.

Schweitzer, B. and Youngs, D.D. A new professional role in the care of the pregnant adolescent. *Birth and the Family Journal*, 1976, **3**, 27–30.

Shah, F., Zelnik, M., and Kantner, J.F. Unprotected intercourse among unwed teenagers. *Family Planning Perspectives*, 1975, **7**, 39–44.

Spanier, G.B. Sources of sex information and pre-marital sexual behavior. *The Journal of Sex Research*, 1977, **13**, 73–88.

Thornburg, H.D. A comparative study of sex information sources. *Journal of School Health*, 1972, **42**, 88.

Torres, A. Does your mother know? *Family Planning Perspectives*, 1978, **10**, 280–282.

Vadies, E. and Hale, D. Attitudes of adolescent males toward abortion, contraception, and sexuality. *Social Work in Health Care*, 1977, **3**, 169–174.

Wallston, B.S., Wallston, K.A., Kaplan, G.D., and Maides, S.A. Development and validation of the Health Locus of Control (HLC) Scales. *Journal of Consulting and Clinical Psychology*, 1976, **44**, 580–585.

Zelnik, M. and Kantner, J.F. Contraceptive patterns and premarital pregnancy among women aged 15–19 in 1976. *Family Planning Perspectives*, 1978, **10**, 135–142.

Zelnik, M. and Kantner, J.F. Sexual and contraceptive experiences of young unmarried women in the U.S., 1976 and 1971. *Family Planning Perspectives*, 1977, **9**, 55–71.

Zuehlke, M.E., Rogel, M.J., and Petersen, A.C. Adolescent sexuality: The concerns and their treatment. Manuscript submitted for publication in Coates, T.J. (Ed.), *Behavioral Medicine: A Practical Handbook*. Research Press, in press.

Part IV
Management

10.
The Delivery-Abortion Decision Among Adolescents*

Lorraine V. Klerman, Dr. P.H.,
Associate Professor of Public Health,
The Florence Heller Graduate School for Advanced Studies in Social Welfare,
Brandeis University,
Waltham, Mass.

Michael B. Bracken, Ph.D.,
Senior Research Associate in Epidemiology, Obstetrics, and Gynecology;
Director, Perinatal Epidemiology Unit,
Yale University Medical School,
New Haven, Conn.

James F. Jekel, M.D., M.P.H.,
Professor of Public Health,
Department of Epidemiology and Public Health,
Yale University Medical School,
New Haven, Conn.

Maryann Bracken, M.A.,
Associate in Research,
Department of Pediatrics,
Yale University Medical School,
New Haven, Conn.

Therapeutic abortions were performed on over 300,000 women under the age of 20 in 1977. During the same period, almost 600,000 gave birth to live infants. Because such a large number of young women, and often their male partners and families, face decisions about the outcomes of the adolescents' pregnancies, it is important for those who advise them to be knowledgeable about the consequences of these decisions and about factors that may influence them.

Current medical research indicates that therapeutic abortion is a low-risk procedure for the pregnant adolescent, and that even multiple abortions need

*The research reported in this paper was supported by a grant from the Joseph P. Kennedy, Jr., Foundation, Washington, D.C.

not have a significant negative effect on subsequent pregnancies. Studies of psychological impact suggest that the most common reaction is one of relief. Feelings of guilt or loss may be experienced in the immediate postabortion period but these are usually transient and can be reduced if the abortion decision receives support from significant others. In addition, the abortion experience appears to lead to better contraceptive practice. Finally, the social and economic costs of an abortion are likely to be less severe and shorter term than those of adolescent childbearing and rearing.

In the study reported in this chapter, 70 never-married women 16 to 18 years of age who planned to deliver were matched with others who planned to abort. Those choosing abortion appeared to find the decision more difficult to make. Few in either group considered the adoption alternative. The variables which seemed to have the greatest influence on the decision were: desire for child (the delivery group waited a longer time before confirming the pregnancy and was less likely to have used contraceptives); relationship with sexual partner (the delivery group had stronger and longer relationships); support for the decision (the delivery group was more likely to discuss and receive support for the decision from significant others); role models (the delivery group personally knew single women who were bringing up their own children, including mothers, sisters, and other family members); attitudes toward abortion (the delivery group was more likely to hold antiabortion beliefs); previous pregnancy history (the abortion group had experienced more previous pregnancies); and timing (the abortion group was more likely to think this was the worst possible time to have a baby.) The two groups did not differ on the Block Scale testing ego resilience or the Rotter Internal-External Locus of Control Scale.

Pregnant adolescents face a series of critical decisions about their futures. Perhaps the most important and most immediate is the decision about whether to carry the pregnancy to term or to abort. Physicians, nurses, social workers, and others to whom these young women, their male partners, and their families may turn for advice should be knowledgeable about the problems associated with this decision. This chapter will review the present state of knowledge about adolescent use of abortion and then report the findings of a study that examined the delivery-abortion decision in an adolescent sample.

ABORTION AMONG ADOLESCENTS

Prevalence of Adolescent Abortion

Between 1973, when the *Roe v. Wade* decision of the United States Supreme Court legalized abortion, and the present, the number of abortions performed on adolescents has risen steadily. In 1977, over 300,000 women under the age of 20 underwent abortions: almost 13,000 were 14 and under; over 135,000 were 15–17; and over 189,000 were 18–19 years of age. These figures are even more startling when compared to the number of births experienced in these age groups. There were 1,132 abortions per 1,000 live births in the 14 and under group, 635 in the 15–17s, and 547 in the 18–19s.[12] In 1977, 30.8 percent of all reported abortions were performed on women under the age of 20.[11]

Sociodemographic Characteristics

The use of abortion to terminate a pregnancy is not randomly distributed in the pregnant adolescent population. Those who choose abortion differ from those who carry to term in terms of socioeconomic status. Whether measured by family income, parental occupation, or parental education, the higher the status the more likely the adolescent is to choose abortion. Several studies have also suggested that young women who seek abortions are doing better in school and are more academically motivated that those who do not.[13,27]

In a recent review of social and psychological correlates of pregnancy resolution among adolescents, Olson[27] characterized the abortion patient, in comparison with her term counterpart, as: "likely to be more independent (judging from her partial self-support); more motivated (judging from her school record and academic aspirations); and more optimistic, as the abortion decision itself appears to imply—for implicit in this decision is a belief that the situation and dilemma it presents, can be resolved without compromising the woman's future plans."

CONSEQUENCES OF ABORTION DECISION

Although many adolescents today choose to terminate their pregnancies by abortion rather than carry them to term, this decision should not be made without an understanding of its possible consequences in terms of physical health, psychological well-being, and other factors.

Physical Health

At present, legal abortion is a very low-risk procedure. The Center for Disease Control[11] reported only 15 deaths from such abortions in 1977 or 1.4 deaths per 100,000 abortions, making this procedure less dangerous than childbirth or tonsillectomy. The rate of nonfatal short-term complications is also low.

Of greater concern during the last few years have been the possible effects of abortion, particularly multiple abortions, on subsequent pregnancies. The

1975 Institute of Medicine (IOM) study, *Legalized Abortion and the Public Health*,[23] as well as subsequent studies in this country and elsewhere, have produced conflicting results. Two recent studies,[22,33] however, have suggested that the risk of prematurity, miscarriage, or other suboptimal pregnancy outcomes is not significantly increased by previous abortions.

Psychological Well-being

Considerable apprehension has also been expressed about the possible short- and long-term psychological trauma of abortion in adolescence. The 1975 IOM[23] study, however, concluded that "the feelings of guilt, regret, or loss elicited by legal abortion in some women are generally temporary and appear to be outweighed by positive life changes and feelings of relief." Studies of adolescents reach similar conclusions. Perez-Reyes and Falk,[29] in a follow-up study of 41 adolescents ages 13–16 who had abortions, (61 percent white and 39 percent black), reported that intense feelings of guilt, depression, and anger were confined mostly to the immediate postoperative period. Six months after the procedure, general health was the same or better for 90 percent, and emotional health was the same or better for 75 percent. The MMPI preabortion profile showed elements of a major crisis, that is, the patients as a group tended to be confused, have physical concerns, feel sad, be suspicious of others, be sensitive, worry, and think little of themselves. After the abortion, however, the depression decreased and the profile approached the normative group. The authors suggested that, for adolescents who become pregnant in early adolescence, abortion relieves stress rather than causes it.

This study, however, did not provide comparable data for pregnant adolescents who chose to deliver. Only by contrasting the delivery and abortion outcomes for comparable pregnancies can the "net" effect of one outcome over another be measured in terms of psychological relief or stress. Graves[21] attempted such a comparison using a sample of 15–23-year-old, black, unmarried primigravida abortion and maternity clinic patients at Grady Memorial Hospital in Atlanta. He administered the MMPI before and after abortion or delivery and, for a smaller subsample, again at approximately 1 year postpartum. He concluded that there was no evidence that legal abortions were more or less deleterious to psychological health than carrying the pregnancy to term.

Evans et al.[15] compared never-married 13–19-year-old Anglos and Mexican-American women who came to health providers in Ventura County, California, for pregnancy tests, prenatal care, or abortions. Interviews were conducted prior to delivery or abortion, or at the time of pregnancy test; and 6 months after the abortion, delivery, or initial interview. At the time of the follow-up interview, satisfaction with all decisions (to become a single parent, to marry and deliver, to deliver and give up baby for adoption, and to abort), had increased. While a large number of adolescents in the abortion group (N=184) who had initially favored another alternative came to believe that abortion was the right choice for them, 20 percent indicated that they wished they had chosen to deliver. The authors stated that these young women could have been recognized prior to the abortion by their youth, poorer educational background, ethnic group (Mexican-American), and ambivalence about their decision.

These studies of adolescents are congruent with studies of older women which indicate some transient depression after abortion but no permanent psychological impairment.[17] Moreover, research findings suggest that the emotional sequelae of abortion are affected by the decision process leading to the abortion. Support from significant others, partners for older women and mothers for younger ones, has been shown to be significantly related to more favorable immediate postabortion reactions.[5] Women who report more difficulty deciding to abort also report more guilt[28] and anxiety[6] postabortion.

Contraceptive Use

Another issue that has concerned many who counsel adolescents has been the possibility that young women who once used abortion as a device to prevent childbirth might continue to use this method rather than the more socially sanctioned methods of contraception. The Evans et al. study[15] found that teenagers whose first pregnancies were terminated by abortion, increased their use of effective contraception over the preabortion level, to a point where more than four out of five sexually active adolescents reported consistently using a highly reliable method. Their contraception was equal to those who had delivered, and higher than those who had not become pregnant. Darney[14] found that the rate of contraceptive acceptance at hospital discharge among women 17 and under was higher for those who had aborted than for those who had delivered. This was true for both whites and blacks and for all ages except 14 and under. On the basis of age-specific pregnancy rates in New York City from 1971–1973, Tietze[35] concluded that easy access to legal abortion had led to more general and effective fertility regulation.

Social and Economic Costs

The risks of negative abortion consequences, which impact largely on the pregnant adolescent herself and are usually of short duration, need to be balanced against the well-documented short- and long-term effects of early child rearing on the adolescent mother, her child, her sexual partner, her family, and society. Disruption of education, economic dependency, low-paying employment, unsuccessful marital careers, and high fertility are among the problems experienced by women who become mothers in their teens.[10,19,26] Although most recent evidence indicates that the child of an adolescent mother is not at high risk biologically, as long as the mother receives adequate prenatal care, the mother's educational and economic deficits appear to have a negative impact on the child's cognitive, social, and emotional development and school achievement.[3]

FACTORS INFLUENCING THE ABORTION DECISION

Early studies[18] which attempted to compare samples of young women who decided to abort with those deciding to deliver, experienced difficulties in interpreting their findings. Differences in sociodemographic characteristics between the two groups were so large that the more subtle differences were obscured. More recent research has provided information useful to the practitioner. One such study was conducted by Fischman[16] in 1972–1973 using a sample of black urban never-married adolescents, 13–18 years of age, who were experiencing their first pregnancy and receiving services at the Baltimore City Maternity and Infant Services Project. Two hundred and twenty-nine young women were interviewed, of whom 66 percent delivered and 34 percent aborted. The investigator reported that adolescents who delivered had better relationships with their parents, especially their mothers, than those who aborted. Those who delivered also reported a longer and more stable relationship with their male partners, who were more likely to be working full-time and to be older than aborters' male partners. Over half of the sample claimed they had not involved anyone in their decision-making process. Among those who had, women delivering were more likely to have been influenced by their male partners, and those who aborted by family members.

Adolescents choosing abortion were more likely to be attending school, to be at the appropriate grade level, and to come from families of higher socioeconomic status than those who delivered. Although religious affiliation did not affect decision making, a belief that religion was important frequently led to a delivery decision. Dislike of baby-sitting was more often associated with an abortion decision.

As part of a 1974–1975 study of unplanned and unwanted conceptions in Michigan, Rosen[31] administered questionnaires to 432 unmarried 12–17-year-olds (250 white and 182 black). Thirty-five percent of the total group chose abortion and 65 percent delivery, including a small group of whites (N=43) who gave up the infant for adoption. The investigator focused on the role of parents in decision making. She found that few respondents sought advice from either parent (12 percent from mothers; 2 percent from fathers) when they first thought they might be pregnant, but one-third consulted a girl friend or the male partner. Parental help was more often sought (23%) in finding a place to confirm the pregnancy. Once the adolescents were sure they were pregnant, 43 percent came to a decision about termination without involving a parent. The mother's influence was most important for the white adolescent who chose adoption and for the black who chose abortion. White adolescents who planned to keep their infants were influenced primarily by their male partners. Girl friends were less influential at this juncture.

In all study groups mother's influence was associated with conflict. Among whites, mother's influence was also negatively associated with feeling of competence. The author suggested that "conflict and lack of perceived competence led to utilization of the mother as a resource . . . The less conflict a girl had and the more competence she felt, the more independent and autonomous she could be and was." [Rosen, 1980]

The study about to be described builds upon previous research on the delivery-abortion decision among adolescents, but since the authors were particularly interested in the psychological and social factors influencing decision making, a matching procedure was used to control several major variables in other domains (marital status, race, age, welfare status, and previous pregnancies).

METHOD

The total study sample was selected by requesting an opportunity to interview all single, never-married women 16 years of age and older, making their first visit to the Yale-New Haven Hospital's prenatal clinic during a one-year period. For each such woman entered into the study, a single, never-married woman seeking an induced abortion in the same hospital for other than medical reasons, was individually matched on race, age ($\pm$ 2 years), welfare status, and gravidity (none versus one or more previous pregnancies), and interviewed. A total of 249 individually matched pairs of women completed the questionnaire. Refusal rates in the prenatal clinic were 6.7 percent and 2.4 percent in the abortion clinic. This report focuses on the 153 women 16–18 years of age within the larger sample. Analyses of the total study sample and a more detailed account of the study methodology have been previously reported.[7,8] In reviewing the findings presented here, it is important to note that, except for refusals, the sample of women *delivering* is representative of the hospital's total prenatal clinic population; while because of the matched design, the sample of women experiencing *abortions* does not represent the total abortion population. The latter was more likely to be white, not on welfare, and pregnant for the first time than the matched sample studied.

Two versions of a questionnaire were developed: one for the delivery and one for the abortion group. Both included items on sociodemographic characteristics, reaction to pregnancy, attitudes toward abortions, and other areas that might affect the delivery-abortion decision. In addition, two measures of psychological functioning were included in the questionnaire: a shortened 18-item version of the Block Scale to test ego resilience or the potential for coping with stressful situations[4] and a shortened 8-item version of the Rotter Internal-External Locus of Control Scale to distinguish those who might be able to make decisions for themselves from those who might rely more on others.[32]

The questionnaire was self-administered and then reviewed by the interviewer who completed the form, and, if necessary, resolved any obvious ambiguities in the answers. This procedure capitalized on the advantages of both approaches. Self-administered forms are often completed quickly and their anonymity produces more reliable answers. At the same time, the interviewer's review is particularly important in a group of young, poorly educated women, if missing data are to be kept to a minimum. Interviewers are also able to probe for more valid responses.

STUDY RESULTS

Sociodemographic Characteristics

Because of the matching procedure, the 79 adolescents who decided to deliver, and the 74 who decided to abort, were almost identical in sociodemographic characteristics. All were single and never married. They ranged in age from 16 to 18.* The mean age of those delivering was 17.3 and of those aborting 17.4 Seventy-two percent of the combined group was black; 53 percent was on welfare; 44 percent was Protestant and 13 percent Catholic; and 52 percent stated that their fathers provided the primary support for their families. Sixty-three percent of the combined group was experiencing a first pregnancy; 28 percent a second; 7 percent a third; and 2 percent a fourth or higher order pregnancy.

Difficulties in Making Decision

Adolescents who decided to abort found their decision somewhat more difficult to make than those who decided to deliver. Each group, however, reported that the reasons for favoring and for contraindicating their decision

*Young women under 16 were excluded because of the greater likelihood that their pregnancy would be terminated for medical reasons. Only those choosing to abort for nonmedical reasons were selected for this decision-making study. Because the full study matched on age using ± 2 years the subset of adolescents (18 years of age or less) utilized here has, by chance, slightly more respondents in the delivery group. This does not materially influence any of the findings. The data were analyzed using the chi square statistic for categorical data and t-tests or one-way analysis of variance procedures for continuous variables. Results are described as "significant" using a value of $p < 0.05$.

were more "evenly balanced" than "one-sided." Almost a third of the young women (31.8%) changed their minds once or twice about continuing the pregnancy or having the abortion, 18 percent changed their mind even more frequently, but 50 percent did not change their mind at all. There was no significant difference between the two pregnancy outcome groups on this dimension.

Relatively few adolescents in either group completely denied the pregnancy by putting all thoughts of it out of their minds, although the abortion group was slightly more likely to repress pregnancy thoughts. When asked about their first reaction to the thought of continuing the pregnancy or having an abortion, adolescents in both groups indicated that they felt neither particularly relieved nor distressed, i.e., they were initially somewhat ambivalent about the outcome of their pregnancy. Nonetheless, the delivery group was significantly more accepting of the idea of delivery than the abortion group was of its choice.

The questionnaire also contained several items which indirectly suggested the difficulties the adolescents had experienced in making their pregnancy decision. For example, young women delivering were significantly more likely to report difficulty in falling asleep and midnight waking than were those aborting. These are usually assumed to be clinical indications of depression.

Adoption

This sample of adolescents barely considered the adoption as an alternative to parenting or abortion. Both groups reported that when they were deciding what to do about their pregnancy, they hardly thought about adoption. Only nine adolescents sought professional advice in this area and they felt they received unbiased information. When the young women in the delivery group were asked about their plans for their infant, 89.6 percent said they definitely, and 3.9 percent probably, would keep it and 2.6 percent were unsure. Only 1.3 percent probably and 2.6 percent definitely would place for adoption.

In response to a question about why adoption was not considered in the pregnancy decision making, most adolescents indicated that they did not wish to go through the entire pregnancy only to "give up" the infant. There was no indication that anticipated difficulties in placing infants caused the adolescents to rule out adoption, although this might have been a factor in a predominately black sample.

Factors Affecting Decision

Seven types of variables discriminated between the group that decided to deliver and the group that decided to abort. The variables which seemed to influence the decision most were: (1) desire for child; (2) relationship with sexual partner; (3) support for decision; (4) role models; (5) attitudes toward abortion; (6) previous pregnancy history; and (7) timing of pregnancy. The two groups did not differ on the measures of psychological functioning.

Desire for Child. Although no question was specifically asked about the adolescent's desire for a child, several items provided inferential evidence. In general, pregnancies in both groups were greeted with sadness and anxiety. Nonetheless, the young women delivering were significantly less sad than those who chose to abort. Also, adolescents in the delivery group felt less urgency about having their pregnancy confirmed by a physican. The delivery group waited an average of 8 weeks after suspicion of pregnancy, in contrast to 4.7 weeks for the abortion group.

The reported use, or nonuse, of birth-control methods also hinted at the desire for a child, although in an indirect manner. The adolescents in the delivery group were significantly less likely to have used a method of birth control *during the time they had known their sexual partner*. Women in the abortion group were less likely to have used the pill but were more likely to have used contraceptive methods requiring the partner's cooperation, such as condoms, rhythm, or withdrawal. The data on use of birth-control methods *at the time they became pregnant* were similar; fewer adolescents in the delivery group practiced any contraception, while more adolescents in the abortion group used some method e.g., rhythm, withdrawal, condoms, pill, or IUD.

Relationship with Sexual Partner. The adolescent's relationship with her sexual partner had a clear and significant relationship with her pregnancy decision. In the delivery group, 19 percent reported that the baby's father was a fiancé; 78 percent said he was a regular boy friend; and only 3 percent admitted that he was a casual acquantance. In the abortion group, however, only 7 percent of partners were fiancés; 84 percent were regular boy friends; and 10 percent casual acquaintances. Another indication of the influence of a relationship was its longevity. Fifty-seven percent of the delivery group, compared with 42 percent of the abortion group, had been involved with the putative father for 12 or more months.

Despite these differences in the formal characterization and duration of the relationship, no differences between the pregnancy outcome groups could be detected using a 4-item scale assessing the closeness of relationship with partner. Both groups reported quite high levels of sharing and understanding and low irritability and loneliness within their relationship. Perhaps in these adolescents a close relationship with their partners was more important in predicting whether sexual intercourse would occur. After conception a decision to deliver appeared to be associated more with the "permanence" than with the "closeness" of the relationship.

Support for Decision. The adolescents were asked if they had discussed their pregnancy with their mother, father, male partner, best girl friend, physician, or clergyman and how those people felt about their continuing the pregnancy or having the abortion. If they had not talked to them, the young women were asked how they thought they would feel. Young women in both groups most frequently discussed their pregnancy decision with, in rank order, their sexual partners, girl friends, and mothers. They less often talked with fathers and physicians; and least frequently talked with clergymen. Only 49 of the adolescents reported visiting a Planned Parenthood agency for assistance. Almost all of them felt they had received support for their respective decisions from that source.

In general, adolescents planning to deliver were significantly more likely than those planning to abort to discuss their decision with significant others. The important exception, however, was physicians; young women planning to abort were more likely than those planning to deliver to discuss their plans with a physician. Moreover, adolescents who planned to deliver received more support for their choice from significant others than did those who planned to abort. Young women in the delivery group were strongly supported, in rank order, by partners, best girl friends, mothers, physicians, clergymen, and fathers. Those in the abortion group received somewhat weaker support, in rank order, from physicians, best girl friends, mothers, fathers, and partners. The strong support of the adolescent's partner for their decisions to deliver contrasted sharply with their broad opposition to abortion decisions. It is interesting to note that older single women appear to have more support for decisions to abort from their partners than do adolescents.[7] Young women in the abortion group were significantly more likely to state that people with whom they discussed their pregnancies were somewhat neutral about abortion, while those in the delivery group reported that the people with whom they discussed their pregnancies were somewhat "one-sided" against abortion.

Fifteen percent of the adolescents reported that their mothers tried to persuade them to have an abortion. This proportion was the same for both groups. Approximately equal numbers in both groups also stated that girl friends (14%), sexual partners (8%), and physicians (5%) tried to persuade them to abort.

Role Models. A greater percentage of adolescents who chose to deliver personally knew single, never-married women who were bringing up their own children. Ninety-one percent of the delivery group had such a friend, compared to 76 percent of the abortion group. Indeed, 85 percent of those who decided to deliver had more than one such friend, compared to 65 percent of the aborting group. Similarly, young women choosing delivery were more likely to have a mother, sister, or other family member who was bringing up children despite being unmarried. Moreover, adolescents in the delivery group were significantly more likely than those in the abortion group to believe that people important to them felt positively about unmarried child rearing.

Only 54 percent of adolescents in the abortion group and 49 percent in the delivery group personally knew any single, never-married women who had experienced an induced abortion. This difference, however, was not significant. A higher percent of young women in the abortion group knew other relatives or friends who had experienced an induced abortion but, again, the differences were not marked. Interestingly, no one in the entire study had a mother who had herself admitted to having had an abortion, although it is highly unlikely that this was the case.

This study does not indicate whether the influence of role models operates primarily by providing social approval for a decision to seek abortion, or whether knowing significant others who have experienced an induced abortion provides easier access to abortion services. In another area, however, the adolescents' decision reflected their perception of the opinions of others. Those in the delivery group were less likely than those in the abortion group to feel that people important to them favored induced abortion for single, never-married women.

Attitudes Toward Abortion. Striking and significant differences were found between the two pregnancy outcome groups in attitudes toward abortion. Adolescents in the delivery group were significantly more likely than those in the abortion group to believe that, "women who have abortions are killing their child," and that a woman's "career or social life is not important enough to permit abortion." Surprisingly, the two groups were almost identical in expecting that few women would feel guilty after an abortion.

Although the adolescent groups were too small to permit more detailed analyses of attitude constructs, such analyses were conducted in the larger study with revealing results. Women aborting their first pregnancy, including many adolescents, held the most positive attitudes toward abortion. Women who had previously delivered all their pregnancies and were delivering again were the most negative in their attitudes toward abortion. Women who had previously aborted but were now delivering, however, had the same favorable attitudes about abortion as women presently aborting.[7]

Previous Pregnancy History. Adolescents in the abortion group had experienced more previous pregnancies than those currently delivering. Even in this relatively young group of women, 26 had already undergone an abortion (44 percent of the delivery group who were pregnant previously and 50 percent of the abortion group who were pregnant previously). Among those who had been pregnant before, a higher percentage of the abortion group had developed pregnancy complications, although it is not clear how much this influenced their decision to terminate the present pregnancy. Worry about abortion side effects was not very great in either group, although, as might be expected from a sample of women waiting for an abortion, it was significantly higher in the group deciding to abort.

Timing. In general, all these adolescents considered it a poor time in their lives to be pregnant. Adolescents who decided to abort, however, in comparison to those who decided to deliver, were significantly more likely to think this was the worst possible time to have a baby.

Psychological Functioning

The two groups did not differ on either the Block Scale testing ego resilience[4] or the Rotter Internal-External Locus of Control Scale.[32] Both groups scored near the midpoint of the scales.

DISCUSSION

The results of this study suggest that adolescents who decided to deliver found it easier to make their decision than those deciding to abort. Some women delivering, consciously or unconsciously, wanted a child. Their non-usage of contraception, their less saddened response to the pregnancy, their apparent lack of urgency in seeking medical advice—all point to a relatively more positive attitude toward childbearing. Also, those who had a longer relationship with the putative father, if not necessarily a closer one, tended to decide to deliver. This may have been to strengthen the relationship or to initiate marriage, since most partners were reported to oppose abortions. Socioenvironmental factors also played a role, as shown by the association between knowledge of other single mothers and feelings about the timing of the pregnancy and the decision to deliver.

Adolescents who decided to abort appear to have had more difficulty with their decision. They talked to fewer people, received less support from the important people in their social networks, and knew relatively few women who aborted. Almost all the partners of these adolescents strongly opposed abortions, and their mothers appeared unwilling to admit to any abortions they had experienced. The aborting adolescents shared some of the moral feelings against abortion felt by the delivering group, although not as strongly. Abortion seemed a more independent, almost lonely, decision with which these adolescents were somewhat less happy after the decision was made. It is certainly a mistake to believe that the easier availability of abortion led to simple and less conflictful decisions in this population.

The present research also underscores the special role of the partner in the decision-making process. Adolescents delivering had been in a longer relationship with their partner and had practiced contraception less, suggesting a desire for pregnancy to stabilize the relationship. Contraception, when it was used, was less likely to involve the partner; moreover, the partner was much more likely to oppose a decision to abort than to deliver. These data, as well as the findings of other studies,[25,34] suggest that the male partners may view pregnancy and childbearing positively, perhaps as symbols of masculinity or adulthood.

Another interesting finding of this and other studies[2,7,24] is the reversibility of the delivery-abortion decision. Half of adolescents who previously delivered now chose to abort and almost half who previously aborted now chose to deliver. Moreover, for the present pregnancy, both groups of young women were very indecisive and half changed their minds during the pregnancy. These findings strongly suggest that the decision about pregnancy outcome in this population is related more to circumstances surrounding the particular pregnancy than to any stable characteristic of the adolescent herself.

Prior reproductive history is another factor affecting the decision. The young women in the abortion group were likely to have a larger number of pregnancies and live children than those in the delivery group. But this factor alone cannot account for most of the difference, and socioenvironmental factors probably play a more important role. A switch from one pregnancy outcome to the other may be the result of a change in sexual partner from one with an antiabortion bias to one more supportive of abortion; or from one with whom the young woman wishes to establish a permanent relationship to one she does not wish to marry. Educational and vocational opportunities may account for the importance of the pregnancy being at the "worst possible time," although retrospective modification of feelings to rationalize a decision must be suspected in this situation.

An adolescent's ideas about abortion may be revised from one pregnancy to the next. By the time this cohort of adolescents reaches the end of its reproductive life, almost all will probably have experienced both abortions and deliveries. This interpretation is supported by the inability of the psychological test results in this and other studies[30] to show any consistent personality pattern in young women who decide to abort rather than deliver. Rosen et al.[30] have also noted that personality factors have little explanatory or predictive value in studies of this type. They believe that this is because personality consists of a set of fairly stable properties and processes, while fertility behaviors are situationally specific.

Another tentative conclusion from this study is that stated attitudes toward abortion at the time of one pregnancy probably do not have much reliability in predicting behavior during subsequent pregnancies. It is more likely that attitudes expressed during a pregnancy are a reaction to that pregnancy experience and form an ego-defensive role which supports the decision that has been made. In the psychosocial literature, there has been considerable interest in the role of behavior in the formation of attitudes (rather than vice versa), and these data tend to support that theory.

One aspect of the decision-making process that was not explored adequately in this study was the pregnant adolescent's awareness of, and concern about, the consequences of early parenting for herself and significant others, including her infant. Other research[20] has suggested that young women and their families approach the task of child rearing rather casually, often in contrast to their attitudes toward marriage, which they perceive, correctly, as likely to involve significant difficulties.

CONCLUSIONS

The relatively uninformed nature of the decision making by the adolescents in this study underscores the need both for additional resources to be devoted to the prevention of pregnancy, and for greater availability of information about the consequences of the range of pregnancy outcomes (abortion, adoption, single parenthood, parenthood within marriage), and of counseling to assist in making the decision.[9]

Unfortunately since this study was conducted, the Hyde amendment restricting the use of federal funds for abortion has been passed and upheld by the Supreme Court. Many states have followed the federal lead and decided not to allow state funds to be used for abortions.[1] Information about these policies may make adolescents reluctant to seek advice about pregnancy termination, even in areas where state or local public funds, or private resources, might be available to finance abortions. More than ever before it is essential for the helping professions to reach out to pregnant adolescents, and those to whom they turn for advice—parents, male partners, and girl friends. They need to know that nonjudgmental, unbiased advice is available, and that in most instances, resources can still be found whether the decision is for an abortion or for a delivery.

REFERENCES

1. Alan Guttmacher Institute. *Abortions and the Poor: Private Morality, Public Responsibility*. New York, 1979.
2. Aries, N. and Klerman, L.V. Evaluating service delivery models for pregnant adolescents. *Women and Health* (forthcoming).
3. Baldwin, W. and Cain, V.S. The children of teenage parents. *Family Planning Perspectives* **12**: 34–43 (1980).

4. Block, J. *The Challenge of Response Sets*. New York: Appleton-Century Crofts, 1965.
5. Bracken, M.B., Hachamovitch, M., and Grossman, G. The deicison to abort and psychological sequelae. *Journal of Nervous and Mental Diseases* **158**: 154–162 (1974).
6. Bracken, M.B. A causal model of psychosomatic reactions to vacuum aspiration abortion. Social Psychiatry **13**: 135–145 (1978).
7. Bracken, M.B., Klerman, L.V., and Bracken, M. Abortion, adoption, or motherhood: An empirical study of decision making during pregnancy. *American Journal of Obstetrics and Gynecology* **130**: 251–262 (1978).
8. Bracken, M.B., Klerman, L.V., and Bracken. M. Coping with pregnancy resolution among never-married women. *American Journal of Orthopsychiatry* **48**: 320–334 (1978).
9. Cain, L.P. Social worker's role in teenage abortions. *Social Work* **24**: 52–56 (1979).
10. Card, J. and Wise, L. Teenage mothers and teenage fathers: The impact of early childbearing on the parent's personal and professional lives. *Family Planning Perspectives* **10**: 199–205 (1978).
11. Center for Disease Control. *Abortion Surveillance 1977*. Atlanta, Georgia, 1979.
12. Center for Disease Control. Teenage childbearing and abortion patterns—United States, 1977. *Morbidity and Mortality Weekly Report* **29**: 157–159 (1980).
13. Chilman, C. Teenage pregnancy: A research review. *Social Work* **24**: 492–498 (1979).
14. Darney, P.B. Post abortion and post partum contraceptive acceptance among adolescents. Paper presented at Annual Meeting of the American Public Health Association, Miami Beach, Florida, 1976.
15. Evans, J.R., Selstad, G., and Welcher, W. Teenagers: Fertility control behavior and attitudes before and after abortion, childbearing, or negative pregnancy test. *Family Planning Perspectives* **8**: 192–200 (1976).
16. Fischman, S.H. Delivery or abortion in inner-city adolescents. *American Journal of Orthopsychiatry* **47**: 127–133 (1977).
17. Ford, C.V. Castelnuovo-Tedesco, P., and Long, K. Abortion: Is it a therapeutic procedure in psychiatry? *Journal of the American Medical Association* **218**: 1173–1178 (1971).
18. Ford, C.V., Castelnuovo-Tedesco, P., and Long, K. Women who seek therapeutic abortion: A comparison with women who complete their pregnancies. *American Journal of Psychiatry* **129**: 58–64 (1972).
19. Furstenberg, F.F. *Unplanned Parenthood*. New York: Free Press, 1976.
20. Furstenberg, F.F. Teenage parenthood and family support. Paper prepared for the National Research Forum on Family Issues sponsored by the White House Conference on Families, Washington, D.C., April 10–11, 1980.
21. Graves, W.L. Sequelae of unwanted pregnancy. A comparison of unmarried abortion and maternity patients. Paper presented at the Population Association of America, Montreal, Canada, April 27–29, 1976.
22. Harlap, S., Shiono, P.H., Ramcharan, S., et al. A prospective study of fetal losses after induced abortions. *New England Journal of Medicine* **301**: 677–681, 1979.

23. Institute of Medicine. *Legalized Abortion and the Public Health*. Washington, D.C.: National Academy of Sciences, 1975.
24. Jekel, J.F., Tyler, N.C., and Klerman, L.V. Induced abortion and sterilization among women who became mothers as adolescents. *American Journal of Public Health* **67**: 621–625 (1977).
25. Ladner, J.A. *Tomorrow's Tomorrow: The Black Woman*. Garden City, N.J.: Doubleday & Co., 1971.
26. Moore, K.A. Teenage childbirth and welfare dependency. *Family Planning Perspectives* **10**: 233–235 (1978).
27. Olson, L. Social and psychological correlates of pregnancy resolution among adolescent women: A review. *American Journal of Orthopsychiatry* **50**: 432–445 (1980).
28. Osofsky, J.D. and Osofsky, H.J. The psychological reaction of patients to legalized abortion. *American Journal of Orthopsychiatry* **42**: 48–60 (1972).
29. Perez-Reyes, M.G. and Falk, R. Follow-up after therapeutic abortion in early adolescence. *Archives of General Psychiatry* **28**: 120–126 (1973).
30. Rosen, R.H., Ager, J.W., and Martindale, L.J. Contraception, abortion, and self-concept. *Journal of Population* **2**: 118–139 (1979).
31. Rosen, R.H. Adolescent pregnancy decision-making: Are parents important? *Adolescence* **15**: 43–54 (1980).
32. Rotter, J.B. Generalized expectancies for internal versus external control of reinforcement. *Psychological Monographs* **80**: 1–23 (1966).
33. Schoenbaum, S.C., Monson, R.R., Stubblefield, P.G., et al. Outcome of the delivery following an induced or spontaneous abortion. *American Journal of Obstetrics and Gynecology* **136**: 19–24, 1980.
34. Thompson, K. A comparison of black and white adolescent's beliefs about having children. *Journal of Marriage and the Family* **42**: 133–139 (1980).
35. Tietze, C. Contraceptive practice in the context of a nonrestrictive abortion law: Age-specific pregnancy rates in New York City, 1971–73. *Family Planning Perspectives* **7**: 197–202 (1975).

11.

Method Discontinuance in Teenage Women: Implications for Teen Contraceptive Programs*

Joel W. Ager, Ph.D., Professor,
and
Fredericka P. Shea, M.S.,
Associate Professor,
Center for Health Research,
College of Nursing,
Wayne State University;

and

Samuel J. Agronow, Ph.D.,
Research Associate,
C. S. Mott Center for Human Growth and Development,
School of Medicine,
Wayne State University

The problems of program and method discontinuance in a teen contraceptive program are examined. The discussion is based primarily on results from the authors' study of 257 teens who had enrolled in such a program to obtain birth control. Of these, 143 were followed up over an 18-month period after program enrollment. The major purposes of the research study were to assess the incidence of, reasons for, and contraceptive consequences of, program dropout and method discontinuance. Over the time period studied, an initial rap questionnaire and three interviews were given.

Of 219 teens for whom initial interviews were obtained, 176 received a method; 43 (20%) were initial program dropouts. Of the 143 teens followed over the 18-month period, only about 37 percent either practiced effective

*The research reported was supported by Grant No. 09361 from the Center for Population Research of the National Institute of Child Health and Human Development.

We wish to acknowledge the contributions to the study of our research assistant, Nancy Newman, our interviewers, Archie Shew, Donald Carter, and Mary Berger Ward, and also the support of the Center for Health Research staff.

contraception, almost always the pill, or were not at risk over that interval. Of the 63 percent who were not continuously practicing effective contraception, 28 percent became pregnant. For the noncontinuers a number of distinctive patterns of contraceptive usage are identified and discussed. The main reasons for discontinuance reported by the teens involved either side effects attributed to the pill or side effects feared.

Based on the findings a number of program implications are discussed. Recommendations are made in the areas of method prescription, contraceptive counseling, follow-up of program and method discontinuers, minimizing the deterrent effects of the required rap sessions and medical exams, scheduling of clinic session, payment policies, transporation and clinic locations. The problem of identification of potential program and method discontinuers is also discussed.

INTRODUCTION

There has been a dramatic increase in recent years in the number and availability of programs designed to meet the contraceptive needs of sexually active teenagers (Caplan, 1973; House and Goldsmith, 1972; Minkowski et al., 1974). Still, the unmet need for such services remains great, as evidenced by the continuing rise in unplanned teen pregnancies over the same period (Jaffe and Dryfoos, 1976; Marinoff, 1972; Morris, 1974).

There are two major problems facing such programs as they try to effectively meet this need. These are the related problems of recruitment and retention.

For most teens it is probably the case that enrollment in the health-care system, which would include the private physician as well as the family-planning clinic, is probably a necessary first step in initiating effective contraceptive practice. The most effective contraceptive methods (e.g., pill, IUD, diaphragm) are available only through the health-care system. Also the counseling and support provided by such programs may be crucial for the effective use of other, theoretically less effective, methods (e.g., condom or foam, cream and jelly). It is too often the case that neither the need for, nor availability of, such services is recognized by the teens as they become sexually active. This is particularly true for the younger teens (and their parents). In our study we found that the teens on the average have been sexually active for about a year before enrolling in the teen program. The recruitment problem then is that of bringing teens into the health-care system as (or preferably before) they first become sexually active.

Initial entrance into the health-care system either through a clinic or private physician is just the first step. Once started on an effective program of contraception the question now is one of continuance—both program and method continuance. With regard to a teen contraceptive program, the teen may continue in the program until age 18 and then transfer to an adult program, or she may at some point drop out of the program. The critical question is whether or not program drop-out also entails increased risk of an unplanned pregnancy. If the teen drops out because she has switched to another clinic or to a private physician, or because she is no longer sexually active, program drop-out may not mean increased risk. In addition, continuance in the program does not necessarily mean that the teen is using the method effectively. She may, for example, often forget to take the pill, putting her at substantial risk even though she would be regarded as a program continuer using an effective method. It is the problem of continuance, both program and especially method continuance, which is the focus of the present paper.

Our discussion of the problem of method and program discontinuance is based on our recently completed study of a sample of 257 teens from a Planned Parenthood teen program. We were able to follow 143 of these teens for a period of 18 months after their enrollment in the program; the results to be reported are based primarily on this subgroup. The purpose of the study was to investigate the incidence of, the reasons for, and contraceptive consequences of, drop-out from the program. For reasons explained later, focus of the research shifted from the study of program discontinuance to that of method discontinuance and its consequences. We found, for instance, in this sample, that about 40 percent continued on an effective method, usually the pill, over the 18-month period. For those who discontinued, the most frequent reasons given were experienced or feared side effects of the pill. As to the consequences of method discontinuance, almost 30 percent of those who discontinued their method became pregnant during the 18-month period; none of the continuous users did so.

In this chapter we will first present the background and the procedures for the study. Next, those results most relevant to programs are presented. Finally, the implications of the study results for program planning and policy are discussed.

OBJECTIVES AND BACKGROUND

Objectives of the Study

The primary objective of the study was to investigate the incidence of, reasons for, and consequences of method discontinuance among teens enrolled in a contraceptive program. A second objective was to identify variables that might predict method discontinuance. Originally we planned to study program drop, however, the teen center program unexpectedly terminated about six months after data collection began. Consequently, that objective shifted to those mentioned above.

Selected Literature

The literature on teen sexual and contraceptive practices is quite extensive. As a result, the literature selected for presentation here should not be considered exhaustive. This review is organized along the topics of teen coitus, contraceptive practices, pregnancy, contraceptive programs, and the problems of program discontinuance.

Teenage Coitus

The incidence of teenage coitus is substantial and increasing (Kantner and Zelnik, 1972; Sorensen, 1973; Zelnik and Kantner, 1977). Precise rates of teenage coitus are difficult to determine. In their 1976 random sample of unmarried women 15–19, Zelnik and Kantner (1977) report the following cumulative percentages of teens who had at least one coital experience at each age: 18 percent at 15, 25.4 percent at 16, 40.9 percent at 17, 45.2 percent at 18, and 55.2 percent at 19. These percentages underestimate the total number of women at each age who are sexually active because married 15–19-year-old women, many of whom had had premarital sex, were excluded (Kantner and Zelnik, 1972; Zelnik and Kantner, 1977).

Not only is teen coitus increasing, it is starting earlier (Kantner and Zelnik, 1972). Cutright (1972) argues that the increased rate of teen pregnancies is attributable to an increase in teen fecundity due to improved health rather than an increased rate of coitus.

Teen Contraceptive Practice

Despite the earlier onset and increased frequency of teen sexual activity, there has not been a corresponding increase in the practice of effective contraception (Kantner and Zelnik, 1973). However, Zelnik and Kantner (1977) did find an increase in teens' use of effective contraceptives from 1971 to 1976. In general, the incidence of unprotected coitus is high among teens, and when a method is used it tends to be relatively ineffective (e.g., rhythm or withdrawal), particularly when teens initiate sexual activity (Kantner and Zelnik, 1973; Reichelt and Werley, 1975; Zelnik and Kantner, 1977).

Numerous reasons have been advanced to explain the relatively low rate of effective contraceptive usage. Teen sexual and contraceptive knowledge is lacking (Furstenberg, Gordis, and Markowitz, 1969; Kantner and Zelnik, 1972; Thornburg, 1972). Further, many teens are misinformed about contraception. Low- and high-risk intervals during the menstrual cycle (Kantner and Zelnik, 1972; Presser, 1974), and the belief that condoms break easily are areas of misinformation (Reichelt and Werley, 1975). Several studies found that the teens' sources of information about sex are often unreliable. Teens cite peers as their main source of information (Thornburg, 1972) and the mass media and parents as secondary sources. Few teens report school education programs or health professionals as important sources of information (Reichelt and Werley, 1975).

The nature of teen sex, episodic and often unplanned, poses another problem for the effective use of contraceptives (Johnson, Burket, and Rauh, 1971; Marinoff, 1972; Rauh, Burket, and Brookman, 1975). The pill requires some planning, produces side effects, and is often not recommended when coitus is infrequent (Rauh, Burket, and Brookman, 1975).

Discontinuance rates for teen pill users are reported to be high (Gordis et al., 1970). Furthermore, to the extent teens place emphasis on spontaneity in sex, use of effective contraceptives which require planning is less likely (Shah, Zelnik, and Kantner, 1975). Contraceptive counseling appears to be essential for teens so that a method compatible with their needs can be suggested (Baldwin, 1976; Jorgensen, 1976; Urban and Rural Systems Associates, 1976).

Teenage Pregnancy

In 1976, live births registered to women under 20 totaled 570,672. Of these, 442,540 were first births (Tietze, 1978). Between 1960 and 1974, the illegitimacy rate for women 15–19 increased 52 percent (Tietze, 1978). Because illegitimacy rates exclude births legitimized by marriage, they underestimate the number of unplanned pregnancies. For married women 15–19, it has been estimated that at least one-half of first births are premaritally conceived (National Center for Health Statistics, 1970; Whelan, 1972; Zelnik and Kantner, 1974). Zelnik and Kantner (1978a; 1978b) report that almost 80 percent of first pregnancies, in their sample, were conceived out of wedlock. Abortion is another reason the illegitimacy rate underestimates the rate of teenage unplanned pregnancies. In 1977, women 15–19 years old had 397,720 abortions (Forrest, Sullivan, and Tietze, 1979). Teens account for one third of all abortions in the United States.

Consequences of Early Childbearing

Interest in, and concern about, teen pregnancy arises from the deleterious consequences of early childbearing both for some teens and their children. Babies born to teens are more apt to be stillborn or die within the first year (National Center for Health Statistics, 1973a). Nortman (1974) reports mortality 41 percent above average in children 1–4 years old whose mothers were teens. Also, babies of teens tend to be of lower birth weight and thus incur a greater risk of cerebral palsy, epilepsy, mental retardation, and congenital anomalies. Oppel and Royston (1971) report that babies born to teens were observed to have received less adequate maternal care, and perform more poorly on IQ tests. Poorer prenatal care, particularly for the unwed teen mother, probably contributes to the increased risks of childbearing for both the teen and child (Dott and Fort, 1976).

Negative consequences for the health and social development of the teen mother have been reported. Maternal mortality is 50 percent higher for teens compared to women 20–24 years old (Menken, 1972). Pregnancy complications are also more frequent (Maternal and Child Health Service, 1972). Teen mothers are likely to disrupt or discontinue their education (Furstenberg, 1976; National Education Association, 1970; Sarrel and Davis, 1966) and then face restricted job or career possibilities with attendant economic limitations (Presser, 1971). When teens marry, the young family tends to be disadvantaged (Card and Wise, 1978; Coombs et al, 1970; Trussell, 1976). Teen marriages also tend to produce more, closely spaced children (Trussell, 1976; Trussell and Menken, 1978). At the same time, teen marriages are more likely to end in divorce (National Center for Health Statistics, 1973b).

Teen Contraceptive Programs

In response to the high rate of unplanned pregnancies, the need for sex education and contraceptive services for teens seems evident. In several metropolitan areas teen centers, often operated by affiliates of Planned Parenthood, provide sex education through rap sessions and offer contraceptive services (Caplan, 1973; House and Goldsmith, 1972; Minkowski et al, 1974). Recommendations for making programs more responsible to the specific needs of teens have been proposed by Furstenberg, Masnick, and Ricketts (1972), and Urban and Rural Systems Associates (1976).

The unmet need is still great. Jaffe and Dryfoos (1976) estimate that approximately 2 million of the 4 million sexually active teen girls are not practicing effective contraception. They further estimate that half of the 2 million will become pregnant in a given year, and 600,000 will bear the child.

Of the teens that practice effective contraception, most obtain their methods (usually the pill) through teen clinics. While some segments of the public view such programs as leading to increased sexual activity and promiscuity among teens, many studies have found that the majority of girls, prior to entering a teen contraceptive program, have been sexually active for a year or more (Akpom, Akpom, and Davis, 1976; Goldsmith et al., 1972; Reichelt and Werley, 1975; Settlage, Baroff, and Cooper, 1973).

Contraceptive Program Discontinuance

It is important to look at how successful teen contraceptive programs are in both recruiting and retaining the teen clients. The two problems are related.

242 Part IV / Management

Presumably many of the same factors that lead to dropout of those enrolled may operate to inhibit others from enrolling in the first place.

A number of studies have looked at reasons for drop-out from adult family-planning programs (Ager, Werley, and Shea, 1973; Hall and Reinke, 1969; Jorgensen, 1973; McCalister and Thiessen, 1970; Sear, 1973; Siegel et al., 1971; Speidel and Wiener, 1970; Tietze and Lewit, 1971). In two of these studies (Ager, Werley, and Shea, 1973; Sear, 1973) program dropouts were further analyzed in terms of the consequences of drop-out for contraceptive practice. The need for elucidating the conceptual and empirical relationships among the variables related to dropout has been emphasized by Bracken and Kasi (1973).

The problem of drop-out from teen programs is in some respects more serious than for adult programs. First of all, the majority of teens attending initial "rap" sessions are sexually active. Secondly, in most cases any resulting pregnancy would be unplanned and unwanted. Third, the consequences of unplanned teen pregnancies are usually more serious for the woman, the child, and society.

METHOD: SUBJECTS, DESIGN, AND INSTRUMENTS

The original study sample consisted of 257 teen girls, 13–17 years of age, from a Planned Parenthood teen program. Only teens who indicated that obtaining a contraceptive was one of the reasons for attending the initial rap were included.

The median age of the teens was 16.1. About 70 percent of the study teens were black and most lived in Detroit. In religious affiliation, 56 percent were Protestant and 18 percent Catholic with the remainder divided between other and none.

Over an approximately 18-month interval the teens were given one questionnaire and three interviews. The initial questionnaire was given just prior to the required sex education or "rap" session and included the usual background questions, a brief section on sexual and contraceptive history, and a 15-item sexual and contraceptive knowledge inventory adopted from the one used by Reichelt (Reichelt and Werley, 1975).

The first interview usually took place at about the time of the medical exam. Areas covered included a detailed sexual and contraceptive history, attitudes of the teen and her perception of her partner's attitudes toward the various types of birth control, opinions about the teen program including things that made it difficult to use, and a section consisting of 45 personality and attitude items. Teens who were classified as drops received a series of questions relating to their reasons for dropping from the program and their intentions to come back in the future.

The second (supply) interview was orginally to be given at the teen center at the time of the first supply visit, about two months after rap. Because the teen center closed, many teens had to be brought to the university for the interviews. Consequently the supply interview was usually obtained anywhere from four to eight months after the medical interview. The supply interview contained a sexual history update and covered experiences with the prescribed contraceptive, feelings about the teen center program, things that could have made it easier to use birth control when they first started having sex, influences of peers on decision to enroll and to continue in the teen program, and Miller's Personal Style Inventory. Dropouts at this juncture were asked, in addition, questions concerning reasons for drop and intentions to return to the clinic.

The annual exam interview used a time-line approach. The purpose of this technique was to obtain information on the chronology of events relevant to the teen's sexual and contraceptive history, including pregnancy and pregnancy termination, along with a chronology of those other events which we felt might influence sexual and contraceptive behavior. We hoped in this manner to be able to place the target sexual behaviors in the larger context of the variety of important events that occur to teens during adolescence. In addition to the time-line data, detailed information on the teen's postrap contraceptive history, relationships with significant boyfriends and parents, and a measure of adolescent self-esteem (Coopersmith, 1959) were also obtained.

Of the original cohort of 257 teens, we obtained medical interviews from 219, supply interviews from 175, and annual interviews from 143. The 114 teens for whom we did not obtain annual interviews were about equally divided among those who did not agree to be interviewed initially or at a subsequent interview, and those who were lost to follow-up through the family moving, the phone being disconnected or changed to an unlisted number, or the teen leaving home. The major difference between the 143 teens for whom we obtained annuals and the 114 for whom we did not, was race. In the final sample of 143 there were 21 percent whites compared to 30 percent in the original sample of 257. The final sample also contained significantly fewer teens who had been pregnant prior to rap and more teens who had not been sexually active prior to rap.

The results discussed below are primarily based on the 143 teens who constituted the completed sample.

RESULTS

Introduction

The presentation of the results of our study follows the teens' chronological progression through the program. First we look at the status of the teens at the time they enter the program at the initial rap session. We then examine program drop-out during the interval between the rap session and the initial medical interview. Our focus then shifts to the problem of method continuance over the next 18 months. A presentation of other findings with program implications concludes this section.

Sample at Time of Rap: Background, and Prerap Sexual and Contraceptive History

The background information on the 257 teens who were eligible for inclusion, and who consented to participate in the study, was obtained from a questionnaire the teens filled out prior to their first rap session. Their ages ranged from 13 to 17 with a median age of 16. The racial breakdown was 68 percent black, 31 percent white, and 1 percent Latino. Religious affiliation was given as Protestant 56 percent, Catholic 18 percent, and 26 percent in the category other or none. Based on answers to the questions about occupation of head of household, education of parents, and residential location, our impression is that this sample came from predominantly middle-class rather than lower class background.

Most of the teens, 89 percent, had had sex prior to rap. This finding agrees with other studies of clinic populations (Goldsmith et al., 1972; Reichelt and Werley, 1975) and would strongly argue against the notion of some that availability of contraceptives and teen programs fosters teen-age sexual activity. Of these, 62 percent had used, at least at some time, some form of birth control. Of the methods, withdrawal was the one most frequently used (53%), then condom (43%), rhythm (35%), pill (30%), and finally, spermicides (19%). This pattern of pre-rap contraceptive usage is similar to that reported in other studies (e.g., Finkelstein, 1972). A sizable number of the teens, 19 percent, had been previously pregnant; of these a little over half (56%) had had an abortion, and 44 percent had borne the child.

Drop-out at the Time of the Initial Medical Examination

The first juncture at which teens could drop out of the program was between rap and the initial medical interview which was typically scheduled from 1 to 2 weeks after rap. Of the 257 teens for whom we have rap data, 38 were lost to follow-up (see Figure 11-1). Of the 219 teens for whom we had the first (medical) interview, all but 17 of them (8%) made an appointment for the medical exam prior to receiving a method. A variety of reasons were given by those who did not make an appointment. These included going to another physician, not being sexually active, fear of pill side effects, and concern about the medical exam itself. An additional 26 teens made an appointment

Flowchart of status at first interview:

- Original cohort of consenting teens, 13–17 years of age: **257**
  - Had first interview: **219**
    - Initial continuers: **176**
      - Early returners: 1–4 weeks: **152**
      - Late returners: 4–12 weeks: **24**
    - "Good" drops: **16**
      - Sexually inactive at time of rap: **7**
      - Went to other MD: **6**
      - Was pregnant at rap: **3**
    - "Bad" drops: **27**
      - Regularly used ineffective method: **7**
      - Sporadic or no use of birth control: **20**
  - Missed first interview or refused: **38**

Criterion groups based on pattern of contraceptive behavior over approximately 18 months following rap

	Early returners: 1–4 weeks	Late returners: 4–12 weeks	Sexually inactive at time of rap	Went to other MD	Was pregnant at rap	Regularly used ineffective method	Sporadic or no use of birth control	Total
A1 Continuous use of effective contraception[a]	42	2						44
A2 Effective contraception except when sexually inactive	6	1	1		1			9
B1 Effective, ineffective, effective	11	2						13
B2 Ineffective, effective	1	1				2	4	8
B3 Effective, ineffective	15	2	1	2	1			21
B4 Ineffective, effective, ineffective							2	2
B5 Episodic use of pill	6	1	1				1	9
B6 No use of effective contraception	3	1				3	1	8
B7 No use of contraception	1		2				1	4
C1 Effective, ineff., preg., eff.	2							2
C2 Ineffective, preg., eff.	2					1	1	4
C3 Effective, ineff., preg.	5	4					2	11
C5 Episodic, preg., episodic	5						1	6
C6 Ineffective, preg., ineff.		1					1	2
Sub-totals	99	15	5	2	2	6	14	143

[a] Effective methods were defined as pill, IUD, diaphragm and the condom/foam combination

Figure 11-1. Contraceptive patterns of teens over 18-month interval following initial rap session.

but did not keep that or any subsequent appointments. Again, the reasons given were varied; they included among others, lack of transportation ($n=5$), inconvenient clinic hours ($n=4$), moving from the area ($n=3$), fear of pill and/or exam ($n=4$), and having their menses at the time their appointment was scheduled ($n=5$). In all, the attrition between rap and the first interview was 43 of 219 teens (20%). Of those 176 who did return for the medical examination and received a method, 152 (86%) were classified as "early returners." The late returners obtained their method anywhere from 4 to 12 weeks after rap. During the rap-medical interval most of the late returners were at risk of becoming pregnant.

The 43 teens who discontinued the program were further categorized as "good" drops and "bad" drops following the distinction used in an earlier study of dropouts from an adult clinic (Ager, Werley, and Shea, 1973). Good drops are those who are at little or no risk following drop (see Figure 11-1). It is for this reason that those who were discovered to be pregnant at the time of rap are categorized as good drops. The bad drops include those who are at risk of an unplanned pregnancy following program discontinuance. These teens continued to be sexually active but used either ineffective methods or no method at all.

Because the teen program itself was terminated shortly after the medical interviews were obtained, further evaluation of program drop at later junctures was precluded. As a result, our focus shifted to the incidence of, reasons for, and consequences of, method discontinuance as discussed below.

Contraceptive and Sexual History of the Teens over 18 Months Following Rap

We will now look at the patterns of contraceptive behaviors shown by our teens for approximately 18 months following rap. These data are based on the 143 teens for whom we were able to obtain final (annual) interviews.

The three major categories (A, B and C) and the 14 subcategories of contraceptive patterns are shown as rows in the lower part of Figure 11-1. The A categories included 53 out of 143 teens (37%) who were at little or no risk during the period. The A_1 group used effective contraception continuously; the A_2 group used effective contraception when they were sexually active.

The B categories represent those teens who were at risk during the interval but who did not get pregnant. Of course, the amount of absolute risk defined by the frequency of unprotected, or partially protected, intercourse differed considerably among individuals and to some extent between groups. (We are currently developing a risk scale taking into account both total frequency of sex and type of method used over the 18-month period.) You will note that the

44 teens (31%) in groups B_1–B_4 used an effective method at some time during the interval while groups B_5–B_7 (21 teens, 15%) never did.

Finally, the C groups are numbered so that their contraceptive use patterns during the time they were not pregnant correspond as closely as possible to the B groups. We note that the C groups include only those who became pregnant during the 18-month interval following rap and specifically exclude those who were discovered to be pregnant at rap. Altogether 25 of the 143 teens (17%) became pregnant during the 18-month interval. This group included 19 of the 114 initial acceptors of a method. It is interesting to note that these initial continuers were almost as likely to become pregnant as the initial program drops. However, none of the 9 "good drops" became pregnant whereas 6 of 20 of the "bad drops" did. Looking at the pregnancy rate from another point of view, we see that 25 of the 90 teens (28%) who were at risk during the 18 months (the B and C groups) became pregnant during this period.

We now turn to the relationship between initial program drop and method discontinuance. By collapsing the categories in Figure 11-1, we show in Table 11-1a the relationship between four initial program groups and the three main criterion groupings descriptive of the full 18-month period. In interpreting this table, however, one must bear in mind that bad drops by definition cannot be in the no-risk (A) group. Table 11-1b is presented to correct for this by comparing those teens who either continued using a method, or obtained a method later, against those who either stopped using a method or who never got a method.

Over the 18-month period (see Table 11-1a) it would appear that the bad drops were more likely (30%) to become pregnant than those in the other three groups (15%), although this difference is not statistically significant. On the other hand, when one examines the contraceptive status of all 143 teens at the end of the 18 months (see Table 11-1b) there is virtually no difference in the percent of drops using effective contraception (15 of 29, or 52%) and the effective initial continuers (50 of 114, or 52%). We are not suggesting that initial receipt of a method through the teen program makes no difference, but rather that such initial use does not ensure effective method continuation.

It seemed to us that the method discontinuance and pregnancy rates were high; certainly higher than we expected. What were the reasons for discontinuance? The reasons as reported by the teens are given in Table 11-2. Included in this tabulation are only those teens who discontinued the pill and were subsequently at risk. Those teens in group A_1 who discontinued one effective method but then changed to another effective method (e.g., from pill to IUD) or those in group A_2 who after discontinuing an effective method did not have sex are excluded. Also those teens in the B and C groups who began using an

Table 11-1. Relationship between program discontinuance and method discontinuance for the 143 teens.

TABLE 11-1a

	EARLY RETURN	LATE RETURN	GOOD DROP	BAD DROP	
A LITTLE OR NO RISK	48	3	2	0	53
B RISK	37	8	7	14	66
C PREGNANT	14	4	0	6	24
TOTALS	99	15	9	20	143

TABLE 11-1b

	RETURN	GOOD DROP	BAD DROP	
CONTINUED OR GOT METHOD LATER	59	3	12	74
STOPPED METHOD OR NO METHOD (AT RISK)	55	6	8	69
TOTALS	114	9	20	143

effective method later in the 18-month period and never discontinued, are also excluded.

The major reasons given by the 66 teens (see Table 11-2) can be further grouped into method reasons (e.g., experienced and feared pill side effects), program reasons (mostly related to the closing of the teen center program), and situational reasons (e.g., stopped having frequent sex or breakup with a boyfriend). Of the reasons listed, by far the most frequently cited (38 of the 66 teens, 58%) are those relating to side effects of the pill. These reasons were also the major ones found for drop out in our previous study on adults (Ager, Werley, and Shea, 1973). Of course, it is difficult to determine the

Table 11-2. Reasons[a] given by 66 teens who discontinued pill and were subsequently at risk.

	FREQUENCY	PERCENT OF 66 TEENS GIVING REASON
Experienced side effects	28	42
Feared side effects[b]	11	17
Stopped having (much) sex	8	12
Broke up with boy friend[c]	6	9
Teen center too far	4	6
Had no money or didn't want to pay	5	8
Teen center closed—didn't know new location or number	3	5
Didn't have time for appointment	2	3
Mother discouraged use	2	3
Boyfriend discouraged use	4	6
Wanted to get pregnant	3	5
No definite reason, e.g., got tired of taking, just wanted to stop	7	11
Lost pills	2	3
Not ascertained	1	2
	86	

[a]Some teens gave two reasons for a single stop; in other cases the teen gave different reasons for two separate stops.
[b]Ten of these teens did not report experienced side effects.
[c]Five of these teens are in addition to those giving the previous reason, i.e., stopped having sex.

extent to which such reasons are those actually leading to discontinuance or, rather, are after-the-fact rationalizations for discontinuance. Further, we have to keep in mind that the side effects reported are those attributed to the pill by the teens; certainly in some cases the reported side effects (e.g., weight loss) may be unrelated to pill usage. The same general comments may apply to the feared side effects reported.

The 13 (20%) teens who said they stopped using a method because they weren't having sex or broke up with their boyfriends are those who in reality had only a decrease in frequency of sex. (Those who stopped having sex completely after discontinuance would be in group A_2 and are not included in Table 11-2). These 13 teens apparently felt that continuing the pill was worthwhile only when they were having sex frequently and/or on a regular basis.

Some of the program reasons given by the teens (e.g., had no money or didn't know the new location of the clinic) are unique to this sample. Free supplies were available to the teens at the adult clinic after the teen center closed, although some teens apparently did not know this. Overall, program reasons for discontinuance did not appear to be as important as the method reasons and were about as important as the situational reasons, at least in terms of the frequency with which they were cited.

It would be useful to be able to predict future contraceptive behavior including use-effectiveness from information obtained at rap or at time of the medical exam. For example, teens predicted to be prone to method discontinuance could be given more extensive counseling or might be designated for more systematic follow-up.

To determine whether or not membership in the three main criterion categories was predictable, we used a Linear Discriminant Function Analysis (LDFA). The predictors used in the LDFA included the background variables of age and race, attitudes of teen toward contraception, the teen's perception of her boyfriend's and mother's attitudes toward contraception, a sexual development scale based on average age at which certain events occurred (first sex, menarche, etc.), scales of acceptance of sexuality, risk-taking and self-esteem, and a dichotomous variable of whether or not serious method side effects were reported.

The results of this analysis were disappointing. Not surprisingly from our earlier discussion of reasons for discontinuance, the side effects variable did predict group membership. Teens in the relevant pregnant groups (C_1–C_3) were most likely to report side effects, the B_1–B_4 groups next most likely, and the A groups least likely. Variables from the rap or the medical interview did not discriminate between the three groups in this analysis. It should be noted, however, that other investigators have found psychological and background variables which predict contraceptive behavior groups. For example, Mindick and Oskamp (1980) report that the Future Events Test significantly distinguished between clinic returners and drops.

Another approach to the problem of predicting contraceptive behavior was undertaken by one of us (SJA) with some suggestive results (Agronow, 1979). For a subset of 107 teens for whom the measures were appropriate, self-esteem, risk-taking, and report of side effects were used as predictors of risk versus no risk of pregnancy in the postrap interval. Risk-taking and self-esteem were combined to define the two categories of high self-esteem/low risk-taking versus low self-esteem or high risk-taking. The data are shown as a three-way contingency table (Table 11-3). The main result of interest in this table is that there appears to be no relationship betwen reported side effects and risk for the high self-esteem/low risk-taking group, whereas there is a strong relationship between these variables for those who are either low on self-esteem or high on risk-taking. The above result suggests that the predictors of contraceptive behavior may be different for various personality groups.

Table 11-3. The effect of self-esteem/risk taking on method continuance in the presence and absence of side effects.

CONTRACEPTIVE BEHAVIOR	HIGH SELF-ESTEEM-LOW RISK TAKER		LOW SELF-ESTEEM OR HIGH RISK TAKER		
	NO SIDE EFF.[a]	EXPR. SIDE EFF.	NO SIDE EFF.[a]	EXPR. SIDE EFF.	N
Continuous Use No Risk	13	4	21	4	42
Discontinue At Risk	14	6	21	24	65
N	27	10	42	28	107

Chi-square = 10.25, df=3, p<.05
[a]Excludes 13 persons who never got a method and 18 persons who got the method late.

Other Findings with Program Implications

In the initial interview the teens were asked to rate on a four-point scale (not important to very important) 15 possible problems they might have encountered in using the teen center program. Among the problems were four related to transportation (e.g., no car, taxi too expensive), two items dealing with waiting time and clinic hours, and six items concerned with attitudes of others toward their participation in the program (e.g., mother disapproves).

Problems with transportation were the ones most frequently rated as "very important," with 23 percent rating the item "taxis too expensive" and 17 percent the item "having no car." Disapproval of parents was also a significant problem. "The father disapproves" or "father might find out" were both rated as a very important problem by 19 percent of the group, while the percentages for the corresponding items for mothers were 16 and 15 percent respectively. Only 1 percent rated either "boyfried disapproval" or "friends finding out" as very imporatnt. The program-related items, "too long waiting times," "inconvenient clinic hours," and "clinic location," were rated as very important problems by 13, 10, and 10 percent of the teens, respectively.

Although only 10 precent of the sample rated clinic location as an important problem, we were struck by the extent to which the teens seemed to live relatively close the two clinics. We, of course, expected that more teens would come from nearby areas than from further away; it was the extent of this phenomenon that surprised us. The teen clinics were set up to serve a tri-county metropolitan area. With the exception of one other small program in a relatively remote part of one of the counties, they were the only teen programs operating at the time. Various outreach efforts had also been made to inform teens throughout the area of the programs' existence.

To look at the phenomenon more systematically we located the teen's residences on large-scale maps of the area and then determined the mileage to the teen center by the most convenient route. The distance to the teen center was then available as a variable in subsequent analyses.

Looking at the plots of residences on our maps it was obvious that the vast majority of the teens for each clinic came from surrounding neighborhoods. With regard to the question of the relationship between the teen's distance from the clinic and likelihood of remaining in the program, we found no significant difference between initial returners and initial program dorps. However, with regard to the relationship between distance from clinic and the 18 months contraceptive criterion, we have found that the teens who became pregnant lived significantly further away from the clinics.

DISCUSSION

Introduction

Our discussion will focus on those results which we feel have the most direct implications for teen contraceptive programs. At the outset it must be borne in mind that our sample and program are not necessarily representative in all respects to teens and teen programs in general. Nevertheless, the problems of high rates of program dropout and method discontinuance are probably common to most (Gordis et al., 1970; Mindick and Oskamp, 1980). Some of our discussion stems directly from the data and some is more speculative. In either case what follows represents our present conclusions based not only on our experience over two years with the teens but also on our reading of the research literature.

Choice of Method

The choice of method for teens is often a difficult one because of the episodic nature of their patterns of sexual activity. Unlike older women, both married and unmarried, who tend to have relatively stable sexual patterns within continuing relationships, the teen is more likely to be involved in shorter term relationships. Periods of relatively frequent coitus alternate with periods within which there is little or no sexual activity.

As is probably the case in most teen programs, almost all the teens received an oral contraceptive. This is not just due to advocacy of the pill on the part of the program physicians and other staff; for almost all of the teens the pill was their method of choice even though they frequently expressed reservations about possible side effects. The teens' choice of the pill may be, of course, in part due to their relatively limited knowledge about the other methods (Taylor, 1979). As we have seen, however, about half of these teens discontinued the pill at some point during the 18 months. Others who remained on the method did not always use it effectively. For many it was probably perceived or feared side effects which led them to discontinue. For others, a change in their pattern and frequency of sex, perhaps because of a breakup with their boyfriend led to discontinuance. A number of teens asked "why should I be taking these pills when I'm not having sex" or as it was more often put, "I'm not having that much sex." Unfortunately, when the pill was discontinued the teens did not change to another effective method even when they resumed having sex, but rather went back to the ineffective methods or to no method at all.

Given the seemingly high rates of method discontinuance with the pill perhaps more attention should be paid to the desirability of alternative methods at least under some circumstances. For example, a teen is probably a poor candidate for the pill if she is having sex infrequently and expresses fears about its safety, or if her mother or boyfriend have discouraged her initiating its use. In this case, even foam, cream or jelly might prove to have a greater use effectiveness. The condom/foam combination may offer a viable alternative to the pill particularly when the partner is supportive. For older or more mature teens the diaphragm/foam combination might be considered. If there are no contraindications the IUD might be the method of choice for younger teens or those assessed as having lower motivation to contracept (Kulig et al, 1980; Rauh, Johnson and Burket, 1976).

There are admittedly specific disadvantages with each of the methods including the possible health hazards associated with the most effective methods, the pill and IUD (Droegemueller and Bressler, 1980). As these authors express it, "The safe, simple, inexpensive, totally effective, easily reversible contraceptive, without side effects and not used at the time of sexual act—in short the ideal contraceptive—is yet to be developed" (p. 329). On the other hand, the costs and health hazards of unplanned teen pregnancies are usually even greater. More research, we feel, is needed on use effectiveness of all these methods under various combinations of sexual activity patterns and personal characteristics of the individual teen.

Counseling Implications

The time which the teen center physicians, nurses, and counselors have to spend with the teens, either individually or in groups, is limited. Consequently it is desirable that this time be used efficiently to promote effective contraceptive practice. A strategy which we feel may be useful is one which systematically prepares teens for the situations and experiences which could cause them to terminate use of effective methods. Such preparation is based on a large body of research in psychology which suggests that attitude change can be prevented by "innoculating" subjects with information which could produce such change (McGuire, 1968). Application of this strategy to the prevention of maladaptive behavior change in health-care settings has been reported by Johnson and Leventhal (1974) and Johnson (1977).

We foresee a similar methodology being employed by teen programs. We have identified a number of common situations which tend to lead to method termination (e.g., experience of side effects, infrequent sex, difficulty in getting supplies, or the influence of others discouraging use). It is first of all, necessary to point out to the teens how such situations can arise. Development of film dramatizations similar to those currently used to help teens understand their sexuality, we feel, would be useful tools in this endeavor. For example, one such dramatization could show a teen choosing to get the pill from the teen center but then experiencing side effects which force her to make a decision to terminate it. It is then necessary to illustrate the potential consequences of method termination. In our film this could be accomplished by having a girl friend or sister of the teen become pregnant. Finally, it is necessary to provide the teen with viable alternatives to that of simply terminating the method. In the film the teen could be shown returning to the teen center to talk to her counselor about receiving either another method or another type of pill prescription.

It is important to stress with the teen that when situations in her life arise, or problems with the method arise that may lead to discontinuing the method, that the teen center staff are available for advice and consultation. The teen should understand that such nonjudgmental counseling is available even if the teen should become pregnant. At no time should the teen feel that there is an onus attached to stopping a method or becoming pregnant in so far as support for her from the program is concerned.

Follow-up After Initial Enrollment

The relationship we have observed between program drop and pregnancy or risk of pregnancy suggests that teen programs should vigorously follow up those teens who appear to be program dropouts. Reasons for drop out should be assessed. These reasons may suggest ways of getting the teens back into the program. As suggested above, development of counseling and referral services for those teens who have dropped out because of pregnancy would also be particularly desirable.

Though our findings suggest a strong need to follow teens who drop from the program, they also suggest the necessity of more continuous and systematic contact with those teens who appear to be program continuers. More than half of our teens showed patterns of alternating method use and nonuse, but most of these would *not*, by most criteria, be labeled program drops. By systematic follow-up of these teens, instances of method discontinuance can be identified, and method change and/or further counseling provided.

We do not underestimate the time, money, and effort these suggested follow-up procedures entail. Teens are often hard to contact and some break appointments repeatedly. For example, of the 27 teens who we classified as initial "bad drops," 25 made an appointment for a medical exam but failed to keep it. Our experience in getting teens to participate in research interviews was similar. It was often necessary to call numerous times just to contact a teen; further, it was not unusual for the teen to break several appointments for an interview before finally appearing.

Our experiences, however, also suggested several remedies for the above problems. We were quite successful in obtaining interviews, both because of persistence of our interviewers, but also because of the personal rapport which we tried to develop between interviewer and teen. Whenever possible we tried to have the same interviewer who initially contacted a teen also interview that teen. We believe such a strategy would be useful for teen-center counselors. It may be desirable for individual counselors to be made responsible for follow-up of the teens they see on initial intake. Included in this responsibility would be careful record keeping so that the counselor is able to identify when the teen has deviated from the program's time schedule for return.

Though the innoculation and follow-up procedures we have suggested may strain already limited resources, our research strongly suggests that monies put toward these areas may greatly enhance the success of these programs.

Implications for Structure and Format of Programs

We now wish to raise some questions about the utility of certain components of the typical teen program. In doing so our intention is not to criticize such programs, but rather to suggest alternative approaches which might increase the effectiveness of such programs in both enrolling and retaining teens in need.

The first question concerns the requirement that teens attend a rap session prior to scheduling the medical examination after which they receive a method. At the rap session the teens are not only given information about, and demonstrations of, the various methods, but are also urged in the discussion to explore more generally the meaning of their own sexuality. That this is very useful educational experience for the teens we have no doubt. Our concern is that for some teens the requirement may act as a barrier for coming to the teen center in the first place. Not only does the rap involve more time for the visit, it also restricts, to some extent, the number of times per week that the teens can be scheduled for initial enrollment. Further, for some teens there may be a reluctance to discuss in a group setting sexual topics in general and their own sexuality in particular. Although we have no direct evidence on this, our guess is that the deterrent effect of the rap requirement is not negligible.

Our suggestion would be that initial rap attendance be voluntary; that is, the teens would be strongly urged to attend but not required to do so prior to scheduling them for their medical exam. Those teens not attending rap initially would be encouraged to do so at a later point in the program. For these teens, information about the various methods would be given in the counseling session before the method was prescribed, as is the case with adult family-planning clinics and private physicians. Whether or not the rap session is a mandatory requirement, we feel that the emphasis of such sessions should be primarily on the methods themselves and their use.

Our second question concerns the requirment of a pelvic examination prior to the prescribing of a method. The major purposes of the exam are to; (a) check for cervical cancer through the Papanicolaou Smear test, and (b) to check for vaginal infections. The second purpose is method related in that if vaginal infections are found both the IUD and pill may be contraindicated (Droegemuller and Bressler, 1980). Of course, if either a diaphragm or IUD were to be fitted the pelvic exam would be necessary anyway.

There is little doubt that for a sizable number of teens the pelvic exam represents a barrier to both enrolling in a program and to receiving an effective method (Urban and Rural Systems Associates, 1976). Further, giving the pelvic exam routinely greatly increases the cost of delivery of contraceptive services to teens and limits the times and sites at which such services are provided. On the other hand, it is usually argued that the overall incidence of contraindications to the IUD and pill identifiable through the exam would make the requirement both cost effective and a part of good clinical practice.

Given that the pelvic exam should be a requirement for all teens seeking a method, there are some things that can be done to minimize both its deterrent effect and its cost. First of all, fears and anxieties the teen might have prior to the exam may be alleviated through the use of Johnson's technique of sensation training (Johnson, 1977; Taylor, 1979). Presumably such preparation would also serve to relax the teen so that discomfort during the exam is lessened. Other procedures designed to lessen the discomfort of the exam are described by Taylor (1979). It is important that the experience of the exam be as trauma free as possible, not only for the sake of the teen herself, but also because her perceptions of the clinic experience, including the exam, may have considerable influence on those of her friends who might be in contraceptive need and considering program enrollment. Secondly, there seems to be no reason why the pelvic exam could not be administered by appropriately prepared nonphysician health providers such as nurse clinicians or nurse practitioners. These nurses could also fit IUDs and diaphragms, as well as prescribe oral contraceptives under physician supervision. More extensive use of such nonphysician personnel would serve to reduce costs and make possible expansion of the services provided.

Factors Which Would Make Services Easier to Use for Teens

Two of the most frequently reported problems in using the services by our teens were that there were too few days and hours available for convenient scheduling of appointments and that the rap and the medical examination appointments took too long. These problems have been reported in other studies (Urban and Rural Systems Associates, 1976) and, of course, are not unique to teen programs or even to family-planning clinics. The consequences of too few clinic hours or too long waiting times go beyond the inconvenience to the teen clients. To the extent these problems exist, or are perceived by the teens to exist, they may act as barriers to both initial enrollment and to program continuation. Greater use of nurse practitioners in the provision of services as discussed above might make possible arranging more flexible clinic hours as well as the more prompt delivery of services.

Another problem for some teen programs involves payment for services (Urban and Rural Systems Associates, 1976). If such payment is required, it should be based on the teen's ability to pay rather than on family income. Such fees should be nominal. Further, it is crucial that the payment policies be made clear to the teens. The perception that the services are expensive, even if that is not the case, may be enough to deter the teen from seeking such services.

Getting to and from the teen clinic was cited by a substantial number of our teens as a problem. A number of things might be done to make transportation less of a problem. For one thing the teens could be encouraged to come to the center with other girl friends or with their boyfriend. For some teens, parents might be able to provide a ride. Well-marked bus routes to the clinic and bus schedules could be made available.

As noted previously, our results suggest that providing more clinic sites closer to the teens' homes would greatly increase the utilization of teen program services. For one reason, the aforementioned transportation problems would be minimized. For another, it is likely that the availability of such services would become better known. There are, of course, a number of practical problems in implementing a delivery system based on the establishment of satellite clinics. Among the primary ones are availability of sufficient funds and trained personnel. A related consideration is the range and level of services and personnel which would be required for each satellite clinic. As noted before, elimination of mandatory rap sessions, and/or use of nurses to perform a wider range of medical services when they are necessary, would go a long way toward making possible the delivery of contraceptive services to teens through such multiple clinic sites.

Predicting Program Method Discontinuance

We have had limited success in identifying the demographic and psychological characteristics of those who were most likely to discontinue the programs. Part of the reason for this problem may reside in the diversity of reasons for terminating a method, and part in the need to understand the complex nature of interactions among psychological and situational variables. Fishbein and Ajzen (1975) have suggested that only very specific knowledge of both attitude and situation can yield adequate prediction of behavior. When these interactions were examined carefully by one of us (Agronow, 1979), prediction of method discontinuance was greatly improved. The relationship which we have reported between self-esteem/risk taking, experience of side effects and method discontinuance provides a little of the flavor of this approach. It was not expected that either self-esteem alone or risk taking alone would predict method discontinuance. Specifically, only those teens both high in self-esteem and low in risk taking were expected to be sufficiently motivated to continue effective method use after experiencing side effects. The results bore this hypothesis out.

It seems to us that it is important that we be able to identify those teens who are least likely to be successful contraceptors so that particular attention could be given to them. Where follow-up procedures are employed, counselors assigned such teens might be alerted in advance. Also, preparatory materials could be developed for these teens in programs which choose to use our innoculation techniques. In short, for the effort needed to identify such teens there would be, we feel, a sufficient payoff in terms of improved method and program continuance and better allocation of program resources.

Conclusions

We do not underestimate the difficulties of improving contraceptive effectiveness among teens. Much of the difficulty lies not in lack of availability of services, but rather in the ambivalence concerning use of contraception on the part of teens themselves. Problems cited by the teens in using services may be, in many cases, simply rationalizations for their not adopting, or discontinuing, effective contraception. Nevertheless, we feel that it is critical that teen programs entail as few barriers to use of such services as possible.

We have emphasized that to bring the sexually active teen into the health-care system is only the first step. Ensuring continuity of effective practice is equally important. We must bear in mind that the teens in the present sample did, after all, enroll in the program in order to obtain a method; presumably their motivation to contracept is on the average higher than for the majority of those sexually active teens who do not obtain contraceptives from a private physician or clinic. As teen programs expand to include more teens, we might expect that the average motivational level of those enrolled would decrease. Consequently both program and method discontinuance might be expected to increase unless successful program procedures to decrease discontinuance are instituted. Innovative attempts to implement such procedures would seem to be an essential part of any teen program.

REFERENCES

1. Ager, J.W., Werley, H.H., and Shea, F.P. Correlates of continuance in a family planning program. *JOGN Nursing*, 1973, **2**, 15–23.
2. Agronow, S.J. *The Utility of Person and Situation Variables as Predictors of Teen Contraceptive Behavior*. Unpublished doctoral dissertation, Wayne State University, 1979.
3. Akpom, C.A., Akpom, K.L., and Davis, M. Prior sexual experience of teenagers attending rap sessions for the first time. *Family Planning Perspectives*, 1976, **8**, 203–206.
4. Baldwin, W.H. Adolescent pregnancy and childbearing—Growing concerns for Americans. *Population Bulletin*, 1976, **31**, 1–36.
5. Bracken, M. and Kasi, S. Factors associated with dropping out of family planning clinics in Jamaica. *American Journal of Public Health*, 1973, **63**, 262–271.
6. Caplan, H.M. Teen rap session. In Sarah Lewit (Ed.), *Advances in Planned Parenthood* (Vol. **8**). Princeton: Excerpta Medica, 1973.
7. Card, J.J. and Wise, L.L. Teenage mothers and teenage fathers: The impact of early childbearing on the parents' personal and professional lives. *Family Planning Perspectives*, 1978, **10**, 199–205.
8. Coombs, L.C., Freedman, R., Friedman, J., and Pratt, W.F. Premarital pregnancy and status before and after marriage. *American Journal of Sociology*, 1970, **75**, 800–820.
9. Coopersmith, S. A method for determining types of self-esteem. *Journal of Abnormal and Social Psychology*, 1959, **59**, 87–94.
10. Cutright, P. The teenage sexual revolution and the myth of an abstinent past. *Family Planning Perspectives*, 1972, **4**, 24–31.
11. Dott, A.B., and Fort, A.T. Medical and social factors affecting early teenage pregnancy: A literature review and summary of the findings of the Louisiana Infant Mortality Study. *American Journal of Obstetrics and Gynecology*, 1976, **125**, 532–536.
12. Droegemueller, W., and Bressler, R. Effectiveness and risks of contraception. *Annual Review of Medicine*, 1980, **31**, 329–343.

13. Finkelstein, R. Program for the sexually active teenager. *Pediatric Clinics of North America*, 1972, **19**, 791–794.
14. Fishbein, M., and Ajzen, I. *Belief, Attitude, Intention, and Behavior: An Introduction to Theory and Research*. New York: Addison-Wesley, 1975.
15. Forrest, J.D., Sullivan, E. and Tietze, C. Abortion in the United States, 1977–1978, *Family Planning Perspectives*, 1979, **11**, 329–341.
16. Furstenberg, F.F., Jr. The social consequences of teenage parenthood. *Family Planning Perspectives*, 1976, **8**, 148–164.
17. Furstenberg, F.F., Gordis, L.T. and Markowitz, M. Birth control knowledge and attitudes among unmarried adolescents: A preliminary report. *Journal of Marriage and the Family*, 1969, **31**, 34–42.
18. Furstenberg, F.F., Jr., Masnick, G.S., and Ricketts, S.A. How can family planning programs delay repeat teenage pregnancies? *Family Planning Perspectives*, 1972, **4**, 54–60.
19. Goldsmith, S., Gabrielson, M.O., Gabrielson, I., Mathews, V., and Potts, L. Teenagers, sex and contraception. *Family Planning Perspectives*, 1972, **4**, 32–38.
20. Gordis, L, Finkelstein, R., Fassett, J.D., and Wright, B. Evaluation of a program for preventing adolescent pregnancy. *New England Journal of Medicine*, 1970, **282**, 1078–1081.
21. Hall, M.F. and Reinke, W. Factors influencing contraception continuation rates: The oral and intrauterine methods. *Demography*, 1969, **6**, 335–346.
22. House, E.A. and Goldsmith, S. Planned Parenthood services for the young teenager. *Family Planning Perspectives*, 1972, **4**, 27–31.
23. Jaffe, F.S. and Dryfoos, J.G. Fertility control services for adolescents: Access and utilization. *Family Planning Perspectives*, 1976, **8**, 167–175.
24. Johnson, J.E. The effects of preparatory information on the recovery of surgical patients. *Sigma Theta Tau Monograph Series 76, A tripartite research conference*, 1976, **2**, 6–19.
25. Johnson, J.E. A better way to calm the patient who fears the worst. *RN*, 1977, **40**, 47–52.
26. Johnson, J.E. and Leventhal, H. The effects of accurate expectations and behavioral instructions on reactions during a noxious medical examination. *Journal of Personality and Social Psychology*, 1974, **29**, 710–718.
27. Johnson, L.B., Burket, R.L., and Rauh, J.L. Problems with contraception in adolescents: The successful use of an intrauterine device. *Clincial Pediatrics*, 1971, **10**, 315–319.
28. Jorgensen, V. One-year contraceptive follow-up of adolescent patients. *American Journal of Obstetrics and Gynecology*, 1973, **115**, 484–486.
29. Jorgensen, V. Selection and management of contraceptives in the adolescent patient. *Fertility and Sterility*, 1976, **27**, 881–885.
30. Kantner, J.F. and Zelnik, M. Sexual experience of young unmarried women in the United States. *Family Planning Perspectives*, 1972, **4**, 9–18.
31. Kantner, J.F. and Zelnik, M. Contraception and pregnancy: Experiences of young unmarried women in the United States. *Family Planning Perspectives*, 1973, **5**, 21–35.

32. Kulig, J.W., Rauh, J.L., Burket, R.L., Cabot, H.M., and Brookman, R.R. Experience with the copper 7 intrauterine device in an adolescent population. *Journal of Pediatrics*, 1980, **96**, 746–750.

33. Marinoff, S.C. Contraception in adolescents. *Pediatric Clinics of North America*, 1972, **19**, 811–819.

34. Maternal and Child Health Service. Adolescent Profile. *Maternal and Child Health Information*, No. *26*, 1972.

35. McCalister, D. and Thiessen, V. Prediction of the adoption and continued use of contraception. *American Journal of Public Health*, 1970, **60**, 1372–1381.

36. McGuire, W.J. The nature of attitude and attitude change. In G. Lindzey and E. Aronson (Eds.), *The Handbook of Social Psychology*, (Vol. 3, 2nd Ed). Reading, Mass: Addison-Wesley, 1968.

37. Menken, J. The health and social consequences of teenage childbearing. *Family Planning Perspectives*, 1972, **4**, 45–53.

38. Mindick, B and Oskamp, S. *Contraception use effectiveness: The fit between method and user characteristics*. Final progress report for Contract Number 1-HD-82842, 1980.

39. Minkowski, W.L., Weiss, R.C., Lowther, L., Shonick, H., and Heidbreder, G.A. Family planning services for adolescents and young adults. *Western Journal of Medicine*, 1974, **120**, 116–123.

40. Morris, L. Estimating the need for family planning services among unwed teenagers. *Family Planning Perspectives*, 1974, **6**, 91–97.

41. National Center for Health Statistics. Interval between first marriage and legitimate first birth, United States, 1964–1966. *Monthly Vital Statistics Reports*, **18**(12), Supplment, March, 1970.

42. National Center for Health Statistics. A study of infant mortality from linked records, by age of mother, total birth order, and other variables, United States. *Vital and Health Statistics*, Series 20, No. **14**, 1973(a).

43. National Center for Health Statistics. Teenagers: Marriages, divorces, parenthood, and mortality. *Vital and Health Statistics*, Series 21, No. *23*, 1973(b).

44. National Education Association. Pregnant teenagers. *Today's Education*, 1970, **59**, 1–26.

45. Nortman, D. Parental age as a factor in pregnancy outcome and child development. *Reports on Population/Family Planning*, **16**, 1974.

46. Oppel, W.C. and Royston, A.B. Teen-age births: Some social, psychological, and physical sequelae. *American Journal of Public Health*, 1971, **61**, 715–756.

47. Presser, H.B. The timing of the first birth, female roles and black fertility. *Milbank Memorial Quarterly*, 1971, **49**, 329–361.

48. Presser, H.B. Early motherhood: Ignorance or bliss? *Family Planning Perspectives*, 1974, **6**, 8–14.

49. Rauh, J.L., Burket, R.L., and Brookman, R.R. Contraception for the teenager. *Medical Clinics of North America*, 1975, **59**, 1407–1419.

50. Rauh, J.L., Johnson, L.B., and Burket, R.L. The reproductive adolescent. *Pediatric Clinics of North America*, 1976, **20**, 1005–1020.

51. Reichelt, P.A. and Werley, H.H. Contraception, abortion and venereal disease:

Teenagers' knowledge and the effect of education. *Family Planning Perspectives*, 1975, **7**, 83–88.

52. Sarrel, P.M. and Davis, C.D. The young unwed primipara: A study of 100 cases with 5-year follow-up. *American Journal of Obstetrics and Gynecology*, 1966, **95**, 722–725.

53. Sear, A.M. Clinic discontinuation and contraceptive need. *Family Planning Perspectives*, 1973, **5**, 80–88.

54. Settlage, D.S.F., Baroff, S., and Cooper, D. Sexual experience of younger teenage girls seeking contraceptive assistance for the first time. *Family Planning Perspectives*, 1973, **5**, 223–226.

55. Shah, F., Zelnik, M., and Kantner, J. Unprotected intercourse among unwed teenagers. *Family Planning Perspectives*, 1975, **7**, 39–44.

56. Siegel, E., Thomas, D., Coulter, E., Tuthill, R., and Chipman, S. Continuation of contraception by low-income women: A one-year follow-up. *American Journal of Public Health*, 1971, **61**, 1886–1900.

57. Sorensen, R.C. *Adolescent Sexuality in Contemporary America: Personal Values and Sexual Behavior Ages 13–19*. New York: World, 1973.

58. Speidel, J.J. and Wiener, L. Continuance of family planning in a health department clinic. *American Journal of Obstetrics and Gynecology*, 1970, **108**, 1134–1140.

59. Taylor, D. Contraceptive counseling and care. In R.T. Mercer (Ed.), *Perspectives on Adolescent Health Care*. Philadelphia: Lippincott, 1979.

60. Thornburg, H.D. A comparative study of sex information sources. *Journal of School Health*, 1972, **42**, 88–91.

61. Tietze, C. Teenage pregnancies: Looking ahead to 1984. *Family Planning Perspectives*, 1978, **10**, 205–207.

62. Tietze, C. and Lewit, S. The IUD and the pill: Extended use-effectiveness. *Family Planning Perspectives*, 1972, **8**, 184–191.

63. Trussell, T.J. Economic consequences of teenage childbearing. *Family Planning Perspectives*, 1976, **8**, 184–191.

64. Trussell, J. and Menken, J. Early childbearing and subsequent fertility. *Family Planning Perspectives*, 1977, **10**, 209–218.

65. Urban and Rural Systems Associates. *Improving Family Planning Services for Teenagers*. San Francisco, 1976.

66. U.S. Bureau of the Census. Fertility Indicators: 1970. *Current Population Reports*, Series P-23, No. *36*, 1971.

67. Vener, A.M. and Stewart, C.S. Adolescent sexual behavior in middle American revisited: 1970–1973. *Journal of Marriage and the Family*, 1974, **36**, 728–735.

68. Whelan, E.M. Illegitimate and premaritally conceived first births in Massachusetts, 1966–1968. *Social Biology*, 1972, **19**, 9–28.

69. Zelnik, M. and Kantner, J.F. The resolution of teenage first pregnancies. *Family Planning Perspectives*, 1974, **6**, 74–80.

70. Zelnik, M. and Kantner, J.F. First pregnancies to women aged 15–19: 1976 and 1971. *Family Planning Perspectives*, 1978(a), **10**, 11–20.

71. Zelnik, M. and Kantner, J.F. Contraceptive patterns and premarital pregnancy

among women aged 15–19 in 1976. *Family Planning Perspectives*, 1978(b), **10**, 135–142.

72. Zelnik, M. and Kantner, J.F. Sexual and contraceptive experience of young unmarried women in the United States, 1976 and 1971. *Family Planning Perspectives*, 1977, **9**, 55–61.

12.

From Macho To Mutuality: Helping Young Men Make Effective Decisions About Sex, Contraception, and Pregnancy

Peter Scales, Ph.D.
Human Services Consultant,
Denver, Colorado

and

Douglas Beckstein, B.A.,
Program Developer,
Santa Cruz, California

This paper reviews research and theory on young men's decision making about sexuality, contraception, and pregnancy. It considers how the socialization of young males continues to be based upon myths that restrict "acceptable" male behaviors in sexual decision making, and perpetuate a macho orientation to relationships. The paper discusses research findings demonstrating that sexual experience continues to be perceived as a crucial rite of passage for young men, and describes the implications of these factors for decisions made about contraception, and, although the literature is sparse, on pregnancy resolution. Throughout the paper, references are made to organized programs intended to counter the limitations of macho socialization and encourage mutuality in decision making. The paper concludes with a summary and series of recommendations for organizations and adults concerned with the sexual health of young men.

INTRODUCTION

In the fall of 1978, the federal Office for Family Planning awarded approximately $250,000 to 16 programs around the country meant to increase sexual health-care services to men, particularly teenage men. Although this was a relatively insignificant sum in the overall $135 million allocation for family-planning services (about .2 percent of the total), the orientation of these supported programs marked a significant change in efforts intended to reach men.

In the early 1970s, the former Office of Economic Opportunity had supported a few projects that concentrated on the distribution of condoms to men, particularly in poor areas. Pamphlets on men's roles in family planning were produced, such as "It's a Man's World," and studies were made of the extent to which free condom distribution programs were a meaningful addition to pregnancy prevention approaches.[1,2] Men's involvement with sexual and contraceptive decisions was thus viewed largely in terms of condom use or non-use. The 1978 effort, however, considered men not simply as potential users of condoms, but as supporters of their partner's contraceptive use and as sexual people with a full range of sexual health-care needs and a variety of ways in which they could be "involved" in family planning. These programs, housed primarily in Planned Parenthood affiliates and city and county health departments, were concerned with other issues as well as family planning, including sexually transmitted diseases, testicular cancer, increasing awareness of prostate problems, and a host of health issues especially affecting men, such as high blood pressure, ulcers, and heart attacks.

This orientation developed in the mid-1970s as the burgeoning women's movement increasingly prompted men to reassess and reconsider their attitudes toward women, work, love, and themselves. While no single event or publication had the galvanizing impact on men's issues comparable to what Friedan's *The Feminine Mystique* had done for the women's movement in 1963, the mid-1970s did see a gradual increase in the number of books and articles written about men and sexuality, and a concomitant deepening of the realization that pregnancy prevention approaches that ignored the male role in sexual and contraceptive decisions were undercutting their own effectiveness. Indeed, as Luker noted, only since the early 1960s and the development of the pill has contraception been seen as a woman's responsibility, and, by extension, "her fault if something goes wrong." As she observed, until that time, (about 1976) "most contraceptors were men wearing condoms." As pill use became more prevalent, however, "family planning" programs focused more on women and female methods.[28] Then, too, a central theme of the women's movement was that women's liberation entailed greater control over their own bodies and their own reproduction. Thus, as the pill became the method of choice and contraception became more politicized, men were excluded from the mainstream of family-planning services, both in clinics and in the counseling offered by other agencies.

However, statistics on teenage pregnancy, and increasing concerns raised about the side effects of various female methods, prompted many professionals in the mid- to late 1970s to become disillusioned with static approaches that attempted to provide contraception to women without understanding the male partner and the relationship in which contraception might play a part. In addition, the research dealing with the consequences of adolescent pregnancy (largely supported by the Center for Population Research within the National Institute of Child Health and Human Development) also began describing the impact of early pregnancy, not only on young women, but also on the male partners who had been largely ignored in earlier research. All of these developments heightened professional concern with the theoretical understanding of (1) how young men make sexual and contraceptive decisions; (2) how they influence their partners at a variety of decision-making points; and (3) how their lives are affected by pregnancy and the various resolutions of pregnancy. In addition to the new theoretical interest, concern was raised over the practical ways in which "male responsibility" could be increased by educational and service programs. This represented a dramatic change from the earlier years of the decade, when, as late as 1975, a major theoretical article on sexual decision making among women treated men only in a footnote, noting that a compaarable theory also needed to be proposed for men.[31] By the late 1970s, when the Family Impact Seminar sponsored a study that included teenage pregnancy's effects on both the male's and female's parental families, both research and program orientations had acknowledged the importance of determining and responding to the male perspective on sexual decisions.

Several problems, however, still confront those concerneed with young men. Among these are: (1) the low priority that special program funding for men has in the overall federal response to adolescent pregnancy and the comparable lack of private sector support for similar efforts; and (2) the remaining misunderstandings among educators, youth workers, social service, and health-care professionals about (a) men's sexual health and psychology, and (b) model program approaches for providing sexual health care appropriate for men. This chapter begins to address these issues, first by reviewing men's sexual psychology as the framework for decision making, including a description of moral development theories as a basis for understanding men's decisions. Data are then presented on the teenage male as a maker of, and contributor to, decisions made about sex, contraception, and pregnancy. Finally, descriptions of model-program approaches are provided, and recommendations are presented for enhancing the ability of the professional to better understand and meet the sexual health-care needs of today's young man.

SEX-ROLE EXPECTATIONS OF AMERICAN MEN

"The male is in crisis. Buffeted by the women's movement and constrained by a traditional and internalized definition of 'masculinity,' men literally don't know who they are, what women want from them, or even what they want from themselves." Levine goes on to divide this crisis into two categories: (1) sex-role identity, and (2) sex-role strain. The sex-role identity framework, according to Pleck, assumes that men have an inner need to validate them-

selves as males and to identify with personality traits that are masculine. To
the extent that the culture makes it difficult for men to achieve that identity—
for example, by confusing the definition of masculinity—men develop problems in understanding themselves and others' expectations of them. The sex-
role strain paradigm, on the other hand, denies any such inner drive and
suggests that men's problems "stem from a culture that pressures them to
conform to a set of personality traits that are narrow and restrictive, to an
ideal of masculinity that is not only arbitrary but dysfunctional as well."[25]

Throughout life, men are taught specific rules of behavior that define the
traditional male role. When carried to extremes, this behavior has been labeled "macho." It must be remembered though, that the word "macho" does
not invariably have negative connotations. For example, among Hispanic
youth, "macho" may also connote a high degree of responsibility on the part
of the man who is a good provider, a caring father, and a loving husband.
Nevertheless, the male who is extremely reluctant and afraid to deviate from
social-role demands, to show weakness and tenderness, is often called "macho." From the earliest ages, boys are taught, for example, not to act like
girls. They may even be punished if they display traditional female behavior,
and might be labeled a sissy. The narrow definition of masculinity requires
that a "real man" be strong, cool, brave, and tough. A real man is expected
to use his head and hide his feelings. A real man is competitive and wants to
win or succeed at any cost. The man is the major breadwinner whose worth
in this definition is measured by the status of his job and the size of his
paycheck.

Men pay a high price in trying to measure up to this rigid macho role. For
example, men die on the average eight years earlier than women,[41] and the
cause is more likely to be cancer, heart problems, TB, or emphysema (and at
a 40 to 450 percent higher rate than women).[20] Men often ignore their bodies'
distress signals, and deny their need for help, until an absolute crisis is
reached. Since they resist treatment during the earlier stages of distress, their
hospitals stays tend to be longer than women's.[20] Men succeed in suicide
three times more often than women.[19] They dare not fail even in their own
self-destruction!

Male Sexual Myths

through no fault of my own, I reached adolescence . . . now I had to prove
myself with girls . . . to get a girl friend though, a boy had to have some
asset beyond the fact that he was alive . . . Boys were the ones who had to
take the initiative and all the responsibility. (I hate responsibility so much
that if my heart didn't beat of itself, I would now be a dim memory) . . .
Finally, through what surely could only have been the direct intervention of

the almighty, I would find myself on the dance floor with a girl . . . God how I envied girls at that moment. Wherever *it* was on them, it didn't dangle between their legs like an elephant's trunk. No wonder boys always talked about sex. That thing was always there. Every time we went to the john, there *it* was, twitching around like a fat little worm on a fishing hook . . . It was there, with a life and mind of its own, having no other function than to embarrass me.[24]

For years, traditional approaches to sex education, both in the schools and in community youth-serving agencies, were tailored for young women, since they were the ones who got pregnant and because they experienced a definite demarcation between nonrisk and risk status: menstruation. Sex education for, young men often involved little more than a rap by the coach on "responsibility," after which they returned to shooting baskets for the rest of the class hour. Topics such as masturbation, erections, wet dreams, rape, and the condom, among others, were rarely covered. The mistaken assumption in these approaches was that young men already knew all about sex and that only young women needed their questions answered.

Neither the school nor parents have prepared teenage men to be sexually responsible and knowledgeable. For example, a recent representative study of 1400 Cleveland parents discovered that only 1 percent of the mothers and 2 percent of the fathers had ever discussed wet dreams with their sons. Only 8 percent of the mothers and 2 percent of the fathers had discussed contraception with their sons. The most disturbing finding of this 1978 study was that, despite failing to educate their sons on contraception, 60 percent of the mothers and 70 percent of the fathers wanted to communicate to their sons that it was acceptable for them to have premarital intercourse![32]

Young teenage men rely more on sexual myths they learn from their friends on the street than on factual information from adult sources. The dictionary defines a myth as "a notion based more on tradition than on fact, an imaginary story of heroes and gods who accomplish superhuman tasks." Even though myths are not based on fact, many young men do not question macho myths because the myths are a vital part of the evolving definition of their masculinity, a definition that is based on accomplishing superhuman tasks of control and achievement.

Bernie Zilbergeld, in his book *Male Sexuality*, discusses many myths in detail. Some of these following myths may seem nonsensical to the reader, but, unfortunately, many young men consider some of these to be the "rules of the game." These are among the myths that educators, health-care professionals, and social-service workers must help young men dispel:

- Men should not express compassion, caring, trust, or feelings of tenderness; it's sexual performance that counts;

- Men must take charge and orchestrate sex;
- Men always want and are always ready for sex;
- Sex equals intercourse;
- Sex requires an erection;
- The only good sex is a "hard-driving fuck";
- Sex should be natural;
- The sexual revolution has eliminated the above myths.[48]

These myths are only an introduction to the vast amount of misinformation that young men believe. Unfortunately, they serve as the backdrop for young men's sexual decision making. In the next section, we describe some of the research on these and other important aspects of young men's decision making.

A Look at the Research

The framework within which young men make their sexual decisions is derived from several basic influences and the balance or imbalance among them:

- The extent to which the young man has accepted the importance of sexual experience as a measure of his emerging manhood.
- The extent to which his standards of sexual permissiveness are based on traditional thought about the relations of the sexes or are responding more to emerging egalitarianism.
- The cognitive moral level at which he predominantly reasons about sexual decisions and the extent to which his reasoning is dominated by either pole of personal gain or mutuality with his partner.
- His style of reasoning about relationships, his style of communication, the extent to which his interests in a relationship are short-term and act-centered or more long-term and person-centered, and the extent to which he is willing to assert and/or share power in a relationship.

The Importance of Sexual Experience

The extension of men's denial of dependency is exaggerated independence, and an extreme importance placed on self-reliance and experience (or the appearance of it), particularly sexual experience. Further, as noted in the earlier discussion of myths, "experience" means intercourse, and thus, for many young men, acceptable sexual behavior usually includes penis-vagina contact as a goal. The most recent Gallup Youth Survey, conducted October 1978, reported that, despite an increase in the 1970s in the proportion of teenage girls who had had intercourse, boys by 66 to 52 percent found premarital intercourse more acceptable than girls did.[3] Research has consistently shown that boys' sexual standards, more so than girls', are affected by their peer group more than by similarity to mother's or father's standards.[26] Teevan, for example, found that boys were significantly more likely than girls to report their sexual standards were "permissive" if they thought their peers' standards were also permissive.[39] Miller and Simon also reported, in a random sample of 2000 white Illinois teenagers, that males who were highly involved with their peers were more likely to be sexually experienced than males with low peer involvement, regardless of how extensively they were involved with their parents.[29] A review of the literature suggests that girls still feel more private and personal about their first sexual experiences. Teenage men much less frequently report that they were "in love" or had special, close feelings for their first sexual partner,[36] and at least one study has confirmed that boys more frequently tell their friends about their sexual experiences than girls do[8] (however, only 32 percent of males, compared with 62 percent of females, said in another study that they had discussed contraception with their friends).[40] The importance to young men of being accepted by their male peers results in sexual posturing: not only do most boys brag about their sexual exploits, but many also lie about their prowess. It has been said that there are three kinds of men: Those who kiss and tell; those who kiss and don't tell; and those who don't kiss but tell anyway. For many young men, it is more important to be accepted by other men than respected by women. In addition, young men often posture about their knowledge. Freeman et al. found that the males in their sample of black urban youth were significantly more likely than females to say they knew about sex than their peers, even though studies typically show young men to know very little![16]

Young men still seem more concerned with the *event* of first intercourse as a rite of passage than as the first chance to get to know another person in this intimate way. A study of over 1000 New York City teenagers, for instance, found that only one-quarter of the girls, but half of the boys, said "having sex" was an important goal in their lives.[34] They seem far less than young women to be concerned about the feelings between the partners and the moral goodness of their behavior. A study of 165 university students, for example, found that both sexes had about the same number of fears and concerns surrounding their first intercourse, but that women were significantly more worried about whether they were doing the "right thing," and men were significantly more concerned with whether they were doing it right, about their performance as lovers.[5] Some young men may be showing more concern, as Lieberman noted. He reported on an American Public Health Association study including several hundred young men, 40 percent black, many of whom stated that they had sexual experience because it "was expected of me." However, 80 percent of the sexually experienced males said they engaged in sex to "please and satisfy" a girl friend. This was the highest proportion responding to any reason for involvement, and far higher than the agreement given by girls to a comparable item.[27] Unfortunately, however, even this concern for the partner can be viewed as a reflection of concern for the man's technical skills as a lover, i.e., the myth that "it's sexual performance that counts." Concern over their experience, particularly relative to the *imagined* experience of their peers, is an important issue in young men's sexual psychology. Thus, it should not be surprising to note that teenage men are far more likely than women to state that their virginity is due to lack of sexual opportunities rather than to a series of negative decision made about potential sexual experiences that presented themselves. For example, in the American Public Health Association study, nearly eight times as many males as females reported this reason for virginity.[4]

Influencing Sexual Decisions

Together with these differences in concern over sexual experience are differences between the sexes in the influence they exert in relationships. For example, Peplau, Rubin, and Hill studied over 200 Boston area couples ("typically a sophomore woman dating a junior man") and reported that a whopping 95 percent of the women waited for the man to make the first sexual move in their relationships![30] While that figure may be inflated due to some women being unable to admit their own sexual assertiveness, it is an eye-opening reminder that whether a situation a couple is in becomes defined as "sexual" may depend more on the man's behavior than the women's. She may, of course, redefine the situation as nonsexual, but there is a good chance that if a man makes no sexual overtures, then nothing sexual will happen. These researchers also reported that, despite the overwhelming assent their research sample gave to egalitarian relationships, fewer than half said their decision making about sex was equal. Of the remainder, the students said by two to one that the man had more say regarding the type and frequency of sexual behavior. Interestingly, the higher the woman's educational aspirations, the more both sexes were likely to say the couple had equal power.

Unfortunately, many young men may exert their influence by lying. Sorensen studied over 400 teenagers nationwide in an attempted national probability study. Methodological problems weakened this study, but his findings are provocative, and until further Zelnik and Kantner data on young men is published in 1982, they are the most recent findings for a national sample. Sorensen reported that 30 percent of his teenage men (white) agreed it is "all right" to tell a girl you love her if that's what it takes to have sex with her.[38]

In a more recent local study, 70 percent of over 1000 Chicago area teenage males, mostly black, agreed with a similar statement.[14] It is not surprising then, to note that recent research with about 150 clinic-attending women aged 12–17, suggests that low female influence on sexual decisions is related to more frequent couple intercourse *and* less regular contraceptive use, i.e., the greater the woman's power over sexual decisions, the lower the risk of prenancy.[22] However, this research did not consider the stage of moral development at which the individuals were reasoning. In several college samples, for instance, D'Augelli and D'Augelli found that a man's reasoning at a level oriented to "law and order" (i.e., responsibly living up to socially defined roles) contributed more to a couple's *low* level of intercourse than even the degree of the female's guilt. Thus, although these men were dominant in setting the sexual standards for the couple, the risk of pregnancy was lessened because of their stage of moral reasoning.[12]

Moral Development and Sexual Decisions

Research in this area has been based on the work of Kohlberg, whose studies in turn have been based on the developmental concepts of Piaget. According to Kohlberg, moral reasoning involves stages of development that parallel the development of cognitive abilities as described by Piaget. The person moves from a "concrete" perception of the world based on absolutist terms to a more "abstract" perspective in which varying viewpoints are perceived and complexities are appreciated and amenable to reconciliation. In addition, an increased understanding of the symbolic meanings of language and behavior allows the person to anticipate the effects of behavior, and to manipulate those effects as desired. Studies of moral development and sexual decisions have so far, however, been based on relatively small and nonrandom samples; thus, much of the following discussion is speculative. Nevertheless, the finding of these studies are provocative. They have suggested, for example, that teenagers, particularly males, reason at lower levels of moral maturity when considering sexual issues than nonsexual ones.[18,23,44] Gilligan et al observed that the downward shift in reasoning appears to be from a "law and order" orientation to ones in which behavior is done primarily to please others or in which the individual tries to "get" what he can without regard to the other.[18] That young people should regress when considering sexual decisions is not surprising when one considers that young people generally receive little training in making sexual decisions. What seems to make sexuality and its related decision so different and problematic than learning how to agree in a family, to manage money, to be effective on the job, to succeed at school, etc., is that adults not only expect increased "experimentation" with all the latter issues, but also give frequent feedback on decisions made about them, while discouraging both practice and feedback on sexual decisions. As Hacker notes, the result of this lack of training is that each decision the young person makes is "essentially novel."[21] For many, the first few years following puberty are filled with decision points that are arrived at without a clear and consistent repertoire of problem-solving skills. In addition, as described earlier, males are more likely to have learned to be narrowly concerned with the act of having sex, than with the much more complicated process of developing a relationship. Unfortunately, the data discussed here indicates that men, who may be functioning at lower levels of sexual maturity than women, most often hold the sexual balance of power in teenage relationships.

The Gilligan et al. study of high-school juniors found that half of these teenagers functions at moral level 3, in which "good behavior equals social conformity."[18] D'Augelli and D'Augelli call this the level of Personal Concordance, at which sex is commonly an expression of love or special feeling. Another one-quarter of the teenagers functioned at level 2, at which the primary motivator is self-interest and "looking out for number one." A young man at this level might well use sexual "lines" in order to get sex. Another study reported that, while chronological age does not have a purely linear association with moral maturity, rough age gradations are possible: 8th graders (about 13–14 years old) are just beginning to move from level 2 to level 3 reasoning; 10th graders (about 15–16 years old) function predominantly at level 3; and 12th graders (about 17–18 years old) are more likely to be reasoning at level 4, in which behavior is motivated by a desire to live up to a socially defined role.[44] This "law and order" level is oriented toward responsibility, and according to D'Augelli and D'Augelli, the person at this level is motivated to be a "responsible member of society by following its rules or by recognizing and willingly accepting the consequences of a sexual relationship." The Gilligan data, however, indicate that while older teenagers may be functioning largely at level 4, many of them function at much less mature levels when considering sexual issues.

Moral Development and Sexual Permissiveness

In a study of college-age men and women, Jurich and Jurich tested subjects on both their moral development levels and also their standards of sexual permissiveness.[23] They reported that the highest levels of moral maturity were associated with more egalitarian standards of permissiveness. The highest moral stage was associated with the standard of "nonexploitative permissiveness without affection," meaning that intercourse is considered acceptable for both sexes without the precondition of love so long as neither partner tries to manipulate or hurt the other. Those who believed in the double standard, abstinence, or permissiveness without affection, showed the *lowest* moral maturity. That is, those either behaving traditionally or exploitatively were less mature; those behaving in a more egalitarian manner were more mature.

Of course, individual standards and moral stages are only partial influences on sexual decisions. Decisions are made and enacted in relationships, and both the kind of relationship and the style of a couple's communication about sexual decisions are very important. D'Augelli and D'Augelli, for example, described a general basis of "relationship reasoning" that they belive parallels Kohlberg's stages of moral maturity.[12] Relationship reasoning is viewed as "the person's interpersonal plan, a cognitive schema for contructing a personally rewarding social life." They posit three levels of relationship reasoning: egoistic (at which the optimal relationship is one that provides the most immediate benefits for the individual); dyadic (at which the partner's expectations are fulfilled and one strives to enact one's socially defined role in the relationship); and interactive (at which the optimal relationship is one that develops its own understanding of what is moral in that relationship through "mutual effort and discussion in genuine reciprocity").

PARTNER INFLUENCE ON DECISION MAKING

Early Sexual Intercourse, Communication, and Contraceptive Use

Certainly, sophisticated, consensual decision making does not characterize most teenagers, particularly at the time surrounding the first intercourse, when individual anxieties and excitement in the relative absence of communication is more likely than reasoned communication based on the ability to see the other person's point of view ("role-taking"). The elements affecting the first few months following initial intercourse are especially critical to understand, since 50 percent of all first teenage pregnancies occur within these first 6 months following a woman's first intercourse.[45] Unfortunately, until more Zelnik and Kantner data on young men becomes available later in 1982, most of the data on the first intercourse refers to women's first intercourse. Only 40 percent of women report using contraception at that first intercourse. For those who do not, a pattern is set that continues high risk of pregnancy: for 75 percent of the noncontraceptors, there is a 1-year lag between the first intercourse and the first use of contraception.[46]

If contraception is used, it is likely to be a "male method": fully two-thirds of use at the first intercourse is either withdrawal or use of the condom, and among those who have only had intercourse once, these methods account for 75 percent of first-time use. Unfortunately, condom use drops off dramatically with age and experience, most likely because pill use by women leaps correspondingly. Blacks are particularly undisposed to using a condom.[46]

The national data indicate the median age of a woman at her first intercourse is 16.3 years for whites and 15.6 for blacks (both younger than the 1971 figures).[47] The data presented earlier suggests that most of these teenagers are reasoning at a moral level at which behavior is done to please others and win their approval. Zelnik and Kantner reported that the male partners for the first intercourse tend to be 2 to 3 years older than the females.[47] She may perceive him as experienced, knowledgeable, and unlikely to be satisfied by a woman who will not have intercourse. Meanwhile, he has learned to value experience—turning down a sexual opportunity goes against his typical upbringing. Thus, he may escalate a potentially sexual situation, either by asserting himself or simply by failing to discourage a woman's initiative, even if he doesn't particularly want a sexual experience. He may also assume that, like most women who contracept, she is on the pill. She may in turn assume that, if this experienced and knowledgeable young man doesn't mention contraception, then everything is all right. In the worse case, he may try to reassure her by saying he'll "pull out." In Finkel and Finkel's study of urban males, however, less than one-third knew that a woman can still get pregnant even if the man withdraws before coming.[15] She, too, may reassure him. Hacker studied a small group of 38 young people and reported that "a number" of the males trusted a female partner who said she was protected, "despite real uncertainty."[21]

The common thread throughout these speculations is that so much ego-centered assumption rather than communication seems to occur. About 60 percent of Sorensen's sample of males, for example, "always, usually, or sometimes" just trusted to luck that the girl wouldn't get pregnant, and only 1 in 10 always made sure the female was using contraception.[38] In Arnold's study of inner-city youth who had obtained condoms in a neighborhood store, only 17 percent said they had discussed birth control with their partners.[1] Some young men may believe, as half of Finkel and Finkel's sample did, that contraception is only the woman's responsibility. Others may feel that using a condom is "too much hassle." Still others, such as 20 percent of the men in the Freeman et al. study, may feel that "sex without birth control shows more love."[16] Many young men probably do not even worry about the possibility of pregnancy. Nearly 40 percent of Sorensen's sample never worried about it, and, when only those with intercourse in the previous month were asked, only half of the boys, compared with over 80 percent of the girls, said they had worried about a pregnancy.[38] In many cases, they may not have worried simply because they were unaware of the risk of pregnancy. They may not feel the need for contraception if intercourse is not frequent and regular. Freeman et al., for example, reported that, in their study of black urban males who had taken a family-life course, 44 percent disagreed that birth control needs to be used if sex is only occasional.[16] It is no coincidence that in the American Public Health Association study, the best contraceptors among white teenagers had the highest knowledge of pregnancy risk.[4]

Ignorance, negative attitudes about contraception, lack of awareness of pregnancy risk, lower moral reasoning level in sexual situations, and a general lack of communication about sex and contraception, thus comprise an important constellation of factors that discourage contraceptive use. It is especially significant when considering the research findings that suggest the partner's influence is one of the most powerful contributors to contraceptive use or nonuse. Delamater and Maccorquodale, for example, studied a student and nonstudent sample including over 350 "sexually active," white males between the ages of 18–23. They found that, for both men and women, one of the two strongest predictors of contraceptive use was discussing contraception prior to intercourse; for men, the proportion of times together that a couple actually had intercourse was also positively related to use.[13] Venham found that in a sample of college females, the boyfriend's encouragement to use contraception was the best predictor of effective contraceptive practice.[42] In Thompson and Spanier's study of "sexually active" youth aged 17–22, including 131 males, partner's influence was a more important predictor of contraceptive use for both sexes than either peers' or parents' influence. For women, peer influence was also significant. Peer influence was measured by questions such as "I have discusses contraception thoroughly with my partner," and "my partner and I have carefully planned our contraceptive pattern."[40] Jorgensen, King, and Terry studied about 150 clinic attendees aged 12–18 and reported that, in addition to peer influence, the woman's satisfaction with the couple's communication about their sexual relationship was an important predictor of contraceptive use.[22] For teenagers, this partner influence may be especially critical: Rosen, Ager, and Martindale studied over 1000 women with "unwanted" conceptions and found that only married white women over age 18 reported a greater male influence on their decision to keep, adopt, or abort than did teenagers. Unmarried women over 18 of both races reported the least male influence on their decision.[33] Finally, a study of Consumer Reports readers found that one third of the 1000 male respondents (median age of 30) said they had discontinued condom use because their partners didn't like them.[11]

It should be noted that the multiple regressions used to predict contraceptive use in the above studies typically yield low coefficients. The Thompson and Spanier and Jorgensen, King, and Terry studies reported the highest percentage of variance in contraceptive use explained in the literature, 34 and 26 percent respectively.[40,22] It is clear that much of the explanation for teenage use or nonuse of contraception remains uncharted and speculative. It is equally clear, however, that communication between the partners is one of the key contributing factors. Another factor is the relative ignorance young men have about contraception and the unfortunate myths surrounding "male methods."

Male Contraceptive Methods

Although there are four "men's" methods (condom, vasectomy, abstinence, and withdrawal), only the condom and abstinence are appropriate to encourage among teenagers. Withdrawal is indeed better than no protection at all, but it is extremely difficult to perform correctly, and even then drops of sperm are included in the first drops of semen even prior to ejaculation. Vasectomy must be considered permanent sterilization and thus is also inappropriate.

The Condom. The first latex condom was developed around 1883. During World Wars I and II, the armed forces distributed condoms to the troops for venereal-disease prevention. Condom use grew, and it remained the most popular method of birth control in the United States until about 1965, when the pill and the IUD began cutting into condom sales. These two women's methods became so popular that many young men assumed that every woman was protected, thus discouraging their use of a condom. In 1970, condom sales hit an all-time low.[9] During the 1970s, a new generation of young men did not perceive their peer group using the condom in as great a proportion as earlier, and thus the condom because perceived as old-fashioned and unattractive. Hence, women sometimes labeled men who didn't use condoms as "irresponsible;" yet, birth control had become a "women only" issue that excluded men's involvement. Many family-planning clinics were designed to serve women and thereby excluded young men. Clinic staff often believed that men didn't like condoms, so clinics that did distribute condoms frequently stocked only the cheapest brand. Although most clinics stock numerous kinds of pills, few clinics even today stock as many brands of condoms, thus perpetuating a double standard that discourages the male's participation by limiting his options.

Condoms Give No Feelings. The most common reason given by young men for not using condoms is that they reduce pleasure. In growing up, most men learn that condoms give no feelings years before they've ever used one! They listen to the older boys, mimic their words and their behaviors, and come to realize that "real men" aren't supposed to like condoms because they "give no feelings." Many young men have walked around with condoms in their pockets but never used them. In our counseling, some of us will be comfortable debunking this myth simply by pointing out the above points. Others may add that different kinds of condoms may actually increase sensation. Still others might point out that, if sensation is decreased, a young man might gain better control over his ejaculation and thus be able to enhance his love making. Further, the condom is still a major means of protection against sexually transmitted diseases.

Abstinence. Periodic or complete abstinence can also be encouraged. If neither a young man nor a young woman is protected, they simply should not have sex. More importantly, the decision to have a sexual experience with someone should be made on the basis of emerging intimacy and sharing with that person, and not on the basis of feeling pressure to conform to macho stereotypes. Increasingly, young men are learning to say "no" because of how they feel about their partners. The ability to do this depends on several factors: (1) the young man's self-esteem (if how he feels about himself is derived largely from his sexual exploits, it will be difficult to turn down sexual opportunities); (2) the extent to which saying "no" is perceived as congruent with his definition of manhood (despite our encouragement of "personhood," it is still crucial for young people to develop a firm gender identity, and if a young man feels that *not* having sex is an acceptable part of "manhood," it will be easier for him to make that choice); and (3) the young man's skill at moral reasoning and communication about sex with his partner. For adults working with young people, enhancement of these three factors means providing opportunities for young men to raise their self-esteem in nonsexual ways, and serving as role models for young men so that they are encouraged to emulate nontraditional behavior. They can help young men rehearse their decision making and communication skills through theater groups, role playing, problem solving, and perhaps even by training older boys to serve as "big brothers" to younger ones with similar issues to confront.

The importance of adults as role models cannot be stressed too much. Machismo exists for many men, not because it holds strong appeal, but because we have not defined a new role for young men who are sensing and trying to come to terms with their sexuality and their wholeness. Until we help them feel good about themselves in other ways, what else can we expect? We need to model the behavior we hope to encourage. Staff who make sexist remarks and cheap double entendres, engage in bathroom humor and macho bravado about their sexual exploits, imagined and real, encourage the same behavior in the young men with whom they work.

Male Involvement in Pregnancy Resolution

The national statistics indicate that about 1 million teenage women get pregnant each year, with about 570,000 giving birth, 350–400,000 having abortions, and the remainder having miscarriages or still births. Ironically, men, at least 7 million of whom are sexually active, appear to be more involved at the point of pregnancy resolution than they are at the point of pregnancy prevention, but the literature on men's involvement at this stage is not extensive. Cahn studied several hundred New York City clinic patients and found that, while 6 in 10 females had discussed birth control with their boyfriends, more than three-fourths of women obtaining abortions had discussed the abortion with their boyfriends.[6] Sorensen reported that marriage was the preferred outcome of an unplanned pregnancy for the males in his study.[38] It is clear that about one-third fewer teenagers today are marrying to "legitimize" the pregnancy—in fact, it is this changed pattern of "cover-up" marriages that has been responsible for the increase in teenage "illegitimacy" since the mid-1960s, a period when the total births and birth rates to teenagers have been declining.[37]

The influence of the male partner was studied by Rosen, Ager, and Martindale.[33] The greatest result of his involvement, for teenage women of both races, was for the woman to decide to keep the child: 70 percent of white teenagers and 60 percent of black teenagers who chose to keep the child said their boyfriends had influenced them. For white girls the boyfriend was the most common influence for this decision. For black girls the decision to keep was influenced as often by their mother. If they aborted, however, the mother had equal influence for whites and far greater influence for blacks.

If the young man does not desert the woman and if he remains in a relationship with her, he, too, feels the deleterious impact of an early pregnancy. For example, a 15-year study of several hundred thousand people showed that men who became fathers after age 24 were three times more likely than fathers under age 18 to have completed college by age 19. Eleven years after their expected graduation from high school, these younger fathers were significantly overrepresented in bluecollar occupations.[7] For those teenage couples who marry, either before or after the pregnancy outcome (46 percent of whites and 17 percent of blacks),[46] the picture is equally bleak. Although there are fewer of these marriages today (due solely to drops among whites) those who marry have a two to three times greater likelihood of divorce than those who are over 20 at first birth, and the marriage makes it even more likely than early childbirth alone that the mother will drop out of school, thus further depressing the young couple's economic resources.[37]

Furstenberg prepared a pilot study for the Family Impact Seminar, interviewing 15 families on the impact of their daughter's pregnancy.[17] Some data was included on the young man. The woman's family of origin is most often the place where the new mother returns: 5 years after delivery, about 36 percent of the young women were living with their parents, with nearly one fourth of these having left the home for marriage and returned when the marriage dissolved. Even amongst the women who married 1 year after delivery, one third of them were living with their parents. A major deterrent to marriage for this sample was that living with the family of origin provided a great deal of support, particularly in raised status of the new mother in her family and provision of child care. Furstenberg notes that, in some cases, when the new father "entered a bid to help" support the child, it might be accepted. By extension, his family of origin would also be accorded the "privileges of kinship." However, it is clear that not all fathers made this offer and certainly that not all families easily incorporated him. Furstenberg concluded that "some sharing of rights" between the two families is evident, but that the teenage mother and her family have the final say concerning how much contact the new father will have.

Abortion

The popular media consider abortion to be only a woman's concern: "There is a common belief that the only feelings that a man has about abortion are relief when he can avoid an unwanted marriage and/or responsibility."[10] Dr. Roger Wade, who has counseled thousands of male partners of women who obtained abortions, reports that men usually feel confused, worried, and upset in this situation. The feeling of being excluded from the decision is a frequent complaint.[43] When men are allowed to participate in rap sessions and counseling to explore their feelings, they "express relief from boredom, tension, and the sense of being an outsider during a lengthy, solitary waiting period." According to the National Abortion Federation, 40 percent of those who call their abortion hotline are men and "they are mainly concerned with [the woman's] safety." Some men are also troubled by the fact that they have no legal say in their wife's or girl friend's decision to have an abortion.[10]

If social-service professionals want to improve their impact on preventing teenage pregnancy, they must not exclude men from abortion counseling and services. Men can be supportive of their partner in many ways, beyond simply providing transportation to the clinic, to a mutual role in the actual decision, and to their supportive presence should an abortion be chosen.

MODEL PROGRAMS THAT ENCOURAGE MALE PARTICIPATION

During the 1970s, the Office for Family Planning expanded birth-control clinic services for "women in need." Although greatly improving access to services for millions of women, this focus reinforced the stereotype that men do not play a role in pregnancy prevention. Up to the late 1970s, family-planning facilities often ignored men since policy frequently required that only "patients" be provided with contraception.

In 1978, OFP funded 16 demonstration projects intended to explore ways of involving teenage men in the prevention of pregnancy. These projects consisted of three main types: (1) men-only clinic services; (2) mixed clinics (a women's clinic allowing male-partner participation); and (3) community-based outreach projects. Planned Parenthood affiliates, health departments, and one university received the funding.

Besides the standard medical screening done in a clinic for men, most programs provide an education component for males. A wide variety of community outreach methods have been used, as illustrated by the following list:

- Workshops on sexuality offered at high schools and colleges
- Community talks
- Special hotlines to answer questions
- National Condom Week
- Condom Couplet Contest
- Training for health professionals
- Media such as PSAs, posters, films, pamphlets
- Frisbees with printed messages
- Father-son workshops
- Condom distribution programs
- Condom "six-packs," a sampler with instructions
- High-school newspaper contests
- Yearbook ads
- Pharmacy surveys
- Theater groups of teens performing for their peers
- Ads on mass transit
- "Rubber rallies" at discos, roller rinks, rock concerts
- T-shirt giveaways
- Matchbooks with printed messages

Each of the federally funded programs was unique, since there were no guidelines limiting program design. The following are highlights from just a few such programs.

The Male's Place

A successful hotline operation in San Jose, the primary callers to its "Healthline" are young men 13–19. Although most of their work is done over the phone, there is also a "drop-in" center. The staff does sell condoms and foam, but it is primarily an educational resource. They have made numerous community presentations, including schools and YMCAs. One of their recent projects is working with labor unions to encourage greater parent-child, especially father-son communication about sex.

The Men's Reproductive Health Clinic

This center is located in San Francisco and serves an economically and racially varied clientele. Treatment is provided for sexually transmitted diseases, and birth-control counseling, blood tests, physicals, and other services are offered. The clinic is free, confidential, and most important in such a diverse setting, multilingual in English, Chinese, and Spanish. A survey of clients indicated that the topics on which men wanted more information included men's birth-control methods, how to maintain an erection longer, the process of sexual arousal in women, prostate cancer, and sexually transmitted diseases. Although only a small percentage of their clients have been teenage men, this is likely to change with continued visibility and acceptance in the community.

Chicago Planned Parenthood

One of the earliest programs in the country, the Male Motivation/Education program was launched in 1971, and by 1975, had reached over 20,000 young men with family-planning information. Street fairs and festivals, as well as community agencies, have been the sites of rap sessions, limited to 25 teenage men, on male-female communication, homosexuality, contraception, masturbation, and other topics. A theater group has also been used. A principal lesson learned in this program has been that young people should be involved in the design of the program wherever possible, and that it is often necessary to go to young men "on their own turf" first, before expecting them to come to a center or agency.

Condom Promotion

Both National Condom Week, started by a pharmacist group in California, and the Condom Couplet Contest, a project of the Center for Population Options, have been designed to promote the purchase and use of condoms. Condom Week is celebrated around Valentine's Day each year, and has been the stimulus for "rubber discos," festivals devoted to the condom, and other events. The Condom Couplet Contest invites people to create a "rubber rhyme" and win a prize—one year's winner from this annual event was "from using a condom you will learn, that no deposit means no return!" "Condom six-packs" are another interesting idea, originally developed by Planned Parenthood of Wisconsin. They stuffed a plastic bag with six varieties of condoms plus detailed instructions on proper use, thus allowing the young man to sample different condoms and select those that meet his unique needs.

Project RAM

Project RAM (Reaching Adolescent Minds) is a program of Denver's Human Services, Inc. It was one of the federal demonstration projects, and was originally aimed at 12–19-year-old males (it now focuses on females also). A unique feature of this project is that adolescent men themselves are involved as educators and community activists. The project frequently uses "Theater for Communication" in its workshops and outreach to group homes, schools, churches, and other community groups. These plays, often acted by young men, portray the importance of male involvement in family planning.

Male Involvement Project

Florida State University's project focuses on the older teenage man, 17–19 years of age, primarily college freshmen and sophomores. Unlike many programs, the university setting of this project has encouraged a considerable amount of research. After each workshop, testing has been done. Among 210 participants to date, attitudes towards contraceptives changed in a positive direction on 12 of 15 scales used, including increased feelings that male contraceptives are "happy, effective, fun, convenient, practical, natural, and safe."

Job Corps

The federal Job Corps program has also tried some demonstration projects. In one such program in Kingston, Pennsylvania, a male clinic was run by peer educators. Although peer counseling itself is not unique, the mixing of a men's clinic and the peer approach has had some impact. The project administrator reports that there has been a more than 100 percent increase in the number of initial clinic visits by women in the corps, with a declining number of pregnancies among those enrolled.

Boys Clubs

Youth serving agencies are often ignored by health professionals in trying to reduce teenage pregnancy. Some, however, are already involved in projects and many more appear interested. At the Frederick Douglass Boys' Club in

New York, for example there is a comprehensive sexuality program that deals with a wide range of issues. Staff lead two sessions per week in the evenings. An innovative aspect to this program is that trained staff react to spontaneous sexual remarks and deal with them as teachers when such comments arise naturally in conversation.

Father-Son Workshops

Two community groups that have conducted father-son workshops since 1979 are the Men's Resource Center in Philadelphia (sponsored by the United Church of Christ), and Planned Parenthood of Austin, Texas. The Philadelphia program targets young adolescents, 12 and 13 years old, who have different needs than the older adolescent. This program begins on a Friday night and concludes the following day. The Austin program for somewhat older teenagers is a two-and-one-half-day program allowing uninterrupted discussion and examination of the father-son relationship. It is held in a retreat setting. Each group discusses male sexuality, sex roles, and relationships with women, and uses recreational games to help relieve tension. These groups do charge between $15 and $25 for participation, a fee that may be unreasonable in using this approach with low-income groups.

Youth Involvement and Leadership

In addition to these approaches, an increasing number of groups are including teenagers as leaders in the educational projects. These have included providing teenagers with the opportunities to design brochures, develop surveys of the community, perform in dramatic groups, write radio and TV scripts, plan and run conferences, and train adults. In many cases, the teenagers are paid for the experience. In all cases, they are given a chance to develop interpersonal skills, perform satisfying, interesting tasks, and work with other young people and committed adults. Especially for young men, this may be a valuable approach. Young men often do not respond well to a direct appeal to their need for sex information, but do respond well to a challenge and to a different experience. In the process of exercising their creativity and skills, they become part of the health-care system in a relatively nonthreatening manner.

CONCLUSIONS AND RECOMMENDATIONS

The simplistic approach to dealing with young men and sexual decision making is to blame the victim for his behavior, but the problem is much deeper. Young men grow up imprisoned in sex roles that are emotionally and physically unhealthy, and only long, painful experience seems to counteract these constraints. We continue to reinforce the myth that in sex as well as work, "it's performance that counts." Lying to young women to "score," or to friends that he did indeed score, is accepted behavior among many young men. Adults need to examine their programs to detect bias against men comparable to the bias that for years has reduced the effectiveness of family-planning centers in reaching men. Community agencies, and youth-serving groups in particular, need to offer young men opportunities for reasoning about sexual issues in nonthreatening situations to counteract the tendency for men to reason at less morally mature levels than women when considering sex. Positive attitudes toward contraceptives and toward nonmacho behavior are best nourished by the example that adult male staff set. Accomplishing the goal of effective modeling may require agencies to devote more time and funding to training their staff in their understanding of issues that are important to men, as well as the resources that are available for program development. Efforts need to be made to conduct more father-son workshops, for the father is the most important model of appropriate male behavior. Services need to become more comprehensive, including not just contraceptive counseling but also physicals, opportunities to gain job experience while educating themselves and others about sexuality, discussions of ejaculatory control, female arousal, homosexuality, and other concerns of young men. In many cases, needs assessments and basic research will need to be conducted; many times our efforts are based on assumptions rather than sound knowledge of the context in which young men are functioning.

Most important, our efforts must be based on talking about men's *rights* as well as on talking about their responsibilities. Too often, we point the finger of blame at the "irresponsible," "uncaring," "selfish" man thought to be "incapable" of the prevention of unplanned pregnancy. Yet if we adults were consistently labeled irresponsible, uncaring, or selfish, we, too, would reject whatever else that labeling, accusatory person had to say. If we want teenagers to listen to us, we must approach them in ways that are ego-enhancing rather than ego-deflating. They do not, for example, have only the responsibility to use a condom, they also have the right to, even if the woman is on the pill, in order to protect themselves from sexually transmitted diseases. They do not have only the responsibility to say "no" to unprotected intercourse, but also the right to protect themselves and their partners from becoming unwanted parents. Other rights include the right to believe that "caring means sharing," the right to express physical and verbal affection for other men, the right to friendships that don't include sex (we men are often so preoccupied with "getting it on" that our relationships with women often end up one-dimensional); the right to enjoy physical self-pleasuring, including masturbation; the right to respecting oneself and other enough to treat women as equals, not as objects of macho derision and humor in the locker room; the right to express sexual likes and dislikes; the right to change feelings about someone; the right to be as free as possible of jealousy; and perhaps most crucially, the right to make mistakes and be human, and look at the "failing" with a sense of humor. If we truly want to promote a social force that encourages men to develop and grow from macho to mutuality in all their relationships, then we will need to counter the grim finalities of stereotypical male roles that prohibit failure and lightheartedness and that limit the sources of self-worth. The more we broaden the socially accepted behaviors and attitudes that comprise a "real man," the less likely it will be that men will use sex as one of the main proving grounds for their worth, locked in battles of quiet desperation. The challenge for those who care for young people and want to reduce macho posturing in favor of relaxed mutuality, is that we ourselves have almost as far to go as the young people with whom we work. The first great hurdle in helping young men make effective decisions about sex, contraception, and pregnancy, in helping them move from macho to mutuality, is whether we can accept the risk of self-disclosure and change.

TEN OF THE BEST EDUCATIONAL MATERIALS FOR TEENAGE MEN AND MEN'S PROGRAM STAFF

1. *Teenage Father*, Children's Home Society, 5429 McConell Avenue, Los Angeles, CA 90066, film, $350 (an Academy Award winner).
2. *Am I Normal?*, Momentum Media, 7 Harvard Square, Brookline, MA 02146, film, $350.
3. *Male Sexuality*, Bernie Zilbergeld, Boston: Little, Brown, 1978, $2.95 paperback book, good for staff and teenagers with good reading ability.
4. *Male Involvement Newsletter*, Florida State University, 215 Stone Building, Tallahassee, FL 32306, $5/Year for 6 issues, news and resources for staff.
5. *Sex and Birth Control for Men*, Tom Zorabedian, Emory University Family Planning Program, 80 Butler Street, Atlanta, GA 30303, $1.00 magazine good for all reading levels.
6. *Vasectomy/Prostate Pelvic Model*, Jim Jackson, 33 Richdale Avenue, Cambridge, MA 02140, $95 (the best unbreakable male pelvic model, and considerably cheaper than others available).
7. *Sports Project Posters*, Family Planning Clearinghouse, Box 2225, Rockville, MD 20852, free posters of famous athletes encouraging family planning.
8. *Rock Project Trigger Tapes*, Center for Population Option's Rock Project, 1111 Kearny Street, San Francisco, CA 94133, $5.00 for tape

and discussion guide that stimulates discussion on sexuality by using interviews and songs of rock stars.

9. Being a Man: a Unit on Instructional Activities on Male Role Stereotyping, David Sadker, Government Printing Office, Pueblo, CO 81009, $2.10 for this curriculum useful in staff planning.

10. *A Man's Guide to Sexuality*, Planned Parenthood Federation of America, 810 Seventh Avenue, New York, NY 10019, pamphlet good for young men at all reading levels.

REFERENCES

1. Arnold, C.B. The sexual behavior of inner city adolescent condom users. *Journal of Sex Research* **8**: 298–309 (1972).
2. Arnold, C.B. and Lubin-Finkel, M. Free condom distribution projects for adolescent males. In M.H. Redford, G.W. Duncan, and D.J. Prager (Eds.).
3. *Behavior Today* **9**(41): 7 (October 23, 1978).
4. Brown, S.S., Lieberman, E.J., and Miller, W.B. Young adults as partners and planners. Paper presented at annual meeting of the American Public Health Association, Chicago, IL, November 16–20, 1975.
5. Buder, J., Scales, P., and Sherman, L. Virgins may be vanishing, but the double standard persists. Syracuse, NY: Institute for Family Research and Education, unpublished paper, 1977.
6. Cahn, J. Adolescents' needs regarding family planning services. New York: Planned Parenthood of New York City, unpublished paper, 1975.
7. Card, J. and Wise, L.L. Teenage mothers and teenage fathers: The impact of early childbearing on the parents' personal and professional lives. *Family Planning Perspectives,* **10**(4): 190–205 (1978).
8. Carns, D.E. Talking about sex: Notes on the first coitus and the double sexual standard. *Journal of Marriage and the Family,* **35**(4): 677–688 (1973).
9. Castleman, M. Uncovering the condom comeback. San Francisco, unpublished paper, 1980.
10. Collier, J.L. Abortion: How men feel about it. *Glamour*, February 1980: 165.
11. Condoms, *Consumer Reports*, October 1979: 583–589.
12. D'Augelli, J.F. and D'Augelli, A.R. Moral reasoning and premarital sexual behavior: Toward reasoning about relationships. *Journal of Social Issues,* **33**(2): 1977.
13. Delamater, J. and MacCorquodale, P. Premarital contraceptive usage: A test of two models. *Journal of Marriage and the Family,* **40**(2): 235–249 (1978).
14. Chicago; Outreach is the name of the game. *The Family Planner,* **8**(2): 2–4 (1977).
15. Finkel, M.L. and Finkel, D.J. Sexual and contraceptive knowledge, attitudes, and behavior of male adolescents. *Family Planning Perspectives,* **7**: 256–260 (1975).
16. Freeman, E.W. et al. Adolescent contraceptive usage: Comparisons of male and female attitudes and information. *American Journal of Public Health,* **70**(8): 790–797 (1980).
17. Furstenberg, F. Accommodating to early parenthood: Sources and consequences of

family support to the teenage childbearer. In T. Ooms (Ed.), *Teenage Pregnancy in a Family Context: Implications for Policy*. Philadelphia: Temple University Press, 1981.

18. Gilligan, C., Kohlberg, L., Lerner, J., and Belenky, M. Moral reasoning about sexual dilemmas. *Technical Reports of U.S. Commission on Obscenity and Pornography*, 1. Washington, D.C.: U.S. Government Printing Office, 1970.

19. Goldberg, H. *The Male: From Self Destruction to Self Care*. New York: William Morrow, 1979.

20. Goldberg, H. *The Hazards of Being Male*. New York: Nash Publishing, 1976.

21. Hacker, S.G. *The Effect of Situational and Interactional Aspects of Sexual Encounters on Premarital Contraceptive Behavior*. Ann Arbor: University of Michigan Ph.D. Dissertation, 1976.

22. Jorgensen, S.R., King, S.L., and Terrey, B.A. Dyadic and network influences on adolescent exposure to pregnancy risk. *Journal of Marriage and The Family*, **42**: 141–155 (1980).

23. Jurich, A.D. and Jurich, J.A. The effect of cognitive moral development upon the selection of premarital sexual standards. *Journal of Marriage and the Family*, **36**: 736–741 (1974).

24. Lester, J. On becoming a boy. *Ms. Magazine*, July 1973.

25. Levine, J. Everyman's blues: Harping on the male role crisis. *Psychology Today*, November 1979.

26. Libby, R.W., Gray, L., and White, M. A test and reformulation of reference group and role correlates of premarital sexual permissiveness theory. 27. *Journal of Marriage and the Family* **40**: 79–94 (1978).

27. Lieberman, E.J. From innocence to experience. Paper presented at annual meeting of the American Public Health Association, Miami Beach, October 17–21, 1976.

28. Luker, K. *Taking Chances–Abortion and the Decision Not to Contracept*. Berkeley: University of California Press, 1976.

29. Miller, P. and Simon, W. Adolescent sexual behavior: Context and change. *Social Problems*, **22**: 58–76 (1974).

30. Peplau, L. Rubin, Z., and Hill, C. Sexual Intimacy in Dating Relationships. *Journal of Social Issues*, 33(2): 86–109 (1977).

31. Reiss, I.L., Banwart, A., and Foreman, H. Premarital contraceptive usage: A study and some theoretical explorations. *Journal of Marriage and the Family*, **37**: 619–620 (1975).

32. Roberts, E.J., Gagnon, J., and Klein, D. *Family Life and Sexual Learning*. Cambridge, MA: Project on Human Sexual Development, 1978.

33. Rosen, R.H., Ager, J.W., and Martindale, L.J. Contraception, abortion, and self-concept. *Journal of Population*, **2**(2): 118–139 (1979).

34. Ross, S. *The Youth Values Project*. Washington, D.C.: Center for Population Options, 1978.

35. Rothstein, A. Men's reactions to their partners' abortions. *American Journal of Obstetrics and Gynecology* **128**: 831ff. (1977).

36. Scales, P. Males and morals: Teenage contraceptive behavior amid the double standard. *Family Coordinator* **26**(3): 210–222 (1977).

37. Scales, P. and Gordon, S. Preparing today's youth for tomorrow's family. *Impact 79* **1**(2): 3–8 (1979).
38. Sorensen, R.C. *Adolescent Sexuality in Contemporary America.* New York: World, 1973.
39. Teevan, J.J. Reference groups and premarital sexual behavior. *Journal of Marriage and the Family* **34**: 283–291 (1972).
40. Thompson, L. and Spanier, G.B. Influence of parents, peers, and partners on the contraceptive use of college men and women. *Journal of Marriage and the Family* **40**: 481–492 (1978).
41. U.S. Department of Health, Education, and Welfare, National Center for Health Statistics. *Monthly Vital Statistics Report: Final Mortality Statistics 1977.* May 11, 1979: 2.
42. Venham, L. *Coeds and Contraception: An Examination of Self-Image and Significant Other Influence.* Columbus, OH: Ohio State University, 1972.
43. Wade, R. *For Men About Abortion.* Boulder, CO: Author, 1977.
44. Wilson, W.C. Adolescent moral development and sexual decisions. *Top of the News* **34**(2): 145–153 (1978).
45. Zabin, L.S., Kantner, J.F., and Zelnik, M. The risk of pregnancy in the first months of intercourse. *Family Planning Perspectives* **11**(4): 215–226 (1980).
46. Zelnik, M., and Kanter, J.F. Contraceptive patterns and premarital pregnancy among women aged 15–19 in 1976. *Family Planning Perspectives* **10**(3): 135–144 (1978).
47. Zelnik, M. and Kantner, J.F. Sexual and contraceptive experience of young unmarried women in the United States, 1976 and 1971. *Family Planning Perspectives,* **9**(2): 55–74 (1977).
48. Zilbergeld, B. *Male Sexuality.* Boston: Little, Brown, 1978.

13.
Intervention With Families of Pregnant Adolescents

Karen Authier, M.S.W. and A.C.S.W.,
Director of Social Services,
Nebraska Psychiatric Institute,
University of Nebraska College of Medicine;

and

Jerry Authier, Ph.D.,
Associate Professor of Medical Psychology,
Department of Family Practice,
University of Nebraska College of Medicine

The pregnant adolescent is part of a family system. Even adolescents who are not residing with their families at the time of professional intervention are products of family systems. Since all family members influence, and are influenced by, the dynamics of their family systems, the family system within which the adolescent is functioning will be an influential, or even a determining factor, in the adolescent's resolution of the crisis of pregnancy. In turn, the family is affected by the adolescent pregnancy. The circular nature of the family interactional system implies that when the adolescent, who has accommodated to her family system in either a positive or negative manner, becomes pregnant, the family unit responds and accommodates to the pregnancy in a positive or negative manner. The adolescent subsequently responds and accommodates to the family's reaction to the pregnancy in a positive or negative manner, ad infinitum. Although the professional can choose to ignore the adolescent's family system, the adolescent will bring her family with her into treatment; if not in person, then as part of her framework for decision making, her learned pattern of response, and her understanding of herself and her situation.

Direct assessment of the family is an important strategy for intervention with the pregnant adolescent. The context of the family as an interactional system: family rules, roles, patterns, flexibility of response, and the concept of loyalty, all have a bearing on the outcome of the crisis for the adolescent. The location of the family unit in reference to the family life cycle is another factor which the professional must consider. The professional also must plan for intervention which takes into account the changing nature of the family. By approaching adolescent pregnancy as a family crisis, as well as an individual crisis, the professional uses a family crisis intervention model. The alternatives of relinquishment, abortion, or parenthood are examined as part of a family process, with acknowledgment that the adolescent, as an individual, has rights and needs that are distinct and different from family needs and expectations. While the decision to abort, or relinquish the child, may move the family toward resolution of the crisis, the decision to become a parent, however, creates still another crisis for the adolescent's family, with the addition of a new dependent member to the family unit. Intervention with the adolescent and her family is directed to the goal of facilitating a resolution of the pregnancy serving the best interests of the adolescent, while promoting continuing healthy family functioning.

THE PREGNANT ADOLESCENT AS PART OF A FAMILY UNIT

If we view the family as more than a backdrop for the enactment of the behavior and developmental processes of individual members, we appreciate the centrality of family intervention to any intervention approach with the pregnant adolescent. Certainly there are a few pregnant adolescents who are completely without family, but this group would encompass a very small number of young women. The majority have some contact or sense of relationship with their family even if the relationship is conflictual, tenuous, or estranged. However, many programs or professionals providing services for the pregnant adolescent work only tangentially, if at all, with the adolescent's family. Moroney[28] has pointed out that policies and programs usually are designed to serve individuals with specific problems or needs, e.g., the pregnant adolescent, and, therefore do not address the needs and problems of the family as a whole. This chapter will stress the importance of recognition by professionals of the significance of her family to the adolescent even when, or perhaps especially when, their influence is vigorously denied by the adolescent, and the importance of intervention with the family unit whenever possible.

The unmarried pregnant adolescent is in a unique dilemma in regard to her family of origin. As part of the normal developmental processes of adolescence she is struggling to establish her own identity and emancipate from the family. For some young women the act of conceiving may even be motivated in part by a desire to establish an adult identity by becoming a mother. For the primigravida, however, pregnancy and childbirth also traditionally provide the impetus for a young woman to reestablish linkages with her family, particularly her mother.[2] Hence, the dilemma: the developmental need to separate from family, countered by the desire of the primigravida to look to her family for emotional support. The dilemma heightens the sense of crisis not only for the adolescent but for her family as well.

This chapter will present information regarding the pregnant adolescent within the framework of the family system, and will discuss the treatment of adolescent pregnancy as a family crisis. The three basic options for resolution of the crisis (abortion, relinquishment for adoption, and parenthood) will be examined as they relate to the family unit.

The Family as a System

Many leading theorists in the field of psychotherapy have documented the role of the family system as a significant factor contributing to the direction of individual development and behavior.[4,20,25,27,40,41] Some general principles of family dynamics take on special meaning when applied to work with the pregnant adolescent.

A family is a system of relationships and the pregnant adolescent is a part of her family system. She affects, and is affected by, changes within the system. Failure to take into account the dynamics of the family system may result in ineffective or even destructive intervention by a professional.[27] Professionals who inadvertently discount the power of the family system may be used by the system, or become puzzled and frustrated when the family and/or the adolescent make seemingly inexplicable decisions, or assume self-defeating positions.

The behavior of individual family members is directed toward maintaining the state of balance in the family system. However, the intent of the individual member's behavior in respect to the family system is not always easily discernible, and, in fact, may be paradoxical. The act of conceiving, and the actions of the adolescent and other family members in response to the pregnancy, may represent efforts to preserve or reestablish equilibrium in the system. Some families use crises as a means of keeping the focus off inadequacies, the lack of real intimacy, or other sources of conflict. The pregnancy and subsequent reactions may keep the system in a state of upheaval that enables members to avoid facing more painful or more sensitive issues in the system, such as marital conflict between the adolescent's parents.

As a system, a family attempts to maintain a state of equilibrium or balance within the system. Events such as pregnancy of an unemancipated child may cause a crisis by creating disequilibrium in the system, which then must make adjustment to reestablish the state of balance. Families have differing capacities for responding to change within the system. The degree of flexibility in the response capacity of a family system, which may be determined by assessing previous patterns of family response to stress or change, is an important indicator of the ability of the family to cope with the changes brought about by the pregnancy of the adolescent member. A family which has demonstrated the capacity for flexibility in adapting to stress or change can be predicted to cope with the demands of the adolescent pregnancy in a more constructive manner than a family with limited and rigid response patterns. A family which approaches change with willingness to explore new and untried options for response will suffer less disruption than a family which can accept only a narrow range of options.

Rules, Patterns, Roles, and Loyalty. The family is governed by rules and expectations that are often unspoken, sometimes at odds with overt instructions given to members, and usually not readily apparent to an observer outside the system. Patterns of behavior based on the family rules are established, and roles are assigned to various members to perpetuate the patterns. Patterns may be passed down from one generation to the next. Boszormenyi-Nagy and Spark[4] reported clinical observation of a family where the role of an unwed mother had been passed down to daughters through several generations. They hypothesized that the young women occupying that role through successive generations were fulfilling an important function in preserving the stability of the family. They also pointed out that a rebellious child in the family, who may well be a pregnant adolescent, paradoxically could be attempting to keep the family together. Once a child assumes the rebellious role, or the role of challenging the surface rules and values of the family while adhering to the covert rules, the system exerts subtle pressure to make relinquishment of that role painful and difficult for the child. In some instances, the rebellious role is needed to counterbalance the role of an overly conforming sibling who seems to do no wrong. In other instances, a stance of exaggerated sexuality on the part of an adolescent may provide a vicarious outlet for a family whose other members maintain an overt attitude of strict repression of sexuality.

Insight into the principles of family dynamics is extremely important to professionals who may identify the adolescent's behavior as self/destructive and try to modify this behavior. Unless intervention with the total family system is successful, the adolescent probably will continue in the self-destructive behaviors expected by the family. Many professionals readily can recall young pregnant women whom they assisted in obtaining an abortion, or arranging a relinquishment, only to have the drama reenacted within the space of a few years.

Triangulation. Several family theroists have explained interactional patterns within the family system as a series of interlocking triangles. Triangles develop as a vulnerable family member is drawn in to alleviate tension between the two members of a dyad.[5] The member added to the dyad to form the triangle alternates between attempting to form a closer liaison with one member of the original dyad, and attempting to minimize the stress of the position by staying out of the conflict which existed between the members of the dyad. The concept of triangulation is relevant to work with the pregnant adolescent since the adolescent may be the child whom the parents have chosen to complete their triangle, or the adolescent may conceive in an attempt to offer the infant as another point for family triangulation.

The professional should be alert to his/her own possible role as a part of a family triangle. When the stress within a family overrides the alternatives within the system, it may turn to an outsider for relief. Since pregnancy of an adolescent member often places unusual stress on the mechanisms a family normally uses to cope, the circumstances may lead to triangulating an outsider, who may be a friend, extended family member, or a professional. In such circumstances the professional may be compromised and seduced into helping preserve the preexisting family balance, rather than functioning as a change-agent.

The Myth of Togetherness. Families appearing as completely free of conflict, and as caricatures of an "all for one and one for all" model of family living, may not be all that they seem. Such families see healthy conflict as a threat, and stifle natural individual differences in order to avoid dreaded conflicts. The facade of togetherness is all-important. Lidz[25] described the phenomena as pseudomultuality, characterized by a "predominant absorption in fitting together, at the expense of differentiation of the identities of the persons in the relations." Minchin[26] uses the term "enmeshed" to describe families where identities are blurred. The fragile exterior of such families may be threatened when an adolescent member becomes pregnant, but the system will exert powerful pressure for resolution of the crisis in a manner that preserves the facade. The family cannot tolerate individual differences of opinion on significant issues and will not easily allow the pregnant adolescent to work through her own conflictual feelings. Happiness and contentment are the accepted norms, and the real pain of life experiences is denied by common agreement. A clue to the lack of positive strength in the family might be preoccupation with secrecy by either parents and/or siblings excluded from knowledge of the pregnancy.

Family Loyalty and the Adolescent

Boszormenyi-Nagy and Spark[4] offer convincing arguments regarding the power of loyalty to the family of origin in maintaining important family patterns and roles. The entry of children into the developmental phase of adolescence poses a challenge for the maintenance of loyalty. In order for the adolescent and her family to arrive at a healthy resolution of this phase, both must accept a new balance in which the adolescent forms new loyalty ties to peers and potential sexual partners, while maintaining a sense of loyalty to the family of origin. Boszormenyi-Nagy and Spark[4] refer to the task of establishment of a new balance as "negotiation of compromises." Since the task is stressful and requires some flexibility of the family system, some adolescents attempt to short-circuit the process through dramatic acts, such as running away or becoming pregnant. In some cases the adolescent may believe that by assuming the role of parent herself she automatically will be accepted by her parents as an adult in her own right. Unfortunately, the pregnancy and birth of a child may only offer new battlegrounds for the continuance of old struggles.

In considering the concept of family loyalty, it is important to remember the significance of paradox, and recognize that loyalty can be demonstrated by attitudes and behaviors that on the surface appear intensely negative or hostile but covertly serve a purpose in preservation of the family unit. For instance, a young woman who becomes pregnant as a result of a sexual relationship which has no potential for long-term emotional commitment may appear to be disloyal to her family's value system. Another interpretation of her behavior, however, might be that she is demonstrating loyalty to the family by communicating that she will not establish serious emotional commitments that would compete with family ties.

The scapegoat role in the family system, which may be assigned to the adolescent who becomes pregnant, also can be examined in respect to the concept of family loyalty. An example from clinical experience: A sexually active adolescent daughter who was the youngest child in the family became pregnant. The parents, who had lectured all their children about the immorality of premarital sex, railed against their daughter for bringing shame to the family. They refused to sanction either abortion or relinquishment and jointly assumed the role of martyrs in committing themselves to rearing their grandchild for their "irresponsible daughter." Friends, neighbors, and relatives expressed sympathy for the self-sacrificing parents and disapproval of the young woman. Thorough exploration of this family system revealed other possible agendas; the daughter was rescuing her parents from a decreasing sense of family and individual purpose which was facing them with the prospect of having their last child eventually marry and leave the unit. By producing a child outside of marriage, the adolescent avoided transferring her loyalty to another family unit. The grandchild provided her parents with a new source for displacement of their own unresolved marital conflicts and renewed their roles as parents. Actually, neither the parents nor the daughter were victims. As a result of the new set of transactions, the daughter was given a continuing license to manipulate her parents within unspoken, but understood limits. In this situation, the pregnant adolescent used her pregnancy and her position as family scapegoat to wield power and influence the balance of the family system, a phenomena which has been discussed in the literature.[4,35]

Another example of the importance of family loyalty in consideration of an adolescent pregnancy is provided by Zilbach.[41] Two teenage daughters sequentially provided their mother with babies to care for, thus compensating for the emptiness and longing for a child the mother experienced following a hysterectomy that occurred shortly after the birth of the youngest of the two daughters. Intervention with similar families, whose members may regard pregnancy as evidence of family loyalty, must be with full cognizance of the meaning of the pregnancy.

The Cohesive Family

Although the discussion to this point emphasizes family dysfunction, there is no intent to imply that all families which contain a pregnant adolescent are characterized by pathological functioning. Family functioning can be plotted on a continuum which ranges from severe pathology to total absence of pathology. Few families, including families with pregnant adolescents, are found at either end of the continuum. Therefore, professionals working with the families of pregnant adolescents generally will be working with families which have some identifiable strengths, as well as some areas of dysfunction. Certainly, some assessments of the state of the American family cite the increase in the number of adolescent pregnancies as evidence of deterioration of the family unit.[28] There are claims in the literature, particularly psychoanalytic literature, that pregnancy outside marriage is symptomatic of pathology, the result of family etiological factors including detached or seductive fathers, lack of murturing by the mothers, competitive and hostile relationships with sexually frustrated mothers, and conflictual relationships between the parents. However, the literature has produced mixed descriptions of the family of the pregnant adolescent.[9,17,22,31,39] Family dynamics may play a part in placing some adolescents in a position of greater risk to become pregnant. However, many adolescents who are sexually active and who become pregnant are from families with positive emotional environments; many adolescents from extremely pathological families do not become pregnant. Although there may be psychosocial and familial implications, reproduction is still a biological phenomena.[15]

For a healthy, cohesive family, the pregnancy may cause temporary disruptions, but this will be manageable and temporary. The pregnancy will not be used to intensify or accelerate preexisting conflicts. In general, the healthy family has a preponderance of positive mechanisms for handling stress and providing support for individual members,[14] it is resilient, and has a repertoire of response patterns which indicate depth and flexibility. Role expectations provide a framework of predictability and stability for the interactional system, but individual differences are accepted, respected, and valued. Although different levels of communication exist, they are clear, direct, open, and consistent. Family members have accurate and realistic perceptions of the distinction between what the family system can provide for them and what they must provide out of their own inner resources. There is an atmosphere of give and take, with an unspoken understanding that members can trust the system to compensate them justly for what they contribute to it.

The Developmental Stage of the Family Unit. Consideration of intervention should include attention to the family developmental stage. If the young woman chooses to rear her child, there actually will be two families; her family of origin and her family of procreation. Each is at different stages of development.

Just as every individual moves through a series of developmental tasks from birth through old age, every family passes through recognizable stages shaped by developmental tasks. The epigenetic principle[11] which provides one conceptual base for looking at the family life cycle, stresses that successful completion of the tasks of one phase is a prerequisite to satisfactory transition to the next phase. Family developmental tasks relate to developmental stages and tasks of various members as they interact within the family system and to the norms and expectations of society. Duvall,[10] an early theorist in the concept of the family life cycle, defined a family developmental task as a "growth responsibility that arises at a certain stage in the life of a family, successful achievement of which leads to satisfaction and success with later tasks, while failure leads to unhappiness in the family, disapproval by society, and difficulty with later family developmental tasks." (p. 45).

The family enters the adolescent phase of development when the oldest child enters adolescence.[10] That child and his/her parents are breaking new ground in the area of family relationships. Benedek[3] referred to the onset of adolescence as a "crossroad in their development" for parents, as well as children.

The onset of adolescence may precipitate uneasy feelings on the part of parents perhaps due to the sexual theme pervading this stage of development for parents and adolescents.[1,3] The emerging youthful sexuality of their children provides an unwelcome counterpoint for what the parents may regard as the fading of their own sexual attractiveness. The vitality and optimism of the adolescent may seem to the parents to be a cruel contrast to their own declining vigor and decreasing options. Anthony[1] noted that "psychologically speaking the adolescent is on his/her way up when the caretaking adults are on their way down." (p. 317) Some parents may react inappropriately to those contrasts with resentment and with punitive responses to normal adolescent behavior. Other parents may push their adolescent into precocious behavior in an attempt to vicariously revive their own youth. Some parents combine both messages and place the adolescent in a double bind. Other parents deny the obvious sexual development of their children. Anthony[1] declared that "the emergence of biologic sexual maturity in children invariably seems to take the family off guard as if it were completely unprepared for this natural and long expected event." (p. 314) Pregnancy makes the arrival of sexual maturity difficult to ignore while some parents even continue to deny its sexual significance. Parental reactions can set the stage for adolescent pregnancy or interfere with the successful resolution of the problems a pregnancy presents for the adolescent and the whole family unit.

A primary task of a family is to allow for the transition to independent living for the adolescent, while maintaining a sense of caring and respect for each other and a sense of continued identification with the family unit. The difficulty of the task can be inferred from the strife and tension that often accompany this stage of family development. Pregnancy of the adolescent can heighten the strain of these years, or perhaps may even be a byproduct of the strain in some instances.

As they work at the task of separating from their family, many adolescents become critical of parents and other family members. Friedman[12] humorously described the developmental task of the parent of an adolescent as "learning to build a new life, having been thoroughly discredited by one's teenager." (p. 28) For the pregnant adolescent who needs advice on alternatives, or the adolescent mother who needs advice and assistance with child rearing, her own need to prove herself as an adult may make her ambivalent, negative, or seemingly unpredictable in her response toward her parents' efforts to assist her. In fact, parental overtures of assistance may be motivated by genuine concern for the adolescent, or in part by a desire to regain control, to rebuke the adolescent, or to prove that the adolescent is inadequate.

The family officially leaves the teenage phase of development when the first child (not necessarily the oldest) leaves home to embark on a life of his/her own. Depending upon the choices made by the adolescent regarding resolution of the pregnancy, it may signal entry of the family into a new phase of development; the "empty nest" or launching phase which changes the direction of the family from expansion to contraction.[10] If the adolescent becomes a parent and leaves home, the family may be forced precipitously into this stage of development, one which they had not planned on entering for several years. A lack of readiness and of emotional preparation for the tasks of the new phase is a causative factor in the stress of the adjustment to the new phase.

The first child to leave home and the last child to leave home are standard bearers for the beginning and end of the launching phase which may continue over a period of years. In a family with more than one child the parents must continue to repeat the simultaneously rewarding but painful task of sending their children out into the world. The process may be more painful than rewarding when the parents believe their adolescent is assuming a parental role at too early an age.

The developmental phase of the adolescent's family is made more ambiguous if she stays in it to rear the child. Her parents may have resolved their feelings regarding their approaching empty nest and the resulting decrease in responsibility. The prospect of facing the same tasks with the new addition that they faced with the birth of their own children may seem like an onerous burden at their stage of life. Just as the end of their active parenting responsibilities are in sight, they are forced to readjust to resumption of roles for child care which could extend through old age.

IMPLICATIONS OF VARIANT FAMILY STYLES

Another dimension to assessment of family dynamics and stage of the family life cycle is added when working with those adolescents who live in nontraditional families, including single-parent families, blended or stepparent families, foster families, or extended family. In her sample of young women attending a special school for pregnant adolescents, LaBarre[22] reported over 30 percent living in single-parent families and approximately 18 percent who had been reared by extended family members, friends of the family, or neighbors. In her sample of pregnant white adolescents, Grow[17] reported 27 percent were from single-parent families.

Although the nontraditional nature of the family unit provides no guide as to the emotional climate of the family, there are some implications for intervention. If the young woman is living with a single parent or blended family (a stepparent), it is important to consider involvement of both natural parents if they are available and concerned. Ingram[19] reports beneficial results in treatment of adolescents from involving both parents and their current spouses if they have remarried. Children of divorced parents sometimes assume responsibility for assuring that their parents maintain a relationship which ostensibly is focused on their problems or behavior. The pregnancy can serve that function. Although the daughter's assumption of such a role may be based in part on her own unwillingness to accept the reality of parental divorce, she also may be responding to equal unwillingness on the part of one or both parents to give up their broken relationship. As a crisis, the pregnancy may serve the purpose of providing an excuse for the parents to persist in their still conflictual relationship. In addition, in a single-parent family, the relationship between the daughter and the custodial parent may be magnified. The intensity may take the form of dependency masked as conflict.

The pregnant adolescent living in a blended family may be confused as to her role in a family system which has conflicting or ambiguous expectations regarding emotional investment, commitment, and loyalty. The confusion will have implications for the decisions the adolescent makes regarding the pregnancy. Work with the blended family may involve sorting out and resolving those issues related to emotional investment, commitment, and loyalty ignored or avoided as the family was being formed.

If the young woman is living with extended family, friends of the family, or a foster family, it is important to evaluate the desirability of working with the adolescent and her natural family as well as the family with which she is living and which probably will remain her support system during and after the pregnancy. If the young woman is not living with her natural parents, one can begin with the assumption that her relationship with her natural parents is problematic in some way. Even if work with the natural parents, in conjunction with work with the girl, is not possible, the adolescent will need to work through her relationship with those parents in absentia.

The adopted status also poses unique considerations for work with families of pregnant adolescents. The adolescent and her adoptive parents may have some sense of recreating history with an opportunity to resolve the pregnancy in the same or a different manner than the adolescent's natural mother. Pannor and Nerlove[30] have noted the higher vulnerability of adopted children to the stresses of adolescence compared to nonadopted children, and the greater anxiety of adoptive parents in dealing with stresses than nonadoptive parents. They cite "compulsive pregnancy" as one possible outcome. The pregnancy of the adopted daughter may reawaken the adoptive mother's unresolved feelings of sandness and/or inadequacy surrounding her own infertility. Those feelings may lead to jealousy and resentment of the adopted daughter. Adoptive parents may have greater need to be perfect parents[30] and, therefore, may be more likely to blame themselves for their daughter's plight. The self-blame, however, may be mixed with fear that their daughter may be following the pattern of her birthmother, whom they imagine as promiscuous. A focus of intervention with adoptive parents and daughters would be to assist the family to deal openly with the issues so that resolution of the current crisis can take place with limited contamination by the past.

THE TREATMENT OF ADOLESCENT PREGNANCY AS A FAMILY CRISIS

A crisis occurs for an individual when that individual experiences disequilibrium as a result of a situation which cannot be resolved through use of available problem-solving behaviors or resources.[7,32] The crisis-provoking situation can be an event that impinges on an individual or family from without, such as job loss, divorce, or death, or it can have an internal focus, such as progression to a new developmental or maturational stage, or a change in role.[16] Pregnancy and the addition of a child to a family are events that are natural stimuli for development of crises. The potential for intensified crisis response often is greater when the pregnant indivdual is an adolescent due to the coalescence of several factors, including the developmental stage of the individual, negative family reactions, societal attitudes, and the frequently unplanned nature of the event. Understanding the pregnant adolescent as part of a system leads to the conclusion that not only is she in crisis, but the family as an interactional system is also in crisis.

Crisis intervention is an approach which is utilized to assist an individual in the process of resoving the situation provoking the crisis and to enable the individual either to return to a previous level of dunctioning, or move to a higher level of functioning. By applying principles of crisis theory and intervention to the family unit, the helping professional acknowledges the significance of the family system to the functioning of the individual and acknowledges the fact that when individuals are in crisis, their families are in crisis also. Umana et al.[38] differentiated family crisis intervention from traditional crisis intervention by the emphasis placed on consideration of "the family rather than the individual as a the unit in crisis" and maximization of "the active role of the family in crisis management." (pp. 6,7) Recognition of adolescent pregnancy as a precipitant of crisis implies a need for family crisis intervention.

Crisis theory delineates sequential phases of the crisis reaction. Caplan[7] perceives four phases of response to the crisis-producing event. In phase one, there is an attempt to utilize problem-solving behaviors and resources which previously have been effective in reducing tensions and returning the system to a steady state. If those behaviors do not produce the desired result, the crisis progresses to phase two, during which there are continuing unsuccessful efforts to bring the system back to a steady state. The lack of success produces a snowballing effect of increased discomfort which stimulates additional efforts for tension reduction. As the tension increases, the system moves into phase three, during which the family is most likely to seek help from resources outside the family as they mobilize and experiment with new behaviors and resources previously untried. According to Caplan,[7] if the family does not resolve the crisis in phase three through use of outside assistance or through discovery of new alternatives on their own, they move toward phase four which is a "point of no return," and options for either avoidance or successful resolutions are no longer available. When families reach stage four, symptoms of individuals, or of the entire unit, appear as indicators of the dysfunction within the system.

Pregnancy of an adolescent member, therefore, can be either a symptom displayed by one member as a result of inadequate resolution of a previous developmental or life crisis, and/or the stimulus which provokes a crisis for the individual and the family. A family that has a history of difficulty in resolving crises will have greater difficulty resolving the crisis caused by the pregnancy of an adolescent member. In general, families who have greater flexibility as evidenced by a greater repertoire of responses, or greater willingness to expand their responses, will be more likely to reach positive resolution of a crisis than rigid families with fewer available responses and less willingness to consider new response patterns. Assessment of the family's past handling of crises will provide clues as to the degree of difficulty they will have resolving the crisis of pregnancy of the adolescent member and thereby guide the professional to an appropriate intervention approach. Families with a history of adequate resolution of previous crises may require only strategic crisis intervention of brief duration, usually one to two months.[23] Families with a history of inadequate resolution of crises may require intensive intervention in response to the crisis followed by long-term intervention to modify long-standing problems of family functioning. Therefore, the distinction should be made between relatively healthy families who are having difficulty with a specific crisis, such as the pregnancy of an adolescent member, and families whose difficulty in managing the current crisis is part of a deeply engrained pattern of dysfunction. This is important so that the professional neither attempts major restructuring of families who are basically healthy, nor applies a band-aid approach to families who require major restructuring. It is the opinion of the authors that initial assessment of the family can be completed quickly, usually in the first session, and results shared with the family regarding implications and recommendations for treatment.

Professionals intervening with the families of pregnant adolescents in crisis generally can utilize the same modalities they include in work with families who seek their help for other reasons. However, utilization of crisis theory necessitates intervention on an immediate basis to take advantage of the disequilibrium caused by the crisis since it is during this period of disequilibrium that families are most receptive to change. If intervention is not immediate, the intense crisis reaction will be time limited; the system will strive to achieve a new equilibrium, either positive or negative, in approximately four to six weeks, after which families may be more resistant to efforts to help them change. Therefore, unless the family chooses to use the crisis to resolve additional long-standing problems, the intervention can be completed within a time frame of two months.

LaBarre[22] viewed the young woman's awareness of pregnancy, either suspected or confirmed, along with the realization that she must tell her family, as the onset of the crisis. She also found that most families reached out for help and began moving toward resolution of the crisis one to two weeks after learning of the pregnancy. During the first several days prior to reaching out, the families seemed to be immobilized by the initial shock reaction and intense feelings of grief, anger, hopelessness, and disbelief. When the first contact with a professional occurs at this point of intense personal and interpersonal disequilibrium, it is important to utilize an active, directive approach in working with the family.[33,38] At this point it is appropriate to assist family members in identifying and ventilating feelings, focusing and clarifying communication, and assessing and understanding the reality of the situation. Although later session may focus on intervention with individuals or subgroups within the family, it is extremely important to schedule a session for the entire family during the early phases of intervention.

With the help of the professional, the family moves to a problem-solving phase. Timing is an important factor at this point. If problem solving is introduced too quickly, the family may resist out of a need to come to some closure at the affective level before moving to the cognitive level. Some families, however, who are more comfortable at the cognitive than the affective level of interaction will push precipitously into the problem-solving stage. With those families the task is to enable them to express the uncomfortable or painful feelings which have the power of subverting later plans if ignored. In contrast, other families prefer to dwell indefinitely at the affective level with shouts and tears, in order to avoid the hard work of the problem-solving phase. Assessment of family communication style in the first few sessions will provide clues as to where individual families are likely to have difficulty. For instance, the professional can ask family members to describe how they feel about the current situation. Response with feeling words would suggest that the family is aware of feelings and is using an affective approach. A response which is cognitively phrased and descriptive of the content of the situation would suggest a cognitive approach to problems.

It is important that professionals have a sense of self-awareness regarding their own style and comfort with affective or cognitive approaches. Those who have difficulty with expression of feeling may be tempted to utilize premature reassurance in the initial stages of intervention. Also, professionals trained in the "medical model" may move to the problem-solving stage too quickly.

After the intense emotional reactions of the crisis have been partially defused, the family can begin realistic consideration of options and alternatives. Although pregnancy is an intensely personal experience for any woman, it would be naive to believe that decisions regarding the pregnancy are made in a vacuum and not shaped by the family context. Indeed, Umana et al.[38] regard the family as the force "having the greatest impact on the production, maintenance, and resolution of a particular crisis." (p. 6) Understanding of the significance of family factors does not imply that the adolescent listens passively to the family's advice and then acts accordingly. Rather there is a realization that an act of defiance against family wishes is also a product of the dynamics of the system. Since family dynamics have the potential for interfering with a rational and thoughtful use of the problem-solving process, the professional must be prepared to intervene to manipulate the system so as to encourage change. While the term manipulate has negative connotations in popular usage, in this context the term is used to refer to skilled use of intervention techniques which encourage a family to discontinue use of habitual, destructive patterns of behavior.[20] For example, families in which members are pressured into acting within narrow, stereotyped roles will have difficulty approaching the problem-solving task with sufficient openness to allow exploration of available options.

The professional must address the question of the composition of the unit that will be involved actively in the intervention. While involvement of all family members living in the household is imperative, there should be consideration of additional individuals who constitute the functional family for the adolescent. These may include siblings who have moved out of the family home, noncustodial natural parents, stepparents, grandparents, aunts, uncles, or other extended family. A primary decision will center on possible involvement of the baby's father and/or his family. Since the pregnancy places the adolescent at a demarcation point between family of origin and family of procreation, the adolescent should be offered the choice of having the father involved in the intervention process with her family. Clearly, there are many instances in which involvement of the father is neither possible nor advisable, but the question should be raised with the adolescent and her family. If the adolescent desires the father's involvement, and her family objects, the professional is provided with important material regarding family issues which require attention in order for the problem-solving tasks to be accomplished successfully.

Available Options

The adolescent and her family will consider three basic options, with some variations, during the problem-solving phase: (1) abortion; (2) relinquishment/adoption; and (3) assumption of the role of parent. The third option, assumption of the role of parent, requires the additional choices of marriage or single parenthood. Some families may consider one or more options unavailable because of strong beliefs and preferences. Nevertheless, a similar process is involved in assisting the adolescent and her family to explore all possible options, or the various alternatives available within the parameters of any one. The professional assumes an educator role and guides the adolescent and her family through the decision-making process, while teaching skills necessary for decision-making. The process includes thorough exploration and assessment of available options whose positive and negative aspects are considered and tallied. Some families have accepted myths about issues such as adoption procedures, rights and responsibilities of the father, public assistance, or abortion procedures, and need accurate information. At times it is necessary to provide concrete information about community resources as well, such as medical clinics, transportation, legal consultation, school programs, and financial assistance. The professional may assist the family in mobilizing needed resources with an awareness that practical needs must be met before the family can direct its efforts to reorganization in response to the crisis.

Chesler and Davis[8] present some suggested crisis-intervention strategies to resolve those which are intensified by inability of the family and the adolescent to agree on its resolution. They suggest guiding the adolescent and her family through a negotiation or bargaining process in which both sides achieve some "trade-offs" to arrive at a mutually agreeable solution. That process is more likely to succeed when there is a positive emotional foundation from which the negotiation process can proceed. They identify assertiveness as an important skill to teach in arriving at crisis resolution. Through use of assertive behavior, individuals are able to express their strong feelings without inflicting or imposing solutions.

The expression of conflict regarding resolution of the pregnancy must be considered carefully within the context of the assessment of the family structure and rules. When an adolescent seems at risk for being pressured into a solution against her wishes, she may need an advocate who can explain her rights and support her in her right of self-determination. However, before leaping into the role of advocate, the professional should consider where that role will place him/her in relation to the family system. Some adolescents will assume stances of rebelliousness, martyrdom, or helplessness as part of an ongoing family script. In such instances, the professional who is seduced into rescuing the adolescent merely helps the family maintain their dysfunctional system. As an alternative to rescue, the professional can choose to intervene at the process, rather than the content level, and utilize strategies designed to assist the family members in modification of dysfunctional roles, expectations, or patterns.

A Decision to Abort. Current data indicate that approximately one-third of the adolescents who become pregnant chose abortion as a solution.[37] The polarization of values makes consideration of this option extremely sensitive. Some families unanimously will rule our abortion even if that is the only topic about which they seem to agree.

A belief that the adolescent has a right to choose abortion without parental consent, or refuse abortion despite family pressure, does not negate the importance of assessment of family feeling. Chesler and Davis[8] emphasized the importance of helping pregnant adolescents understand that successful problem solving requires some consideration of the feelings and anticipated response of significant others. They stressed the adolescent's need for emotional support during and subsequent to the decision to abort. An adolescent who chooses to abort without parental consent, may be in need of counseling to help her resolve possible feelings of disloyalty to family values. Even if the adolescent maintains an attitude of bravado and rebelliousness, it is quite probable that she has not reached a level of genuine comfort with her decision.

The literature reveals some findings regarding the families of adolescents who choose to abort in comparison with families of adolescents who carry pregnancies to term. There is some indication that those who abort are more likely to come from intact, two-parent homes, with higher family income.[29] Some studies have suggested that adolescents who abort are likely to have achieved a degree of financial independence from parents and are less likely to be influenced in the decision regarding the pregnancy by their mothers, who, nevertheless, support their decision.[29] Other studies indicate that adolescents are more likely to perceive their decision to abort as externally determined.[24] The perception of external locus of control regarding the abortion decision is consistent with the adolescent's difficulty with, or ambivalence about, accepting responsibility for her own behavior. This is a normal developmental characteristic. However the findings also would seem to reflect that real pressures are exerted by some parents on adolescents who may feel powerless to oppose their wishes. Therefore, the issue of real or imagined powerlessness or helplessness of a family member may need to be addressed as part of the intervention.

The Decision to Relinquish. Whereas the early literature on pregnant adolescents reflected the prevalence of relinquishment as resolution of the pregnancy, current literature reflects an emphasis on abortion or adolescent parenting. The change is in keeping with solutions currently in vogue. Of those adolescents who carry their pregnancies to term, approximately 90 percent choose parenthood over relinquishment.[9]

Tasks for the family where relinquishment is the decision may include dealing with mourning over loss of the child, guilt associated with a sense of abandoning a part of the family, fantasies regarding heredity factors, such as the child's appearance or personality traits, concerns regarding the child's future which is placed in the control of unknown others, and questions regarding the future rights of the adopted child to seek the birthmother. The professional can assist the family by using a model of grief resolution as a basis for intervention in relation to the relinquishment. The family can be prepared to anticipate resurgence of feelings of sadness on the birth date of the child. If the intervention surrounding the relinquishment is successful, the family will achieve a sense of acceptance of the placement of the child, and perhaps even a degree of satisfaction over contributing to another family's happiness in the process of resolving their family's crisis.

Some families may consider intrafamily adoption as an option with the adolescent's parents, siblings, or extended family adopting the child. The professional has a responsibility to help the family assess this option with consideration of future implications for potential conflict regarding "owner-ship" of the child and for the family chains of relationships and loyalties. Some families may interpret this option as an opportunity for the adolescent unselfishly to bestow a child as a gift on some less fortunate family member who is unable to conceive. Although such interpretations may be at variance with the professional's own norms, it is not necessarily an unhealthy resolu-tion, and, in fact, may be a positive resolution for families, particularly those whose cultural traditions support that option.

The Decision to Become a Parent. The decision to assume the role of parent as an outcome of pregnancy may be further complicated by marriage versus single parenthood issues. There are estimates that one half to one third of teenage marriages occur subsequent to conception.[22] Other adolescents marry and then conceive, either purposefully or accidentally. Although preg-nant adolescents who are married bear the burden of coping with three simultaneous crisis stimuli, adolescence, marriage, and pregnancy changing to parenthood, societal concern and programs seemed to be focused more on the unwed pregnant adolescent. Intervention with the family of a married adoles-cent is usually focused on the marital couple. However, the work with the marital couple may be directed to helping them resolve issues with their families of origin.

In spite of the increasing acceptance of unwed mothers and an awareness of the high rate of divorce for teen marriages, there is still significant pressure for pregnant adolescents to marry, and numerous variations possible for a conflict regarding the issue of marriage. In some instances both the young woman and her family may be anxious to arrange a marriage, but the boyfriend and/or his family may be unwilling. In other cases the young woman and her boyfriend may decide to marry, but one or both families are in opposition. Also, the family or families may push the prospective parents toward marriage when one or both believe that marriage is unwise.

If there is a conflict surrounding the issue of marriage, the professional can help the family examine the agendas, expectations, fears, and hopes as part of the decision-making process. Involvement of the father and his family during the intervention process is extremely important if marriage is an issue. If the father is also an adolescent, it is likely that the marriage will depend on some degree of support from one or both sets of parents. A session with the young couple, and both sets of parents, should be arranged with the goal of making explicit the expectations of all parties.

Premarital counseling with the young couple is an important aspect of the intervention. Both parties bring to the marriage expectations and unfinished business derived from their own families of origin. Since adolescents are still in process of emancipation from their families, such factors can be expected to be extremely important in their adjustment to marriage. Issues that would be explored in premarital counseling under any circumstances, such as sexuality, family planning, financial issues, and division of responsibilities, are even more important when working with the adolescent couple. Unfortunately, however, the decision to marry is usually made without professional counseling. Professionals generally become involved only at the point the young marriage is in crisis, or even after it has been dissolved.

If marriage has been ruled out, the continuing relationship between the adolescent and the father may still remain an issue. The rights and responsibilities of the father and his family in respect to financial support, child care, and decision making must be negotiated with all parties. For instance, the decision of the adolescent mother to name the baby for the father, or to allow the father to name the baby, might provoke renewed uproar in her family.

An area of anticipated conflict between the adolescent and her parents is the extent of emancipation of the young mother from her own family. The infant is a tangible reminder that the adolescent has been sexually active. Parental fears that their daughter will again become pregnant may be exaggerated, perhaps with the intent of placing the daughter in the "bad girl" role. However, there is a solid statistical basis for those fears since adolescent mothers are likely to conceive again within several years of the first pregnancy.[31] The adolescent, however, tends to believe that rearing the child has earned her the perogatives of adult independence and rebels against parental injunctions regarding her social life inclusive of her sexual activity. Since her parents usually are supplying financial support and assistance in child care, they may choose to wield those factors as weapons to threaten or provoke guilt in their daughter.

When marriage is not considered, or selected as an option, the adolescent and her family will need to consider carefully the implications that the addition of the adolescent's child will have on the total family unit. Depending on the age of the adolescent, the alternatives of the adolescent's emancipating and establishing a new residence with her child may be considered.[14]

Although emancipation provides a solution to some issues and affirms the adolescent in her new adult role, other problems are exacerbated around the need for financial stability and the burdens of child care.

There is a central question that should be raised and resolved if the adolescent is to add her child to the existing family unit: whose child will this be? The professional can assist the family in anticipating and planning for the inevitable conflicts that will arise in areas such as allocation of responsibility for child-care tasks, identification of the primary nurturing figure for the child, and agreement on child-rearing philosophy and practices. Realistic consideration of those issues will provide a framework for decision-making revolving around the larger decision regarding assumption of the parenting role.

THE CRISIS OF THE ADDITION OF THE NEWBORN TO THE FAMILY

If the problem is resolved by the decision either to abort or adopt, the family unit can begin the process of reorganization. If the decision of parenthood is selected, however, the process of adjustment and reorganization continues around the task of assimilating the new infant into the family. The birth of a child precipitates a crisis in all families, but there are unique aspects to the resolution of the crisis when the parent is an adolescent. According to Hill's[18] schema of family crisis, the pregnancy and birth of a child to an unmarried adolescent has the potential of displaying dual characteristics; a crisis of addition, and a crisis of demoralization for the family.

The choice of marriage, which may occur prior to, or subsequent to, the birth of the baby, provides still another crisis for the adolescent which must be resolved along with the developmental crisis of adolescence and the crisis of pregnancy and parenthood. Although the marital couple will probably be the unit targeted for intervention, the families of both parties may be instrumental in adjusting to their new roles of husband/father and wife/mother. It is important to note however that data supports the assumption that married mothers, including adolescent mothers, who live separate from either family are less likely to receive support and assistance from their families than unwed adolescent mothers living with their families.[13]

If the adolescent becomes a single parent, she must make the same transition that every primigravida makes from the role of daughter to the role of mother. That transition has unique aspects when it is attempted with the daughter/mother remaining in the household with her family. Schaffer and Pine[34] refer to the task as resolution of the need to move from a position of being mothered to a position of being a mother. The professional must assist the entire family in supporting the adolescent in that difficult transition. An incentive for the adolescent is the establishment of a new relationship with her own mother, based on mutual sharing of experiences of pregnancy, birth, and mothering and a reaffirmation of the shared female identity.[2,22] According to Ballou,[2] "the resolution of ambivalent feelings toward the mother is one of the major object-relation tasks of pregnancy." (p. 31) She sees the difficulty of this task as dependent upon the degree of ambivalence in the daughter/-mother relationship. Since adolescent girls are notoriously ambivalent toward their mothers, one must predict that the task will be difficult for many pregnant adolescents. One aspect of the resolution of the mothered/mothering dilemma, and arrival at a new, more mature daughter-mother relationship, seems to be temporary regression of the pregnant woman to a dependent relationship with her mother.[2,21,34] Since adolescents are working on the developmental task of establishing independence, they may have difficulty accepting a dependent role if their mothers increase their nurturing behaviors. However, they may be resentful, without insight regarding the source of their resentment, if their mothers do not supply nurturance. The confusion of the tasks of pregnancy and parenthood with the tasks of adolescence requires special awareness and skill on the part of the professional in helping the adolescent and her family achieve the required delicate adjustments and balances.

In addition to tasks that need to be resolved at the intrapsychic and interpersonal levels, there are many practical issues as well. The resolution of practical issues, in fact, may provide the arena for resolution or continuation of interpersonal issues. For instance, purchase of necessities such as baby clothes and furniture, or selection of sleeping space for the baby, may be utilized as indirect means to communicate intended role definitions in relation to the infant.[6] The adolescent's mother who takes charge of all preparations for the baby and makes the bulk of purchases of clothing, furniture, and other necessities, or insists that the baby sleep in her room so that the adolescent can rest, is usurping the mothering role. On the other hand, the adolescent's mother who does nothing to prepare or provide for the infant is not providing the support necessary to help her daughter adequately assume the mothering role.

While some programs and interventions seem to be premised on the belief that certain resolutions of the crisis of adolescent pregnancy and/or parenthood are preferable to others, there appears to be no one course of action or pattern that will satisfy the need of all families. In a recent study of a very small sample of adolescent mothers living with their families, Furstenberg[13] reports findings which indicate that satisfactory resolution of role distinctions and division of labor can result from various patterns. Therefore, interventions that are to be successful should be directed toward clarification of communication patterns, resolution of role ambiguity, improvement of family problem-solving skills, integration of cognitive and affective messages, and other tasks related to improvement of processes within the family. The content of the decisions then belongs to the family.

BIBLIOGRAPHY

1. Anthony, E.J. The reaction of parents to adolescents and their behavior. In E.J. Anthony and T. Benedek (Eds.), *Parenthood: Its Psychology and Psychopathology*. Boston: Little, Brown, 1970.
2. Ballou, J.W. *The Psychology of Pregnancy: Reconciliation and Resolution*. Lexington, Mass.: Lexington Books, 1978.
3. Benedek, Therese. Parenthood during the life cycle. In E.J. Anthony and T. Benedek (Eds.), *Parenthood: Its Psychology and Psychopathology*. Boston: Little, Brown, 1970.
4. Boszormenyi-Nagy, I. and Spark, G. *Invisible Loyalties*. New York: Harper Row, 1973.
5. Bowen, M. Theory in the practice of psychotherapy. In P.J. Guerin (Ed.) *Family Therapy: Theory and Practice*. New York: Gardner Halsted Press, 1976.
6. Bryan-Logan, B.N. and Dancy, B.L. Unwed pregnant adolescents: Their mothers' dilemma. *The Nursing Clinics of North America*. 1974, **9**(1), 57–68.
7. Caplan, G. *Principles of Preventive Psychiatry*. New York: Basic Books, 1964.
8. Chesler, J.S. and Davis, S.A. Problem pregnancy and abortion counseling with teenagers. *Social Casework*, 1980, **61**(3), 173–179.
9. Chilman, C.S. Teenage pregnancy: A research review. *Social Work*, 1979, **24**(6), 492–498.
10. Duvall, E.M. *Family Development (3rd. Ed.)*. Philadelphia: J.B. Lippincott, 1967.
11. Erikson, E.H. *Childhood and Society*. New York: W.W. Norton, 1950.
12. Friedman, D.B. Parent development. *California Medicine*, 1957, **86**(1), 25–28.
13. Furstenberg, F.F. Burdens and benefits: The impact of early child bearing on the family. *Journal of Social Issues*, 1980, **36**(1), 64–87.
14. Furstenberg, F.F. and Crawford, A.G. Family support: Helping teenage mothers to cope. *Family Planning Perspectives*, 1978, **10**(6), 322–333.
15. Garmenzy, E. Book review—The unmarried father: New helping approaches for unmarried young parents. *Minnesota Welfare*, 1972, **24**(1), 22–23.
16. Gartner, R., Fulner, R., Weinshel, M., and Goldklank, S. The family life-cycle: Developmental crises and their structural impact on families in a community mental health center. *Family Process*, 1978, **17**(1), 47–58.
17. Grow, L.J. *Early Childbearing by Young Mothers: A Research Study*. New York: Child Welfare League of America, 1979.
18. Hill, R. Generic features of families under stress. *Social Casework*, 1958, **39**, 139–150.

19. Ingram, G. Families in crisis. In R.E. Hardy and J.G. Cull (Eds.) *Therapeutic Needs of the Family*: Problems, Descriptions, and Therapeutic Approaches. Springfield, Ill.: Charles Thomas, 1974.
20. Jackson, D.D. and Weakland, J.H. Conjoint family therapy: Some considerations on theory, techniques, and results. *Psychiatry*, 1961, **24**, 30–45.
21. LaBarre, M. Pregnancy experiences among married adolescents. *American Journal of Orthopsychiatry*, 1969, **38**(1), 47–55.
22. LaBarre, M. Emotional crisis of school-age girls during pregnancy and early motherhood. *American Journal of Orthopsychiatry*, 1972, **11**, 537–557.
23. Langsley, D.G., Kaplan, D., Pittman, F., Machotka, P., Flomenhaft, K., and DeYoung, C. *The Treatment of families in Crisis*. New York: Grune & Stratton, 1968.
24. Lewis, C.C. A comparison of minors' and adults' pregnancy decisions. *American Journal of Orthopsychiatry*, 1980, **50**(3), 446–453.
25. Lidz, T. Schizophrenia and the family. *Psychiatry*, 1958, **21**, 21–27.
26. Minuchin, S. The use of an ecological framework in treatment of a child. In E.J. Anthony and C. Kaupernic (Eds.) *The Child in His Family*. New York: Wiley-Interscience, 1970.
27. Minuchin, S. *Families and Family Therapy*. Cambridge: Harvard University Press, 1974.
28. Moroney, R.M. *Families, Social Services, and Social Policy: The Issue of Shared Responsibility*. Rockville, MD: National Institute of Mental Health, U.S. Department of Health and Human Services, 1980.
29. Olson, L. Social and psychological correlates of pregnancy resolution among adolescent women. *American Journal of Orthopsychiatry*, 1980, **50**(3), 443–445.
30. Pannor, R. and Nerlove, E. Fostering understanding between adolescents and adoptive parents through group experiences. *Child Welfare*, 1977, **56**(8), 537–557.
31. Phipps-Yonas, S. Teenage pregnancy and motherhood: A review of the literature. *American Journal of Orthopsychiatry*. 1980, **50**(3), 403–431.
32. Rapoport, L. Working with families in crisis: An exploration in preventive intervention. In H.J. Parad (Ed.) *Crisis Intervention: Selected Readings*. New York: Family Services Association, 1965.
33. Rosenberg, B.N. Planned short-term treatment in developmental crises. *Social Casework*, 1975, April, 195–204.
34. Schaffer, C. and Pine, F. Pregnancy, abortion, and the developmental tasks of pregnancy. *The American Journal of Child Psychiatry*, 1972, **11**, 511–536.
35. Stierlin, H. Counter transference in family therapy with adolescents. In M. Sugar (Ed.) *The Adolescent in Group and Family Therapy*. New York: Brunner Mazel, 1975.
36. Strean, H.S. Reconsiderations in casework treatment of the unmarried mother. *Social Work*, 1968, **13**(4), 91–100.
37. Tietze, C. Teenage pregnancies: Looking ahead to 1984. *Family Planning Perspectives*, 1978, **10**(4), 205–207.
38. Umana, R.F., Gross, S.J., McConville, M., and Turner, A. *Crisis in the Family: Three Approaches*. New York: Gaines Press, 1980.

39. Vincent, C.E. *Unmarried Mothers*. New York: Free Press of Glencoe, 1961.
40. Whitaker, C.A. The symptomatic adolescent: An awol family member. In M. Sugar (Ed.), *The Adolescent in Group and Family Therapy*. New York: Brunner Mazel, 1975.
41. Zilbach, J.L. Family development and familial factors in etiology. In J.D. Noshpitz (Ed.), *Basic Handbook of Child Psychiatry (Vol. 1)*. New York: Basic Books, 1979.

14.
The Emotionally Disturbed Pregnant Adolescent

Howard D. Eisman, Ph.D.,
Chief Psychologist,
Coney Island Hospital,
Brooklyn, N.Y.

and

Frederick L. Covan, Ph.D.,
Chief Psychologist,
Bellevue Psychiatric Hospital,
New York, N.Y.

Adolescence is a very stressful period for most in American and European culture. The adolescent stresses occur at the same time that the parents of adolescents are undergoing their own mid-life crises. These conditions can interact with one another creating unstable and intolerable family conditions. Some adolescents attempt to resolve interpersonal and intrapsychic conflicts with impulsive action. Pregnancy can be one result of such acting out. This chapter describes basic adolescent conflicts and sources of abrasive and destructive interaction between adolescents and parents. It discusses the manner in which pregnancy can be used as a "solution" to a difficult family situation.

Five case histories are presented. The examples were selected to be representative of the more common cases the worker in this field is likely to find. The case histories include that of a schizophrenic adolescent, an adolescent abusing alcohol, a suicidal adolescent, and two adolescents in the same family, one schizophrenic, one neurotic, both becoming pregnant for different reasons. In each case, the motivation for the pregnancy and the background of the emotional disturbance are discussed with emphasis upon adolescent stresses and familial conflict.

Treating the pregnant adolescent is difficult, because most tend to use symbolic action acting-out instead of introspection as a way of dealing with their feelings. The difficulties this causes in attempting to do individual therapy is discussed. The manner in which therapy groups can be helpful for the pregnant adolescent is presented, and the importance of family therapy, either as primary therapy or as an adjunct to other therapeutic modes, is emphasized.

INTRODUCTION

Pregnancy can be a conflict free, accepted event for some adolescents, but a destructive and disruptive one for others. It is a particularly difficult problem for most emotionally disturbed adolescents. A pregnancy can exacerbate existing depressions and psychoses, worsen latent or borderline conditions, or considerably strengthen an already pathological life-style. Depressed, schizophrenic, neurotic, and character disordered adolescents can all be adversely affected by pregnancy. Getting pregnant can be a symptomatic expression of an individual's severe pathological disturbance and cause great hardship.

This chapter will discuss the personal and familial stresses suffered by the adolescent, present five case histories of emotionally disturbed pregnant adolescents, and discuss each case with emphasis on adolescent and family conflict. Suggestions for the most effective treatment methods will then be presented.

ADOLESCENT STRESS

The period of pain, uncertainty, inner turmoil, and tumultuous relationships which we call adolescence has long been described in Western novels and poetry. It was first included in scientific study in the early years of this century. G. Stanley Hall (1904) wrote extensively of the adolescent's behavior, and Freud in 1905 postulated an explanation for these beahviors (Freud, 1961). Freud's view was that puberty, with its strong biological drives, brings about a reactivation or recapitulation of impulses long repressed, and once again there is an Oedipal struggle. This results in the adolescent's inner chaos, family conflict, and eventual resolution through identification with the same sexed parent. This recapitulation perspective was elaborated by Peter Blos (1962) who emphasized a "second individuation stage."

These views were contradicted by anthropological studies showing the absence of adolescent difficulties in some non-Western societies in which sexual roles and social responsibilities of children and adolescents are different from our own (Mead, 1939). Also the turmoil of adolescence lasts long after puberty and is often at its worst long after all physical changes have been completed (Stone and Church, 1957).

A social psychological approach to adolescence was taken by Lewin (1954) and Rel (1969). Here, societal factors are emphasized along with inner conflict. Lewin described the adolescent as having an ill-defined place in our society, neither adult nor child. An adolescent is allowed some responsibilities but not others, and is seen as an adult in some ways and still a child in others. Not really belonging fully to the social system, the adolescent becomes part of an outgroup culture, much as do other minority groups. The adolescent feels uncertain, inferior, and incompetent; her peers, who are similar to her and have the same feelings, are seen as a safe haven, while adults are seen as an occupying army.

What all theorists agree upon is the type of life an adolescent lives and experiences. They are enormously self-centered. They are most concerned about their appearance. They worry about their interaction with their peers and what their peers think of them. Their feelings about themselves alternate considerably over short periods of time. An adolescent can feel elated and grandiose about her abilities in the morning and then be severely depressed and feel incompetent by the afternoon. The intensity of these feelings is a new experience for the adolescent and it can lead to confusion. The causes for such severe flip-flops often seem trivial; a slight from a friend or being caught doing something embarrassing.

Adolescents become quite irreverent and iconoclastic about much of adult values. They are quick to reject hypocrisy and conformity in their society. But they follow adolescent fads slavishly and then drop them suddenly. There are many forms of allegiances in adolescents. One classical form, religious asceticism as a part of early adolescence, has been frequently described (Freud, 1946), but it seems less common nowadays than in previous years.

In the early years of adolescence girls develop crushes on popular figures which are mercurial and change rapidly. Some distant, idealized figure, usually an entertainer who projects a child-adult image can become a cult figure for adolescents as they search for icons upon which to project their uncertain, chaotic identity.

Much of this behavior has been considered a search for identity (Erikson, 1963). Adolescents try to find ways of making themselves unique, clear-cut individuals. Thus, in early adolescence distinctive clothing becomes important along with particular types of hair cuts and similar items of personal grooming. The adolescent may also "adopt" a personality, trying to imitate some distinctive adult manner, usually a popular figure. Thus, one sees many exaggerations of speech and walk along with theatrical mannerisms of various sorts. Teams and organizations of peers are very important, especially if jackets or other badges of membership are involved. In their attempts to become individuals, adolescents become very trendy, almost compulsive in their devotions to the latest styles. This paradox is understandable when one considers that there is no real opportunity for any but the rare adolescent to distinguish herself in any other manner. Having no alternatives, many early adolescents turn to the garish and the florid in styles. Older adolescents have more real choices. They are involved in making scholastic or career decisions.

Great amounts of affection and acceptance are needed by the adolescent. In the face of all the self-doubt and awkwardness adolescents feel, they need considerable support. This support can come from their peers, who know what they are going through, and is thus of great value. Support can also come from the family, but this can be difficult. The adolescent is embarrassed by her strong needs and doesn't want to be treated as a child. Thus, messages she may send out requesting affection can be mixed with expressions of hostility for her parents and siblings. Antagonism and love are mixed together and the adolescent can only expect family support to be inconstant. The strong need for some manner of gaining consistent love, unambivalently given and unambivalently received, is a powerful adolescent motivator.

The adolescent also has to separate from her family despite the continuing attachment. Independence is a major issue in adolescence. Young adolescents want privacy at home and complete freedom to conduct their own affairs. Older adolescents want to be the ones able to make basic decisions about their lives. At both age levels, ambivalence about this independence is the rule. The adolescent is frequently so unsure about her ability to handle her independence that she feels the need for help. The involvement of adults, especially parents, can be experienced as meddling and a threat to her independence and can bring on a murderous rage, but the adolescent continues to request help, either overtly or covertly. Often parental involvement is invited by a burst of acting out. An adolescent in real trouble once again unequivocally requires family protection and the ambivalence about independence is resolved.

Conflict is not always the rule. In lower class adolescents who have a narrower range of life-style choices and more emphasis on early maturation, less conflict exists (Stone and Church, 1957). There is less of a gap between parents and children.

Offer (1969) believes that the idea of "Sturm und Drang" associated with adolescents is the result of studies of disturbed adolescents. His own study of normal adolescents led him to conclude that many made a rather smooth voyage through this period with minimal destruction of family ties and little personal discomfort. Redl (1969) does see adolescents as being under extremely strong pathogenic pressures, but many are capable of effectively standing up to such pressures. These adolescents are not much disturbed during this period, and it may be assumed that their families may not be much disturbed either.

Other family situations exist where little conflict is manifested, but for pathological reasons. These may be very authoritarian families where the children have no room whatever to exercise individuality, or families in which there is a very closely knit core group. In these latter families, there may have never been any clearly defined parental role or child role; everyone identified with everyone else. The children frequently had to care for parents incapable of caring for themselves, and the children were in turn cared for by these same parents or by their siblings. A group symbiosis was formed. The family group existed as the most powerful entity in the lives of all its members, with personal identification subordinate to family identification.

FAMILIES IN STRESS

Adolescence occurs at a time when most parents are at a crisis stage themselves. If a couple have a child when they are 24, they will be 39 years old when she becomes 15. Thus, the parents of many adolescents are themselves undergoing life changes and emotional upsets at the same time that their adolescent children are undergoing their crises. This makes for a particularly difficult state of affairs.

The clashes are inevitable. The adolescent children are developing sexually and exhibiting this development in the most obvious and florid fashion just when the parents are worrying about a diminution of their own sex drives. Adolescent romances flourish, while parents feel the fire gone from their own relationship and are perhaps fearful that their own romantic fantasies will never actualize. Adults with middle-aged spread and sagging musculature see children developing ideal figures and flaunting them!

Parents who are beginning to regret the predictable stable patterns their lives have taken, face children with a new adventure every day. Their conservatism is challenged by their child's radicalism. They, who have given up believing that they can make any significant mark in the world, converse with offspring who voice the most grandiose plans. The parents suffer disquieting thoughts about how they have settled into their own hopefully comfortable niche, praying the world's problems would not find them, and they hear the insistent demands of their adolescent children that the world be changed.

The conflict between the adolescent and her family is not just one of a growing person having to find and battle adult resistance. The phases of adolescent development of necessity incite adults into less than mature behavior themselves. For parents, an adolescent child is not just one who battles, challenges, provokes, and disregards them. The adolescent child is a stimulus for the stirring up of old memories, old desires, and fantasies long forgotten. They experience a profound undermining of the life they have set up for themselves. The life is no longer satisfying, and as they look at their children they become aware of how fast time is passing; they, too, are in crisis.

Parents can respond in a number of ways. They can try to be authoritarian and insist that their child follow their instructions. They can identify with the adolescent and covertly encourage the developing sexuality and rebelliousness. They can leave the field, either becoming psychologically detached, or abandoning home completely. These are not necessarily mutually exclusive choices, and many parents manage to do two or even three of these either simultaneously or sequentially.

The actual leaving of home does occur. A father quitting his banking job and running off to Tahiti with his daughter's 17-year-old classmate has become a stereotyped joke. But the stresses of waning sexuality, disenchantment with marriage and job, advancing years, and a sexually blooming daughter do lead to such behavior. In cases where the male parent may not be the natural parent of the difficult adolescent, often the case in disorganized, lower class families, such departures are frequent.

In fact, the threat of a parent departing is one form of pressure on the adolescent and an opportunity to act out further. In a tenuous family situation, it may become very obvious that the conflicts resulting from one child's adolescence may be the straw that breaks the camel's back. The adolescent is in a position to keep her father or send him packing, while mother is pleading with her to back off. She herself has mixed feelings about what she wants to do, and the power she can wield in the family makes her alternately euphoric and frightened.

The reawakening of an adolescentlike state in parents is not the only reason for the conflicts which develop. Parents begin to worry about being useless when children reach the point of leaving home. There is nothing left for them but old age. Children may be holding the parents together; it is the children which they have in common. When the children leave, the parents look at each other and see two strangers. Marriages often break up when the last child leaves home. Parents with such feeling may be ambivalent at best about their adolescent child's development. They may, indeed, be interested in retarding such development as much as is possible. Or, for some, they may have fantasies of again having a baby in the house, a helpless docile infant which needs them.

The stresses and tensions which arise as a result of the adolescent in the family are not only manifested in the relationship between the adolescent and her parents, but also in the relationship of the parents to each other. Conflicts about the adolescents' behavior can arise between the parents as well. One might be inclined to identify with the adolescent while the other will fight every action tooth and nail. Most likely, this sort of conflict will be manifest by extreme inconsistency on the part of all parties with positions and allegiances changing drastically daily. In cases of this sort, adolescence in a child may be a catalyst for a long-latent conflict between the parents to emerge with a vengeance.

These situations wherein the parents regress or lose effectiveness cause further distress in the adolescent. While experiencing an unpredictable world of psychological chaos, sharp mood swings, lack of any sense of inner organization, the adolescent is then also faced with unpredictable, sometimes emotionally upset parents who are unable to provide any structure at all to her world. She is left feeling even more confused, and is thus likely to act out against the parents even more, perhaps causing a further deterioration in their ability to respond adequately or to manage their own lives and their relationship with each other.

ADOLESCENCE AND PREGNANCY

Although adolescents seem to be endlessly talking about themselves and show a preoccupation with themselves unmatched at any other period of life, most of them don't really reveal much of their feelings. Denial is the most prevalent defense, and adolescents express their feelings by acting out (Toolan, 1969). Feelings are experienced in a confused manner and dealt with in an indirect way through actions which have symbolic significance. There are certainly numerous exceptions to this style. Some adolescents can be quite introspective and articulate about their feelings, others can be all too inarticulate. But many resort to acting out. This is a particular problem for those attempting to do therapy with adolescents, as they can lead the therapist through a merry chase of verbiage, hyperbole, fantasies, and challenges without directly expressing what is bothering them.

An adolescent dissatisfied with her life, feeling overwhelmed by strong needs, seeks to take some significant action to alleviate the uncomfortable state. A blind impulsive action—without regard for long-term consequences— can result. The pressures which she is seeking to alleviate might have had a lifetime to develop, but they are strongly exacerbated by the stresses of adolescence and the family conflicts that arise during this period. Most acting out has a powerful element of familial conflict as part of it. The adolescent may be doing the acting out, but other family members indirectly foster it and may also derive some reduction in their own discomfort as a result.

Pregnancy in almost all adolescents can be seen as some form of acting out. The adolescent who gets pregnant is motivated by an inner discomfort, but it often seems that family, friends, school, and perhaps her subculture are all involved in some way in motivating her for a pregnancy. The adolescent with a history of, or a potential for, emotional disturbance is subject to the same pressure. She can go about getting pregnant in a different manner from the normal adolescent, and her ability to deal with the consequences may be limited, but the basic psychological mechanisms behind pregnancy are similar in the emotionally disturbed girl and in the normal girl.

Pregnancy can be a most powerful disruptive force in an already shaky adolescent. It is a factor in the high rate of adolescent suicide (Otto, 1969) and it can exacerbate latent pathological processes so that severe psychoses and depressions can result. This is not always the case. There are adolescents in which the pregnancy is the result of an already well-developed pathological life-style and it might be accepted with apparent equanimity. It resolves their conflicts—for the moment.

This chapter will present five cases of emotionally disturbed pregnant adolescents. The cases were selected to be representative of the more common cases the worker in this field is likely to find. The motivation for the pregnancy and the background of the emotional disturbance are discussed with emphasis upon adolescent stresses and familial conflict.

CASE HISTORIES

Case history: A Schizophrenic Girl

Sharon became pregnant in her 16th year. She was the youngest of five children. Her parents were born in Europe and are members of an ultra-orthodox Jewish sect. The family lives in a middle-class area of two-family houses. The members of this sect, Hassidic Jews and followers of a particular family of revered rabbis, all live in the immediate neighborhood making a very closely knit community.

Little is known of the early life of Sharon's parents. Both were young children in Rumania during the holocaust. Neither were in concentration camps, but the circumstances of their survival is not known as they were disinclined to speak much about themselves as children during the interviews. They and their families were brought to this country in the late 1940s through the efforts of the sect to which both families had connections. Their families had known each other in Rumania, but they themselves were unacquainted. A marriage was arranged for them through the efforts of their families (with the approval of the sect's rabbi), when Sharon's mother was 18 and her father 21. All sect marriages are arranged in this way, and the participation of the particular rabbi who was involved was considered a great honor.

Sharon's father continued night school after marriage eventually obtaining both an accounting degree and a law degree. He worked exclusively for sect members. He also worked without fee for the sect's rabbi, handling the sect's finances and legal matters. He was a well-known and respected figure in the community.

Sharon's mother was busy with the children born to her over the years, and maintaining their household. Sect women rarely worked outside the home. All dressed very modestly, with longish dresses (never pants!), long sleeves, and a high neckline. The men dressed in dark, usually black business suits and a dark hat, in a modern but conservative style. Since sect members dressed in modern fashion and had secular as well as religious education, the sect considered itself modern and moderate.

Premarital intercourse is forbidden to males and females. Sect members marry early. When adolescents show sexual stirrings, it is considered time to arrange a marriage, which can take a very long time to finally materialize. Chastity until marriage is a firm rule. An unchaste man is seen as having acted in an unpious manner; an unchaste women has suffered a tragedy.

Sharon's childhood was first described by her parents as being unremarkable. As they got more comfortable, they were more revealing. They had always been a bit worried about her because of her tendency to go her own way. She would wander beyond the confines of her own neighborhood. She played hookey from class in grade school on occasion, and she engaged in rough play. All of these behaviors were most unusual in young girls of this sect. She showed curiosity about proscribed items, and she was know to have read books and seen television shows which were forbidden to her. In recent years, she tried to get her parents to discuss basic tenets of their religious faith with her, not quite arguing with them, but certainly raising some disquieting questions. She had been insistent about picking out her own clothing in recent months, and she refused to shop in the local stores because they sold "old lady's stuff." The clothing which she did buy was seen as immodest, even gaudy, by ther parents although it was essentially conservative. In her high school—a small all-girl school run by the sect—she was seen as outspoken and challenging, questioning much of what she was taught, particularly the religious material. Her attitude was mentioned to the parents by the major rabbi of the sect; she was seen as being rebellious, but still very much a sect member in good standing.

Sharon was impregnated by a 17-year-old sect member whom she had known since childhood. Both claim that each was the first lover for each other. Intercourse took place on three occations. No birth control was used. Both adolescents knew about birth-control devices, but they had no access to them, and they also had no intention of having intercourse on any of the occasions. Birth-control devices as well as abortion are prohibited by the sect. Abortion is seen as a heinous destruction of human life and not available as an alternative under any conditions.

Sharon never reported her pregnancy to her parents, and being busy they noticed nothing. They began wondering about her at about her third month of pregnancy when she showed signs of erratic and bizarre behavior. A physical examination revealed the pregnancy. Sharon first insisted that she could not be pregnant then began to voice bizarre fantasies about being impregnated by "the evil one." She became unusually talkative. Her speech was tangential and often did not make sense. She appeared preoccupied. No psychiatric consultation had yet been made.

Sharon's parents were busy trying to rectify a disastrous situation. Abortion was out of the question. An attempt was made to arrange a marriage with Sharon's lover—but he refused. Rabbis were brought in to resolve the issue, and they ordered a marriage. All of these negotiations were known to Sharon, her siblings, friends, and probably the whole community. Her former lover agreed to the marriage, but with many recriminations on the part of his family. They were inclined to see Sharon as an experienced seductress of their innocent boy.

Sharon's bizarreness became more apparent as the marriage was arranged. She claimed that she spoke regularly to God. She saw God, at first in numerous forms, but finally He appeared to her in the form of a German Shepherd dog. She proclaimed to all, family, friends, and strangers that "God is a German Shepherd dog." She also took a kitchen knife to her stomach on several occasions, saying that God had told her to kill the evil within her. When she actually scratched her abdomen with the knife, she was taken to a private psychiatrist. She was then promptly hospitalized, diagnosed as "acute schizophrenic episode."

When her hospitalization became known to her future husband and his family they canceled the marriage arrangement. There was much pleading from the sect's rabbis, but they remained adament.

Sharon was in the hospital a brief period of time. Medication was administered. She ceased to voice her bizarre thoughts. Her parents insisted she return home, and she was discharged.

Once home, the family faced the dilemma. Sharon would have to have her child, but it would be placed for adoption. The problem then would be one of Sharon's marriageability. Within her community, Sharon would be seen as a most unfortunate woman. She could not expect a marriage to a respectable, eligible member. Someone handicapped was a possibility. A physical handicap, perhaps with luck, only a slight one. A limp. A speech defect . . . the discussion continued.

Sharon was a passive participant to these discussions. She seemed bland and indifferent at first, but she began to speak of German Shepherd dogs again. All the knives were locked up and Sharon was forbidden to leave the house. She did, however, and she was gone all night and then returned with no comprehensible explanation as to where she had been. She was again hospitalized with the same diagnosis.

Sharon was once again quieted with medication. The delusion about God remained as a preoccupation. She would not speak much about her pregnancy except as part of her whole delusional system. Her family visited and these visits would agitate her. The family was insistent about a quick discharge, as every day spent in a mental institution worked against her, and their, reputation.

Sharon was released to a Day Treatment Center. This placement required considerable therapy for her family. They agreed to participate as it was preferrable to inpatient hospitalization for Sharon. Sharon's parents became more helpful in their attitude toward her. Her older siblings, now married, were brought into the family therapy and they acted to stabilize the family. The parents had a chance to voice their own fears and sadness over the situation, and their reaction to the covert chastisement by the community which they felt. Expression of these pent-up feelings resulted in the reduction of their desperate attempts to undo the pregnancy and corresponding loss of face, and they began to see Sharon as a suffering daughter who needed their love and support. There was no discussion of how they might have covertly encouraged her behavior, as this would have increased their resistance to the therapy.

Once this change in parental attitude had been accomplished, Sharon was herself brought into the family sessions. The goals were to have the parents and Sharon understand one another's feelings and to have the parents show their support of her. Sharon's agitation and self-destructiveness diminished rather quickly, but her delusional system lingered for 2 months before it completely disappeared.

Sharon's family and the subculture in which they live have righteous, highly structured lives with rules for even the most minor aspects of daily activity. A departure from these standards is seen as evil. In such a tightly knit, highly structured, and very restrictive environment, there are bound to be some feelings of rebellion in all members. Most individuals repress and suppress these feelings in themselves, but certain family members become selected as "rebels." They are the ones who are seen as sinful and profligate as other family members project the unacceptable impulses, feelings, and ideas they have onto the "rebel." The attempts made to correct the "rebel" lead to this person seeing herself as the kind of person she is accused of being. The "rebel" incorporates the image the other family members have of her into her own self-image. In this manner, and with other covert reinforcements, the "rebel" is encouraged to act out the secret wishes of the other family members.

Sharon seems to have been such a "rebel." As the youngest child entering her adolescence at a time of great social permissiveness in the host American society, with her parents in mid-life, with all her siblings out of the household, and no longer mitigating forces, Sharon was particularly vulnerable to any covert messages to express the sexual urges she so strongly felt.

But pregnancy without hope of abortion was tragic for her as it left her facing the strongest possible social and familial condemnation. Her parents could only try to frantically salvage some respectability from the situation by trying to arrange a marriage. Sharon was left with the guilt and self-hatred without any parental or social affection or support. She had to face a marriage she had never even considered and probably didn't want. These pressures brought on a reactive psychosis which included some secondary gain. She had to be removed from the family household, the marriage arrangement was canceled, and she could safely express some of her hostility. Seeing God as a dog is a particularly harsh insult to an extremely pious Jewis family, and a German dog yet!

CASE HISTORY: ALCOHOL ABUSING GIRL

Margaret was brought to the emergency room of a general hospital by the police. They were called by her neighbors who complained that she was loudly yelling profanities in the hall of their apartment house. She became abusive when asked to stop. She resisted the police, who brought her to the hospital in handcuffs. At the hospital, she had alcohol on her breath, she yelled threats at the medical personnel, and she also threatened to kill her child. She refused to answer questions, she was hostile and agitated, continued to be abusive, and she was then placed in a psychiatric ward.

She was six months pregnant at the time. She gave her age (later confirmed) as 18½ years, although she looked older. At first she voiced fears that she would kill her one-year-old son. She felt that she did not give this child adequate care. She described herself as having become agitated when she saw her former boyfriend, the father of her son and of the child she was carrying, with another woman who also appeared to be pregnant. She went on a drinking binge after this, finally winding up in the condition in which she was hospitalized.

Margaret described a long history of drinking. She started drinking mildly when she was 12, and by the time she was 13 she was finishing six-packs in her school basement with her friends. She would drink even more on weekends. In recent years, she has become a binge drinker. When upset, she drinks heavily for two or three days. She sometimes blacks out, and she usually experiences a change of personality from her shy, quiet, pleasant, and docile self.

Margaret is of Irish background. Her father, a bus driver, separated from her mother when Margaret was four. This man is considered to be crazy by Margaret's family. After the separation, he threatened to kidnap Margaret and her older sister. He would break into their apartment and weep to his children. On other occasions, he would break in and leave large, threatening messages on the walls, windows, and mirrors. His appearances gradually diminshed, and her natural father ceased to be a part of Margaret's life. She has not seen him in many years and has no idea as to his whereabouts.

Margaret's mother is a practical nurse. She has worked sporadically. She drinks heavily and is considered to be an alcoholic. Between her drinking and her employment, she has never adequately taken care of her household. After divorcing Margaret's natural father, she remarried and had a son.

The stepfather is a bartender who also drinks heavily, but he keeps his jobs. He also manages the household; he does the cooking and supervises the three children. He can be quite a martinet, but goes through periods when things lapse and he does nothing at all in the house. He frequently leaves Margaret's mother for periods of two or three days after an argument and returns with no word of explanation as to where he has been. It is suspected it is a woman friend with whom he lives during these absences. He is much closer with his natural son than he is with his stepchildren. He has had frequent quarrels with Margaret's older sister over the years while Margaret has always been quite frightened of him.

Margaret's 21-year-old sister and her child live with Margaret, Margaret's child, her stepfather and her 11-year-old stepbrother in one apartment. Of the group, only the stepbrother and the young children are not heavy drinkers. Margaret's mother recently underwent an operation to correct a slipped disk and has been since confined to a wheelchair. Margaret's sister moved in to help, taking her child and leaving her husband, who objected strongly to the move. Margaret, who has lived sporadically with the father of her child over the past 3 years, now considers her mother's apartment her permanent home and has no plans to leave.

Margaret was confined to this apartment for long period of time in the past. She had kidney problems when she was 7 and did not attend school, but obtained home instruction. This happened again when she was 13. She felt deprived as she could not socialize with other children. Margaret's stepfather cared for her physical needs, but her older sister and her mother were her only company.

She met the father of her son when she was 15; he was 22 and had his own apartment. She moved in with him when she was 16, but returned to her mother's home whenever they quarreled and whenever her mother became ill; both frequent events. Her boyfriend has never been loyal. He always went out openly with other women. He, too, is a heavy drinker and while drunk he stabbed the mother of one of his other girl friends. She was not seriously injured and he was let off on probation. Margaret feels she has had enough of this relationship and she does not intend to return to him.

The day after Margaret was admitted, her sister and her mother came to the ward and insisted that she be released. Both were drunk and their request was refused. They reappeared later and stated that they had made arrangements for

Margaret at another hospital. As this could not be confirmed, Margaret was not released. However, Margaret was calming down quickly; she was completely oriented, showed good reality testing, and adequate social judgment. There were no signs that she had ever mistreated or neglected her child, and she firmly denied every having had any thoughts of hurting it. There was no further reason for her to be hospitalized, and she was released after 3 days.

Margaret was referred to an outpatient treatment facility for alcohol abusers. She made one visit, describing herself as a moderate drinker, wanting help with her habit, but has not yet returned for treatment.

In this family, Margaret, her sister, and her mother have spent a good deal of time together. (All three have dependent children.) In fact, much of the time of her critical social formative years was spent restricted to the home. There seems to be little differentiation between Margaret, her mother, and her sister. They form a symbiotic system. They cannot stay separated from each other for long; they use every excuse to live with each other. When together, they nurse each other, care for each other's children, and make it possible for each of them to drink without neglecting their children. Margaret's stepfather is excluded from this symbiotic system. He is on the periphery, but he is important in that he keeps the family's household together.

It was necessary for Margaret and her older sister to avoid developing any real life outside this symbiotic system in order to remain a part of it. They could not live with responsible, caring men nor have any independent careers of their own. Identifying with one another, each had to be a mother. Having infant children, with only welfare as support if they lived away from the family, kept them dependent on the family system. Drinking further limited their competence.

Each is partly a maternal caretaker and partly a dependent child in this symbiotic system. Margaret, identifying with her mother and sister almost completely, is not experiencing the pressures of adolescence in the same way as most girls her age. No separation from her mother has ever taken place nor is one in process. She shows no overt desire for independence. Her misgivings about her situation are expressed indirectly when she goes on a drunken binge. She leaves the house and her child and she expresses her hostility for both. These binges are a safety valve, allowing Margaret to express some of her pent-up feelings without having to take any responsibility for having them. Once this explosion has subsided, Margaret can meekly return to the symbiotic system and resume her place in it.

CASE HISTORY: A SUICIDAL ADOLESCENT

Josephine was treated for a severe depression on a psychiatric inpatient service after she spontaneously aborted in her first trimester. She was withdrawn, anhedonic, and tearful; she showed psychomotor retardation and a slowing of association. She had been hospitalized for a suicide attempt and taken to an emergency room when she told her mother about it.

Josephine, of Italian-American background, was almost 19 at the time. She had a history of psychiatric contacts since she was 12, and had treatment off and on since that age. Her parents have been legally separated for the past 5 years. Their relationship had always been a tumultuous one and they lived together only sporadically through most of Josephine's life. Her father was in the construction business and in general was a wheeler-dealer and hustler. Although his fortunes wax and wane, he usually has a good deal of money.

This girl is the older of two children. She has a 10-year-old brother who was conceived after her parents had a long separation. Josephine was an obese child and continued to be heavy during her adolescence. She also developed a bad case of acne which she still has. She has lost weight on occasion, and she has been told that she could be attractive, but most of the time she has been obese, poorly groomed, and unattractive.

She had few friends in school and had a very poor attendance record. She missed two years of grade school because of a phobia. She never did enjoy school, did not do well, nor did she make any close friends. She finally returned to school after she was put into therapy for the first time and the therapist used a behavior modification program.

Josephine felt that she didn't belong. She saw herself as awkward, inarticulate, and ugly. Everyone else seemed happy and carefree to her, and she was embarrassed about her unhappy feelings. She felt that she was basically different from her peers and avoided social contacts with both boys and girls her own age. In fact, she dreaded the prospect of any such contact and spent as much time as possible at home playing with her baby brother.

Her mother and father were always fighting. They would separate, reconcile, and separate again. Although Josephine lived with her mother during the separations, she was very close to her father. He visited her often, and whether he was living apart, or in the household, he lavished gifts on her. It was he who first started her in psychotherapy because he wanted her to be outgoing, attractive, and popular, as he was. He would pay the bills after he found a therapist in whom he felt confidence, and he encouraged Josephine to go. As soon as Josephine would complain about the therapist or become upset, her father would terminate therapy and search for another therapist. Thus, at the time of her hospitalization, Josephine had already been in individual therapy with four different therapists and had had brief consultations with at least as many more.

Josephine's mother devoted her life to visiting her own mother and complaining about the misfortunes life had inflicted on her. She was constantly derogating Josephine's father, blaming him for all of her and Josephine's problems. She had always been a dependent person, had never worked, and was supported by her husband during their separations. Josephine's mother presented a picture of a fussy, hypersensitive, self-centered, self-pitying, and ineffectual person. In addition, she was hypochondriacal. Life to her seemed to be one perpetual anxiety attack. She never really took care of her children. She enthusiastically encouraged Josephine to first play with, and then care for her younger brother. She expected the same solicitous care from Josephine when she herself felt ill and voiced her resentment when she didn't get it. She also resented the time, money, and energy Josephine's father lavished on Josephine while neglecting her. There were many quarrels with Josephine.

As Josephine grew older her father began to see her less frequently. He always came running in an emergency and tried to do something about her problems, but his gradual distancing of himself was obvious. Her brother was growing up and no longer needed nor wanted the great attention he was getting from Josephine. She grew more depressed. She gradually stopped attending school when she was 16. She became morose at that time and made a suicidal gesture, swallowing some aspirins. She blamed her behavior on her constant fights with her mother. Her father and the therapist she had at that time had Josephine placed in a residential treatment facility, a school for disturbed children. Josephine seemed to improve there, but when she did not want to return there the next year, her father removed her. She tried school again, but could not stay. She was fighting with her mother. Her father obtained a small studio apartment for her at a building he owned. She did not have to pay any rent. He created a clerical job for her at his construction firm, but she worked only sporadically from the beginning and eventually stopped completely.

She sat in her small apartment with nothing to do. She dreamed of running a small boutique. She told this to her father, and he rented a store so that she could start one. She became frightened of the responsibility and convinced him to abandon the idea. The emptiness and loneliness she felt were painful. She would go to therapy twice a week to tell her therapist about how she felt, but she could not mobilize herself to do anything at all.

She spent much time thinking, and she devised a plan to end her loneliness. She would have a child. She was sure her father would continue to give her financial support so that she could devote herself to caring for her child. She would have someone to love and someone who loved her. Her life would have a purpose. She remembered the times she took care of her younger brother as being the only happy times she ever had. It was the only thing she ever remembered herself to be good at. She had fantasies of taking her child to the zoo, to amusement parks, and visiting her father. The child in her fantasies was a beautiful, playful, good-natured, trouble-free little angel. These fantasies took much of her time, but she told no one about them, not even her therapist.

Approaching 19, never having had a date, still a virgin, and frightened of social contact, Josephine resolved to get pregnant. She had no idea of where to even meet a man. She had heard of singles' bars, so she wandered about her neighborhood, selected a likely looking bar and entered. She ordered and drank two drinks in rapid sequence then looked around. She saw an attractive looking man in his twenties, and she approached him and made him an offer. If he promised to not ask her her last name or her phone number, she would come to his apartment and let him make love to her. He was not to follow her back to her apartment. At first, he thought she was kidding, but Josephine stoically repeated her offer. He agreed, then excused himself for a moment and went to talk to some friends. His friends laughed and joked amongst themselves and leered at Josphine. She waited until he came back to her.

Once at his apartment, Josephine insisted that it all be done in pitch blackness. She was passive during the sex, said nothing, hurried home afterwards and threw up. Nevertheless, she returned to the same bar a week later and the scenario was repeated, as it was for a number of weeks thereafter. Josephine always felt disgusted and dirty after the sex. Finally, the man insisted upon bringing a friend along. He would not make love to her unless she did it with his friend first. She refused at first but finally agreed. She felt so bad afterwards that she made an emergency session with her therapist and finally told him what she was doing.

The therapist became upset and without giving her a chance to say another word, he rattled off a long list of reasons why her behavior was self-destructive. She left the session feeling more depressed than ever. During her next session, she tried to convince the therapist that her having a child would be good for her. She clearly articulated her belief that this love object would fill up her life and give her something to live for. The therapist described to her how difficult it would be to care for a child, and how destructive her exceptionally strong personal need for it would be to the child. She would see it as an extention of herself, and this child would not be able to become an individual. His arguments didn't matter to Josephine. She asked what else her life had to offer. Besides, she added, with a smile, she was already pregnant. She would not consider an abortion.

She was quite happy pregnant. She told her father that she had been impregnated by a married man with whom she had had a torrid love affair. She would not name him, nor even tell him about the child. Her father first exploded, but when he calmed down, he was sympathetic. He offered to pay all her bills and find her a larger place to live. Josephine began looking for children's furniture.

Josephine spontaneously aborted in her first trimester. He initial reaction was one of quiet calm. She reassured her father, the only family member who knew she had been pregnant, that she was all right. But she stopped eating, did not sleep well, and spent most of her time crying. She had dreams of delivering a baby. These dreams upset her even more. She would get upset when she saw babies on her shopping trips. These trips discontinued, and her father had to bring her food. Her heart would sink every time she heard a baby cry, and she did not know if the cries she heard were real or in her imagination.

It became obvious to Josephine's father that she could no longer care for herself. He insisted that she move back with her mother on a temporary basis. Josephine did not want to do this, preferring to live with him instead. He told her that he was so frequently absent that he could not really care for her. She reluctantly moved back with her mother, explaining that she was very depressed, but not revealing why.

She lived with her mother for about a week, then she made her suicide attempt. On an afternoon when her mother and brother were out, she went to the medicine chest and ingested every single pill which she found. She then went into her mother's bedroom and locked the door behind her. She passed out. Her mother became suspicious when she returned, shouted for Josephine to unlock the door, and when this drew no response, easily pushed in the door herself. She managed to awaken Josephine (most of the pills were minor tranquilizers), then she called the police and got her to a hospital.

Josephine was eventually referred to a Day Hospital Program. She was active during the day in group therapy and in many activity groups. Her parents were also seen regularly. An attempt was made to try to develop her strengths and find interests which could lead to employment. Treatment is still in progress.

Josephine has to be taken at her word for her reasons for wanting to have a child. She felt lonely, empty, and unloved. A child gave her life a purpose, and she had a love object, an unthreatening one which she could control. It gave her a chance to be a mother, the only comfortable role she had had in life. She would have a closer relationship with her father whom she knew would accept and take a strong interest in her child. The child would structure her life in the manner in which she felt most comfortable. The great pain and degradation which she suffered in order to get pregnant shows just how important the child was to her. Her loss was profound. She had lost her only hope. She felt she had little to live for.

CASE HISTORY: A SCHIZOPHRENIC AND A NEUROTIC ADOLESCENT

Sandra and Debra Smith are two black adolescent sisters, both of whom became pregnant. Their histories demonstrate the complex manner in which familial processes can be directly and indirectly involved in adolescent pregnancies.

Mr. and Mrs. Smith had been married for 17 years. He was a subway train engineer, and she an office clerk. Their oldest child was Sandra, 17, and their other child was Debra, 14 years old. Mr. Smith stated that he had been doing what he thought was the "right thing" in getting married. Theirs was apparently a cold, humorless, loveless relationship. However, they were comfortable, and the two salaries allowed for a pleasant standard of living.

Mr. Smith was 54, worked an evening shift from 4:00 P.M. to midnight, with frequent overtime. When not working, he was often out with friends or at home, sleeping during the day. During weekends he usually became drunk.

He impressed the interviewer as being a highly rigid man of average intelligence. He was constricted with respect to the expression of emotion, and he was limited in his range of emotional experience. He, thus, exerted considerable energy in attempting to control this element of his life. His own childhood had been rather bleak; orphaned at seven and raised by an uncle who was a harsh disciplinarian and forced him to work long hours after school and on weekends. Mr. Smith appeared to be chronically depressed, and his affective rigidity was a defense against overwhelming depression.

Mr. Smith's work and social pattern had existed almost since the beginning of the marriage, and he obviously had little interaction with his family. He strongly adhered to the belief that his role was totally that of a breadwinner. Moreover, he was closed to the notion that he might have an alcohol problem. When the girls were younger, he was described as having been somewhat more involved with the children, usually expressing his affection very physically, i.e., through hugs and having them sit on his knee.

Although there was no report to overt sexual play between Mr. Smith and the girls, Mrs. Smith expressed the idea that she disapproved of the way he used to "touch" the girls. This is noteworthy in light of the highly unusual and symbolic nature of the sexual partners Sandra chose, or at least fantasized about, as will be described.

Mrs. Smith was 40 and had worked for the same company as a clerk since graduating from high school. Her only extended absences had been maternity leaves for four months each.

Mrs. Smith had few heterosexual experiences before she met her husband. Her willingness to marry Mr. Smith, whom she said she never loved, was a means of getting away from her parents. Like her husband, she was an emotionally controlled person with little tolerance for any lack of structure in her life. Her relationship with both children was quite distant. Her few social contacts were through her church and she was very concerned about moral behavior. Clinically, she appeared moderately depressed and frustrated. It was felt that her obesity was a reflection of her suppressed anger and depression.

Sandra, their 17-year-old daughter, had been referred to an outpatient clinic at age 13 for truancy and running away from home. At that time, she was diagnosed as a childhood schizophrenic. She reported command hallucinations saying that she was bad and telling her to leave home. During these absences, she often rode buses to the end of the line and told stories of having had sexual relations with the drivers. Sandra had begun her menses at age 11, and by the time she was seen she was sexually developed, looking older than her chronological age. Although these escapades were never confirmed, she became pregnant and had an abortion at 14. The men she chose as sexual partners, at least those she reported, had much in common with her father.

Sandra's schizophrenia is not in itself a reason for her pregnancy. The fact of her schizophrenia is relevant only so far as it explains the primitiveness of her defense against conflict. The content of adolescent conflict is usually the same in neurotic and more severly emotionally disturbed individuals. What differs is the manner in which the conflicts are resolved. Thus, Sandra appears to have developed a strong eroticized attachment for her father, perhaps related to the overly sexualized nature of their early interaction. Her attachment to him was too threatening to be conscious; a bus driver served as a satisfactory substitute, enabling her to act out her conflict without awareness of the significance.

Sandra was treated with individual, family, and chemotherapy and she appeared to go into a remission. However, cooperation with treatment on her and the family's part was inconsistent at best. After a five-month absence from the clinic, she returned and was found to be three months pregnant. Her parents were furious and forced her to have the baby as "punishment." During the pregnancy Sandra settled down, stayed at home, and attended school. She was the focus of much of the parents' attention, both positive and negative, of which her younger sister Debra was jealously aware. After Sandra's baby was born, it was kept at home for several months and then placed in a foster home since Mrs. Smith wanted to work and did not feel Sandra was capable of caring for the baby. After the baby was placed, Sandra began to deteriorate. She dropped out of school and began staying out late, often not coming home at all. The parents gave up trying to manage her and began to focus their controlling techniques on Debra who by now was 14. Debra deeply resented, and was jealous of, her older sister. She realistically felt Sandra received much more attention because of her behavior. Debra also believed that Sandra was favored, misperceiving her parents' inability to enforce her curfew as the granting of special privileges.

Debra also began staying out all night. Her parents referred her to outpatient treatment. She was a sexually developed, postpubescent 14-year-old, but she seemed immature in her emotional development. She presented herself as angry and distant. She had poor peer relationships and was rather isolated. It was felt that she suffered an underlying depression. She was placed in individual therapy.

Debra told her therapist that she wanted a baby to prove to her mother that she was as good as her sister, Sandra, and she was now a woman. It was thus most important to her that she be granted the same "privileges" as her sister, her own child being one of them. The child would also be someone to love her. These reasons, which are frequently motivations for adolescents to get pregnant, are usually unconscious. In Debra's case they were quite conscious and seen by her as valid reasons for having a baby. Her therapist was forced to question the soundness of her reasoning rather than deal with her feelings and motivations. What transpired was more frequently a debate than psychotherapy. Her therapist was very experienced, but the situation left little alternative.

Debra was soon happily pregnant by her steady boyfriend. She had the baby. Unlike her sister, she did not place the child in a foster home. She kept the child. Her mother quit her job to care for Debra's child. Sandra's child was taken out of the foster home and joined Debra's under Mrs. Smith's care.

The baby had a positive effect on Debra. She stopped staying out late, and she developed several friendships. She returned to school and began to apply herself. She remained in therapy. On the other hand, Sandra did not relate to her child, nor did its existence in her household appear to have any effect upon her behavior. Her life remained much the same.

The different postpartum reactions of these sisters is characteristic of the effect having a baby can have on two types of emotional disturbances. Pregnancy and birth, although motivated by neurotic needs, can have a very beneficial effect on an adolescent such as Debra. It provides an organizing focus to her life and a reason for achievement which the adolescent has been unable to feel for herself alone. While this behavior is motivated by forces outside the adolescent rather than a result of inner maturation, it is still adaptive and can eventually become self-fulfilling. Her schizophrenic sister did not have the ability to mobilize in this way, and a child only added to the chaos of her life.

TREATMENT CONSIDERATIONS

The motivation for an emotionally disturbed adolescent pregnancy almost always arises out of the youngster's interaction with her family. This is one of the reasons that family therapy must always be considered as a mode of therapy. In addition, the type of adolescent who gets pregnant tends to have an acting-out personality, and these types of people present difficulties in individual therapy. They tend to neither talk about themselves nor introspect (Redl, 1969) and the pressures of individual therapy can even lead to further acting out. The family can be seen as a collective ego, perhaps a stronger one. Family therapy can direct itself to the interactional conflicts which the pregnant adolescent is inclined to resolve by her own acting out. But classical family therapy is not always a viable alternative. Often an adolescent is just too alienated or rebellious to contribute anything but raw hostility, or to be willing to attend at all. Other emotionally disturbed adolescents may be too delusional or depressed to participate. This can also be the case for parents; one or both parents may be uncooperative or too disturbed to become part of the therapy. The therapist must not be doctrinaire as to what "family therapy" is supposed to be. A major effort must be made to involve as much of the family in the adolescent's treatment as is possible, and the involvement should serve the purpose of removing the adolescent from the role of scapegoat or safety valve for the collective family conflict. This is the broad goal; exceptional flexibility is necessary to implement it.

Group therapy is another effective modality for reaching the emotionally disturbed pregnant adolescent. Peer groups allow the adolescents to gain a more articulate and stable sense of self. Inappropriate self-perceptions and ineffective modes of social interaction are brought to light as other group members challenge and perhaps mimic the adolescent's assumptions about herself and her behavior. Adolescent groups can be surprisingly supportive. It is frequently easier for adolescents to speak about their feelings in group than in individual therapy with an adult (Redl, 1969). There are intrinsic limitations to how far this process can go, and Ackerman (1958) strongly recommends a combination of group and individual therapy.

Some youngsters are so disturbed that neither family therapy, group, or individual therapy can be considered a strong enough intervention in the existing crisis. In such cases, it is often necessary to consider a therapeutic residential placement. This can never be an ideal solution since it works against resolution of the basic conflicts; the dynamics of the problem are avoided rather than dealt with directly. But therapeutic residential placement does remove the youngster from an abrasive situation. This physical removal sometimes sufficiently reduces the intensity of the family conflicts so that acting out is no longer necessary. It is important with residential placement, as well as with group therapy for the adolescent, that ongoing therapeutic work with the family also continue.

The emphasis placed on family and group therapy and residential placement is not meant to negate the potential of individual therapy with pregnant adolescents. It is just that this is a particularly difficult treatment modality with this population. Their inclination to act out rather than to introspectively consider their feelings has been discussed. The adolescent can be belligerent to the therapist, act evasive, and show undependable attendance patterns. The therapist can be challenged, manipulated, derogated, insulted, and dismissed. The adolescent spins long tales of unreality while the therapist wonders what to say. It is a frequent occurrence for a therapist to listen to an adolescent reveal all of her feelings and conflicts, tearfully pleading for help, and then not appear for subsequent sessions. When the therapist finally contacts her and a new appointment is made, the youngster claims not to remember anything of what was previously discussed. Frequent requests are made for the therapist to aid the adolescent in some acting out (asking for money to buy drugs, for example). The therapist is always being tested.

For these reasons, individual therapy is a thankless, time consuming, and expensive process with pregnant adolescents. It is virtually impossible with some. In all cases, it calls for a highly trained, thoroughly experienced therapist. Inexperienced therapists can be driven to distraction, and their efforts may be, in fact, harmful. In those facilities where experienced therapists exist, and in those cases where families have the money for private practitioners, it definitely should be considered. The therapist who can finally reach the pregnant adolescent in a close relationship can be a most powerful, beneficial force, perhaps the most powerful one available.

REFERENCES

Ackerman, Nathan W. *The Psychodynamics of Family Life*. New York: Basic Books, 1958.

Blos, Peter. *On Adolescence: A Psychoanalytic Interpretation*. New York: The Free Press, 1962.

Erikson, Erick. *Childhood and Society*. Second Ed. New York: W.W. Norton, 1963.

Freud, Anna. *The Ego and the Mechanisms of Defense*. New York: International Universities Press, 1946.

Freud, Sigmund. Three essays on the theory of sexuality. in Strachey, J. (Ed.) *The Complete Psychological Works of Sigmund Freud*. Standard Edition 19, London: Hogarth Press, 1961.

Hall, G. Stanley. *Adolescence: Its Psychology and Its Relations to Physiology, Anthropology, Sociology, Sex, Crime, Religion, and Education*. I and II, New York: Appleton, 1904.

Lewin, K. Behavior and development as a function of the total situation. In Carmichael, L. (Ed.) *Manual of Child Psychology* New York: John Wiley & Son, 1954.

Mead, Margaret. *From the South Seas*. New York: William Morrow, 1939.

Miller, Derek H. *Adolescence: Psychology, Psychopathology, and Psychotherapy*. New York: Jason Aronson, 1974.

Offer, Daniel. *The Psychological World of the Teenager*. New York: Basic Boods, 1969.

Otto, U. Suicide attempts among Swedish children and adolescents. In Caplan, G. and Lebovici, S. (Eds.) *Adolescence: Psychosocial Perspectives*. New York: Basic Books, 1969.

Rel, F. Adolescents—just how do they react? In Caplan, G. and Lebovici, S. (Eds.) *Adolescence: Psychosocial Perspectives*. New York: Basic Books, 1969.

Stone, L. Joseph and Church, Joseph. *Childhood and Adolescence: A Psychology of the Growing Person*. New York: Random House, 1957.

Toolan, J.M. Depression in children and adolescents. In Caplan, G. and Lebovici, S. (Eds.), *Adolescence: Psychosocial Perspectives*. New York: Basic Books, 1969.

15.

Identifying Needs, Gaining Support for, and Establishing an Innovative, School-Based Program for Pregnant Adolescents

Ann M. DeRose, M.Ed.,
Principal,
Lee Adolescent Mother's Program (LAMP),
Fort Myers, Fl.

This chapter deals with establishing a school-based program for adolescent mothers within the school system in a rural or semirural area. It includes information on how to determine whether or not there is a need for this type of program, and how to set it up including sources of referrals, enrollment, orientation techniques, and planning a curriculum that will meet as many of the adolescent mother's needs as possible.

The chapter details considerations in the selection of a staff and volunteers, selection of a school plant, problems encountered in transporting these young mothers and their children, along with suggestions for involving the young father and the young mother's family in the program.

Motivational attendance, rather than enforcing an attendance policy, is addressed, as are the problems of classroom discipline, home visits, hospital visits, and special counseling sessions in which the student's options are discussed with regard to getting a job or, if qualified and motivated, going ahead with a college education.

It is written to be of assistance to someone who is contemplating initiating a program of this type, and also includes suggestions and methods for creating community and media support.

Since its inception in September 1972, the Lee Adolescent Mothers Program (LAMP) has been attended by more than a thousand pregnant adolescents. There are thousands more we have not been able to reach for one reason or another. However, in one sense, we consider LAMP a success because it has not only survived a number of setbacks and attacks, but has attracted increasing support from both educators and residents in Lee County. We feel LAMP's most important accomplishment has been to reduce the number of repeat pregnancies by adolescent mothers who deliver their first baby at 15 or younger to 20 percent, as compared to the national average of 95 percent.

We do not consider LAMP in its present form either the perfect or ultimate cure-all for the problem of adolescent pregnancy. As the number of girls enrolled in LAMP grows, so LAMP must grow and adapt to handle the larger numbers. Nor will we consider LAMP a true success until each and every pregnant adolescent in Lee County—married or not—knows LAMP is available to her and feels free to decide for herself, without any form of official interference, whether she wishes to enroll.

At this point, it would be relevant to describe the area served by LAMP. Lee County has several times been declared by pollsters to be the fastest growing metropolitan area in the nation. This fact is regarded by its residents as a mixed blessing.

The 1020-square-mile county is located 150 miles across state from Miami and 125 miles south of Tampa. According to the 1980 U.S. Census, it has a population of 201,903 with approximately 32,000 students enrolled in its public-school system.

Lee County is a county of excesses of wealth and poverty, and all the problems associated with rapid growth. The problems associated with the poor and the young are often brushed aside in an effort to project a "fun in the sun" image which befits a tourist area. The fact that young people living in Lee County have serious problems is largely overlooked, but Lee County has the highest incidence of infant mortality (31.7%) in the state for mothers under the age of 19. Lee County also has the state's highest incidence of teenage pregnancies. Last year 312 babies were born to unwed mothers, 188 to white mothers, 124 to nonwhite mothers. These two facts established the need for a program such as LAMP in Lee County.

For the most part, Lee County can best be described as rural, and it has a large seasonal and migrant population. It has remained basically untouched by the turmoil and awakening social awareness of the 1960s. It is outwardly serene, and its residents are quietly determined to retain the small-town atmosphere, morality, and social hierarchy which is peopled by old families who consider charitable activities the duty of the privileged class.

Blacks were and are quiescent and complacent, remaining on their side of the tracks. It was understood that drug traffic, gambling, prostitution, Saturday night shootings, and adolescent pregnancies were a part of the way "they" lived. "They" were those people residing in the well-defined poverty areas of the county, areas to the south, east, and the central-city area.

Fort Myers, the county seat, is where the LAMP program is based. It is the oldest of the communities within Lee County and is closest to being the geographic center.

In 1972, the pregnant teen was no problem to either the school system or the community because she was invisible. Her invisibility was fostered by subtle and sometimes overt pressure to leave school. Health care was provided by the County Health Department and granny midwives delivered the baby. Thes midwives, there were two, enjoyed almost professional status in the black community.

The pregnant white wasn't discussed. She was the truly invisible nonperson. Her options were simple. She could marry the baby's father, go to live with a relative in another town or state, or go to a maternity home. If she didn't marry, her baby was adopted and she returned home to pick up the threads of her life, but seldom to complete her education.

This was the social and economic climate in Lee County in 1972 when Title 1X of the Education Amendment addressed the issue of sex discrimination as practised by education institutions receiving Federal Aid. Actually, this was the second blow in as many years to Lee County's traditional way of life. On January 29, 1970, after a seven-year battle ending in the U.S. District Court, Lee County was ordered to totally desegregate its faculty and student population. Dunbar High School, the pride of the black community, had been closed and reopened as a community school. Its students has been assigned to four other county high schools to comply with the ratio of 80/20 ordered by the court.

These facts, coupled with the concern and dedication of Lee County School Superintendent Ray L. Williams, a responsive and caring school board and other personnel, coupled with the availability of Title XX funds, combined to provide the framework for LAMP, a special program aimed toward preventing the pregnant adolescent from being forced to "drop out."

Superintendent Williams directed a task force composed of school administrators and guidance personnel. This task force located an unused building, the 2000-square-foot bandroom on the campus of the Dunbar Community School, arranged to utilize special education buses, worked with the local health department and other community organizations, and applied for seed money through a Title 1V A grant of the Social Security Act.

As a result of their efforts, LAMP began that September with a staff of two certified teachers, a bus driver/aide, some books, supplies, baby beds, and a list of 12 potential students.

The announcement of LAMP's birth was not widely proclaimed for the general fear was that it would be considered a reward for those requiring its services, or as a waste of tax dollars by the general population of Lee County. Because of the religious and social structure of Lee County, it took courage for those administrators and school-board members to even support LAMP.

Sadly, even some of the educators within the system regarded LAMP with disdain and distaste, resenting the school board's support. Thus, while the majority of school administrators and personnel were supportive, others in key positions not only refused to cooperate in its operation but in some instances tried, and still try, to defeat it. These people either do not refer students, intimidating them with a mass of unnecessary and involved paperwork, or subject them to unnecessary confrontations with authority figures. (I mention this not to be negative, but to point out some of the bottlenecks and problems other educators may face in starting a program such as LAMP.)

I first joined LAMP as its head teacher in September of 1974 after the original staff had quit in a "silent" demonstration protest. The student and the program had needs. Those who were in a position to implement its expansion and efficiency chose to view LAMP as simply a program to keep the girls out of public view and so were happy to maintain the status quo.

At that time, it was decided to change the basic format of the program. LAMP's philosophy and goals were stated. A logo was designed, printed, and distributed to develop a broader base of support from the community.

REFERRALS

Ninety percent of the LAMP students are referred to us by agencies other than the school system. Ideally, since it is a school-based program, the girls should be sent to us by school personnel, but this is true in only roughly 10 percent of the cases.

This is not entirely the fault of school personnel. In most cases, the girls drop out of school before enrolling in LAMP and do so without stating the real reason for their action. School personnel, therefore, seldom learn the girls are pregnant until later.

Our largest number of referrals, between 80 and 85 percent, comes from the Improved Pregnancy Outcome Program (IPOP), a federal program administered by the Lee County Health Department. LAMP gets many referrals from IPOP because that's the place the students first learn they are pregnant. In fact, they go to the Health Department for verification of their pregnancy.

The remainder of our referrals come from friends, private physicians, community agencies, lay people, and the self-referring student herself.

Because most of our referrals do not come from within the school system, we have found it necessary to form a close liaison with various service agencies. In addition to making contact with every possible civic and service organization, a concerted effort must be made to see all the physicians in the area served by the program. The doctors should be made aware of your program and what it has to offer the pregnant teen. They should also be given an adequate supply of brochures and descriptive materials so they can pass these on to their patients.

When the administrators of a school will cooperate, we try to get posters in home economics classes, health classes, and the gym. The curriculum in home economics and health classes lends itself to discussion of programs such as LAMP, and the gym is an excellent place because that's usually the center for social functions where the girls gather.

In addition, in establishing a network with the service and civic agencies in your community, it is equally important to establish a good working relationship with the media. Each time a story concerning LAMP has appeared in any of our local papers, or on one of the local radio and television stations, we have received a number of phone calls either from people wishing to help or girls needing help.

However, a suggestion: It is important to be discerning in your relationship with the media. Bad publicity can destroy the program and corrode the support of school board members who, at least in Florida, must answer to the voters, and of school personnel who must answer to the board.

It's not difficult to figure out who is unbiased or sympathetic to your program. Just watch the individual reporters and how they cover their stories. This is especially important when it comes to the education reporter who covers the school system.

We cannot give enough credit to the fine people working as volunteers, and the service agencies in our community. Without them and an understanding media, LAMP would find it difficult, if not impossible, to survive.

One final comment on referrals. Our experience has been that by the time the girls are referred to us, they are four to five months pregnant. This gives us very little time to work with them, especially since teens nearly always deliver early. One of our goals at LAMP is to locate and enroll the girls sooner. The earlier we get the girl, the more time we have to work with her on all aspects of her pregnancy, including nutrition. The earlier we get her, the healthier she is and the better her chances are of giving live birth to a healthy baby.

ENROLLMENT

The enrollment procedure should be as simple as possible. Ideally, the only requirement would be that the student is pregnant. These girls and their families are experiencing enough emotional turmoil and heartache so every effort should be made to expedite the student's admission to the program.

Each LAMP student must be enrolled in a Lee County school. Since the majority have dropped out, they must return to their home schools and be reenrolled. This is just a formality since they aren't required to attend classes. They then withdraw from that school and enroll in LAMP. They are transferred to LAMP by a form listing their special needs and academic schedule. A letter requesting confirmation of the pregnancy is sent to the physician, and upon receipt of these two forms a staff member visits the student's home to explain the program. There she advises the student of her alternatives, which include remaining in her home school, attending adult education classes, or attending LAMP. The applicant, her parents or guardian, and the staff member then sign a form indicating their commitment to the LAMP program and LAMP's commitment to the girl.

Additionally, at the time of the initial home visit, the girl and her parents or husband are invited to tour our campus. We also inform the girl and her family of the income scale for determining her eligibility for breakfasts and lunches at LAMP, either without charge or for reduced prices. This is vital when considering the importance of proper nutrition to the young mother and the child she is carrying. If eligible, the staff worker gets the necessary paper signed.

Another form which must be signed is one requesting special student transportation. Basically, this means she is eligible to ride on buses for exceptional students. It is important because insurance coverage on the regular school buses does not cover pregnant students and their babies.

Any person or agency contemplating beginning a program similar to LAMP should know that our program is funded under Exceptional Student Education and subject to provisions specified under Federal Law 94-142 (the aid to the handicapped law). At the time of her enrollment, the student and her parents receive a copy of the School Board's Procedural Safeguards which are consistent with Federal Law 94-142.

Further, at the time of the initial home visit, the staff worker gets the guardian/parent to sign a form entitled "Notification of Recommendation for Placement in an Exceptional Student Program." Although merely a formality in our instance, it is required by Florida Statutes (Section 230.23(4)(m)(4F.S) and basically indicates that the parent/guardian agrees to the placement of the girl in LAMP.

In Lee County we find several drawbacks to our enrollment procedure which others may be able to avoid. First, our procedure takes two to three weeks to complete. This period of time would not be critical when dealing with the average student, but for the pregnant girl, it can total one-quarter of her total attendance time.

The second drawback in our system is that it forces the girl to return to her home school to reenroll. Many are reluctant to do so because they fear being seen and exposed to ridicule by fellow students or intimidated by school personnel. Some just don't have the transportation.

Girls who are pregnant for the second or third time are especially vulnerable to intimidation from the school. We've had several who've even expressed the fear we might not readmit them to the program.

Repeat pregnancies may be a problem for staff members themselves who might feel the girl should have "learned her lesson the first time." It is important for the coordinator or director of the program to work with her people so they approach repeat pregnancies with understanding and compassion. I have found it helps to remind them that even the most intelligent and sophisticated of women have repeat and unplanned pregnancies, and also that it is impossible to change a human being's entire life-style in the three or four months we have them in the program. This is expecially true at LAMP because most of our girls remain in the same social environment. However, when viewed in this light, the staff can consider the repeat pregnancy both a challenge and an opportunity to further help the pregnant teen.

Having a sensitive staff worker personally help the student reenroll has been an important factor in getting a greater number of girls to attend LAMP. The student should be allowed to reenroll directly at the program's center without being forced to return to her home school. Her records are already on file, so all she should have to do is present a verification of pregnancy which would make her eligible for immediate admission.

It cannot be stressed too strongly that the girl must be admitted as quickly and painlessly to the program as possible. It should also be pointed out that this is one area where an unsympathetic school administrator can discourage the girl from taking advantage of the program. He or she can do this by not informing the girl of the program's existence or require a complicated and involved enrollment procedure, coupled with special conferences, where she and her parents are confronted with authority figures in the school system.

We deal quite often with students from outside the county who have moved here to have their babies. As a rule, they have come to live with relatives until after the delivery. In such cases, the girls must submit a health certificate showing they have received the required immunizations, a birth certificate, declaration of domicile, and a letter from their parents or guardian giving the person with whom they are living supervisory authority. They are also required to pay $50 tuition, although in hardship cases the superintendent of schools can waive this fee.

Because of our student's special situation, LAMP maintains an open entry/exit policy. Students can enter at any time during the school year upon completion of the enrollment procedure. They may withdraw at any time after the delivery of the baby, although we prefer and encourage them to remain six weeks postpartum or until the end of the quarter or semester. In this way, we can be assured the mother keeps her medical appointments, at which time the physician discusses and prescribes a birth-control method.

Equally important, this postpartum period gives our staff an opportunity to observe the student, to be sure she is emotionally ready to leave. We observe her as a mother to be sure that bonding with the child has taken place and that there is no evidence of rejection which might be the forerunner of child abuse. Further, we can see that she puts into practice the theories of child care we have taught her, and we also have time to observe the baby to ascertain that there are no physical problems.

We feel this follow-up is especially important in cases where the girls have placed their children for adoption, or where the baby has died. LAMP gives them a chance to work through their grief. The other girls are supportive and understanding and the grieving mother helps care for other babies. She does not run away from her problem, but faces it and deals with her grief in a positive and supportive environment.

This open entry/exit policy means we have a constant flow of new students, which has required a more flexible approach to curriculum and attendance along with innovative methods of orientation.

ORIENTATION

On the new student's first day in the LAMP program she is immediately assigned a big sister, given an intake packet, and views a slide presentation which describes LAMP.

Big Sisters

We select big sisters on the basis of information we have on each of the girls, trying to match them by backgrounds and needs. We try to avoid placing the new girl with someone she knows or someone from her own neighborhood, because part of her adjustment requires making new friends and broadening her social horizons.

By utilizing a big-sister program, the new student immediately has a friend. The big sister explains that our butterfly symbol means a new life, a new beginning, and that one has a choice of living as a caterpillar or a beautiful, free-flying butterfly. She takes her little sister on a tour of the campus and introduces her to the others. She also explains how to complete the various forms in the intake packet.

Intake Packet

When beginning the program, we developed an intake packet which is distributed to each student in a tote tray. (Incidentally, because we have a very small sum of money to use on these tote trays, we found cat-litter trays a perfect and less costly investment! We still use them.) The intake packet includes the following items.

Student Handbook. This includes a letter welcoming the student to LAMP, outlines the program's guidelines and rules and includes a list of various telephone numbers of organizations the student may need to contact. These include LAMP, the Drug Abuse Council, the Children's Home Adoption Information, a day-care center, and the Lee County Health Department.

We recommend keeping the rules and regulations to a minimum and involving the students in reworking them. This makes the girls feel truly involved in the program and, in many instances, they have valuable insights which prove helpful.

Personal Information Questionnaire. This calls for personal information such as address, phone number, names of people who live with the student, names of brothers and sisters at home, names of members of family who work and what they do, what the student does for relaxation, if the student has a pet and, if so, what it is.

Coat of Arms. This exercise is adopted from a text entitled *Personal Coat of Arms*, by Simon, Howe, and Kirschenbaum. The student is given a diagram in the shape of a coat of arms, or more recently an African shield. She is to consider it as a sign she would hang over her business if she owned one. It is divided into seven sections and calls for the student to settle on one word that states a value in which her family believes. She is then asked to draw pictures of the greatest skill she possesses at the time, what occupation she would most like for a career, the place she expects to live 10 years from now, a flag representing the student using her favorite colors, and finally the personal motto the student would like to live by.

Writing Assignment. This is done after the student studies a series of pictures cut from magazines. She is asked to project herself into anyone of them and then write an essay. The instructions include questions to be answered, such as what kind of family the student has, how her life has shaped her personality, what problems she has, how her face reflects her emotions, if anyone else can help ease her burdens and, if so, how.

Autobiography. This assignment requires the student to write in composition form the story of her life to date, including her school background, her hobbies, her travel experiences, her pets, favorite foods and colors, and her career hopes.

Pretest Package. This deals specifically with the student's potential parent effectiveness and includes among others questions the student will face during the parenting course. These include how she feels about being a mother, whether she feels she should spank her child, is disciplining teaching or punishing, and whether or not she should feel guilty if she is not with her child.

The Lamplighter. This bulletin, published and distributed each Monday, serves many purpose. It lists the girls who are having birthdays and contains uplifting slogans, but also contains the class assignments for each week from each teacher. This is important because if the student is absent, she still knows exactly what assignments she has missed and what she needs to make up. Or, if she is in the hospital or at home following delivery, she can keep up with her class. On the first Monday of each month an additional page is added. This is a calendar which tells the other students who's delivered, who's overdue, what girls are due to deliver that month, and the dates of special events and classes.

Observation Book. One of the most important segments of the intake packet is also the simplest. It consists of sheets of blank paper stapled into a construction paper cover. In this students are encouraged to write about their feelings and problems. At first we make no comment concerning grammar, punctuation, or spelling because we are interested in content. We use the observation book technique because at this point we are strangers to the girl, and it is often much easier for her to write down her feelings, her problems, and concerns than it would be to tell us about them in a face-to-face situation. She may fear being overheard, and also may fear rejection from us.

The observation books are turned in every Friday and read over the weekend. Sometimes these books reflect problems where we can help. If this is the case, on Monday we'll arrange a private conference with the student. If that's not possible because of schedule conflicts, then we sometimes drive her home after class or take her along on special home or hospital visits, or even take her out to lunch to get her away from the classroom environment. Then we can relate as woman to woman, not as student to teacher.

Sometimes students write about being abused by their boyfriends or families, which prompts us to call the abuser in for discussion and counseling. In many instances we've had to go to the young father's or the parents' job sites in order to talk with them. We do this because often it is the only way we can establish face-to-face contact, and it is important to keep in mind we are dealing with the whole person and all aspects of her life, not just the time she spends in class.

At the time of orientation the student is also given a butterfly name tag and assigned a seat. Beacuse of the amount of writing and self-examination involved, we give students two days to complete entry papers. This also gives the staff time to work up an academic schedule, to complete staffing and paper work, and to notify the home school that the student is officially enrolled in LAMP.

CURRICULUM

Most of our students are "turned off" to school. They were not required to attend, and they could elect to remain at home, to sleep late, and keep up with their favorite TV soap opera. The challenge to the LAMP staff is to offer something just as interesting.

The curriculum has to meet the student's health needs and social adjustment problems, as well as individual academic requirements. Many of our students have a history of poor attendance prior to pregnancy and had fallen behind in school work. Most had given up hope of regaining this lost ground.

The staff discovered that given the opportunity, most students welcome the challenge when enabled to progress in subject areas at their own rate of speed. As they see themselves beginning to catch up on credits, feelings of hopelessness begin to dissipate, and they look forward to being able to graduate and even get a job.

Be aware, however, that just as critics of this type of program feel it rewards the pregnant girl, these same people oppose her moving ahead academically at her own speed. There are two reasons for this. First, they feel the program should be punitive in nature, and second, they feel all students should conform in academic achievement. To be effective, you must either surmount or evade the red tape such people will attempt to throw in your path.

As educators, we cannot throw away the golden opportunities this period offers. This is the one time when the girl is truly motivated, and she must be encouraged so she will move ahead, complete her education, and become self-supporting.

From the standpoint of the material we must cover (we offer more than 33 subjects in grades 6 through 12), the first problem is to fit everything in. Flexibility and creative utilization of time are key elements. We accomplished a great deal by scheduling special units dealing with personal and social adjustment, scheduling academic classes around these units, and assigning a great deal more academic homework than is usually done in the home school.

Homework frees valuable class time so we can provide the special educational training these girls need. This is the one time in the girl's life when she has the time and motivation to do homework. Being pregnant, her social life is limited, and doing homework helps pass the long hours at home.

In addition to required curriculum, five special activities are scheduled in order to expose the student to as many new and positive experiences as possible. These are scheduled simultaneously for a two-hour time period one day a week and students are rotated through them moving in an assigned group every six weeks.

Classes include (1) Foods For Fun, such as cooking for children and cake decorating; (2) Flower Arranging and Home Decorating; (3) Crafts such as knitting, crocheting, and liquid embroiders; (4) Social Awareness, which in the past has involved students in projects such as organizing concerned renters' groups, local political campaigns, and currently working on organizing a community cooperative nursery; (5) Journalism. Students in this block compile and edit our school newspaper *The Delivery*; and (6) Basic Etiquette and Child Safety. This course helps train young mothers to be aware of their own behavior.

We offer "something special" daily, a guest speaker, a special film or group activity. Recently students performed their own version of *Othello*, making their own costumes and building the limited scenery.

Parent effectiveness training, special health classes, LaMaze instruction, and Transactional Analysis are also required as part of the students' training.

Health classes include general hygiene, infant and child care, bathing and feeding, breast-feeding and its alternatives, birth control and nutrition. In this class we have speakers from the LaLeche League, Right to Life groups as well as speakers who discuss abortions, masturbation, and homosexuality, and speakers from Parents Anonymous who discuss their group and the support it provides in helping prevent child abuse. We expose the young mothers to all philosophies and beliefs because we feel they have the right to make their own, informed decisions.

Throughout the entire time they're with us, we take every "teachable moment" and every opportunity to discuss and offer alternatives to sexual intercourse. For this, we use Sol Gordon's book *You Would If Your Loved Me* and do a lot of role playing.

LAMP is fortunate in that we share the campus with the Dunbar Community School, Children's Personal Development Center (CPDC), Title 1 reading programs, Latch Key and a Title XX day-care center. CPDC is a program for socially maladjusted grade-school children. LAMP students enrolled in psychology classes earn extra academic credits by spending an hour a week at CPDC observing and writing case studies. This has proven to be a very valuable experience and they often become so involved with these youngsters that they help them in special projects such as baking cookies or teaching crafts.

A special arrangement with the Adult and Community Education Center enables LAMP students to be assigned to typing and business classes. Their special instruction and well-equipped laboratory have become a very important part of our program.

Special Units

Education should change a person's life for the better, and help the individual cope with life more effectively. To this end, assertiveness training is perhaps the most important course we offer our students. In this, we rely heavily on specially trained volunteers and a series of films.

Special instructors from the local community college speak to the girls. We fell this is the most important segment of our curriculum because many of the girls learn for the first time that they have the right to say "no," that their feelings are important, and that they don't have to say "yes" to be popular. They also learn that because men approach life from a different perspective, what to a woman may be merely a friendly gesture may be interpreted by a man as a come on. We feel this special unit is one of the main reasons we have such a low percentage of students involved in repeat pregnancies.

Assertiveness training is not only a part of the weekly curriculum, it is also emphasized during a special unit we call women's week entitled "A Celebration of Women." During this week we schedule special units dealing with jobs and careers, the role of women in today's world and sex stereotypes. We invite women in politics, medicine, the media, and other aspects of the career world to speak to our girls, but we look for women with positive attitudes and women who have overcome difficult handicaps.

Special Projects

These are designed to foster creativity, to bring the students out of themselves and make them aware of others, and also relieve the monotony of regular school classes. We give birthday parties at the county nursing home with the girls baking the cookies and presenting the program. There are parties for the children in the Title XX nursery, and we have a Mothers' Day Tea where the students' mothers are invited. At the end of the school year, we have a very special graduation program for all students who have been in LAMP or are in LAMP and are graduating that year.

LAMP Anthologies. Each student is asked to write a poem, a short story, or just a paragraph about someone or something that has had a significant impact on her life. These writings are edited, printed, and bound into the

From LAMP With Love Christmas Anthology. Each year these are presented by the students as a very personal gift to the student's loved ones and the very special friends of LAMP.

Baby Book. A meaningful special project has been the preparation of a baby book. Copied from the more expensive "store bought" versions, the student uses her own ideas to create a personal information book that deals with her prenatal days, the baby's family tree, the birth and early growth information, along with significant events and happenings in the lives of the infants and the new mothers. The student who places her child for adoption may also choose to make a modified book and pass this on to her baby's adoptive parents as a gift of love.

Family Night. One of our most important special projects is Family Night held twice a year in the Spring and Fall. The young fathers and the girls' families are invited to the program which we try to make informal, entertaining, and informative.

The students make invitations, prepare the refreshments, and decorate the classrooms. They host the program which includes a slide presentation which the students have made depicting a typical school day at LAMP. Families and students enjoy seeing themselves on the screen. The camera is never far from us. We keep it loaded with slide film, and during the year we try to take slides whenever an appropriate opportunity occurs.

Our theme song, Carol King's touching rendition of *You've Got A Friend* introduces our program. We show two films. One is *The Story of Eric* which is a very sensitive film depicting a couple going through LaMaze childbirth and concluding with the baby's birth. The second is an amusing film on birth control entitled *Happy Family Planning*.

The staff is on hand to talk with and answer any questions the families and fathers may have. We do get quite a few of the fathers. We've found, whether they'll admit or not, that their natural curiosity is aroused about seeing a baby being born which lures them to the program and encourages them to participate.

ATTENDANCE POLICY

Our basic philosophy is to motivate students to attend as opposed to punishing them or forcing them to do so. We try always to keep in mind that our students have unique medical problems along with family and home pressures, all of which can discourage them from coming to class. We are also keenly aware of the students' negative reactions to the orthodox school system. With these factors in mind, we do not try to enforce an attendance policy.

This is not to say that we consider attendance unimportant. Far from it! We consider each day a girl attends class a victory, because we face formidable competition from television soap operas and the basic fact that it's much easier for her to stay at home than it is to get dressed and come to school.

Furthermore, there is nothing to be gained from dropping a student with a poor attendance record because this would indicate that we have failed to meet the girl's needs. If the program and the curriculum are properly structured, each moment she is in attendance provides a learning experience that we hope will prove valuable to her in the future, as well as keeping her interest in LAMP alive.

To this end we have devised a relevant innovative curriculum. We plan lessons far enough ahead, and publish them in *The Lamplighter*, so that the student is able to catch up on work that is missed. This helps prevent the student's getting so far behind that she becomes discouraged.

As an attendance incentive we frequently hold surprise drawings with valuable prizes on unannounced days. These are donated by local businesses, private citizens, or support agencies and have included cash ranging from $1.00 to $10, baby clothes, maternity outfits, cosmetics, games, household furnishings, garden plants, restaurant coupons for free food, theater tickets, craft supplies, and ticket books for the county bus system.

Responsibility is a key word in our approach to the attendance policy. With regard to curriculum, we enforce the rule that school work is due each Friday, and it is the individual student's responsibility to get it to the appropriate teacher. We also attempt to foster a sense of responsibility by encouraging them to call and tell us why they can't attend when they're absent.

We believe that we accomplish these goals to a very rewarding extent because we make sure LAMP girls understand that we care about them as people and that when they are absent we really miss them. We go one step further by emphasizing that we also want to help to resolve the problems that make it difficult for them to attend.

CLASSROOM DISCIPLINE

Very often we do have problems, but there is little need for formal discipline. The students know the rules and are treated as adults. A mutual commitment is made by students and staff to principles as outlined in Dr. William Glasser's book *Reality Therapy: A New Approach to Psychiatry* (1965; Harper & Row). Five basic elements are as follows:

1. School must be a good place.
2. Everyone must know the rules.
3. Everyone must help make and agree with the rules.
4. Rules must be changeable.
5. Rules must be enforced consistently.

Consistent with Dr. Glasser's reality therapy approach, we have prepared a hand-out which serves as a guide to both students and staff. We try to be constant in our efforts to implement the following:

1. BE PERSONAL
   Emphasize role before goal.
2. DEAL IN THE PRESENT
   "What are you doing?"
3. GET A VALUE JUDGMENT
   "Is what you're doing good for you, your baby, the class, the school?"
4. MAKE A PLAN
   If the response to 3 is no, then ask how the student plans to change.
5. GET A COMMITMENT
   "That's a good plan. Now do you really mean to follow it?"
6. NO EXCUSES
   Do not accept excuses for a broken commitment. Perhaps the plan was unrealistic from the start.
7. NO PUNISHMENT
   There must be a logical and reasonable consequence. Punishment degrades the student as a person. Consequently we uphold the student's worth, while communicating to her that she is responsible for her actions.

When we do have problems, we avoid confrontation in the presence of peers. We try to take the student aside privately to find the underlying cause of the deviant behavior. However, this behavior may be indicative of problems totally unrelated to school.

In one recent instance, a student absolutely refused to do any work whatsoever or to participate in class activities. In talking with her, we learned she had not had a bowel movement in four days and was suffering a great deal of discomfort from constipation. We explained to her that this was a common occurrence during pregnancy, explained how it could affect her behavior, encouraged her to drink a lot of water, and contacted the clinic which prescribed medication and gave her proper diet information. Two days later, she felt great.

Common sense is another important facet of discipline in the LAMP classrooms. Teachers must be constantly aware of, and alert to, potential health and safety problems. They must be able to pick up on subtle innuendos and undertones that signal potential personality conflicts, or neighborhood disputes that might result in physical confrontations.

We try to keep in mind that students are human, as are the staff, that we work under unique pressures, and that constant recrimination and punishment does more harm than good. To avoid this we try to deal with the here and now, to reassure the student that she is accepted and wanted. We point out that she is entitled to make mistakes and to have a bad day, as are staff members, and that we accept and care for her as a fallible human being and ask the same acceptance for ourselves.

Perhaps humor is one of the most important facets of our discipline. It enables the staff to place incidents in the proper perspective and many times to defuse a possibly explosive situation.

STAFF

Because programs such as LAMP deal with girls and families in crisis and in semirural areas similar to Lee County, such programs represent change, and the staff must be selected with great care.

Academically, the teaching staff must be certified and we prefer teachers certified in several academic areas. We also look for teachers who are interested in continuing their own education and who are willing to attend at least one or two relevant courses, workshops, or in-service training sessions each year.

In general, we seek both academic and support people who have some medical background, an interest in alternative education, and who read and are aware of recent education innovations such as varied learning styles.

It doesn't matter whether the person is male or female. In fact, male staff members can be a very important adjunct simply because they are male. As I write this, I am thinking of an older male volunteer who worked with our program. He was able to express his feelings without embarrassment and to help in many areas the girls considered strictly female. The girls saw him cooking, changing babies, typing, writing poetry, and holding and rocking the babies. He was a very caring person and showed genuine affection and respect for the young mothers as individuals.

This was a new experience for most of the girls, for many had never been able to relate to any man, whether it be father, uncle, friend, lover, or husband. Furthermore, in the majority of their relationships with men, most had suffered degradation and a loss of self-esteem and had seen their mothers do the same. But here was a man who did for them because he cared and expected nothing in return. It gave them a new perspective on the man/

woman relationship, helped them decide what they would look for in future relationships, and reinforced their feelings of self-worth because there was this bright, educated, successful man who cared about them as people.

Many other attributes weight heavily in decisions concerning staff. I look for people with a strong commitment to the program; for people with an understanding and compassionate approach to the girls and their loved ones; for people who possess a generous dollop of common sense, all of which must be coupled with a highly developed, fully operative sense of humor.

The one type of person eliminated from consideration is the moralist. We need people who can accept the girls just as they are when they enter the program, and work from there. If there's any preaching to be done, we prefer it be done by setting an example of kindness, caring, and responsible action, not sermonizing!

Along these lines, each staff member and volunteer must be evaluated to determine whether he or she will fit in with the others. Staff and support people must not necessarily be in total agreement with one another on all phases of the program. They must, however, be able to accept, appreciate and respect both the other person and that person's right to a differing opinion.

Without this, there can be no sharing, no genuine exchange of affection between staff members, which is vital. Our program goes far beyond the three Rs and home economics. If it is to be truly effective, we must teach the girls how to actually live, love, and function in the real world. It is important, therefore, that staff members be able to touch and react to one another openly and honestly.

This encourages students to emulate the staff and to see the worth in an honest, open, accepting relationship. It also frees them from some inhibiting, repressive conceptions. It removes homosexual connotations, for example, from an embrace between two women or two men. In like manner, it helps them understand that men and women can hug and express affection without any sexual connotation. This is important, because it frees the girls from stereotypes and allows them to show warmth not only to their babies, but to their parents. It helps them understand the importance of touching and the verbal expression of caring.

From the standpoint of numbers, the academic staff should, ideally, be in a ratio of one teacher for every 8 or 10 girls. You need also a coordinator, a secretary/aide, housekeeper/aide, and a bus driver.

Volunteers are the backbone of our staff and can actually make or break the program. We use them for answering the phone and other clerical work. Retired teachers help by coaching students behind in academics; volunteers teach arts and crafts; retirees work one-on-one with students who have reading problems. In Lee County, we have made extensive use of the Community Coordinating Council, an agency which matches the skills of the volunteer to the organization needing those skills.

With regard to constantly upgrading the staff's effectiveness, it is important that the coordinator make it a top priority to keep abreast of any workshops and seminars offered by school systems, state agencies, and child advocacy groups, along with workshops on various funding sources and grant writing. These should either include or be supplemented by in-service training workshops for the entire staff in areas of reality therapy, transactional analysis therapy, health, and first aid.

And finally, our staff is encouraged to socialize together. In off hours, staff members and their families have dinner parties, special celebrations, picnics, and swim parties. This gives us time to unwind and to get to know one another in a different dimension. It helps us build and maintain the cohesiveness we need in the classroom. When we get together like this, we come back to school with a close feeling that carries over to the student. As in a good family situation, the way the staff members get along reflects on the success of the program.

CONFIDENTIALITY

Program coordinators and their staffs must be aware of each student's legal right to confidentiality. School records, accordingly, should be clearly marked *Confidential Information*. This is required by the Federal Law entitled Privacy Rights of Parents and Students, adopted 6/7/76. U.S. Statutes, Sec.20, USC 1232CG.

Some students do not feel so strongly about the need for confidentiality. They are willing to take the risk of exposure and discrimination so that other girls and their families will learn about the LAMP program. These are the girls who are willing to speak at civic clubs or to be photographed and interviewed by members of the media. Since they do have the legal right to confidentiality, we make sure to obtain a signed waiver at the time of the initial home visit in order to protect both the school and the media in the event they volunteer later for public appearances.

Failure to protect a student's confidentiality can have dire results. One LAMP student had her baby, the child was adopted, and the young mother returned to the general school population. She made a fine adjustment, excellent grades, and was getting on well with the business of her own life. A very attractive girl, she was nominated for the teen board of a local department store. The store, in checking her grades with the school board was told she had been a LAMP student. Based entirely on this piece of information, the department store dropped her from consideration.

Not only was this rejection a terrible, and unnecessary, grief to the girl and her parents, it placed the school board in legal jeopardy. The parents decided not to sue, but only because they felt court action would lead to further discrimination and humiliation for their daughter.

To further a feeling of belonging, and because we're proud of them, we like to keep a family album containing picture of all our mothers and fathers and their babies. If they do not wish to have their photographs included, we respect their right to say so and we keep foremost in our minds the grief and hardship violating a girl's confidentiality can have . . . for her!

HOME AND HOSPITAL VISITS

We make no specified number of home visits per student. There is, of course, the initial home visit at the time the student is enrolled in LAMP.

We also make home visits if the girl is ill, if there is a special problem in the home such as the illness of another family member, if we feel it would be helpful to the girl, or if she simply asks that we do so.

We do make at least one visit after the baby has been delivered. If the baby was delivered by a midwife, we visit the girl at her home, otherwise we visit her in the hospital. At the time of this postpartum visit, we carry a goody bag containing items that have been donated, layette items such as sheets, blankets, bootee sets knitted or crocheted by volunteers, shampoo, cologne, and always her books and her homework assignment.

Of course, if the baby is stillborn or adopted, we don't bring the gift pack. Instead, we bring her a butterfly necklace as a symbol of our caring and also to remind her that like the caterpillar she can turn her life into something new and beautiful.

If needed, or if the girl goes into labor while in class, one of us will go with her to the hospital. Sometimes the other girls act as support persons during labor. They are qualified to do this because of their LaMaze training. In fact, sometimes two girls who have become especially close in LAMP will decide to act as support persons for one another.

The girls are encouraged to come to class when they are in the early stages of labor. This serves many purposes. First, it gives all the girls the opportunity to become involved in the miracle of birth, and they have a chance to put their learning to use. Second, it helps allay their fears by knowing exactly what to expect, and they are less afraid.

Participating and helping the girl in labor also brings the girls closer. It helps the young mother, because the time passes more quickly and she has less time and inclination to dwell on the pain. I must point out that this is feasible in our case only because we are 1½ miles from the hospital and two blocks from the local midwife. We are also on the same campus as the Migrant Health Services staff.

The size of our staff, and the number of girls enrolled, also determines the frequency of home and hospital visits. When we were smaller, it was simple for the coordinator or the teachers to make these. As our enrollment has increased, we have had to turn this over to our social worker except in unusual circumstances.

There are several things to keep in mind in connection with these visits. First is the importance of documentation. Whoever makes the visit should file a written report including her observations. These can be of real help to the other teachers and staff people in understanding both the girl, the problems she encounters, and the way she reacts or resolves these problems. It may also help the staff avert problems that might otherwise arise. For example, if hostility is a way of life in the girl's family, it helps to be aware of this and to understand when the student brings this method of reacting, or problem solving, to school.

The second is equally important. The coordinator and her staff should avoid becoming too involved and therefore overextend themselves. There's a tendency to do this, especially because you become emotionally involved with these girls. It is important, however, to pull away when you begin to feel overburdened, for that's the only way you can maintain your perspective. It's also important for each member of the staff to keep some time for himself or herself.

SPECIAL COUNSELING

At some time during their stay in LAMP, we call each girl in for a special counseling session. At this time, we make available information concerning the accelerated learning program available through adult and community education. We also try to provide job counseling and direct students to our school's occupation specialists who further help her develop employability and skills. Many times we are able to help the girl directly because community employers and friends call us when they have job openings. Sometimes these employers are parents of former students or have had a friend who has gone through the program.

The coordinator should investigate to see the kinds of special employment programs available in the community as well as using the state employment and vocational school placement services.

Of course, if during this counseling session we find a girl with academic talent and a desire for further education, we explore possible scholarships and especially the CETA program (Comprehensive Education and Training Act) that provides jobs so that she can be paid while attending college.

INVOLVEMENT OF YOUNG FATHERS

To be truly effective, we must help the young father, for he has problems of his own that have been largely ignored by educators and workers in the mental-health services. We invite fathers to make the initial visit to the LAMP campus with the student and we encourage him to sign her enrollment forms.

We welcome the father's participation in special events, and, when feasible, encourage him to share her homework assignments, especially those that deal with pregnancy and child development. We encourage him to attend LaMaze classes with her and we let him know we are available for job and academic counseling. We also provide emotional support if the need arises, encouraging him to share his fears and his outlook, as a man, on life. These sessions have been enlightening for all of us.

If they need job counseling, we refer them to the appropriate agencies, such as the state employment service, the army recruiter, Job Corps, CETA Job Training, and very often encourage them to return to school.

The most important facet in dealing with young fathers is being sure they do not feel threatened. They should feel LAMP is as much their home as the girls' and they are not only welcome and accepted, but that the staff cares about them, too.

INVOLVEMENT OF THE STUDENTS' FAMILIES

We encourage the girls to take home hand-outs containing transactional analysis exercises, information on prenatal care, child care, labor and delivery, the emotional aspects of pregnancy, and birth-control information. We try to educate the family as well as the young mother to overcome any superstitions and fears surrounding childbirth and child care. Some of our girls, for example, still bring their babies to class with a piece of broom straw tied in the child's hair to ward off evil spirits. We've had a number of infants who've suffered eye infections because the family believes the baby's urine is sterile and should be used to clean the baby's eyes.

In educating the family, we also encourage the girls to pass along information concerning budgeting, proper nutrition, and available community resources.

TRANSPORTATION

Just getting the girl to the LAMP campus in this semirural area can be a problem as severe as finding her and encouraging her to enroll. Because of the special education designation under which we operate, most students residing within the city limits are able to ride the special education bus. Realistically, however, it can only serve the largest concentration of students which, in our case, is within a 5-mile radius of our campus.

Attendance remains a problem for those girls who live in outlying areas of the county. These girls must take whatever school buses are available in order to make connection with the special education bus. In some instances these girls must change buses as many as three times each way and spend a total of 4 hours daily traveling to and from school. As the girl's pregnancy advances, this can be very tiring.

Another problem arises once the chid is born. Mothers in the outlying areas cannot bring their babies to school with them on regular buses because the school board's insurance coverage insures infants only on the LAMP bus. We have resolved some of these problems by helping the girls to organize car pools or to utilize public transportation.

Anyone contemplating initiating a program such a LAMP should investigate federal programs that might provide special transportation for students classified as migrants. We have made use of these programs and are investigating other avilable federal grants.

SCHOOL PLANT

There are two things to keep in mind. The first is that a program of this sort does not necessarily have to be housed in a school building. It can be a storefront, a private home, a church, a hospital, an abandoned warehouse, a government complex, or even a National Guard armory. A lot of communities do have old scholls they've closed down, but don't be limited in your thinking. The most important thing is that the program be in a site that is centrally located and easily accessible.

The second thing to remember is that you can accomplish miracles with a little paint and some imagination. You must have heat, air conditioning, and running water. Carpeting is also essential, both for using the floor during LaMaze exercises and also because it cuts down the noise when you have babies in the center.

As a minimum, you need adequate space to provide the following:

1. A clinic area which students can utilize for special health needs and where they can be examined by the school nurse.
2. A learning resource area.
3. Academic study areas.
4. Space for baby cribs.
5. Restroom facilities.
6. A private room for counseling.
7. An infant center with diaper pails and a changing table.
8. A reception area with work space for a secretary.
9. A conversation center with rocking chairs, for students always hold their babies for feeding.

Ideally, you will have a kitchen with laundry facilities for home econonics classes and preparing infant formulae. When we began we didn't have a kitchen, but we contacted the Florida Home Ecnomics Extension Agent and she graciously allowed us to use their kitchen on special occations. Laundry was sent to a nearby wash center or taken home by a staff member.

If possible, try to find a place that has room for a flower and vegetable garden. If not, use window boxes. A package of marigold seed is cheap, but it can produce a spot of beauty regardless of its surroundings, and this shows the girls they can make their lives beautiful with very little money. It also helps them appreciate nature and adds a new dimension to their lives.

When we began, a survey of the county revealed a 2800-square-foot building built in 1927. However, although decrepit, it was located in the heart of dowtown Fort Myers and with a minimal amount of money and work could be converted into a comfortable, adequate facility.

School personnel, the building teacher, and students from the vocational school program, along with interested volunteers, supplied the skill, knowledge, and supplies. They built bookshelves that served as room dividers providing a nursery area, social studies, math and language areas, as well as a conversation center. The floor was covered in a soft green carpet and colorful curtains brightened the interior. A tour of the school's warehouses resulted in the necessary tables, soft padded chairs, and teachers' desks.

Volunteers and school personnel donated cribs and used baby baskets were purchased from a local hospital. Despite its furnishings, which could best be described as "Good Will" or "early marriage," the center had a cheerful and homelike atmosphere, which is of prime importance for any program of this type.

SUPPORT GROUPS

We have received a great deal of support from state and federal agencies, and also from community organizations such as the March of Dimes, the local health department, the Salvation Army, the Children's Home Society, Planned Parenthood Association, the Lee County Migrant Health Department, and local women's clubs, church groups, and Edison Community College, 4H, Home Economics Extension Services, and the Abuse Counseling Treatment Center, to mention only a few.

The coordinator should contact every group concerned with prevention or teen sexuality. This would include Planned Parenhood and the National Alliance Concerned With Responsible Adolescent Parenting. Check to see if they have local or state chapters for they can be very helpful. We have both the state and local Alliance. These organizations not only serve as advocacy groups, but also disseminate information, and present an annual conference which offers speakers and special workshops of interest to people working with teenagers. This group was instrumental in the passage of recent legislation in Florida which mandated that all adolescents remain in school until their 16th birthday regardless of whether they are pregnant, married, or not.

POSSIBLE FUNDING SOURCES

Federal grants are available through the office of Adolescent Pregnancy Prevention in Rockville, Maryland. There also are vocational grants, Title XX grants, state and federal monies as well as local foundations. The coordinator must be willing and prepared to do a great deal of research.

SUMMARY

In determining whether there is need for a program of this sort in your community, I would suggest you not rely on school statistics because they seldom reflect the real situation. Again, this is not because of inefficiency on the part of the school staff, but because the girls drop out of school without telling officials the real reason. For a more accurate assessment, I would recommend a poll of private physicians, your local health department staff, and migrant health services people.

One of the most effective ways to gain support for a program, once you have determined there is a need, is to do some research and come up with dollar figures that show how much money the community will save by educating these girls. Comparing the cost of your proposed program to the cost of maintaining these young mothers and their children on welfare will make it clear that a staggering amount of tax moneies can be saved in the long run.

You can also gain support by pointing out that the suicide rate among these girls is extremely high and that their children are far more likely to have medical problems and neurological defects, both of which can be prevented by proper diet and prenatal care your program will provide.

To establish the program, you will need a nucleus of support people within the school system and the community. Making public appearances before civic and church groups is an important step. For this purpose, produce a slide presentation or movie you can show or, better still, take along some of your students. Let them tell people first-hand about their experiences in the program, and what having the opportunity to continue their education means to them and their future. You can't help but win support when your audience sees for itself the good the program accomplishes.

Along these same lines, be sure to maintain and continue close contact with professionals dealing with the same problem on local, state, and national levels. They can be a rich source not only of information and ideas, but other kinds of support as well.

You can take a program of this sort as far as energy and imagination permit, but if it is to be successful you must never forget it is not simply an academic program, or a school. It is truly a happening, where love and sharing can take place and where there is the genuine openness that leads to personal growth.

It is also an opportunity to redirect a young woman's life script, a script created and imposed by generations of role stereotyping. It is the opportunity to make her aware of the magnitude of choices and alternatives open to her, and also to enable her to make responsible decision concerning these options.

And finally, it is a chance to support these young mothers as they begin to take charge of their lives and their children's lives, and, it is hoped, to begin to break the vicious circle of welfare, poverty, and ignorance. It is personally rewarding to share their joy when they learn for the first time that they do not have to accept what they previously perceived to be their "lot in life."

BIBLIOGRAPHY

1. The Exceptional Student Act which is consistent with the requirements stipulated by Federal Law 94-142, sections 121a.561, 121a.504(b)(1)(i), 121a.344(a)(3), 121.504(b)(1)(ii), 121.500(a)(b)(c) and Floridat State Board of Education Administrative Rules 6A-1.955(6)(a), 6A-6.331(7)(a), 6A-6.331(1)(d), and 6A-6.331(6).
2. Schmuck, R.A., Runkel, p.j., Arends, J., and Arends, R. *The Second Handbook of Organizational Development in Schools*, Palo Alto, Calif.: Mayfield Publishing, 1977.
3. Gordon, Sol C., Ph.D., *You Would If You Loved Me*, New York: Bantam Books, 1978.
4. *Acquaintance Rape*, ODN Productions (Movie), 79 Varick Street, New York, NY 10010.
5. "Carol King Tapestry," A&M Records, Hollywood, CA.
   The Story of Eric, Centre Films, Hollywood, CA. (movie)
   Happy Family Planning, Planned Parenthood, New York. (movie)
6. Glasser, William M.D., *Reality Therapy: A New Approach to Psychiatry*, New York: Harper & Row, 1965.
7. CETA is an acronym for Comprehensive Education Training Act which was adopted in 1973. It is a federally subsidized employment and job training program for the economically disadvantaged.

16.
Pregnant Adolescents in Maternity Homes: Some Professional Concerns

Ernie Lightman, Ph.D.,

and

Benjamin Schlesinger, Ph.D.,
Faculty of Social Work,
University of Toronto,
Canada

Recent trends in the English-speaking, industrialized countries indicate that a decreasing number of unmarried mothers are choosing to enter maternity homes. The pattern for such women appears to be increasingly in the direction of keeping their children (75–90%), resulting in fewer adoptions; in addition, the unmarried mother is now likely to be living on her own or with friends.

In the 1950s, the social work literature still had articles dealing with "homes for unmarried mothers," but by the 1970s such content was rare. With the passage of time, the growing availability of alternative options for the unmarried mother, including abortion and keeping the child, have combined with changing public perceptions of illegitimacy and woman's place in society; the result has been declining admissions to maternity homes, and an associated need for these homes to adapt to new functions or to confront the possibility of closure.

It thus is a question of some interest to consider the nature of the client group which was served by maternity homes in the 1970s. Who are the women who enter maternity homes rather than dealing with their pregnancy in some other way? What personal or situational factors induce these women to follow this particular approach, and what supports are available to them as they implement their decisions?

This paper presents some demographic data related to nonmarried mothers in Canada. Nearly 10 percent of all births annually are to single mothers. We then review the existing Canadian studies related to nonmarried mothers, and present the highlights of their findings.

During the six-month period of February to July 1978 we completed a study of intake into 10 maternity homes in the province of Ontario. There were 246 nonmarried mothers admitted to these homes. Three profiles were developed.

A general profile of the typical admission; a profile of the single mother who intends to have her child adopted "The Adopter"; and a profile of the "Keeper," the single mother who plans to keep her child. A discussion of the implications of the findings to the helping professions raises a series of questions dealing with present practices and research dealing with single mothers. The findings are compared with an American study by Grow (1979) which found similar trends related to nonmarried mothers.

INTRODUCTION

In Canada in 1977, there were 351,799 births. Of these, 34,634 were to nonmarried women, constituting 9.8 percent of all births in 1977.[10] Of all the births to single mothers, 49.6 percent were to women aged 19 years and under. If we examine the total births to women under the age of 19 years in 1977, we find that 36,294 births, or 10.3 percent of all births were to Canadian women under the age of 19 years. Thus 47.3 percent of all births to women under the age of 19 years were to single women.[10] Table 16-1 contains this data.

In 1978 the province of Ontario had a population of 8.3 million people. During that year there were 9974 births to nonmarried mothers. Of these, 5220, or 52.3 percent, were to women under the age of 20 years. These births constituted 8.2 percent of all births in the Province in 1978. In Ontario 88 percent of the mothers kept their children.

In examining admissions to maternity homes in Ontario, Schlesinger and Storey[9] found the following trends:

1. From 1974–75 the number of homes decreased from 13 to 12 homes.
2. Total residents declined from 1248 in 1974, to 1097 in 1975.
3. In 1976, 946 women, in 1977, 1002 women, and in 1978, 879 women were admitted to maternity homes in Ontario.

The trend to date indicates a declining population coming to maternity homes in Ontario, with the exception of 1977, when an increase was noted.

Table 16-1. Births to Canadian women aged 19 years and under in 1977—total births and births to nonmarried mothers.

AGE GROUPS	TOTAL BIRTHS	SINGLE WOMEN	% OF TOTAL BIRTHS
Under 15 years	323	296	91.6
15–19 years	35,971	16,800	46.7
Total	36,294	17,196	47.3

Source: Statistics Canada, Catalogue #84-204, October 1979.

HISTORICAL BACKGROUND IN CANADA

Legal rights and services for unmarried parents and their children is a relatively modern phenomenon, with the first piece of effective legislation being enacted in 1921. Originally, the unwed mother had no rights or services, and consequently concealed or even destroyed her offspring. In 1826 the first piece of legislation on this subject was passed in Upper Canada, an Act "to prevent the destroying and murdering of bastard children." The law was a punitive one, making provision to try a mother for the murder of her child, or in the case of concealment, for a lesser offense. The following year the Guardianship Act took the child into account, specifying that an illegitimate child could be place placed with a guardian. However, exploitation and cruelty towards these children were rampant and the Act was generally ineffective. The Illegitimate Children's Act in 1914 attempted to make the father liable for the child's maintenance. The Act enabled the mother to present an Affidavit of Paternity to the court. However, as there was no provision in the legislation to make the father legally responsible, action could rarely be taken. Finally, in 1921, through the efforts of both the medical and social work professions, The Children of Unmarried Parents Act was passed marking a new approach to children born out of wedlock. The Act, no longer referring to such children as illegitimate, focused on aiding the unmarried mother to provide for her child. Affiliation orders made between the Province of Ontario and the putative fathers were now legally binding, requiring the father to contribute to the cost of his child's maintenance. In practice the mother was also financially responsible; however, the new Act provided her with the right to appear for statutory guardianship with a provincial child welfare officer. If she were still unable to care for the child, or in the case of abandonment or neglect, the Children's Aid Society was given a mandate to assume guardianship. In turn, it could transfer the guardianship role to adoptive parents.

In the following years sociologists sought explanations of illicit pregnancy. The shift from an emphasis on moral deficiency and bad companions, to the role of environmental or cultural factors, seems to be consonant with the willingness of the community to assume responsibility for the social problem of illegitimacy. Earlier, moral judgments were reflected in the external applications of labels—the scarlet "A" as implied in the terms "illegitimate" and "bastard" in legislation—and in the absence of social supportive services. However, a recognition of poverty, broken homes, and their concomitant influences brought about a change in public attitude. In the 1950s Sigmund Freud's explanations of all behavior as purposive became "vogue," contributing to the development of a psychological interpretation of illegitimacy. Thus, the out-of-wedlock pregnancy was accepted as symptomatic and purposeful; an attempt by the personality to ease an unresolved conflict. Attention also became focused on societal attitudes. While illicit pregnancy continued to be censored, a "fun morality" which includes premarital sex is implicitly condoned, if not encouraged, by our mass media. Nevertheless, although our society continues to see the unmarried mother as a "role violator," in theory at least neither our legislation, nor our services, reflect any moral judgment. Rather, they recognize the social, emotional, and financial problems which are likely to beset the unmarried parent.

The most important decision to be made by the unmarried mother is the disposition of her child. In some cases the unwed mother, because she lacks the capacity to plan realistically or to foresee the consequences of her action, will require assistance in planning for the future care of her child. She is faced with a number of alternatives. If she chooses to keep the baby she may return with him to her parents' home, marry the putative father (or another man), or set herself up independently. On the other hand, she may decide to place him for adoption.

THE UNMARRIED MOTHER

Many studies on unwed mothers have included surveys of her expressed needs for service. The tangible services concerning housing, finances, employment, and vocational training are repeatedly given priority. However, there are inconsistencies in requests for help regarding personal or social adjustment. First, there is a discrepancy between the number of unmarried mothers requesting casework and counseling service and the number of mothers whom the interviewers evaluate as needing this type of help. Secondly, while the agency is required to interpret services in the community and provide tangible aid, the amount of casework service which can be given to the unmarried mother is limited to the amount of assistance the client desires and is willing to accept. The proximity of the birth of the child when the girl comes to the agency also influences the completeness of the service given, as priority must be afforded to those things which are of prime concern.

A prevalent concept in the recent literature on unmarried motherhood is the repetition of illicit pregnancy when the circumstances around conception are not adequately dealt with. In recognition of this possibility, either because of psychological factors or more practical ones such as the use of appropriate birth-control methods, social work offers continuing casework services; its goals are the prevention of recidivism as well as a more constructive redirection of the girl's future life. It has been recognized that for some girls an examination of motivation may be harmful or unfeasible. However, there are several areas around personal and social adjustment which might provide focus for casework service.

For any individual, entry into a new role may be experienced as a crucial event. For the unmarried girl who becomes pregnant the problem is twofold:

She is faced with the transition to a changed status; and her new role of mother is an unexpected and may be an unwanted one. The role of the unmarried mother is also an ambiguous one. While the married, widowed, separated, or divorced woman finds both a socially recognized status and role behavior anchored in the social system, the unmarried mother is socially recognized only as a role "violator;" the role of mother in our society prescribes the counter-role of father, and both roles to be within wedlock. Should the unmarried mother be an adolescent, she may also experience role conflict, for the pregnant teenager must orient herself simultaneously to two roles which would ordinarily occur in sequence. Consequently, her perceptions and reactions to individuals and events may be alternately governed by each of these roles.

The girl's relationship with her family may be another area of concern. The literature on illegitimacy indicates that many unmarried mothers have family backgrounds which are characterized by early deprivation in terms of primary interpersonal relationship. Often, as a result of her experiences, the girl also has extremely negative feelings towards men. Although the Children's Aid Societies tend to be largely staffed by women, male caseworkers have been assigned to unwed mothers. Although they may be at a disadvantage in some aspects of the client-worker relationship, male workers are in a unique position of being able to demonstrate positive male attributes. The client is thus given a concrete opportunity to test her attitudes toward men. In addition to her personal feelings and adjustments towards her family, the unmarried mother must make several practical decisions. Since her confinement, future plans, as well as the disposition of her child, may involve her family, she must evaluate the emotional and practical support which they can offer.

The School and the Unmarried Mother

During this period, fraught with uncertainty and change, schooling could provide some continuity; yet most schools require unwed mothers to drop out of classes as soon as their pregnancy becomes known. The reasons given for exemption from attendance are given as the possible impact on the girl and her inability to function in a school situation, or her detrimental influence on the morals of the school. Whether school officials in fact fear that pregnancy is "catching," or if these rationales are cover-ups for moral biases, is a moot question. The important point is that education, an important prerequisite for self-maintenance in our rapidly changing technological society, becomes interrupted for these girls and often leaves them with little motivation to return to school after the birth of the baby. Thus, not only are they deprived of the stabilizing experience of involvement in a study program but also of the social contact which school ordinarily provides and stimulates. While most maternity homes offer educational programs, for those who stay in the community there are few alternatives. However, an emphasis on helping the school-age unwed mother to complete her education has not been put into practice in some areas in Canada. A bolder and more recent program, unique to Canadian education, was reported in the February 1971 issue of *Chatelaine* magazine:

> Some 100 girls averaging sixteen and a half years, have taken advantage of the opportunity of continuing their education at a school operated by the adult education department of the Calgary School Board, which supplies a building, services and bus tickets. Students pay a tuition fee of $5 a month. There's a full-time teaching staff and many community agencies co-operate to help the students. In addition to regular academic subjects covering grades seven to twelve, there are also classes in business education, home economics and sewing.

This type of program offers the girls an opportunity to continue their education and focus on their potential for achievement. Those programs which relate to the student's imminent life-style—as do, for example, courses in home economics, sewing, and business education—and an environment which is task-oriented, nonthreatening, informal, and highly supportive have been found to be most conducive to learning.

The unwed mother who works may not find her routine as disrupted as that of the student. Interestingly, in contrast to the student, it is rarely suggested that pregnancy will interfere with her individual functioning as a worker. Employers also seem to be more tolerant of unmarried pregnant women, allowing them to continue working for longer periods before delivery. This attitude has become more widespread with the Women's Equal Employment Opportunity Act (December 1970) prohibiting dismissal because of pregnancy.

CANADIAN STUDIES

The Family and Children's Services of the City of London and County of Middlesex carried out a Longitudinal Study to find out more about how the unmarried mother and her child fared in the community, and to learn also of the kind of problems she is likely to encounter.[6]

The study concerned itself specifically with interpersonal relationships, the emotional and economic adjustments of the unmarried mother, and how the first born child of an unmarried mother, and retained by her, fared in the community. Fifty-nine unmarried mothers, mostly white, and ranging between the ages of 17 and 19 years, were chosen. They represented a cross-section of the general population of the area served by the Agency as far as socioeconomic factors were concerned. Personal follow-up interviews were conducted at 6, 12, and 18 months after the baby's birth.

Information gathered indicated that most of the mothers had relatively long-term and probably meaningful relationships with the fathers of their children. The data found only about one out of five of the fathers assumed any financial responsibility toward the mother, or for the care of their child. It also showed more than two-thirds of the mothers were self-supporting and one in four had married either the father of the child, or another man. This could indicate that having a child out of wedlock is not necessarily associated with inability to become self-supporting, nor is it a hindrance toward future marriage.

The study found that most of the unmarried mothers and their babies lived in adequate accommodations. A large number resided in publicly subsidized low-rental housing. The lack of male staff in the recreational centers which were accessible to those single-parent, female-led families, was apparent. It was recommended by the author that more thought should be given to such a lack. The assumption underlying this is related to the fact that there are few male role models in public housing, but also such males could provide a nonthreatening and caring support to the unmarried mother.

The mothers who lived alone with their children experienced a very lonely existence, while those who had a good relationship with their parents were able to create a better emotional atmosphere for the grandparents, the mother, and the child. Most of the mothers had the major responsibility for caring for their children. Mothers complained that the lack of day-care facilities was a serious problem. They also complained about the amount of financial assistance they were receiving. Only a few mothers felt that they had received adequate personal help in the form of guidance or advice, psychological or emotional support, or opportunities for satisfying social contacts.

The study also indicated that at the 12-month period the mothers experienced a critical time. It was at this point that outside help diminished, including help received from their own family. Only a few of the mothers had regrets regarding their marital status at the time of the baby's birth, although many stated that they experienced an unsatisfactory social life as most of their time was spent in caring for the child.

The author of the report found that marriage was offered to some of the mothers by men other than the putative father. Many of the mothers indicated that they saw marriage as their ultimate goal, closely followed by happiness and financial security. Much optimism was expressed in regard to obtaining these goals. Some even stated their willingness to return to school so as to complete their educational program. They did not see that as a major problem.

The author stated that in her opinion there was a significant hard-core minority, perhaps 25 percent, where the potential for adequate child care was lower than for the group as a whole, and where the danger of future child neglect was prominent. The most outstanding needs of the mothers were for financial and emotional assistance.

The community from which the Longitudinal Study was drawn does carry a comprehensive range of services for the unmarried mother and her child through the Family and Children's Services Department. Services provided include counseling follow-up if the mother keeps her child, and adoption for the child, if indicated. Other services, such as maternity home care, prenatal care, financial assistance, and income maintenance, although provided under other auspices (private and public), are clearly coordinated for the recipient by the Family and Children's Services social worker.

The Children's Aid Society of Metropolitan Toronto (CAS) has carried out surveys of the unwed mother who keeps her child and who functions as a solo-parent in the community.[1] In one such study, mothers from the CAS and CCAS (Catholic Children's Aid Society) participated. The results revealed that over 70 percent of the CCAS and CAS groups, and 60 percent of the Control group, were no more than 20 years of age or younger. It also indicated that 80 percent of these young mothers were primary full-time caring person of the child or children, and that 37 percent of them were living on their own with the child/children.

Income, or lack of it, tended to be a problem to the mothers. About 80 percent of these young mothers were living on an income of $4000 or less. This inadequate amount did not allow them the pleasure of securing baby-sitters; neither did it allow them the opportunity to indulge in any kind of recreation. The average educational level of most of these mothers was grade 10. Other information obtained from the study, revealed a large percentage of the mothers retained only a few, in some cases none, of their old friends. Many of them were raising their children in an isolated environment, and a large percentage felt that their role as a mother inhibited their social life. Only about 30 percent felt that their mothering role minimally inhibited their social life. Seventy percent of the mothers stated their desire to see on-going groups for Single Parents as part of Agency program.

Gordon[2] carried out a project within the Central Branch Agency of the Children's Aid Society of Metropolitan Toronto. She contacted 29 unwed mothers in their homes who had kept their babies, to find out how they were faring in the community as solo-parents. It was the aim of the unstructured interview to examine the unwed mothers "concerns and supports" and the gaps they encountered in community resources. As it turned out, it was discovered at the initial interview that the mothers were more interested in reporting the failures of the community to come up with a comprehensive and coordinated approach to basic needs, rather than dealing with what the investigator wanted to find out.

In Vancouver, of 90 single mothers, Poulos[5] ranked the most frequent problems they said they faced:

Rank Order

1. Day Care
2. Income Management
3. Personal Adjustment
4. Living Arrangements
5. Child rearing and care
6. Getting along in the community
7. Employment
8. Sex education
9. Job Training
10. Family Court Action
11. Health

Finding suitable day-care facilities for their children has been felt as a problem by 80 percent of the mothers interviewed. Older mothers (over 25 years of age) considered this more of a problem than the younger ones, (72 as opposed to 53 percent). Age of child did not seem to influence the felt severity of this problem. Those who were self-supporting found day care to be a far greater problem than those who were not self-supporting, (83 as opposed to 45 percent). The simplest explanation for this would seem to be a greater number of the former group were probably employed, or wanted to seek employment. An alternate explanation may be the cost of day care.

Seventy-five percent of the mothers experienced problems with budgeting. Slightly more of the younger mothers found this to be so than the older mothers, (76 and 66 percent respectively). Of those mothers who were not self-supporting, 86 percent found this area to be problematic and 62 percent of those who were self-supporting agreed. Those with older children (older than one year) found it more difficult than those whose children were younger than one year (78 and 65 percent respectively).

Seventy-one percent of the mothers had experienced problems in the area of personal adjustment. Again, older mothers found this slightly more problematic than the younger mothers (77 as opposed to 64 percent). Those with older children were more affected by this problem than those with infants (75 and 60 percent). Fifty-five percent of the mothers had difficulty in finding suitable housing. This did not vary according to mother's or child's age or financial situation.

Child rearing and care has been a problem for 69 percent of the mothers interviewed. As would be expected, this is slightly more of a problem for the older mothers and for those mothers with children over one year of age.

Fifty-nine percent of the mothers have experienced difficulties in their community relations and activities. This did not vary greatly according to mother's or child's age.

In 1975, Youtz[11] reported on a study of 181 teenage single mothers who were receiving Ontario Family Benefits allowances (welfare). Their average age was 18.6 years. He concluded that, on the whole, unmarried teenagers in receipt of Provincial Benefits were managing quite well to raise their children, despite their relative youth and their dependence on social assistance. Employing measures of parental functioning, life satisfaction, social activity, and expectations for the future, he found that children in these families were well cared for by their mothers and that the mothers themselves were, on the whole, satisfied with their life situation. In addition, qualitative materials indicated that mothers received considerable support from their own parents and relatives whether they lived with them or not. For instance, the vast majority of women relied upon their mothers to babysit for them, and a number indicated that they received modest amounts of financial assistance in addition to their Provincial Benefits allowance. Many women who did not receive cash gifts, received gifts of clothing or household articles from relatives and friends. In addition, substantial proportions of women indicated that they often sought the aid of parents or other relatives in finding housing, securing work, or dealing with their children's problems. These findings strongly suggested that most mothers are part of a family network that provided considerable security through mutual support for its members. Among this group of young women there were relatively few of the isolated, bitter, apathetic "welfare mothers" characterized in much of the literature on poverty.

The data also suggested that these young mothers may be financially better off than many older deserted and divorced women, heading families and receiving Provincial Benefits.

Maternity Homes Study in Ontario

It is a question of some interest to consider the nature of the client group which is served by maternity homes in the 1970s. Who are the women who enter maternity homes? What personal or situational factors induce these women to follow this particular approach and what supports are available to them as they implement their decisions?

Methodology

Each member of the Maternity Homes Association has traditionally collected its own data upon intake. For purposes of the study, an instrument was developed which basically combined the questions found on the individual forms used by the Homes.

The questionnaire was largely precoded so as to enhance its statistical reliability as well as to facilitate data analysis. In addition, the nature of the information sought was such that a precoded closed instrument was deemed to be appropriate (i.e., there were no attitudinal or motivational questions; the information being collected was purely of a demographic descriptive nature).

The original questionnaire was pretested at one home in Metropolitan Toronto over a period of 2 months, and the draft form was revised in the light of preliminary results. In addition, the administrators of all homes were invited to scrutinize the form and their suggested changes were also incorporated. The data was to be collected for 6 months, from February to July 1978, by all members of the Maternity Homes Association of Ontario. The form was to be administered on intake by the director of the home or her designate, although there were minor variations in this regard.

Forms were completed by most of the homes during the 6-month period, and a total of 246 completed questionnaires were ultimately received by researchers from 10 maternity homes. It is believed that this number represented an adequate and reasonable sample of all clients at Maternity Homes in Ontario and the findings could be safely generalized to this extent. It is clear, however, that not all nonmarried mothers choose to enter a maternity home in response to their pregnancy, and no interferences can properly be drawn from the present findings to the total population of nonmarried mothers. This was a study of that portion of nonmarried mothers who chose to enter maternity homes. This is of particular importance to professionals inasmuch as the decision to enter a maternity home will be influenced by a variety of factors which includes geographical residence. as well as the location of the various homes, along with the support network which may be available. The support network includes family, friends, as well as the putative father. Potential lack of access to abortion facilities may also influence the decision to enter a maternity home, as is the fact that these homes are administered under religious auspices.

The validity of responses was discussed with the administrators of the maternity homes at a meeting in Toronto in September 1978. In general, the reported results were felt to be reasonable and consistent with the experience of the staff. A very limited number of items were questioned as to validity; it was suggested that at the point of intake, a meaningful trust relationship had not yet been established with the respondents, and administration of the form at a slightly later point might have enhanced the comfort of the respondent in replying to the questions. For example, respondents were asked if the present pregnancy was the first; the administrators suggested that at the point of intake the clients may have been unwilling to be fully candid. Previous abortions may in fact have been more common than reported in this study.

It should be noted that there was no guarantee of confidentiality to the respondent vis à vis the director of the home. This may, in principle, have influenced the results. The names of the respondents were not recorded on the questionnaires and were not made available to the researchers. A consent form was signed by each respondent prior to completion of the questionnaire, and the ethical requirements of the University of Toronto, Office of Research Administration were met in full.

Three Profiles

We developed three profiles of women at the time of admission to the maternity homes. The first one is of the average pregnant and unmarried woman, the second deals with the women who decided to adopt, and the third profile describes the woman who decided to keep her child.

1. The Single Mother.
The average woman was white, 19 years of age, with a range of 14–42 years. Almost half of the women were still in school, the average grade was 10. A little over half the women were Catholic, and 40 percent Protestant. Three-quarters lived in their parents' home and 92 percent were Canadian citizens, with English spoken at home. A little less than two thirds had a blue-collar job, in 38 percent of the cases, a white-collar job. Nearly half the women's mothers were full-time homemakers. For 87 percent, this was their first pregnancy. The putative father was known for an average of 1½ years by our sample. His average age was 21 years, with a range from 15–55 years. His average education was grade 11. Nearly one-half of the fathers were still in contact with the women at the time of admission to the home. Thirty-nine percent planned to maintain contact with the mother after delivery of the baby.

Of the total sample, 37 percent planned to keep their child, and 50 percent planned to put the child up for adoption. As far as further education was concerned, 39 percent planned to return to school, and 22 percent to work.

A surprising finding was that nearly one-quarter of the women were presently under psychiatric treatment, or had such treatment in the past.

Adoption or Retention Among Single Mothers

In analysis of the data, it was found that 90 (37 percent) of the women were planning to keep the child, 124 (50 percent) intended to give the child up for adoption, while the remaining 32 (13 percent) said they had unspecified plans at the time of admission to the maternity homes. It was felt that a comparison of the "Adopters" and "Keepers" would be of interest to social workers who are involved with single mothers at the time of pregnancy, birth, and future planning for this family unit. Two profiles were developed which clearly differentiated the backgrounds and social characteristics of these two groups of single mothers.

2. The Adopters' Profile. From our data, the following conclusions emerged in relation to the adopters. The "adopter" was more likely to be in school, and was planning to return to school after the birth of the child. She would be living at home with her parents in a two-parent family unit. Her parents were paying some board to the maternity home, and her parents were involved in decisions concerning the baby. The adopter appeared to have little contact with the putative father, and was not planning any future contact. The putative father's family was not involved in the woman's decisions and plans related to the baby.

Her friends were not nonmarried mothers, nor did she report any serious illness, or handicap, or psychiatric treatment in her past. The adopter was not in contact with a social-work agency, and was not planning to relate to a social agency after the birth of her child.

3. The Keepers—Profile. The single mother who planned to keep her child will have left school and will have done so at a slightly younger age than the adopter. It is less probably that she was living at home with her parents. She was residing permanently in public housing, an apartment, or some other situation that does not involve home ownership. Over three-quarters of this group reported they have other nonmarried mothers as friends. The woman who was planning to keep her child reported serious illness or handicaps and was three times as likely to have undergone psychiatric treatment in the past. The family structure at home was primarily a parent unit which involved divorce or separation. The "keeper" was more likely to be in contact with the putative father and his family and to have them involved in her own decisions for the future. This woman was in contact with some social work agency in the past with much greater frequency, including the payment of board on her behalf to the home, and was planning to retain such contact with the agency in the future.

A Comparative Study

In the United States Grow (1979)[3] compared pregnant nonmarried mothers who keep their children and those who surrender them for adoption. The study included 210 white single mothers in Milwaukee, of whom 182 kept their children. She reported that more of the keeping, than surrendering, mothers were from parental homes broken by divorce or separation, were more often nonstudents, had less education, had sought help earlier, had known the putative father longer and were more likely to have maintained contact with him. The keeping mothers were younger than their counterparts and were more likely to have lived with parents or relatives during pregnancy. Grow also points out that women who opted for adoption were now in the minority and indeed may be reflecting traditional values of previous decades. They were more likely to have grown up in smaller cities and towns, were less likely to have considered the possibility of abortion, and were more likely to believe that children should be reared in two-parent homes. Although no differences were found in the religious affiliation of the two groups, women who surrendered their babies were far more likely to be regular churchgoers. This fits with their more conventional views on abortion and the family.

The women who kept their children were more likely to have received support from family and friends during pregnancy. They were also more likely to have maintained contact with the putative father, suggesting that some entertained the prospect of eventual marriage to him, or at the least some financial assistance from him. That the keeping mothers are younger than their counterparts may reflect less cautiousness than would be true for older women, as well as less awareness of the responsibilities entailed in childrearing. Since fewer of them were attending school, they were less likely to have career plans, and perhaps viewed the prospect of childrearing as less of a change in life-style than it would be considered by the women who chose adoption. In addition, since more of the keeping than surrendering mothers had lived in one-parent homes themselves, they may have been less likely to see a continuation of this one-parent pattern as a handicap for themselves and their child.

It is of great interest that our profiles in Canada appeared to match in some respects those found in this American study. We must, however, note that the American sample included subjects from social agencies and one maternity home, while our population were all residents in maternity homes.

Societal Implications

In examining the phenomenon of increased adolescent pregnancy and sexuality, Schlesinger[7] developed the "pregnant alphabet."

A. stands for action in the community. It is time that besides talking, slogans, conferences, and reports, communities begin with action.

B. the basic issues which underlie the simple or complex topic of adolescent sexuality. We cannot discuss nor examine in a community, adolescent sexuality without examining the basic issues of that community in relation to the political system the religious system, the culture, the economics, etc., of this community. In other words, we have to consider under "B" the sexual politics in our community.

C. stands for control. We have to ask our community: "What type of control do we want in our communities in relationship to sexual behaviour?" There is a range of control from the idea of China, with a political, almost total control over the sexuality of adolescents, to the American view of laissez faire: "Do what you want when you want it, but just don't bother me."

D. in the alphabet, stands for the double standard. The double standard signifies responsibility for adolescent women and irresponsibility for young adolescent men. If our communities continue with this double standard then, frankly speaking, we won't get very far. Instead of the double standard, we must establish a new standard which should be "equality between human beings."

E. in the alphabet, stands for education. This education in the present context, is primarily sex education. May we humbly suggest that we have not really considered many practical questions of introducing sex education into our communities. How do we start? Who will teach? What approaches are best for my community and yours? What shall we transmit? It is so easy to talk about sex education, but we do have to remember that there are different values in each community. A textbook or training material appropriate for one community may be wholly inappropriate for another.

F. stands for father. Let's not leave out the father in adolescent fertility. The father is mentioned very few times in discussions of adolescent sexuality. Discussions of his conduct are usually negative and often jocular. We consider adolescent fertility and pregnancy as part of a family. Babies born out of wedlock are born to two people, a mother and father. Social work especially at times tends to leave out that third party, the father. The shadow of this family is the unmarried father. It is time that we include him, not simply in a punitive way, but more hopefully, in a positive way. He also has feelings and emotions. He also may be an adolescent. The experience of fatherhood has affected him also, and he may need help.

G. stands for grownups—adults. We see grownups as models, not as judges; as examples, not as hypocrites. "Do as I say, not as I do" seems to express the situation in many parts of the world. We should not be surprised that youngsters reply: "You do not act as you advise. Why should I act as you tell me to do?" It is time that we grownups who represent the community to adolescents do a little introspection and ask ourselves: "What type of examples are we setting for our adolescents?"

H. is for health. We need, of course, physical and mental health services. Sometimes we feel we overdo the building of clinics and the building of hospitals, while we fall short on some of the novel approaches to health. For example, the whole paramedical field in working with adolescents has yet to be explored in many countries. Let's face it—we do not have enough trained doctors to do all the work, nor do doctors want to provide some of the health and quasi-medical services which adolescents need.

I. stands for involvement in our community—involvement with adolescents. By involvement, we mean that professionals, volunteers, and institutions, doctors, teachers, social workers, religious groups, social groups and cultural groups should integrate their work, rather than follow a piece-meal approach. One person is interested in the adolescent's head, another is interested in his mouth (nutrition), etc. None of them sits down and talks with a young man and young woman as persons. There is competition for the adolescent rather than collaboration in a holistic approach. Adolescents are human beings, total persons, with total needs.

J. stands for justice for adolescents. We mean justice which is not punitive, but is therapeutic. Many laws, regulations of social agencies and community policies are punitive. Often they are unenforceable. We need to re-examine them from the viewpoint both of community values and justice for the intended adolescent.

K. stands for kindness. It is time that we began to show kindness toward adolescents. They are worthwhile beings who need love. We should stop rejecting some of them because of their behaviour. They need understanding, not accusations; they need warmth, not coldness; they need to be included, not isolated in our communities.

L. stands for limits. "Are there limits to the acceptable sexual behaviour of adolescents within a community?" It is time that we reintroduce one small word into our communal vocabularies: the word is "NO." Sometimes we adults of the community appear to want to leave all decisions about sex up to adolescents to do as they choose. Maybe there are times when we should say "NO." All of us who have worked with children know that even adolescents do want some limits. We are moving toward a situation in many communities where the adolescents do not know whether there are any limits at all.

M. stands for media. There are universal complaints of how television, radio and newspapers are being misused. We can use the media positively for adolescent education. We don't mean we should have ads saying every minute "A pill a day keeps the babies away!" or "Technicolour condoms will save you from V.D.!" We are talking about a positive approach to use what we now know. One of the most effective, positive efforts would be to educate not only the adolescents, but also the parents, through our media.

N. stands for national goals of the community. Does our national government support communities trying to help adolescents or are we working in a vacuum? For example, a government may announce a sex education policy, but there is no implementation. What is the good of a beautiful document 220 pages long, if it is not implemented by a national programme? A document alone cannot stop my teenager or yours from getting pregnant.

O. is for openness. It is time that we open our minds to new ideas. We need not accept every new idea, but let us examine them. For example, we have learned that we, who live in an "industrialized country" can learn a lot from the work being done with adolescents in the so-called "non-industrial countries." There is much to learn from other countries or from the efforts of other communities in our own country.

P. stands for parents. We must get parents involved in our work with adolescents. How? When? What are the objectives? What is the purpose? How do we use parents? We need to help parents for their own sake, as well as for the sake of their adolescent children. Adolescent sexuality, adolescent pregnancy (even the prospect of it) is a major force for anxiety, depression, frustration, and general social and psychological maladjustment among parents. Often they need help as much, or more, than their own teenage child. Helping the parent with his child often helps the parent as well.

Q. stands for quality of life. What kind of "quality of life" do we have in our communities, yours and mine? Is there respect for human beings? Do people care for each other? Is the individual adolescent considered as a human being? Is there some affection?

R. stands for research. Research should not be for the sake of research only, but for helping communities to discharge their responsibilities to their adolescent citizens. Let us do research. For example, what kinds of adolescents live in your community and mine? What are their beliefs? What do they believe is the quality of life in their community? What are their standards?

S. stands for services. We can overservice a community. To open one is very easy. When you try to close one, there are vested interests which oppose it. As a result, we have many unneeded service units which overlap or duplicate each other. Yes, we do need services, but let us examine the type, the needs and the costs.

T.   stands for truth. Can we have a true dialogue between adults and adolescents without lies, sham and hypocrisy? What, really, is the truth in human sexuality?

U.   is for underlying causes of pregnancy. These include boredom, poverty, unemployment, a difficult home life, misinformation about sexuality, and the effects of morality in your community on the lives of adolescents.

V.   stands for values. Whose values? Are we supposed to impose our generation's values on the adolescent? What values does the adolescent have? It's very nice and easy to talk about throwing out old values, but what worries us is that we have no truly new values to substitute. It's as if we propose to throw old values in the garbage can as well. Suddenly, we have no place to put the garbage. It is so easy to reject this or that basic community value without substituting anything in its place. We cannot live in a valueless society. Yes, the adolescents are proposing a few warmed-over old values. What they call new values are nothing more than old values with a new accent. We now have to consider, at the community level, whether we (or the adolescents themselves, when they become older) would want these to be a permanent part of the community culture. Sexual values are not in a vacuum; they must be consistent with other moral, religious, psychological, and social values.

W.   stands for women. It is time that we begin to recognize their rights, their sexual rights and their expectations. We must recognize that they have the entire spectrum of adult needs, that they want to and must be encouraged to participate as equals.

X.   stands for experimental. We need experimental programmes. We need innovative programmes that do not cost much, but which have imagination. There are some very beautiful innovations that need to be tried, as in utilizing the arts, plays, literature and the whole area of creativity. We have done a little outreach work here and there, but not nearly enough. The construction of a building for adolescents gives honour to the country, but may accomplish less than small experimental programmes done without fanfare, without trumpets, and without monuments for the youngsters that they don't need.

Y.   stands for youth. Do we want to dominate the adolescents? Do we want to work against them, for them, or with them? Working with them is the only fruitful alternative. This is probably the first generation in history where we adults and adolescents have the opportunity of working together as two generations rather than continuing the intergenerational conflicts of the past. Both generations should seek cooperation not authoritarianism, partnership not patriarchial benignity, dialogue not monologues, self-help not external aid, understanding not deaf ears, and open-mindedness, not unresponsiveness.

Z. is for zip. It is a slang term which suggests zest, a high morale and readiness. We must become front-line soldiers in our communities in the fight to liberate adolescents, and this fight includes their sexual liberation also. It takes a great energy, great fortitude and courage to take this stand. Right now there are a few pioneers who are fighting almost a lone battle on the national level. What is needed is this same spirit in our local communities. When the words, "sex," "adolescence" and "fertility" are mentioned in local discussion there should be leaders who will stand up and be counted. It is a difficult position to stand on a podium and shout aloud to your neighbours: "We need change!" Such persons are accused of all kinds of subtle and not-so-subtle motives.

Professional Implications

1. Our profile of the "keeper" in our study raises the question "Is the wrong woman keeping the child?" On paper, the profile appears to indicate that this teenager comes from a disadvantaged background. One considers what strengths she brings to the role of mother. Her social and psychological profile is one related to unmet needs in her own upbringing, and one has to question her motivations in wanting to keep her baby.

2. What are the "conscious" or "unconscious" reasons for a decision to keep the child? We assume that the pregnancy was not a result of a conscious decision to become a mother, but was a result of her sexual experimentation and sexual intercourse without any prevention. It is sometimes difficult to find out the reasons for "keeping." Do professionals really investigate these reasons?

3. Among professionals there appears a shift from literally forcing teenagers to have their babies adopted in the 1960s, to an acceptance on the part of teenagers to keep the babies. What responsibility do professionals have in setting limits, goals, and protection for the baby and mother? Are we sitting back and not getting involved in the decision making of the keepers? With increasing emphasis on civil and human rights in the 1970s we may have moved away too much from any authority in facing the dilemma of the "keepers."

4. What type of support is offered to the "keepers" after they leave the maternity homes? This support should include child-care help, retraining, education, health education, vocational training, and social supports to make the life of the "keepers" a viable one.

5. At this time we have only a few longitudinal studies which explore the

first three years of motherhood and of the teenage single mother and her child.[8] What happens to the mother and child in all spheres of life? How does the baby manage? How many babies are coming back into care during the 18–24 months period? Are health and welfare agencies monitoring the utilization of services of the single mother and her child?

6. Do we assume that everything is all right with the "adopters" after they relinquish their child? We assume that she, too, requires follow-up services to work out her loss. How much are professionals involved in working with the "adopters" after they have given up their child?

7. What type of preventive programs help teenagers not to become pregnant? What innovative approaches have worked in reducing unwanted pregnancies?

8. What about the "putative father," are we forgetting him in our efforts in working with the teenage mother? We have almost no studies which examine the father. Can we not involve him more in the decison-making[4] aspect of the "keepers" and the "adopters"? If he still has contact with the keeper, why not involve him much more in the total plan for the "keeper" after she leaves the maternity home. We assume that many fathers do care, and want a part to play in the life of the mother and child.

9. Should the maternity homes become multiservice centers to enable us to help, not only the resident, but the nonresident pregnant teenager during the pre-, and postnatal period. These services would include educational, social, parenting help, and mothering skills during the first year of the baby's life.

10. We need more research in depth in examining the "keepers" and the "adopters," including longitudinal studies which would examine the lives of teenage single mothers and their children.

CONCLUSIONS

During a session at the American Orthopsychiatric Association Annual Meeting in Toronto, Canada, April 7–11, 1980, the topic was the plight of the adolescent mother.

Some of the issues which emerged were:

1. Adolescent teenage single mothers have inconsistent, unpredictable behavior.
2. Many flee into pregnancies because their lives are hectic, and difficult ones.
3. When the baby becomes a toddler, many problems arise at that time for the teenage mother.
4. Many "keepers" are troubled teenagers.

5. Many "keepers" are poor teenagers who are dependent on welfare for their day-to-day existence.
6. We need imaginative programs to help the "keepers."

The meeting at Ortho felt that the cycle of deprivation does not start with the pregnant teenager, but started in her own life cycle, as she grew up in a deprived family. Can we, as professionals, break this cycle by our intervention in order to help both the single teenage mother and her child into a different life-style than she experienced in the past?

The findings of studies in many ways constitute a challenge to both public and private health and welfare agencies. Clearly, these mothers are in need not only of social services and adequate financial assistance, but also other community services, including those dealing with health, housing, education, recreation, and religion. It is pretty certain that unless these mothers receive such help, their future and the future of their babies is likely to hold continuing poverty, dependence, and poor opportunity.

The results of these studies have awakened social agencies to the strong and urgent needs of teenage unmarried mothers who are coping with adverse circumstances in raising their children. They have also brought home to the minds of social workers a greater understanding, and an acceptance of the need for social programs to help these mothers alleviate their problems.

It is not unique for social agencies to be conscious that an unwed mother is in a state of crisis. This is true also of the girl's family and of the father of the child, if they are brought into the situation. Locked up in their own emotional involvement, these individuals often find themselves temporarily immobilized and unable to act reasonably in the best interest of all. It is, therefore, the responsibility of the community to help these mothers cope with their problems.

In Metropolitan Toronto, the Children's Aid Societies do provide a range of comprehensive services for unmarried mothers who keep their children—similar to those provided by the Family and Children's Services of London and Middlesex. The agencies have recently placed girls and their new babies together in foster homes for a few weeks after leaving the hospital, in an effort to help the young mother adjust and learn to look after her infant. A few of the maternity homes in Toronto are experimenting with new approaches, such as out-resident services, which include group educational programs, and half-way houses. Self-help groups, like "Parents Without Partners," offer social and recreational opportunities for the single parent, but few unmarried mothers take advantage of them.

The helping professions in Canada working with unmarried mothers have recognized the need for preventive measures in terms of family life and birth-control education. These measures are important. However, in light of the fact that we are unable to eradicate the problem of illegitimacy, we have an obligation to ensure the prevention of unwanted out-of-wedlock pregnancy.

Many of the services now offered to unmarried mothers are fragmented throughout the community. In addition to the community social agency where she may have made her initial request for aid, the unmarried girl may find herself in contact with a number of authorities: The Department of Welfare when seeking financial assistance; a housing authority, should she apply for a public housing project apartment; with hospital clinics and/or private doctors for medical care for herself and the baby; with school officials concerning continuing education; and possibly legal authorities regarding the baby's paternity or support. One recommended solution to the problem is a multiservice facility which would provide, in a single setting, personnel of various professional disciplines who could work together with, or on behalf of, the unmarried mother and where appropriate, the putative father. In addition to medical casework, psychiatric and legal services, an educational program could be offered. Besides regular school courses designed to further the young woman's general education, vocational training, instruction in child care, homemaking and family budget counseling could prepare the woman who intends to keep her child for her new role. It has also been suggested that these mothers be involved in programming on a daily basis similar to the day-care program of many mental-health facilities. Such a multiservice facility would foster close cooperation among the various disciplines concerned with providing total service to the young mother, and would prevent unnecessary duplication. The availability of all these services in one setting might also spur their utilization by young mothers reluctant to initiate the many different contacts now necessary. Finally, the energy and economic resources of both the unwed mother and the community agencies could be conserved.

REFERENCES

1. Children's Aid Society of Metropolitan Toronto. *Study of Single Parents*. Toronto, 1974.
2. Gordon, C. A Project in the Area of Unmarried-Parent Services. Toronto: Children's Aid Society of Metropolitan Toronto, 1972.
3. Grow, L.J. Today's unmarried mothers: The choices have changed. *Child Welfare*, 1979, **58**, 363–371.
4. Mishna, F. and Sinclair, D. *Unmarried Mothers: A Review of the Literature*. Toronto: Faculty of Social Work, University of Toronto, 1978.
5. Poulos, S. *A Problem Inventory of Single Mothers*. Vancouver: Children's Aid Society of Vancouver, 1969.
6. Pozsonyi, J. *A Longitudinal Study of Unmarried Mothers Who Kept Their First Born Children*. London, Ontario: Family and Children's Services of London, and Middlesex, 1973.

7. Schlesinger, B. Community responsibilities. In D.J. Bogue (Ed.) *Adolescent Fertility*. Chicago: Community and Family Study Center, 1977.

8. Schlesinger, B. *The One-Parent Family: Perspectives and Annotated Bibliography*. Toronto: University of Toronto Press, 1978 (4th Ed.).

9. Schlesinger, B. and Storey, A. Unmarried mothers in Ontario: A review and commentary. In B. Schlesinger (Ed.) *One in Ten: The Single Parent in Canada*. Toronto: Faculty of Education, Guidance Centre, University of Toronto, 1979.

10. Statistics Canada. *Vital Statistics: Birth 1977*. Ottawa: 1979, (Catalogue #84204).

11. Youtz, R. *Unmarried Teenagers on Provincial Benefits*. Toronto: Ministry of Community and Social Services, 1975.

17.
Adoptive Placement: Developmental and Psychotherapeutic Issues

Joanne G. Greer, Ph.D., Deputy Chief,
National Center for the Prevention and Control of Rape,
National Institute of Mental Health

Prior to 1970, over 90 percent of unwed teen mothers relinquished their infants. By 1980 over 90 percent were retaining legal custody, although the infant himself might be in the grandmother's care or in paid foster care. The practice of infant adoption has thus become relatively rare. This paper advocates a return to the routine and serious consideration of adoptive placement for the infant when the teenager cannot or will not abort. Issues regarding both maternal and infant welfare which are pertinent to decision making about adoption are discussed. A brief overview of some of the counseling needs of the birthmother (natural mother) of an infant placed for adoption is given. Special preventive mental-health service needs of the adopted child and his adoptive family are briefly noted. In conclusion, the paper notes the almost total lack of federally or privately funded major research studies on adoption, and the evident lack of interest and even understanding regarding adoption among federal policy makers. The position is taken that adoptive placement represents a level of commitment to the infant which is feasible and potentially satisfying for the young girl who cannot bring herself to abort but is not able or willing to mother.

INTRODUCTION

The delivery of the neonate introduces a realignment of priorities in case management for the pregnant adolescent. Prior to the arrival of the newborn infant on the scene, both American law and pluralistic American ethics display ambivalence about the reality of the infant's personhood. Consequently, the welfare of the mother, who is unequivocally a person, takes precedence over the welfare of the gestating fetus, whose personhood is disputed by many members of the reference group society. In times past, this attainment of personhood was sometimes delayed even into the neonate stage, and societies which thought in this fashion permitted infanticide of the neonate, if, for example, he or she were defective or of an undesired sex. In present-day

386

U.S. society, in spite of its extreme pluralism of ethical, religious, and philosophical belief, death wishes toward the neonate are restricted to passive expressions, such as withholding of life-support systems, and the neonate capable of survival without technological interventions is acknowledged to have the full rights of a person.

If, then, in spite of the relative undesirability or inconvenience of the event, two persons of equal dignity now exist, it follows that neither can be exploited for the welfare of the other. This principle is extremely important in formulating suggested plans for the mother and child. The birthmother must not be shamed or pressured into building her future around the consequences of an accidental or forced sexual encounter, or even of a nonviable relationship. The child must not be treated as an incidental piece of property to be disposed of routinely, even into a blatantly threatening environment. In certain cases, these principles will lead to the conclusion that adoptive placement of the infant is the least harmful arrangement for one or both members of the birth dyad.

THE NEEDS OF THE BIRTHMOTHER

Young unmarried girls, like adult women, get pregnant as a result of any of a number of diverse factors. Deliberate action, failure of contraceptive routine, lack of contraceptive services, alcohol or drug use, "acquaintance rape" while parked in the local lover's lane, physiological ignorance, are just examples of the many nonpsychopathological, nonsocioeconomically related factors which may result in teen pregnancy. Public health researchers have paid most attention to the problems of the girl who is sexually at risk due to a dangerous, neglectful, or impoverished environment, or due to lack of sex education or contraceptive services. Mental-health theorists, on the other hand, have been fascinated with the psychopathological elements sometimes implicit in early pregnancy: (1) the daughter's possible "acting out" of her mother's promiscuous urges; (2) the expression of ownership of the body by its defiant use against parental norms; (3) testing the adolescent body's sexual potency; or (4) the creation of a baby as a transitional object to ease the process of separation from mother in late adolescence.

If young girls get pregnant for such varied reasons (and the above list makes no claim to be complete), then it makes little sense to have one case management strategy for all teen pregnancies. Yet another piece of data opposing uniform management is found in subcultural variations. Prior to the new sexual morality of the 1970s, adoptive placement of the white infant was usually demanded by the grandparents. The black culture has traditionally been more accepting of the illegitimate child, but this value was little understood and even criticized by nonblacks. It is probable that the current reluctance of human services workers to recommend adoption is partly based in a distaste for both the past coercion of white girls and the past devaluation of the culture of black girls. The significance of an unwed pregnancy in the Hispanic family, currently the other large U.S. subpopulation, has not received sufficient study by public health or mental health planners. The knowledge necessary to design appropriate services for Hispanics is simply not generally available at this time. One must also keep in mind that subcultural behaviors and values change over time, particularly when several subcultures mingle rather freely. For example, in a Michigan study, Raye H. Rosen (1975) found that pregnant black teens who sought their mother's counsel were most likely to abort, while black girls who did not were likely to keep and rear the infant. Obviously the mothers were giving advice contrary to the traditional black view of abortion as genocide. Similarly, middle-class blacks with sickle-cell trait are starting to use legal adoption of healthy black infants to have a family, rather than taking a chance with natural parenthood. This obviously opens up options for black unwed mothers and their infants not previously available.

The girl in advanced pregnancy (i.e., too late to consider abortion), comes to the human services worker with a unique story of conception, a unique heredity and environment, a unique subculture, and a unique set of physical, mental, and emotional qualities. What does she need? Obviously her needs will also be unique in their particulars, but we can indulge in a few generalities: (1) She needs physical health care, a safe delivery, and postpartum services; (2) she needs a solution for future economic and emotional care for the infant; and (3) she needs to preserve or reestablish progressive developmental trends in her own adolescent life: career preparation and emotional maturation.

In most, although not all, counties in the U.S., medical service and delivery are available at no fee, through public-health clinics, for teen mothers, who are officially high-risk mothers due to their age. Under Title V of the Social Security Act, all high-risk pregnancies can receive free care, free delivery, and free medical care for the infant up to age 12 months. However, the federal funds appropriated are totally inadequate, and the individual states and counties actually administer the program, with varying degrees of conscientiousness and varying supplements of state and local funds. Alternately, the middle-class girl or the girl with good quality state Medicaid coverage will also have access to private care.

The economic future of the girl who keeps her infant, or the infant who is kept, is rather grim. Eight out of 10 women who assumed a mother's role at age 17 or younger have never finished high school. Seventy percent get pregnant again within two years. Women whose first birth is in the teen years are much less likely to ever work and much more likely to be on welfare. Obviously the birth represents either an acute disorganizing influence or, alternatively, a full-blown symptom of latent personal disorganization already present. Humanitarians state that such statistics are not necessary, and, given proper support services, need not occur. Comprehensive support programs are reported elsewhere in this volume, and certainly they do make a difference in many cases. But some girls cannot reach such a program, while a minority of those enrolled do not profit from programs. Realistically, even successfully utilizing a good mother-infant support program is still a life far different from that of a 12 to 17-year-old nonmother. Career goals are lowered, and the girl faces essentially the same life as a young widow 10 years her senior, but with less education and no job skills, while having on the average far fewer economic or emotional resources. Few birthfathers acknowledge the baby and visit it, fewer still will establish a common household or contribute to child support. Indeed, where the birthfather himself is 14 to 17, advocating an attempt at support seems ludicrous. Cohabitation arrangements are notoriously unstable, and the ultimate rupture is deeply hurtful to all three persons. In some states it is even counterproductive, making mother and baby ineligible for welfare or other free services.

It appears clear that becoming a mother at age 12 to 17 is seldom an asset. One purpose of this chapter is to point this out, and to point out the obligation to counsel the teen primipara about her risks and her options. To many counselors and parents abortion is a welcome option for the high-risk teen pregnancy, negating at least on the surface a jarring unwelcome event. But, if one judges by actions rather than verbiage, this option is clearly repellent to many pregnant teens, because, in point of fact, approximately half of them do not seek it.

The greatest need of the perhaps defiant birthmother is for help in identifying her own needs, which are then accepted with respect by a counselor who searches for options to fulfill those needs. Few responsible adults would consider a junior high or high-school girl an optimal mother, at least in a society as complex and stressful as ours. Logically, for the girl under 18, the burden of proof should be put on the decision to keep, not on the decision to place for adoption (or the decision to abort if possible). The girl must be helped to assess her own values, ambitions, resources, and current competencies for mothering in a realistic way. Particularly to be emphasized is the fact that mothering must start when the infant is born, that he cannot wait for her to grow up. Love is not enough; a girl may love deeply the infant she relinquishes.

The circumstances of the very young pregnant adolescent who relinquishes her infant touch on deep human taboos: sexual violation of a person the adult perceives as a child, sexual and maternal drives in the (perceived) innocent, and the abandonment of infants by the females who bear them. It is little

wonder that such work is stressful even to seemingly sophisticated professionals. To women counselors, the idea of "abandoning" an infant is so highly
emotional, often so repugnant, that a subtle communication of values will
take place unless guarded against. What the adult counselor would do is not
necessarily what the client should do. The counselor also fears the crisis of
anger and blame which may well surface in the girl who relinquishes her baby
as she painfully assimilates her loss. On the other hand, the natural charm of
the infant and the initial fun of being grown up may serve to modulate the
depression of a partially unwilling mother, making her much easier to manage
in the short run. Unfortunately, for many immature girls the delights of playing dolls with a real live baby wear thin, usually around the toddling stage,
and the marginally adequate caregiver may become a child abuser, or in extreme cases a murderess. It is the task of the helper (1) to promote realistic
assessment of the willingness and ability to accept an 18-year commitment to
support and mother the child, and (2) to promote in the client the cognitive
and emotional maturity and the flexibility to face painful decisions and carry
them out.

ADOPTION COUNSELING BEFORE THE BIRTH

Statistically, the one-parent home is at a disadvantage in child rearing. In a
1979 survey done for the Charles F. Kettering Foundation by the National
Association of Elementary School Principals, 18,244 school children, grades
1–12, were studied. Even though only 18 percent came from one-parent families, the ratio for dropouts was nine to five, for expulsions was eight to one,
and the ratio for disciplinary actions was three to two, all to the disfavor of
the one-parent child. Turnbull (1980) among others, states that he has found
male-identity problems in boys reared by mothers only.

It is difficult for the unwed teen mother to establish a relationship with a
male willing to marry her and function as a permanent father figure for her
child. Not surprisingly, these girls have a high rate of repeated unwed pregnancies. In a society where the double standard is still alive and well, it is
difficult to refuse the current lover the free gifts of intercourse and paternity
which were obviously enjoyed by his past rival. The young woman who does
succeed in acquiring a husband may find her child a stumbling block to the
new relationship. The child, whether male or female, acquires a somewhat
higher probability of rape, seduction, or child abuse than in the female-headed
household of any socioeconomic class.

The probability of the birth of a "special" child, borderline retarded, developmentally disabled, or physically impaired, must be at least alluded to. The
probabilities of such births are much higher for unmarried adolescents, due to
their physical immaturity, poor observance of prescribed regimens, and high

level of emotional stress. An infant with a very low Apgar score or with birth defects may be a contraindication for retention of custody by a very young mother. Such an infant will require a specially mature dedication in his caregiver, and demands greater financial and personal sacrifices than a healthy infant. Many of these infants are adoptable, and in an increasing number of states the adoptive parents receive special casework or medical subsidies.

None of this discussion is meant to imply that girls should be forced to relinquish their infants as girls were in the past. But the adolescent mother is immature and inexperienced, unknowledgeable regarding the sorrows and burdens of adult life. She probably overvalues the freedom of legal emancipation and instant adulthood and the romance of the mother-infant dyad. Her choice cannot be informed if she is not made aware of the reality-based limits of the freedom ahead, and the unreality of the media presentations of motherhood. If she is going to falter on the long road ahead, it is only fair to her and to the infant to discourage her from trying, at least for the present. Adoptive placement will be better for both.

The type of counseling which is being advocated here cannot be carried on in a 5-minute addition to obstetrical visits, or in 45 minutes by the hospital bed. What is needed is a developmentally oriented counselor who is frequently and dependably available throughout the pregnancy in a structured setting such as a special school program or the old-fashioned maternity residence. Currently such counseling programs are not widely available, particularly outside of large urban areas. Moreover, some of the available school programs assume the girl will keep her baby, and orient the program to child care training and job training, not to decision making. The possibility of relinquishment may not be thoroughly discussed, or treated with sympathy, in such a milieu.

SHORT-TERM NEEDS OF THE INFANT

Parenting competently has two components: the ability and the will to perform. Bromwich and Parmalee (1979) distinguished these two components carefully in a controlled experimental study of parenting of premature infants, and their observations on an infant-parent dyad who failed to profit from high quality, intensive parent training seem relevant:

. . . the infant was not given a high priority by his immature teenage mother who found it difficult to cope with day-to-day decisions about her own life and seemed to possess very little confidence in herself in the parenting role. When this young mother, quite fond of her little boy, found herself in the (test) situation in which she had no reasonable alternative to spending ten minutes with him, she showed herself capable of very positive interaction and both parent and infant evidenced mutual pleasure in their interaction with each other. However, in the home (according to all observations) this same mother left her child largely to his own devices.

In addition to immaturity the teen mother may suffer from clinical depression. An infant with a chronically depressed, inattentive mother will have suffered severe damage before 12 months of age. Current work with "nonorganic failure-to-thrive" infants demonstrates clearly that the infant can sink into a depression so deep he/she refuses to eat or chew food, precipitating life-threatening weight loss. Intervention strategies are sometimes, but not always, successful. As in any other mental-health intervention, some persons have enough hope, trust, and flexibility left to be accessible to helpers, while others do not. Other teens may be incapable of altruistic involvement with a helpless infant because their own needs for nurturing have never been adequately met. Young women with childhoods of physical abuse or neglect do not always make poor mothers; sometimes they are determined to give their baby all the love and opportunities they missed. Others seem caught up in a phenomenom Fraiberg (1980) terms "Ghosts in the Nursery": the parent seems determined to repeat the tragedy of her own childhood suffering with her baby, who becomes a silent actor in a reenactment of the past.

A baby cannot wait "on hold" while his child-mother grows up. No baby can wait until the successful therapy of his mother's mental-health problems is completed. The helper must assess the availability of the new mother or the mother-to-be to the baby. If her availability is deficient, then her accessibility to rapid intervention must be assessed. The baby inevitably represents a sort of rebirth of the self, and may become a new focal point for old conflicts. If those conflicts are available to therapeutic intervention to the extent that they will not interfere radically with mothering, then bonding may occur. On the other hand, if the young mother views the baby in a magical way, and has no grasp of good parenting as giving to the infant rather than using the infant, the future bodes no good. Social workers, psychologists, medical personnel, and program administrators must jointly face up to this responsibility, and not hide behind the letter of the law in avoiding active advocacy for the neonate.

Current legal procedures for removing infants from even a physically dangerous environment are clearly inadequate. Every large city newspaper carries several news items each year on the deaths of physically abused infants who were previously known to the local child protection services. It is even more impossible to quickly remove an infant suffering emotional neglect. When finally removed or abandoned, it will be placed, not in a permanent adoptive home, but in a temporary foster home. Perhaps mother will return someday, perhaps not. Perhaps the foster mother will offer long-term love and security, but most foster children are not so lucky, and stay at an average of six foster homes. The baby cannot tell us of its fate for many years.

Sorosky, Baran, and Pannor (1978) interviewed both the birthmother and the grown son from a dyad that stayed together off and on for 6 years prior to final adoptive placement. The unwed mother meant well and loved her son, but was unaware of the minimally necessary conditions for his emotional security and normal development:

> . . . the father abandoning me when I was six months pregnant . . . I was . . . for the first nine months on welfare. I felt I had to place him in foster care for a while . . . When Tim was four I married, just to have security and keep Tim with me. The marriage was a disaster, and we separated and divorced when Tim was five. That time, placing Tim in a foster home was most difficult. He kept asking why, why? . . . . When he was six years old I finally gave up and signed the papers to place him for adoption.

The authors also present Tim's memories of the same events: "I don't know how far my memories go back, but my mother is in the picture, leaving me, over and over again. I am scared and crying, and I don't understand what to do to be good enough for her to let me stay." Unfortunately Tim also had a poor adoptive placement, with an elderly, rigid couple. He stated, "I have had one lousy deal from beginning to end." (Sorosky et al., 1978)

Case histories such as Tim's should convince any person of common sense that an infant needs a permanent caregiver from the very beginning. Scholarly research reaches the same conclusion. In his classic works, *Attachment and Loss*, and *Separation, Anxiety, and Anger*, John Bowlby (1969, 1973) describes research studies on the paramount significance of a reliable "attachment figure" to the young child. Appropriate response by the attachment figure has two components in Bowlby's terminology: accessibility and appropriate response. Only when the attachment figure is both physically accessible *and* can be counted on for an appropriate response at the child's approach can that person be said to be actually available to the child. Bowlby's data from extensive child observation maintained his hypothesis that the child who lacks an attachment figure who consistently responds in a supportive and protective way will grow up to see the world as comfortless and unpredictable, and "will respond either by shrinking from it or by doing battle with it." (Bowlby, 1973)

State or federal programs can supply teen mothers with medical care, support checks, public housing, and special education programs. They can supply medical intervention for the infant. But they cannot supply the magic that makes a mother able to be a reliable attachment figure to an infant, nor, operationally, do they seem to see the infant's emotional well-being as their responsibility. In many ways the U.S. law still treats children as property, and often there is no legal way to fend off disaster from an infant. But for the human services worker, lacking legal resources which undeniably would make the job easier, there still remains the ethical obligation to utilize ingenuity and persuasiveness to make the best possible arrangement for the infant.

THE NEEDS AND STRENGTHS OF THE ADOPTIVE COUPLE

In adoption planning it is a fact of life that both the birthparents and the prospective adoptive parents have been traumatized by prior life events, and this will almost certainly affect their parenting. The birthmother, and perhaps the future stepfather, may feel extreme ambivalence toward an unplanned or unwanted child from a teen pregnancy. At the other extreme, the adoptive parent is prone to overprotect and overidealize the child because he fills an aching void in the parent's personal history. The child's natural psychological function as a potential embodiment of the parent's ego ideal and an object for the parent's generative impulses can be heightened and intensified by the pain of the long wait for his arrival. A feeling of unreality surrounds the first weeks after receiving the infant, and the adoptive mother may visit the crib over and over again to convince herself that the sleeping baby is really there.

The adoptive parents naturally have a rather high level of anxiety. After all, they have waited a number of years for their baby, and they regard him as their only chance at parenthood. No parent will be careless with the safety of the child just because another pregnancy is possible, but the adoptive parent is certain that pregnancy, or even another adoption, is probably not possible. Consequently there may be a rather excessive preoccupation with the health and safety of the baby until the parents settle down.

It is safe to say that a family formed around an unplanned child, whether a genetic family or an adoptive family, is a high-risk family, and could likely profit from at least intermittent social and psychological services. Child-guidance clinics, parent training, special home-school liaison, and other like services are very helpful but seldom available. These services are expensive, and public-agency budget analysts find it harder to justify preventive mental-health services than treatment services or incarceration for youngsters in trouble. In studies done in the 1960s, adopted youngsters made up about 30 percent of psychiatric clinic child clients, although they were only about 2 percent of the child population. However, the author is not aware of any diagnostic data on these children and the nature of their distress. Undoubtedly the integration of the disclosure of adoptive status is traumatic to at least some adoptees, and can be made more traumatic by poor timing of disclosure. However, any statistically valid comparison of treatment encounters for adopted and nonadopted children would have to be controlled for prenatal conditions (usually far less than optimal in unwed mothers), average higher income of adopting couples, and average higher education of adopting couples. These latter two factors, along with a natural hypersensitivity about their performance as parents, would most likely lead adoptive couples to seek therapeutic services more freely than the average parents. Further, the adoptive couple has already interacted with various human-services professionals during the adoptive process, and if the experience was good will be more prone to seek such help again, according to classic consumer behavior theroies. In addition, although it is known that the adopting couple have their own adjustments to make to instant parenthood, little or no help is available to them to deal with their fears, lack of confidence, or other such problems. The only socially acceptable strategy for most parents is to seek guidance for themselves by using the child as an index patient.

Placement studies of adoptive couples have become much more sophisticated and selective in recent years. Until the easy availability of abortion, there were more relinquished babies than there were adoptive families, but currently there are many more applicant couples than babies, with most agencies refusing to give third or even second children. The applicant couples are also generally still in the prime parenting years, because infertility diagnosis has become both quicker and more definitive. The common practice of the pre-1950 era, of placing infants with infertile couples in their forties or even fifties, has ended, and couples are routinely rejected for infant placement consideration if either of them will be over 35 at the projected time of placement. The infant benefits from having a family which is structurally indistinguishable from a "natural" family and he/she has parents who are not emotionally traumatized by decades of waiting, hoping, and medical manipulations. The author is aware of one DES daughter who lost her uterus at age 20 and was a happy adoptive mother at age 22. This type of deliberate speed in decision making is important for both infant and parent mental health. The baby who waits too long in foster care may form poor quality attachments. Parents who wait too long for a baby to love may fear to love when the baby comes, or, on the other hand, may smother him with overprotection.

Choice of adoptive parents should take into consideration whether a couple has the potential to offer the child a philosophical, ethical, or religious framework within which he/she can more easily come to accept and understand the birthparents. For example, parents who subscribe to such philosophical concepts as "the brotherhood of men" or "the fatherhood of God" (or their feminist equivalents!) offer the child a form of enduring kinship to both themselves and the absent birthparents. Parents who can maintain a compassionate concern for the birthmother will be able to speak sincerely and respectfully of her hard choices and the reality of her love when the child is old enough to deal with his/her early losses through adoption. Such parents are also less likely to be plagued with unconscious guilt at having taken over another person's child.

Persons who counsel the participants in an existing adoption require special information, if not special training. They must have an understanding of rather complicated legal and psychological issues, and they must have the habit of thinking in family systems, since in effect they are dealing with the welfare of an augmented and segmented family. The birthmother's jealousy, the adoptive mother's guilt, the child's curiosity and insecurity at his unique parentage, are all natural reactions to a rather unusual situation. All participants continue to exist for one another psychologically, even if they have never met. The mental health of all requires that they acknowledge their feelings about one another. It is to be hoped that they can come to appreciate one another's contributions and become reconciled to each other's limitations.

There is an acute need for research on the adoptive process and participants, in order to better select the participants and to better meet their emotional needs. A 1980 computer search of the research grants records of NIMH since 1965 found only 16 funded studies, of which 8 utilized the adoptees as convenience subjects in "heredity versus environment" studies of topics such as schizophrenia. There were two studies on transracial adoption, three on transnational adoption, and two on adoptive parents. There were none on birthmothers or adoptees.

NONTYPICAL ADOPTION PRACTICES

The "typical" adoption consists of placement of a healthy newborn infant directly from the hospital nursery into the care of adoptive parents of the same race and nationality, with the placement controlled by an agency subject to state regulation and national licensing. Genetic parents and adoptive parents are matched to the extent possible on physical appearance, intelligence, social background, religion, and ethnic extraction. If a genetic parent has a particular talent which may be inherited, adoptive parents are sought who share at least the interest if not the actual talent. Because of the usual age gap between the genetic parents and the adoptive parents, matching for educational attainment takes into account the genetic grandparents as well.

White couples who had been unable to adopt white children, and also a minority of whites who wished to make a philosophical statement in their personal lives, adopted black or interracial children with increasing frequency in the early 1970s. This practice came to be opposed by black social workers and psychologists and by other groups advocating preservation and enhancement of black identity for all black children. As a result the practice is now less common. The hoped-for recruitment of black adoptive parents for these children has been only a modest success to date, and consequently many black youngsters are reared in foster care or institutional care, particularly after infancy. It is not clear whether the relative infrequency of formal adoption by blacks is due to lack of economic means or to cultural factors as well. The passage of the Child Welfare Act of 1980 (Public Law 96-272) will be a start toward removing the economic barriers to formal adoption. The Act sets a ceiling on the number of children a state can have in foster care over 24 months, and mandates a timetable of due process to either reunite the child with his/her genetic family, or, failing that, place him/her in adoption, subsidized if necessary. Dependence on foster care as a solution for abandoned children will be discouraged by limitations on foster care matching funds for each state, and by providing federal matching funds for families adopting "special children"; i.e., handicapped, older children, minority children, or sibling groups.

When white American infants became scarce during the 1970s, the adoption of foreign infants was another solution frequently sought by white couples for their childlessness. The practice continues, but the availability of newborns is nil, the children being from 6 to 24 months or even older when they arrive stateside. These children often have multiple, serious health problems, including parasitic infestations and chronic malnourishment, and require the parent to nurse as well as parent until their health is restored. Because of the serious challenges presented to the adoptive parents, the most respected agencies dealing in placement of foreign infants try to discourage parents who seem not to have the personal and financial resources to offer quality care. Financial resources are important because in transnational adoptions the placement itself is costly, and because the child cannot benefit from any tax financed program for seven years after arrival. The parents must pay for legal services in two countries, professional fees to two placement agencies, and at least two international air fares. Further, they must be prepared to hospitalize the child as soon as he/she arrives, at their own personal expense. This may not always be necessary, but it must be prepared for. The fact that these adoptions take place at all will give the reader some insight into the desperate wish for a child on the part of the adoptive parents.

Severely handicapped infants were always considered unadoptable until the last few years, and were placed in institutional or foster care. This was often the case even if the infant were born to a married couple, because the parents were not able to cope with rearing the child. The push for deinstitutionalization has resulted in the establishment of community-based multifaceted support programs for families with severely handicapped infants, and these programs have also made it easier to place a handicapped infant for adoption. Adoptive parents receive casework from the adoption agency and/or the local program for handicapped infants, and they may receive medical subsidies as well. Some programs, such as the New Hope program of the Edna Gladney Maternity Home in Fort Worth, Texas, are even placing infants with severe incurable conditions such as spina bifida. Naturally the selection and social support of such an adoptive couple will be costly, but it will be less costly and more humane than institutionalization.

The practice of "private adoption" by physicians and lawyers historically preceded the establishment of state licensing laws and national accrediting groups for adoption agencies. In the past such physicians and lawyers typically had permanent professional ties with the families involved in the adoption and provided an otherwise unavailable service. In contrast, modern-day private adoption ranges from an attempt to evade current legal protections for infant and birthmother to blatant black marketeering in infants for profit. Users of private adoption tend to be persons who are not acceptable as adoptive parents to licensed adoption agencies, but who have the financial means to purchase a baby at fees ranging up to $25,000. Girls placing their babies through private adoption are exposed to heartless exploitation. They are not counseled regarding their rights to change their original plans and keep the infant after his birth, and in some cases they have been threatened and intimidated if they attempted to renege on the plan after receiving support money. They receive no information about the persons who will have custody of their infant, and no assurances that they will be fit parents. Theoretically, private adoption could be used in some states to stock brothels with child prostitutes, as is done in some Third World countries. For the unwary adoptive parents who seek private adoption, there is no guarantee regarding the infant. They may receive an infant with severe congenital defects, fetal alcohol syndrome, prenatal drug addiction, or other severe unidentified problems. The placement may turn out to be illegal, and the infant may be taken from them either by child protection workers or by legal action of the birthmother. Obviously the only person to profit by private adoption is the person who receives the placement fee. In response to these problems, some states have attempted to regulate private adoption, while others have outlawed it. The practice is a legal anachronism which should be completely banned, with severe penalties for violations.

THE MOURNING PROCESS OF THE BIRTHMOTHER AFTER RELINQUISHMENT

Present-day U.S. society seems to shun the thought that generativity in and of itself is rewarding. The idea that in birthing a woman makes a sublime contribution to the service of the species is considered old-fashioned and even sexist. Giving birth has become a self-focused act, and one which should be avoided unless it is self-aggrandizing. Little wonder that adoptive placement is regarded with horror by many women, and abortion is preferred. One is struck by the reasoning that "a child of mine who cannot live with me can give me no joy, and therefore he cannot and must not exist at all." The girl who chooses to bear a child and place it for adoption is often considered a passive victim of circumstances and social pressure.

If she chooses adoption, the birthmother should be encouraged to think of herself as an active, significant planner in her infant's future, and to feel that they both continue to exist for each other, as indeed they do, from a psychological point of view. Her wishes about the adoptive couple, such as religion or ethnic group, should be respected, and they are one form of the expression of her concern. Obviously the girl who chooses adoption requires sophisticated social and psychotherapeutic services to handle her crisislike emotional tasks surrounding relinquishment and placement. She will also need more leisurely, insight-oriented therapy to deal with themes of loss in the months following separation from the baby.

The teenager pregnant out of wedlock faces the same psychological terrors regarding pregnancy and labor as any other young primipara. It seems too much for her to give up the same comforting expectations: "Soon I shall have a baby of my own; soon I shall be a woman in every sense." If actually keeping the baby is unreasonable or undesirable in the long run, helping figures must be provided to minimize the very real trauma. Sadly, the maternal and child-health clinic or the private obstetrician often regard such a case as closed after the completion of postpartum check-ups. While site-visiting a clinic in a small Southern town, the author was told of a recent client who gave up her newborn infant and returned to high school. She then telephoned her attending midwife every day for six months to talk of the baby. The midwife grew impatient and referred her to the Community Mental Health Center. The CMHC rejected her as a client because she was obviously not mentally ill and the Center's resources were already overcommitted to chronic patients. She was left to work through her loss alone.

The birthmother may feel she should be grateful to the adoptive parents. Actually she has good reason to resent their enjoyment of the infant born out of her months of discomfort and her possibly difficult or even dangerous labor. Acknowledgement of the reasonableness of her ambivalent feelings will facilitate completion of the acute mourning phase. Her counselor's acceptance of her anger at her pain and her difficult choices will reassure her that the feelings will not overwhelm her, that things will get better, that she can live with her decisions.

Currently, it is well understood that advice to forget, without any help to work through the pain of loss, is unwise. In the past, many girls, trying to prove their maturity and avoid causing trouble to family or friends, repressed their sad feelings and even their memories. One birthmother commented: "Suppressing emotions doesn't destroy them. They manifest themselves in many ways, such as unconscious fear of sex, tenseness and uneasiness around children, a vague fear of discovery, guilt." Another woman recalled her anger that no one at the hospital took time to share her pride in her son's health, because they knew he would be placed for adoption. (Silverman, 1978)

The birthmother who decides, either for her own sake or the sake of the child, to relinquish her infant, is as needful and deserving of services as the one who keeps her infant. We are accustomed to offer support to the woman whose infant dies, but her loss is only a little more permanent than the birthmother's. If the birthmother ever sees her child again, he/she will be grown, and the joy of nurturing him/her will have been someone else's. Given the current oversupply of potential adoptive parents, perhaps one selection criterion should be sufficient compassion to maintain voluntary contact with the placement agency. Agency staff can then respond to the birthmother's inquiries and allay her periodic anxiety about her child's development and his safety.

The experience of unwed motherhood and adoptive placement of the infant is a heavy emotional burden for a teen to carry into adulthood and marriage. As a response to this need, in recent years mutual support groups for birthmothers such as CUB (Concerned United Birthparents) have been organized. One role of such groups has been to sensitize professionals to the unwitting callousness in some adoption procedures, and to help humanize them. These groups also provide the birthmother with the helpful counsel of other women who have gone through the same experience. Such relationships help her to work through her grief, which may resurface periodically, for example when she bears another child of the same sex.

DISCLOSURE OF ADOPTION

The decision to tell a loved child that he/she was adopted is a difficult one for parents. However, placement agencies have routinely urged them not to conceal the adoption, and to incorporate it into the child's first sex instruction, around age three to five. This strategy is presented as necessary to avoid the crisis of confidence in the parents which may occur with accidental or malicious disclosure from other sources. This advice is probably based on a statistically small sample of perhaps transiently upset adopted children, or perhaps a sample of truly disturbed adoptees who found the disclosure a confirmation of long perceived misfit. More recently, some mental-health workers who have had occasion to form therapeutic relationships with adoptees have ventured the opinion that disclosure before the end of the latency period is inadvisable and causes significant difficulties vis-à-vis "family romance fantasies" common to this developmental period. Latency-age children commonly fantasize that they are adopted and their "real" parents are different, and better, than their caregivers. The adopted child must deal in reality, with two pairs of parents, the known and the unknown, both "real" in their own way. (Wieder, 1977)

The experience of one adoptive mother of a newborn infant is perhaps relevant. Following the directives of placement workers, she communicated the facts of adoption in an extremely positive light, utilizing the recommended theme of the "chosen baby," when the child reached age three. The introduction of two daddies and two mommies into the story created such cognitive confusion that the net effect was a two-to three-year delay in the grasp of where babies come from. The child was finally able to rephrase the essential message in his own words around age six: "you mean I didn't come out of your body?" His reaction was rage and grief at this breaching of the bond with his only known mother, an experience no six-year-old should have to endure.

For the older child who knows of his adoption, the recent upsurge in TV programs and news stories on the topic of adoption has the effect of constantly nagging the child about his differentness in a public sort of way. Such programs are more likely to be appreciated by the teen adoptee rather than the younger child. On the positive side, they do create opportunities for family discussion of the adoption, and repeated assurances of the love of both mothers. The topic of the birthfather is another potential source of grief for the adopted child, and is difficult to avoid with the sexually knowledgeable child. But, as noted below, the integration of knowledge about the birthfather will also be a problem when the unwed mother retains custody.

Attempting the maintenance of secrecy about the adoption is possible for some affluent and geographically mobile couples. The stresses of such a strategy should not be undertaken lightly. A minimum risk strategy might be to disclose in childhood, but on a slower timetable, doling out both sexual and adoption information so that the full integration of the communication falls in the latter part of the latency period, and is assimilated in the teens, with access to professional help on demand. Parents who are at ease with their decisions and actions, and who plan them carefully, are best able to carry out disclosure in a nontraumatic way. Amazingly, it is the exception rather than the rule for parents to receive professional guidance and support in this task.

In considering the problems of disclosure in adoption, it must not be forgotten that the unwed mother who keeps her child will also have a disclosure problem someday. Only an undesirable vagueness about the past will serve to avoid the issues of chronology and paternity. If indeed they are avoided, the child will be sure to imagine birth circumstances at least as difficult as the reality, based on the mother's evasiveness. The unplanned or unwanted child will suffer narcissistic injury from disclosure in either case. What is needed is (1) an optimal strategy for sharing the information the child is due, and (2) an infancy and childhood experience most likely to produce the strong ego the child needs to withstand personal blows from fate.

It is noteworthy that having been unplanned or unwanted by the mother is a particularly painful experience for a girl. Separation from the birthmother is also more likely to trouble a female than a male adoptee. About 90 percent of adult adoptees who initiate searches for their birthmothers are women.

SEARCHING FOR THE GENETIC PARENT OR CHILD

Current legislation regarding the disclosure of information about past adoptions is in a state of flux. A discussion of these legal issues is beyond the scope of this paper, and is outside the author's area of expertise. In general, it is to be hoped that the final legislation will reflect concern for the emotional and developmental needs of all concerned in addressing whether to disclose, when to disclose, and how to disclose. Protection of the privacy of the birthmother from her adult child, as promised by the placement agency, should be an absolute commitment of society unless she herself waives her right and expresses a wish to be found. Conversely, the birthmother cannot demand the companionship of her adult child, or even knowledge of its whereabouts, against its wishes. A certain number of children are going to react to having been relinquished with permanent alienation; many others will regard the genetic bond as unimportant. Some children die in childhood or adolescence; others may be institutionalized. Both potential seekers must also be sure they are ready to deal with the person they actually find, who may be quite different from the person they fantasized.

The feelings of the adoptive parents are due deep respect and consideration from both the birthmother and the adult child. If the adoption has been successful, consideration for these feelings may be a major factor in the child's willingness or unwillingness to make contact. However, enough reunions have occurred in recent years to demonstrate that the psychological parents of the successful adoptive home maintain their primacy in the typical case. Some genetic relatives may see each other only infrequently once their curiosity and their anxiety about each other have been satisfied. A few adult adoptees have been fortunate enough to find themselves with two extended families accepting both the adult adoptee and each other, in a true fairy-tale ending to the story.

Currently available computer technology makes the creation of a bank of data on searching birthmothers and children for cross-matching quite possible. It is likely that such a service will develop if there is sufficient demand, and if successful it may decrease pressure for legal access to records. Even if records were unsealed, the matching service may still be necessary as well. In our mobile society, an 18-year-old name and address is often useless.

THE BIRTHFATHER

Disclosure to the birthfather has become a legal and ethical issue since the mid-1970s. In a few landmark legal cases, a rejected suitor succeeded in stopping the adoption of an infant he had fathered, and ultimately obtained custody. One can certainly feel sympathy for a young man in this position. However, the welfare of the infant still has first priority. If there is a good chance that the birthfather will persevere and win custody, the baby would be best served by being given into his temporary custody immediately, contingent on his presenting a reasonable care plan. Placement in foster care during prolonged legal battling results in presenting a one- or two-year-old child to strangers as he screams with anguish for his foster mother. For such a child, his real psychological mother dies. He never sees her again, and he never knows why he was abandoned and given away. Unfortunately he cannot read the documents which say that the court, at long last, has decided that he belongs to these other caregivers instead. Such behavior by the courts appeared reasonable in past decades, when it was believed that the infant's needs were mostly physical. With the burgeoning of infant research since Anna Freud's pioneering work during World War II, we now know better. The sine qua non of infancy is a stable one-to-one relationship.

The Model State Adoption Act designed during 1979 by the Health Care Financing Administration evoked rage from advocates for infants and unwed mothers precisely because it treated the infant like a parcel left at the post office, a piece of property whose ownership was temporarily in doubt. The law allows a generous time period for the birthfather to be notified of the birth and to prevent adoption while he considers applying for custody. During this period the infant is placed in temporary foster care. No placement could be made until after the period of the first months of life, during which vital capacities for relating begin to develop in close interaction with the caregiver. The infant is left without an object on which to exercise his genetic predilection for permanent bonding; fed, sheltered, diapered, but unloved. Meanwhile the birthmother's former sex partner can meet her again in court, with no consideration for her reasons for avoiding voluntary contact with him. Critics of the Act noted that even a rapist had a right to claim "his" baby. The act also condones and even encourages private adoption, with its possibilities for baby-selling and placement with unfit adoptive parents. Thus, hypothetically, the birthmother could ask to place the infant through a licensed agency, and the birthfather could hold out for a profit-making placement.[1]

Clearly there can be circumstances in which the birthfather is due consideration, but they should bear some reasonable relationship to the circumstances of the conception, the continuing voluntary relationship between the birthparents, and his willingness to support mother and child together if the mother wishes. The real agenda of the federal agency proposing this bill to

[1]In response to an onslaught of criticism from birthmothers, adoptive parents, infant advocates, and placement workers, Congress on May 19, 1981 rejected the "Model Act" and ordered further study of the issues for an 18 month period.

the states was to free the time of state adoption caseworkers from infant casework, so that they could work on placement of abandoned school-aged children, thus relieving state and federal governments of their foster-care support. Ironically, much of the placement of infants is, or can be, subsidized by fees paid by the adoptive parents, except where the placement is of a nature to place continuing financial hardship on the adoptive family. This piece of legislation is a good example of what happens when legal and financial experts who are ignorant of psychological issues assume the lead in planning programs for children. No research on adoption options and their relative success was carried out, and the relevance of general research on infant development was ignored, as was the issue of the birthmother's psychological need for privacy. Under this act she would be forced to keep custody, even if she did not want it, unless she were willing to enter into negotiation with the birthfather and to face the possibility that he, and not an adoptive couple, would receive her child. Her only other option would be to declare from the beginning that she had been so promiscuous that she had no idea who the father was.

SOME CONCLUDING REMARKS

In a presentation before the 1980 national meeting of the American Orthopsychiatric Association, Benjamin Schlesinger presented data from a study of about 800 teen mothers, in which he found that the unwed mothers who kept their babies were more likely to come from a broken home, to have left the parental home, to live in public housing, to have had a serious physical illness, to have a psychiatric history, and to be younger, when compared to girls who relinquished their babies for adoption. He concluded that the wrong girls were making use of the option of keeping the infant, i.e., the girls who were least likely to be adequate mothers. He concluded by stating that the unwillingness to promote the idea of adoption to such teen mothers constitutes an abandonment of a sense of responsibility on the part of professionals. The author of this paper most heartily concurs with this opinion.

It is true that the past decade of developments in policy, law, and social work practice with regard to teen mothers and their infants constitutes one of the largest and most poorly controlled experiments ever performed on human beings. When these infants are grown up, when their mothers are middle-aged, then the policy makers will know whether they have brought about a miracle of human liberation or a disaster of human suffering. More than likely it will be some of both, while there will be still other participants in the experiment who would have fared about the same under any arrangement. It is hoped that the realization will grow that the system is dealing with individuals, who have individual strengths and weaknesses, and individual needs. The author strongly believes that the best service delivery system will be one that offers the girl and her infant the widest range of options to benefit both of them. The social costs of bearing and rearing infants as a teen mother are high for the girl, for the infant, for the grandparents, and for the girl's adult marriage and career potential. In addition, the majority of teen mothers and their infants make use of welfare and Medicaid, often for many years. Some girls ultimately place their child in tax supported foster care, while retaining custody until the child's emotional and developmental problems make it unadoptable. Thus, the program costs to the state and federal taxpayer for teen motherhood are major and are constantly growing, taking funding from other needed projects.

In light of all these considerations, it is time for service delivery researchers, policy makers, and program planners to make a serious reassessment of the possibility of facilitating and promoting the option of adoptive placement for the infants of teen unwed mothers.

CITED AND RECOMMENDED READINGS

Bedger, Jean E., Buben, Judith N., Hughes, Margaret, et al. *Child Abuse and Neglect: An Exploratory Study of Factors Related to the Mistreatment of Children.* Chicago, Illinois: Council for Community Services, 1976.

Blehar, Mary. *Development of Mental Health in Infancy.* Washington, D.C.: National Institute of Mental Health. DHHS Publication No. (ADM) 80-962.

Bohman, Michael. *Adopted Children and Their Families: A Follow-up Study of Adopted Children, Their Background, Environment, and Adjustment.* Stockholm, Sweden: Proprius, 1970.

Bowlby, John. *Attachment and Loss.* New York: Basic Books, 1969.

Bowlby, John. *Separation, Anxiety, and Anger.* New York: Basic Books, 1973.

Bromwich, Rose M. and Parmelee, Arthur H. "An Intervention Program for Pre-term Infants." *Infants Born at Risk.* Jamaica, New York: Spectrum Publications, 1979.

Deutsch, Helene. *The Psychology of Women: A Psychoanalytic Interpretation Volume Two: Motherhood.* New York: Grune and Stratton, 1945.

Chilman, Catherine S. *Adolescent Sexuality in a Changing American Society: Social and Psychological Perspectives.* Washington, D.C.: U.S. Government Printing Office #017-046-00050-1 (1979).

Elmer, Elizabeth. "Studies of Child Abuse and Infant Accidents" in *Mental Health Program Reports*—5, J. Segal (Ed.), Washington: Department of Health, Education, and Welfare # HSM 72-9042 (1971). pp. 58–85.

Fertility and Contraception in America: Adolescent and Pre-Adolescent Pregnancy: Hearings Before the Select Committee on Population, Ninety-fifth Congress, February 28–March 2, 1978, Volume II. Washington: U.S. Government Printing Office (1978).

Fraiberg, Selma. *Clinical Studies in Infant Mental Health: The First Year of Life.* New York: Basic Books, 1980.

Friedman, Alfred S., et al. *Therapy with Families of Sexually Acting-Out Girls*. New York: Springer Publishing Company (1971).

Jaffee, Benson and Fanshel, David. *How They Fared in Adoption: A Follow-up Study*. New York: Columbia University Press, 1970.

Rosen, Raye H. "Adolescent Pregnancy Decision Making: Are Parents Important?" *Adolescence*, 1980, **15**, 43–54.

Silverman, Phyllis S. *Living as a Birthparent: When You Have Lost a Child Through Adoption*. Cambridge, Mass.: American Institutes for Research in the Social Sciences, 1978.

Sorosky, Arthur D., Baran, Annette, and Pannor, Reuben. *The Adoption Triangle: The Effects of the Sealed Record on Adoptees, Birthparents, and Adoptive Parents*. Garden City, New York: Anchor Press/Doubleday, 1978.

Tancredi, L.R. "Child Abuse." *Legal Issues in Psychiatric Care*. New York: Harper & Row, 1975.

Turnbull, Jame M. "Masculinity of Father-Absent Boys." *Medical Aspects of Human Sexuality*, 1980, **14**, 149–163.

Williams, Gertrude J. and Money, John. *Traumatic Abuse and Neglect of Children at Home*. Baltimore Md.: Johns Hopkins University Press, 1980.

Wieder, Herbert. "The Family Romance Fantasies of Adopted Children." *The Psychoanalytic Quarterly*, 1977, **46**, 185–200.

Wieder, Herbert. "On Being Told of Adoption." *The Psychoanalytic Quarterly*, 1977, **46**, 1–22.

Winnicott, D.W. "A Clinical Study of the Effect of a Failure of the Average Expectable Environment on a Child's Mental Functioning." *The International Journal of Psycho-Analysis*, 1965, **46**, 81–88.

18.
Adolescent Girls as Mothers: Problems in Parenting

*Babette R. Bierman, M.S.W., L.C.S.W.,
Clinical Psychiatric Social Worker,
The Johns Hopkins Center for Teen-Aged
Parents and Their Infants;

**Rosalie Streett, B.S.
Education Director,
The Johns Hopkins Center for Teen-Aged
Parents and Their Infants

This chapter addresses how becoming a mother while still an adolescent* affects both the teenaged girl and her child. Clinical impressions, observations, and conversations with hundreds of young women who are enrolled in The Johns Hopkins Center for Teen-Aged Parents and Their Infants form the bases for this discussion. Although the problem of early childbearing and child rearing has serious implications for society, both in humanitarian and economic terms, this chapter devotes itself only to how teen pregnancy and parenting impacts upon the adolescents, their babies, and the professionals who interact with them.

The basic conflict between being a parent and being an adolescent is examined, beginning with the pregnancy and spanning the course of the first three years of the child's life. Problem areas, such as denial, feeding, language development, limit-setting, play, and medical care are highlighted. Recommendations are made for effective intervention programming. Both theoretical discussion and case vignettes are employed to illustrate the young women's adolescent development and the difficulties encountered in accomplishing developmental tasks when faced with the added burden of parenthood.

Adolescence has long been ignored by our society but today we acknowledge adolescence as one of the more significant stages of development. This period

This chapter was supported by grants from The Educational Foundation of America and the Health Care Financing Agency, #11-P-90513/3-03.

*We limit the term adolescent pregnancy to those pregnant at age 17 years or below.

407

is characterized by physical, sexual, social, ideological, and vocational adjustments, and of striving for independence from parents in the search for identity. In order to pass successfully through this developmental phase, the teenager must devote herself to the tasks of gaining control over her impulses—both sexual and aggressive, separating from her parents, finding a new love object, and working toward appropriate educational and vocational goals.[7,8,15,16,18] The achievement of these tasks takes enormous psychic energy and a singleness of purpose almost fanatical in nature. Perhaps Anna Freud[13] most succinctly described the characteristics of this age when she wrote:

"Adolescence is by its nature an interruption of peaceful growth; the upholding of a steady equilibrium during the adolescent period is in itself abnormal. It is normal for an adolescent to behave for a considerable length of time in an inconsistent and unpredictable manner, to fight his impulses and to accept them, to ward them off successfully and to be over-run by them; to love his parents and to hate them, to revolt against them and to be dependent on them; to be deeply ashamed to acknowledge his mother before others and, unexpectedly, to desire heart to heart talks with her; to thrive on imitation of and identification with others while searching unceasingly for his own identity; to be more idealistic, artistic, generous and unselfish than he will ever be again, but also the opposite; self-centered, egotistic, calculating.

Freud[13] further refers to the multitude of feelings present at different times and in different degrees. She speaks of the adolescent's inability to bear frustration, especially in feelings of love-hate. She discusses the adolescent's experience of isolating words from affect, her narcissistic withdrawal, tendency for projection, intermittent feelings of hopelessness, acting-out tendencies, and lack of insight. She also notes that adolescents may change rapidly from one of these emotional positions to the next, exhibit all simultaneously, or in quick succession.

This chapter will address how becoming a mother during this developmental process affects both the teenage girl and her child. Our clinical impressions, observations, and conversations with the hundreds of young women who have enrolled in The Johns Hopkins Center for Teen-Aged Parents and Their Infants since 1976 will form the bases for the discussions.* Although adolescent pregnancy and parenthood have serious implications for society,

---

*The Hopkins Center is a facility which enrolls young women who are 17 years or less at the time of their pregnancy. Most of the girls in the program are inner-city residents, the majority of whom are black. The teenager is eligible to remain in the program until her child's third birthday. While attending the Center, she receives comprehensive services—her child's and her own primary medical care, social-work services, educational intervention, psychological services, and family planning.

both in humanitarian and economic terms,[21] this chapter will devote itself only to how teen pregnancy and parenting impact upon the adolescents, their babies, and the professionals who interact with them.[25]

Being a parent and being an adolescent are two roles that are in basic conflict. Pregnancy and parenting, considered functions of adults, thrust the youngster abruptly from her current stage of adolescent development into a new, adult role. All too frequently, from the moment she becomes pregnant, her actions are judged differently. One now looks for adult behavior and begins to view her during her pregnancy, delivery, and forever after as a parent, but no longer as an adolescent. She is expected no longer to put her own needs first, nor may she behave impulsively and irresponsibly anymore. Because she has committed an adult act, says society, she must now carry the full burden of adulthood. Unfortunately, this is rarely the case. These young people continue to behave as teenagers who happen to have babies. Their developmental tasks still must be fulfilled and the problems associated with them addressed. In fact, the problems are often exacerbated by the pregnancy and subsequent birth of the baby.[18]

CASE ILLUSTRATION

The following case illustrates the basic conflict between adolescence and parenthood. Andrea was so successful as an adolescent that she was unsuccessful as a parent. Now a bright, ebullient college sophomore, she gave birth to her son Allen 2 years ago when she was 17 and in the middle of her senior year in high school. At the time of Allen's birth she was member of several after-school clubs, listed in *Who's Who Among American High School Students*, and an honor student bound for college. Her parents are married and employed. She has several siblings both older and younger than herself.

The baby's father, Martin, was 19 years old when the child was born, and already enrolled in his sophomore year in college. Andrea and Martin had been dating for 2 years prior to her pregnancy, and had been engaging in sexual intercourse with sporadic use of condoms for several months before Andrea became pregnant. Neither teen-ager wanted a child at that time, but when Andrea discovered that she was pregnant, both decided against abortion or adoption. They felt they could cope with child rearing without too much difficulty and planned to rely heavily on both sets of grandparents, although all were working.

After Allen's birth, Andrea sought family day care for him while she went to school. She was a loving, stimulating parent for the first few months of Allen's life. She spoke of some feelings of resentment at not being able to go to an out-of-state college, but quickly amended her statement, claiming that her baby was more important and it really didn't matter anyway.

As the months went by, Allen became increasingly mobile and demanding.

Some of Andrea's friends were preparing to leave for college, and the reality of being a parent and the resultant limitations of the role, became painfully apparent to the young woman. She manifested her frustration and disappointment by becoming angry with her son when he "made too much noise," threw things, made a mess, or got into her possessions. She began to slap his hands frequently and displayed an almost indifferent attitude toward him. As Allen's verbalizations decreased, his temper tantrums increased. The mother's anger towards her baby was now apparent even to herself.

Andrea viewed any attempts by clinic staff at reflection, or discussion of her behavior, as intrusions into her heavily defended position and resisted all intervention. She continued to take excellent physical care of her son, but much of the joy was going.

Shortly after Andrea began her first semester in a local junior college, she terminated her relationship with the baby's father, enlarged her circle of friends, and involved herself even more fully in a rich social life. She found her classes difficult but stimulating and her son difficult and unstimulating. Andrea allowed more and more of Allen's care to fall to her mother and siblings and she began arriving at Allen's day-care home progressively later each week. Martin's involvement with his son significantly decreased with the breakdown in his relationship with Andrea.

Continued attempts by concerned staff members to help Andrea see the importance of the interaction with her child through play, feeding, bathing, and bedtime have proven fruitless. Andrea's only contacts with the Center are for her son's well-baby appointments, which she keeps fairly regularly. Allen is always clean, well fed, and clothed. Although Andrea is still rather short-tempered with him, one would not classify her as an abusive parent. All appears well to a casual observer. However, when one has seen the progressive changes in the relationship, it is apparent that the now minimal mother/child interactions bear no resemblance to the nurturing attention first lavished on the baby. The bubbly, verbal, exuberant 6-month-old is now a low-average functioning 21-month-old, with a disinterested teenage mother.

Discussion

Andrea's story typifies a serious, but subtle, problem of teenage parenting. This young woman, were she not burdened prematurely with a child, would be viewed as a highly motivated adolescent, attempting to accomplish appropriate developmental tasks. She has a close peer group, realistic educational and vocational goals which she is pursuing, and she is striving toward independence.

Andrea also manifests other very common adolescent behaviors which, were she not parenting a toddler, would be viewed in perspective as transient traits. She tends to be idealistic, expecting people to live up to her unrealistically high standards. She behaves impulsively at times without thinking through the consequences of her actions. She is prone to wide emotional swings, making her responses to her son and others inconsistent at best. And lastly, Andrea is self-centered. Perhaps it is her inflexible self-centeredness, coupled with impulsivity, which are most incompatible with effective parenting.

Professionals working with adolescent parents may find this type of teenager a very real challenge. How does one help the young woman achieve a harmonious blend of meeting her child's needs while not sacrificing her own very real and appropriate needs? Compounding the difficulty of counseling Andrea is her unwillingness to perceive these need conflicts as a problem. She is bound by her developmental stage; intruding upon its progress is threatening. Therefore, Andrea avoids any contact with the Center except when mandated by medical needs and by Women, Infant and Children's Nutrition Program (WIC) eligibility requirements.

Not only is this parenting problem too subtle and threatening for Andrea to deal with, but frequently professionals also do not confront the problem. When there is no overt problem, the child is developing within normal limits, his health is good, and his mother is back in the mainstream of society, all looks superficially adequate. This is especially true when one is working with a high-risk population who present a multiplicity of complex problems. Nevertheless, we maintain that the "Andreas" must be scrutinized and offers of help extended. It appears that, for the most part, both parent and child cannot achieve the fulfillment of their developmental tasks. Either the parent or the child is sacrificed in the process[17] and oftentimes both.

More often the mothers we see are not as successful as Andrea in terms of being adolescents. The problems of being a teenager and a parent at the same time interact in such a complicated way that neither can be dealt with very well.

The ensuing problems begin to surface with the pregnancy itself, and although there are many problems specific to the particular mother/child dyad, there are some which arise repeatedly. We shall try to address these in chronological order below.

1. Problems During Pregnancy and During the Hospital Stay.
Denial, a defense mechanism used by adults as well as children, is frequently employed by adolescents, and often marks the beginning of a teenage pregnancy. it is not unusual for a pregnant adolescent to forget the date of her last menses and ignore two or more missed menstrual periods. She may then postpone a pregnancy test until her mother initiates the confrontation and insists that she schedule one. In fact, a large number of young

women do not begin prenatal care until the second or third trimester, and even with such a late beginning, may miss many appointments. In extreme cases, teenagers appear at the hospital in labor, never having received prenatal care, and having denied the pregnancy for the entire nine months. Fear of parental disapproval, of the physical exam, and of exposing her body contribute to denial and subsequent procrastination.

Long-range planning and follow-through are also problems for teenagers. When denial is coupled with procrastination, the result may be diapers and other baby equipment unpurchased in advance of the baby's birth. It may mean that despite many attempts made by well-meaning adults, young parents may leave the hospital with WIC and Medical Assistance forms buried in a diaper bag, acknowledged but forgotten demands of an adult world.

It is imperative that we constantly keep in focus that the young woman is still a child in many ways and is not attuned to being responsible for someone else or even fully responsible for herself. She is still struggling with ambivalent feelings concerning full care for her own needs. Although she emerged from the hospital as an "adult" in the eyes of the community, she is not an adult in reality. She probably still needs reminding to clean her room, wash the dishes, and fulfill other household chores. Yet we now expect that this overwhelmed youngster will soon negotiate the labyrinth of social and medical services, return to school, arrange child care for her baby, fulfill social, educational, and parental expectations, and provide for the physical and emotional needs of her infant.

Pregnancy, to some extent, feeds into a teenager's narcissism. Attention is drawn to the expectant adolescent mother. New clothes are purchased for her, and she becomes a focus of attention both at home and in school. She may be given a baby shower at which time gifts are lavished upon her and food is prepared especially for her. This is frequently the first time in a long while that she has been the honored guest at a party. Many teachers report that some behavior problems in school disappear during pregnancy only to return with the infant's birth when attention and care prevously given to the pregnant teenager now shifts to the baby.

2. Ongoing Parenting Problems. When the young mother comes home from the hospital with her baby, a whole new set of difficulties awaits her. One of the most common problems during the first few months concerns infant feeding. Regardless of careful instructions given prenatally and in the hospital, many young mothers begin feeding solids within the first two weeks. Some of the early feeding problems can be attributed to the guidance of well-meaning relatives with whom the young mother comes into conflict very early over her mothering role. Who is responsible for the care and well being of the baby? What happens when a teenager disagrees with her mother about what is best for the infant? How can the new mother be considered both a child and an adult in her home?[18] An additional contributing factor in feeding problems is the anxiety of the young parent. In her desire to perform her parenting role adequately, and feeling uncertain of the components involved, she may use feeding and the symbolic "fat baby" to allay her anxiety and prove her adequacy as a mother.

The baby may unwittingly add to her feelings of inadequacy by crying for extended periods of time. To stop the nerve-shattering sound, and because teenagers normally have difficulty bearing frustration, she learns very quickly the magical effects of putting a bottle in her baby's mouth. However, every cry of the baby is not a call for nourishment, and the baby, finding sucking comforting, may drink much more formula than he/she needs or is good for him/her.

Another source of difficulty during the early months may be the pediatric examination. The teenager's inability to separate her own feelings and needs from the needs of her child, often make these visits stressful events. It is not uncommon for the adolescent to abandon her baby on the examining table when an inoculation is necessary. She may state that she "can't bear to look" while her new baby is being hurt. It is as if the teenager feels it is she who is on the table getting the shot. This identification with her baby does not allow her to function as the baby's mother to comfort her child and allay his anxieties. At times staff members have had to comfort the young mother while the physician or nurse is giving her infant a shot or drawing blood. In order to help the girl parent effectively, we need to help her understand how necessary it is to hold and comfort her child. We need to help her get some insight into how this strong identification with her baby is preventing her from seeing him/her as a separate individual with his/her own needs, fears, and feelings.[12]

Guidance over a prolonged period of time may be in order to help the teen mother understand the effect her fears have upon the development of her child's personality. She may not understand the profound implications that result from her approach to fear-producing situations, new foods, sleep disturbances, and other areas of the baby's life.[4] Additionally, she may have borne a child at this time in order to relive her own mother/child experience, thus making close identification with her infant even more troublesome to deal with.

Later, as the baby approaches the toddler stage, this same mother may laugh and tease him about the immunization or other frightening aspects of a medical examination. Again, it is incumbent upon the professional staff to help her explore this response to her child's distress and her refusal to identify and empathize with his fears. The teen mother may be expressing her own fears of medical treatment and bodily harm through this strange and heartless behavior.

In fact, some girls behave altogether differently in the medical exam situation than they do with other staff members. Medical providers occasionally report that the adolescent appears distant and uninvolved during the examination and that the mother has difficulty communicating with them. This may be due to the doctor or nurse being seen by the teenager as an authority figure who elicits this type of passive behavior.

Not only are feeding and medical problems apparent in the early months, but the baby's beginning signs of aggressive behavior raises unresolved dependence/independence issues in the young parent. When the baby, at about six months of age, begins to exhibit more independent behavior, a formerly adequate young parent may start to lose her temper and become unable to cope. She may now begin to tire of the novelty of playing mother; dressing, bathing, and feeding her possession may not offer the gratification that they did earlier. Coupled with her boredom come the child's new fine and gross motor abilities and aggressive behavior. He begins to grab, pull her hair, tap her face, spit, and throw. The young parent frequently interprets these as negative behaviors, purposely planned by an "evil" child and designed to annoy her.

Sometimes there is a note of pride in the teenager's voice as she relates how bad her child is (especially her baby boy). However, accompanying her half-smile and proud tone, may be a slap and a harsh, "No!" Other teenagers completely ignore all aggressive behavior well into the toddler years and allow the child to move unrestricted without any limits at all. It appears that the adolescent's tenuous hold over her own impulses and her concern about controlling her own aggressive behavior, might stop any display of normal agressiveness on her toddler's part. At other times she may get pleasure out of watching her child act out his aggression when she should be controlling it. Confused messages from a confused young parent are bewildering to a baby and mark the beginning of inconsistent and inappropriate limit-setting which can contribute to future difficulties.

The problems of discipline and a child's aggressive behavior, though they begin at about six months of age, reach a climax during the toddler years when the child is behaving in much the same way as his immature mother. According to Peter Blos,[8] adolescence is the second individuation, and conflicts with authority, wide emotional swings, a lack of impulse control, and dependence/independence issues may parallel the behavior of the toddler. While the teenager may be trying to control her temper with her own mother, or in peer situations at school, her baby may be pulling toys away from his playmates and saying "No" to every command his mother gives. At the same time that the teen parent may be racing in tears to her room in a door slamming fit of rage, her baby may throw down his toy and fly into a temper tantrum. Since the adolescent is struggling with her own aggressive behavior, it is doubly difficult for her to cope with that same behavior in her child.

Perhaps a parent further removed from her teenage years might handle these difficult situations by encouraging the child to expend energies in a creative activity. The wild running around the house, toy throwing, and unsafe climbing that we frequently see in children of adolescents may be diverted into jungle gym climbing, block building, and ball throwing under supervision. Tantrums are probably handled more constructively with language and patience, than with a matching tantrum on the part of the mother.

Language is a key area in which teen parents and older parents differ in their handling of their children. Language deficits in babies have been noted as early as 12 months of age in babies who are attending the Hopkins Center. By 36 months these deficits may be quite startling. Since oral communication is dependent on speech patterns set up very early in life, a look at how the child's early attempts at speech are handled is in order.

Two of the first consonant sounds that appear in normal development are *b* and *d*. Quite naturally, one of the first syllables spoken by babies is *da-da*. This, when repeated over and over again, may elicit negative reinforcement from the teenage mother. Girls frequently report feelings of anger at their children for saying "dada" when it is they (the teenage mothers) who provide all of the child care.*

Here a little education goes a long way. When the baby is about four months old, parent educators, social workers, and health providers would be wise to prepare young mothers for this phenomenon so those early attempts at sound production will be encouraged, praised, and imitated.[23]

Not only are these first speech attempts often thwarted by adolescent parents, but later, when the child is capable of more complex verbalizations, the young mother may not aid in the baby's verbal achievement. We believe there are several contributing factors which cause this to occur.

1. The mother's age-appropriate self-centeredness and impulsivity restrict her ability to communicate effectively with her child. She is far too involved in her own development to be a consistent stimulator and receptor of her child's thoughts. Her responses are therefore sporadic, abbreviated, and inconsistent.

---

*Many of the young mothers we have talked with have known the father of the baby for several years prior to the pregnancy, but for some the relationship wavers and falters after the child's birth. The young father may come to see the baby, take the child to his parents' home, and contribute something to the baby's support, but often the relationship between the couple shifts and begins to disintegrate. Very often the only way for the relationship to continue is for the girl to move from her parents' home.

2. When the child becomes able to express ideas, he then presents a threat to the parent's power and authority. Young parents, because of the inherent role conflicts of child, adolescent, and parent, may find this area too difficult to address and better left undeveloped.

3. Often parents want their children to speak, but a lack of understanding of the development of language makes them ineffective teachers. Education and modeling of communication patterns may be in order here. For those parents who "would if they could," teaching them how to encourage language can make a significant difference.

Many parents believe that being around other children and watching television are speech-producing activities. Teaching these parents the limitations of such activities and the productive strategies of parent/child interaction will prove an effective intervention.

4. Language learning and teaching are best achieved through an ongoing, consistent, relationship between the child and his primary caregiver.[15,19,23] When a teenager becomes a parent, she is frequently unable to provide that relationship. Her child's care may be shifted among several caregivers, all of whom have different speech patterns and different expectations of the child. None of them may spend enough time with the baby to learn his subtle cues and anticipate his needs. The child may therefore cease his attempts to communicate verbally and resort to earlier behaviors—pulling at the caregiver's arm, pointing, grunting, and crying to indicate needs.

Limited language skills have long-term consequences for cognitive development and a child's later success in school, in relationships with others, and in coping with life events.[6,26] Since poor language skills are common to children of teenagers, it is essential that those who work with teenage parents address language development and develop effective intervention strategies.

CASE ILLUSTRATION

The following vignette of Joanne and her daughter Kelly illustrates an extreme example of language deprivation and show how an immature, emotionally deprived young mother of average intelligence was unable to allow her child to separate and individuate until some of the mother's needs were addressed.

Joanne lives with her employed mother, unemployed stepfather, and several siblings. She is the next to the youngest in her family. At the time she became pregnant 3 years ago she was 16 years old and in the ninth grade. John, the father of the baby, was 19 and in an apprentice program. Joanne did not return to school after Kelly's birth, but remained home spending her days in the dilapidated roach-infested rowhouse rented by her family. She spent her days watching television, listening to music, composing songs, reading, daydreaming, and sometimes crying. Her child was constantly with her. At first she breast-fed her and then weaned her abruptly to the bottle after a few weeks. The infant was usually on her mother's lap, fondling her mother's breasts while sucking either her bottle or pacifier. Very few words passed between them.

At 18 months of age Kelly seemed terrified of the physical examination and her mother seemed unable to find the words or actions to comfort her. Although we had provided all of Kelly's medical care since birth no one in the clinic had ever heard her speak. Joanne agreed at this time to intervention from our clinical staff for she was bored with her life at home and did not know why her child acted so "strangely" at the clinic and was shy with strangers. She did not seem to realize the extent of the delay her child exhibited in speech, play, and independence.

Weekly home visits were made by the parent educator and social worker who visited together and soon realized how deprived this young mother felt, both physically and emotionally. There was very little food in the house and it was bought and distributed in such a way that Joanne was never sure when food would be available. It was noticed that she frequently fed herself first before offering food to her child. There was no set time for meals and Kelly often ate on her mother's lap. At 18 months of age she was still being fed by her mother and frequently meal time was an unpleasant experience for both of them. The only scheduled event in Joanne and Kelly's life was a daily telephone call from John during his lunch hour at work. During these calls Joanne spoke animatedly while her child stood immobilized staring out of the window.

The rest of the day and night were completely unstructured. Sometimes both mother and child slept at home, sometimes at John's mother's home with John. Kelly had an unassembled crib in her father's house but she slept in bed with her parents even while they were having intercourse.

There were no visible toys or baby equipment on the first floor of the home where this mother and child spent most of their day. Fragile objects well within the child's reach did not seem to arouse her curiosity. She appeared to make no attempt to investigate her surroundings but seemed totally dependent on her mother. Her mother's breasts were her toys.

Many hours were spent in Joanne's house working with both mother and child in an effort to help them separate and grow. Joanne was given elaborate step-by-step instructions on how to play with Kelly, with specific instructions on what toys to buy or make. Toys were made in her home and she was accompanied on trips to the toy store. She was shown how to make books, and taught how to read to her child to engage her interest and encourage speech. Joanne was also taught the importance of a routine for eating and sleeping and encouraged in her effects at structure. At the same time we were helping Joanne learn the rudiments of basic parenting, we were tending to her needs. She was tutored in math, given emergency food on several occasions, and counseled intensively. The counseling consisted of encouraging her to verbalize her feelings, desires and concerns. In time, she began to express her ambivalent feelings toward her emotionally inaccessible mother, her hatred of her stepfather, resentment toward her younger sister, and her feeling of discomfort and confusion about the homosexuality of her older sister and sexual deviance of an older brother. She had warm memories of her deceased blind grandfather who had been her primary caregiver. She also spoke fondly of her alcoholic father whom she visited periodically.

As Joanne's need for attention, concern, and nurturance were met, she began to explore what she wanted for herself. She made two abortive attempts to return to school and finally, nine months ago, joined a nonresidential Job Corps program where she is still involved. She had problems in allowing her child to be cared for out of her home and thus resorted to using various relatives. For a short time Joanne had accepted placement for Kelly in a licensed Family Day Care Home. When her child showed some attachment to the provider, she abruptly removed her from this home and returned to letting relatives take over the care of her child. Her mother has neither supported her return to school nor her use of Family Day Care.

Kelly is now 32 months old. She has developed some speech, but as she is still shy and reticent with strangers, it is difficult to get an accurate evaluation of her speech. Her motor skills appear adequate and she displays an interest in her surroundings, although she approaches new tasks and objects with excessive caution. Joanne is unwilling to accept that there is any evidence of developmental delay in her child at this time. This young mother is now more interested in pursuing her own social, vocational, and educational interests.

Discussion

Joanne's pregnancy came at a time when she was unhappy in school and at home. Her struggle for identity was clouded by an indifferent mother and two siblings with negative sexual adjustments who only contributed to the inherent problem she was facing. As a major task of adolescence is to sort out one's sexual identity and resolve heterosexual and homosexual feelings,[14] we might speculate that Joanne's pregnancy was her affirmation of her identity as a woman.

Pregnancy is often viewed by adolescents as a way of separating from parents and a chance to be seen on equal terms.[3,25] In reality it may turn into a flight toward greater dependency, especially if the girl plans to return to school or employment. Not only does she increase her dependency on her parents, she frequently, and perhaps unconsciously, resorts to dependence on the parent substitute, welfare.

Joanne's inseparable early attachment to her child is perhaps an extreme example, but it clearly represents the behavior, on a more moderate scale, of many teenagers who see their children as the love object who will provide a missing part of their lives. Joanne's attachment was prolonged because of her own needs for the symbiosis. Since she had not individuated herself, she could not encourage this in her baby, or watch her daughter develop as an individual in her own right.[2,20] Kelly had not made the step from her mother to the usual toys appropriate for her age, nor did she develop language as a means of self-expression. She appeared arrested at a very early stage of development and was not encouraged to move forward. Subsequent psychological testing in the clinic revealed her to be of average intelligence.

The inability to engage in play or verbal interaction with a baby is a frequent finding among teenage mothers. The adolescent mood swings, preoccupation with her own fantasies, and self-centeredness often make her inaccessible to her child, or accessible only on an inconsistent basis.

Joanne, because of her own deprivation, was blocked in her ability to play spontaneously and verbalize with Kelly. To become involved for a prolonged period of time in such activities may be very threatening to an adolescent struggling for adult identity. Rather than enjoy the fun and throw herself into a game with her baby, she assumes a parent role to safeguard herself from her own infantile feelings she is trying so desperately to control.

Not only was Kelly language-deprived, but she was play-deprived as well. Play is a primary means through which a child learns. What and how he/she plays determines in large part, who he/she will be in later years.[22,24] Through the play situation, a child develops motor, social, and language skills and discovers that it is pleasurable to learn.

One might assume that a very young parent might be a perfect playmate for her baby because the mother is young and energetic. Unfortunately, this is rarely the case. One is more likely to see babies deposited in front of television sets, expected to play alone, or sent off to play with other children. It is the exception to observe a rich, consistent quality of interaction between mother and baby. Adolescents are more often seen dominating the play, not allowing the child to exercise its own will and determine the course of the game. Others may play for an extremely short period of time before abruptly walking away. Another play pattern often seen is "silent play." Here the young parent presents a toy and offers no verbal clues relating to either the toy or its function. At other times, the play may be composed of a series of maternal teasings; joking and giving unclear directions to the baby or taking the toy away, seemingly playfully, but with hostility beneath the surface. As a result the child learns that his mother is not a reliable source of information and may cease to consider her as a learning resource.

The choice of toys also poses problems. Usually those selected by a young mother are unsuited to the child's age. One frequently gets the impression that a particular toy was purchased because of its appeal to the mother, not because of its value to the child. Often girls buy large, child-sized stuffed animals appropriate to adorn their own rooms. They certainly were not bought for the baby because a baby's response is usually fear of the enormous creature.

Further problems with toy selection are safety factors. Because a young mother may care more about the toy's appeal to herself than to her child, she may not notice that the chosen toy may have parts too small to be safe and may not be structurally durable for rough handling by a child.

As stated earlier in the discussion of Joanne, to play is to momentarily regress. A teenager, whose childhood years are not just faded memories, but are still close to the surface, may have difficulty deliberately regressing and interacting with her baby.[1] The lure to regress to a dependent state is a source of constant struggle for an adolescent.[14] Being placed in the position of companion to a young child may be intolerable for her. The only way some mothers can deal with these ambivalent feelings is to do what Joanne did and separate completely from the parenting role.

Joanne illustrates another problem area for adolescent parents discussed earlier in this chapter. Feeding difficulties may be encountered as early as the second week, when some anxious mothers begin pushing solids into ther babies. Uncertainty about the quantity a baby needs to eat often continues throughout the first few years. A parent who has a problem separating her own self from her child's may expect the baby to eat portions the same size as hers. Or, to the contrary, she may underfeed solids to her baby and rely mainly on the bottle as the sole source of nourishment long after it is appropriate. Perhaps relying so heavily on the bottle is an unconscious wish to keep the child in an infantile, dependent state. The ramifications of this practice, however, may be that the hematocrit and weight begin to drop seriously.

Not only is quantity a problem, but quality of foods and scheduling of meals are also issues of concern. It would appear that unless grandparental supervision and involvement in meal planning are considerable, teens are frequently poor nutritionists. Meals may be erratically served, not conforming to any schedule, nor served in any consistent place. They also may replicate the types of meals that adolescents like to eat, i.e., quick snack-type foods like pizza, hot dogs, hamburgers, potato chips, and sodas. Unless the young mother has a preference for liver and green vegetables, the baby will rarely be exposed to such fare.

Additional feeding difficulties commonly observed are:

1. Not allowing the baby to finger feed when it is age-appropriate;
2. Not assisting the baby with meals when he is just begining to feed himself;

3. Insisting that the baby eat with utensils before it is developmentally appropriate;
4. Engaging in a power struggle with the baby over types and amounts of foods eaten;
5. Feeding many between meal snacks and then insisting he eat his regular meal as well.

Some of the poor feeding practices that adolescent parents indulge in are due to sheer ignorance of proper nutrition. Others reflect the developmental stage of the parent. Her own impulsivity, inconsistent behavior, and lack of ability to care for her own primary needs may make it nearly impossible for her to perform feeding tasks adequately. Here again, one sees that a teenage parent is an adolescent first and a parent second.

CASE ILLUSTRATION

Betty's story is a graphic illustration of feeding difficulties with a toddler, not an unusual one in a teen parent population.

Betty, a tall, thin 20-year-old is today a teacher's aide in an elementary school. She awakens at 5:30 each morning to ready herself and her 3½-year-old son Thomas for school, before catching the three buses she must take to get to work. They live alone in a charming apartment, tastefully decorated and furnished with items paid for over the last 3 years. Thomas is a healthy, bright-eyed, verbal youngster. It has not always been this way for Betty and her son.

Four years ago when she was 16 years old Betty had an unplanned pregnancy after having unprotected sex a few times with a boy she had known for 2 years. She was living at home with her parents, four siblings, and her older teenaged sister's new baby. Both of Betty's parents were employed, and were absent from the home for long hours, leaving the teenagers alone. There were school absences, unsupervised parties, and un-eaten meals.

At her parents' urging, Betty remained in school. During her pregnancy she attended a special school for pregnant students, and after Thomas' birth, returned to her regular school to complete her senior year. During this year, her relationship with Thomas' father ended, although the young man continued to visit the baby sporadically. She also obtained an after-school job, and began to plan for college to achieve her ambition of becoming a registered nurse. Upon graduation, Betty was hired as a temporary aide in an elementary school, doing both clerical jobs and some classroom assistance.

While Betty was out of the home, Thomas' care fell to various family members and neighbors. Meals became more erratic and mimicked those of the teenagers who were his primary caregivers. He stayed up late, slept late, snacked on junk foods. Although he was cherished by all of his relatives, his physical and emotional needs were not always understood.

Just before Thomas turned 2 years old, Betty's mother gave birth to another child, an unplanned birth with 15 years difference between the baby and the next oldest sibling. Because Betty had a child, the care of the infant seemed to fall on her shoulders. She resented this and found she was having difficulty in managing her own son as he grew into toddlerhood. She had very little time alone with him.

In order to be alone with her son, she moved to the basement of her parents' home. She partitioned the large room into two smaller ones and purchased suitable furniture. Soon her siblings began to spend more and more time in the basement, once again infringing upon her privacy.

After Thomas' second birthday, his growth pattern began to show a marked decline. In addition, his speech was slightly delayed, although Betty read to him and tried to encourage speech. Her communication with Thomas was either in the form of orders or questions, never just an easy conversation. He was constantly asked to perform.

When first informed of the growth and speech problems, Betty seemed unable to comprehend the problem. However, in time, and with professional staff intervention, consisting of weekly visits with the staff social worker, she made many painful and time-consuming changes in the best interest of her child. Although it angered her family, Betty learned to insist that all candy feeding was to stop and that the food which she prepared for Thomas was the only food to be given at meals. This new rule was not an easy one to accomplish. Her younger sibling secretly offered Thomas candy, and openly teased him by offering and withdrawing it. Her parents, when they tired of the boy's crying, supplied him with tidbits to quiet him. The grandparents were also seen by the social worker and their help elicited.

Betty was taught by our educator how to encourage language in a more skillful manner, and was helped to find a good day-care placement for Thomas. She eagerly complied with this plan and kept her son in day care. The social worker accompanied Betty to the day-care center on occasion to observe with her how her child interacted with his peers and to consult with the day-care staff on his progress.

Several months after Thomas was enrolled in day care, Betty, with her parents' approval, moved into her own apartment quite a distance away. She has been on her own for nearly a year, and although her job ended for the summer, she did not return to her parents. She thought about enrolling in a nursing program, but decided to postpone it so that she would not again have to be dependent on her parents. Betty has been rehired by her former school, this time as a full-time staff member with all the benefits of employment. Thomas is in another day-care center close to her apartment. He speaks fluently, participates actively, and there is no question that he is thriving emotionally and physically. Betty says she has not given up, but only postponed, her goal of becoming a registered nurse.

Discussion

Many young mothers we have worked with have gone back to school or work after the birth of their babies, but it is rarely achieved as smoothly as Betty's return. We can speculate that the support of her family, especially her parents, made this possible. They also provided role models with which she could identify, since they both worked and had marketable skills; mother as a nurses' aide and father as a bus driver.

Betty also illustrates two common problems observed in adolescent parenting:

1. An increased dependence on the family in order that the teen-ager may return to school or work, and the inherent conflict this dependency produces.

2. The often divergent approaches to child rearing practiced by the various family members/caregivers, the teen parent, and the recommendations of health providers and other professionals.

The teenager may experience real conflicts as to whose advice she will heed. Most commonly, she will raise her child as she was raised, particularly in the areas of feeding, bowel training, and discipline. The persistence of early patterns in mothering, and its extremes, are well documented in Selma Fraiberg's "Ghosts in the Nursery."[12] Intervention in the form of education can raise the possibilities that there may be other strategies that the adolescent parent can employ, but education alone will not necessarily be successful in changing patterns.[18] The conflict that is stirred up when the adolescent must depend heavily on her mother sometimes results in a premature flight from home without having evaluated her readiness for this move. Too often the move results in further frustration, alienation, and depression.

Another common problem, discussed earlier in this chapter, is the delayed speech of many babies born to teenagers. Thomas was no exception. His motor skills were precocious and strongly encouraged by his mother. She praised him for sitting, walking, crawling, and even dancing. However, his language development was slow, and he made his needs known by using his body—pointing, grabbing at Betty's sleeve, or pulling her to what he wanted. His few two-word utterances were "gimme milk" or "want candy." To Betty and to many other adolescent parents, early motility seems more important than early speech. Perhaps the characteristic behavior of some adolescents to rely on acting-out behavior to express themselves[1] may contribute to their difficulty in encouraging expressive and receptive speech in their children.

Another reason for Betty's and Joanne's not encouraging language in their children may be due to a lack of understanding of child developmental stages. The issue of inappropriate expectations has been frequently cited and pervades all areas of teenaged parenting. DeLissovoy[10] states that the majority of parents he interviewed were "impatient, insensitive, irritable, and prone to use physical punishment with their children."

Concrete examples of this problem can be seen in the areas of toilet training, feeding, walking, and discipline. Occasionally expectations are too low, especially in the area of language. But more frequently we have observed that an adolescent expects her baby to behave in an adult manner—not crying when he falls, is afraid, or frustrated; accepting parental limits stoically; sitting quietly for extended periods of time; and generally reacting with the same pseudosophistication that his mother might assume. Not only may she expect the child to behave as an adult, but she may also dress him as one. Designer jeans, warm-up suits, bracelets, and other trappings of teen attire are worn by even the youngest infants.

It seems that the girl's need to appear more mature is transferred onto her baby, and the child must also appear grown-up for his age. Just as the mother may be denied her adolescence, so the baby is denied his infancy.

Recommendations and Conclusion

Professionals who work with teenage mothers must keep in mind that these are adolescents first and parents incidentally and often accidentally. Regardless of how elaborate an intervention program is, the foremost aspect of the services must address the adolescence of the participants.

Parenting education, to be effective, begins first by aiding the girls in their understanding of their own needs, goals, and feelings. We believe that only after a teenage mother has dealt with her own needs, and has related her feelings to her child's, can she take the next step of providing consistent, empathic, ongoing care of her child. Due to the nature of her developmental stage, an adolescent cannot receive theoretical information on child development in a lecture format and apply this knowledge practically. A small discussion group with a supportive leader encouraging active participation of each member appears to be a good means toward the end of reconciling adolescence with parenthood. A planned but unobtrusive curriculum covering such topics as adolescent and child development, health care, nutrition, parenting, family planning, and related topics is essential to fill demonstrated gaps in information. A format which encourages goal-setting and responsibility is useful in promoting growth in parenting skill.

For some girls, this type of group experience will not be sufficient and more intense individual counseling may be essential. The counselor, usually a social worker, is perceived by the teenager as the person who is there to help the girl first and only peripherally the baby. Thus the social worker may be viewed differently from other staff members in a center whose first priority may be the baby.

No program for teenage parents, in our view, can have maximum effectiveness without close ties to the community. Since school-age parents require a myriad of services, strong linkages must be established for referral purposes. Whoever does the referring must also be responsible for the follow-up since, as stated previously, adolescents frequently procrastinate and deny, even around critical issues. There will be times when a staff person may find that the only way to ensure that a referral is acted upon is to take the young parent there herself.

We recognize that the goal is to help the adolescent mother assume responsibility for herself and her child, but we also recognize that when one is able to do this fully, one is called an adult. Until the time that teenagers are able to assume adulthood, they need help from society, to be certain that early parenting does not result in shattered lives for both mother and child.

BIBLIOGRAPHY

1. Adams, B., Brownstein, C., et al. The pregnant adolescent: A group approach. *Adolescence*, Vol. **XI**, No. 44:467–485, 1976.
2. Anthony, E. and Benedek, T., (eds.) Parenthood during the life cycle. *Parenthood–Its Psychology and Psychopathology*. Boston: Little Brown, 185–205, 1970.
3. Barglow, P. Some psychiatric aspects of illegitimate pregnancy in early adolescence. *American Journal of Orthopsychiatry*. **38**:4, 672–687, 1968.
4. Beckwith, L. Caregiver—Infant interaction and the development of the high risk infant. In: *Intervention Strategies for High Risk Infants and Young Children*. Edited by Tjossem, T., Baltimore: University Park Press, 119–139, 1974.
5. Beck, L. Relationship between infants' vocalization and their mothers' behaviors. *Merrill Palmer Quarterly*, Vol **27**, 211–226, 1971.
6. Bernstein B. In: *Economy, Education and Society*. Edited by Helsey, A.H., Florid, J., and Anderson, C.A., New York: Free Press, 288–314, 1961.
7. Bergen, M. Some observations of maturational factors in young children and adolescents. *Psychoanalytic Study of the Child*, Vol. **XIX**, 275–286, 1964.
8. Blos, P. *On Adolescence: A Psychoanalytic Interpretation*, New York: Free Press, 1962.
9. DeLissovoy, V. Child care by adolescent parents. *Child Today*, Vol. **2**, 22–25, 1973.
10. Epstein, A. *Adolescent Parents and Infants Project: Preliminary Findings*. Mimeo. Ypsilanti, Michigan: High Scope Education Research Foundation, 1978,
11. Fraiberg, S., Adelson, E., and Shapiro, V. Ghosts in the Nursery: A psychoanalytic approach to the problems of impaired infant/mother relationships. *Journal of the American Academy of Child Psychiatry*, Vo. **14**, No. 3, New Haven: Yale University Press, 1975.

12. Fraiberg, S. The Magic Years—*Understanding and Handling the Problems of Early Childhood.* New York: Scribner and Sons, 1958.
13. Freud, A. Adolescence. *Psychoanalytic Study of the Child,* Vol. **XLLI**, 255–278, 1958.
14. Freud, A. *The Ego and the Mechanisms of Defense.* New York: International Universities Press, 1946.
15. Jones, E. *Some Problems of Adolescence.* Papers on Psychoanalysis. London: Baillere, Tindall, 1950.
16. Josselyn, I. *The Adolescent and his World.* Family Service Association of America, New York, 1975.
17. LeBow, M. Helping teenage mothers. In: *Helping Parents Help Their Children.* Edited by Arnold, L., New York: Brunner-Mazel, 1978.
18. Levenson, P., Atkinson, B., Hale, J., and Hollier, M. Adolescent parent education: A maturational model. *Child Psychiatry and Human Development.* Vol. **9**(2), 1978.
19. Lewis, M. *How Children Learn to Speak.* New York: Basic Books, 1959.
20. Mahler, M. The mother's reaction to her toddler's drive for individuation. In: *Parenthood–Its Psychology and Psychopathology* Edited by Anthony, E. and Benedek, T., Boston: Little Brown, 1970.
21. Moore, K. Teenaged Childbirth and Welfare Dependency. *Family Planning Perspectives,* Vol. **10**, 233, 1978.
22. Oppel, W. and Royston, A. Teenage births: Some social, psychological and physical sequelae. *American Journal of Public Health,* Vol. **61**, 751–756, 1971.
23. Rheingold, H., Gerwitz, V., and Ross, H. Social conditioning of vocalizations in the infant. *Journal of Comparative and Physiological Psychology,* Vol. **52**, 68–73, 1959.
24. Sarril, P. and Davis, C. The unwed primipara. *American Journal of Obstetrics and Gynecology,* Vol. **95**, 722–725, 1953.
25. Williams, T. Childbearing practices of young mothers: What we know, how it matters, why it's so little. *American Journal of Orthopsychiatry,* **44**:1, 70–75, 1974.
26. Yarrow, L., Goodwin, M., Manheimer, H., and Milowe, I. Infancy experience and cognitive and personality development at ten years. In: *The Competent Infant: Research and Commentary.* Edited by Stone, L.J., Smith, H., and Murphy, L. New York: Basic Books, 1973.

19.
The Second Time Around: Birth Spacing Among Teenage Mothers

Katherine Darabi, Ph.D.,
Assistant Professor,
Center for Population and Family Health,
Columbia University;

Elizabeth H. Graham, M.S.W.
Executive Director,
Northside Center for Child Development;

and

Susan Gustavus Philliber, Ph.D.,
Associate Professor,
Center for Population and Family Health,
Columbia University

National studies have demonstrated that young women who begin childbearing as teenagers have a greater number of children overall, and have these children more rapidly than do women who postpone childbearing. In the present study we have analyzed data from a sample of teenage mothers in order to identify the characteristics of women who have a second live birth within 30 months of the first. The data for the study come from structured interviews with 93 black and Hispanic women who were teenagers when they delivered their first children on the wards of a New York hospital in 1975. By two and a half years after the first birth, almost a quarter of these teenagers (24%) had delivered a second child.

The variables used included a variety of family background characteristics, measures pertaining to the womens' living situations at the time their first children were born, and experiences and attitudes subsequent to the first birth. Of these, only two variables showed statistically significant relationships to the probability of a second birth within 30 months of the first: living arrangement and return to school. Interestingly, these are the same variables found by other researchers to be related to rapid subsequent pregnancies among teenagers. Whether we are explaining repeat pregnancies or repeat childbearing, it appears that married women and women who do not return to school are at highest risk.

Demographers and family planning program administrators have recently become concerned with rapid repeat pregnancies to teenage childbearers. Despite the negative personal consequences attributed to early childbearing, the younger a woman is when she bears her first child, the more rapidly she will become pregnant again, and the greater her completed fertility. These differences do not appear to be due to a greater desire for children, since teenage mothers also have more unplanned and nonmarital births than their peers who postpone childbearing (Trussell and Menken, 1978).

Despite the higher subsequent fertility of teenage mothers *relative to older women*, it is important to remember that many young women do not have rapid second pregnancies after the first birth. Several studies have shown that by one, and even two years after the first birth, the majority of teenagers have had no subsequent pregnancies (Jekel et al., 1973; Furstenberg, 1976, Zelnik, 1980). While there are few studies that focus on women who have a second birth within this time interval, these rates are, of course, even lower. In a study by Furstenberg (1976), for example, as long as five years after the first birth, only a slight majority of teenage mothers (54%) had had a second or third child. Among single teenage mothers 63 percent still had only one child five years after the first birth.

In addition, if we assume that the most deleterious effects of teenage childbearing occur to single mothers, then it is encouraging to note that unmarried teenagers are *less* likely than married teens to have rapid second pregnancies. Furstenberg (1976) and Jekel et al. (1973) analyzed data from samples of black teenagers who delivered their first children in Baltimore and New Haven hospitals respectively. In both studies married women had higher rates of rapid subsequent pregnancy.

In the Trussell and Menken analysis of data from the 1973–74 National Survey of Family Growth (NSFG) marital status at first birth had relatively little effect upon subsequent fertility of black or white teenage mothers at 5, 10, or 15 years after the first birth. However, in most categories teenage women who were married at the time of their first birth had higher subsequent fertility than women who bore their first children out-of-wedlock. Although Zelnik (1980) reached different conclusions concerning the role of marital status *after* the first birth all of the women in his sample were unmarried at the time of their first pregnancies.

In order to plan more effective postpartum counseling programs, it would be useful to identify other characteristics of teenagers who are at greatest risk of rapid subsequent pregnancies. This task has been begun by some of the authors cited previously. Jekel et al. (1973) and Furstenberg (1976) examined cumulative probabilities of subsequent pregnancy among women who returned and did not return to school after the first birth. In both studies the lowest cumulative percentages of subsequent pregnancy occurred to single women who had returned to school and remained there.

Trussell and Menken (1978) found a similar relationship between completed years of schooling and the pace of subsequent fertility. After controlling for age at first birth in the NSFG sample, they still found pronounced differences in family size 10 years after the first birth by mother's educational attainment. The greatest differences due to education occurred for women who were 15 to 17 years old when they delivered their first children.

Aside from education and marital status, what other variables characterize women who experience rapid subsequent pregnancies? Few clear-cut conclusions can be drawn. In the NSFG sample, racial differences in completed fertility after 10 years disappeared after a control age at first birth was introduced. However, in Zelnik's 1980 analysis of premaritally pregnant teenagers, black women experienced higher cumulative rates of repeat pregnancy than whites at every follow-up interval. Since Zelnik did not control for age in this analysis, we do not know whether black-white differences exist even within age at first birth categories.

Neither the Furstenberg nor the Jekel et al. analyses included white women, but Furstenberg did compare the subsequent pregnancy experiences of women in several different employment and socioeconomic status categories. He reported no significant differences in the likelihood of rapid subsequent pregnancy due to interest in employment, actual employment, job prestige, welfare status after the first birth, or socioeconomic status of the woman's family of origin. Jekel et al. looked at two of these variables and reported that women who were employed were less likely to have had a subsequent pregnancy within 15 months, but that no differences appear by welfare status.

From the studies described above we might conclude that married teenagers and women who do not return to school after the first birth are at highest risk for a rapid second pregnancy. Further research is necessary to draw conclusions about the roles of race, employment, socioeconomic status, and other variables on the timing of subsequent pregnancies or on subsequent live births.

We might make a variety of hypotheses about such influences on the timing of a second pregnancy or birth. For example, since some studies suggest that there is a correlation between a mother's and daughter's ages at first birth (Presser, 1978), perhaps daughters are also influenced by their mothers' fertility in the timing of subsequent births. While we have cited research on black-white differences in subsequent fertility, it may be that within minority groups there are differences between Hispanics and blacks. Similarly, there may be family or partner pressures to bear a second child sooner if the first child is female. It may also be true that women who planned the birth of their first children are less likely to experience rapid subsequent births. Finally, there may be circumstances surrounding the birth of a first child which led to the postponement of a second child. An explanation of these and other factors would enhance our understanding of rapid subsequent births among teenage mothers.

We turn now to information gathered from a sample of young urban mothers about their birth experiences. It is our purpose to broaden our knowledge of factors related to rapid subsequent births among teenage mothers by exploring selected hypotheses, and by comparing the case histories of a young woman who postponed a second birth, and one who delivered her second child less than two years after the first.

METHODOLOGY

For the statistical analyses to follow, we have chosen to focus on the occurrence of a second live birth. While the occurrence of subsequent pregnancies to teenagers is certainly important, whether or not these pregnancies are carried to term, the addition of a second child is an event of more lasting importance and impact for the young mother. Indeed, a case might be made that how a young woman chooses to handle a second rapid pregnancy is cause for a study in and of itself. Our data do not permit us to explore this distinction and it has been virtually ignored by others.

The data presented here come from structured interviews with 93 black and Hispanic women who were teenagers when they delivered their first children on the wards of a New York hospital in 1975. The sample thus controls for parity, and variability in socioeconomic status is limited, since all women were ward patients.

Respondents were identified from hospital delivery records and were interviewed in their homes with their children who ranged in age from two and a half to four years. The total sample of 282 women from which these teenagers come, represents 51.5 percent of all women delivering their first children in the target hospital in that year. A comparison of delivery records for interviewed and noninterviewed women shows no significant differences between the two groups in age, ethinicity, marital status, or economic status. However, interviewed women were slightly more likely to have completed high school than were those who could not be located.

These teenagers come from large families where teenage childbearing and single parenthood were common. One-third of their mothers had borne a first child by the time they were 17. In addition, 40 percent of the young women grew up in homes where at least one parent was absent. The majority of their parents never finished high school and relied upon public assistance to support the family.

These patterns of economic deprivation appear to be repeated in the teen-ager's own lives. When they became pregnant, a majority of the young women we interviewed had not completed high school. Eighty percent were receiving welfare soon after delivery, and those who had worked, generally had low-prestige, poor-paying jobs.

THE PROBABILITY OF A SECOND BIRTH

In Table 19-1 we present the cumulative probability of a second live birth among these young women at 12, 18, 24, and 30 months. By two and a half years after the first birth almost a quarter of the teenagers (24%) had delivered a second child.

In Table 19-2 we examine differences in the probability of a second live birth within 30 months among women by various family background char-acteristics. While all of the relationships in Table 19-2 are nonsignificant, the differences are in expected directions. Since Hispanic women in the United States have higher fertility than black women, it is not surprising to find that they are more likely to bear a second child within 30 months of the first. Similarly, women whose fathers were unskilled workers have a higher cumulative probability of a second live birth than women whose fathers had higher prestige jobs. However, there was very little difference for another measure of socioeconomic status: amount of time on welfare during child-hood.

Presser (1978) has suggested that a woman's age at first birth is associated with the age at which her mother initiated childbearing. Such a correlation might lead us to expect a similar relationship between mother's age at first birth and daughter's timing of the second birth. In our sample this was not the case. Although respondents who came from large families had a slightly higher probability of rapid subsequent childbearing, those whose mothers were teenage parents had a slightly *lower* probability than those whose moth-ers bore their first children while in their twenties.

Table 19-1. Cumulative probability of a second live birth among teenage mothers.

MONTH	CUMULATIVE PROBABILITY
12	.032
18	.118
24	.194
30	.237

Table 19-2. Cumulative probability of a second live birth within 30 months by selected family background variables.

VARIABLE	CUMULATIVE PROBABILITY
Ethnicity	
Hispanic	.300
Black	.189
Father's Occupational Prestige	
Unskilled worker	.269
Skilled worker	.091
Amount of Time on Welfare During Childhood	
Never or hardly ever on welfare	.261
On welfare some or most of the time	.233
Respondent's Mother's Age at First Birth	
Teenager	.200
Over age 19	.306
Respondent's Mother's Total Live Births	
0–3	.200
4+	.267
Religion	
Protestant	.176
Catholic	.326

In line with Trussell and Menken's findings from the NSFG, Catholic women in our sample were more likely to have a second birth within 30 months than were the Protestants, although again the difference is not statistically significant. Furthermore, in our study religion is confounded by ethnicity, since the Hispanic women are much more likely than the blacks to be Catholics.

In Table 19-3 there is a statistically significant difference that is similar to findings from other studies. A higher proportion of women who were living with a husband or boyfriend when the first child was born had a second live birth within 30 months of the first. It is interesting to note that only this expanded definition of living arrangements is statistically significant; legal marital status follows the same direction but the differences in probabilities of a second birth are not as great. Among the other variables in Table 19-3 we find that younger teenagers and women whose first births were unplanned are slighly more likely to have rapid subsequent births. A slightly larger proportion of the women whose first children were females delivered again within 30 months. These latter differences are small and not statistically significant, but the differential by sex of the first child parallels studies among adults showing that couples are more likely to stop having children after the birth of a boy than after the birth of a girls (Dawes, 1970).

Table 19-3. Cumulative probability of a second live birth within 30 months by selected variables pertaining to the birth of the first child.

VARIABLE	CUMULATIVE PROBABILITY
Sex of First Child	
Male	.209
Female	.260
Age at First Birth	
Under 18	.282
18–19	.204
Living Arrangements[1]	
Living with husband or boyfriend	.394
Not living with husband or boyfriend	.150
Marital Status	
Ever Married	.324
Never Married	.196
Whether First Birth Was Planned	
Yes	.167
No	.277

[1]Chi square of second live birth status by the independent variable significant at $p<.05$.

Table 19-4 includes variables pertaining to women's experiences after the first birth and their attitudes toward its timing, subsequent events, and their first child's development. Of these, only school return is statistically significant. This variable, like living arrangements, has appeared in other studies. In regard to employment status, our findings support Furstenberg's conclusion that working is not significantly related to the occurrence of a rapid subsequent pregnancy. However, in our study, the women who have not been employed since the first birth do have a slightly higher probability of a second birth within 30 months.

Somewhat surprisingly, neither attitudes toward life changes and the timing of the first birth, nor perceptions of the first child's development, were significantly related to occurrence of a second birth within 30 months. In fact, women who wished the first birth had been later, and women who thought their children were developing at about the same rate, or more slowly than other children, were actually somewhat more likely to have a second birth within 30 months.

Taken together then, Tables 19-2 to 19-4 offer only two variables with statistically significant relationships to the probability of a second birth within 30 months of the first: living arrangement and return to school.

The first of these factors seems clear enough. Women living with a male partner are more likely to be involved in an ongoing sexual relationship, and

Table 19-4. Cumulative probability of a second live birth within 30 months by selected variables pertaining to experiences and attitudes subsequent to the first birth.

INDEPENDENT VARIABLES	CUMULATIVE PROBABILITY
School Return[1]	
Returned to school since first birth	.140
Didn't return to school since first birth	.389
Employment Status	
Worked since first birth	.182
Not worked since first birth	.316
Attitudes Toward Life Changes Since First Birth	
Life became better	.261
Life stayed same or worsened	.233
Attitude Toward Timing of First Birth	
About right or wish it had been earlier	.205
Wish it had been later	.283
First Child Ever Hospitalized	
Yes	.240
No	.246
Perception of First Child's Development	
Faster than other children	.192
Same or slower than other children	.316

[1]Chi square of second live birth status by the independent variable significant at $p < .05$.

are thus rather constantly exposed to the risk of pregnancy. However, in previous research, the education variable has not been so clearly interpretable, since failure to return to school may itself be caused by a second pregnancy.

To examine the time order of these events we looked at the dates of school return relative to second pregnancies in our sample. The vast majority (78%) of women returned to school *before* their pregnancies rather than afterwards. In addition, it is interesting to compare the pregnancy outcomes of women who return before and after their pregnancies. Of the women who returned to school before their second pregnancies, 90 percent did not carry to term. Of the women who returned to school after or during their pregnancies, 33 percent did not carry to term. This suggests two possibilities. First, it is more often school return which leads a woman to postpone pregnancy rather than vice versa. Secondly, after a woman has returned to school she is significantly less likely to carry a subsequent pregnancy to term.

The meaning of these statistical findings is perhaps more clear when presented in the context of case studies of the young women they represent. The particular importance of the marital status and school variables are illustrated by the cases of Carmen and Jeanette.

Carmen is an 18-year-old Hispanic mother of two children, 3-year old Carlos and 20-month-old Chico. She was married to Carlos' father shortly after she became pregnant, but they are now separated, and she and her children are living with another man. This young family is supported by the man's part-time earnings as a salesman. Their income is also supplemented by public assistance.

Neither of Carmen's pregnancies was planned, nor was she using contraception. "I guess it's just nature," she explains. Carmen dropped out of the ninth grade when she became pregnant. She believed she would no longer be accepted in school, and said she decided to leave because "I was planning to get married." She has neither worked nor returned to school since her pregnancy. If permitted to choose among work, school, or staying at home, Carmen would select employment. However, she feels completely ill-equipped to enter the labor market, and restricted by childcare responsibilities. Despite this, Carmen is satisfied with the timing of her child's birth.

Jeanette is a black high-school student from a working-class family. She became pregnant the first time after her parents were separated. She had just completed the seventh grade and was working for the Youth Corps when her pregnancy was diagnosed. She returned and remained in regular school until midway into her second trimester before transferring to a special school for pregnant girls.

Jeanette's boyfriend Joseph had completed the 10th grade when she became pregnant. Their relationship ended when the baby was only three months old, and Joseph is now incarcerated. One year later, Jeanette's second pregnancy was terminated by voluntary abortion. Neither pregnancy was planned. However, she asserts that they were both the result of method failure. Jeanette is satisfied with the timing of her daughter's birth and believes that the quality of her life has improved since then. At some future date, she would like to have another child, but her current priority is the pursuit of a career as a teacher. She is now a high-school senior and reports that she has always enjoyed school and been a good student. Jeanette enjoys the support of both her parents in this effort to avoid permitting early parenthood to appreciably alter her educational goals. Having a child, she said, has sometimes made it difficult to maintain a good attendance record. But, because of her excellent academic standing, the school has allowed her to continue.

Immediately after her daughter's birth, Jeanette secured a summer job in a local youth organization. Currently she is looking for after-school work to supplement the family income.

Although her family was intact during her formative years, Jeanette's parents are currently separated, and she, her child, and her two brothers, live with their mother. Jeanette's relationship with Deborah's father terminated when the baby was quite young. However, she possesses a wide circle of family and friends who have helped her raise her child. She believes it is important that she provide a positive role model for her child—a model which combines raising a family and pursuing a career.

Discussion

National studies have demonstrated that young women who begin childbearing as teenagers have a greater number of children overall, and have these children more rapidly than do women who postpone childbearing. This is a fact of some demographic importance, since such patterns contribute to overall rates of population growth. Early, rapid, and repeated childbearing have negative impacts on the health and welfare of young women as well.

Despite these real causes for concern, it is important to remember that many teenagers do not have a rapid subsequent pregnancy and that even when they do, not all of those pregnancies result in live births. In our sample, 76 percent of adolescent mothers had not experienced a subsequent birth at 30 months after their first. Among those who had delivered a second child within that time frame, only a few were still teenagers. This latter point is often neglected in research on this topic.

It is useful to delineate the characteristics of those young mothers who have a second child soon after bearing their first children as teenagers, because of the negative personal and social consequences which may accompany this event. In a society that frowns on teenage childbearing, it is important to understand what explains this behavior "the second time around."

Interestingly, we have found few variables to be related to rapid repeat childbearing among teenagers. For example, none of the variables measuring experiences with the first child was related to having a second birth within 30 months. Rather, the same two variables seem consistently important, whether we are explaining repeat pregnancy or repeat childbearing among young mothers. These are living arrangement and return to school after the first birth. It is difficult to suggest direct program uses for these findings since these variables are not easily amenable to change.

The importance of the school return variable may be that it indicates an ability to both plan for the future and to act upon those plans. In data not reported here, we note that 82 percent of the teenagers in our sample reported they were not trying to get pregnant the first time, and that 86 percent reported an unplanned pregnancy the second time around. Thus, well over a majority of the teenagers were either not using any contraception, or were using it ineffectively even after they knew they could become pregnant. Perhaps the explanation of the effect of school return on subsequent births is that a minority of future-oriented women are able to both go back to school and postpone childbearing to accomplish that.

The implication of these findings is that the occurence of an unplanned pregnancy or live birth is an insufficient deterrent for a repetition of the event. Therefore, service providers must not assume that teenagers who have delivered an unplanned child will be more motivated to plan their families following that event, or even that they will have a clearer understanding of the likelihood of becoming pregnant. We must find better ways of communicating this information and of encouraging young women to plan for the future.

BIBLIOGRAPHY

Dawes, R.M. Sexual heterogeneity of children as a determinant of American family size. *Oregon Research Bulletin* **10**(8), 1970.

Furstenberg, Frank F. *Unplanned Parenthood*. New York: The Free Press, 1976.

Jekel, J.F., Klerman, L.V., and Bancroft, D.R. Factors associated with rapid subsequent pregnancies among school-age mothers. *American Journal of Public Health* **63**(9): 769–773 (1973).

Presser, Harriet B. Social factors affecting the timing of the first child. Paper presented at Conference on the First Child and Family Formation, Asilomar, Pacific Grove, CA. March 1976 Proceedings. W.M. Miller and L.F. Newman, eds. Chapel Hill: University of North Carolina. Carolina Population Center, 1978.

Trussell, James, and Menken, Jane. Early childbearing and subsequent fertility. *Family Planning Perspectives* **10**(4): 209–218 (1978).

Zelnik, Melvin. Second pregnancies to premaritally pregnant teenagers, 1976 xxxx. *Family Planning Perspectives* **12**(2): 69–76 (1980).

Index

Index

interpersonal factors, 200-201
intrapsychic factors in, 197
male use of, 196-197
methods of, 55-62, 252-253
prevention programs in use of,
 201-202, 203-255, 241-242
promotion of, 282-284
race and use of, 196
side effects of, 165-168
success in using, 154
unreliable use of, 189
variables affecting use of, 179-180,
 180-181, 182-183, 195, 257-258

Emotional disturbance
alcohol abuse, 325-327
schizophrenia, 321-325, 331-334
suicidal tendencies, 328-331
treatment considerations, 334-336

Family unit
adolescent loyalty to, 294-296
adolescent pregnancy as crisis in,
 300-304
as a system, 292-294
burden of the newborn, 309-311
cohesiveness, 296
developmental stage, 297-299
pregnant adolescent and, 291-292
stress of, 318-320
variant styles, 299-300
Fertility
demographic determinants in, 141-142
psychopathology in, 142-143
rational decision making in, 143-144

Johns Hopkins
studies of adolescent sexuality, contraception, and pregnancy, 29

Medicaid funding
abortions, 2, 10, 29
Hyde amendment, 42
Medical risks

drugs, syphilis, and alcoholism of
 mother, 126
gynecological age, 125
infant prematurity and low birth
 weight, 121-122, 124-126
maternal anemia, 123-124
mortality of infant, 125-127, 135
poor nutrition, 125
Men
abortion and, 280
contraceptive methods, 277-278
involvement in pregnancy resolution,
 278-280
moral development and, 272-274
partner's influences upon, 274-277
promotion of contraceptives, 282-284
sex role expectations, 266-267
sexual decisions of, 271-272
sexual experiences of, 269-271
sexual myths, 267-268

Needs
access to abortion services, 44,
 366-367
day care facilities, 371
early sex education, 42-43, 53-54
employment and earnings as, 133
family planning clinics, 42-43
income, 370, 388
infant, 391-394
maternity homes, 372-374
prenatal care, 134
programs for parents and child, 45,
 372

Parental rights
involuntary termination of, 16
voluntary termination of, 16
Parenting problems, 411-423
second births, 428-437
Personality profiles
adoptees, 375
emotional needs, 387, 392
keeper's, 375, 381